THIRD EDITION

Human Resource Selection

Robert D. Gatewood
University of Georgia

Hubert S. Feild
Auburn University

THIRD EDITION

Human Resource Selection

Robert D. Gatewood
University of Georgia

Hubert S. Feild
Auburn University

The Dryden Press
Harcourt Brace College Publishers
Fort Worth   Philadelphia   San Diego   New York   Orlando   Austin   San Antonio
Toronto   Montreal   London   Sydney   Tokyo

Publisher Elizabeth Widdicombe
**Director of Editing, Design,
  and Production** Diane Southworth
Acquisitions Editor Ruth Rominger
Editorial Assistant Dona Hightower
Project Editor Matt Ball
Production Manager Marilyn Williams
Art Director Bill Brammer
Marketing Manager Lisé Johnson

Copyeditor Anne Lesser
Indexers Billie R. Najour and Cynthia Searcy
Compositor Octavo Design & Production
Text Type 10/12 Janson Text

Cover Image Phototone

Address for Editorial Correspondence
The Dryden Press, 301 Commerce Street, Suite 3700, Fort Worth, TX 76102

Address for Orders
The Dryden Press, 6277 Sea Harbor Drive, Orlando, FL 32887
1-800-782-4479, or 1-800-433-0001 (in Florida)

ISBN: 0-03-074667-1

Library of Congress Catalog Card Number: 93-72126

Printed in the United States of America
3 4 5 6 7 8 9 0 1 2 090 9 8 7 6 5 4 3 2 1

The Dryden Press
Harcourt Brace College Publishers

The Dryden Press Series in Management

Kuehl and Lambing
Small Business: Planning and Management
Third Edition

Kuratko and Hodgetts
Entrepreneurship: A Contemporary Approach
Second Edition

Kuratko and Welsch
Entrepreneurial Strategies: Text and Cases

Lewis
Io Enterprises Simulation

Luthans and Hodgetts
Business
Second Edition

McMullen and Long
Developing New Ventures: The Entrepreneurial Option

Matsuura
International Business: A New Era

Mauser
American Business: An Introduction
Sixth Edition

Montanari, Morgan, and Bracker
Strategic Management: A Choice Approach

Northcraft and Neale
Organizational Behavior: A Management Challenge
Second Edition

Penderghast
Entrepreneurial Simulation Program

Sandburg
Career Design Software

Sawyer
Business Policy and Strategic Management: Planning, Strategy, and Action

Schoderbek
Management
Second Edition

Schwartz
Introduction to Management: Principles, Practices, and Processes
Second Edition

Varner
Contemporary Business Report Writing
Second Edition

Vecchio
Organizational Behavior
Second Edition

Walton
Corporate Encounters: Law, Ethics, and the Business Environment

Wolford and Vanneman
Business Communication

Wolters and Holley
Labor Relations: An Experiential and Case Approach

Zikmund
Business Research Methods
Fourth Edition

The Harcourt Brace College Outline Series

Pentico
Management Science

Pierson
Introduction to Business Information Systems

Sigband
Business Communication

All of us have been involved in the selection program of an organization at one time or another. We have either been applicants to schools or businesses; or we have been on the other side, one of the organization members making decisions about applicants. From either perspective, a common reaction to selection is uneasiness and uncertainty. How many times have we heard an applicant say something like, "I wonder what he was looking for?" or an organization decision maker mutter, "How can I tell the difference among these people? I hope I made the right choice."

The procedure of selection is familiar to most of us. We all know that it is necessary to collect information from applicants about themselves. Such devices as applications, interviews, and various kinds of tests are used for this purpose. We also know that this information is then used to make comparisons among applicants in the hopes of identifying strong future performers. Even so, the question often arises, "If selection procedures are so commonly known, why do uneasiness and uncertainty still occur?"

We think there are two reasons: (a) there are some inherent features of selection—in evaluating applicants and predicting future performance—that cannot be totally controlled, and (b) even though selection procedures are well known, the more important parts of selection, such as what characteristics of applicants should be examined, which devices should be used to gather information, and how information should be combined to identify desirable applicants, are not well understood. Understanding the variables in each of these aspects is critical to building an effective selection program and, to a lesser extent, being comfortable with its operation. We think of these aspects as the technical components of selection—technical in the sense that psychometric procedures, statistical analyses, the conceptual framework of selection, the findings of previous empirical research, and the various legal constraints all contribute to a scientific understanding of the field.

It is the purpose of this book to present this technical information in a manner that will be useful and, we hope, interesting to those who are or will be involved in the development and implementation of a selection program for an organization. In our writing, we have summarized the most important research in selection, with an emphasis on the conclusions and only minimal discussion of the research steps and procedures. We have incorporated these results into recommendations for the actual development of a selection program. This book, therefore, is intended to be both generally informative and directly useful to those working in selection. The text is divided into the following five sections which systematically present the technical aspects of selection.

Part *I: An Overview of Human Resource Selection*. This section presents the nature of selection programs and their legal context. Chapter 1 describes the purpose of selection—the identification of high-performing individuals—and outlines the major steps that must be taken to develop an effective selection program, concluding with the limitations that must be addressed in these programs. Chapter 2 presents the legal constraints that must be considered in selection by discussing laws, federal guidelines, court cases, and methods used to determine discrimination.

Part II: *Foundations of Measurement for Human Resource Selection*. These chapters treat the psychometric measurement concepts that are basic to selection. Chapter 3 introduces the topic of measurement and discusses its definition and nature. Chapter 4 is devoted entirely to the importance of reliability and methods of estimating reliability. Chapter 5 discusses types of validity and focuses on the interpretation, and meaning of empirical validation. Chapter 6 presents the methods and strategies of setting cutoff scores.

Part *III: Job Analysis in Human Resource Selection*. This section describes the first steps in developing a selection program. Chapter 7 gives an overview of job analysis in selection and the implementation of a job analysis program in an organization. Chapter 8 thoroughly describes the most common job analysis methods and how they are used. Chapter 9 discusses the identification of worker knowledge, skills, abilities, and other employee specifications using the various job analysis methods. The emphasis is on how these data are translated into selection instruments.

Part IV: *Predictors of Job Performance*. This section, composed of seven chapters (10–16), is the longest. Each chapter discusses major selection instruments. The discussion in each chapter reviews the research about the validity of the instruments and treats their appropriate construction and use.

Part V: *Criteria Measures*. This section presents only one topic. Chapter 17 is an overview of the essential characteristics and methods of measuring work performance for use as criterion data in validation. This is a critical component in developing a complete selection program.

New to This Edition

The third edition of *Human Resource Selection* includes a number of changes from the previous edition. For example, implications for HR selection of the Civil Rights Act of 1991 and the Americans with Disabilities Act have been added. A new chapter on decision making in HR selection has also been incorporated. Chapters on the selection interview and personality measurement have been rewritten to include the latest developments on these selection measures. Finally, each of the chapters has been revised to include current research on topics relevant to HR selection.

Acknowledgments

One of the nicest aspects of writing a book is that it presents a formal opportunity for the authors to thank individuals who have had positive influences on both them and their text.

Robert Gatewood would like to thank two couples for long term contributions. Maurice and Sophie Gatewood, my parents, have, of course, guided me from the start. However, their support during my teens, early twenties, and the last five years were especially necessary. Robert and Evelyn Perloff directed most of my graduate and early professional activities. From them I learned not only technical knowledge, but also professional and ethical behavior that has been even more lasting. I also thank Jodi Bill for her help in revising my chapters, and Cindy Searcy and Billie Najour for their work on the indexes.

Hubert Feild would like to thank Hubert and Bernice Feild, my parents. Their love, support, and sacrifice will always be remembered. Bob Teare and Bill Owens served as important role models early in my career. Their work with me will always be appreciated. I am indebted to Art Bedeian, Bill Giles, Stan Harris, Bill Holley, and Kevin Mossholder for their encouragement, and to Achilles Armenakis for his support and our "miles of therapy" through the cemetery. Finally, sincere appreciation is also given to Boyd Childress for his help in locating numerous literature sources cited throughout this text. And to Amy Prewett for her help in revising several of my chapters. All of these individuals have meant so much to me.

Several people have been instrumental in the writing of all editions of this book. We thank the following reviewers for their time and comments, which improved the manuscript:

James A. Breaugh—University of Missouri at St. Louis
Kenneth P. Carson—Arizona State University
Cynthia F. Cohen—University of South Florida
Fritz Drasgow—Univeristy of Illinois, Champaign
Jerald Greenberg—Ohio State University
Hank Hennessey—University of Hawaii, Hilo
Mark L. Lengnick-Hall—Wichita State University
Mary Lewis—PPG Industries
Betty Jo Licata—Gannon University
Lyle F. Schoenfeldt—Texas A&M University
Brian Steffy—Franklin and Marshall College
Patrick Wright—Texas A&M University

James Breaugh has read every draft of all three editions and provided detailed reactions and advice that helped define the present content. We especially thank Mark Lengnick-Hall who wrote Chapter 6—Strategies for Selection Decision-Making.

Others provided aid, support, and assistance that ranged from discussing the interpretation of relevant research to drinking beer and sharing humor late on Friday afternoons: Archie Carroll, James Lahiff, Jim Ledvinka, Dwight Norris, John Veres, and Wiley Boyles. Art Bedeian got us started on the first edition and had confidence in two relatively new book writers.

The people at Dryden were, of course, the main force behind this effort. Special thanks goes to those who pushed the third edition through its writing, development, and production: Matt Ball and Marilyn Williams (both of whom provided the most help, encouragement, and demands); Ruth Rominger, Lisé Johnson, and Dona Hightower, who were instrumental in the development and production of the final product.

To all of the above individuals, we simply say, "Thank you. We have benefited from and sincerely appreciate your efforts."

Robert D. Gatewood
Athens, Georgia

Hubert S. Feild
Auburn, Alabama

Robert D. Gatewood received his Ph.D. in industrial psychology from Purdue University and is currently Chair of the Department of Management at the University of Georgia. He refuses to talk about how he arrived at a management department via psychology (something about an operation in Sweden). Bob has written several articles (some of which have actually been read) appearing in journals such as *The Academy of Management Journal, Academy of Management Review, Journal of Applied Psychology, Personnel Psychology,* and *Journal of Occupational Psychology.* He has acted (literally) as a trainer and consultant for several organizations, some of which are still in business. Not considering Pan American, Eastern Airlines, and several S&L's; the list of those surviving his recommendations includes PPG Industries, Westinghouse, Gulf Power Company, and Ford Motor. Although he claims his research interests are in selection, job loss, and recruitment; there is little evidence of this. He would be delighted, however, to discuss these topics with anyone interested for the standard consulting fee.

Hubert S. Feild received his Ph.D. in industrial psychology from the University of Georgia and is the Edward L. Lowder Professor of Management at Auburn University. (That position lets him teach more classes than anyone else.) Hubert has the nickname of Junior and the middle name of Spottswood. This explains a lot about his behavior. Junior has authored many articles in journals such as the *Academy of Management Journal, Journal of Applied Psychology,* and *Personnel Psychology.* Unlike Bob Gatewood's articles, however, none of Junior's has ever been read. Spottswood has been a consultant to, among others, SONY, PPG Industries, West Point Pepperell, and the U.S. Commission on Civil Rights. Unlike Bob Gatewood, he has gotten paid for his time, if not his effort. However, none of these companies has asked him back . Presently, Hubert is simplifying his life. He is down to six shirts, three pairs of pants, two pairs of shorts, and three shoes (not pairs).

Chapter 5

Chapter 6

PART THREE

Job Analysis in
Human Resource
Selection
283

Chapter 7

Chapter 8

Appendix to Chapter 8

Chapter 9

Chapter 10

Chapter 11

I

An Overview of
Human Resource Selection

A recent major concern of management has been the development of ways to increase the productivity of organization members. Many diverse methods have been introduced. There are programs that stress, for example, the improvement of communication, the proper use of rewards, and the redesign of work activities in order to improve performance. An assumption of many of these programs is that workers and jobs are suitably matched and that the purpose of the program is to enable the worker to use his or her job talents more effectively. Stated another way, the assumption of many of these programs is that the selection process of the organization has been successful in placing individuals in appropriate jobs, and the main concern now is to motivate these individuals to use their talents to the fullest.

Stated either way, the importance of selection in job performance is clear. It is the basis for the development of other programs devoted to maintaining or increasing the productivity of employees. If employees do not have the appropriate talents for the jobs to which they are assigned, programs to improve performance will be less than successful. In some cases, such programs may actually lead to a drop in performance. For example, many job redesign programs actually increase the complexity of the job in order to provide an opportunity for higher levels of achievement and felt responsibility. If, however, a worker is poorly suited for the job, an increase in its complexity may make a difficult situation even worse.

Unfortunately, there is ample evidence, both anecdotal and empirical, that many selection programs in organizations do not function as well as they should. An appropriate match between worker talents and job demands is frequently not achieved. That is the down-side. The up-side, at least for us, is that often selection programs can be improved fairly easily, and that creates the purpose for this book. Our basic viewpoint is that selection programs can be useful if (a) proper steps are taken to develop selection instruments that collect job-related information from applicants, and (b) this information is then used appropriately in making selection decisions. As you probably have guessed, the purpose of this book is to go into much (some say much-too-much) detail over how to accomplish these two objectives.

You have also probably guessed that this first section will present a general treatment of selection. (The word *Overview* in the section title also might have given a hint.) We know it's not nice to disappoint readers early in a book (that usually happens later), so a general treatment is what is coming. The two chapters in this opening section should give you an understanding of these four specific topics:

1. The importance of selection in conjunction with other human resource functions, especially recruitment.

2. The steps to be taken in developing a useful selection program.

3. The inherent difficulties and constraints of selection that must be addressed in developing a program.

4. The specific legal demands upon selection. These take the form of laws, executive orders, court decisions, and guidelines for selection practices.

1

An Introduction to Selection

Definition of Selection

Selection is one area within the field of human resource management (HRM). Selection is critical for the management of organizations because "choosing . . . employees . . . is necessary in all organizations, and the quality of choices often affects organizations for decades."[1] The definition of human resource (HR) selection that we use in this text reflects the many factors operating in this area.

> **Selection** is the process of collecting and evaluating information about an individual in order to extend an offer of employment. Such employment could be either a first position for a new employee or a different position for an existing employee. The selection process is performed under legal and environmental constraints to protect the future interests of the organization and the individual.

Our definition of selection is more inclusive than traditional ones that describe it as the process of choosing qualified individuals to fill positions in the organization. We now amplify the main parts of this definition.

Collecting and Evaluating Information

A basic objective of selection is to separate, from a pool of applicants for a job, those that have the appropriate knowledge, skills, and abilities (KSAs) to perform well on the job. We cannot assume that everyone who applies for a job is qualified to actually perform it. Therefore, in order to separate the qualified applicants from those who are not, the selection specialist must systematically collect information from the applicants about how much of the necessary knowledge/skills/abilities (KSAs) each possesses. The term KSA is shorthand for the job-related factual information and the ability to perform job activities possessed by the individual. If we said all that each time, this book would be about 50 pages longer. How bad would that be?

This systematic collection of information from applicants can range from being fairly simple to being very complex. For some jobs, a brief interview may provide all the data necessary to evaluate the applicant. However for complex jobs such as managerial ones, it may be necessary to use interviews, tests, job simulations, or other measures to properly assess job candidates. A major purpose of this book is to discuss the various devices that are used to evaluate applicants.

Our use of the term *selection* does not include all offerings of employment that may occur within a firm. We make a distinction between selection and hiring. Selection, as we have just said, occurs when job-related information is collected from applicants and offers of employment are given to those who apparently possess the necessary KSAs to do well on the job. Often, however, offers of employment are given with no evaluation of the applicant's job-related qualifications. We refer to this type of employment as hiring. One example of such employment is when family members, friends, or relatives of customers are given jobs. This is hiring because employment is based primarily on one's relationship to a member of the organization and not on the possession of job-related qualifications. Such hiring is not necessarily inappropriate nor does it always lead to employing incompetents. It is simply not selection as discussed in this text. Hiring also often occurs when a company desperately needs individuals to fill unskilled or semiskilled positions. This has most commonly happened in manufacturing, textile, food processing, and some service organizations with high turnover and many positions. For one reason or another, the organization has a need to fill openings within a very short period of time. As a result little or no evaluation is done of the applicants' KSAs. Availability is the critical variable.

Initial Job and All Internal Movement

Selection is often only equated with offers of employment to individuals who are taking their first job with the organization. Internal movement of existing employees (e.g., through promotions and transfers) is commonly thought of differently. This distinction between the initial job and internal movement is usually made for two reasons: The applicant pools are different and so is the nature of the information collected from candidates For the initial job, all applicants, naturally, are external to the organization. Very little is known about them. In internal movement situations applicants are current employees and a great deal is known about them. Thus evaluation of external applicants is done through application forms, interviews, and tests, whereas evaluation of internal applicants is accomplished via conversations among higher-level managers and a review of the performance records of the candidates.

Our view is that such a distinction between initial employment and internal movement decisions is not appropriate and may actually be detrimental to the overall staffing within the organization. Conceptually, the task is the same in both of these types of employment decisions. There are more applicants than positions available. Therefore, it is necessary to collect information about the job-related skills of the applicants and identify those individuals with the best skills. Logically, the accuracy of internal movement decisions will increase if more information is collected.

Basing promotion and transfer decisions on such variables as seniority, non-systematic opinions of others in the organization, and ill-defined reputations of candidates is similar to what we describe earlier as hiring.

Thus selection here applies to all evaluation decisions that place individuals in jobs. Matching the KSAs of individuals with the demands of the job is desirable, good, and should lead to a stronger economy. Can you see the flag waving in the background?

Constraints and Future Interests

From an organization's viewpoint, the selection decision is ideally made in circumstances in which the organization has a great deal of influence or control over the number of applicants that seek the job, the information that can be gathered from these applicants, and the decision rules used by the organization in evaluating this information. However, as for so much else, the world is not perfect for selection. For example, there are great fluctuations in the number of applicants, frequently due to general economic or educational conditions over which the organization has little control. There are also numerous federal and state laws and administrative rulings that restrict the information that can be gathered from applicants and the way this information can be evaluated. Equal Employment Opportunity laws and guidelines regarding discrimination in selection are a good example.

There is also a growing realization that the usefulness of the selection, decision should be viewed in terms of effects over time. One factor frequently mentioned in this connection is the match of the individual's talents and needs with the organization's talent demands and job characteristics.[2] It is generally recognized that the interests of both parties must be treated in the selection process or the result will be less than optimal. Rapid and costly turnover, lower performance levels, and friction between an employee and the organization are among the results of a mismatch of interests.[3]

Now that you have a better understanding of what is meant by selection, our next task is to provide a clear overview of the various parts of this subject. To do this the first chapter of a textbook frequently follows one of two patterns: It either traces the history of the subject matter back to the Greeks, Romans, and Egyptians, or it elaborates on how the subject relates to all that is important and how the subject must be treated for the correct ordering of the universe. We could only trace selection back to the Chinese, somewhere around 200 B.C. That reached only the Romans. Falling short of the Greeks and Egyptians, we had to adopt the second pattern for this chapter. The following section therefore describes how selection relates to other HRM activities, what HRM specialists must do to develop an effective selection program, and, finally, the problems inherent in the selection process. We know you will be amazed. We hope you will gain a better understanding of the complexity of this field and the technical knowledge it requires. In the meantime, we will dig farther into history. Plato's *Republic* seems like a good prospect.

Selection Related to Other Management Activities

Strategic planning specifies the future objectives of the organization, taking into account both its own strengths and weaknesses and those of the competition, and environmental factors that are external to the organization. It is hoped that strategic planning will identify the firm's competitive advantage and allow it to use this advantage to its overall benefit. It has been argued that one way HRM can help a firm obtain its competitive advantage is by lowering labor and production costs and/or by increasing sources of product and service differentiation.[4] To continue our overview of selection, we discuss the part HRM can play in strategy formulation and also the relationship of selection to other HRM activities.

Strategy and HRM

Recently it had been argued that HRM should become an integral part of the strategic planning process. The human capital of the firm can either be a strength or a weakness in a firm's achievement of objectives. Therefore, HRM should become part of the planning process in the same way that information about the firm's technology, financial status, and research and development achievements are. Knowing the assets and liabilities of employees and labor markets helps determine the feasibility of various objectives that are being considered.

To illustrate how HRM and strategy may be integrated, writers have developed categorization schemes in which business strategies are linked to specific types of HRM practices. For example, one such scheme consists of the two dimensions of Corporate Growth Expectations and Organization Readiness (availability and obtainability of human resources).[5] Another lists four commonly known strategic types of firms (*Analyzers, Defenders, Prospectors,* and *Reactors*) and describes HRM practices that should be used by each type in order to better attain its strategic position.[6] One of these types, *Prospectors,* are companies that thrive on product innovation and the creation of new markets. These firms pioneer strategies that identify emerging trends in the external environment. They emphasize innovation in products and services at the cost of internal efficiency.

To coincide with this strategy, the HRM system must produce creative experts who are both independent producers and thinkers on the leading edge of new ideas.[7] Selection must concentrate on individuals with developed skills, specialists in various areas of the firm. Also selection of external applicants is encouraged at all levels of the organization because of the heavy strategic emphasis on innovation that often can only be obtained from individuals who are new to the firm.

In contrast, *Defenders* are firms that have narrow product/market domains. They rarely make fundamental changes in their operations, instead focusing on reliability and consistency. For this strategy, selection should concentrate on external entry only at early career stages, and individuals who are selected should have general abilities. Selection for subsequent positions is from among internal candidates as it becomes important to maintain continuity in the organization's operations. Related work in this area has discussed these four strategic types in

terms of the other HRM activities that are critical to the management of necessary employee competencies and behaviors.[8]

Thus in the most sensible of worlds, selection programs are developed to fit
the overall goals of the organization. We know, however, that many times such
a fit is not explicitly made. Instead selection is carried out in order to refill a
vacant or soon-to-be vacant position. Also, unexpected growth can create the
need for more employees.

Selection and Other HRM Functions

Whether selection is linked to business strategy or designed to meet immediate
needs, it is closely related to other HRM activities. As Exhibit 1.1 indicates, there
are four such HRM activities: recruitment, initial training, compensation, and
job performance measurement. For example, training is designed to teach necessary job skills and abilities to those individuals who have accepted a job offer as
a result of the selection process. The content, length, and nature of training are
affected by the level of skills and abilities of the individuals selected. If these skills
and abilities are well developed for the job, then minimal training should suffice.
If necessary job skills and abilities are low, then training should be more extensive. Compensation and selection interact because, on the one hand, the specific
qualifications possessed by the one selected may affect the amount that he or she
is paid. On the other hand, the salary offer that is determined through the
recruitment and selection activities of the organization affects the applicant's
decision to accept the offer or not. As we frequently point out later, selection and
work performance measurement are also linked. The purpose of selection is to
identify those individuals who will perform well on the job. Work performance
data are used to examine the effectiveness of the selection program. This topic is
discussed in both Chapter 5, "Validation of Selection Measures," and Chapter
17, "Measurement of Job Performance."

EXHIBIT 1.1   INTERACTION OF SELECTION AND OTHER HRM FUNCTIONS

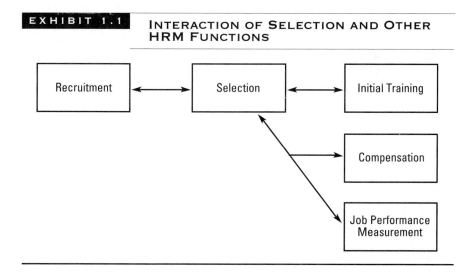

Selection and Recruitment

Selection is more closely related to recruitment than it is to these other HRM areas because both are concerned with processing individuals to place them in jobs. Other HRM areas deal with individuals after they have been placed. Until recently, recruitment and selection were often conducted as separate activities. Recruitment was the process of attracting a group of individuals to an organization. Selection began after recruitment was completed and was the process of reducing this group down to those suitable for employment. Sara Rynes, in an extensive review of recruitment, points out that this is a naive viewpoint.[9] At the very least, the selection requirements applied to applicants affect the recruitment sources used and some of the specific information about the job that is included in the recruitment message. Correspondingly, the applicant pool obviously serves as the limiting factor in selection. If this pool is inappropriate for the position, the effectiveness of the selection program is limited. Although a complete treatment of recruitment is beyond the scope of this book, we summarize some of its major characteristics to indicate its critical importance to selection.

Purposes of Recruitment   In terms of HR selection, recruitment has three major purposes:

1.   To increase the pool of job applicants with minimum cost.

2.   To meet the organization's legal and social obligations regarding the demographic composition of its work force.

3.   To help increase the success rate of the selection process by reducing the percentage of applicants who are either poorly qualified or have the wrong skills.

It has been demonstrated that the value of selection to the organization increases as the pool of qualified applicants grows. Essentially, a larger pool means that there are more very well qualified applicants for the same number of positions. An effective selection program can identify these well-qualified individuals and use them to fill the openings. If the recruitment program produces a small number of applicants relative to the number of available positions, the situation approaches what we have referred to as hiring rather than selection.

Later in this text, we discuss the various laws and directives that focus on eliminating discrimination due to non–job-related worker characteristics. As we shall see, an organization's compliance with such laws and directives has often been determined by the demographic characteristics of those selected. However, the demographic characteristics of those selected are directly related to the characteristics of the applicant pool. If the recruitment program does not provide a demographically balanced set of applicants, it is unlikely that the selection program will produce a demographically balanced set of selectees.

The third purpose of recruitment refers to the costs of selection. Processing applicants can be very expensive. Even the initial steps of the selection program require staff time, materials, and physical facilities. If the recruitment program produces applicants who do not match the requirements of the open positions, the result can be disastrous. The money spent on evaluating unsuitable candidates is totally wasted. Moreover, the extra time needed for looking further is an added cost to the organization.

Given this close interrelationship between recruitment and selection, you are probably ready to ask us, "What is the best way to carry out recruiting so it meets these objectives and helps selection?" In response, we say to you "That's a difficult question . . . ugh, why don't you ask your instructor?" The reality is that recruitment is one of the least studied of the HRM activities so there are not many definite guidelines, but we summarize here what has been done. There are four parts of recruiting that an organization can control: recruitment sources, recruiter, administration, and content of the message. Much of our discussion is based on the work of James Breaugh and Sara Rynes.[10] If you want more detail, read their material.

Recruitment Sources   There are two general forms of recruitment: external and internal. As the terms imply, *external recruitment* is of potential workers who are currently not members of the organization, and *internal recruitment* is of those who are current members. External recruitment is one of the main ways of bringing into the organization individuals who have new skills/abilities and different ways of approaching job tasks. Of course, the negative side is that these individuals are unfamiliar with the organization's policies, work methods, and performance standards. Because applicants produced by external recruiting methods are new to the organization, little or nothing is known of their job-related skills/abilities. The selection program must elicit all such information.

The major sources of external recruitment are presented in Table 1.1. These vary in a number of important characteristics that affect their use by organizations. One characteristic is cost of use. Generally speaking, advertising, especially when only local media are used, and employee referral sources are relatively inexpensive, meaning that cost per each person contacted or each applicant is usually low. Sources that require a good deal of travel and personnel time, such as college recruiting, are much more expensive. Another important characteristic is the amount of information that can be given to potential applicants. This is generally directly related to cost. The best example of this is recruiting using mass media. The cost of television and newspapers is a direct function of the timing and length of the recruitment message. Therefore, most companies restrict the amount of information given to recruits, even though it is possible to provide much more. College recruitment is usually quite expensive for the number of individuals contacted. However, it can provide detailed information specific to the questions of those contacted. A third factor is predictability of numbers who apply. It is commonly thought that advertising and employment agencies are less consistent in terms of both numbers and qualifications of applicants generated than are sources more directly under the control of the organization, such as school recruiting and employee referral. Such variability can be caused by time of year, general economic and employment factors, amount and intensity of competitors' recruiting efforts, and applicants' perceptions about the specific media or agencies used. A major part of the design of

TABLE 1.1	SOURCES OF EXTERNAL RECRUITMENT

Advertising

A message containing general information about the job and the organization is placed in various media, e.g., newspapers, radio, television. These media can have either a local, regional, or national audience and can serve the general public or a specific segment of population.

Associations and Unions

Many occupations have state, regional, or national associations that hold meetings, publish newsletters, and represent the interests of the occupation. Such associations frequently have job placement units.

College and Secondary Schools

Organization members are sent to schools to meet with individuals or groups of students to provide specific information about the organization or the job and to answer any questions. They may also perform the first review of applicants.

Employee Referral Programs

A word-of-mouth technique in which employees are provided with information about job openings and asked to refer individuals to the company. Often the employee is given a bonus if the individual who is referred is employed. Should the applicant be rejected, the employee is given a brief explanation.

Employment Agencies

Contact is made with organizations whose main purpose is to locate job seekers. The company provides information to the agency about the job, which is then passed along by the agency to its clients. Clients can be either employed or unemployed. Agencies can be either public or private. Fees may be charged to either or both the client seeking a job and the company seeking applicants.

Walk-ins

Unsolicited individuals initiate contact with the organization. The number depends on such factors as the level of the positions open, the image of the company, the frequency of job openings, and the physical proximity of the labor market.

---

recruitment programs is deciding which combination of recruiting sources to use for specific jobs.

Internal recruitment, in contrast, uses only two methods: job posting and review of internal personnel records. Job posting is a formal method of notifying members of the organization about job openings and the proper method of applying for these openings. Most often information about the job such as title, job activities, and necessary qualifications of applicants are printed and posted on bulletin boards or published in flyers and company newsletters. Employees who feel they are qualified are encouraged to apply for the position. Such applicants are then processed through the selection program.

Review of internal personnel records is the process in which an organization tries to identify a few employees who are thought to be qualified for another job. Data banks called "talent banks" or "succession banks" are kept for this purpose. These are data files in which information such as performance evaluations, academic and training programs completed, assessment center evaluations, and self-reported skills and abilities for each employee are kept.

Almost all studies have found differences among various recruitment sources in terms of future turnover, absenteeism, job attitudes, and performance. Generally, it has been found that internal sources are superior in these results to external sources. However, internal sources frequently yield disparities in the gender or ethnic composition of the applicant pool.[11]

Therefore, a variety of sources must usually be chosen. In our opinion, three important features to consider are the nature of the job being recruited, the image of the company in the external labor market, and the attitudes of current employees. Complex jobs would seem to require sources that allow detailed information to be given about the job, company and selection qualifications. The image of the organization is a function of the effectiveness of its advertising. A strong, positive image increases the interest of applicants. Similarly, poor attitudes of present employees would be expected to limit employee referral.

Therefore, the recruitment sources should be chosen to fit the particular situation. The number and quality of applicants reached vary considerably across sources. Similarly, the demographic mix of respondents to various sources also differs. A company should mix the sources to ensure that both sexes and the appropriate ethnic groups in the labor market are contacted.

Recruiter   There is some evidence that the recruiter has an effect on the success of the recruitment process. After all, this is the first real contact an applicant has with the organization. How a recruiter is received by the applicant should affect the applicant's future behavior toward the company. Three types of characteristics of recruiters have been examined: demographics, functional job held, and personality and behavioral traits.

Regarding demographics, there is some evidence that gender, ethnicity, and age can all affect applicant reactions. For example, women applicants have changed their opinions of fit with an organization because of not being able to get an interview with a woman on a site visit, seeing no women in high positions in the organization, or feeling that the company is a "men's club."[12] Similarly, one study found that black applicants preferred black recruiters, but that race made little difference to white applicants.[13] Another study found that an older recruiter was less favorably received than a younger one.[14] One might conclude that applicants develop a more favorable reaction if they are in contact with recruiters who are similar to them or who can serve as examples that individuals like them can succeed in the organization.

The functional job area of the recruiter also seems to be important. The choices are to have the recruiter actually be an individual from the work unit seeking applicants or be an HRM specialist who recruits for all units of the organization. The data seem to indicate that the work unit member is more favorably received. This may be because he or she is looked at as the manager or coworker and is given more credibility or is seen as more representative of the job conditions.

Personality traits and interpersonal behaviors of the recruiter apparently have the greatest effect on recruits.[15] Such characteristics as warmth, enthusiasm, supportiveness, concern, empathy, and personableness have been linked to the applicant's perception of job characteristics, regard for the job and company, likelihood of job acceptance, and expectations of receiving a job offer. Recruiters' knowledge about the job is also important, but less so than the first set of characteristics.

Administration of Recruitment   The small amount of research on administration definitely indicates that the promptness of follow-up contacts with applicants between the various stages of recruitment is positively related to the applicants staying in the recruitment pool.[16] Prompt responses by the company could indicate to the applicant that the company is efficient and, therefore, a desirable place to work or that the applicant has very favorably impressed the company and has a good chance of getting a job offer. No relationship between expenditures on recruiting in the form of dinners, receptions, gifts, hotels, etc., and applicant response has been found.[17] However, ignoring such items when competing firms in the same industry are doing this, as is the situation with recruitment by large accounting firms, would probably not be a wise decision. Finally, there are preliminary data that suggest increasing the information which must be supplied by the applicant, for example, transcripts, more letters of reference, certificates, or writing samples, reduces the number of applicants.[18] There was no noticeable change in quality of applicants, however, indicating that both highly qualified and weaker individuals dropped from the recruitment pool.

Content of the Message   An obvious question in the design of recruitment programs is the effect of various kinds of information on recruits both in the short and long term. Traditionally, the message in recruitment programs has been regarded as an opportunity to sell the organization as a favorable place to work, and it has, therefore, been universally positive. The excellence of pay, coworkers, physical facilities, advancement, benefits, and job challenge have been stressed. Because no work situation is without negative aspects, false expectations can be instilled in recruits that cannot be fulfilled in actual employment.

This happens to some degree in most recruitment. Many now think that it is unproductive to create false expectations in the applicant. Once selected, some individuals find the differences between their expectations and the actual job are unpleasantly large. Such discrepancies can cause a lack of commitment to the organization and rapid job turnover. Obviously, in such cases the whole cost of selection must be repeated as other applicants are processed. In place of such recruitment activities, John Wanous recommends "Realistic Job Preview" (RJP).[19] In realistic recruitment activities the applicants are shown the negative aspects of the job as well as the positive. For example, Southern New England Telephone made a film for potential operators that made clear that the work was closely supervised, repetitive, and sometimes required dealing with rude or unpleasant customers. Such information led to a self-selection process whereby those candidates who regarded these job aspects negatively removed themselves from further consideration by the organization. Those that remained made up a recruitment pool of individuals for selection with fairly accurate expectations of job demands and characteristics.[20] Wanous has written guidelines for the development and implementation of RJPs.[21]

Although several studies have shown a reduction in turnover associated with the use of RJPs, the size of the reduction has usually been fairly small. An RJP's contribution to the organization is related, therefore to the magnitude of the existing turnover and the value of the job to the firm. Most writers agree that while RJPs do reduce turnover, they should not be regarded as a primary solution.[22] Changes in compensation, supervisory behavior, and job assignments are more effective long-term solutions.

A related issue is the effect of the specificity of the information contained in the recruitment message. One approach recommends a more general description of the company and the job in the hopes of attracting a large number of potentially interested individuals which can then be reduced through additional recruitment and selection. The opposing viewpoint suggests that greater specificity in terms of job qualifications, job tasks, and so on, will increase the percentage of appropriately qualified applicants. This could reduce the overall expense of recruitment without diminishing the number of qualified recruits.

The choice of these two approaches may depend on when in the recruitment process the message is given. Reactions to early recruitment messages seem to be related to the image of the company held by the applicant. Recruitment messages at this time usually contain information only about the organization and little about specific jobs. Image seems to be influenced by the arrangement and use of some general but important topics in the advertisement itself.[23] Recruitment messages that are given later contain information about specific jobs and qualifications. It seems that specificity in qualifications does reduce the number of less-qualified candidates. The effect of specificity in the job description is more complex and interacts with the specificity of qualifications.[24] One strategy is that if the purpose of recruitment is to maximize the response rate from qualified individuals, the message should have a vague job description and specific applicant qualifications.

Organizational Recruitment Practices   The last topic we discuss in this section is the results of a survey conducted by Sara Rynes and John Boudreau of the college recruiting practices carried out by *Fortune* 1000 companies.[25] We present only part of their extensive findings. One somewhat surprising result was that college recruitment was not treated as a major HRM activity in most companies. While approximately 16 percent of both the HRM budget and time were spent on this, little was done in terms of either planning or evaluation of effectiveness. For example, only one-third of the respondents reported having regular meetings to discuss college recruiting. Another third met whenever it was necessary; and the remaining third did not hold formal planning meetings. Evaluation was most often based on meeting recruiting deadlines and recruiter feedback of applicant quality. Very few firms collected future performance or tenure data of recruits.

Many of the recruitment practices examined in the previously discussed studies were part of the regular programs of these companies. In general, respondents said that recruitment messages were accurate rather than favorable in their descriptions. In addition, the most important criteria used in selecting recruiters were strong interpersonal skills, enthusiasm for the company, and credibility with students and coworkers. However, most received little or no training, with less than half of the companies offering standardized training programs. In those programs that were given, an average of 30 percent of the time was devoted to interpersonal skill training, another 20 percent focused on traits to look for in applicants, and 10 percent was given to designing interview content. Recruiters were evaluated primarily on procedural grounds such as the keeping of appointments, timeliness of reports, and taking of notes.

Because this survey was conducted on *Fortune* 1000 companies and treated only college recruiting, it is unknown how representative these findings are of recruiting in general. It is possible to guess, however, that because of their resources and constant demand for recruits these companies have comparatively sophisticated recruitment practices. If that is the case, it seems that the tie-in between recruitment and selection is underestimated by many organizations. It would, at least, be useful to have more training given to recruiters in how to develop the content of recruitment and the methods of evaluating the qualifications of recruits.

Developing a Selection Program

A good deal of work must be completed by organization members, especially personnel specialists, before the selection process is implemented. We contend that the adequacy of these developmental steps, illustrated in Exhibit 1.2, strongly influences the adequacy of the selection process. If little attention and effort is devoted to the development of the selection program, then its usefulness will be limited. If these developmental steps are seriously addressed, the usefulness of the selection process improves. Another way of viewing this issue is that a selection process itself can be implemented quite readily. An application form can quite easily be printed or purchased; interviews can be conducted without too much prior work; employment tests (with names that sound like they should produce useful information for selection) can be purchased and administered to applicants. The crucial issue, however, is not whether an organization can collect information from applicants and then decide which are to be given employment offers. Obviously this is possible. Rather the issue is whether the organization can collect information from applicants about individual characteristics that are *closely* related to job performance and *effectively* use these data to identify the best applicants for employment offers. Many who study human resource selection think that it is the developmental steps of the selection program that provide a better match between applicant and job.[26] The following paragraphs briefly describe these steps.

Job Analysis Information   If the purpose of the selection program is to identify the best individuals to perform a job within the organization, then

EXHIBIT 1.2

STEPS IN THE DEVELOPMENT OF A SELECTION PROGRAM

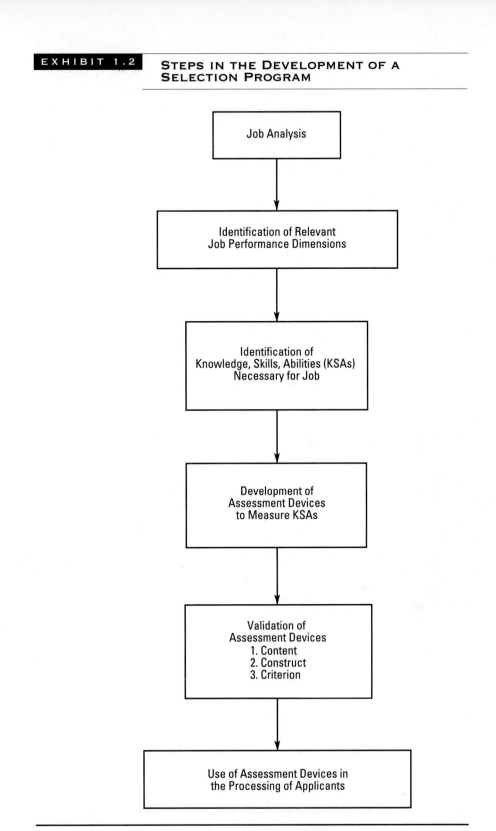

Job Analysis

Identification of Relevant
Job Performance Dimensions

Identification of
Knowledge, Skills, Abilities (KSAs)
Necessary for Job

Development of
Assessment Devices
to Measure KSAs

Validation of
Assessment Devices
1. Content
2. Construct
3. Criterion

Use of Assessment Devices in
the Processing of Applicants

information about the job would be the logical starting point in the development of this program. *Job analysis* is the gathering of information about a job in an organization. This information should be descriptive of the tasks or activities, the results (products or services), the equipment, material, and individuals, and the environment (working conditions, hazards, work schedule, etc.) that characterize the job. Such information is, of course, essential to all HRM activities: selection, compensation programs, training, performance appraisal, and career development, etc. For selection it serves two main purposes. The first is to convey to potential applicants information about the nature and demands of the job. This helps minimize inappropriate expectations. The second purpose is actually the more critical for the development of selection programs. The job analysis information provides a database for the other steps in the developmental process.

Identification of Relevant Job Performance Measures   One of the major purposes of selection programs is to identify those applicants who will be successful on the job under consideration. We assume actual differences among workers can be measured on aspects of the job that are important to the performance of that job. In other words, there is some way that the organization can tell how successful the workers are on the job. At first this may seem relatively easy to do: find out how much work an employee finishes and how well it is done. However, there are a number of factors present in organizations that make this measurement of job performance difficult: many jobs do not produce tangible products; jobs are interdependent so that it is difficult to determine how much any one individual has contributed; jobs are paced by machines or assembly lines with little opportunity for an employee to do more or less. Under such circumstances, it is the immediate superior's judgment of job performance that is gathered. In other cases variables such as being on time for work duties, or consistently coming to work, or completing an extensive training program might be indicants of job success. Frequently, more than one variable is identified as important in job performance. In any case, the information provided by the job analysis should help measure job performance.

Identification of Worker Characteristics   Using both the job analysis information and the job performance data, the HR specialist must identify the KSAs and other employee characteristics that a worker should possess in order to perform the job successfully. These KSAs become the basic pool of characteristics to be evaluated in applicants. This identification is an extremely difficult task. As we discuss in Chapter 9 there are a few methods that attempt to identify these KSAs in terms of a limited number of predetermined variables. In most cases, however, HR specialists rely on their judgment. Work requirements, worker attributes, worker characteristics, or job requirements are all terms that are frequently used in the same context that we have used the term KSAs.

Development of Assessment Devices   After the KSAs of primary interest have been identified, it becomes necessary either to find or construct the appropriate selection devices for collecting information from applicants. These instruments can be classified into the following groups: application blanks, biographical data forms, and reference checks; the selection interview; mental and special abilities tests; personality assessment inventories; and simulation and performance measures. There are two basic principles for choosing the selection device(s) to be used. The first is that the device must be representative of the KSAs identified previously. This might appear to be relatively simple but in fact is frequently quite complex and difficult. There are numerous application forms, personality inventories, and leadership questionnaires that are available from various organizations. Deciding among these must be done by considering both test construction principles and the similarity between KSAs measured by the device and those necessary for the job.

The second principle is that the assessment device should be able to differentiate among applicants. The assumption in selection is that applicants possess *different amounts of the KSAs necessary for job performance.* The purpose of the assessment device is to measure these differences (usually by means of differences in numerical scores). It is in this way that promising applicants can be distinguished from unpromising applicants. If all, or nearly all, applicants performed about the same on these assessment devices, the selection decisions would be very difficult, as the applicants would appear to be equal. Obviously there would be difficulty in choosing a few applicants from a larger group of equals. The problem of lack of differentiation occurs in the use of interviews that emphasize general questions about career goals and self-assessment of strengths and weaknesses, personality inventories that are transparent in purpose (for example, scales that measure the amount of social interaction preferred or attitudes toward stealing or dishonesty), and simple math or clerical tests. Knowledge of how tests are constructed and information from job analysis and job performance analysis will help the professional deal with this problem.

Let us briefly summarize the steps completed at this point. Information has been collected describing important aspects of both job activities and outcomes. This information has been used to identify a set of KSAs that a worker needs to succeed on the job. A set of selection instruments has been identified that will measure the amount of the KSAs possessed by applicants. If these steps are performed with care, we should reasonably expect to obtain the information needed to choose the right applicants. Frequently, however, the developmental work of the selection program stops at this point. If this happens, the difficulty is that there is very little evidence to verify the accuracy of the steps taken, Robert Guion likens these first steps to the development of hypotheses.[27] That is, the HR specialist has formulated testable statements as to the worker characteristics that should be related to successful job performance. The last steps in the development of a selection program can be viewed as a testing of these hypotheses. Technically referred to as *validation,* these steps focus on the collection and evaluation of information to determine whether the worker characteristics thought to be important are, in fact, related to successful job performance. If they are, then the selection program should be useful to the organization. If, on the other hand, it turns out that the identified worker characteristics are not related to job performance, it is better to learn this as early as possible so that alternatives can be developed.

Validation Procedures   There are several ways to validate the selection process. In *empirical validation,* for example, two types of data are collected: (1) the scores on the selection devices of a representative sample of individuals, and (2) measures of how well each of these individuals is performing on important parts of the job. The purpose of validation is to provide evidence that data from the selection instruments are related to job performance.

Statistical data analysis, usually correlational analysis, is the most straight-forward manner of producing this evidence. Since empirical validation involves calculating correlation coefficients between scores on the selection instruments and scores on the job performance measure, this information can be used to assess the usefulness of the selection program.

In addition to empirical validation, other validation procedures, such as *content* and *construct,* can be used. No matter which type is employed, it is really only after the valuation phase has been completed that one has evidence that the information collected by the selection devices is indicative of job performance and, therefore, is useful in choosing among applicants. It is these steps from job analysis to validation that we referred to previously in stating that much developmental work must precede the installation of the selection program. If all these steps have not been completed, then, in Guion's terms, the organization is using a set of selection instruments that are thought to be useful for the identification of potentially successful workers, but there is no real evidence to support this.

If the instruments are not related to job performance, their use can be costly in two different ways. One is that less than a preferred group of workers is being selected for employment. This obviously could have serious economic effects on the organization. For example, it has been estimated that if selection for most white-collar jobs in the federal government was based on valid tests of cognitive ability, this could result in either output gains or payroll savings of several hundred million each year.[28] Despite these financial returns, organizations often choose not to fully carry out these steps in the development of their selection programs. Less time-consuming and less rigorous procedures are adopted. In such cases long-term consequences and costs are downplayed or ignored.

Recent work has described variations of the model of selection presented in these steps. In these variations, selection is tied more directly into strategic planning. As a result, the KSAs that are measured in applicants may be based not only on specific jobs but also on more general work roles, work-team interactions. and broad knowledge and skills that can be applied in a variety of organizational activities.[29] In all cases, however, selection is still tied to either present or anticipated work activities and is dependent on proper measurement of individual characteristics.

Constraints in Developing a Selection Program

If we assume that the primary purpose of a selection program is to choose from among a number of applicants those who have a high possibility of performing well on the job, the essence of selection is *prediction* or forecasting. Specifically, a major concern is using the information gathered from the selection devices to determine differences among applicants on job-related KSAs and on the basis of this information to choose those applicants that will do well on the job under consideration. In HR selection, as in medicine, stock market analysis, meteorology, and economics, prediction is an uncertain activity. Even with a well-developed selection program, not all of the predictions about future job performance are going to be correct. There are a number of factors that greatly affect the selection process and must be considered by HR specialists.

Limited Information on Applicants

The quality of selection decisions, as in other areas of managerial decision making, depends in part on the accuracy and completeness of data gathered from the applicants. In general, the greater the amount of accurate data obtained, the more complete the assessment of the applicants' characteristics. However, in selection the extensiveness of the data collected is often severely limited by the cost of obtaining the data. The organization incurs costs for such items as materials and facilities, staff time, travel expenses for staff and applicants, and data storage and analysis. These costs usually limit the amount of data collected, especially early in the processing of applicants. For example, a college campus interviewer frequently spends only 30 minutes with each applicant and part of this time is devoted to the presentation of information about the organization. In other cases either application forms and/or resumes are extensively used as major screening devices for many positions. However, in both cases the selection devices used can obtain only limited, basic information about applicants. Especially when there is a large number of applicants for a few positions, difficult decisions about the acceptability of applicants must be made from limited information. Such limitations affect the accuracy of the decisions.

Measurement of Jobs, Individuals, and Work Performance

A basic assumption of this book is that the development of a selection program requires the measurement of characteristics of jobs, individuals, and work performance. By **measurement** we mean quantitative description, that is, the use of numbers. Numbers are used to represent such information as the amount of time spent in a certain job activity, or the level of mathematical knowledge needed to perform a certain task, or the score of an applicant on a verbal skill test, or the quality of a worker's performance in preparing an advertisement. Numbers are necessary because they facilitate comparison of people; they transmit information more succinctly than words; and they permit statistical manipulation which provides even more information about the selection program. For example, assume that there are 12 applicants for an entry-level position in the loan department of a bank. All are interviewed and complete a brief test on financial terms and financial analysis.

Quantifying the performance of each candidate on each of the two selection instruments is the most practical way of comparing the 12. If scores are not developed, the selection specialist is placed in an extremely complex situation; differences must be determined among the 12 using descriptive information such as "He seemed able to express himself pretty well," or "She knew most of the financial terms but did not seem comfortable judging the risk of the loan." Obviously, when there are such statements about a number of individuals, the difficulty in identifying the most promising of the applicants is enormous.

A comment is necessary at this point to make sure that we do not give you a false impression. We have mentioned that it is important to use selection instruments that generate scores about the characteristics of applicants in making selection decisions. That is not to say, however, that selection decisions are usually made by counting the scores and offering employment only to those who score the highest, even though some maintain that the best results occur if this is done. It is more common for other factors also to enter into the decisions, for example, a desire to balance the demographic composition of the work force or an intuition about a specific applicant. In this type of situation, our position is that these factors should come into play after the applicants have been measured on the selection devices and a group has been identified that is appropriate for the job. These other factors can then aid choice from among this group. Very different results can occur, and much less desirable, if these other factors are used early in selection, before the applicant pool has been measured. In such situations, a great number of errors can be made before the selection instruments are even used.

The problem of measurement for the HR specialist, however, is to ensure that the numbers generated are actually accurate descriptions of the characteristics of the applicant, the job, or the job performance under study. We address specific measurement issues throughout this text, especially in Chapters 3–5. For now we can say that the measurement of many KSAs is difficult and not as precise as we would wish.

Other Factors Affecting Work Performance

A third issue to keep in mind regarding selection programs is that many factors affect work performance. The primary purpose of selection is to enhance the probability of making correct employment decisions—extending offers to those who will perform well in the organization, and not extending job offers to those who will not do as well. Typically any evaluation of the adequacy of the selection program should be made in terms of job performance.

However, it is apparent that the KSAs of those hired are not the sole determiners of job performance. Practitioners and researchers have identified numerous other factors in an organization that affect individual performance. Among these organizational factors are training programs for employees, appraisal and feedback methods, goal-setting procedures, financial compensation systems, work design strategies, supervisory methods, organizational structure, decision-making techniques, work schedules, and sociotechnical work systems design.[30]

The implication of these findings for the evaluation of selection programs is clear. A selection program focuses on a few of the many variables that influence performance. Often it is difficult to assess adequately its effectiveness. At times, a thoughtfully developed program might seem to have only a minimal measurable relationship to performance. It is possible in such cases that one or more of these other variables is adversely affecting performance levels and negating the contribution of the selection program. The conclusion is that it is advisable in judging selection programs to examine several other organizational systems before an accurate diagnosis of deficiencies can be made.

Plan of This Book

The major purpose of this book is to discuss each of the steps necessary in the development of selection programs within organizations. We will concentrate on the characteristics of the data that should be gathered and the types of decisions the HR specialist should make at each step. We incorporate recent research about selection and discuss its implications for the development of HR selection programs. There is not one blueprint for the development of selection programs, and we do not wish to give that impression. The steps we refer to are different stages in the accumulation and processing of information about jobs, individuals, and job performance. At each step the HR specialist must make a number of decisions about the kind of data that are needed and what must be done to these data. The particular selection needs of the organization will dictate the appropriate actions; we hope this book will provide information necessary for evaluating options at each stage.

The book is divided into five parts. The first two chapters present an overview of the selection program and its legal environment. Chapters 3–6 are devoted to the major measurement issues in selection. These chapters provide the basic information necessary to quantify characteristics of applicants, jobs, and job performance within the legal direction of the courts. The next three chapters, 7–9, explain job analysis and the identification of KSAs and other important employee characteristics. This information is the basis of selection. Chapters 10–16 discuss in detail the various selection instruments. They present common forms of each instrument, indicate measurement concerns, and suggest the most appropriate use for each instrument. Chapter 17 summarizes the methods of measuring job performance for use in selection programs.

References

[1] George T. Milkovich and John W. Boudreau, *Personnel/Human Resource Management: A Diagnostic Approach* (Plano, Tex. Business Publications, 1988), 399.

[2] John P. Wanous, "Effects of a Realistic Job Preview on Job Acceptance, Job Attitudes, and Job Survival," *Journal of Applied Psychology* 58 (1973): 327–332.

[3] Steven L. Premack and John P. Wanous, "A Meta-Analysis of Realistic Job Preview Experiments," *Journal of Applied Psychology* 70 (1986): 706–719.

[4] Patrick M. Wright and Gary C. McMahan, "Theoretical Perspectives for Strategic Human Resource Management," *Journal of Management*, 18 (1992): 295–320.

[5] Cynthia A. Lengnick-Hall and Mark L. Lengnick-Hall, "Strategic Human Resources Management: A Review of the Literature," *Academy of Management Review* 13 (1988): 454–470.

[6] Jeffery A. Sonnenfeld and Maury A. Peiperl, "Staffing Policy as a Strategic Response: A Typology of Career Systems," *Academy of Management Review* 13 (1988): 588–600.

[7] Sonnenfeld and Peiperl, "Staffing Policy as a Strategic Response: A Typology of Career Systems," *Academy of Management Review* 594.

[8] Patrick Wright and Scott Snell, "Toward an Integrative View of Human Resource Management," *Human Resource Management Review* 1 (1991): 203–225.

[9] Sara L. Rynes, "Recruitment, Job Choice, and Post-Hire Consequences: A Call for New Research Directions," in *Handbook of Industrial and Organizational Psychology*, 2d ed., Vol. 2., eds. M. D. Dunnette and L. M. Hough (Palo Alto Calif.: Consulting Psychologists Press, 1991), 399–444.

[10] Sara L. Rynes, "Recruitment, Job Choice, and Post-Hire Consequences: A Call for New Research Directions," in *Handbook of Industrial and Organizational Psychology*, 2d ed., Vol. 2., eds. M. D. Dunnette and L. M. Hough (Palo Alto Calif.: Consulting Psychologists Press, 1991); James A. Breaugh, *Recruitment: Science and Practice*, (Boston: PWS-Kent, 1992).

[11] Jean P. Kirnan, John A. Farley, and Kurt Geisinger, "the Relationship Between Recruiting Source, Applicant Quality, and Hire Performance," *Personnel Psychology* 42 (1989): 293–308.

[12] Sara L. Rynes, Robert D. Bretz, Jr., and Barry Gerhart, "The Importance of Recruitment in Job Choice: A Different Way of Looking," *Personnel Psychology* 44 (1991): 487–521.

[13] Rodney E. Wyse, "Attitudes of Selected Black and White College Business Administration Seniors Toward Recruiters and the Recruitment Process," *Dissertation Abstracts International* 33 (1972): 1269–1270A.

[14] Donald P. Rogers and Michael Z. Sincoff, "Favorable Impression Characteristics of the Recruitment Interviewer," *Personnel Psychology* 31 (1978): 495–505.

[15] Steven D. Maurer, Vince Howe, and Thomas W. Lee, "Organizational Recruiting as Marketing Management: An Interdisciplinary Study of Engineering Graduates," *Personnel Psychology* 45 (1992): 807–834.

[16] Richard D. Arvey, Michael E. Gordon, Douglas P. Massengill, and Stephan J. Mussio, "Differential Dropout Rates of Minority and Majority Job Candidates Due to 'Time Lags' Between Selection Procedures," *Personnel Psychology* 28 (1975): 175–180. Rynes et al., "The Importance of Recruitment in Job Choice: A Different Way of Looking."

[17] M. Susan Taylor and Thomas J. Bergmann, "Organizational Recruitment Activities and Applicants' Reactions at Different Stages of the Recruitment Process," *Personnel Psychology* 40 (1987): 261–285.

[18] Wayne F. Gersen, "The Effects of a Demanding Application Process on the Applicant Pool for Teaching Positions," *Dissertation Abstracts International* 36 (1976): 7773A

[19] John P. Wanous, *Organizational Entry: Recruitment, Selection, and Socialization of Newcomers* (Reading, Mass.: Addison-Wesley, 1980), 34.

[20] Wanous, "Effects of a Realistic Job Preview on Job Acceptance, Job Attitudes, and Job Survival," 329.

[21] John P. Wanous, "Installing a realistic Job Preview: Ten Tough Choices," *Personnel Psychology* 42 (1989): 117–134.

[22] Glen M. McEvoy and Wayne F. Cascio, "Strategies for Reducing Employee Turnover: A Meta-Analysis," *Journal of Applied Psychology* 30 (1987): 342–353.

[23] Robert D. Gatewood, Mary A. Gowan, and Gary L. Lautenschlager, "Corporate Image, Recruitment Image, and Initial Job Choice Decision," *Academy of Management Journal*, 36 (1993): 414–427.

[24] Nancy A. Mason and John A. Belt, "Effectiveness of Specificity in Recruitment Advertising," *Journal of Management* 12 (1986): 425–432.

[25] Sara L. Rynes and John W. Boudreau, "College Recruiting in Large Organizations: Practice, Evaluation, and Research Implications," *Personnel Psychology* 39 (1986): 729–757. For related information, see also *Recruiting and Selection Procedures, Personnel Policies Forum Survey No. 146* (Washington, D.C.. The Bureau of National Affairs, May 1988).

[26] Robert M. Guion, "Personnel Assessment, Selection, and Placement," in *Handbook of*

Industrial and Organizational Psychology, 2d ed., Vol. 2, eds. M.D. Donnette and L.M. Hough (Palo Alto, Calif.: Consulting Psychologists Press, 1991), 327–398.

[27] Ibid.

[28] Frank L. Schmidt, John E. Hunter, Alice N. Outerbridge, and Marvin H. Trattner, "The Economic Impact of Job Selection Methods on Size, Productivity, and Payroll Costs of the Federal Work Force: An Empirically Based Demonstration," *Personnel Psychology* 39 (1986): 1–29.

[29] Charles C. Snow and Scott A. Snell, "Staffing as Strategy," in *Personnel Selection in Organizations*, eds. N. Schmitt and W. Borman (San Francisco: Jossey-Bass, 1992), 448–478.

[30] Raymond A. Katzell and Richard A. Guzzo, "Psychological Approaches to Productivity Improvement," *American Psychologist* 38 (1983): 468–472.

2

-business necessity
-stock / flow analyses

Legal Issues in Selection

As we discussed in Chapter 1, the development of a selection program is a formidable task even when we deal only with the measurement issues. It becomes even more complex when we add the legal policies that must be considered. These legal policies influence the records that must be kept on all employment decisions, the determination of fair treatment of all applicants, and the methods for identifying the job relatedness of selection devices.

If these legal policies are not attended to in the development and use of selection programs, the organization will be vulnerable to charges of discrimination. A court judgment against the organization in such a case can be extremely costly. Courts can order organizations to make back pay settlements to individuals they had not hired, to pay punitive damages, to change selection devices and decision rules, and to maintain specified percentages of women and minority group members in future employment patterns. It is imperative that HR specialists have a thorough understanding of the legal guidelines for selection decisions. Actually, every selection program should have the following major objectives: (a) to maximize the probability of making accurate selection decisions about applicants, and (b) to ensure that these selection decisions are carried out in such a manner as to minimize the chance of a judgment of discrimination being made against the organization. The two are not mutually exclusive objectives and overlap considerably in necessary procedures and data. Chapter 1 presented the major considerations important for meeting the first objective. This chapter does the same for the second objective by discussing the following:

1. The basic principles of federal regulation of HR activities

2. An overview of the specific laws and executive orders appropriate to selection

3. The types of evidence that are used in deciding when discrimination has occurred

4. The *1978 Uniform Guidelines on Employee Selection Procedures*

5. Major court cases in selection

6. The most important legal issues to consider in developing and implementing a selection program

Federal Regulation

Many HR specialists incorrectly think that federal laws and directives designed to regulate the actions of organizations are a recent phenomenon in American business. Such regulation can actually be traced back to the creation of the Interstate Commerce Commission (ICC) in 1887. For many years coping with government regulation has been a part of business activities. What is different in recent years is the nature of that regulation. Traditionally, regulation was confined to a given industry. For example, the ICC regulates the railroad and trucking industries and the Federal Communications Commission (FCC) regulates the radio, telephone, and television industries. For the most part these traditional agencies act to increase competition and to prevent a monopoly from developing. One of their major purposes is to promote the well-being of the industry by preventing domination by a few members. In this sense, industry companies are actually the constituents of the regulatory agency because the agency works on their behalf.

Regulatory Model

Newer regulatory agencies have a very different approach. James Ledvinka and Vida Scarpello present a regulatory model of this approach (see Exhibit 2.1). Understanding this model is useful to HR specialists, enabling them to explain and even anticipate actions of regulatory agencies.

The thrust of federal regulation for HR activities is equal employment opportunity (EEO). The major characteristic that differentiates regulation in this area from traditional regulation is that it is not specific to one industry but, rather, is applied to many. Rather than being directed to the well-being of a particular industry, as in the past, regulation is now addressed to social and economic problems, as shown in the left column of Exhibit 2.1. It is important to recognize that EEO regulation is directed to the solution of national issues such as employment inequalities. Also, the constituents of EEO regulatory agencies are not business organizations but rather political and social groups devoted to the solution of employment problems. Realizing this is key to understanding the changes in regulation as well as the apparent disregard of business interests.

The various components of this regulation process are depicted in Exhibit 2.1. As Ledvinka and Scarpello explain the model:

> . . . (1) regulation begins with the social political problems, which cause lawmakers to pass laws; (2) those laws empower agencies to take the regulatory actions that trigger management responses; and (3) the courts oversee this process by settling disputes between the parties to it.[1]

EXHIBIT 2.1   REGULATORY MODEL OF EEO

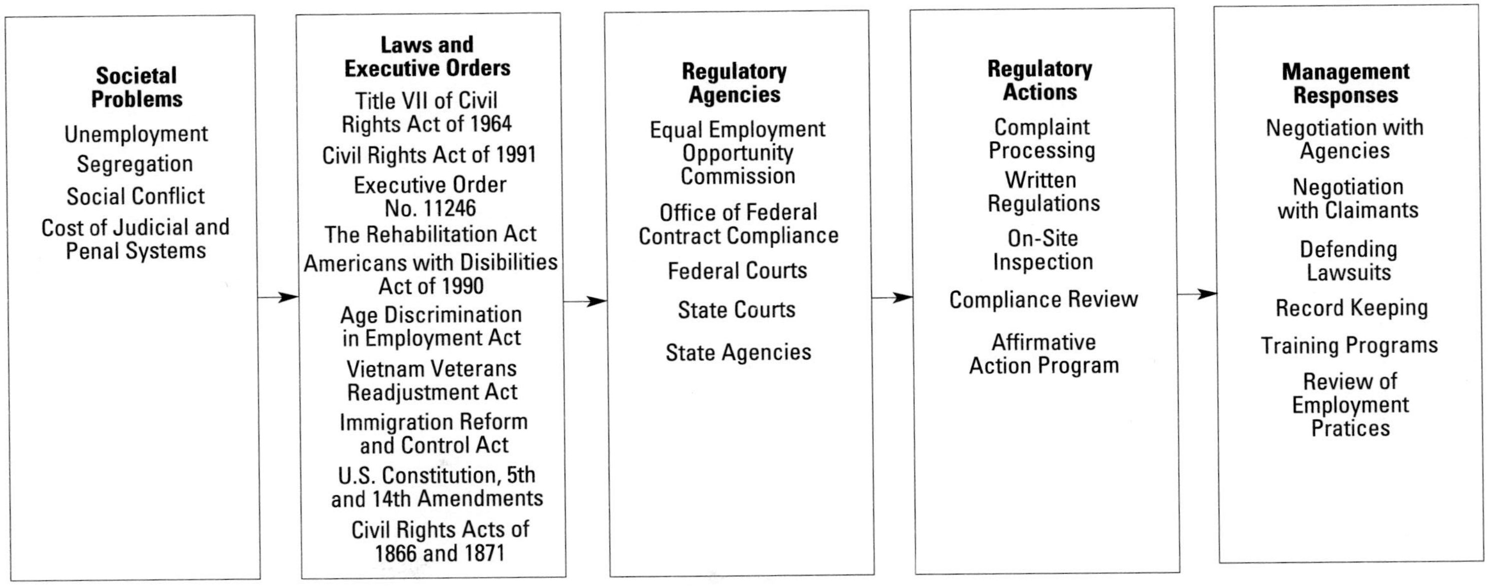

Societal Problems

Unemployment

Segregation

Social Conflict

Cost of Judicial and Penal Systems

Laws and Executive Orders

Title VII of Civil Rights Act of 1964

Civil Rights Act of 1991

Executive Order No. 11246

The Rehabilitation Act

Americans with Disbilities Act of 1990

Age Discrimination in Employment Act

Vietnam Veterans Readjustment Act

Immigration Reform and Control Act

U.S. Constitution, 5th and 14th Amendments

Civil Rights Acts of 1866 and 1871

Regulatory Agencies

Equal Employment Opportunity Commission

Office of Federal Contract Compliance

Federal Courts

State Courts

State Agencies

Regulatory Actions

Complaint Processing

Written Regulations

On-Site Inspection

Compliance Review

Affirmative Action Program

Management Responses

Negotiation with Agencies

Negotiation with Claimants

Defending Lawsuits

Record Keeping

Training Programs

Review of Employment Pratices

SOURCE: Adapted from James Ledvinka, and Vida G. Scarpello, *Federal Regulation of Personel and Human resources Management Second Edition* (Boston: PWS-Kent Publishing Co., 1991), P. 18.

To fully understand EEO regulation it is necessary, therefore, to be familiar with two factors: (1) the laws and executive orders that state general principles and empower regulatory agencies, and (2) court decisions that interpret these general principles in specific situations. We treat both of these topics, starting with the laws and directives and discussing the court cases later in the chapter.

EEO Laws and Executive Orders

EEO laws are federal laws whose purpose is the elimination of discrimination in HR management decisions. EEO executive orders are statements made by the executive branch of the government intended for the same purpose but aimed at organizations that do business directly with the government. The scope of both EEO laws and executive orders is broader than selection decisions, although selection decisions have received a great deal of publicity, especially early in the history of the enforcement of EEO laws.

Ledvinka and Scarpello list 22 separate federal laws and execute orders that taken together would be considered EEO law.[2] Additional ones have been added recently. Most of these contain directives for several areas of HR employment decisions. In this book we examine those that have the most impact on selection while acknowledging that they have broader impact on HR management. Table 2.1 lists eleven laws and one order with a brief summary of the major provisions of each.

Title VII Civil Rights Acts of 1964   Under Title VII private employers, unions, employment agencies, joint labor-management committees that direct apprenticeship and training programs, and state and federal governments are prohibited from discriminating on the basis of *sex, race, color, religion,* or *national origin.* This law has been amended several times. In 1972 enforcement powers were strengthened and coverage was expanded to include governmental and educational system employers as well as private employers with more than 15 employees. A 1978 amendment prohibited discrimination based on pregnancy, childbirth, or related conditions. The only employers not covered by Title VII are private clubs, religious organizations, and places of employment connected with an Indian reservation.

The Equal Employment Opportunity Commission (EEOC) is the enforcement agency for Title VII. Basically it acts in response to a charge of discrimination filed by one of the EEOC commissioners, by an aggrieved person or someone acting on behalf of an aggrieved person. In most cases, the charge of discrimination must be filed within 180 days of the alleged act. After the EEOC has assumed jurisdiction, the first step is the no-fault settlement attempt, an invitation to the accused to settle the case without an admission of guilt. If this option is not accepted, the case will be taken to the second step, that of investigation. During this period the employer is prohibited from destroying any records related to the charge, and is invited to submit a position paper regarding the charge, which becomes part of the investigatory data. At the completion of this phase, the district director of EEOC issues a statement of "probable cause"

TABLE 2.1	MAJOR EEO LAWS REGARDING SELECTION	
Law	**Demographic Characteristics**	**Employers Covered**
Title VII Civil Rights Act of 1964	Race, color, religion, sex, or national origin	Private employers with at least 15 employees, governments, unions, employment agencies, employers receiving federal assistance
Civil rights Act of 1991	Race, color, religion, sex, or national origin	Same as Title VII
Executive Order No. 11246	Race, color, religion, sex, or national orgin	Federal contractors and subcontractors
Age Discrimination in Employment Act of 1967	Age (over 40 years)	Private employers, governments, unions, employment agencies
The Rehabilitation Act of 1973	Physical and mental disability	Federal contractors, federal government
Americans with Disability Act of 1990	Physical and mental disability	Private employers, labor unions, employment agencies
Vietnam Veterans Readjustment Act of 1974	Vietnam era veterans, disabled veterans	Federal contractors, federal government
Immigration Reform and Control Act of 1986	Citizenship, national origin	Private employers with 4 employees, governments
U.S. Constitution Fifth Amendment	All demographic characteristics	Federal government
U.S. Constitution Fourteenth Amendment	All demographic characteristics	State and local governments
Civil Rights Act of 1866	Race, national and ethnic origin	Private employers, unions, employment agencies
Civil Rights Act of 1871	All demographic characteristics	State and local governments

or "no probable cause." In the case of a "probable cause" decision, an attempt is made at conciliation between the two parties. This usually involves some major concessions on the part of the employer regarding the employment practice under question. If it fails to obtain a conciliation agreement, the EEOC can either undertake litigation itself or issue a right-to-sue notice to the charging party, informing this party that he or she may bring his or her own action in federal court. However, the individual may file a private suit even without an EEOC right-to-sue notice.

Civil Rights Act of 1991　This act amends the Civil Rights Act of 1964 and strengthens other federal civil rights laws. A major impetus for its passage was the Supreme Court's decision in *Wards Cove Packing Co. v. Atonio*, (1989), which we discuss later in the chapter. This decision significantly increased the plaintiff's burden of proof in many discrimination cases. Frank Landy, past president of the American Psychological Association's Society for Industrial and Organizational Psychology division, interpreted the *Wards Cove* decision this way:

> This turned out to be a big deal. It meant the plaintiffs all of a sudden were responsible for doing studies of various kinds, gathering data, or demonstrating a problem with the test. Part of the previous logic had been that the person most able to bear the burden of litigation—the employer—ought to have the burden . . . [it] greatly increased the cost and difficulty . . . of bringing a successful civil rights suit.[3]

Therefore, one major part of this act was to codify the principles of proof established in cases previous to *Wards Cove* and, in essence, to negate the Supreme Court's opinion in *Wards Cove*.

This act also allows victims of intentional discrimination, including sexual harassment, to sue for both compensatory and punitive damages. Punitive damages may be recovered against a respondent (but not a government or its agency) if the complainant demonstrates that the respondent engaged in a discriminatory practice with malice or "reckless indifference." The sum of compensatory damages is capped at between $50,000 and $300,000 depending on the number of employees with the company.

Another part of the act, section 106 (1), makes it unlawful for an employer "in connection with the selection or referral of applicants or candidates for employment or promotion, to adjust the scores of, use different cutoff scores for, or otherwise alter the results of, employment-related tests on the basis of race, color, religion, sex, or national origin,"[4] This prohibits race norming: the practice of ranking test scores of minorities separately from nonminorities, choosing high scorers within each group and thereby creating or maintaining a more diverse work force.

Selection specialists have been mixed in their views of norming. Supporters point to the major benefit of helping employers hire a qualified but diverse work force backed by the opinion that selection tests measure no more than 25 percent of how well people perform in jobs.[5] Detractors have pointed out that minorities usually score lower than nonminorities on many valid selection tests and any adjustment in the ranking of applicants can be expected to lower overall job performance.

Title II of the act is based on Congress's findings that even though the number of women and minorities in the work force has grown dramatically, they continue to be underrepresented in management and decision-making positions. The so-called glass ceiling effect, then, refers to artificial barriers that impede their advancement to these higher positions. Under the act, a Glass Ceiling Commission was established to study the manner in which business fills these higher positions, the developmental and skill-enhancing practices used to foster necessary qualifications for advancement into these positions, and the compensation programs and reward structures utilized in the workplace. Finally, the act allows for more extensive use of jury trials, and addresses issues such as coverage of government employees (Title III), awarding of expert fees, and coverage of U.S. citizens in foreign countries.

Executive Order 11246   This order is directed toward contractors doing business with the federal government. Originally enacted in 1965 and amended in 1968, it prohibits the same discriminatory acts as Title VII. In addition, it requires contractors to develop *affirmative action plans.* These are formal, specific HR programs that are designed to increase the participation of protected groups. We discuss affirmative action plans later in the chapter. An affirmative action program is not a requirement of Title VII.

Enforcement of executive orders is the responsibility of the Department of Labor, specifically the Office of Federal Contract Compliance Programs (OFCCP). Investigations by the OFCCP are not dependent on charges of discrimination being filed but, instead, are a product of the OFCCP's administrative review of contractors. The review usually begins with a request to the contractor to forward the affirmative action plan. When this is received an office review and an on-site visit are conducted. If deficiencies are found, the contractor is usually informed of them by the OFCCP and an attempt is made to adjust them. If the attempt fails, a formal deficiency letter is drawn up and formal conciliation attempts are undertaken. If these fail, the OFCCP issues a show-cause letter formally stating that the contractor is not in compliance with the executive order. Noncompliance can adversely affect the contractor's participation in government business. If the deficiencies are not corrected at this time, an administrative hearing procedure before an administrative-law judge can be initiated. The whole procedure can take several years. The government's position is that during this time it can deny the contractor any two contracts, regardless of total size.

Age Discrimination in Employment Act of 1967 (ADEA)   This act, amended in 1978, 1984, 1986, and 1987, has the intention of promoting employment of older persons based on their ability and eliminating barriers to employment based on age. The underlying premise of the act is that there are large individual differences among workers of all ages; some older workers are superior to some young workers. Age, therefore, is not a valid indicator of ability to perform. The act prohibits discrimination against individuals who are 40 years old or older. It also, in essence, has prohibited mandatory retirement policies, except as applied to executives who are guaranteed an annual retirement compensation of $44,000. This act applies to private industry, federal and state governments, employment agencies, and labor organizations.

Enforcement of the ADEA resides in the EEOC, and is usually initiated by the filing of a charge of discrimination. However, the EEOC has the authority to review organizations when there is no charge. The act also provides for trial by jury. This is thought to be potentially beneficial to the person bringing suit because the plaintiff's age and other personal characteristics may elicit a sympathetic reaction from the jury.

The Rehabilitation Act of 1973   This act, directed toward the federal government and federal contractors, requires both nondiscrimination in employment practices and also affirmative action toward the disabled. The Americans with Disabilities Act (ADA) of 1990, which we discuss next, essentially replaces the Rehabilitation Act whose major importance is that its wording is very similar to critical sections of the ADA. Therefore, court decisions regarding the Rehabilitation Act have important bearing on the ADA of 1990.

Americans with Disabilities Act of 1990   This act, which is expected to have a major impact on selection, prohibits discrimination against qualified people with disabilities in all areas of employment. Title I, which addresses employment and is enforced by the EEOC, went into effect July 1992 for employers with 25 or more workers. July 1994 is the effective date for employers of 15 or more employees.

An individual with a disability is someone who (1) has a physical or mental impairment that substantially limits one or more major life activities, (2) has a record of such an impairment, or (3) is regarded as having such an impairment. It is estimated that as much as 25 percent of the labor force and at least 900 disabilities are covered under the act.[6] It is worth noting that some groups are specifically excluded under ADA: homosexuals, bisexuals, transvestites, transsexuals, pedophiles, exhibitionists, voyeurists, other sexual behavior disorders, compulsive gamblers, kleptomaniacs, pyromaniacs, and those currently using illegal drugs. Furthermore, active alcoholics who cannot perform their job duties or who present a threat to the safety or property of others are excluded. However, those individuals who have been rehabilitated and are no longer using drugs are covered.

ADA's impact on selection   ADA prohibits private employers, employment agencies, labor organizations, and joint labor-management committees from discriminating against a "qualified individual with a disability" in regard to applying for a job, hiring, advancement, termination, compensation, training, or any other terms, conditions, or privileges of employment.[7]

Interpreting potential effects of the ADA on HR selection necessitates further defining "qualified individual with a disability." Qualified refers to an individual with a disability who, *with or without reasonable accommodation,* can perform the "essential functions" of the employment position held or desired. What exactly are "essential functions"? Although not specifically defined, they are fundamental job duties of the position. It is up to the employer to determine what those essential functions are. Donna Denning has pointed out that the concept of essential functions means that the job can no longer be considered only as it exists—the traditional premise of job analysis—but also as the job might exist with accommodation.[8]

The ADA also prohibits the use of qualification standards, employment tests, or selection criteria that tend to screen out individuals with disabilities unless the standard is job-related and consistent with business necessity. Specifically, Section 102 states that tests must be selected and administered to ensure that "test results accurately reflect the skills, aptitude, or whatever other factor . . . that such test purports to measure, rather than reflecting the [impairment]."[9] This may require that the test administration be modified in accordance with the disability of the applicant.

Selection Testing Alternatives for ADA It is important that employers provide enough employment test information to applicants to help them decide if they will require accommodations. This information should be exchanged early in the application process[10] and should include what is required by the test, how information is presented, response format, and time limits. Test accommodation may be relatively simple and inexpensive, such as larger type for impaired sight, or it may require greater effort and/or cost to the employer, especially with regard to determining whether the accommodation (for instance, increasing time for speed tests) compromises the psychometric properties of the test. In other words, reliability, validity, and norms of the test could be significantly altered due to an accommodation. If the employer determines that accommodation of the existing testing procedure is not reasonable, substitute methods for determining KSAs should be explored. Some of these methods might include structured interviews, work samples, job trials, rehabilitation expert evaluation, or certificates and references.

The ADA also prohibits pre-employment inquiries about a person's disability. If a disability is obvious to the employer, questions about the nature or severity of the disability can't be asked unless they are limited to the performance of specific job-related functions. This disallowance, in effect, places responsibility on the disabled person to bring any relevant disability to the employer's attention. However, employers may ask that individuals with disabilities request in advance any accommodations necessary to take employment tests. Generally, the disabled person is responsible for informing the employer that accommodation is needed. Pre-employment medical examinations are restricted to those that are job related, consistent with business necessity, and undergone only after an employment offer has been made to the applicant. Furthermore, the employment offer may be contingent on the results of the examination *only* if the examination is required of all employees, regardless of disability, and if the information obtained is kept confidential and maintained in separate files. It is important to note that the ADA does not consider drug testing a medical examination.

Reasonable Accommodation Key to understanding a major purpose of the ADA, employers are required to make "reasonable accommodation" to physical or mental limitations of an otherwise qualified individual with a disability unless such accommodation would impose an "undue hardship" on the business. Common examples of reasonable accommodation are making facilities readily accessible (ramps, larger rest rooms); job restructuring; alterations in work schedules or equipment; job reassignment; modifications of examinations and training materials; and providing interpreters. Although there exist no hard and fast rules concerning whether an accommodation would impose an undue hardship, generally the nature and cost of the accommodation as well as the size, type, and finances of the specific facility and those of the parent employer are considered. Accommodation will be judged on a case-by-case basis and will be related to both the job itself and the nature of a disability.

As we mentioned, reasonable accommodation is not specifically defined in the ADA and the reasonableness of the accommodation is judged against imposition of an undue hardship. Elliot Shaller has offered his opinion of requirements that is based on legislative history and the interpretation of the Rehabilitation Act of 1973 as well as other state statutes.[11] First, an employer is not required to create a job for a disabled employee or maintain quotas. Second, reasonable accommodation does not require preferences be awarded to persons with disabilities. However, if the choice is between a disabled individual who without reasonable accommodation cannot perform a task as fast or well as a nondisabled person but with accommodation could perform better, the employer risks ADA liability if the nondisabled applicant is hired. Third, an employer is not required to hire a "shadow" employee, someone who actually performs the majority of essential functions of the disabled employee's position. Fourth, if an employee can be accommodated by a relatively simple and inexpensive redesign or piece of equipment, the employer will likely be required to make such accommodation.

The Vietnam Era Veterans Readjustment Act of 1974 This act, also under the direction of the Department of Labor (OFCCP), relates only to government contractors. Veterans covered are either those who served during the Vietnam War (not necessarily in Vietnam, however), defined as the period between August 5,1964, and May 7, 1975, or those who have a compensable disability rated at 30 percent or more by the Veterans Administration.

A contractor is required under the act to list all employment openings at the local office of the state employment agency. These listings must be made before, or at least at the same time as, others being released through any other recruitment mechanism. Compliance reviews may be made by the OFCCP even without the filing of a charge. Enforcement can be through court ruling or administrative sanctions, which can include such penalties as termination of or debarment from contracts, or the withholding of progress payments.

Immigration Reform and Control Act of 1986 Employers for the first time face civil and criminal sanctions for knowingly employing any alien not authorized to work in the United States. Antidiscrimination provisions were added to address concern that the employer sanctions might lead to discrimination against "foreign-looking" job applicants.

Regarding employment, the act states that it is unlawful for a person or other entity to hire or continue to employ an alien knowing that the alien is unauthorized. The company is required to verify authorization by attesting that it has examined any of the following documents produced by the individual being employed: a U.S. passport, certificate of U.S. citizenship, certificate of naturalization, unexpired foreign passport with the proper endorsement of the attorney general, resident alien card, or specified combinations of social security card, certificate of birth in the United States, documentation evidencing authorization of employment in the United States, driver's license, and documentation of personal identity.[12] A company has complied with these requirements "if the document submitted by the individual reasonably appears on its face to be genuine."[13]

Regarding discrimination, rules issued by the Department of Justice ban only those immigration-related employment practices in which an employer "knowingly and intentionally" discriminates.[14] In terms we will explain later in this section, unintentional discrimination that creates adverse impact is not covered by this act. Also, it is not an unfair employment practice, to prefer to select, recruit, etc., an individual who is a citizen or national of the United States over another individual who is a noncitizen if the two individuals are equally qualified. The antidiscrimination provisions apply to any employer with four or more employees.

Complaints are processed by the Office of Special Counsel for Unfair Immigration-Related Employment Practice in the Justice Department. Complaints must be filed within 180 days of discriminatory action and the special counsel must investigate each charge within 120 days. All cases are heard by an administrative-law judge. An employer guilty of discrimination may be assessed back pay for up to two years, along with civil fines of up to $2,000 for subsequent violations.

Constitutional Amendments and Civil Rights Acts of 1866 and 1871 In addition to these recent EEO statutes, discrimination complaints can be pursued on the basis of the Fifth and Fourteenth Amendments to the Constitution and the Civil Rights Acts of 1866 and 1871, which were part of reconstruction after the Civil War. Both constitutional amendments prohibit the deprivation of employment rights without due process. The Fifth covers the federal government and the Fourteenth addresses state and local governments. Unlike the EEO statutes, protection under these amendments applies to all citizens, not only to specific demographic groups. Therefore, discrimination charges can be filed for actions not covered by EEO statutes, for example, discrimination against homosexuals. Pursuit of a charge requires that the plaintiff establish discriminatory intent by the accused, not merely unequal effects of employment actions. This, of course, is often difficult to do.

The Civil Rights Act of 1866 states that "all persons . . . shall have the same right, to make and enforce contracts . . . as is enjoyed by white citizens. . . ."[15] Because of this wording, discrimination charges have been limited to racial and, to a lesser extent, ethnic and national background complaints. Sexual, religious, and other forms of discrimination are not considered to be appropriate. Charges can be filed against private employers, unions, and employment agencies. Whereas Title VII requires a minimum of 15 employees in an organization, no such limitation exists with this act. The Civil Rights Act of 1871 is very similar to provisions of the Fourteenth Amendment. By its wording, it applies to state and local governments. It does not apply to purely private business or federal agencies unless there is state involvement in the questioned employment practices. Thus this act has been applied to police and fire departments, public schools, colleges, hospitals, and state agencies. A broad range of bases for discrimination is applicable, for example, ethnicity, gender, sex, religion, age, sexual preference, citizenship, physical attributes.

This brief review of the important EEO laws highlights the major points of the regulatory model. These laws are clearly addressed to societal problems; they focus on safeguarding the fair treatment in employment of groups that traditionally have not had access to the American dream of success. These laws created agencies designed to monitor the compliance of organizations in various industries and to represent the claims of individuals who feel they were unfairly treated. Such actions require the employment practices of organizations to be evaluated. In most cases the well-being of the organization itself is not of major concern.

Employment Discrimination

The previously cited laws and orders clearly prohibit discrimination in selection and other HR actions. The difficulty for managers of organizations is to identify when discrimination is present. As we have said, laws state principles. Putting these principles into operation is another step. As the regulatory model indicates, this step is partially based on court decisions in discrimination cases and partially on actions by regulatory agencies such as the EEOC. The court decisions set legal precedent and yield specific comments about the treatment of evidence of alleged discrimination in specific situations. These legal precedents serve as benchmarks for subsequent legal interpretation. In 1978 the EEOC published the *Uniform Guidelines on Employee Selection Procedures* which, while being neither law nor court decisions, are important because they represent the joint statement of the agencies empowered by law to enforce the EEO laws. The *Uniform Guidelines* describe what evidence will be considered in judging discrimination and how an employer may defend a selection program. In addition, the guidelines are given "great deference" by the courts when considering discrimination cases. We now discuss the definition and evidence of discrimination.

Discrimination Defined

Disparate Treatment The first form of discrimination is *disparate treatment.* This form of discrimination describes those situations in which different standards are applied to various groups of individuals even though there may not be an explicit statement of intentional prejudice. Examples are such practices as not hiring women with young children while hiring men with such children, or hiring minority group members to fill cleaning jobs in a restaurant while similarly qualified whites are made cashiers or waiters. The effect of such decisions, even though they may be prompted by the employer's idea of good business practice, is to subject a specific group to negative treatment because of a personal characteristic.

Adverse Impact The second form of discrimination is that of *adverse impact.* In this form organizational selection standards are applied uniformly to all groups of applicants, but the net result of these standards is to produce differences in the selection of various groups. Two classic examples of such discrimination are the requirement of a high school diploma, which had been used extensively for entry-level positions, and of height minimums, for example 5′6″, which have been used for police and some manual labor positions. Both standards are usually applied to all individual applicants consistently, and, therefore, at first might not seem to be discriminatory.

The problem is that such standards have been demonstrated to have the effect of disqualifying from employment a much larger percentage of some groups than others. For example, traditionally, more whites have high school diplomas than do most minority groups. Therefore, the requirement of a diploma would limit the percentage of minority applicants in comparison to white applicants. Similarly, a minimum height requirement usually limits the number of women, Orientals, and Hispanics who would be eligible to apply even though they otherwise could be found to be acceptable for employment. A number of frequently used and, seemingly valid, selection requirements have been the subject of adverse impact discrimination charges, including arrest records, type of military discharge, various educational degrees, scores on some tests and interviews, years of previous work experience, and financial history. The use of each of these has been linked to the disqualification of a high percentage of at least one demographic group of applicants.

Evidence Required

One major consequence of these two forms of employment discrimination is their differential effect on both plaintiffs and defendants when charges are brought to court. That is to say that the legal burdens for both plaintiffs and defendants are different depending on whether the case is heard as disparate treatment or adverse impact discrimination. In discussing this, we frame our points within Title VII litigation because that is the most prevalent.

In both types of cases there is a logical sequence of events that should occur. To start, the burden of proof is on the plaintiff to present arguments and facts that, if not rebutted, would convince the judge or jury hearing the case that the employer has engaged in practices in violation of Title VII. If this is done, the plaintiff is said to have established a *prima facie case* of discrimination. If this is not done, the case should be dismissed for lack of grounds. Once a prima facie case has been established, the burden of proof switches to the defendant. It is necessary to present arguments and facts that rebut the charges and provide a legally permissible explanation for the employment practices under question. If this is done, the burden shifts back to the plaintiff who has a final opportunity to attack the defendant's evidence and otherwise challenge previous arguments.

Disparate Treatment Cases   As indicated in Table 2.2, there are major differences in specific data, evidence, and arguments that must be made during this general trial process for the two types of discrimination cases. For disparate treatment cases, a guideline for establishing a prima facie case was specified in the *McDonnell Douglas v. Green (1973)* case and is commonly known as the McDonnell Douglas rule. In this the plaintiff must show that the following conditions exist:

1. He or she belongs to a racial minority;

2. He or she applied and was qualified for a job for which the company was seeking applicants;

3. Despite these qualifications, he or she was rejected;

4. After this rejection, the position remained open and the employer continued to seek applicants from persons of the complainant's qualifications.[16]

This rule reflects a basic premise of disparate treatment cases: the employer's *intention* to discriminate must be shown. The demonstration that a specific, qualified member of a demographic group was passed over and a member of a different demographic group, with equal or fewer qualifications, was selected, suffices to prove intention if not rebutted.

If intent to discriminate is shown, in order to rebut, the employer must provide a legitimate, nondiscriminatory reason for rejecting the plaintiff. This is relatively easy to do. For example, in the McDonnell Douglas case, the reason was that Green had participated in a protest by illegally stalling his car during a shift change at the McDonnell Douglas plant. In other cases, arguments have been made and accepted that the qualifications of the plaintiff were inferior to those of individuals selected. In general, if the argument is clear and specific, the employer meets its burden of proof. The employer does not have to persuade the judge that it actually used this as the basis for rejecting the plaintiff. It is up to the plaintiff to prove that the employer did *not* use it. To the extent that the employer's reasons include some objective data, the argument is usually more acceptable. The argument is less acceptable, however, if the reasons are based on subjective judgments, especially if these are made without clear definition and procedures.

If the company is successful, the plaintiff must then refute these statements. In essence this means that he or she must show that the company's defense is really a pretense and that discrimination was being practiced. Examples of evidence that courts have accepted are statements made by company managers which were sexual or racial slurs, records that the company's treatment of the plaintiff was inconsistent with that of individuals of other demographic groups, and statistics showing the demographic group of the plaintiff was underrepresented in the company's work force. If the data presented are not acceptable, the plaintiff is unsuccessful in countering the defense of the company.

Adverse Impact Cases   In trials of this form of discrimination, as also shown in Table 2.2, the focus for establishing a prima facie case shifts from the intention of the employer to an evaluation of the impact of an employment decision on various demographic groups. That is, evidence mainly addresses whether or not various groups have been affected in the same manner by employment decisions. For this reason, statistical data are a major part of these cases. Intention of the employer is normally not addressed, only the results of decisions. Statistics, which we discuss in the following section, are used to analyze the pattern of selection decisions over a period of time. If these analyses do, in fact, indicate that a pattern of adverse impact has occurred, the prima facie case has been established.

Once a prima facie case has been accepted, the company has the opportunity of presenting evidence to show that the results of the selection process in question are job-related and not, therefore, illegal discrimination. To do this,

TABLE 2.2	PRESENTATION OF EVIDENCE IN TITLE VII DISCRIMINATION CASES	

Sequence of Steps	Disparate Treatment	Adverse Impact

Plaintiff	demonstrates that
	    he/she belongs to a minority
	    he/she applied and was qualified
	      for the job
	    he/she was rejected by the
	      company
	    the job remained open
		demonstrates statistically that this HRM practice affects various groups differently in comparison to their distribution in the relevant labor market

Defendant	provides a clear and specific job-based explanation for actions	demonstrates at least one or the
		    following:
		    business necessity
		    bona fide occupational qualifica-
		      tion
		    validation data

Plaintiff	proves that the defendant's argument is a pretext and the true reason for rejection was prejudice	proves that an alternative practice is available which has less adverse impact

the company traditionally has three options: proving *business necessity, bona fide occupational qualifications* (BFOQ), or *validity.*

We have discussed validation generally in Chapter 1 and go into detail about its procedures in Chapter 5. The requirements for the other two defenses are very strict and have application in limited cases. Business necessity has been viewed by the courts primarily in terms of safety to either workers or customers of the organization. It is necessary to present evidence that if the selection requirement were not used, the risk to members of these groups would be substantially raised. Ordinarily, business necessity has not been judged by the courts in terms of economic costs or profits. Therefore, demonstrating that not using the selection requirement would result in great cost or loss of business to the firm has not been acceptable.

A BFOQ defense means that *no* person of a particular sex, race, color, religion, or national origin can adequately perform the given job. This defense has mainly been related to sex or religious discrimination and has been applied to jobs such as rest room attendants and church ministers and administrators. Conceptually, it would be very difficult to frame a BFOQ defense for race, color, or national origin.

If the company is successful in defending the adverse impact, the plaintiff has a chance to present another argument to refute this defense. The nature of this is to establish there is another selection procedure that could be used which would have less adverse impact. This topic is not well developed, however, because courts seldom get to this stage in the weighing of evidence.

As we mentioned in our discussion of the Civil Rights Act of 1991, the Supreme Court decision made in June 1989 concerning the *Wards Cove Packing*

Company, Inc. et al., Petitioners v. Frank Atonio et al. case (No. 87-1387) marked a major change in the evidence needed by both parties in adverse impact cases. The court held that the defendant's burden of proof should be less demanding than what has traditionally been required, and more similar to evidence characteristic of disparate treatment. This allowed organizations to use defenses other than the ones cited previously. Also, the court stated that a stronger burden of proof should be required of the plaintiff to "persuade" the court of discrimination. The effect of this decision was to greatly increase the difficulty of the plaintiff in proving that discrimination occurred. The Civil Rights Act of 1991 returned the burden of proof of both the plaintiff and the defendant to that specified previously in this section, specifically negating the *Wards Cove v. Atonio* decision.

The Use of Statistics

As should be evident from the previous discussion, statistics are used in cases of both forms of discrimination. In disparate treatment cases, statistics are mainly used to assist the plaintiff in rebutting the defendant's explanation of the selection practice under question. In adverse impact cases, statistics are most often used by the plaintiff in demonstrating that a pattern of adverse effect has occurred. There are two main types of statistics that have been used: *stock* and *flow* statistics.

Stock Statistics   Statistics are used in discrimination cases mainly to compare proportions of various demographic groups on the results of selection decisions. Stock statistics compare groups at one point in time. For example, the most common stock comparison is between the percentage of a specific demographic group in the work force of the organization and the percentage of that same demographic group in an appropriate comparison group, such as total applicants or the general, available labor force. Here is a specific example:

$$\frac{\text{number of women managers in organization}}{\text{total number of managers in organization}} \quad \text{vs.} \quad \frac{\text{number of appropriately skilled women managers in labor force}}{\text{total number of appropriately skilled managers in labor force}}$$

If the percentage of women managers in the company's work force is significantly smaller than the percentage in the comparison group, in this case the labor force, then evidence of discrimination in selection practices exists.

Relevant Labor Market   The term that is applied to the comparison group is relevant labor market (RLM). To better understand the various statistical comparisons that are used in discrimination cases, it is important to know more about the concept of RLM.

EEO laws require employers to keep and update various records about the composition of their work force and the results of managerial decisions. One of

EXHIBIT 2.2　　FORM EEO-1

441:274　　　　FEDERAL LAW: REPORTS AND RECORDS　　　　No. 591
SF 100 Page 2

Section D—Employment Data

Employment at this establishment—Report all permanent full-time or part-time employees including apprentices and on-the-job trainees unless specifically excluded as a set forth in the instructions. Enter the appropriate figures on all lines and in all columns. Blank spaces will be considered as zeros.

JOB CATEGORIES		Number of employees										
		OVERALL TOTALS (SUM OF COL. B THRU K)	Male					Female				
			WHITE (NOT OF HISPANIC ORIGIN)	BLACK (NOT OF HISPANIC ORIGIN)	HISPANIC	ASIAN OR PACIFIC ISLANDER	AMERICAN INDIAN OR ALASKAN NATIVE	WHITE (NOT OF HISPANIC ORIGIN)	BLACK (NOT OF HISPANIC ORIGIN)	HISPANIC	ASIAN OR PACIFIC ISLANDER	AMERICAN INDIAN OR ALASKAN NATIVE
		A	B	C	D	E	F	G	H	I	J	K
Officials and Managers	1											
Professionals	2											
Technicians	3											
Sales Workers	4											
Office and Clerical	5											
Craft Workers (Skilled)	6											
Operatives (Semi-Skilled)	7											
Laborers (Unskilled)	8											
Service Workers	9											
Total	10											
Total employment reported in previous EEO-1 report	11											

(The trainees below should also be included in the figures for the appropriate occupational categories above)

Formal on-the-job trainees	White collar	12											
	Production	13											

NOTE: Omit questions 1 and 2 on the Consolidated Report.
1. Date(s) of payroll period used:　　　　　2. Does this establishment employ apprentices?
　　　　　　　　　　　　　　　　　　　　　1. ☐ Yes　2. ☐ No

SOURCE: Bureau of National Affairs, Inc., Policy and Practice Series: Fair Employment Practices, section 441-273.

these records is Form EEO-l (see Exhibit 2.2), which must be filed only by employers with 100 or more employees. In this form, data must be reported for nine specific job categories as well as for the total organization. For each job category, the company must report the number of individuals in each demographic group that constitutes at least 2 percent of the labor market for that job category. Therefore, the specific demographic groups reported may vary for firms in different parts of the country.

In stock analyses, the data from Form EEO-l, or similar data, are compared to the RLM and this result is used as evidence. It is in this context that the RLM becomes important. The RLM has two components: geographical location and skill level. The geographical location is that region from which applicants for the specific job category would likely come, absent any discrimination.[17] In general, determination of this region depends on the scope of the employer's recruiting efforts, the interest among prospective employees in working for the employer in question, and the availability of public transportation.[18] Typically, the geographic region will be its smallest for lower-paying jobs and its broadest, sometimes nationwide, for high-level executive positions.

Within a region there is still the issue of who shall be counted. At this point, skill level becomes important. Skill level means the special qualifications needed to fill a specific job. Obviously, the number of individuals qualified to serve as electrical engineers is greatly different from that in the general population. The courts recognize that, in calculating stock statistics, it would not be relevant to compare the demographic composition of the company in each of the nine EEO-1 job categories with that of the population as a whole. In general, as the skill level of the job category increases, the percentage of minorities in that job category decreases. Table 2.3 describes some of the relevant labor markets that have been used in selection discrimination cases.

The labor market chosen for comparison has frequently been the subject of intensive debate between plaintiffs and defendants in court cases. This is because the percentage of various demographic groups can change radically depending on which combination of geographical region and skill level is used. For example, the percentage of female engineers nationally is 4.4, whereas the percentage of female engineers in the Atlanta metropolitan area is 6.4 and the percentage of female clerks is 77.4.

The difficulty in using a relevant labor market is an operational one of gathering the appropriate data. In the large majority of cases, existing data in the form of census, chamber of commerce, industry, and similar reports are used. In these reports, geographical units are usually reported in three forms: (1) the nation, (2) a state, or (3) Standard Metropolitan Statistical Area (SMSA), which is the region surrounding a central city or town. Appropriate skill level is expressed in terms of numbers reported as holding or qualified to hold specific jobs. In the U.S. census data, several different types of sales, technician, managerial, and so on, jobs are reported. The selection of an RLM, in many cases, becomes a judgment as to the most appropriate geographical region and the most similar types of jobs available in existing data sources.

Flow Statistics   The second type of statistics used are referred to as flow statistics. The term is used because this type of statistic compares proportions taken at two points in time. A common flow statistic in selection is the following:

$$\frac{\text{number of minority applicants selected}}{\text{number of minority applicants}} \quad \text{vs.} \quad \frac{\text{number of nonminority applicants selected}}{\text{number of nonminority applicants}}$$

The comparison is made from numbers gathered at two different points in time, before and after selection has taken place. The purpose of the comparison is obviously to determine how minority members fared in the selection process in comparison to nonminority members. If the percentage for the minority group is significantly smaller than the percentage for the nonminority group, evidence of discrimination is present. Because the comparison is made between groups that are both being acted upon by the company, the RLM is usually not an issue.

TABLE 2.3	SOME RELEVANT LABOR MARKETS USED FOR STATISTICAL COMPARISONS

General population data
Labor force data (civilian, nonfarm, or total)
Qualified labor market data
Actual applicant flow data
Qualified actual applicant flow data
Employer's own work force composition (promotion cases)
Employer's own qualified and interested work force composition (promotion cases)

Statistical Tests of Significance   In making the comparison between the proportions previously discussed, the final step is for the court to decide whether any difference between the proportions is important enough to matter. This is the crux of deciding whether evidence of discrimination exists or not. If the proportions are close enough, insufficient evidence exists and the case should be dropped. If the proportions are different enough, sufficient evidence exists. To assist in making this decision, the courts have used statistical tests. The most commonly used tests are the *Four-Fifths Rule* and the *Standard Deviation Rule*, which are applied to analyses of demographic groups that constitute at least 2 percent of the labor force.

The Four-Fifths Rule uses the basic flow statistic that was previously explained:

$$\frac{\text{number of minority applicants selected}}{\text{number of minority applicants}} \quad \text{vs.} \quad \frac{\text{number of nonminority applicants selected}}{\text{number of nonminority applicants}}$$

The ratio of any group must be at least 80 percent of the *ratio of the most favorably treated* group. For example, if 60 percent of white applicants are selected, then the selection proportion of any minority group should be at least 48 percent (.80 × .60). Let us say that there are numerous entry-level retail clerk positions to be filled for a large department store. Through recruiting, 120 white applicants are processed and 72 (60 percent) are selected. Through the same recruiting process, 50 blacks apply for the positions. If blacks were hired at the same rate as the whites, we would expect that 30 black applicants would be selected (50 × .60). However, according to this guideline, exact parity is not expected. The minimum number of black hires would be expected to be 24 (30 × .80), which is 80 percent of the 60 percent hire rate of whites. If the ratio is smaller, the *initial* conclusion is that discrimination in selection has occurred.

The other statistical test, The Standard Deviation Rule, can be applied to both flow and stock analysis comparisons. Here is the formula for the Standard Deviation Rule:

$$\text{S. D.} = \sqrt{\frac{\begin{array}{c}\text{total minority}\\\text{applicants}\end{array}}{\text{total applicants}} \times \frac{\begin{array}{c}\text{total nonminority}\\\text{applicants}\end{array}}{\text{total applicants}} \times \begin{array}{c}\text{total}\\\text{persons}\\\text{selected}\end{array}}$$

For example, let us assume that 200 individuals were selected from an applicant pool of 500. Of these 500 applicants, 200 were black and 300 were white. Applying these data to the formula yields the following:

$$\text{S.D.} = \sqrt{\frac{200}{500} \times \frac{300}{500} \times 200}$$

$$= \sqrt{.4 \times .6 \times 200}$$

$$= \sqrt{48}$$

$$= 6.93$$

If blacks were selected in the same proportion as they were represented in the applicant pool, one would expect that 80 blacks would have been selected (200 hires × .40 of applicants). The Standard Deviation Rule provides a rule of thumb to judge whether or not the number of blacks actually hired is roughly representative of their proportion in the applicant pool. The genera rule is that the number selected should be within a range defined by ± standard deviation units from the expected number selected. In this case the expected number hired is 80 and one standard deviation is 6.93. Two standard deviations would be approximately 14. The acceptable selection range would therefore be 80 ± 14, or the range of from 66 to 94 blacks selected. Obviously, in most cases the lower boundary of the range is given the most importance. According to this type of analysis, if fewer than 66 blacks were in the group of 200 selected, evidence of discrimination would exist.

The Uniform Guidelines on Employee Selection Procedures (1978)

The *Uniform Guidelines on Employee Selection Procedures (1978)*, reprinted in the appendix to this chapter, represent a joint statement of the Equal Employment Opportunity Commission, the Civil Service Commission, the Department of Labor, and the Department of Justice as to the characteristics of acceptable selection procedures. As such, these guidelines are not themselves legally binding. However, because they represent the viewpoints of the federal agencies charged with the enforcement of EEO laws, the guidelines serve as a primary reference for court decisions and have been cited in various cases. The most important aspects of the *Uniform Guidelines* are summarized in this section.

Determination of Adverse Impact   The *Uniform Guidelines* clearly state that the central issue in judging discrimination in selection is the use of any selection procedure that has adverse impact. However, it must be noted that in certain cases the *Uniform Guidelines* provide exceptions to this. When large numbers of applicants are being selected, discrimination could be indicated even if comparison proportions of applicants are within the Four-Fifths rates. Statistically significant differences in selection rates could be determined because of the large sample sizes. In addition, enforcement agencies would naturally be quite concerned with differences in which large numbers of individuals are affected. Conversely, in cases in which very small numbers of applicants are processed, the Four-Fifths Rule may not always be accepted as determining discrimination. With small samples, differences in decisions about one or two applicants could greatly change the comparison ratios. This factor is thus taken into account and differences greater than the four-fifths ratio allows may not be viewed negatively.

Selection Methods   The *Uniform Guidelines* also state that *any* method of selection which results in an employment decision is covered. Many individuals have incorrectly assumed that only scored selection tests are addressed in the guidelines. This is clearly incorrect as the following indicates:

> When an informal or unscored selection procedure which has an adverse impact is utilized, the user should eliminate the adverse impact or modify the procedure to one which is formal, scored, or quantified measure.[19]

Defense of Selection Program   The *Uniform Guidelines* are not concerned, except with respect to record keeping, with selection programs that do not demonstrate adverse impact. For those selection programs that do have adverse impact, the options of the organization are specified. First, the organization may cease use of the selection device(s) under question and adopt other procedures that do not result in adverse impact. If this is not acceptable, the organization may defend its practices in one of the ways we have discussed previously. If validation evidence is used, it should specifically address the use of the selection instrument with all groups for whom the test is to be used. At a minimum this means that statistical validation should include a representative number of women and minorities. In criterion validation the steps should address the issue of "test fairness" or the comparative performance of various groups on the test. A large portion of the *Uniform Guidelines* are in fact devoted to the steps, data, and procedures of validation strategies. An added provision, however, is that the organization should demonstrate there are no other alternative selection programs that are both valid and have less adverse impact.

Selection Requirements   There are several other aspects of selection programs that are specifically addressed. Skills and abilities easily learned during a brief training program are not acceptable as selection requirements. Requirements drawn from higher-level jobs are permissible only if it can be documented that a majority of individuals move to the higher-level job within a reasonable time period. This time period is not precisely defined but the *Uniform Guidelines* state "a reasonable period of time will vary for different jobs and employment situations but will seldom be more than five years."[20] The various forms of selection cutoff scores are also discussed. The least stringent cutoff is a score above which all applicants are judged equally acceptable. Scores on selection devices may also be grouped according to the magnitude of the score with the first applicants considered for selection to be those with scores in the highest group. Selection proceeds down score groups until all open positions are filled. This could result in selection being completed before some score groups are even considered. An even more severe version of this is to rank all applicants individually and proceed down this list of individuals. The *Uniform Guidelines* indicate when these latter two forms of cutoff scores are used, and if adverse impact results, the organization must not only demonstrate the validity of the selection devices but also justify the contention that scores above a minimum are indicative of higher job performance.

Job Performance Measures   In a discussion of measures of job performance that are useful in the demonstration of validity, the *Uniform Guidelines* allow a variety of such measures, for example., production quantity or quality, supervisors' ratings, turnover, and absenteeism records. Whatever ones are used, however, they must represent important work behaviors or work outcomes that are free from factors that would unfairly alter the scores of any particular groups. We discuss performance measures in Chapter 17 to fully develop this issue. The *Uniform Guidelines* also permit validation evidence to be gathered by means of a multiunit study or evidence borrowed from other companies, as long as data are produced indicating the similarity of the job being considered. The necessary procedures of such job analysis will be discussed in Chapters 8 and 9.

Record Keeping   Another major requirement of the *Uniform Guidelines is* record keeping. All organizations are required to keep information about the demographic characteristics of applicants and hires and to produce such information if requested. This requirement applies only to the groups that constitute at least 2 percent of the relevant labor market. All organizations are technically required to record such data; however, if adverse impact is not characteristic of the selection program, the probability of a request by an enforcement agency for this documentation is remote. Organizations with fewer than 100 employees should record by sex, race, and national origin, the number of persons selected, promoted, and terminated for each job level. Data are also necessary indicating the number of applicants for both entry-level positions and promotion. These data should also be categorized by sex, race, and national origin. Finally selection procedures should be described. Organizations with more than 100 employees must develop records indicating whether the total selection process for each job, or any part of that selection process, has had adverse impact on any group that constitutes at least 2 percent of the relevant labor market. In cases in which there is an insufficient number of selections to determine whether there is an adverse impact, the organization should continue to collect, maintain, and have available the information on individual components of the selection process until the information is sufficient to determine if adverse impact has occurred or until the job changes substantially. In the latter case, presumably a new round of record keeping would begin.

In summary, the *Uniform Guidelines of Employee Selection Procedures* direct HR specialists as to appropriate selection program features and records. The determination of adverse impact as indicated by the Four-Fifths Rule is of primary importance. If such impact is determined, using required organizational records, the company must either cease the selection procedure and adopt a nondiscriminatory one or produce evidence of the job relatedness of the selection program with the adverse impact.

Affirmative Action Programs

Another aspect of EEO laws and regulations that has importance for companies is Affirmative Action Programs (AAP). Generally, this term applies to a set of specific actions taken by an organization to meet the objectives of EEO law. For example, an organization's AAP in selection of women and minority college graduates might include identifying and visiting colleges with large proportions of women and minority students, staffing recruiting teams with women and minority members, developing internship programs, and training interviewers and other selection decision makers in appropriate techniques. An Affirmative Action Plan is a written document produced by the company that explicitly states steps to be taken, information to be gathered, and the general bases of decision making for each area of HRM. It is to serve as a guideline for actions to ensure that EEO principles are implemented within the organization. Such a plan is to be under the direction of a top-level manager and to be communicated to all within the organization.

Basically, there are three situations in which a company would adopt an AAP: (1) being a government contractor, (2) having lost a court discrimination case or having signed a consent decree, or (3) voluntarily attempting to implement EEO principles. We discuss each of these.

Federal Contractor   Most of the EEO laws and executive orders dealing with federal contractors contain the requirement of affirmative action for those with contracts of at least $10,000. The Office of Federal Contract Compliance Programs (OFCCP), a subdivision within the Department of Labor, is usually set up as the regulatory agency. It can review the employment practices of contractors and levy specified penalties if it finds a contractor to be out of compliance with AAP requirements. There are three main activities that must be carried out by a contractor in an AAP.[21] The first is a utilization analysis. Conceptually, this is similar to previously described stock statistical analyses because it requires a comparison of the company's work force to the relevant labor market. If there is a smaller percentage of a specific demographic group in the company's work force than there is in the labor market, that group is said to be underutilized. The complete determination of underutilization, however, also includes additional information such as the size of the minority unemployed group, the availability of promotable and transferable minorities within the company, the existence of appropriate training institutions, and the degree of training that the contractor may deliver.

The numerical results of a utilization analysis are important because they indicate the discrepancy between the work force and the available labor force. This discrepancy then serves as the basis for the second activity, determining the "goals" that a company should strive to achieve in its employment practices. For example, if Hispanic skilled craft workers constitute 8 percent of the RLM and only 2 percent of the company's work force, the company would be expected to set a specific numerical goal to achieve a balance between the two numbers or, at least, to reduce the discrepancy substantially. In addition, a timetable should be developed that would indicate the dates at which the company expects to achieve milestones in reducing the discrepancy. As an example, the percentage in the company's work force would be expected to increase by 2 percent for each of the next three years. A major debate on this topic is to what extent these goals are considered to be desirable ends to be achieved within the specified timetable and to what extent they are considered to be "quotas" that must be achieved. This has historically been a source of conflict between contractors and OFCCP regulators. Theoretically, the contractor is to "put forth every good faith effort to make his overall affirmative action program work."[22] Obviously, the term "good faith effort" is open to interpretation and disagreement. It is a common opinion that pressure has often been exerted on contractors to give preferential treatment to women and minorities to reduce underutilization.

The third major aspect of these AAPs is the actual steps to be taken. Among these are the publication of job openings through meetings with various minority organizations, taking ads in media with a high percentage of minorities as a target audience, and publicizing the company's affirmative action policy. Also included are reviews of selection practices and instruments for unnecessary adverse impact, and training organization members in the objectives of the AAP and procedures necessary to fulfill its objectives.

Court Order and Consent Decree   In this situation, the company is legally required to engage in HRM actions that will directly, and in a specified period of time, lead to a balance between its work force and the relevant labor market. The activities just discussed relative to AAPs for government contractors become part of the AAP for companies in this situation. However, even less freedom of action exists for these companies. Usually, they are required to meet their numerical employment goals. To do so, they may give preferential treatment to underutilized groups and undertake actions to prepare them to perform well in their jobs.

For example, part of the consent decree signed by AT&T in its sexual discrimination case required the company to implement numerical promotion quotas.[23] One of the major points of the case was that AT&T failed to promote women managers at the same rate as comparable male managers. To rectify this, the company adopted a timetable that specified how many female managers would be promoted within each of several six-month time periods. In many cases the promotions were of more than one level, with some as great as four levels. In addition, the company was required to change selection practices, work team composition, and equipment design for skilled craft positions. This was not only to select more females for these jobs but also to take steps so that artificial barriers to adequate work performance were eliminated. In such circumstances, the primary purpose of the HRM activities is to meet the mandated numerical employment goals. The AAP is the vehicle for achieving this.

Voluntary AAP The most controversial AAPs have been those initiated by an organization without the direct requirement of a court or government agency. The problem with these is the potential conflict between their results and the wording of Title VII of the Civil Rights Act of 1964. Part of this act expressly states that it is "an unlawful . . . practice . . . to fail or refuse to hire . . . any individual with respect to . . . race, color, religion, sex, or national origin."[24] Further it is written that "nothing contained in this title shall be interpreted to require any employer . . . to grant preferential treatment to any individual. . ."[25]

The potential difficulty with a voluntary AAP is that in order to be fair to those who are the traditional victims of discrimination, the company may bend over backward and discriminate against other groups by violating the parts of Title VII just cited. We have already mentioned that in the two previous AAP situations a company is in the direct review (some would say control) of a court or government agency and can legitimately grant preferential treatment to specific groups to meet goals or quotas. In voluntary AAPs, any preferential treatment given one group may be translated into disparate treatment against another group. Because white males are usually the group negatively affected in such instances, the term *reverse discrimination* has been used.

The resolution of such conflicts between voluntary AAPs and disparate treatment of other groups has been the subject of specific court rulings. The most complete of these has been *Weber v. Kaiser Aluminum and Chemical Corp.*[26] In 1974 Kaiser and the United Steelworkers of America entered into a collective bargaining agreement, which included an AAP, for 15 plants. Until 1974, Kaiser selected as craft workers only persons who had prior craft experience. Because blacks had long been excluded from craft unions, few were able to qualify. As a result, in the Grammercy plant less than 2 percent of the skilled craft workers were black in an area with a labor force of 39 percent blacks. Therefore, Kaiser changed its selection policies. Rather than hiring already-trained outsiders, Kaiser established a training program for its production workers to fill craft openings. Selection of craft trainees was made on the basis of seniority with the requirement that at least 50 percent of the new trainees were to be black until the percentage of black skilled craft workers approximated the percentage of blacks in the surrounding labor force.

The first group of 13 trainees contained seven black and six white members. Some of the least senior black selectees had less seniority than did several rejected white production workers. One of these white workers, Weber, brought suit alleging violation of Title VII. In 1979, the Supreme Court decided the case in favor of the company. Focusing on the narrowness of its enquiry, the Court ruled that the specific features of the Kaiser program were within the spirit of Title VII. The following statements summarize the Court's viewpoint:

> . . . the plan does not unnecessarily trammel the interests of white employees. The plan does not require the discharge of white workers and their replacement with new black hires. . . . Nor does the plan create an absolute bar to the advancement of white employees; . . . Moreover the plan is a temporary measure; it is not intended to maintain racial balance, but simply to eliminate a manifest racial imbalance. Preferential selection . . . will end as soon as the percentage of black skilled craft workers . . . approximates the percentage . . . in the local labor force.[27]

These characteristics of being temporary, not having a permanent adverse impact on individual white workers, and correcting a manifest imbalance have been taken to be essential in voluntary AAPs. This was made clear in a following case, *Lilly v. City of Beckley*.[28] In 1975 the city of Beckley, West Virginia, undertook to remedy the lack of minority and women employees in city departments. In April 1976 a formal AAP was adopted to achieve this. This case arose over selection decisions made in the police department in January 1976, before the formal AAP was adopted. Lilly applied for a patrol officer position at this time and passed the essay test portion of the selection program but failed the interview. He was told that his chance of obtaining employment would be much greater if he were a minority member. Accordingly, he brought suit against the city. The city's argument in the case was that it was operating under an informal AAP pursuant to the formal adoption of the AAP in April 1976. The Fourth Circuit Court of Appeals compared the circumstances of this informal AAP with the Supreme Court's comments about the Kaiser plan and found for Lilly. In essence, the informal plan was rejected for lack of specific goals and timetables, evidence that it was to remedy past discrimination, and that it did not result in the hiring of unqualified applicants and unnecessarily trammel the interests of the white majority.

Selection Court Cases

In this section we review some of the major court decisions about selection practices. The cases presented in this section are not all of the major cases that deal with selection issues. Rather, they are a cross section chosen to represent demographic issues (age, ethnicity, gender, disability, etc.), measurement issues (job-relatedness, test construction, principles, etc.), and different selection applications (entry level and promotion). The purpose of the section is both to familiarize you with the manner in which courts review discrimination charges and to present important decisions that affect selection practices in organizations.

Griggs v. Duke Power (1971)   The first landmark case decided by the Supreme Court under Title VII was *Griggs v. Duke Power*.[29] The case began in

1967 when 13 black employees filed a class action suit against Duke Power, charging discriminatory employment practices. The suit centered on recently developed selection requirements for the company's operations units. The plaintiffs charged that the requirements were arbitrary and screened out a much higher proportion of blacks than whites. The requirements, which were implemented in 1965, included a high school diploma, passage of a mechanical aptitude test, and a general intelligence test. When the requirements were initiated, they were not retrospective and so did not apply to current employees in the company's operations units. There was no attempt made by the company to determine the job relatedness of these requirements.

A lower district court found in favor of the company on the grounds that any former discriminatory practices had ended and there was no evidence of discriminatory intent in the new requirements. An appellate court agreed with the finding of no discriminatory intent and in the absence of such intent the requirements were permissible.

The Supreme Court, in a unanimous decision, reversed the previous decisions. The court ruled that lack of discriminatory intent was not a sufficient defense against the use of employment devices which exclude on the basis of race. In North Carolina at that time 34 percent of the white males had high school degrees whereas only 12 percent of the black males did. The court acknowledged that tests and other measuring devices could be used, but held that they must be related to job performance. Duke Power had contended that their two test requirements were permissible because Title VII allowed the use of "professionally developed tests" as selection devices.

Because there were employees already working in the operational units of the company who did not have a high school diploma or had not taken the tests and were performing their duties in a satisfactory manner, Duke Power had no evidence relating these requirements to job performance. The court stated that if "an employment practice that operates to exclude Negroes cannot be shown to be related to job performance, it is prohibited."[30]

Two important precedents were set by the *Griggs* case, both of which are related to burdens of proof. The applicant carries the burden of proving the adverse impact of a particular selection device. Once adverse impact has been determined, the burden shifts to the employer to prove the validity or job relatedness of the device. The court said that the *EEOC Guidelines* were entitled to deference for proving validity.

United States v. Georgia Power (1973)   While the Supreme Court held in the *Griggs* decision that employment tests must be job-related, attention was directed in later cases to the question of just what an employer must do to demonstrate job relatedness, and the extent to which the *Guidelines* define that. For example, in February 1973, the Fifth Circuit Court of Appeals upheld the 1970 *EEOC Guidelines* in *United States v. Georgia Power.*[31]

In 1969 the attorney general brought suit against the Georgia Power Company for discrimination against blacks. Evidence was presented that at that time only 543 of the company's 7,515 employees were black (7.2 percent) despite the existence of a large pool of black applicants. Moreover, while blacks were classified exclusively as janitors, porters, maids, and laborers, almost all white employees occupied higher positions.

Beginning in 1960, in order to qualify for employment, all new employees were required to have a high school diploma or evidence of equivalent educational accomplishment. Then in 1963, all new employees were required also to pass a battery of tests developed by the Psychological Corporation. This requirement was instituted less than one month after the discontinuance of formal job segregation. In 1964 the company imposed the diploma requirement on all incumbent employees who wanted to transfer from the position of janitor, porter, or maid, but did not add that requirement for transferring from elsewhere in the company's structure. No study of these tests to determine job relatedness had been conducted prior to the filing of the suit.

Recognizing its obligation under *Griggs* to provide proof of the job relatedness of its test battery, the company began a validation study after the initiation of the suit. An official of the company conducted a validity study using an all-white sample. The study collected supervisors' ratings on employees who had earlier been hired on the basis of the tests to be validated, and then compared those ratings with the test scores. This sample was admittedly small and excluded the 50 percent of the applicants who failed the test. Nevertheless, statistical evidence was produced by Georgia Power that supported the relationship of their selection test scores to the job performance ratings of supervisors, thereby demonstrating job relatedness.

The court, however, held that the validation study did not meet the minimum standards recommended for validation strategy by the *EEOC Guidelines*. One failure was the absence of blacks from the validation study. With an applicant population that was one-third black, the court concluded that such a study could at least have been attempted. The court also held that there were black employees in three of the company's job classifications in numbers as large as some of the all-white samples used by Georgia Power; therefore, the company could have attempted separate validation studies and, even though the studies would have been conducted on different job categories, some data could have been generated indicating whether the tests treated both races equally.

The *EEOC Guidelines* also required that the sample of subjects be representative of the normal applicant group for the job or jobs in question. Since there was an absence of blacks in the sample, the court ruled that this requirement had not been fulfilled. Also, according to the *Guidelines*, tests must be administered under controlled and standardized conditions. In this case, the court found that testing of new applicants was uniform, but that testing of incumbents was not.

Finally, the court held that even without regard to the *Guidelines*, the validation study was not a proper way of determining whether these tests predicted job success because it did not validate the actual testing procedure used by the company. The company required a preset passing score on each of three tests by any applicant before he or she would be considered for employment. However, the Georgia Power study evaluated the three-test battery by weighting the numerical test scores twice as high as the verbal and calculating a composite score on the battery. Therefore, the court concluded that not only did the study not meet the minimum requirements of the *Guidelines*, but also that the study was irrelevant because it was not conducted on the actual practice followed by the company in administering its testing program. Also, in accordance with the *Griggs* decision, the court struck down the company's use of diploma requirements on the grounds that there was no evidence relating the possession of a diploma to job performance.

Spurlock v. United Airlines (1972)   The case of *Spurlock v. United Airlines* involved a demonstration of the job relatedness of selection instruments other than tests.[32] In this case, Spurlock filed suit against United Airlines after his application for the job of flight officer had been rejected. Spurlock charged the airline with discrimination against blacks and offered as evidence the fact that only 9 flight officers out of 5,900 were black. In the suit, Spurlock challenged two of the requirements for the job: a college degree and a minimum of 500 hours of flight time.

United contended that both these selection requirements were job-related. Using statistics, United showed that applicants with a greater number of flight hours were more likely to succeed in the rigorous training program which flight officers must complete after being hired. Statistics also showed that 500 hours was a reasonable minimum requirement. In addition, United contended that, because of the high cost of the training program, it was important that those who begin the training program eventually become flight officers.

United officials also testified that the possession of a college degree indicated that the applicant had the ability to function in a classroom atmosphere. This ability is important because of the initial training program and because flight officers are required to attend intensive refresher courses every six months.

The court accepted the evidence presented by United as proof of the job relatedness of the requirements and, in a significant ruling, stated that when a job requires a small amount of skill and training and the consequences of hiring an unqualified applicant are insignificant, the courts should closely examine selection instruments which are discriminatory. On the other hand, when the job requires a high degree of skill and the economic and human risks involved are great, the employer bears a lighter burden to show that selection instruments are job-related.

Connecticut v. Teal (1982)   The central issue in the case of *Connecticut v. Teal* was whether discrimination occurred in a multistep selection program even though the total program did not demonstrate adverse impact.[33] Four black employees of the Department of Income Maintenance of the state of Connecticut were provisionally promoted to Welfare Eligibility Supervisor and served in that capacity for almost two years. According to departmental policy, to gain the position permanently an individual had to participate successfully in a multistep selection process. The first step was a passing score on a written examination. This exam was administered to 48 black and 259 white applicants. Of these, 26 blacks (54%) and 206 whites (80%) passed. The four black individuals serving as provisional supervisors did not pass.

Even though the rate of passing for blacks was below the recommended Four-Fifths ratio, the remaining parts of the selection program were conducted in such a way as to ensure nondiscrimination in the final selection. Forty-six persons in total were promoted, 11 of whom were black and 35 of whom were white. This meant that 23 percent of the black applicants were promoted and 14 percent of the whites. The department argued that, as a consequence, no discrimination against blacks in selection was demonstrated.

The court disagreed with this position, pointing out the adverse impact of the written test. The decision stated that Title VII prohibits employment practices which deprive "any individual of employment opportunities." Therefore, the focus of the statute is on the individual, not the minority group as a whole. Title VII does not permit the victims of discriminatory policy to be told they have not been wronged because other persons of their race or sex were hired. The Department, therefore, had to ensure that each part of the selection program was nondiscriminatory.

Watson v. Ft. Worth Bank & Trust (1988) This case addressed the important question of whether or not discrimination cases focusing on the interview could be heard as adverse impact cases even though traditionally these cases have been tried as disparate treatment.[34] Clara Watson, a black woman, was hired by Ft. Worth Bank & Trust as a proof operator in August 1973, and promoted to teller in January 1976. In February 1980, she sought to become supervisor of the tellers in the main lobby; a white male, however, was selected for the job. Watson then sought a position as supervisor of the drive-in bank, but this position was given to a white female. In February 1981, after Watson had served for about a year as a commercial teller in the bank's main lobby and informally as assistant to the supervisor of tellers, the man holding that position was promoted. Watson applied for the vacancy, but the white female who was the supervisor of the drive-in bank was selected instead. Watson then applied for the vacancy created at the drive-in; a white male was selected for that job. The bank, which had about 80 employees, had not developed precise and formal criteria for evaluating candidates for the positions for which Watson unsuccessfully applied. It relied instead on the subjective judgment of supervisors who were acquainted with the candidates and with the nature of the jobs to be filled. All the supervisors involved in denying Watson the four promotions were white.

The U.S. District Court that heard the case addressed Watson's claims under the standards that we discussed as being applied to disparate treatment cases. It concluded that Watson had established a prima facie case but that the bank had met its rebuttal burden by presenting legitimate and nondiscriminatory reasons for each of the promotion decisions. Finally, Watson had failed to show that these reasons were pretexts and her case was dismissed.

Watson appealed the decision on the basis that the district court had erred in failing to apply adverse impact analysis to her claim. From our previous discussion, we understand the significance of this argument. Under disparate treatment the burden of proof required of the bank to defend its practices is lighter than under adverse impact processes. If the case were heard as adverse impact and Watson established a prima facie case, the bank would most likely have to provide validation evidence as a defense. Given its situation with no defined criteria and no scored selection instruments, this would be difficult to do. The Fifth

Circuit Court of Appeals, however, held that "a Title VII challenge to an allegedly discretionary promotion system is properly analyzed under the disparate treatment model rather than the disparate impact model.[35] In so ruling, citations were given to various courts of appeals decisions which held that disparate treatment analysis was proper when subjective criteria (the interview) was of issue. In essence, this court said that adverse impact analysis should only be applied to objective selection devices (e.g., tests) and disparate treatment to opinion or judgment devices. The implication for selection practices is obvious: the use of interviews and related instruments would be easier to defend in discrimination cases; they should, therefore, be extensively used. Anything else would be far riskier.

The Supreme Court, however, took an opposing view and remanded the case to the court of appeals for further consideration of the adverse impact argument. In so doing, the Supreme Court made several important statements. One was that the ultimate legal issue in the two forms of discrimination cases was not dissimilar. Also the ruling stated the following:

> We are persuaded that our decisions in *Griggs* and succeeding cases could largely be nullified if disparate impact analyses were applied only to standardized selection practices. However one might distinguish "subjective" from "objective" criteria, it is apparent that selection systems that combine both types would generally be considered subjective in nature. Thus, for example, if the employer in *Griggs* had consistently preferred applicants who had a high school diploma and who passed the company's general aptitude test, its selection system could nonetheless have been considered "subjective" if it also included brief interviews. . . . If we announced a rule that allowed employers so easily to insulate themselves from liability under *Griggs*, impact analysis might effectively be abolished.[36]

OFCCP v. Ozark Air Lines (1986)　This case concerns the Rehabilitation Act of 1973 and the refusal of the airline to employ a disabled person as an airline technician.[37] Gary Frey, because of a childhood accident, had a nonfunctioning left ear. His right ear was unimpaired. Ozark agreed that Frey had the necessary qualifications for the position but refused to hire him because of his hearing disability and his failure to prove that he could carry out the job duties without endangering himself and others. Because Ozark Airlines was regarded as a federal contractor, the case was decided by the OFCCP.

Frey won the decision and was also awarded back pay. In so doing, the OFCCP argued that it was Ozark's burden to prove that Frey's employment would have endangered him and others, not the burden of Frey and OFCCP to prove that he could do the work successfully. Secondly, it stated that a disabled person is "qualified for employment if he is capable of performing a particular job with reasonable accommodation to his or her handicap."[38] The only evidence that Ozark submitted was the testimony of its personnel director who, responding to questioning as to whether he had given any thought to accommodating

Frey or putting restrictions on his duties, stated that this was not possible because of limitations in the union contract. A related Ozark argument that the noise levels of the facility would endanger Frey's remaining hearing was also dismissed. Citing specific decibel levels, the OFCCP commented that Ozark failed to show that Frey's hearing could not be protected by wearing ear protectors.

Auto Workers v. Johnson Controls (1991)   In this case, the Supreme Court attempted to strike a balance between fetal protection and sex discrimination.[39] Johnson Controls manufactured car batteries that required significant exposure to lead. Health experts have noted for years specific health risks involved with such exposure, including risk of harm to a fetus. Prior to the Civil Rights Act of 1964, Johnson Controls did not employ any female in a battery-manufacturing job. In 1977 it changed its policy to allow females in these positions but required them to sign a statement that acknowledged their advisement of prenatal risk. In 1982 Johnson changed its policy back to one of virtual female exclusion based on the fact that eight females became pregnant while maintaining high blood lead levels, the critical level noted by the Occupational Safety and Health Act for individuals who are planning to have a family. Only those women whose inability to bear children was medically documented were allowed for consideration.

A class action suit was filed, among them a man who had been denied leave of absence to lower his lead level so he could become a father. The plaintiffs challenged Johnson Controls' fetal-protection policy as sex discrimination under Title VII. The District and Court of Appeals ruled for Johnson Controls, concluding that business necessity was an appropriate framework for its defense. Furthermore, the Circuit Court ruled that discrimination against women for the battery jobs was a BFOQ—the industrial safety was part of the essence of the business.

The Supreme Court decided for the plaintiffs, however, ruling that the company's fetal-protection policy explicitly discriminates against women on the basis of their sex and childbearing capacity, rather than fertility alone. This, said the Court, is clearly in violation of section 703 (a) of the Civil Rights Act of 1964, which prohibits sex-based classifications in terms and conditions of employment. Furthermore, Johnson Controls did not, by its policy, equally protect the offspring of all employees, notably men who were planning families. As for the BFOQ issue, the Court held that its case law

> makes clear that the safety exception is limited to instances in which sex or pregnancy actually interferes with the employee's ability to perform the job. This approach is consistent with the language of the BFOQ provision itself (Section 703 (e)), for it suggests that permissible distinctions based on sex must relate to ability to perform the duties of the job.[40]

Furthermore, the Court cited the Pregnancy Discrimination Act's amendment to Title VII, which states that unless pregnant employees differ from others "in their ability or inability to work" they must be treated the same as other employees. In its review of legislative history, the Court felt that Congress "made clear that the decision to become pregnant or to work while being either pregnant or capable of becoming pregnant was reserved for each individual woman to make for herself."[41]

Wards Cove Packing Co. v. Atonio (1989)   As you will recall, this Supreme Court case made it more difficult for plaintiffs to prove adverse impact and served as a major impetus for the Civil Rights Act of 1991, which legislatively overturned the Wards Cove ruling.

This case involved employment at a salmon-packing company.[42] There were essentially two groups of jobs. Cannery jobs were unskilled, low-paying, seasonal positions, which were primarily filled by nonwhites, Filipinos, and Alaska Natives. Noncannery jobs were higher-paying, skilled jobs filled by whites.

The cannery workers brought action against Wards Cove Packing, alleging that its hiring and promotion practices—nepotism, a lack of objective hiring criteria, and separate hiring channels—were to blame for racial imbalances in the work force. First, the Supreme Court took issue with the lower courts' acceptance of statistics that showed a high percentage of nonwhite workers in cannery jobs and a low percentage of these workers in noncannery, higher-level positions. The appropriate comparison, the Court stated, is between qualified job applicants or the qualified population in the labor force and the skilled, noncannery positions. Second, the Court noted that the plaintiff's burden in establishing a prima facie case extends beyond statistical imbalances in the employer's workforce. Specifically, the Court stated this:

> Respondents will also have to demonstrate that the disparity they complain of is the result of one or more of the employment practices that they are attacking here, specifically showing that each challenged practice has a significantly disparate impact on employment opportunities for whites and nonwhites. To hold otherwise would result in employers being potentially liable for the myriad of innocent causes that may lead to statistical imbalances. . .[43]

The Court also ruled that if these burdens are met by the plaintiff, the company will have to show a legitimate business justification; but there is no requirement that the practice be shown to be "essential" or "indispensable," the employer only has a burden of production (of employment practice legitimacy). After this business justification is offered and accepted, "[t]he burden of persuasion however, remains with the disparate-impact plaintiff."[44] Finally, to counter the defendant the plaintiff still may be able to show that other tests or devices without such adverse impact would also serve the employer's legitimate employment interests. However, any alternative practices offered "must be equally effective" as the company's chosen procedures in achieving its goals. As discussed previously, these specifications of burdens of proof essentially increased the demands on the plaintiff while reducing those on the defendant.

The major points of each of these cases are summarized in Table 2.4. We can see that the result of the various court decisions is to identify selection practices that

TABLE 2.4

KEY ISSUES IN MAJOR SELECTION COURT CASES

Griggs v. Duke Power (1971)

1. Lack of discriminatory intent not sufficient defense
2. Selection test must be job-related if adverse impact results
3. Employer bears burden of proof in face of apparent adverse impact

U.S. v. Georgia Power (1973)

1. Validation strategy must Comply with EEOC guidelines
2. Validation must include affected groups
3. Validation must reflect selection decision practices
4. Testing must occur under standardized conditions

Spurlock v. United Airlines (1972)

1. College degree and experience requirements can be shown to be job-related
2. Company's burden of proof diminishes as human risks increase

Connecticut v. Teal (1982)

1. Company must ensure that all parts of a multiple-step selection program have no adverse impact

Watson v. Ft. Worth Bank & Trust (1988)

1. Cases focusing on subjective selection devices, e.g., interviews and judgments could be heard as adverse impact
2. Organization may need to validate interview in same manner as objective test.

OFCCP v. Ozark Air Lines (19S6)

1. In disability cases, organization must prove that individual cannot perform job
2. Reasonable accommodation must be given to disabled individual

Auto workers v. Johnson Controls (1991)

1. Safety exception to BFOQ defense is limited to instances in which gender or pregnancy actually interferes with employee's ability to perform job
2. Company's moral concerns about health of future children is not sufficient to bar women from employment
3. Decisions about children left to future parents

Wards Cove Packing v. Atonio (1989) (negated by Civil Rights Act of 1991)

1. Appropriate reference in order to indicate adverse impact is pool of qualified individuals in labor force, not comparison of skilled and unskilled cannery workers
2. Burden of persuasion in adverse impact case remains with individual who brought case
3. Challenged practice must not be essential to business to meet employer's burden of proof
4. Adverse impact must be shown by applications of specific employment practice

are either acceptable or unacceptable. Unfortunately for selection specialists, most decisions identify unacceptable actions. We, therefore, know more about what *not* to do than what we can do. This is somewhat unsettling. It would be more convenient if the courts could assemble a description of acceptable selection practices. From all that has been said in this chapter, however, you should realize that such an action by the courts is not possible. Selection practices are too varied and too interrelated. In terms of the regulatory model, the main responsibility of the courts and agencies is to stop organizations from perpetuating the societal problems that prompted the EEO laws. It is the responsibility of those who design selection programs to develop the various parts of their programs so they comply with the laws. Government regulation is a major reason why, as we said at the beginning of Chapter 1, selection has increasingly become such a complex activity.

EEO Summary

This chapter has presented the major EEO principles and discussed their impact on HR selection programs. This last section summarizes the major legal concepts regarding discrimination that HR specialists need to be aware of in either reviewing an-existing selection program or developing a new one.

Basis of Discrimination

Charges of discrimination in selection practices must be linked to one of the personal characteristics specified in EEO law. The federal laws and directives identify race, color, religion, sex, national origin, age (over 40), physical or mental handicaps, and Vietnam era veteran status as the covered characteristics. Although this is indeed a long list, it clearly means that, unless there is a state or local law, many of the charges of discrimination that are threatened against private organizations (e.g., discrimination based on homosexuality, hair or clothing style, school affiliation, etc.) are not feasible according to EEO law unless the charge can be linked to one of the specified characteristics. For governmental employers, however, there is a broader accountability because of the wording of constitutional amendments. These amendments do not specify their applicability to specific demographic groups; rather, they apply to all citizens. The specification of these characteristics defines the groups that HR specialists should consider when reviewing the vulnerability of a selection program to discrimination charges. An analysis of possible discrimination can be conducted on those groups with characteristics that are both specified in EEO law and constitute at least 2 percent of the relevant labor market. Although this will constitute a lengthy list, it has the advantage of defining the scope of compliance to EEO law.

Evidence of Discrimination

A charge of discrimination can be brought against an organization with little substantiating evidence other than the fact that an individual was not selected for a position. In many cases such a charge constitutes a public embarrassment for an organization. Also, many times organizations do not wish to bear the cost of legal action, especially if such action may be prolonged. The result is that the organization frequently will negotiate a settlement to the charge. Although this may be a pragmatic solution to a particular situation, it does little to resolve a potentially recurrent problem. It is important for HR specialists to realize that judicial rulings about discrimination in selection practices generally have been based on patterns of selection decisions over a period of time rather than on an isolated instance. A particular selection decision means that one (or a few) individuals have been hired from a pool of applicants. The others have been denied employment. Perhaps several of these rejected applicants differ from the one who was selected on a personal characteristic specified in EEO law, for example, color, race, or religion. This difference and the denial of employment could serve as an *indicator* of discrimination in selection. Courts have generally recognized, however, that each individual selection is favorable to some applicants and unfavorable to others. The crucial information is the pattern that is evident when one views the overall result of a series of decisions. If such data indicate that one group, for example, white males, are selected in more cases than one would expect to find, given the relevant labor market's demographic characteristics, then the usual judgment has been that the questioned selection decision is, in fact, discriminatory. However, if the review of this series of selection decisions indicates that over time the demographic pattern of those selected is similar to the demographic profile of the relevant labor market, the usual judgment is that the questioned selection decision is not an indicant of discrimination. Furthermore, the consequences of a particular selection decision are a natural and nondiscriminatory by-product of the selection process.

Options of the Organization

If, after reviewing selection patterns for specific jobs and applying the appropriate statistical analysis (e.g., the Four-Fifths Rule or the standard deviation test) to the demographic groups specified in EEO law, the HR specialist notes large selection differences, the organization has two options for reducing its vulnerability. The first is to discontinue the current procedures and develop alternative ones that would result in small differences in selection among the various demographic groups. At first this may seem a formidable task, but there are many situations in which such a change is actually fairly straightforward. We previously discussed the interaction between recruitment and selection. Some organizations have found that, especially for entry-level positions, a broadening of recruitment activities to systematically include women and minorities has provided a sufficiently qualified applicant pool to change selection patterns substantially. Other cases would require the reevaluation of selection requirements, such as the number of years of experience and education degrees, to determine their necessity for job performance. Such requirements, especially if they are used stringently at an early stage of the processing of applicants, can have a large effect on the applicant pool. The second alternative, if large selection differences exist, is to conduct a validation study to support the organization's contention that the selection instruments are job-related. As the *Uniform Guidelines* indicate, such studies must conform to common methodological procedures to be maximally useful. Chapter 5 presents the steps in the most common of these validation methods.

A final important point to keep in mind is that there is not a legal requirement either to demonstrate the job relatedness of all selection devices or to hire unqualified applicants in order to increase the "numbers" of specific groups. As has been pointed out previously, proof of job relatedness becomes necessary only if discrimination is evidenced. Looked at another way, if an organization is willing to live with the consequences of selection decisions based on applicant information that is not demonstrated to be related to job performance, then the organization ought to share this risk among all relevant demographic groups. However, if an organization goes through the process of building job relatedness into the data that are used for selection decisions, the organization is not obligated to ignore such work and hire only because the applicant belongs to a certain demographic group. This is a point often overlooked and frequently results in hiring decisions made primarily to increase the employment of certain groups. If these individuals are not qualified for the jobs into which they are hired, their selection is not a service to either themselves or the organization.

References

[1] James Ledvinka and Vida Scarpello, *Federal Regulation of Personnel and Human Resource Management* 2d ed.(Boston. PWS-Kent, 1991), p. 17

[2] Ibid., pp. 30–32.

[3] "Civil Rights Act Is Signed: Interpretation Will Be Next Arena for Debate," *The APA Monitor* 23 (January 1992): p. 12.

[4] Public Law 102-166 102d Congress—Nov. 21, 1991, 105 STAT. 1075.

[5] *The APA Monitor* 23 (Jan. 1992): 13.

[6] An Informational Bulletin on Recent Legal Developments, Paul, Hastings, Janofsky & Walker a law partnership including professional corporations, August 23, 1991. p. 1.

[7] "Provisions: Americans with Disabilities Act," *Congressional Quarterly*, July 28, 1990: 2437.

[8] Donna L. Denning, "What Does Physical Ability Test Validation Strategy Have to Do with Americans with Disabilities Act?" Paper presented at Society for Industrial-Organizational Psychology Annual Conference, April 26–28, 1991.

[9] Act S102; 29CFR S1630.11.

[10] Cheryl Mahaffey, *Accommodating Employment Testing to the Needs of Individuals with Disabilities* (Psychological Services, Inc., August 1992).

[11] Elliot H. Shaller, "Reasonable Accommodation" under the Americans with Disabilities Act—What Does It Mean?" *Employee Relations L.J.* 16 (Spring 1991): 431–451.

[12] *Immigration and Nationality Act*, Sec. 274B, 274C.

[13] Ibid., p. 402.

[14] Ibid., p. 366.

[15] Act of April 9, 1866, Chap. 31, 1, 14 Stat. 27.

[16] *McDonnell Douglas v. Green*, 411 U.S. 792 (1973).

[17] Barbara Lindemann Schlei and Paul Grossman, *Employment Discrimination Law*, 2d ed. (Washington, D.C.: Bureau of National Affairs, 1983), p. 1361.

[18] Ibid., p. 1362.

[19] Equal Employment Opportunity Commission, Civil Service Commission, Department of Labor, and Department of Justice, *Adoption of Four Agencies of Uniform Guide lines on Employee Selection Procedures*, 43 Federal Register 38, 290-38, 315 (Aug. 25, 1978)

[20] Ibid., 1607.5(1).
[21] Ledvinka, *Federal Regulation of Personnel and Human Resource Management*, p. 124.
[22] Revised Order of No. 4, 41 Code of Federal Regulations, Part 60, at sec. 2.10 (1979)
[23] "Landmark AT&T-EEOC Consent Agreement Increases Assessment Center Usage," *Assessment & Development* 1 (1973).
[24] *Civil Rights Act of 1964*, Title VII, sec. 703(a).
[25] Ibid., sec. 703(j).
[26] *Weber v. Kaiser Aluminum and Chemical Corp.*, CA 5th Cir. 1977, 20 FEP Cases 1.
[27] Ibid., p. 7.
[28] *Lilly v. City of Beckley*, 797 F.2d 191, 41 FEP 772 (4th Cir., 1986).
[29] *Griggs v. Duke Power Co.*, 401 U.S. 424 (1971).
[30] Ibid.
[31] *United States v. Georgia Power*, 474 F.2d 906 (1973).
[32] *Spurlock v. United Airlines*, 475 F.2d 216 (10th Cir. 1972).
[33] *Connecticut v. Teal* 457 U.S. 440 (1982).
[34] *Watson v. Ft. Worth Bank & Trust*, 47 FEP Cases 102 (1988).
[35] Ibid., 104.
[36] Ibid., 107.
[37] *OFCCP v. Ozark Air Lines*, 40 FEP 1859 (U.S. Department of Labor, 1986).
[38] Ibid., 1862.
[39] *Auto Workers v. Johnson Controls*, 1991, 55 FEP Cases 365–382.
[40] Ibid, 373.
[41] Ibid, 374.
[42] *Wards Cove Packing Co. v. Atonio*, 1989, 49 FEP Cases 1519–1535.
[43] Ibid, 1526.
[44] Ibid, 1527.

Uniform Guidelines
on Employee Selection Procedures (1978)

Following is the full text of the Uniform Guidelines on Employee Selection Procedures adopted August 22, 1978 by the four federal agencies with EEO responsibilities—The Equal Employment Opportunity Commission, the U.S. Civil Service Commission (now OPM), and the departments of Labor and Justice.

The guidelines, effective September 25, 1978, are preceded by introductory material that does not appear with the Guidelines themselves in the Code of Federal Regulations. However, the introductory material, which was published with the guidelines in the Federal Register, has been described as "legislative history." The guidelines are codified as 29 CFR Part 1607.

The final guidelines culminated nearly six years of effort and give employers one set of government requirements to meet in order to avoid discrimination in testing and other employee selection processes. The bulk of the guidelines consist of the government's interpretation of validation standards.

Introduction

Adoption of Employee Selection Procedures

AGENCIES: Equal Employment Opportunity Commission, Civil Service Commission, Department of Justice, and Department of Labor.

ACTION: Adoption of uniform guidelines on employee selection procedures as final rules by four agencies.

SUMMARY: This document sets forth the uniform guidelines on employee selection procedures adopted by the Equal Employment Opportunity Commission, Civil Service Commission, Department of Justice, and the Department of Labor. At present two different sets of guidelines exist. The guidelines are intended to establish a uniform Federal position in the area of prohibiting discrimination in employment practices on grounds of race, color, religion, sex, or national origin. Cross reference documents are published at 5 CFR 300.103(c) (Civil Service Commission), 28 CFR 50.14 (Department of Justice), 29 CFR Part 1607 (Equal Employment Opportunity Commission), and 41 CFR Part 60-3 (Department of Labor) elsewhere in this issue.

EFFECTIVE DATE: September 25, 1978.

Source: Federal Register, Vol. 43, No. 166 (August 25, 1978) 38290-315.

Supplementary Information

An Overview of the 1978 Uniform Guidelines on Employee Selection Procedures

I. Background

One problem that confronted the Congress which adopted the Civil Rights Act of 1964 involved the effect of written preemployment tests on equal employment opportunity. The use of these test scores frequently denied employment to minorities in many cases without evidence that the tests were related to success on the job. Yet employers wished to continue to use such tests as practical tools to assist in the selection of qualified employees. Congress sought to strike a balance which would proscribe discrimination, but otherwise permit the use of tests in the selection of employees. Thus, in Title VII, Congress authorized the use of "any professionally developed ability test provided that such test, its administration or action upon the results is not designed, intended or used to discriminate".[1]

At first, some employers contended that, under this section, they could use any test which had been developed by a professional so long as they did not intend to exclude minorities, even if such exclusion was the consequence of the use of the test. In 1966, the Equal Employment Opportunity Commission (EEOC) adopted guidelines to advise employers and other users what the law and good industrial psychology practice required.[2] The Department of labor adopted the same approach in 1968 with respect to tests used by Federal Contractors under Executive Order 11246 in a more detailed regulation. The Government's view was that the employer's intent was irrelevant. If tests or other practices had an adverse impact on protected groups, they were unlawful unless they could be justified. To justify a test which screened out a higher proportion of minorities, the employer would have to show that it fairly measured or predicted performance on the job. Otherwise, it would not be considered to be "professionally developed."

In succeeding years, the EEOC and the Department of Labor provided more extensive guidance which elaborated upon these principles and expanded the guidelines to emphasize all selection procedures. In 1971 in *Griggs v. Duke Power Co.*,[3] the Supreme Court announced the principle that employer practices which had an adverse impact on minorities and were not justified by business necessity constituted illegal discrimination under Title VII. Congress confirmed this interpretation in the 1972 amendments to Title VII. The elaboration of these principles by courts and agencies continued into the mid-1970's,[4] but differences between the EEOC and the other agencies (Justice, Labor, and Civil Service Commission) produced two different sets of guidelines by the end of 1976.

With the advent of the Carter administration in 1977, efforts were intensi-

---

[1] Section 703(h), 42 U.S.C. 2000e(2)(h).
[2] See 35 U.S.L.W. 2137 (1966).
[3] 401 U.S. 424 (1971).
[4] See, e.g., *Albemarle Paper Co. v. Moody, 422 U.S. 405 (1975).*

fied to produce a unified government position. The following document represents the result of that effort. This introduction is intended to assist those not familiar with these matters to understand the basic approach of the uniform guidelines. While the guidelines are complex and technical, they are based upon the principles which have been consistently upheld by the courts, the Congress, and the agencies.

The following discussion will cite the sections of the Guidelines which embody these principles.

II. Adverse Impact
The fundamental principle underlying the guidelines is that employer policies or practices which have an adverse impact on employment opportunities of any race, sex, or ethnic group are illegal under Title VII and the Executive order unless justified by business necessity.[5] A selection procedure which has no adverse impact generally does not violate Title VII or the Executive order.[6] This means that an employer may usually avoid the application of the guidelines by use of procedures which have no adverse impact.[7] If adverse impact exists, it must be justified on grounds of business necessity. Normally, this means by validation which demonstrates the relation between the selection procedure and performance on the job.

The guidelines adopt a "rule of thumb" as a practical means of determining adverse impact for use in enforcement proceedings. This rule is known as the "4/5ths" or "80 percent" rule.[8] It is not a legal definition of discrimination, rather it is a practical device to keep the attention of enforcement agencies on serious discrepancies in hire or promotion rates or other employment decisions. To determine whether a selection procedure violates the "4/5ths rule," an employer compares its hiring rates for different groups.[9] But this rule of thumb cannot be applied automatically. An employer who has conducted an extensive recruiting campaign may have a larger than normal pool of applicants, and the "4/5ths rule" might unfairly expose it to enforcement proceedings.[10] On the other hand, an employer's reputation may have discouraged or "chilled" applicants of particular groups from applying because they believed application would be futile. The application of the "4/5ths" rule in that situation would allow an employer to evade scrutiny be cause of its own discrimination.[11]

III. Is Adverse Impact To Be Measured by the Overall Process?
In recent years some employers have eliminated the overall adverse impact of a selection procedure and employed sufficient numbers of minorities or women to meet this "4/5th's rule of thumb." However, they might continue use of a component which does have an adverse impact. For example, an employer

---

[5] *Griggs*, note 3, supra; uniform guidelines on employee selection procedures (1978), section 3A, (hereinafter cited by section number only).

[9] *Furnco v. Waters*, 98 S. Ct. 2943 (1978).

[7] Section 6.

[8] Section 4D.

[9] Section 16R (definition of selection rate).

[10] Section 4D (special recruiting programs).

[11] *Ibid* (user's actions have discouraged applicants).

might insist on a minimum passing score on a written test which is not job related and which has an adverse impact on minorities.[12] However, the employer might compensate for this adverse impact by hiring a sufficient proportion of minorities who do meet its standards, so that its overall hiring is on a par with or higher than the applicant flow. Employers have argued that as long as their "bottom line" shows no overall adverse impact, there is no violation at all, regardless of the operation of a particular component of the process.

Employee representatives have argued that rights under equal employment opportunity laws are individual, and the fact that an employer has hired some minorities does not justify discrimination against other minorities. Therefore, they argue that adverse impact is to be determined by examination of each component of the selection procedure, regardless of the "bottom line." This question has not been answered definitively by the courts. There are decisions pointing in both directions.

These guidelines do not address the underlying question of law. They discuss only the exercise of prosecutorial discretion by the Government agencies themselves.[13] The agencies have decided that, generally, their resources to combat discrimination should be used against those respondents whose practices have restricted or excluded the opportunities of minorities and women. If an employer is appropriately including all groups in the work force, it is not sensible to spend Government time and effort on such a case, when there are so many employers whose practices do have adverse effects which should be challenged. For this reason, the guidelines provide that, in considering whether to take enforcement action, the Government will take into account the general posture of the employer concerning equal employment opportunity, including its affirmative action plan and results achieved under the plan.[14] There are some circumstances where the government may intervene even though the "bottom line" has been satisfied. They include the case where a component of a selection procedure restricts promotional opportunities of minorities or women who were discriminatory assigned to jobs, and where a component, such as a height requirement, has been declared unlawful in other situations.[15]

What of the individual who is denied the job because of a particular component in a procedure which otherwise meets the "bottom line" standard? The individual retains the right to proceed through the appropriate agencies, and into Federal court.[16]

IV. Where Adverse Impact Exists: The Basic Options

Once an employer has established that there is adverse impact, what steps are required by the guidelines? As previously noted, the employer can modify or eliminate the procedure which produces the adverse impact, thus taking the

---

[12] See, *e.g., Griggs* v. *Duke Power Co.* 401 U.S. 424 (1971).

[13] Section 4C.

[14] Section 4E.

[15] Section 4C.

[16] The processing of individual cases is excluded from the operation of the bottom line concept by the definition of "enforcement action," section 16I. Under section 4C, where adverse impact has existed, the employer must keep records of the effect of each component for 2 years after the adverse effect has dissipated.

selection procedure from the coverage of these guidelines. If the employer does not do that, then it must justify the use of the procedure on grounds of "business necessity."[17] This normally means that it must show a clear relation between performance on the selection procedure and performance on the job. In the language of industrial psychology, the employer must validate the selection procedure. Thus the bulk of the guidelines consist of the Government's interpretation of standards for validation.

V. Validation: Consideration of Alternatives

The concept of validation as used in personnel psychology involves the establishment of the relationship between a test instrument or other selection procedure and performance on the job. Federal equal employment opportunity law has added a requirement to the process of validation. In conducting a validation study, the employer should consider available alternatives which will achieve its legitimate business purpose with lesser adverse impact.[18] The employer cannot concentrate solely on establishing the validity of the instrument or procedure which it has been using in the past.

This same principle of using the alternative with lesser adverse impact is applicable to the manner in which an employer uses a valid selection procedure.[19] The guidelines assume that there are at least three ways in which an employer can use scores on a selection procedure: (1) To screen out of consideration those who are not likely to be able to perform the job successfully; (2) to group applicants in accordance with the likelihood of their successful performance on the job; and (3) to rank applicants, selecting those with the highest scores for employment.[20]

The setting of a "cutoff score" to determine who will be screened out may have an adverse impact. If so, an employer is required to justify the initial cutoff score by reference to its need for a trustworthy and efficient work force.[21] Similarly, use of results for grouping or for rank ordering is likely to have a greater adverse effect than use of scores solely to screen out unqualified candidates. If the employer chooses to use a rank order method, the evidence of validity must be sufficient to justify that method of use.[22]

VI. Testing for Higher Level Jobs

Normally, employers test for the job for which people are hired. However, there are situations where the first job is temporary or transient, and the workers who remain are promoted to work which involves more complex activities. The guidelines restrict testing for higher level jobs to users who promote a majority of the employees who remain with them to the higher level job within a reasonable period of time.[23]

---

[17] A few practices may be used without validation even if they have adverse impact. See, *e.g. McDonnell Douglas v. Green*, 411 U.S. 792 (1973) and section 6B.

[18] *Albemarle Paper Co.* v. *Moody*, 422 U.S. 405 (1975); *Robinson* v. *Lorillard Corp.*, 444 F.2d 791 (4th Cir. 1971).

[19] Sections 3B; 5G.

[20] *Ibid.*

[21] See sections 3B; 5H. See also sections 14B(6) (criterion-related validity); 14C(9) (content validity); 14D(1) (construct validity).

[22] Sections 5G, 14B(6); 14C,(9); 14D(1).

[23] Section 51.

VII. How Is Validation to be Conducted

Validation has become highly technical and complex, and yet is constantly changing as a set of concepts in industrial psychology. What follows here is a simple introduction to a highly complex field. There are three concepts which can be used to validate a selection procedure. These concepts reflect different approaches to investigating the job relatedness of selection procedures and may be interrelated in practice. They are (1) criterion-related validity,[24] (2) content validity,[25] and (3) construct validity.[26] In criterion-related validity, a selection procedure is justified by a statistical relationship between scores on the test or other selection procedure and measures of job performance. In content validity, a selection procedure is justified by showing that it representatively samples significant parts of the job, such as a typing test for a typist. Construct validity involves identifying the psychological trait (the construct) which underlies successful performance on the job and then devising a selection procedure to measure the presence and degree of the construct. An example would be a test of "leadership ability."

The guidelines contain technical standards and documentation requirements for the application of each of the three approaches.[27] One of the problems which the guidelines attempt to meet is the "borderline" between "content validity" and "construct validity." The extreme cases are easy to understand. A secretary, for example, may have to type. Many jobs require the separation of important matters which must be handled immediately from those which can be handled routinely. For the typing function, a typing test is appropriate. It is justifiable on the basis of content validity because it is a sample of an important or critical part of the job. The second function can be viewed as involving a capability to exercise selective judgment in light of the surrounding circumstances, a mental process which is difficult to sample.

In addressing this situation, the guidelines attempt to make it practical to validate the typing test by a content strategy,[28] but do not allow the validation of a test measuring a construct such as "judgment" by a content validity strategy.

The bulk of the guidelines deals with questions such as those discussed in the above paragraphs. Not all such questions can be answered simply, nor can all problems be addressed in the single document. Once the guidelines are issued, they will have to be interpreted in light of changing factual, legal, and professional circumstances.

VIII. Simplification of Reporting and Recordkeeping Requirements

The reporting and recordkeeping provisions which appeared in the December 30 draft which was published for comment have been carefully reviewed in light of comments received and President Carter's direction to limit paperwork burdens on those regulated by Government to the minimum necessary for effec-

---

[24] Sections 5B, (General Standards); 14B (Technical Standards); 15B (Documentation); 16F (Definition).

[25] Sections 5B (General Standards); 14C (Technical Standards); 15C (Documentation); 16D (Definition).

[26] Sections 5B (General Standards); 14D (Technical Standards); 15D (Documentation); 16E (Definition).

[27] Technical standards are in section 14; documentation requirements are in section 15.

[28] Section 14C.

tive regulation. As a result of this review, two major changes have been made in the documentation requirements of the guidelines:

(1) A new section 15A(1) provides a simplified recordkeeping option for employers with fewer than 100 employees;

(2) Determinations of the adverse impact of selection procedures need not be made for groups which constitute less than 2 percent of the relevant labor force.

Also, the draft has been changed to make clear that users can assess adverse impact on an annual basis rather than on a continuing basis.

Analysis of Comments. The uniform guidelines published today are based upon the proposition that the Federal Government should speak to the public and to those whom it regulates with one voice on this important subject; and that the Federal Government ought to impose upon itself obligations for equal employment opportunity which are at least as demanding as those it seeks to impose on others. These guidelines state a uniform Federal position on this subject, and are intended to protect the rights created by Title VII of the Civil Rights Act of 1964, as amended, Executive Order 11246, as amended, and other provisions of Federal law. The uniform guidelines are also intended to represent "professionally acceptable methods" of the psychological profession for demonstrating whether a selection procedure validly predicts or measures performance for a particular job. *Albemarle Paper Co.* v. *Moody*, 442 U.S. 405, 425. They are also intended to be consistent with the decisions of the Supreme Court and authoritative decisions of other appellate courts.

Although the development of these guidelines preceded the issuance by President Jimmy Carter of Executive Order 12044 designed to improve the regulatory process, the spirit of his Executive order was followed in their development. Initial agreement among the Federal agencies was reached early in the fall of 1977, and the months from October 1977 until today have been spent in extensive consultation with civil rights groups whose clientele are protected by these guidelines; employers, labor unions, and State and local governments whose employment practices are affected by these guidelines; State and local government antidiscrimination agencies who share with the Federal Government enforcement responsibility for discriminatory practices; and appropriate members of the general public. For example, an earlier draft of these guidelines was circulated informally for comment on October 28, 1977, pursuant to OMB Circular A-85. Many comments were received from representatives of State and local governments, psychologists, private employers, and civil rights groups. Those comments were taken into account in the draft of these guidelines which was published for comment December 30, 1977, 42 FR 66542.

More than 200 organizations and individuals submitted written comments on the December 30, 1977 draft. These comments were from representatives of private industry, public employers, labor organizations, civil rights groups, the American Psychological Association and components thereof, and many individual employers, psychologists, and personnel specialists. On March 3, 1978, notice was given of a public hearing and meeting to be held on April 10, 1978, 42 FR 9131. After preliminary review of the comments, the agencies identified four issues of particular interest, and invited testimony particularly on those issues, 43 FR 11812 (March 21, 1978). In the same notice the agencies published questions and answers on four issues of concern to the commenters. The questions and answers were designed to clarify the intent of the December 30, 1977 draft, so as to provide a sharper focus for the testimony at the hearing.

At a full day of testimony on April 10, 1978, representatives of private industry, State and local governments, labor organizations, and civil rights groups, as well as psychologists, personnel specialists, and others testified at the public hearing and meeting. The written comments, testimony, and views expressed in subsequent informal consultations have been carefully considered by the four agencies. We set forth below a summary of the comments, and the major issues raised in the comments and testimony, and attempt to explain how we have resolved those issues.

The statement submitted by the American Psychological Association (A.P.A.) stated that "these guidelines represent a major step forward and with careful interpretation can provide a sound basis for concerned professional work." Most of the A.P.A. comments were directed to clarification and interpretation of the present language of the proposal. However, the A.P.A. recommended substantive change in the construct validity section and in the definition of work behavior.

Similarly, the Division of Industrial and Organizational Psychology (division 14) of the A.P.A. described the technical standards of the guidelines as "superior" in terms of congruence with professional standards to "most previous orders and guidelines but numerous troublesome aspects remain." Division 14 had substantial concerns with a number of the provisions of the general principles of the draft.

Civil rights groups generally found the uniform guidelines far superior to the FEA guidelines, and many urged the adoption, with modifications concerning ranking and documentation. Others raised concerns about the "bottom line" concept and other provisions of the guidelines.

The Ad Hoc Group on Employee Selection Procedures representing many employers in private industry supported the concept of uniform guidelines, but had a number of problems with particular provisions, some of which are described below. The American Society for Personnel Administration (ASPA) and the International Personnel Management Association, which represents State and local governments, generally took the same position as the ad hoc group. Major industrial unions found that the draft guidelines were superior to the FEA guidelines, but they perceived them to be inferior to the EEOC guidelines. They challenged particularly the bottom line concept and the construct validity section.

The building trade unions urged an exclusion of apprenticeship programs from coverage of the guidelines. The American Council on Education found them inappropriate for employment decisions concerning faculty at institutions of higher education. Other particular concerns were articulated by organizations representing the handicapped, licensing and certifying agencies, and college placement offices.

General Principles

1. Relationship between validation and elimination of adverse impact, and affirmative action. Federal equal employment opportunity law generally does not require evidence of validity for a selection procedure if there is not adverse impact; e.g., *Griggs* v. *Duke Power Co.*, 401 U.S. 424. Therefore, a user has the choice of complying either by providing evidence of validity (or otherwise justifying use in accord with Federal law), or by eliminating the adverse impact. These options have always been present under Federal law, 29 CFR 1607.3; 41 CFR 60-3.3(a); and the Federal Executive Agency Guidelines, 41 FR 51734 (November 23, 1976). The December 30 draft guidelines, however, clarified the nature of the two options open to users.

Psychologists expressed concern that the December 30 draft of section 6A encouraged the use of invalid procedures as long as there is no adverse impact. Employers added the concern that the section might encourage the use of illegal procedures not having an adverse impact against the groups who have historically suffered discrimination (minorities, women), even if they have an adverse impact on a different group (whites, males).

Section 6A was not so intended, and we have revised it to clarify the fact that illegal acts purporting to be affirmative action are not the goal of the agencies or of the guidelines; and that any employee selection procedure must be lawful and should be as job related as possible. The delineation of examples of alternative procedures was eliminated to avoid the implication that particular procedures are either prescribed or are necessarily appropriate. The basic thrust of section 6A, that elimination of adverse impact is an alternative to validation, is retained.

The inclusion of excerpts from the 1976 Equal Employment Opportunity Coordinating Council Policy Statement on Affirmative Action in section 13B of the December 30 draft was criticized as not belonging in a set of guidelines for the validation of selection procedures. Section 13 has been revised. The general statement of policy in support of voluntary affirmative action, and the reaffirmation of the policy statement have been retained, but this statement itself is now found in the appendix to the guidelines.

2. The "bottom line" (section 4C). The guidelines provide that when the overall selection process does not have an adverse impact the Government will usually not examine the individual components of that process for adverse impact or evidence of validity. The concept is based upon the view that the Federal Government should not generally concern itself with individual components of a selection process, if the overall effect of that process is nonexclusionary. Many commenters criticized the ambiguity caused by the word "generally" in the December 30 draft of section 4C which provided, "the Federal enforcement agencies generally will not take enforcement action based upon adverse impact of any component" of a process that does not have an overall adverse impact. Employer groups stated the position that the "bottom line" should be a rule prohibiting enforcement action by Federal agencies with respect to all or any part of a selection process where the bottom line does not show adverse impact. Civil rights and some labor union representatives expressed the opposing concerns that the concept may be too restrictive, that it may be interpreted as a matter of law, and that it might allow certain discriminatory conditions to go unremedied.

The guidelines have been revised to clarify the intent that the bottom line concept is based upon administrative and prosecutorial discretion. The Federal agencies cannot accept the recommendation that they never inquire into or take enforcement action with respect to any component procedure unless the whole process of which it is a part has an adverse impact. The Federal enforcement agencies believe that enforcement action may be warranted in unusual circumstances, such as those involving other discriminatory practices, or particular selection procedures which have no validity and have a clear adverse impact on a national basis. Other unusual circumstances may warrant a high-level agency decision to proceed with enforcement actions although the "bottom line" has been satisfied. At the same time the agencies adhere to the bottom line concept of allocating resources primarily to those users whose overall selection processes have an adverse impact. See overview, above, part III.

3. *Investigation of alternative selection procedures and alternative methods of use (section 3B).* The December draft included an obligation on the user, when conducting a validity study, to investigate alternative procedures and uses, in order to determine whether there are other procedures which are substantially equally valid, but which have less adverse impact. The American Psychological Association stated:

> We would concur with the drafters of the guidelines that it is appropriate in the determination of a selection strategy to consider carefully a variety of possible procedures and to think carefully about the question of adverse impact with respect to each of those procedures. Nevertheless, we feel it appropriate to note that a rigid enforcement of these sections, particularly for small employers, would impose a substantial and expensive burden on these employers.

Since a reasonable consideration of alternatives is consistent with the underlying principle of minimizing adverse impact consistent with business needs, the provision is retained.

Private employer representatives challenged earlier drafts of these guidelines as being inconsistent with the decision of the Supreme Court in *Albemarle Paper Co.* v. *Moody, 422 U.S. 405.* No such inconsistency was intended. Accordingly, the first sentence of section 3B was revised to paraphrase the opinion in the *Albemarle* decision, so as to make it clear that section 3B is in accord with the principles of the *Albemarle* decision.

Section 3B was further revised to clarify the intent of the guidelines that the obligation to investigate alternative procedures is a part of conducting a validity study, so that alternative procedures should be evaluated in light of validity studies meeting professional standards, and that section 3B does not impose an obligation to search for alternatives if the user is not required to conduct a validity study.

Just as, under section 3B of the guidelines, a user should investigate alternative selection procedures as a part of choosing and validating a procedure, so should the user investigate alternative uses of the selection device chosen to find the use most appropriate to his needs. The validity study should address the question of what method of use (screening, grouping, or rank ordering) is appropriate for a procedure based on the kind and strength of the validity evidence shown, and the degree of adverse impact of the different uses.

4. Establishment of cutoff scores and rank ordering. Some commenters from civil rights groups believed that the December 30 draft guidelines did not provide sufficient guidance as to when it was permissible to use a selection procedure on a ranking basis rather than on a pass-fail basis. They also objected to section 5G in terms of setting cutoff scores. Other comments noted a lack of clarity as to how the determination of a cutoff score or the use of a procedure for ranking candidates relates to adverse impact.

As we have noted, users are not required to validate procedures which do not have an adverse impact. However, if one way of using a procedure (e.g., for ranking) results in greater adverse impact than another way (e.g., pass/fail), the procedure must be validated for that use. Similarly, cutoff scores which result in adverse impact should be justified. If the use of a validated procedure for ranking results in greater adverse impact than its use as a screening device, the evidence of validity and utility must be sufficient to warrant use of the procedures as a ranking device.

A new section 5G has been added to clarify these concepts. Section 5H (formerly section 5G) addresses the choice of a cutoff score when a procedure is to be used for ranking.

5. Scope: Requests for exemptions for certain classes of users. Some employer groups and labor organizations (e.g., academic institutions, large public employers, apprenticeship councils) argued that they should be exempted from all or some of the provisions of these guidelines because of their special needs. The intent of Congress as expressed in Federal equal employment opportunity law is to apply the same standards to all users, public and private.

These guidelines apply the same principles and standards to all employers. On the other hand, the nature of the procedures which will actually meet those principles and standards may be different for different employers, and the guidelines recognize that fact. Accordingly, the guidelines are applicable to all employers and other users who are covered by Federal equal employment opportunity law.

Organizations of handicapped persons objected to excluding from the scope of these guidelines the enforcement of laws prohibiting discrimination on the basis of handicap, in particular the Rehabilitation Act of 1973, sections 501, 503, and 504. While this issue has not been addressed in the guidelines, nothing precludes the adoption of the principles set forth in these guidelines for other appropriate situations.

Licensing and certification boards raised the question of the applicability of the guidelines to their licensing and certification functions. The guidelines make it clear that licensing and certification are covered "to the extent" that licensing and certification may be covered by Federal equal employment opportunity law.

Voluntary certification boards, where certification is not required by law, are not users as defined in section 16 with respect to their certifying functions and therefore are not subject to these guidelines. If an employer relies upon such certification in making employment decisions, the employer is the user and must be prepared to justify, under Federal law, that reliance as it would any other selection procedure.

6. *The "Four-Fifths Rule of Thumb" (section 4D).* Some representatives of employers and some professionals suggest that the basic test for adverse impact should be a test of statistical significance, rather than the four-fifths rule. Some civil rights groups, on the other hand, still regard the four-fifths rule as permitting some unlawful discrimination.

The Federal agencies believe that neither of these positions is correct. The great majority of employers do not hire, promote, or assign enough employees for most jobs to warrant primary reliance upon statistical significance. Many decisions in day-to-day life are made on the basis of information which does not have the justification of a test of statistical significance. Courts have found adverse impact without a showing of statistical significance. *Griggs* v. *Duke Power Co.*, supra; *Vulcan Society of New York* v. *CSC of N. Y.*, 490 F.2d 387, 393 (2d Cir. 1973); *Kirkland* v. *New York St. Dept. of Corr. Serv.*, 520 F.2d 420, 425 (2d Cir. 1975).

Accordingly, the undersigned believe that while the four-fifths rule does not define discrimination and does not apply in all cases, it is appropriate as a rule of thumb in identifying adverse impact.

Technical Standards

7. *Criterion-related validity (section 14B).* This section of the guidelines found general support among the commenters from the psychological profession and, except for the provisions concerning test fairness (sometimes mistakenly equated with differential prediction or differential validity), generated relatively little comment.

The provisions of the guidelines concerning criterion-related validity studies call for studies of fairness of selection procedures where technically feasible.

Section 14B(8). Some psychologists and employer groups objected that the concept of test fairness or unfairness has been discredited by professionals and pointed out that the term is commonly misused. We recognize that there is serious debate on the question of test fairness; however, it is accepted professionally that fairness should be examined where feasible. The A.P.A. standards for educational and psychological tests, for example, direct users to explore the question of fairness on finding a difference in group performances (section E9, pp. 43-44). Similarly the concept of test fairness is one which is closely related to the basic thrust of Federal equal employment opportunity law; and that concept was endorsed by the Supreme Court in *Albemarle Paper Co.* v. *Moody*, 422 U.S. 405.

Accordingly, we have retained in the guidelines the obligation upon users to investigate test fairness where it is technically feasible to do so.

8. *Content validity.* The Division of Industrial and Organizational Psychology of A.P.A. correctly perceived that the provisions of the draft guidelines con-

cerning content validity, with their emphasis on observable work behaviors or work products, were "greatly concerned with minimizing the inferential leap between test and performance." That division expressed the view that the draft guidelines neglected situations where a knowledge, skill, or ability is necessary to an outcome but where the work behavior cannot be replicated in a test. They recommended that the section be revised.

We believe that the emphasis on observable work behaviors or observable work products is appropriate; and that in order to show content validity, the gap between the test and performance on the job should be a small one. We recognize, however, that content validity may be appropriate to support a test which measures a knowledge, skill, or ability which is a necessary prerequisite to the performance of the job, even though the test might not be close enough to the work behavior to be considered a work sample, and the guidelines have been revised appropriately. On the other hand, tests of mental processes which are not directly observable and which may be difficult to determine on the basis of observable work behaviors or work products should not be supported by content validity.

Thus, the Principles for the Validation and Use of Personnel Selection Procedures (Division of Industrial and Organizational Psychology, American Psychological Association, 1975, p. 10), discuss the use of content validity to support tests of "specific items of knowledge, or specific job skills," but call attention to the inappropriateness of attempting to justify tests for traits or constructs on a content validity basis.

9. *Construct validity (section 14D)*. Business groups and professionals expressed concern that the construct validity requirements in the December 30 draft were confusing and technically inaccurate. As section 14D indicates, construct validity is a relatively new procedure in the field of personnel selection and there is not yet substantial guidance in the professional literature as to its use in the area of employment practices. The provisions on construct validity have been revised to meet the concerns expressed by the A.P.A. The construct validity section as revised clarifies what is required by the Federal enforcement agencies at this stage in the development of construct validity. The guidelines leave open the possibility that different evidence of construct validity may be accepted in the future, as new methodologies develop and become incorporated in professional standards and other professional literature.

10. *Documentation (section 15)*. Commenters stated that the documentation section did not conform to the technical requirements of the guidelines or was otherwise inadequate. Section 15 has been clarified and two significant changes have been made to minimize the recordkeeping burden. (See overview, Part VIII.)

11. *Definitions (section 16)*. The definition of work behavior in the December 30, 1977 draft was criticized by the A.P.A. and others as being too vague to provide adequate guidance to those using the guidelines who must identify work behavior as a part of any validation technique. Other comments criticized the absence or inadequacies of other definitions, especially "adverse impact." Substantial revisions of and additions to this section were therefore made.

Uniform Guidelines on Employee Selection Procedures (1978) Table of Contents

General Principles

1607.1 Statement of Purpose
  A. Need for Uniformity—Issuing Agencies
  B. Purpose of Guidelines
  C. Relation to Prior Guidelines

1607.2 Scope
  A. Application of Guidelines
  B. Employment Decisions
  C. Selection Procedures
  D. Limitations
  E. Indian Preference Not Affected

1607.3 Discrimination Defined: Relationship between Use of Selection Procedures and Discrimination
  A. Procedure Having Adverse Impact Constitutes Discrimination unless Justified
  B. Consideration of Suitable Alternative Selection Procedures

1607.4 Information on Impact
  A. Records Concerning Impact
  B. Applicable Race, Sex, and Ethnic Groups for Recordkeeping
  C. Evaluation of Selection Rates. The "Bottom Line"
  D. Adverse Impact and the "Four-Fifths Rule"
  E. Consideration of User's Equal Employment Opportunity Posture

1607.5 General Standards for Validity Studies
  A. Acceptable Types of Validity Studies
  B. Criterion-Related, Content, and Construct Validity
  C. Guidelines Are Consistent with Professional Standards
  D. Need for Documentation of Validity
  E. Accuracy and Standardization
  F. Caution against Selection on Basis of Knowledges, Skills, or Abilities Learned in Brief Orientation Period
  G. Method of Use of Selection Procedures
  H. Cutoff Scores
  I. Use of Selection Procedures for Higher Level Jobs
  J. Interim Use of Selection Procedures
  K. Review of Validity Studies for Currency

1607.6 Use of Selection Procedures Which Have Not Been Validated
  A. Use of Alternate Selection Procedures to Eliminate Adverse Impact
  B. Where Validity Studies Cannot or Need Not Be Performed
    (1) Where Informal or Unscored Procedures Are Used
    (2) Where Formal and Scored Procedures Are Used

1607.7 Use of Other Validity Studies
  A. Validity Studies Not Conducted by the User
  B. Use of Criterion Related Validity Evidence from Other Sources
    (1) Validity Evidence
    (2) Job Similarity
    (3) Fairness Evidence
  C. Validity Evidence from Multiunit Study
  D. Other Significant Variables

Documentation of Impact and Validity Evidence

1607.15 Documentation of Impact and Validity Evidence
- A. Required Information
  - (1) Simplified Recordkeeping for Users with Less Than 100 Employees
  - (2) Information on Impact
    - (a) Collection of Information on Impact
    - (b) When Adverse Impact Has Been Eliminated in the Total Selection Process
    - (c) When Data Insufficient to Determine Impact
  - (3) Documentation of Validity Evidence
    - (a) Type of Evidence
    - (b) Form of Report
    - (c) Completeness
- B. Criterion-Related Validity Studies
  - (1) User(s), Locations(s), and Dates(s) of Study
  - (2) Problem and Setting
  - (3) Job Analysis or Review of Job Information
  - (4) Job Titles and Codes
  - (5) Criterion Measures
  - (6) Sample Description
  - (7) Description of Selection Procedures
  - (8) Techniques and Results
  - (9) Alternative Procedures Investigated
  - (10) Uses and Applications
  - (11) Source Data
  - (12) Contact Person
  - (13) Accuracy and Completeness
- C. Content Validity Studies
  - (1) User(s), Location(s), and Date(s) of Study
  - (2) Problem and Setting
  - (3) Job Analysis or Content of the Job
  - (4) Selection Procedure and Its Content
  - (5) Relationship between the Selection Procedure and the Job
  - (6) Alternative Procedures Investigated
  - (7) Uses and Applications
  - (8) Contact Person
  - (9) Accuracy and Completeness
- D. Construct Validity Studies
  - (1) User(s), Location(s), and Date(s) of Study
  - (2) Problem and Setting
  - (3) Construct Definition
  - (4) Job Analysis
  - (5) Job Titles and Codes
  - (6) Selection Procedure
  - (7) Relationship to Job Performance
  - (8) Alternative Procedures Investigated
  - (9) Uses and Applications
  - (10) Accuracy and Completeness
  - (11) Source Data
  - (12) Contact Person

General Principles

§1607.1. Statement of purpose.

A. *Need for uniformity—Issuing agencies.* The Federal Government's need for a uniform set of principles on the question of the use of tests and other selection procedures has long been recognized. The Equal Employment Opportunity Commission, the Civil Service Commission, the Department of Labor, and the Department of Justice jointly have adopted these uniform guidelines to meet that need, and to apply the same principles to the Federal Government as are applied to other employers.

B. *Purpose of guidelines.* These guidelines incorporate a single set of principles which are designed to assist employers, labor organizations, employment agencies, and licensing and certification boards to comply with requirements of Federal law prohibiting employment practices which discriminate on grounds of race, color, religion, sex, and national origin. They are designed to provide a framework for determining the proper use of tests and other selection procedures. These guidelines do not require a user to conduct validity studies of selection procedures where no adverse impact results. However, all users are encouraged to use selection procedures which are valid, especially users operating under merit principles.

C. *Relation to prior guidelines.* These guidelines are based upon and supersede previously issued guidelines on employee selection procedures. These guidelines have been built upon court decisions, the previously issued guidelines of the agencies, and the practical experience of the agencies, as well as the standards of the psychological profession. These guidelines are intended to be consistent with existing law.

§1607.2. Scope.

A. *Application of guidelines.* These guidelines will be applied by the Equal Employment Opportunity Commission in the enforcement of Title VII of the Civil Rights Act of 1964, as amended by the Equal Employment Opportunity

Act of 1972 (hereinafter "Title VII"); by the Department of Labor, and the contract compliance agencies until the transfer of authority contemplated by the President's Reorganization Plan No. 1 of 1978, in the administration and enforcement of Executive Order 11246, as amended by Executive Order 11375 (hereinafter "Executive Order 11246"); by the Civil Service Commission and other Federal agencies subject to section 717 of Title VII; by the Civil Service Commission in exercising its responsibilities toward State and local governments under section 208(b)(1) of the Intergovernmental-Personnel Act; by the Department of Justice in exercising its responsibilities under Federal law; by the Office of Revenue Sharing of the Department of the Treasury under the State and Local Fiscal Assistance Act of 1972, as amended; and by any other Federal agency which adopts them.

B. *Employment decisions.* These guidelines apply to tests and other selection procedures which are used as a basis for any employment decision. Employment decisions include but are not limited to hiring, promotion, demotion, membership (for example, in a labor organization), referral, retention, and licensing and certification, to the extent that licensing and certification may be covered by Federal equal employment opportunity law. Other selection decisions, such as selection for training or transfer, may also be considered employment decisions if they lead to any of the decisions listed above.

C. *Selection procedures.* These guidelines apply only to selection procedures which are used as a basis for making employment decisions. For example, the use of recruiting procedures designed to attract members of a particular race, sex, or ethnic group, which were previously denied employment opportunities or which are currently underutilized, may be necessary to bring an employer into compliance with Federal law, and is frequently an essential element of any effective affirmative action program; but recruitment practices are not considered by these guidelines to be selection procedures. Similarly, these guidelines do not pertain to the question of the lawfulness of a seniority system, within the meaning of section 703(h), Executive Order 11246 or other provisions of Federal law or regulation, except to the extent that such systems utilize selection procedures to determine qualifications or abilities to perform the job. Nothing in these guidelines is intended or should be interpreted as discouraging the use of a selection procedure for the purpose of determining qualifications or for the purpose of selection on the basis of relative qualifications, if the selection procedure had been validated in accord with these guidelines for each such purpose for which it is to be used.

D. *Limitations.* These guidelines apply only to persons subject to Title VII, Executive Order 11246, or other equal-employment opportunity requirements of Federal law. These guidelines do not apply to responsibilities under the Age Discrimination in Employment Act of 1967, as amended, not to discriminate on the basis of age, or under sections 501, 503, and 504 of the Rehabilitation Act of 1973, not to discriminate on the basis of handicap.

E. *Indian preference not affected.* These guidelines do not restrict any obligation imposed or right granted by Federal law to users to extend a preference in employment to Indians living on or near an Indian reservation in connection with employment opportunities on or near an Indian reservation.

§1607.3. Discrimination defined: Relationship between use of selection procedures and discrimination.

A. *Procedure having adverse impact constitutes discrimination unless justified.* The use of any selection procedure which has an adverse impact on the hiring, promotion, or other employment or membership opportunities of members of any race, sex, or ethnic group will be considered to be discriminatory and inconsistent with these guidelines, unless the procedure has been validated in accordance with these guidelines, or the provisions of section 6 below are satisfied.

B. *Consideration of suitable alternative selection procedures.* Where two or more selection procedures are available which serve the user's legitimate interest in efficient and trustworthy workmanship, and which are substantially equally valid for a given purpose, the user should use the procedure which has been demonstrated to have the lesser adverse impact. Accordingly, whenever a validity study is called for by these guidelines, the user should include, as a part of the validity study, an investigation of suitable alternative selection procedures and suitable alternative methods of using the selection procedure which have as little adverse impact as possible, to determine the appropriateness of using or validating them in accord with these guidelines. If a user has made a reasonable effort to become aware of such alternative procedures and validity has been demonstrated in accord with these guidelines, the use of the test or other selection procedure may continue until such time as it should reasonably be reviewed for currency. Whenever the user is shown an alternative selection procedure with evidence of less adverse impact and substantial evidence of validity for the same job in similar circumstances, the user should investigate it to determine the appropriateness of using or validating it in accord with these guidelines. This subsection is not intended to preclude the combination of procedures into a significantly more valid procedure, if the use of such a combination has been shown to be in compliance with the guidelines.

§1607.4. Information on impact.

A. *Records concerning impact.* Each user should maintain and have available for inspection records or other information which will disclose the impact which its tests and other selection procedures have upon employment opportunities of persons by identifiable race, sex, or ethnic group as set forth in subparagraph B below in order to determine compliance with these guidelines. Where there are large numbers of applicants and procedures are administered frequently, such information may be retained on a sample basis, provided that the sample is appropriate in terms of the applicant population and adequate in size.

B. *Applicable race, sex, and ethnic groups for recordkeeping.* The records called for by this section are to be maintained by sex, and the following races and ethnic groups: Blacks (Negroes), American Indians (including Alaskan Natives), Asians (including Pacific Islanders), Hispanic (including persons of Mexican, Puerto Rican, Cuban, Central or South American, or other Spanish origin or culture regardless of race), whites (Caucasians) other than Hispanic, and totals. The race, sex, and ethnic classifications called for by this section are consistent with the Equal Employment Opportunity Standard Form 100, Employer Information Report EEO-l series of reports. The user should adopt safeguards to insure that the records required by this paragraph are used for appropriate purposes such as determining adverse impact, or (where required) for developing and monitoring affirmative action programs, and that such records are not used improperly. See sections 4E and 17(4), below.

C. *Evaluation of selection rates. The "bottom line."* If the information called for by sections 4A and B above shows that the total selection process for a job has an adverse impact, the individual components of the selection process should be evaluated for adverse impact. If this information shows that the total selection process does not have an adverse impact, the Federal enforcement agencies, in the exercise of their administrative and prosecutorial discretion, in usual circumstances, will not expect a user to evaluate the individual components for adverse impact, or to validate such individual components, and will not take enforcement action based upon adverse impact of any component of that process, including the separate parts of a multipart selection procedure or any separate procedure that is used as an alternative method of selection. However, in the following circumstances the Federal enforcement agencies will expect a user to evaluate the individual components for adverse impact and may, where appropriate, take enforcement action with respect to the individual components: (1) where the selection procedure is a significant factor in the continuation of patterns of assignments of incumbent employees caused by prior discriminatory employment practices, (2) where the weight of court decisions or administrative interpretations hold that a specific procedure (such as height or weight requirements or no arrest records) is not job related in the same or similar circumstances. In unusual circumstances, other than those listed in (1) and (2) above, the Federal enforcement agencies may request a user to evaluate the individual components for adverse impact and may, where appropriate, take enforcement action with respect to the individual component.

D. *Adverse impact and the "four-fifths rule."* A selection rate for any race, sex, or ethnic group which is less than four-fifths (4/5) (or eighty percent) of the rate for the group with the highest rate will generally be regarded by the Federal enforcement agencies as evidence of adverse impact, while a greater than four-fifths rate will generally not be regarded by Federal enforcement agencies as evidence of adverse impact. Smaller differences in selection rate may nevertheless constitute adverse impact, where they are significant in both statistical and practical terms or where a user's actions have discouraged applicants disproportionately on grounds of race, sex, or ethnic group. Greater differences in selection rate may not constitute adverse impact where the differences are based on small numbers and are not statistically significant, or where special recruiting or other programs cause the pool of minority or female candidates to be atypical of the normal pool of applicants from that group. Where the user's evidence concerning the impact of a selection procedure indicates adverse impact but is based upon numbers which are too small to be reliable, evidence concerning the impact of the procedure over a longer period of time and/or evidence concerning the impact which the selection procedure had when used in the same manner in similar circumstances elsewhere may be considered in determining adverse impact. Where the user has not maintained data on adverse impact as required by the documentation section of applicable guidelines, the Federal enforcement agencies may draw an inference of adverse impact of the selection process from the failure of the user to maintain such data, if the user has an underutilization of a group in the job category, as compared to the group's representation in the relevant labor market or, in the case of jobs filled from within, the applicable work force.

E. *Consideration of user's equal employment opportunity posture.* In carrying out their obligations, the Federal enforcement agencies will consider the general posture of the user with respect to equal employment opportunity for the job or group of jobs in question. Where a user has adopted an affirmative action program, the Federal enforcement agencies will consider the provisions of that program, including the goals and timetables which the user has adopted and the progress which the user has made in carrying out that program and in meeting the goals and timetables. While such affirmative action programs may in design and execution be race, color, sex, or ethnic conscious, selection procedures under such programs should be based upon the ability or relative ability to do the work.

§1607.5. General standards for validity studies.

A. *Acceptable types of validity studies.* For the purposes of satisfying these guidelines, users may rely upon criterion-related validity studies, content validity studies or construct validity studies, in accordance with the standards set forth in the technical standards of these guidelines, section 14 below. New strategies for showing the validity of selection procedures will be evaluated as they become accepted by the psychological profession

B. *Criterion-related, content, and construct validity.* Evidence of the validity of a test or other selection procedure by a criterion-related validity study should consist of empirical data demonstrating that the selection procedure is predictive of or significantly correlated with important elements of job performance. See section 14B below. Evidence of the validity of a test or other selection procedure by a content validity study should consist of data showing that the content of the selection procedure is representative of important aspects of performance on the job for which the candidates are to he evaluated. See section 14C below. Evidence of the validity of a test or other selection procedure through a construct validity study should consist of data showing that the procedure measures the degree to which candidates have identifiable characteristics which have been determined to be important in successful performance in the job for which the candidates are to be evaluated. See section 14D below.

C. *Guidelines are consistent with professional standards.* The provisions of these guidelines relating to validation of selection procedures are intended to be consistent with generally accepted professional standards for evaluating standardized tests and other selection procedures, such as those described in the Standards for Educational and Psychological Tests prepared by a joint committee of the American Psychological Association, the American Educational Research Association, and the National Council on Measurement in Education (American Psychological Association, Washington, D.C., 1974) (hereinafter "A.P.A. Standards") and standard textbooks and journals in the field of personnel selection.

D. *Need for documentation of validity.* For any selection procedure which is part of a selection process which has an adverse impact and which selection procedure has an adverse impact, each user should maintain and have available such documentation as is described in section 15 below.

E. *Accuracy and standardization.* Validity studies should be carried out under conditions which assure insofar as possible the adequacy and accuracy of the research and the report. Selection procedures should be administered and scored under standardized conditions.

F. *Caution against selection on basis of knowledges, skills, or ability learned in brief orientation period.* In general, users should avoid making employment decisions on the basis of measures of knowledges, skills, or abilities which are normally learned in a brief orientation period, and which have an adverse impact.

G. *Method of use of selection procedures.* The evidence of both the validity and utility of a selection procedure should support the method the user chooses for operational use of the procedure, if that method of use has a greater adverse impact than another method of use. Evidence which may be sufficient to support the use of a selection procedure on a pass/fail (screening) basis may be insufficient to support the use of the same procedure on a ranking basis under these guidelines. Thus, if a user decides to use a selection procedure on a ranking basis, and that method of use has a greater adverse impact than use on an appropriate pass/fail basis (see section 5H below), the user should have sufficient evidence of validity and utility to support the use on a ranking basis. See sections 3B, 14B (5) and (6), and 14C (8) and (9).

H. *Cutoff scores.* Where cutoff scores are used, they should normally be set so as to be reasonable and consistent with normal expectations of acceptable proficiency within the work force. Where applicants are ranked on the basis of properly validated selection procedures and those applicants scoring below a higher cutoff score than appropriate in light of such expectations have little or no chance of being selected for employment, the higher cutoff score may be appropriate, but the degree of adverse impact should be considered.

I. *Use of selection procedures for higher level jobs.* If job progression structures are so established that employees will probably, within a reasonable period of time and in a majority of cases, progress to a higher level, it may be considered that the applicants are being evaluated for a job or jobs at the higher level. However, where job progression is not so nearly automatic, or the time span is such that higher level jobs or employees' potential may be expected to change in significant ways, it should be considered that applicants are being evaluated for a job at or near the entry level. A "reasonable period of time" will vary for different jobs and employment situations but will seldom be more than 5 years. Use of selection procedures to evaluate applicants for a higher level job would not be appropriate:

(1) If the majority of those remaining employed do not progress to the higher level job;

(2) If there is a reason to doubt that the higher level job will continue to require essentially similar skills during the progression period; or

(3) If the selection procedures measure knowledges, skills, or abilities required for advancement which would be expected to develop principally from the training or experience on the job.

J. *Interim use of selection procedures.* Users may continue the use of a selection procedure which is not at the moment fully supported by the required evidence of validity, provided: (1) The user has available substantial evidence of validity, and (2) the user has in progress, when technically feasible, a study which is designed to produce the additional evidence required by these guidelines within a reasonable time. If such a study is not technically feasible, see section 6B. If the study does not demonstrate validity, this provision of these guidelines for interim use shall not constitute a defense in any action, nor shall it relieve the user of any obligations arising under Federal law.

K. *Review of validity studies for currency.* Whenever validity has been shown in accord with these guidelines for the use of a particular selection procedure for a job or group of jobs, additional studies need not be performed until such time as the validity study is subject to review as provided in section 3B above. There are no absolutes in the area of determining the currency of a validity study. All circumstances concerning the study, including the validation strategy used, and changes in the relevant labor market and the job should be considered in the determination of when a validity study is outdated.

§1607.6. Use of selection procedures which have not been validated.

A. *Use of alternate selection procedures to eliminate adverse impact.* A user may choose to utilize alternative selection procedures in order to eliminate adverse impact or as part of an affirmative action program. See section 13 below. Such alternative procedures should eliminate the adverse impact in the total selection process, should be lawful and should be as job related as possible.

B. *Where validity studies cannot or need not be performed.* There are circumstances in which a user cannot or need not utilize the validation techniques contemplated by these guidelines. In such circumstances, the user should utilize selection procedures which are as job related as possible and which will minimize or eliminate adverse impact, as set forth below.

(1) *Where informal or unscored procedures are used.* When an informal or unscored selection procedure which has an adverse impact is utilized, the user should eliminate the adverse impact, or modify the procedure to one which is a formal, scored or quantified measure or combination of measures and then validate the procedure in accord with these guidelines, or otherwise justify continued use of the procedure in accord with Federal law.

(2) *Where formal and scored procedures are used.* When a formal and scored selection procedure is used which has an adverse impact, the validation techniques contemplated by these guidelines usually should be followed if technically feasible. Where the user cannot or need not follow the validation techniques anticipated by these guidelines, the user should either modify the procedure to eliminate adverse impact or otherwise justify continued use of the procedure in accord with Federal law.

§1607.7. Use of other validity studies.

A. *Validity studies not conducted by the user.* Users may, under certain circumstances, support the use of selection procedures by validity studies conducted by other users or conducted by test publishers or distributors and described in test manuals. While publishers of selection procedures have a professional obligation to provide evidence of validity which meets generally accepted professional standards (see section 5C above), users are cautioned that they are responsible for compliance with these guidelines. Accordingly, users seeking to obtain selection procedures from publishers and distributors should be careful to determine that, in the event the user becomes subject to the validity requirements of these guidelines, the necessary information to support validity has been determined and will be made available to the user.

B. *Use of criterion-related validity evidence from other sources.* Criterion-related validity studies conducted by one test user, or described in test manuals and the professional literature, will be considered acceptable for use by another user when the following requirements are met:

(1) *Validity evidence.* Evidence from the available studies meeting the standards of section 14B below clearly demonstrates that the selection procedure is valid;

(2) *Job similarity.* The incumbents in the user's job and the incumbents in the job or group of jobs on which the validity study was conducted perform substantially the same major work behaviors, as shown by appropriate job analyses both on the job or group of jobs on which the validity study was performed and on the job for which the selection procedure is to be used; and

(3) *Fairness evidence.* The studies include a study of test fairness for each race, sex, and ethnic group which constitutes a significant factor in the borrowing user's relevant labor market for the job or jobs in question. If the studies under consideration satisfy (1) and (2) above but do not contain an investigation of test fairness, and it is not technically feasible for the borrowing user to conduct an internal study of test fairness, the borrowing user may utilize the study until studies conducted elsewhere meeting the requirements of these guidelines show test unfairness, or until such time as it becomes technically feasible to conduct an internal study of test fairness and the results of that study can be acted upon. Users obtaining selection procedures from publishers should consider, as one factor in the decision to purchase a particular selection procedure, the availability of evidence concerning test fairness.

C. *Validity evidence from multiunit study.* If validity evidence from a study covering more than one unit within an organization satisfies the requirements of section 14B below, evidence of validity specific to each unit will not be required unless there are variables which are likely to affect validity significantly.

D. *Other significant variables.* If there are variables in the other studies which are likely to affect validity significantly, the user may not rely upon such studies, but will be expected either to conduct an internal validity study or to comply with section 6 above.

§1607.8. Cooperative studies.

A. *Encouragement of cooperative studies.* The agencies issuing these guidelines encourage employers, labor organizations, and employment agencies to cooperate in research, development, search for lawful alternatives, and validity studies in order to achieve procedures which are consistent with these guidelines.

B. *Standards for use of cooperative studies.* If validity evidence from a cooperative study satisfies the requirements of section 14 below, evidence of validity specific to each user will not be required unless there are variables in the user's situation which are likely to affect validity significantly.

§1607.9. No assumption of validity.

A. *Unacceptable substitutes for evidence of validity.* Under no circumstances will the general reputation of a test or other selection procedures, its author or its publisher, or casual reports of its validity be accepted in lieu of evidence of validity. Specifically ruled out are: assumptions of validity based on a procedure's name or descriptive labels; all forms of promotional literature; data bearing on the frequency of a procedure's usage; testimonial statements and credentials of sellers, users, or consultants; and other nonempirical or anecdotal accounts of selection practices or selection outcomes.

B. *Encouragement of professional supervision.* Professional supervision of selection activities is encouraged but is not a substitute for documented evidence of validity. The enforcement agencies will take into account the fact that a thorough job analysis was conducted and that careful development and use of a selection procedure in accordance with professional standards enhance the probability that the selection procedure is valid for the job.

§1607.10. Employment agencies and employment services.

A. *Where selection procedures are devised by agency.* An employment agency, including private employment agencies and State employment agencies, which agrees to a request by an employer or labor organization to devise and utilize a selection procedure should follow the standards in these guidelines for determining adverse impact. If adverse impact exists the agency should comply with these guidelines. An employment agency is not relieved of its obligation herein because the user did not request such validation or has requested the use of some lesser standard of validation than is provided in these guidelines. The use of an employment agency does not relieve and employer or labor organization or other user of its responsibilities under Federal law to provide equal employment opportunity or its obligations as a user under these guidelines.

B. *Where selection procedures are devised elsewhere.* Where an employment agency or service is requested to administer a selection procedure which has been devised elsewhere and to make referrals pursuant to the results, the employment agency or service should maintain and have available evidence of the impact of the selection and referral procedures which it administers. If adverse impact results the agency or service should comply with these guidelines. If the agency or service seeks to comply with these guidelines by reliance upon validity studies or other data in the possession of the employer, it should obtain and have available such information.

§1607.11. Disparate treatment.

The principles of disparate or unequal treatment must be distinguished from the concepts of validation. A selection procedure—even though validated against job performance in accordance with these guidelines—cannot be imposed upon members of a race, sex, or ethnic group where other employees, applicants, or members have not been subjected to that standard. Disparate treatment occurs where members of a race, sex, or ethnic group have been denied the same employment, promotion, membership, or other employment opportunities as have been available to other employees or applicants. Those employees or applicants who have been denied equal treatment, because of prior discriminatory practices or policies, must at least be afforded the same opportunities as had existed for other employees or applicants during the period of discrimination. Thus, the persons who were in the class of persons discriminated against during the period the user followed the discriminatory practices should be allowed the opportunity to qualify under less stringent selection procedures previously followed, unless the user demonstrates that the increased standards are required by business necessity. This section does not prohibit a user who has not previously followed merit standards from adopting merit standards which are in compliance with these guidelines nor does it preclude a user who has previously used invalid or invalidated selection procedures from developing and using procedures which are in accord with these guidelines.

§1607.12. Retesting of applicants.

Users should provide a reasonable opportunity for retesting and reconsideration. Where examinations are administered periodically with public notice, such reasonable opportunity exists, unless persons who have previously been tested are precluded from retesting. The user may however take reasonable steps to preserve the security of its procedures.

§1607.13. Affirmative action.

A. *Affirmative action obligations.* The use of selection procedures which have been validated pursuant to these guidelines does not relieve users of any obligations they may have to undertake affirmative action to assure equal employment opportunity. Nothing in these guidelines is intended to preclude the use of lawful selection procedures which assist in remedying the effects of prior discriminatory practices, or the achievement of affirmative action objectives.

B. *Encouragement of voluntary affirmative action programs.* These guidelines are also intended to encourage the adoption and implementation of voluntary affirmative action programs by users who have no obligation under Federal law to adopt them, but are not intended to impose any new obligations in that regard. The agencies issuing and endorsing these guidelines endorse for all private employers and reaffirm for all governmental employers the Equal Employment Opportunity Coordinating Council's "Policy Statement on Affirmative Action Programs for State and Local Government Agencies" (41 FR 38814, September 13, 1976). That policy statement is attached hereto as appendix, section 17.

Technical Standards

§1607.14. Technical standards for validity studies.

The following minimum standards, as applicable, should be met in conducting a validity study. Nothing in these guidelines is intended to preclude the development and use of other professionally acceptable techniques with respect to validation of selection procedures. Where it is not technically feasible for a user to conduct a validity study, the user has the obligation otherwise to comply with these guidelines. See sections 6 and 7 above.

A. *Validity studies should be based on review of information about the job.* Any validity study should be based upon a review of information about the job for which the selection procedure is to be used. The review should include a job analysis except as provided in section 14B(3) below with respect to criterion-related validity. Any method of job analysis may be used if it provides the information required for the specific validation strategy used.

B. *Technical standards for criterion-related validity studies.*—(1) *Technical feasibility.* Users choosing to validate a selection procedure by a criterion-related validity strategy should determine whether it is technically feasible (as defined in section 16) to conduct such a study in the particular employment context. The determination of the number of persons necessary to permit the conduct of a meaningful criterion-related study should be made by the user on the basis of all relevant information concerning the selection procedure, the potential sample and the employment situation. Where appropriate, jobs with substantially the same major work behaviors may be grouped together for validity studies, in order to obtain an adequate sample. These guidelines do not require a user to hire or promote persons for the purpose of making it possible to conduct a criterion-related study.

(2) *Analysis of the job.* There should be a review of job information to determine measures of work behavior(s) or performance that are relevant to the job or group of jobs in question. These measures or criteria are relevant to the extent that they represent critical or important job duties, work behaviors or work outcomes as developed from the review of job information. The possibility of bias should be considered both in selection of the criterion measures and their application. In view of the possibility of bias in subjective evaluations, supervisory rating techniques and instructions to raters should be carefully developed. All criterion measures and the methods for gathering data need to be examined for freedom from factors which would unfairly alter scores of members of any group. The relevance of criteria and their freedom from bias are of particular concern when there are significant differences in measures of job performance for different groups.

(3) *Criterion measures.* Proper safeguards should be taken to insure that scores on selection procedures do not enter into any judgments of employee adequacy that are to be used as criterion measures. Whatever criteria are used should represent important or critical work behavior(s) or work outcomes. Certain criteria may be used without a full job analysis if the user can show the importance of the criteria to the particular employment context. These criteria include but are not limited to production rate, error rate, tardiness, absenteeism, and length of service. A standardized rating of overall work performance may be used where a study of the job shows that it is an appropriate criterion. Where performance in training is used as a criterion, success in training should be properly measured and the relevance of the training should be shown either through a comparison of the content of the training program with the critical or important work behavior(s) of the job(s), or through a demonstration of the relationship between measures of performance in training and measures of job performance. Measures of relative success in training include but are not limited to instructor evaluations, performance samples, or tests. Criterion measures consisting of paper and pencil tests will be closely reviewed for job relevance.

(4) *Representatives of the sample.* Whether the study is predictive or concurrent, the sample subjects should insofar as feasible be representative of the candidates normally available in the relevant labor market for the job or group of jobs in question, and should insofar as feasible include the races, sexes, and ethnic groups normally available in the relevant job market. In determining the representativeness of the sample in a concurrent validity study, the user should take into account the extent to which the specific knowledges or skills which are the primary focus of the test are those which employees learn on the job.

Where samples are combined or compared, attention should be given to see that such samples are comparable in terms of the actual job they perform, the length of time on the job where time on the job is likely to affect performance, and other relevant factors likely to affect validity differences; or that these factors are included in the design of the study and their effects identified.

(5) *Statistical relationships.* The degree of relationship between selection procedure scores and criterion measures should be examined and computed, using professionally acceptable statistical procedures. Generally, a selection procedure is considered related to the criterion, for the purpose of these guidelines, when the relationship between performance on the procedure and performance on the criterion measure is statistically significant at the 0.05 level of significance, which means that it is sufficiently high as to have a probability of no more than one (1) in twenty (20) to have occurred by chance. Absence of a statistically significant relationship between a selection procedure and job performance should not necessarily discourage other investigations of the validity of that selection procedure.

(6) *Operational use of selection procedures.* Users should evaluate each selection procedure to assure that it is appropriate for operational use, including establishment of cutoff scores or rank ordering. Generally, if other factors remain the same, the greater the magnitude of the relationship (e.g., correlation coefficient) between performance on a selection procedure and one or more criteria of performance on the job, and the greater the importance and number of aspects of job performance covered by the criteria, the more likely it is that the procedure will be appropriate for use. Reliance upon a selection procedure which is significantly related to a criterion measure, but which is based upon a study involving a large number of subjects and has a low correlation coefficient will be subject to close review if it has a large adverse impact. Sole reliance upon a single selection instrument which is related to only one of many job duties or aspects of job performance will also be subject to close review. The appropriateness of a selection procedure is best evaluated in each particular situation and there are no minimum correlation coefficients applicable to all employment situations. In determining whether a selection procedure is appropriate for operational use the following considerations should also be taken into account: The degree of adverse impact of the procedure, the availability of other selection procedures of greater or substantially equal validity.

(7) *Overstatement of validity findings.* Users should avoid reliance upon techniques which tend to overestimate validity findings as a result of capitalization on chance unless an appropriate safeguard is taken. Reliance upon a few selection procedures or criteria of successful job performance when many selection procedures or criteria of performance have been studied, or the use of optimal statistical weights for selection procedures computed in one sample, are techniques which tend to inflate validity estimates as a result of chance. Use of a large sample is one safeguard; cross-validation is another.

(8) *Fairness.* This section generally calls for studies of unfairness where technically feasible. The concept of fairness or unfairness of selection procedures is a developing concept. In addition, fairness studies generally require substantial

numbers of employees in the job or group of jobs being studied. For these reasons, the Federal enforcement agencies recognize that the obligation to conduct studies of fairness imposed by the guidelines generally will be upon users or groups of users with a large number of persons in a job class, or test developers; and that small users utilizing their own selection procedures will generally not be obligated to conduct such studies because it will be technically infeasible for them to do so.

(a) *Unfairness defined.* When members of one race, sex, or ethnic group characteristically obtain lower scores on a selection procedure than members of another group, and the differences in scores are not reflected in differences in a measure of job performance, use of the selection procedure may unfairly deny opportunities to members of the group that obtains the lower scores.

(b) *Investigation of fairness.* Where a selection procedure results in an adverse impact on a race, sex, or ethnic group identified in accordance with the classifications set forth in section 4 above and that group is a significant factor in the relevant labor market, the user generally should investigate the possible existence of unfairness for that group if it is technically feasible to do so. The greater the severity of the adverse impact on a group, the greater the need to investigate the possible existence of unfairness. Where the weight of evidence from other studies shows that the selection procedure predicts fairly for the group in question and for the same or similar jobs, such evidence may be relied on in connection with the selection procedure at issue.

(c) *General considerations in fairness investigations.* Users conducting a study of fairness should review the A.P.A. Standards regarding investigation of possible bias in testing. An investigation of fairness of a selection procedure depends on both evidence of validity and the manner in which the selection procedure is to be used in a particular employment context. Fairness of a selection procedure cannot necessarily be specified in advance without investigating these factors. Investigation of fairness of a selection procedure in samples where the range of scores on selection procedures or criterion measures is severely restricted for any subgroup sample (as compared to other subgroup samples) may produce misleading evidence of unfairness. That factor should accordingly be taken into account in conducting such studies and before reliance is placed on the results.

(d) *When unfairness is shown.* If unfairness is demonstrated through a showing that members of a particular group perform better or poorer on the job than their scores on the selection procedure would indicate through comparison with how members of other groups perform, the user may either revise or replace the selection instrument in accordance with these guidelines, or may continue to use the selection instrument operationally with appropriate revisions in its use to assure compatibility between the probability of successful job performance and the probability of being selected.

(e) *Technical feasibility of fairness studies.* In addition to the general conditions needed for technical feasibility for the conduct of a criterion-related study (see section 16, below) an investigation of fairness requires the following:

(i) An adequate sample of persons in each group available for the study to achieve findings of statistical significance. Guidelines do not require a user to hire or promote persons on the basis of group classifications for the purpose of making it possible to conduct a study of fairness; but the user has the obligation otherwise to comply with these guidelines.

(ii) The samples for each group should be comparable in terms of the actual job they perform, length of time on the job where time on the job is likely to affect performance, and other relevant factors likely to affect validity differences; or such factors should be included in the design of the study and their effects identified.

(f) *Continued use of selection procedures when fairness studies not feasible.* If a study of fairness should otherwise be performed, but is not technically feasible, a selection procedure may be used which has otherwise met the validity standards of these guidelines, unless the technical infeasibility resulted from discriminatory employment practices which are demonstrated by facts other than past failure to conform with requirements for validation of selection procedures. However, when it becomes technically feasible for the user to perform a study of fairness and such a study is otherwise called for, the user should conduct the study of fairness.

C. *Technical standards for content validity studies.*—(1) *Appropriateness of content validity studies.* Users choosing to validate a selection procedure by a content validity strategy should determine whether it is appropriate to conduct such a study in the particular employment context. A selection procedure can be supported by a content validity strategy to the extent that it is a representative sample of the content of the job. Selection procedures which purport to measure knowledges, skills, or abilities may in certain circumstances be justified by content validity, although they may not be representative samples, if the knowledge, skill, or ability measured by the selection procedure can be operationally defined as provided in section 14C(4) below, and if that knowledge, skill, or ability is a necessary prerequisite to successful job performance.

A selection procedure based upon inferences about mental processes cannot be supported solely or primarily on the basis of content validity. Thus, a content strategy is not appropriate for demonstrating the validity of selection procedures which purport to measure traits or constructs, such as intelligence, aptitude, personality, common sense, judgment, leadership, and spatial ability. Content validity is also not an appropriate strategy when the selection procedure involves knowledges, skills, or abilities which an employee will be expected to learn on the job.

(2) *Job analysis for content validity.* There should be a job analysis which includes an analysis of the important work behavior(s) required for successful performance and their relative importance and, if the behavior results in work product(s), an analysis of the work product(s). Any job analysis should focus on the work behavior(s) and the tasks associated with them. If work behavior(s) are not observable, the job analysis should identify and analyze those aspects of the behavior(s) that can be observed and the observed work products. The work behavior(s) selected for measurement should be critical work behavior(s) and/or important work behavior(s) constituting most of the job.

(3) *Development of selection procedures.* A selection procedure designed to measure the work behavior may be developed specifically from the job and job analy-

sis in question, or may have been previously developed by the user, or by other users or by a test publisher.

(4) *Standards for demonstrating content validity.* To demonstrate the content validity of a selection procedure, a user should show that the behavior(s) demonstrated in the selection procedure are a representative sample of the behavior(s) of the job in question or that the selection procedure provides a representative sample of the work product of the job. In the case of a selection procedure measuring a knowledge, skill, or ability, the knowledge, skill, or ability being measured should be operationally defined. In the case of a selection procedure measuring a knowledge, the knowledge being measured should be operationally defined as that body of learned information which is used in and is a necessary prerequisite for observable aspects of work behavior of the job. In the case of skills or abilities, the skill or ability being measured should be operationally defined in terms of observable aspects of work behavior of the job. For any selection procedure measuring a knowledge, skill, or ability the user should show that (a) the selection procedure measures and is a representative sample of that knowledge, skill, or ability; and (b) that knowledge, skill, or ability is used in and is a necessary prerequisite to performance of critical or important work behavior(s). In addition, to be content valid, a selection procedure measuring a skill or ability should either closely approximate an observable work behavior, or its product should closely approximate an observable work product. If a test purports to sample a work behavior or to provide a sample of a work product, the manner and setting of the selection procedure and its level and complexity should closely approximate the work situation. The closer the content and the context of the selection procedure are to work samples or work behaviors, the stronger is the basis for showing content validity. As the content of the selection procedure less resembles a work behavior, or the setting and manner of the administration of the selection procedure less resemble the work situation, or the result less resembles a work product, the less likely the selection procedure is to be content valid, and the greater the need for other evidence of validity.

(5) *Reliability.* The reliability of selection procedures justified on the basis of content validity should be a matter of concern to the user. Whenever it is feasible, appropriate statistical estimates should be made of the reliability of the selection procedure.

(6) *Prior training or experience.* A requirement for or evaluation of specific prior training or experience based on content validity, including a specification of level or amount of training or experience, should be justified on the basis of the relationship between the content of the training or experience and the content of the job for which the training or experience is to be required or evaluated. The critical consideration is the resemblance between the specific behaviors, products, knowledges, skills, or abilities in the experience or training and the specific behaviors, products, knowledges, skills, or abilities required on the job, whether or not there is close resemblance between the experience or training as a whole and the job as a whole.

(7) *Content validity of training success.* Where a measure of success in a training program is used as a selection procedure and the content of a training program is justified on the basis of content validity, the use should be justified

on the relationship between the content of the training program and the content of the job.

(8) *Operational use.* A selection procedure which is supported on the basis of content validity may be used for a job if it represents a critical work behavior (i.e., a behavior which is necessary for performance of the job) or work behaviors which constitute most of the important parts of the job.

(9) *Ranking based on content validity studies.* If a user can show, by a job analysis or otherwise, that a higher score on a content valid selection procedure is likely to result in better job performance, the results may be used to rank persons who score above minimum levels. Where a selection procedure supported solely or primarily by content validity is used to rank job candidates, the selection procedure should measure those aspects of performance which differentiate among levels of job performance.

D. *Technical standards for construct validity studies.*—(1) *Appropriateness of construct validity studies.* Construct validity is a more complex strategy than either criterion-related or content validity. Construct validation is a relatively new and developing procedure in the employment field, and there is at present a lack of substantial literature extending the concept to employment practices. The user should be aware that the effort to obtain sufficient empirical support for construct validity is both an extensive and arduous effort involving a series of research studies, which include criterion-related validity studies and which may include content validity studies. Users choosing to justify use of a selection procedure by this strategy should therefore take particular care to assure that the validity study meets the standards set forth below.

(2) *Job analysis for construct validity studies.* There should be a job analysis. This job analysis should show the work behavior(s) required for successful performance of the job, or the groups of jobs being studied, the critical or important work behavior(s) in the job or group of jobs being studied, and an identification of the construct(s) believed to underlie successful performance of these critical or important work behaviors in the job or jobs in question. Each construct should be named and defined, so as to distinguish it from other constructs. If a group of jobs is being studied the jobs should have in common one or more critical or important work behaviors at a comparable level of complexity.

(3) *Relationship to the job.* A selection procedure should then be identified or developed which measures the construct identified in accord with subparagraph (2) above. The user should show by empirical evidence that the selection procedure is validly related to the construct and that the construct is validly related to the performance of critical or important work behavior(s). The relationship between the construct as measured by the selection procedure and the related work behavior(s) should be supported by empirical evidence from one or more criterion-related studies involving the job or jobs in question which satisfy the provisions of section 14B above.

(4) *Use of construct validity study without new criterion-related evidence*—(a) *Standards for use.* Until such time as professional literature provides more guidance on the use of construct validity in employment situations, the Federal agencies will accept a claim of construct validity without a criterion-related study which satisfies section 14B above only when the selection procedure has been

used elsewhere in a situation in which a criterion-related study has been conducted and the use of a criterion-related validity study in this context meets the standards for transportability of criterion-related validity studies as set forth above in section 7. However, if a study pertains to a number of jobs having common critical or important work behaviors at a comparable level of complexity, and the evidence satisfies subparagraphs 14B (2) and (3) above for those jobs with criterion-related validity evidence for those jobs, the selection procedure may be used for all the jobs to which the study pertains. If construct validity is to be generalized to other jobs or groups of jobs not in the group studied, the Federal enforcement agencies will expect at a minimum additional empirical research evidence meeting the standards of subparagraphs section 14B (2) and (3) above for the additional jobs or groups of jobs.

(b) *Determination of common work behaviors.* In determining whether two or more jobs have one or more work behavior(s) in common, the user should compare the observed work behavior(s) in each of the jobs and should compare the observed work product(s) in each of the jobs. If neither the observed work behavior(s) in each of the jobs nor the observed work product(s) in each of the jobs are the same, the Federal enforcement agencies will presume that the work behavior(s) in each job are different. If the work behaviors are not observable, then evidence of similarity of work products and any other relevant research evidence will be considered in determining whether the work behavior(s) in the two jobs are the same.

Documentation of Impact and Validity Evidence
§1607.15. Documentation of impact and validity evidence

A. *Required information.* Users of selection procedures other than those users complying with section 15A(1) below should maintain and have available for each job information on adverse impact of the selection process for that job and, where it is determined a selection process has an adverse impact, evidence of validity as set forth below.

(1) *Simplified recordkeeping for users with less than 100 employees.* In order to minimize recordkeeping burdens on employers who employ one hundred (100) or fewer employees, and other users not required to file EEO-1, et seq., reports, such users may satisfy the requirements of this section 15 if they maintain and have available records showing, for each year:

(a) The number of persons hired, promoted, and terminated for each job, by sex, and where appropriate by race and national origin;

(b) The number of applicants for hire and promotion by sex and where appropriate by race and national origin; and

(c) The selection procedures utilized (either standardized or not standardized).

These records should be maintained for each race or national origin group (see section 4 above) constituting more than two percent (2%) of the labor force in the relevant labor area. However, it is not necessary to maintain records by race and/or national origin (see §4 above) if one race or national origin group in the relevant labor area constitutes more than ninety-eight percent (98%) of the labor force in the area. If the user has reason to believe that a selection procedure has an adverse impact, the user should maintain any available evidence of validity for that procedure (see sections 7A and 8).

(2) *Information on impact*—(a) *Collection of information on impact.* Users of selection procedures other than those complying with section 15A(1) above should maintain and have available for each job records of other information showing whether the total selection process for that job has an adverse impact on any of the groups for which records are called for by sections 4B above. Adverse impact determinations should be made at least annually for each such group which constitutes at least 2 percent of the labor force in the relevant labor area or 2 percent of the applicable workforce. Where a total selection process for a job has an adverse impact, the user should maintain and have available records or other information showing which components have an adverse impact. Where the total selection process for a job does not have an adverse impact, information need not be maintained for individual components except in circumstances set forth in subsection 15A(2)(b) below. If the determination of adverse impact is made using a procedure other than the "four-fifths rule," as defined in the first sentence of section 4D above, a justification, consistent with section 4D above, for the procedure used to determine adverse impact should be available.

(b) *When adverse impact has been eliminated in the total selection process.* Whenever the total selection process for a particular job has had an adverse impact, as defined in section 4 above, in any year, but no longer has an adverse impact, the user should maintain and have available the information on individual components of the selection process required in the preceding paragraph for the period in which there was adverse impact. In addition, the user should continue to collect such information for at least two (2) years after the adverse impact has been eliminated.

(c) *When data insufficient to determine impact.* Where there has been an insufficient number of selections to determine whether there is an adverse impact of the total selection process for a particular job, the user should continue to collect, maintain and have available the information on individual components of the selection process required in section 15(A)(2)(a) above until the information is sufficient to determine that the overall selection process does not have an adverse impact as defined in section 4 above, or until the job has changed substantially.

(3) *Documentation of validity evidence.*—(a) *Types of evidence.* Where a total selection process has an adverse impact (see section 4 above) the user should maintain and have available for each component of that process which has an adverse impact, one or more of the following types of documentation evidence:

(i) Documentation evidence showing criterion-related validity of the selection procedure (see section 15B, below).

(ii) Documentation evidence showing content validity of the selection procedure (see section 15C, below).

(iii) Documentation evidence showing construct validity of the selection procedure (see section 15D, below).

(iv) Documentation evidence from other studies showing validity of the selection procedure in the user's facility (see section 15E, below).

(v) Documentation evidence showing why a validity study cannot or need not be performed and why continued use of the procedure is consistent with Federal law.

(b) *Form of report.* This evidence should be compiled in a reasonably complete and organized manner to permit direct evaluation of the validity of the selection procedure. Previously written employer or consultant reports of validity, or reports describing validity studies completed before the issuance of these guidelines are acceptable if they are complete in regard to the documentation requirements contained in this section, or if they satisfied requirements of guidelines which were in effect when the validity study was completed. If they are not complete, the required additional documentation should be appended. If necessary information is not available the report of the validity study may still be used as documentation, but its adequacy will be evaluated in terms of compliance with the requirements of these guidelines.

(c) *Completeness.* In the event that evidence of validity is reviewed by an enforcement agency, the validation reports completed after the effective date of these guidelines are expected to contain the information set forth below. Evidence denoted by use of the word "(essential)" is considered critical. If information denoted essential is not included, the report will be considered incomplete unless the user affirmatively demonstrates either its unavailability due to circumstances beyond the user's control or special circumstances of the user's study which make the information irrelevant. Evidence not so denoted is desirable but its absence will not be a basis for considering a report incomplete. The user should maintain and have available the information called for under the heading "Source Data" in section 15B(11) and 15D(11). While it is a necessary part of the study, it need not be submitted with the report. All statistical results should be organized and presented in tabular or graphic form to the extent feasible.

B. *Criterion-related validity studies.* Reports of criterion-related validity for a selection procedure should include the following information:

(1) *User(s), location(s), and date(s) of study.* Dates and location(s) of the job analysis or review of job information, the date(s) and location(s) of the administration of the selection procedures and collection of criterion data, and the time between collection of data on selection procedures and criterion measures should be provided (essential). If the study was conducted at several locations, the address of each location, including city and state, should be shown.

(2) *Problem and setting.* An explicit definition of the purpose(s) of the study and the circumstances in which the study was conducted should be provided. A description of existing selection procedures and cutoff scores, if any, should be provided.

(3) *Job analysis or review of job information.* A description of the procedure used to analyze the job or group of jobs, or to review the job information should be provided (essential). Where a review of job information results in criteria which may be used without a full job analysis (see section 14B(3)), the basis for the selection of these criteria should be reported (essential). Where a job analysis is required a complete description of the work behavior(s) or work outcome(s), and measures of their criticality or importance should be provided (essential). The report should describe the basis on which the behavior(s) or

outcome(s) were determined to be critical or important, such as the proportion of time spent on the respective behaviors, their level of difficulty, their frequency of performance, the consequences of error, or other appropriate factors (essential). Where two or more jobs are grouped for a validity study, the information called for in this subsection should be provided for each of the jobs, and the justification for the grouping (see section 14B(1)) should be provided (essential).

(4) *Job titles and codes.* It is desirable to provide the user's job title(s) for the job(s) in question and the corresponding job title(s) and code(s) from U.S. Employment Service's Dictionary of Occupational Titles.

(5) *Criterion measures.* The bases for the selection of the criterion measures should be provided, together with references to the evidence considered in making the selection of criterion measures (essential). A full description of all criteria on which data were collected and means by which they were observed, recorded, evaluated, and quantified, should be provided (essential). If rating techniques are used as criterion measures, the appraisal form(s) and instructions to the rater(s) should be included as part of the validation evidence, or should be explicitly described and available (essential). All steps taken to insure that criterion measures are free from factors which would unfairly alter the scores of members of any group should be described (essential).

(6) *Sample description.* A description of how the research sample was identified and selected should be included (essential). The race, sex, and ethnic composition of the sample, including those groups set forth in section 4A above should be described (essential). This description should include the size of each subgroup (essential). A description of how the research sample compares with the relevant labor market or work force, the method by which the relevant labor market or work force was defined, and a discussion of the likely effects on validity of differences between the sample and the relevant labor market or work force, are also desirable. Descriptions of educational levels, length of service, and age are also desirable.

(7) *Description of selection procedures.* Any measure, combination of measures, or procedure studied should be completely and explicitly described or attached (essential). If commercially available selection procedures are studied, they should be described by title, form, and publisher (essential). Reports of reliability estimates and how they were established are desirable.

(8) *Techniques and results.* Methods used in analyzing data should be described (essential). Measures of central tendency (e.g., means) and measures of dispersion (e.g., standard deviations and ranges) for all selection procedures and all criteria should be reported for each race, sex, and ethnic group which constitutes a significant factor in the relevant labor market (essential). The magnitude and direction of all relationships between selection procedures and criterion measures investigated should be reported for each relevant race, sex, and ethnic group and for the total group (essential). Where groups are too small to obtain reliable evidence, the magnitude of the relationship need not be reported separately. Statements regarding the statistical significance of results should be made (essential). Any statistical adjustments, such as for less than perfect reliability or for restriction of score range in the selection procedure or criterion should be described and explained; and uncorrected correlation coefficients should also be

shown (essential). Where the statistical technique categorizes continuous data, such as biserial correlation and the phi coefficient, the categories and the bases on which they were determined should be described and explained (essential). Studies of test fairness should be included where called for by the requirements of section 14B(8) (essential). These studies should include the rationale by which a selection procedure was determined to be fair to the group(s) in question. Where test fairness or unfairness has been demonstrated on the basis of other studies, a bibliography of the relevant studies should be included (essential). If the bibliography includes unpublished studies, copies of these studies, or adequate abstracts or summaries, should be attached (essential). Where revisions have been made in a selection procedure to assure compatibility between successful job performance and the probability of being selected, the studies underlying such revisions should be included (essential). All statistical results should be organized and presented by relevant race, sex, and ethnic group (essential).

(9) *Alternative procedures investigated.* The selection procedures investigated and available evidence of their impact should be identified (essential). The scope, method, and findings of the investigation, and the conclusions reached in light of the findings, should be fully described (essential).

(10) *Uses and applications.* The methods considered for use of the selection procedure (e.g., as a screening device with a cutoff score, for grouping or ranking, or combined with other procedures in a battery) and available evidence of their impact should be described (essential). This description should include the rationale for choosing the method for operational use, and the evidence of the validity and utility of the procedure as it is to be used (essential). The purpose for which the procedure is to be used (e.g., hiring, transfer, promotion) should be described (essential). If weights are assigned to different parts of the selection procedure, these weights and the validity of the weighted composite should be reported (essential). If the selection procedure is used with a cutoff score, the user should describe the way in which normal expectations of proficiency within the work force were determined and the way in which the cutoff score was determined (essential).

(11) *Source data.* Each user should maintain records showing all pertinent information about individual sample members and raters where they are used, in studies involving the validation of selection procedures. These records should be made available upon request of a compliance agency. In the case of individual sample members these data should include scores on the selection procedure(s), scores on criterion measures, age, sex, race, or ethnic group status, and experience on the specific job on which the validation study was conducted, and may also include such things as education, training, and prior job experience, but should not include names and social security numbers. Records should be maintained which show the ratings given to each sample member by each rater.

(12) *Contact person.* The name, mailing address, and telephone number of the person who may be contacted for further information about the validity study should be provided (essential).

(13) *Accuracy and completeness.* The report should describe the steps taken to assure the accuracy and completeness of the collection, analysis, and report of data and results.

C. *Content validity studies.* Reports of content validity for a selection procedure should include the following information:

(1) *User(s), location(s), and date(s) of study.* Dates and location(s) of the job analysis should be shown (essential).

(2) *Problem and setting.* An explicit definition of the purpose(s) of the study and the circumstances in which the study was conducted should be provided. A description of existing selection procedures and cutoff scores, if any, should be provided.

(3) *Job analysis—Content of the Job.* A description of the method used to analyze the job should be provided (essential). The work behavior(s), the associated tasks, and, if the behavior results in a work product, the work products should be completely described (essential). Measures of criticality and/or importance of the work behavior(s) and the method of determining these measures should be provided (essential). Where the job analysis also identified the knowledges, skills, and abilities used in work behavior(s), an operational definition for each knowledge in terms of a body of learned information and for each skill and ability in terms of observable behavior and outcomes, and the relationship between each knowledge, skill, or ability and each work behavior, as well as the method used to determine this relationship, should be provided (essential). The work situation should be described, including the setting in which work behavior(s) are performed, and where appropriate, the manner in which knowledges, skills, or abilities are used, and the complexity and difficulty of the knowledge, skill, or ability as used-in the work behavior(s).

(4) *Selection procedure and its content.* Selection procedures, including those constructed by or for the user, specific training requirements, composites of selection procedures, and any other procedure supported by content validity, should be completely and explicitly described or attached (essential). If commercially available selection procedures are used, they should be described by title, form, and publisher (essential). The behaviors measured or sampled by the selection procedure should be explicitly described (essential). Where the selection procedure purports to measure a knowledge, skill, or ability, evidence that the selection procedure measures and is a representative sample of the knowledge, skill, or ability should be provided (essential).

(5) *Relationship between the selection procedure and the job.* The evidence demonstrating that the selection procedure is a representative work sample, a representative sample of the work behavior(s), or a representative sample of a knowledge, skill, or ability as used as a part of a work behavior and necessary of that behavior should be provided (essential). The user should identify the work behavior(s) which each item or part of the selection procedure is intended to sample or measure (essential). Where the selection procedure purports to sample a work behavior or to provide a sample of a work product, a comparison should be provided of the manner, setting, and the level of complexity of the selection procedure with those of the work situation (essential). If any steps were taken to reduce adverse impact on a race, sex, or ethnic group in the content of the procedure or in its administration, these steps should be described. Establishment of time limits, if any, and how these limits are related to the speed with which duties must be performed on the job, should be explained. Measures of central ten-

dency (e.g., means) and measures of dispersion (e.g., standard deviations) and estimates of reliability should be reported for all selection procedures if available. Such reports should be made for relevant race, sex, and ethnic subgroups, at least on a statistically reliable sample basis.

(6) *Alternative procedures investigated.* The alternative selection procedures investigated and available evidence of their impact should be identified (essential). The scope, method, and findings of the investigation, and the conclusions reached in light of the findings, should be fully described (essential).

(7) *Uses and applications.* The methods considered for use of the selection procedure (e.g., as a screening device with a cutoff score, for grouping or ranking, or combined with other procedures in a battery) and available evidence of their impact should be described (essential). This description should include the rationale for choosing the method for operational use, and the evidence of the validity and utility of the procedure as it is to be used (essential). The purpose for which the procedure is to be used (e.g., hiring, transfer, promotion) should be described (essential). If the selection procedure is used with a cutoff score, the user should describe the way in which normal expectations of proficiency within the work force were determined and the way in which the cutoff score was determined (essential). In addition, if the selection procedure is to be used for ranking, the user should specify the evidence showing that a higher score on the selection procedure is likely to result in better job performance.

(8) *Contact person.* The name, mailing address, and telephone number of the person who may be contacted for further information about the validity study should be provided (essential).

(9) *Accuracy and completeness.* The report should describe the steps taken to assure the accuracy and completeness of the collection, analysis, and report of data and results.

D. *Construct validity studies.* Reports of construct validity for a selection procedure should include the following information:

(1) *User(s), location(s), and date(s) or study.* Date(s) and location(s) of the job analysis and the gathering of other evidence called for by these guidelines should be provided (essential).

(2) *Problem and setting.* An explicit definition of the purpose(s) of the study and the circumstances in which the study was conducted should be provided. A description of existing selection procedures and cutoff scores, if any, should be provided.

(3) *Construct definition.* A clear definition of the construct(s) which are believed to underlie successful performance of the critical or important work behavior(s) should be provided (essential). This definition should include the levels of construct performance relevant to the job(s) for which the selection procedure is to be used (essential). There should be a summary of the position of the construct in the psychological literature, or in the absence of such a position, a description of the way in which the definition and measurement of the construct was developed and the psychological theory underlying it (essential). Any quantitative data which identify or define the job constructs, such as factor analyses, should be provided (essential).

(4) *Job analysis.* A description of the method used to analyze the job should

be provided (essential). A complete description of the work behavior(s) and, to the extent appropriate, work outcomes and measures of their criticality and/or importance should be provided (essential). The report should also describe the basis on which the behavior(s) or outcomes were determined to be important, such as their level of difficulty, their frequency of performance, the consequences of error or other appropriate factors (essential). Where jobs are grouped or compared for the purposes of generalizing validity evidence, the work behavior(s) and work product(s) for each of the jobs should be described, and conclusions concerning the similarity of the jobs in terms of observable work behaviors or work products should be made (essential) .

(5) *Job titles and codes.* It is desirable to provide the selection procedure user's job title(s) for the job(s) in question and the corresponding job title(s) and code(s) from the United States Employment Service's Dictionary of Occupational Titles.

(6) *Selection procedure.* The selection procedure used as a measure of the construct should be completely and explicitly described or attached (essential). If commercially available selection procedures are used, they should be identified by title, form and publisher (essential). The research evidence of the relationship between the selection procedure and the construct, such as factor structure, should be included (essential). Measures of central tendency, variability and reliability of the selection procedure should be provided (essential). Whenever feasible, these measures should be provided separately for each relevant race, sex and ethnic group.

(7) *Relationship to job performance.* The criterion-related study(ies) and other empirical evidence of the relationship between the construct measured by the selection procedure and the related work behavior(s) for the job or jobs in question should be provided (essential). Documentation of the criterion-related study(ies) should satisfy the provisions of section 15B above or section 15E(1) below, except for studies conducted prior to the effective date of these guidelines (essential). Where a study pertains to a group of jobs, and, on the basis of the study, validity is asserted for a job in the group, the observed work behaviors and the observed work products for each of the jobs should be described (essential). Any other evidence used in determining whether the work behavior(s) in each of the jobs is the same should be fully described (essential).

(8) *Alternative procedures investigated.* The alternative selection procedures investigated and available evidence of their impact should be identified (essential). The scope, method, and findings of the investigation, and the conclusions reached in light of the findings should be fully described (essential).

(9) *Uses and applications.* The methods considered for use of the selection procedure (e.g., as a screening device with a cutoff score, for grouping or ranking, or combined with other procedures in a battery) and available evidence of their impact should be described (essential). This description should include the rationale for choosing the method for operational use, and the evidence of the validity and utility of the procedure as it is to be used (essential). The purpose for which the procedure is to be used (e.g., hiring, transfer, promotion) should be described (essential). If weights are assigned to different parts of the selection procedure, these weights and the validity of the weighted composite should be reported (essential). If the selection procedure is used with a cutoff score, the

user should describe the way in which normal expectations of proficiency within the work force were determined and the way in which the cutoff score was determined (essential).

(10) *Accuracy and completeness.* The report should describe the steps taken to assure the accuracy and completeness of the collection, analysis, and report of data and results.

(11) *Source data.* Each user should maintain records showing all pertinent information relating to its study of construct validity.

(12) *Contact person.* The name, mailing address, and telephone number of the individual who may be contacted for further information about the validity study should be provided (essential).

E. *Evidence of validity from other studies.* When validity of a selection procedure is supported by studies not done by the user, the evidence from the original study or studies should be compiled in a manner similar to that required in the appropriate section of this section 15 above. In addition, the following evidence should be supplied:

(1) *Evidence from criterion-related validity studies.—(a) Job information.* A description of the important job behavior(s) of the user's job and the basis on which the behaviors were determined to be important should be provided (essential). A full description of the basis for determining that these important work behaviors are the same as those of the job in the original study (or studies) should be provided (essential).

(b) *Relevance of criteria.* A full description of the basis on which the criteria used in the original studies are determined to be relevant for the user should be provided (essential).

(c) *Other variables.* The similarity of important applicant pool or sample characteristics reported in the original studies to those of the user should be described (essential). A description of the comparison between the race, sex and ethnic composition of the user's relevant labor market and the sample in the original validity studies should be provided (essential).

(d) *Use of the selection procedure.* A full description should be provided showing that the use to be made of the selection procedure is consistent with the findings of the original validity studies (essential).

(e) *Bibliography.* A bibliography of reports of validity of the selection procedure for the job or jobs in question should be provided (essential). Where any of the studies included an investigation of test fairness, the results of this investigation should be provided (essential). Copies of reports published in journals that are not commonly available should be described in detail or attached (essential). Where a user is relying upon unpublished studies, a reasonable effort should be made to obtain these studies. If these unpublished studies are the sole source of validity evidence they should be described in detail or attached (essential). If these studies are not available, the name and address of the source, an adequate abstract or summary of the validity study and data, and a contact person in the source organization should be provided (essential).

(2) *Evidence from content validity studies.* See section 14C(3) and section 15C above.

(3) *Evidence from construct validity studies.* See sections 14D(2) and 15D above.

F. *Evidence of validity from cooperative studies.* Where a selection procedure has been validated through a cooperative study, evidence that the study satisfies the requirements of sections 7, 8 and 15E should be provided (essential).

G. *Selection for higher level jobs.* If a selection procedure is used to evaluate candidates for jobs at a higher level than those for which they will initially be employed, the validity evidence should satisfy the documentation provisions of this section 15 for the higher level job or jobs, and in addition, the user should provide: (1) a description of the job progression structure, formal or informal; (2) the data showing how many employees progress to the higher level job and the length of time needed to make this progression; and (3) an identification of any anticipated changes in the higher level job. In addition, if the test measures a knowledge, skill or ability, the user should provide evidence that the knowledge, skill or ability is required for the higher level job and the basis for the conclusion that the knowledge, skill or ability is not expected to develop from the training or experience on the job.

H. *Interim use of selection procedures.* If a selection procedure is being used on an interim basis because the procedure is not fully supported by the required evidence of validity, the user should maintain and have available (1) substantial evidence of validity for the procedure, and (2) a report showing the date on which the study to gather the additional evidence commenced, the estimated completion date of the study, and a description of the data to be collected (essential).

Definitions
§1607. 16. Definitions.
The following definitions shall apply throughout these guidelines:

A. *Ability.* A present competence to perform an observable behavior or a behavior which results in an observable product.

B. *Adverse impact.* A substantially different rate of selection in hiring, promotion, or other employment decision which works to the disadvantage of members of a race, sex, or ethnic group. See section 4 of these guidelines.

C. *Compliance with these guidelines.* Use of a selection procedure is in compliance with these guidelines if such use has been validated in accord with these guidelines (as defined below), or if such use does not result in adverse impact on any race, sex, or ethnic group (see section 4, above), or, in unusual circumstances, if use of the procedure is otherwise justified in accord with Federal law. See section 6B, above.

D. *Content validity.* Demonstrated by data showing that the content of a selection procedure is representative of important aspects of performance on the job. See section 5B and section 14C.

E. *Construct validity.* Demonstrated by data showing that the selection procedure measures the degree to which candidates have identifiable characteristics which have been determined to be important for successful job performance. See section 5B and section 14D.

F. *Criterion-related validity.* Demonstrated by empirical data showing that the selection procedure is predictive of or significantly correlated with important elements of work behavior. See sections 5B and 14B.

G. *Employer.* Any employer subject to the provisions of the Civil Rights Act of 1964, as amended, including State or local governments and any Federal agency subject to the provisions of section 717 of the Civil Rights Act of 1964, as amended, and any Federal contractor or subcontractor or federally assisted construction contractor or subcontractor covered by Executive Order 11246, as amended.

H. *Employment agency.* Any employment agency subject to the provisions of the Civil Rights Act of 1964, as amended.

I. *Enforcement action.* For the purposes of section 4 a proceeding by a Federal enforcement agency such as a lawsuit or an administrative proceeding leading to debarment from or withholding, suspension, or termination of Federal Government contracts or the suspension or withholding of Federal Government funds; but not a finding of reasonable cause or a conciliation process or the issuance of right to sue letters under Title VII or under Executive Order 11246 where such finding, conciliation, or issuance of notice of right to sue is based upon an individual complaint.

J. *Enforcement agency.* Any agency of the executive branch of the Federal Government which adopts these guidelines for purposes of the enforcement of the equal employment opportunity laws or which has responsibility for securing compliance with them.

K. *Job analysis.* A detailed statement of work behaviors and other information relevant to the job.

L. *Job description.* A general statement of job duties and responsibilities.

M. *Knowledge.* A body of information applied directly to the performance of a function.

N. *Labor organization.* Any labor organization subject to the provisions of the Civil Rights Act of 1964, as amended, and any committee subject thereto controlling apprenticeship or other training.

O. *Observable.* Able to be seen, heard, or otherwise perceived by a person other than the person performing the action.

P. *Race, sex, or ethnic group.* Any group of persons identifiable on the grounds of race, color, religion, sex, or national origin.

Q. *Selection procedures.* Any measure, combination of measures, or procedure used as a basis for any employment decision. Selection procedures include the full range of assessment techniques from traditional paper and pencil tests, performance tests, training programs, or probationary periods and physical, educational, and work experience requirements through informal or casual interviews and unscored application forms.

R. *Selection rate.* The proportion of applicants or candidates who are hired, promoted, or otherwise selected.

S. *Should.* The term "should" as used in these guidelines is intended to connote action which is necessary to achieve compliance with the guidelines, while recognizing that there are circumstances where alternative courses of action are open to users.

T. *Skill.* A present, observable competence to perform a learned psychomotor act.

U. *Technical feasibility.* The existence of conditions permitting the conduct of meaningful criterion-related validity studies. These conditions include: (1) An adequate sample of persons available for the study to achieve findings of statistical significance; (2) having or being able to obtain a sufficient range of scores on the selection procedure and job performance measures to produce validity results which can be expected to be representative of the results if the ranges normally expected were utilized; and (3) having or being able to devise unbiased, reliable and relevant measures of job performance or other criteria of employee adequacy. See section 14B(2). With respect to investigation of possible unfairness, the same considerations are applicable to each group for which the study is made. See section 14B(8).

V. *Unfairness of selection procedure.* A condition in which members of one race, sex, or ethnic group characteristically obtain lower scores on a selection procedure than members of another group, and the differences are not reflected in differences in measures of job performance. See section 14B(7).

W. *User.* Any employer, labor organization, employment agency, or licensing or certification board, to the extent it may be covered by Federal equal employment opportunity law, which uses a selection procedure as a basis for any employment decision. Whenever an employer, labor organization, or employment agency is required by law to restrict recruitment for any occupation to those applicants who have met licensing or certification requirements, the licensing or certifying authority to the extent it may be covered by Federal equal employment opportunity law will be considered the user with respect to those licensing or certification requirements. Whenever a State employment agency or service does no more than administer or monitor a procedure as permitted by Department of Labor regulations, and does so without making referrals or taking any other action on the basis of the results, the State employment agency will not be deemed to be a user.

X. *Validated in accord with these guidelines or properly validated.* A demonstration that one or more validity study or studies meeting the standards of these guidelines has been conducted, including investigation and, where appropriate, use of suitable alternative selection procedures as contemplated by section 3B, and has produced evidence of validity sufficient to warrant use of the procedure for the intended purpose under the standards of these guidelines.

Y. *Work behavior.* An activity performed to achieve the objectives of the job. Work behaviors involve observable (physical) components and unobservable (mental) components. A work behavior consists of the performance of one or more tasks. Knowledges, skills, and abilities are not behaviors, although they may be applied in work behaviors.

Appendix
§1607.17. Policy statements on affirmative action (see section 13B).

The Equal Employment Opportunity Coordinating Council was established by act of Congress in 1972, and charged with responsibility for developing and implementing agreements and policies designed, among other things, to eliminate conflict and inconsistency among the agencies of the Federal Government responsible for administering Federal law prohibiting discrimination on grounds of race, color, sex, religion, and national origin. This statement is issued as an initial response to the requests of a number of State and local officials for clarification of the Government's policies concerning the role of affirmative action in the overall equal employment opportunity program. While the Coordinating Council's adoption of this statement expresses only the views of the signatory agencies concerning this important subject, the principles set forth below should serve as policy guidance for other Federal agencies as well.

(1) Equal employment opportunity is the law of the land. In the public sector of our society this means that all persons, regardless of race, color, religion, sex, or national origin shall have equal access to positions in the public service limited only by their ability to do the job. There is ample evidence in all sectors of our society that such equal access frequently has been denied to members of certain groups because of their sex, racial, or ethnic characteristics. The remedy for such past and present discrimination is twofold.

On the one hand, vigorous enforcement of the laws against discrimination is essential. But equally, and perhaps even more important are affirmative, voluntary efforts on the part of public employers to assure that positions in the public service are genuinely and equally accessible to qualified persons, without regard to their sex, racial, or ethnic characteristics. Without such efforts equal employment opportunity is no more than a wish. The importance of voluntary affirmative action on the part of employers is underscored by Title VII of the Civil Rights Act of 1964, Executive Order 11246, and related laws and regulations—all of which emphasize voluntary action to achieve equal employment opportunity.

As with most management objectives, a systematic plan based on sound organizational analysis and problem identification is crucial to the accomplishment of affirmative action objectives. For this reason, the Council urges all State and local governments to develop and implement results-oriented affirmative action plans which deal with the problems so identified.

The following paragraphs are intended to assist State and local governments by illustrating the kinds of analyses and activities which may be appropriate for a public employer's voluntary affirmative action plan. This statement does not address remedies imposed after a finding of unlawful discrimination.

(2) Voluntary affirmative action to assure equal employment opportunity is appropriate at any stage of the employment process. The first step in the construction of any affirmative action plan should be an analysis of the employer's work force to determine whether percentages of sex, race, or ethnic groups in individual job classifications are substantially similar to the percentages of those groups available in the relevant job market who possess the basic job related qualifications.

When substantial disparities are found through such analyses, each element of the overall selection process should be examined to determine which elements operate to exclude persons on the basis of sex, race, or ethnic group. Such elements include, but are not limited to, recruitment, testing, ranking certification, interview, recommendations for selection, hiring, promotion, etc. The examination of each element of the selection process should at a minimum include a determination of its validity in predicting job performance.

(3) When an employer has reason to believe that its selection procedures have the exclusionary effect described in paragraph 2 above, it should initiate

affirmative steps to remedy the situation. Such steps, which in design and execution may be race, color, sex, or ethnic "conscious," include, but are not limited to, the following:

(a) The establishment of a long-term goal, and short-range, interim goals and timetables for the specific job classifications, all of which should take into account the availability of basically qualified persons in the relevant job market;

(b) A recruitment program designed to attract qualified members of the group in question;

(c) A systematic effort to organize work and redesign jobs in ways that provide opportunities for persons lacking "journeyman" level knowledge or skills to enter and, with appropriate training, to progress in a career field;

(d) Revamping selection instruments or procedures which have not yet been validated in order to reduce or eliminate exclusionary effects on particular groups in particular job classifications;

(e) The initiation of measures designed to assure that members of the affected group who are qualified to perform the job are included within the pool of persons from which the selecting official makes the selection;

(f) A systematic effort to provide career advancement training, both classroom and on-the-job, to employees locked into dead-end jobs; and

(g) The establishment of a system for regularly monitoring the effectiveness of the particular affirmative action program, and procedures for making timely adjustments in this program where effectiveness is not demonstrated.

(4) The goal of any affirmative action plan should be achievement of genuine equal employment opportunity for all qualified persons. Selection under such plans should be based upon the ability of the applicant(s) to do the work. Such plans should not require the selection of the unqualified, or the unneeded, nor should they require the selection of persons on the basis of race, color, sex, religion, or national origin. Moreover, while the Council believes that this statement should serve to assist State and local employers, as well as Federal agencies, it recognizes that affirmative action cannot be viewed as a standardized program which must be accomplished in the same way at all times in all places.

Accordingly, the Council has not attempted to set forth here either the minimum or maximum voluntary steps that employers may take to deal with their respective situations. Rather, the Council recognizes that under applicable authorities, State and local employers have flexibility to formulate affirmative action plans that are best suited to their particular situations. In this manner, the Council believes that affirmative action programs will best serve the goal of equal employment opportunity.

Because of its equal employment opportunity responsibilities under the State and Local Government Fiscal Assistance Act of 1972 (the revenue sharing act), the Department of Treasury was invited to participate in the formulation of this policy statement; and it concurs and joins in the adoption of this policy statement.

§1607.18. Citations.

The official title of these guidelines is "Uniform Guidelines on Employee Selection Procedures (1978)." The Uniform Guidelines on Employee Selection Procedures (1978) are intended to establish a uniform Federal position in the area of prohibiting discrimination in employment practices on grounds of race, color, religion, sex, or national origin. These guidelines have been adopted by the Equal Employment Opportunity Commission, the Department of Labor, the Department of Justice, and the Civil Service Commission.

The official citation is:

"Section _____ , Uniform Guidelines on Employee Selection Procedure (1978); 43 FR _____ , (August 25, 1978)."

The short form citation is:

"Section _____ , U.G.E.S.P. (1978); 43 FR _____ , (August 25, 1978)."

When the guidelines are cited in connection with the activities of one of the issuing agencies, a specific citation to the regulations of that agency can be added at the end of the above citation. The specific additional citations are as follows:

Equal Employment Opportunity Commission

    29 CFR Part 1607

Department of Labor

Office of Federal Contract Compliance Programs

    41 CFR Part 60-3

Department of Justice

    28 CFR 50.14

Civil Service Commission

    5 CFR 300.103(c)

Normally when citing these guidelines, the section number immediately preceding the title of the guidelines will be from these guidelines series 1-18. If a section number from the codification for an individual agency is needed it can also be added at the end of the agency citation. For example, section 6A of these guidelines could be cited for EEOC as follows: "Section 6A, Uniform Guidelines on Employee Selection Procedures (1978); 43 FR _____ , (August 25, 1978); 29 CFR Part 1607, section 6A."

II

Foundations of Measurement for Human Resource Selection

The collection of information on job candidates through selection measures is central to any HR selection system. Information is the basis for all decisions concerning the selection of job applicants. Sometimes, however, HR selection decisions turn out to be wrong. Perhaps individuals who were predicted to be outstanding performers actually contribute very little to an organization. Others who were forecast to stay with an organization for a lengthy period of time leave after only several months. And, in cases that are not verifiable, persons who were thought to be very poor employees for a firm and not hired would have been valuable contributors had they been employed. In each of these situations, we would conclude some inappropriate selection decisions had been made. Yet, when we analyze the situation, it may not be the decisions themselves that were wrong, but the data on which they were based that were faulty. Thus it is imperative that managers have sound data on which to base selection decisions. What do we mean by "sound data"? The three chapters in this section address this question. Specifically, the objectives of this section are as follows:

1. To explore the role of HR "measurement" in selection decision making.

2. To examine the concepts of "reliability" and "validity" of selection data as well as their role in choosing useful selection measures and making effective selection decisions.

3

Human Resource Measurement in Selection

Fundamentals of Measurement: An Overview

An important assumption in selection decision making is that information is available with which selection decisions can be made. But what types of information can be used? Where does this information come from? What characteristics should this information have in order to be most useful for selection purposes? These are only a few of the questions addressed in this chapter. Specifically, we focus on (a) the basics of psychological measurement as they apply to HR selection and (b) the locating, developing, and interpreting of measures commonly used in HR selection.

The Role of Measurement in HR Selection

If you have watched competent carpenters build a house or a piece of furniture, you cannot help being impressed by how well the various pieces fit together. For example, when a door is hung in place, the door will have a snug fit with its frame. Or, perhaps, you have watched a rocket lift off for space. It is amazing that we can launch a craft from the Kennedy Space Center, send it thousands of miles into space, have it orbit Earth numerous times, and then days later have the craft land at a precise time and place. Although there are many things that contribute to the success of a carpenter installing a door and a scientist launching a rocket, one of the factors common to the success of both is their ability to employ "measurement." How could a door be made to fit if a carpenter could not determine the exact dimensions of the opening the door was designed to fit? How could a rocket be launched and safely returned to a specified location if a scientist could not measure factors such as time, distance, and speed? The answer is that neither could be done without measurement. As we will see, measurement is also essential to the successful implementation and administration of an HR selection program.

The Nature of Measurement

Let's imagine for a moment that we are in charge of employment for a large company. We have position openings for the job of sales representative. Because of current economic conditions and the nature of the job, many people are interested in applying for the position. As we sit in our office, we see numerous applicants coming in to be screened for employment. Each person completes an application, takes a test, and is interviewed by us. After several days of assessing applicants, we can draw at least one obvious conclusion: *People are different.* As we think about the applicants that enter our office, we notice that some are tall, some are short, some pleasant and agreeable, others serious and even unpleasant. Still other applicants seem intelligent and others rather dull; some seem assertive and outgoing, while others appear very shy and withdrawn. Although our usual system of classifying individuals in these extreme categories may be useful for *describing* people in a gross way, it may not be very useful for choosing among applicants. In a personnel selection context, we will probably find that few people really fall at these extreme points. For example, only a few of our applicants will be extremely bright and only a few extremely dull. For the many others, we will need a means for making finer distinctions among them for the various characteristics (intelligence, assertiveness, etc.) that are of interest to us. We will need to use "measurement" to make these discriminations and to study in detail the relations between applicant characteristics and employee performance on the job.

A Definition   But, what is measurement? Numerous writings have been directed toward the topic; some have emphasized its meaning, others have addressed methods involved in its application. From the perspective of human resource selection, we can offer one definition. Simply put, measurement involves the application of rules for assigning numbers to objects to represent quantities of attributes.[1] Let's explore this definition. Rules suggest that the basis for assigning numbers is clearly specified. For any measure that we might use in selection, say a test, it is important that if different users employ the measure they will obtain similar results. Thus if job applicants take a test, differences among applicants' scores should be due to individual differences in their test performance and not to the way in which different scorers scored the tests. Rules for assigning numbers to our selection measures help to standardize the application of these measures.

A second point in our definition involves the concept of an *attribute*. In reality, when we measure an object, we do not measure the object per se, rather we assess an attribute or property of the object. When we measure *physical* attributes of people, many of these attributes (for example, gender) can be assessed through direct observation. However, when we are interested in assessing *psychological* characteristics, some attributes of people are not so easily observable. Psychological characteristics (such as aggressiveness, intelligence, job knowledge, mathematical and verbal abilities) must be inferred from *indicants* of these objects. An indicant simply represents something that points toward something else.[2] A score on a mathematics test is an indicant of a job applicant's mathematical ability. With our test, we are not measuring the applicant but the mathematical ability of the applicant. Notice in our description we have not talked about how well we measure an attribute. Obviously, if we want to measure mathematical ability, we want an indicant (a test, for example) that is a good measure of this ability. But, our obtaining a good measure of such elusive but nevertheless critical attributes (such as various knowledge, skills, abilities, personality, and other traits) is not always easy. To measure an applicant's physical characteristics is one thing. However, to measure the psychological characteristics of an applicant is a different problem. Yet, in contrast to physical characteristics, it is psychological attributes that will typically be identified as important indicators of how well an applicant can perform a job.

When we use measures (such as tests or interviews) of psychological attributes, we have to draw inferences from these measures. Because inferences are involved, however, we are on much shakier ground than when we can directly observe an attribute. An interviewer conducting a selection interview might believe that the extent of an applicant's eye contact with the interviewer reflects the applicant's interest in the company or the firmness of a handshake reflects the interviewee's self-confidence. But, are these inferences warranted? This is an important question to answer if we are to use in a meaningful way indicants of important psychological attributes in selection decision making. We will see shortly what characteristics we might look for in obtaining a good measure of any attribute in selecting human resources.

A third and final point in our definition of measurement is that *numbers* represent quantities of attributes. Numbers play a very useful role in summarizing and communicating the degree or amount of an assessed attribute. Thus, in this sense, numbers can provide a convenient means for characterizing and differentiating among job applicants. Numbers generally play an important role in the current use of selection techniques.[3]

Criteria and Predictors in Selection Research   A fundamental problem in personnel selection is to choose from a large group of job applicants, a smaller group to be employed. The goal of personnel selection is to designate the individuals who should be hired. These individuals are chosen because the selection techniques predict that they can best perform the job in question. When the term *predict* is used, it is assumed that a selection manager has the information on which to base these predictions. Where does this information come from? Basically, the information is derived from an analysis of the job. A job analysis is designed to identify the attributes needed by incumbents to perform the job successfully. Once the attributes of employee success are known, we can name employee specifications required for the job. We can measure applicants with respect to these specifications and make our predictions accordingly.

Measurement plays a vital role in helping the selection manager make accurate predictions. Predicting who should be hired generally requires the identification and measurement of two types of variables. The first of these is called the *criterion* (or *criteria* when more than one criterion is being considered). A criterion usually serves as a measure or definition of what is meant by employee success on the job. It is the dependent variable to be predicted. Criteria are defined by thoroughly studying the job(s) for which a selection system is being developed. A wide array of variables might serve as criteria. Some criteria deal with employee behaviors. For example, absenteeism, tardiness, number of goods produced, dollar sales, amount of scrap produced in manufacturing tasks, and speed of performance are a small sampling of criteria that depict what some workers *do*. On the other hand, some criteria may be equally important but involve affective reactions to a job as reported by an incumbent, rather than specific behaviors. These reactions are usually recorded on a self-report questionnaire. Job satisfaction, employee morale, and intention to stay with an organization are but a few examples of such criteria. Further, supervisory ratings of employee behavior, such as employee productivity, are also often used.

There are numerous types of criteria that can be predicted. Nevertheless, criteria should not be chosen or measured in a cavalier, unsystematic, or haphazard manner. They *must* be important to the job, and they *must* be appropriately measured. Since criteria are the basis for characterizing employee success, the utility of a selection system will depend to a significant degree on their selection, definition, and measurement.

A second type of variable required in predicting applicants' job success is called *predictor* variables. Predictors represent the *indicants* of those attributes identified through a job analysis as being important for job success. Thus predictors are used to predict our criteria. This book discusses a wide variety of predictors that have been found to be useful in predicting employee performance. Tests, interviews, biographical data questionnaires, application blanks, and assessment centers are just some of the types of predictors you will read about. But, as with criteria, there are two important requirements in developing and using predictors: (a) they *must* be important to the job and (b) they *must* be appropriate measures of attributes identified as critical to job success.

Measurement and Individual Differences   Earlier in this chapter, we noted a basic law of psychology applicable to human resource selection: People are different. Furthermore, we said that one goal of selection is to identify those individuals who should be hired for a job. Measurement of individual differences with our predictors and criteria helps us to meet our goal. Suppose, for instance, you were charged with the responsibility for hiring workers who could produce high quantities of work output. The workers individually manufacture wire baskets. After looking at some recent production records, you plot graphically the quantity of output per worker for a large number of workers. Exhibit 3.1 shows the results of your plot. This "bell-shaped" or "normal" curve is a typical distribution for a variety of biological characteristics such as height and weight, as well as for psychological test scores, when sufficiently large numbers of observations are available.

Our plot suggests several things. First, because there is variability in productivity scores, there must be individual differences among employees in their levels of productivity. Second, relatively few produce a very large or very small number of baskets. Many, however, fall between these two extremes. If we can assume that our quantity of production measure is a suitable criterion, our objective is to obtain a predictor that will detect the individual differences or variance in productivity. If our predictor is a good one, individuals' scores on the predictor will be associated with their productivity scores.

EXHIBIT 3.1   HYPOTHETICAL DISTRIBUTION OF
QUANTITY OF WIRE BASKETS PRODUCED BY
A LARGE NUMBER OF WORKERS

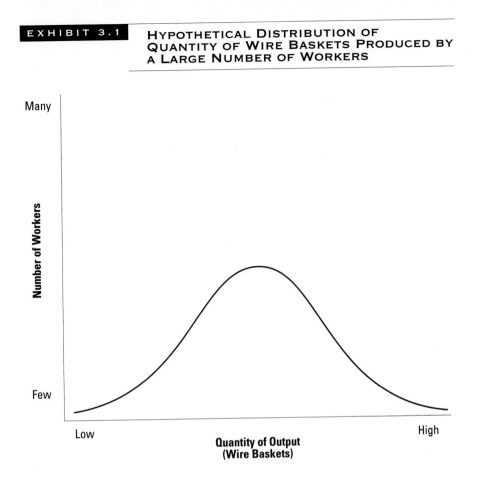

The preceding example highlights the important role of measurement in selection research. Numbers assigned to predictor and criterion attributes enable us to make the necessary fine distinctions among individuals. Subsequent analyses of these numbers help us meet one of our roles: developing a system to successfully predict job performance. Without measurement, we would probably be left with our intuition and personal best guesses. Perhaps, for a very small number of us, these judgments will work. For most of us, however, "deciding by the seat of our pants" will simply not suffice.

Scales of Measurement

Use of predictors and criteria in selection research requires that these variables be measured. Measurement is prerequisite to any statistical analysis to be performed in a selection study. However, the refinement of our distinctions among people is determined by the precision with which we measure the variables. (By "precision," we mean the number of distinct scores permitted by the measure that is used.) In addition, the level of precision will dictate what statistical analyses can be done with the numbers obtained from measurement.

In the context of selection research, a *scale of measurement* is simply a means by which individuals can be distinguished from one another on a variable of interest. Because we use a variety of scales in selection research, our research variables tend to differ rather dramatically in terms of precision. For example, suppose we were developing a selection program for bank management trainees. One criterion we want to predict is "trainability," that is, trainee success in a management training program. We could measure trainability in several ways. On one hand, we could simply classify individuals in terms of who did and who did not graduate from the training program. (Graduation, for example, may be based on trainees' ability to pass a test on banking principles and regulations.) Our criterion would be a dichotomous category, that is, unsuccessful (fail) and successful (pass). Thus, our predictor variable would be used to differentiate between those applicants who could and those who could not successfully complete their training.

On the other hand, we could evaluate trainability by the *degree* of trainee success as measured by training performance test scores. Again, our test might be used to assess how much trainees know at the end of their training program. But, notice that in this case our criterion is not a categorical measure (that is, success or failure) but rather a measure of degree.

Exhibit 3.2 shows the distributions of trainees' scores for the two methods of measuring trainability. Notice that our simple *classification* of success criterion is not as precise a measure as our *degree* of success criterion. Greater individual differences in trainability can be mapped by the latter criterion measure than by the former one. The variable "trainability" is the same in both of our examples. But the two examples differ with respect to the level of measurement involved. *It is the manner in which the variable is measured and not the variable itself that determines level of measurement.* As such, we can draw more precise conclusions with one measure than we can with the other.

There are four types of scales or levels of measurement: (a) nominal, (b) ordinal, (c) interval, and (d) ratio. The degree of precision with which we can measure differences among people increases as we move from nominal to ratio scales. Increased precision provides us with more detailed information about people on the variables being studied. More powerful statistical analyses can then be performed with our data. These analyses, in turn, can help us develop more accurate human resource selection methods.

Nominal Scale   A nominal scale is one composed of two or more mutually exclusive categories. Examples of nominal scale measurement for the variables of applicant sex, applicant race, and job class include the following:

A. *Applicant Sex*
    1. Male
    2. Female

B. *Applicant Race*
    1. Black
    2. White
    3. Other

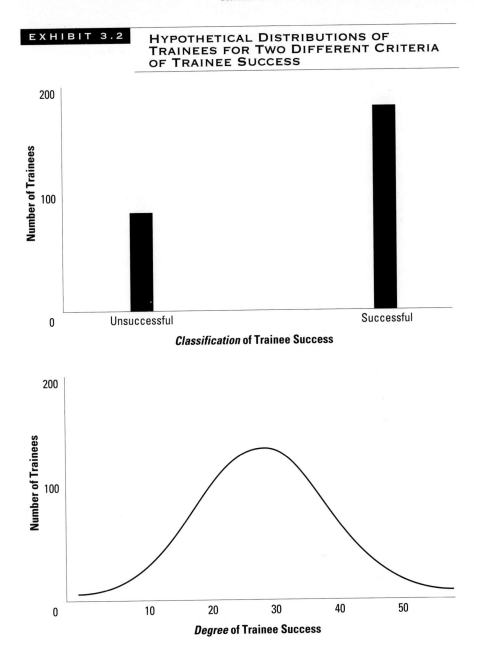

EXHIBIT 3.2   HYPOTHETICAL DISTRIBUTIONS OF TRAINEES FOR TWO DIFFERENT CRITERIA OF TRAINEE SUCCESS

C. *Job Class*
    1. Sales Manager
    2. Sales Clerk
    3. Sales Representative
    4. Salesperson
    5. Other

In nominal scale measurement, all individuals having a common characteristic are assigned to the same category or class. Members in the category are regarded as being equivalent. Persons possessing a different characteristic are assigned to a different category. Since the categories are mutually exclusive, individuals can belong to only one of the classes. Numbers can be given to individuals assigned to the scale categories, however, the numbers serve merely as labels. They carry no numerical meaning. Thus if we are using the variable "applicant sex" in a study, we could assign a code of "1" to all male applicants and a code of "2" to all females. Numerical codes provide a convenient form for distinguishing between categories of "applicant sex." We could use other numbers as well (such as 0 and 1) to identify males and females. Both scoring schemes have the same meaning. The numerical codes themselves do not indicate how males and females differ. The only information we have through our numerical codes is an applicant's sex. Because we cannot state *how* members assigned to nominal scale categories differ, this type of scale is the simplest form of measurement.

Some statistical analyses can be performed with nominal scale data. For example, we can count and obtain percentages of members assigned to our scale categories. Other statistical procedures are possible, but we will not discuss them here since they are beyond the scope of our treatment.

Ordinal Scale   An ordinal scale is one that ranks objects, such as individuals, from "high" to "low" on some variable of interest. Ordinal scales can be found rather frequently in selection research. In developing criteria measures, for instance, supervisors are sometimes asked to rank their subordinates with respect to some attribute. One example of a completed rank-order scale used by supervisors to evaluate their subordinates is shown in Exhibit 3.3.

The ordinal scale provides us with more information than does a nominal scale. Individuals are not only assigned a number representative of a category, as on a nominal scale, but differences between the numbers assigned yield additional information. Numerical differences indicate the relative position of individuals for the variable on which they are ranked. For example, in Exhibit 3.3, we know that W. F. Giles, ranked 1, was highest in quality of work completed. Furthermore, we know that each individual down the scale produces better quality work than the following individual. However, an ordinal scale does not provide information on the *magnitude* of the differences among the ranks. In our personnel ranking example, W. F. Giles may be only marginally more productive in quality of work than A. G. Bedeian ranked 2. However, A. G. Bedeian may be considerably better than W. B. Boyles, the employee ranked 3.

Another example of an ordinal scale often encountered in selection involves test scores. Percentiles are sometimes used to interpret the results of a test. A percentile represents the proportion of persons taking a test who make below a given score. If we know that a job applicant scored at the 76th percentile, we know that 76 percent of the individuals who took the test scored lower and 24 percent scored higher. As in our previous example, we do not know how much better or worse the next individual performed in terms of a specific test score.

From our two examples, we see we can only draw "greater than" or "less than" conclusions with ordinal data; we do not know the amount of difference

EXHIBIT 3.3	EXAMPLE OF AN ORDINAL SCALE OF MEASUREMENT

Ranking of Employees

Below are listed the names of your 10 subordinates. Read over the list and then rank the individuals in terms of their *quality of work completed* on their jobs. By "Quality of Work Completed," it is meant the *minimum* amount of re-work necessary to correct employee mistakes. You should give the subordinate you believe is *highest* in quality of work performed a rank of "1," the employee *next* highest in quality of work a "2," the next a "3," and so on until a "10" is given to the employee who is *lowest* in quality of work completed.

Note:

1 =	Highest Quality
•	•
•	•
•	•
10 =	Lowest Quality

Employee	Rank on Quality of Work Completed
A. A. Armenakis	4
A. G. Bedeian	2
W. F. Giles	1
W. H. Holley	7
R. E. Niebuhr	9
D. R. Norris	5
W. B. Boyles	3
K. W. Mossholder	6
S. G. Harris	8
L. F. Schoenfeldt	10

that separates individuals or objects being ranked. Information relative to magnitude differences is provided by our next two scales.

Interval Scale   With an interval scale, differences between numbers take on meaning. In addition to rank-order information, it is also known how different objects being measured are with respect to an attribute.

The interval scale has an arbitrary but not an absolute zero point. Although an object being measured may be given a score of zero, the score of zero is set by convention. Let's look at an example to clarify the point. Assume we have given a mathematics ability test to a group of job applicants. The test consists of 100 math problems, each item counting one point. Possible test scores can range from 0 to 100 (no items missed). A difference between scores of 40 and 60 would not represent the same difference *in applicants' mathematical abilities* as the difference between 60 and 80. If individuals scored 0, we could say they got 0 items correct. But we could not conclude they did not have any mathematical ability. Such a conclusion would imply that our test covered *all* possible items of mathematical ability; in fact, our test is only a *sample* of these items. Obviously, we cannot make this statement since zero is only set by convention for our specific test. Also, because of the absence of an absolute zero, we cannot state that an individual who scores 80 on our test has twice as much ability as one who scores 40.

Rating scales are frequently used as criterion measures in selection studies. For example, many job performance measures consist of performance appraisal ratings. Most rating scales used in this manner are Likert-type scales such as that shown in Exhibit 3.4. When these ratings are treated as an interval scale, it is assumed that the magnitude of the difference between rating points is the same. Thus raters are expected to view the difference between points 1 and 2 on the scale the same as the difference between points 4 and 5.

Variables measured by interval scales tap the differences, order, and equality of the magnitude of the differences in the data. These scales are more powerful than the nominal and ordinal scales; therefore, more powerful statistical methods can be employed. Interval data can be analyzed by many of the statistical procedures important in personnel research. For example, means, standard deviations, and various correlation procedures can be employed.[4] These procedures are essential for developing the models to be used in selection decision making.

Ratio Scale   As on the interval scale, differences between numerical values on a ratio scale have meaning. In contrast, though, a ratio scale has an absolute zero point. The presence of an absolute zero point permits statements to be made about the ratio of one individual's scores to another based on the amount of the attribute being measured. Thus if one worker produces 100 wire baskets in an hour while another produces 50, we can then state that the second worker produces only half as much as the first.

The numerical operations that can be performed with the data suggest the origin of the name "ratio" scale. Numerical values on a ratio scale can be added, subtracted, multiplied, and divided. Ratios of scale numbers can be used, and the meaning of the scale will be preserved.

Most scales involving physical measurements (such as, height, weight, eyesight, hearing, and physical strength) or counting (such as amount of pay, number of times absent from work, months of job tenure, number of promotions received, and number of goods produced) are ratio scales. There is at least one situation in selection where frequencies are not ratio scales. For instance, if we score a test by the number of items correct and want to draw conclusions with respect to this number, then we have a ratio scale. However, if we want to draw conclusions in terms of the trait or characteristic measured by the test, then we no longer have a ratio scale. In the first case, we have an absolute zero point (with respect to the number of items correct). In the other case, we do not have an absolute zero point; we have an arbitrary one (in terms of the trait measured).

Our earlier discussion of a zero point for interval scales applies to ratio scales as well. We noted that a zero score on a measure such as a mathematics ability test is set by convention; it is not absolute. We can draw ratio scale conclusions about the *number* of mathematical ability items missed but not about the *trait:*

EXHIBIT 3.4

EXAMPLE OF AN INTERVAL SCALE USED IN RATING EMPLOYEE JOB PERFORMANCE

Rating Factors   **Ratings**

1. **Quality of Work**—The extent to which the employee actually completes job assignments.

1	2	3	4	5
Almost always makes errors, has very low accuracy	Quite often makes errors,	Makes errors but equals job standards	Makes few errors, has high accuracy	Almost never makes errors, has very high accuracy

Comments:_____   _____

2. **Quality of Work**—The extent to which the employee produces a volume of work consistent with established standards for the job.

1	2	3	4	5
Almost never meets standards	Quite often does not meet standards	Volume of work is satisfactory, equals job standards	Quite often produces more than required	Almost always exceeds standards, exceptionally productive

Comments:_____   _____

3. **Attendance/Punctuality**—The extent to which the employee adheres to the work schedule.

1	2	3	4	5
Excessively absent or tardy	Frequently absent or tardy	Occasionally absent or tardy	Infrequently absent or tardy	Almost never absent or tardy

Comments:_____   _____

4. **Coworker Assistance**—the frequency with which the employee assists coworkers in the completion of their job assignments.

1	2	3	4	5
Never provides assistance to coworkers	Seldom provides assistance to coworkers	Sometimes provides assistance to coworkers	Often provides assistance to coworkers	Always provides assistance to coworkers

Comments:_____   _____

5. **Use of Work Time**—The extent to which the employee uses time to accomplish job tasks effectively and efficiently.

1	2	3	4	5
Excessively wastes time	Frequently wastes time	Makes adequate use of time	Utilizes time wisely	Exceptionally effective in use of time

Comments:_____   _____

mathematics ability. Even if some students were to miss all of the items on the test, we could say they got "0" items correct, but we could not conclude that they have "0" mathematics ability. Why? Because our test is only a sample of items; it does not cover all possible mathematical ability items. Thus the score of zero on the test is not absolute, and we do not have a ratio scale.

In the field of human resource selection, we simply do not have as many ratio scales available to us as we might like. As we discussed earlier, many of our measures are psychological rather than physical in nature; they do not lend themselves to ratio measurement.

From the preceding discussion, you can probably surmise that interval and ratio scales are the most desirable. Because of the precision of the scales and the statistical manipulations they permit, interval and ratio scales are to be preferred. A number of writers have raised questions about the scale of measurement that many of our selection measures (for example, tests) have. Several earlier writers argued that many of these measures have underlying ordinal scales. But, to treat these measures as ordinal scales would limit our use of many powerful statistical methods. More recently, researchers have suggested that the use of many of our psychological measures as if they approximate interval scale data does not do an injustice to the data. Thus they recommend the application of interval scale statistical methods with those measures that approach interval scale quality. They further recommend that a researcher following this strategy should be constantly alert to the possibility of gross inequalities in measurement intervals (as might occur when a manager is asked to rank subordinates according to some criterion).[5] Table 3.1 summarizes the general characteristics of the four types of scales of measurement.

Standardization of Selection Measures

As discussed in the next section, a variety of measures are used in human resource selection. When we refer to a measure or measurement method in the context of selection, we mean *a systematic instrument, technique, or procedure for assigning scores to a characteristic or attribute of an individual.* A selection measure may provide information to be used as either a predictor (such as a test) or a criterion (such as a supervisor's performance appraisal form). It may also involve any one of our four scales of measurement.

An important characteristic of any selection measure is its ability to detect any true differences that may exist among individuals on the attribute being measured. For example, if there are true differences in knowledge of scheduling techniques among job candidates applying for a shift supervisor's job, then a scheduling knowledge test must be able to detect these differences. If test score differences in scheduling knowledge are found, these score differences should be due to differences in the candidates' knowledge and not due to extraneous factors such as differences in the manner in which the test was given to the job candidates or the way in which it was scored. To help control such factors, "systematic" or *standardized* measures are preferred for use in human resource selection. A predictor or criterion is standardized if it possesses each of the following characteristics:

TABLE 3.1 GENERAL CHARACTERISTICS OF THE FOUR SCALES OF MEASUREMENT

Type of Scale	Example of Scale Use in Selection Reasearch	Scale Characteristics			
		Classification	Order	Equality of Difference	Absolute Zero
Nominal	*Classifying* applicants by their gender	Yes	No	No	No
Ordinal	Supervisory *ranking* of subordinates	Yes	Yes	No	No
Interval	Employee *rating* of job satisfaction	Yes	Yes	Yes	No
Ratio	*Counting* employee number of units produced	Yes	Yes	Yes	Yes

1st   2nd   3rd

1   2   3   4
Very Dissatisfied   Dissatisfied   Satisfied   Very Satisfied

SOURCE: Based, in part, on Uma Sekaran, *Research Methods for Managers* (New York: John Wiley, 1984), p. 134.

1. *Content*—All persons being assessed are measured by the same information or content.

2. *Administration*—Information is collected in the same way each time the selection measure is applied.

3. *Scoring*—Rules for scoring are specified in advance of administration of the measure and are applied the same way with each application.[6]

No matter how many times a measure is administered or to whom it is given, the content, administration, and scoring of a standardized measure is the same. When viewed from the standpoint of professional practice, however, a truly standardized measure is more of an ideal than a reality. Standardization of selection measures is a goal we strive for but do not always attain. Sometimes it may even be necessary to alter the standardization of a measure. For example, it may be necessary to modify the administration of a test in order to accommodate the special needs of a disabled job applicant.

Measures Used in HR Selection

One of the principal roles of a manager involved in HR selection is deciding whether applicants should or should not be employed. Predictor and criterion variables that we defined earlier in the chapter are used by a manager in selection decision making. Predictors are measures (such as a test) that are employed in deciding whether to accept or reject applicants for a specific job. Criteria (such as supervisory ratings of job performance) are employed as part of a research study designed to determine if the predictors are really measuring those aspects of job success that the predictors were designed to predict. This type of research study is known as a "validation study." We have more to say about validity and validation studies in Chapter 5. But, for now, you should understand that criterion measures really help serve as a standard for evaluating how well predictors do the job they were intended to do. Predictors have a *direct* impact on the decisions reached by a manager involved in HR selection decisions. A manager actually reviews an applicant's scores for a predictor and uses this information in deciding whether to accept or reject the applicant. Criteria play an *indirect* role in that they are employed in determining which predictors should actually be incorporated in the selection decision-making process.

We began this chapter by reviewing the impact of scales of measurement on the application and interpretation of data collected by predictors and criteria. The rest of the chapter discusses additional measurement principles that apply to the use of these two types of variables. These principles are very important for understanding the application of the selection techniques and issues you will encounter in the remaining chapters. However, before we can continue our discussion in any meaningful way, it might be helpful to give you a brief overview of the various types of predictors and criteria employed in research involving HR selection. Later chapters will go into greater detail about specific measures. As you read, you should remember that when we talk about "selection measures," we mean *both* predictors and criteria. Now, let's look at some of the more common types of predictors and criteria in use.

Predictors   There are numerous types of predictors that have been used to forecast employee performance. In general, the major types tend to fall roughly into the three categories described here. Keep in mind as you read these descriptions, our intention is not to give a complete account of each type of predictor. We simply want to acquaint you with the variety of predictors currently in use in selection. Subsequent chapters will provide a more detailed review of these measures.

1. *Background information*—Application forms, reference checks, and biographical data questionnaires are generally used to collect information on job applicants and their backgrounds. *Application forms* typically consist of a form asking job applicants to describe themselves and their previous work histories. Questions are usually asked about current address, previous education, past employment, and the like. *Reference checks* are made by the prospective employers contacting individuals who can accurately comment on the applicant's characteristics and background. These checks are often used to verify information obtained from the application form as well as to provide additional data on the applicant. *Biographical data questionnaires* consist of questions about the applicant's past life history. The assumption is that past life experiences are good indicators of future work behaviors.

2. *Interviews*—Selection interviews are also used to collect information about the applicant. The selection interview principally consists of questions asked by a job interviewer. Responses are used for assessing an applicant's suitability for a job.

3. *Tests*—There are literally hundreds of tests that have been used for selection purposes. A variety of schemes have been offered for classifying these measures. We will not review any one system for describing the types of tests that are available, but we can use some of the descriptive labels that have been assigned to give you a feeling for the range of options available. *Aptitude* tests, for example, are used to measure the potential of an individual for doing a job. Abilities measured by aptitude tests include intellectual, mechanical, spatial, perceptual, and motor. *Achievement* tests are employed to assess an individual's proficiency at the time of testing (for example, job proficiency or knowledge). (For the purposes of this book, you will see in Chapter 13 that we have combined aptitude and achievement tests into the general category "ability" tests.) *Personality* tests in the context of selection are used on the assumption that knowing a person's motivation or the manner in which an individual responds to a variety of situations can help predict success in a job.[7]

Most of the tests you will encounter will probably fall into one of these categories. You should keep in mind, though, that you will find some differences among tests within each of these categories. Some may require an individual to respond with a paper and pencil; others may require the manipulation of physical objects. Some will have a time limit; others will not. Some can be administered in a group setting while others can only be given to one applicant at a time.

Criteria   Measurement methods oriented toward criteria can generally be clustered in terms of the type of data they provide.[8] These categories include:

1. *Objective production data*—These data tend to be physical measures of work or as Robert Guion states "simply a count of the results of work."[9] Number of goods produced, amount of scrap left, and dollar sales are examples of objective production data.

2. *Personnel data*—Personnel records and files frequently contain information on workers that can serve as important criterion measures. Absenteeism, tardiness, accident rates, salary history, promotions, and special awards are examples of such measures.

3. *Judgmental data*—Performance appraisals or ratings frequently serve as criteria in selection research. They most often involve a supervisor's rating of a subordinate on a series of behaviors or characteristics found to be important to job success. Supervisor or rater judgments play a predominant role in defining this type of criterion data.

4. *Job or work sample data*—These data are obtained from a measure developed to resemble the actual job. Basically, a job sample represents the job in miniature. Measurements (for example, quantity and error rate) are taken on individual performance of these job tasks, and these measures serve as criteria.

5. *Training proficiency data*—This type of criterion focuses on how well employees respond to job training activities. Often, such criteria are labeled "trainability" measures. Error rates on the job during a training period and scores on training performance tests administered during training sessions are examples of training proficiency data.

Use of Predictors and Criteria   We have mentioned various types of predictors and criteria likely to be encountered in selection research. But, to what extent do organizations use these measurement methods? Two surveys conducted by the Bureau of National Affairs (BNA) shed some light on this question. The first survey, conducted in 1983, was composed of personnel executives in 437 companies who were members of the American Society for Personnel Administration (now the Society for Human Resource Management). The second survey was completed in 1988 by personnel executives in 245 firms who were members of BNA's Personnel Policies Forum.[10] Table 3.2 summarizes the percentage of firms that employed various types of predictors and criteria. For predictors, the BNA researchers found:

TABLE 3.2	PERCENTAGE OF COMPANIES USING VARIOUS TYPES OF PREDICTORS AND CRITERIA IN SELECTION RESEARCH

Predictors	Percentage of Companies[a] 1983[b]	1988[c]	Criteria	Percentage of Companies[a] 1983[d]	1988
Background Information			**Objective Production Data**		
Reference/record checks	97%	96%	Production rate	18%	—
Weighted application blanks	11	—[e]	**Personnel Data**		
Investigation by outside agency	26	—	Length of service	21	—
			Absence/tardiness record	16	—
Interviews			Success in training	16	—
Unstructured	81	—	Pay increases/promotions earned	9	—
Structured	47	—			
			Judgmental Data		
Ability Testing			Actual performance evaluation record	37	—
Skill performance test/work sample	75	63	Research performance evaluation record	31	—
Mental ability test	20	31			
Job knowledge test	22	27			
Physical ability test	6	11			
Assessment center	6	12			
Other Predictors					
Medical examination	52	57			
Polygraph test	6	5			
Personality test	9	17			
Other	3	2			

[a] Percentages will sum to more than 100 percent since companies used multiple selection measures.
[b] These percentages are based on a survey of 437 companies.
[c] These percentages are based on a survey of 245 companies.
[d] These percentages are based on a survey of 68 companies that reported they had validated any of their selection procedures according to the *Uniform Guidelines*.
[e] Data were unavailable in the 1988 survey.
SOURCE: The 1983 survey data were based on the Bureau of National Affairs *ASPA-BNA Survey No. 45 Employee Selection Procedures* (Washington, D. C. Bureau of National Affairs, May 5 1983), pp. 2, 8. The 1988 survey data were based on the Bureau of National Affairs, *Recruiting and Selection Procedures* (Washington, D. C.: Bureau of National Affairs, May 1988), p. 17.

1. Reference checks, interviews, and skill performance tests were the procedures most likely to be used in selection. Assessment centers, physical abilities tests, and polygraph tests were the least likely to be employed.

2. The percentages of firms using the various types of predictors were roughly the same for the years 1983 and 1988.

In addition, the 1983 survey showed that approximately one-third (132) of the organizations used commercially available tests. Of these, 80 percent used standard tests for office/clerical positions; 30 percent used existing tests for professional or technical applicants.

For criteria used in selection or validation research studies (which we discuss later), it was found in the 1983 survey that:

1. Judgmental criteria (supervisory ratings) were most often employed.

2. Objective criteria (pay increases, promotion rates, work samples) were least frequently used.

Earlier studies have documented results similar to some of those reported in the BNA surveys.[11] These studies do not necessarily represent what should or should not be done but only what appears to be common practice. Thus, in sum, reference checks, interviews, and skill tests (as predictors) and supervisory ratings (as criteria) are likely to be the most common measurement methods used in human resource selection research.

Criteria for Evaluating Selection Measures

Now that we have provided an overview of some of the measurement methods used in selection, let's assume that you have already conducted a thorough analysis of the job in question to identify those worker characteristics thought to lead to job success. (In Chapters 7, 8, and 9 we provide some details on the job analysis process.) At this point, you are interested in choosing some measures to be employed as predictors and criteria indicative of job success. One of several questions you are likely to have is "What characteristics should I look for in selecting a predictor or a criterion?"

There are a number of characteristics or qualities you should consider in choosing or developing a selection measure. Although it is not an exhaustive list, a number of characteristics that you should carefully examine are listed in question form in Table 3.3. Some are more critical to predictors, some more essential for criteria, and some important for both types of measures. As you read these characteristics, you might think of them as a checklist to be reviewed for each measure you are considering. Unless you can be sure that a measure meets these standards, you *may* not have the best measure you need for your selection research. In that case, you have at least two options: (a) determine if there are adjustments you can make in your data or with the calculation of the measure itself so it will meet each measurement evaluation criterion or (b) if this option is not viable, find or develop another, more suitable measure.

Each of the characteristics is not of equal importance. Issues concerning reliability, validity, and freedom from bias are obviously more critical than some of the administrative concerns such as acceptability to management. Other characteristics will vary in importance depending upon the specific selection situation. Regardless, the wise selection manager will give serious consideration to each one.

| TABLE 3.3 | CRITERIA TO CONSIDER IN CHOOSING OR DEVELOPING MEASURES FOR USE IN HR SELECTION RESEARCH |

For Predictors:

1. *Does the predictor appear appropriate for the group or problem for which it is to be used?*
   Predictors have been used that are entirely inappropriate for the group or the problem to be addressed. A careful review of the predictor should be made to determine if it is appropriate.

2. *Is the cost of the predictor in dollars or cents or human values less than the cost of making an inaccurate decision?*
   Cost in purchasing or developing a predictor, scoring, and conducting validation studies should be considered. In a validation study, predictor content should be reviewed for offensiveness to applicants or employees.

3. *Has the predictor been "standardized"?*
   Administration and scoring procedures should be the same whenever a predictor is given. Data should also be available on how relevant groups of individuals have scored on the measure so that comparative data are available for interpreting the results.

4. *Does the predictor require highly trained persons for administration and scoring?*
   A predictor that can be administered and scored by persons not having high levels of training is less expensive than one requiring high levels.

5. *Can the predictor be administered to a group rather than just to an individual?*
   Group predictors are more economical than individual predictors. Group predictors can be given to individuals, but many individual predictors cannot be given to groups.

For Criteria:

6. *Is the criterion realistic and representative of the job for which it is chosen to measure success?* All important aspects of the job under study should be covered by the criterion.

7. *Is the criterion acceptable to management?*
   Unless management accepts the criterion to be predicted, there will be very little support for a system that may predict that which is considered to be worthless.

8. *Is situation change likely to alter the criterion?*
   Jobs and situations change. Thus, measures of success today may be inappropriate a year later. Criteria should be periodically reviewed for their relevancy.

9. *Is the criterion uncontaminated and free of bias so that meaningful comparisons among individuals can be made?*
   Unless jobs and work environments are identical, comparisons among individuals will be biased. Opportunity bias occurs when factors are beyond the control of the employee. Examples include differences between sales territories, differences in tools and equipment, differences in work shift, differences in physical conditions of the job. Group bias occurs when a group characteristic is related to employee performance. Examples include age and job tenure which can be related to performance. Rating bias can occur because of many factors that can influence supervisory ratings given to subordinates.

10. *Will the criterion detect differences among individuals if differences actually exist (discriminability)? Are there meaningful differences among individuals actually scored on the criterion?*
    If variance or individual differences in criterion scores cannot be obtained, then no predictor can be found to predict it.

(continued)

TABLE 3.3	(CONTINUED)

For Predictors and Criteria:

11. *Does the measure unfairly discriminate against sex, race, age, or other protected groups?*
    Significant differences among protected groups on a measure do not necessarily mean discrimination. However, any group differences found should be carefully examined for bias or unfairness.

12. *Does the measure lend itself to quantification?*
    For purposes of personnel selection, quantitative data are more desirable than qualitative data. Measures on an interval or ratio scale are most preferred.

13. *Is the measure objective?*
    Specific rules and procedures should be available for scoring individuals on the measure. Different scorers of an individual's performance should obtain the same score.

14. *How dependable are the data provided by the measure (reliability)? Will different results be obtained with each administration of the measure?*
    A measure should provide information that is dependable and accurate. Consistency of measurement is desirable. Thus repeated application of a measure (if the context of measurement is the same with each application) should yield the same scores.

15. *How well does the device measure the construct for which it is intended (validity)?*
    Measures chosen should assess what they are supposed to measure.

SOURCES: Based, in part, on Lewis E. Albright, J. R Glennon, and Wallace J. Smith, *The Use or Psychological Tests in Industry* (Cleveland: Howard Allen, 1963), pp. 34–35, 41–47; Charles H. Lawshe and Michael J. Balma, *Principles of Personnel Testing* (New York: McGraw-Hill, 1966), pp. 35-37; Milton L. Blum and James C. Naylor, *Industrial Psychology: Its Theoretical and Social Foundations* (New York: Harper & Row, 1968), pp. 180–182; G. C. Helmstadter, *Principles of Psychological Measurement* (Englewood Cliffs, N.J.: Prentice-Hall, 1964), pp. 34–35.

Finding and Constructing Selection Measures

The process of identifying selection measures to be used in an HR selection study should not be taken lightly. Identification of measures is not made simply by one's gut instincts and personal whims about what measures are best in a specific situation. As we see in our later chapters on job analysis, systematic work is conducted to identify what types of measures should be used. Thorough analyses of jobs are made to identify the necessary knowledge, skills, abilities, and other characteristics necessary for successful job performance. Then, once we know the qualifications needed to perform the job, we are ready to begin the process of identifying and implementing our selection measures. Obviously, the identification of selection measures is an important one. It is also one where a consultant, usually an industrial psychologist, may be needed. However, whether selection measures are identified by a consultant or by personnel staff within an organization, you need to be familiar with the basic approach. In identifying these measures, we have two choices: (a) we can locate and choose from existing selection measures, or (b) we can construct our own. In all likelihood, we will probably need to take both options.

Locating Existing Selection Measures

There are several advantages to finding and using existing selection measures. Some of these advantages include the following:

1. Use of existing measures is usually less expensive and less time consuming than developing new ones.

2. If previous research has been conducted, we will have some idea about the reliability, validity, and other characteristics of the measures.

3. Existing measures *may* be superior to what could be developed in-house.

In searching for suitable selection measures, you will find that there are many types of measures available. The vast majority of these are intended to be used as predictors, such as tests. A variety of predictors are commercially available, for example, intelligence, aptitude, ability, interest, and personality inventories. Other predictors such as application blanks, biographical data questionnaires, reference check forms, interview schedules, and work sample measures will probably have to be developed. Criteria measures are generally not published and will probably have to be constructed by a user. Sometimes measures other than predictors and criteria are employed in a selection study to describe a sample of employees or to help interpret the data available. For instance, job analysis measures, such as questionnaires, are included in most selection research investigations. Existing job analysis measures can be obtained, and they can usually be found in the research literature. (Some of the more prominent job analysis measures are mentioned later.)

Information Sources for Existing Measures   There are several sources for obtaining information on existing measures that can be used in personnel selection studies. Although most of these sources will not present the measures themselves, they will provide descriptive information on various options to be considered. Each of these sources is described here.

Text and Reference Sources   Several books are available that provide excellent reviews of predictors and other measures that have been used in hiring for a variety of jobs. Some of the books are organized around the types of jobs in which various measures have been used; others are centered around types of selection measures. Still others are organized around the technical aspects of the human resource selection process. Many of the relevant books on personnel selection are cited in this text.

In addition, the *Annual Review of Psychology*, published yearly, should also be consulted. On occasion, reviews of current selection research are published. These reviews offer an excellent, up-to-date look at research on measures and other issues relevant to personnel selection.

***Buros's* Mental Measurement Yearbooks**   The *Mental Measurements Yearbook* is the most important source for information on tests for personnel selection. Historically, a new edition of the *Yearbook* has been published every six years with the most recent edition being the *Eleventh Mental Measurements Yearbook* (1992).[12] (A biennial *Mental Measurements Yearbook* began publication in 1989, with a *Supplement* to be published in alternating years. The most current work is the *Supplement to the Eleventh Mental Measurements Yearbook*.) Previously, Oscar Buros was editor of the *Yearbook*, but following his death, his institute was moved to the University of Nebraska. His work is now being carried on by the Buros Institute of Mental Measurements at that university.

The *Yearbook* consists of critical reviews by test experts and bibliographies of virtually every test printed in English. Because of the completeness of the *Yearbook*, finding appropriate tests can be facilitated through use of its indexes. Beginning with the publication of *The Ninth Mental Measurements Yearbook*, six indexes can be used for locating tests for use in specific personnel selection applications. These indexes are invaluable aids in locating tests and include (a) *Index of Titles*, (b) *Index of Acronyms*, (c) *Classified Subject Index*, (d) *Publishers Directory and Index*, (e) *Index of Names*, and (f) *Score Index*. The *Score Index* is a feature that should be very helpful in finding a desired test. For instance, when someone is searching for an employment test, the search is usually defined in terms of specific variables that need to be measured in a given employment setting. Test titles can be studied; however, titles alone can be misleading. But the scores for variables included in a test often provide specific definitions of the variables the test developer is trying to measure. The *Score Index* can be referenced as a subject index to locate the specific variables purportedly measured by a test. Once the user has identified the desired variables, reviews of tests that measure these variables can be found in the *Yearbook*.

In addition, the Buros Institute has published several supplementary books containing additional bibliographies and reviews. These references include *Tests in Print, Intelligence Tests and Reviews, Vocational Tests and Reviews*, and *Personality Tests and Reviews II*. The latter three volumes also contain master indexes of tests reviewed in the *Yearbook*. Unquestionably, the Buros publications represent some of the most valuable sources for identifying existing tests to be considered for personnel selection applications.

Mental Measurements Yearbook Database   If you are interested in continuous access to the latest reviews of tests compiled by the Buros Institute of Mental Measurements, try the Bibliographic Retrieval Service (BRS), a computer retrieval service available through most major university and many public libraries. The BRS can be used to search the *Mental Measurements Yearbook Database* that contains the latest factual information. critical reviews, and reliability/validity information on all tests reviewed by the Buros Institute. The database is structured so a user can identify a test by focusing on test characteristics such as test name, author, publisher, publication date, intended population for test use, scores yielded, form of administration, reviewers' names, or combinations of these characteristics. The score characteristic is particularly helpful, since it can be searched to locate tests that provide scores on variables of most interest. Once a suitable test(s) has been found, copies of review(s) can be printed either on- or off-line.

Other Reference Sources   PRO-ED, a testing corporation in Austin, Texas, offers a series of testing sources referencing a variety of psychological measures. These sources include the following:

1. *Psychware Sourcebook 1988–1989*—A biennial reference guide describing over 450 computer-based assessment products including software for administering and scoring tests. In addition to product descriptions, product supplier, sales restriction, cost information. and sample printouts of reports are provided.

2. *Tests: A Comprehensive Reference for Assessments in Psychology, Education, and Business*—Describing more than 3,200 tests, this reference includes information on each instrument's scoring procedures, cost, and publisher.

3. *Test Critiques, Volumes I–VI*—A six-volume series that provides evaluations of over 800 tests in three areas: practical applications and uses, technical aspects (validity, reliability, normative data), and a critique of the tests.

4. *Test Critiques Compendium: Reviews of Major Tests from the Test Critiques Series*—A reference that includes reviews from *Test Critiques* of 60 tests used most frequently in professional practice.

5. *Consumer's Guide to Tests in Print*—A descriptive characterization of 148 tests based on the availability of test norms, reliability, and validity information.

6. *Business and Industry Testing: Current Practices and Test Reviews*—A reference that summarizes and reviews 60 tests commonly used in industry.

Educational Testing Service (ETS) of Princeton, New Jersey, has several reference sources available for identifying suitable selection measures. For instance, *Test Collection Bibliographies* is a collection of 200 annotated test bibliographies in specific subject areas such as "Salespersons—Selection and Evaluation" and "Supervisory Management." *Test Collection Database* is a publicly searchable database through BRS Information Technologies. The database has information on over 9,000 tests used to assess abilities, aptitudes, interests, and personality as well as other variables related to various vocational and occupational fields. Use of the database is very similar to that of the *Mental Measurements Yearbook Database* described earlier.

Journals   Several journals are also suitable sources for information on selection measures. In particular, the *Journal of Applied Psychology (JAP)* and *Personnel Psychology* are most relevant. *JAP* has a long history as a major journal in the field of industrial psychology. In general, it is technical and focuses on empirical research in applied psychology. Articles on various predictors, criteria, and other issues related to personnel selection can be found. Any search for measures should definitely include *JAP* as a source.

Personnel Psychology also has a long history of publishing articles concerned with personnel selection and related topics. From 1954 to 1965, *Personnel Psychology* included a special feature called the "Validity Information Exchange." In order to encourage the publication of validation studies completed in the context of HR selection, the Exchange offered an outlet requiring minimal time and effort to prepare a validity study for publication. Although the studies reported in the Exchange are dated, they offer a source for possible ideas concerning selection measures. For a number of years, articles have appeared periodically dealing with measures involved in selection.

The *Annual Validity Review*, started in 1988, is a publication edited by Frank Landy of Pennsylvania State University with the objective of publishing empirical validity studies of psychological measures. Each volume contains roughly 100 studies with technical details about the predictors, criteria, sample, and job family being provided. Other journals such as the *Journal of Occupational and Organizational Psychology*, *The Industrial-Organizational Psychologist (TIP)*, *Educational and Psychological Measurement*, and *Applied Psychological Measurement* will have articles from time to time dealing with the application of selection measures. At times, reviews of specific tests that may be relevant to industrial personnel selection can also be found in the *Journal of Educational Measurement* and the *Journal of Counseling Psychology*. In order to have a thorough search, these journals should be reviewed for possible ideas. *Psychological Abstracts* and *Personnel Management Abstracts* as well as computerized literature searches (for example, PsycLIT or PsycINFO) offered through many libraries and the American Psychological Association can also be employed to identify potential selection measures.

Test Publishers   A number of organizations publish tests that are used in HR selection. Catalogs describing the various tests offered can be obtained from each publisher. A comprehensive list of test publishers and addresses can be found in Buros's *Mental Measurements Yearbook*.

Catalogs obtained from these publishers will present information on the most current tests that are available. Once a test is located that may appear to meet a specific need, a test manual and specimen set can be ordered by qualified users. (Typical costs for specimen sets range from $25 to $75.) The test manual provides information on the administration, scoring, and interpretation of results. In addition, reliability and validity data are also presented. These materials help users decide if a test is appropriate prior to actually adopting it.

However, just because a test is identified for use does not mean that anyone may purchase it. Some test publishers use a scheme (originally developed by the American Psychological Association but later dropped from the association's 1985 revision of its testing standards) for classifying their tests and for determining to whom tests can be sold. There are three levels of classification:

1. *Level A*—This level consists of those tests that require very little formal training to administer, score, and interpret the results. Most personnel practitioners may purchase tests at this level. A typing test is representative of tests in this classification.

2. *Level B*—Tests classified in this category require some formal training and. knowledge of psychological testing concepts to properly score and interpret. Aptitude tests that are designed to forecast individuals' potential to perform are of this type. Individuals wishing to purchase Level B tests

must be able to document their qualifications to correctly use such tests. These qualifications usually include evidence of formal education in tests and measurement as well as psychological statistics.

3. *Level C*—These tests require the most extensive preparation on the part of the test administrator. In general, personality inventories and projective techniques make up this category. A Ph.D. in psychology and documentation of training, such as courses taken on the use of a particular test, are required. Tests in this category tend to be less frequently used in industrial personnel selection contexts than tests in levels A and B.

A more complex approach to describing test selection practices than the classification scheme just described above can be found in the *Standards for Educational and Psychological Testing*, published by the American Psychological Association (APA).[13] Although it is not a source of selection measures per se, APA's *Standards* provides an excellent treatment of the considerations in selecting and using tests.

Professional Associations   Various professional associations may also be a source of selection measures. For example, the American Banking Association has supported research to develop selection measures for use in hiring clerical personnel in banking. The American Petroleum Institute has sponsored research to review the use of tests in selection of clerical personnel. In addition, the American Foundation for the Blind has published a book, *Measures of Psychological, Vocational, and Educational Functioning in the Blind and Visually Handicapped*,[14] that contains a variety of measures for individuals with visual problems. Other trade and professional associations should be contacted as possible sources for selection measures or research on such measures.

Certain management associations may also be able to provide guidance in locating possible selection measures for specific situations. The Society for Human Resource Management (SHRM) and the International Personnel Management Association (IPMA) are two potential sources of information.

Sourcebooks   Several sourcebooks have been published that provide information on little known instruments. Not all of the instruments cited in these references are suitable in the context of personnel selection, but it may be worthwhile to consult them. *A Sourcebook for Mental Health Measures*[15] contains over 1,000 abstracts describing tests, questionnaires, rating scales, and other measures used to evaluate both aptitude and personality variables. *Measures for Psychological Assessment*[16] contains references and bibliographies on 3,000 measures cited in 26 measurement-oriented journals published between 1960 and 1970. Although it is an older reference, *Objective Personality and Motivation Tests*[17] describes a wide array of measures for assessing dimensions of personality. *Assessment Tools for Practitioners, Managers, and Trainers*[18] as well as *Women and Women's Issues: A Handbook of Tests and Measures*[19] may provide some suitable measures in some HR selection contexts.

As a user of selection measures, be a careful, thoughtful consumer when searching for and choosing these measures. As Oscar Buros once wrote, "At least half of the tests currently on the market should never have been published. Exaggerated, false, or unsubstantiated claims are the rule rather than the exception.[20]

Constructing New Selection Measures

There are obvious advantages to using existing selection measures, and when suitable measures can be found, they certainly should be used. But, sometimes, selection researchers may not be able to find the precise measure that they need for their purposes. At this point, they have no choice but to develop their own. In this section, we outline the major steps that should be taken in developing any selection measure.

Before proceeding, we need to note some questions for consideration. Some legitimate concerns that might be raised by HR professionals are whether it is reasonable to expect practitioners to develop selection measures, particularly in light of the technical and legal ramifications associated with them and whether an organization would have the resources in time and expertise to develop such measures. In addition, we might ask, "Can't a little knowledge be dangerous? That is, won't some well-meaning practitioners be encouraged to attempt to develop and use measures that 'appear' to be 'good' but really are worthless?"

Our intention is not to prepare you nor even encourage you to go out to develop selection measures yourselves but to enable you to work productively with a selection specialist or expert. The development of such measures is a complex, resource consuming process for which expert advice is usually required. The risks associated with the process can be quite high. Most HR managers will simply not have the resources or the skills necessary to engage in selection measure development. Thus, consultants will likely be needed.[21] Given that consultants are employed, the material presented in this and related chapters is intended to serve as a means by which the work of a consultant can be monitored and evaluated as well as the literature describing selection measures studied and reviewed. In addition, if consultants are hired, knowledge of the basic issues involved in selection measure development, validation, and application can help bridge any possible communications gap between the organization and the consultant.

Steps in Developing Selection Measures   Although the details may vary somewhat depending on the specific selection measure being developed, there are eight major steps typically taken. These general steps include the following:

1.   Analyzing the job for which a measure is being developed,

2.   Selecting the method of measurement to be used,

3.   Developing the specifications or plan of the measure,

4.   Constructing the preliminary form of the measure,

5.   Administering and analyzing the preliminary form,

6. Preparing a revised form,

7. Determining the reliability and validity of the revised form for the jobs studied, and

8. Implementing and monitoring the measure in the human resource selection system.

Now, let's examine each of these steps.

Analyzing the Job   The first step in the instrument development process is perhaps the most crucial. If this step is inappropriately carried out, then all subsequent steps will be flawed. It is for this reason that we have devoted three chapters (Chapters 7, 8, and 9) to the role of job analysis in personnel selection. The role of job analysis in the context of selection is to determine the knowledge, skills, abilities, and other characteristics necessary to adequately perform a job. From knowledge of these requisite characteristics as well as the activities and conditions wherein they will be used, the developer of a selection measure gains insights and forms hypotheses as to what types of measures may be appropriate. Whether a measure is being developed or whether existing measures are being considered, job analysis *must* be performed as an initial step.

In addition to its role in developing and selecting selection measures, job analysis also provides the foundation for developing criteria measures of job proficiency. We cannot do systematic research on the selection of personnel until we know which of the applicants we have selected have become successful employees. Intimate knowledge of the job gained through job analysis will help us to identify or develop measures of job success. Ultimately, through validation research we will determine the extent to which our selection measures can actually predict these criteria.

As you will see in later chapters, there are many approaches to job analysis. In the context of selection, these can be classified into basically two categories: (a) *work*-oriented methods and (b) *worker*-oriented methods. Under a work-oriented method, the researcher principally addresses the activities and functions performed on the job. Measures are sought that reproduce these features of the job. Thus if typing activities are a central function of a clerk's position, a typing test based on materials like those encountered on the job might be developed. In determining whether adequate coverage of the job has been taken, the job analyst may ask: "If tasks A, B, C, . . . , Z are required on the job, do I have a measure or can I develop one that will require a worker to perform similar tasks?"

Notice that under the work-oriented approach the focus is on the *functions* of the job rather than the human attributes necessary to perform it. Under our second general method of job analysis, the worker-oriented approach, the focus is on the *qualities* of the job incumbent needed to perform it rather than characteristics of the job itself. Under this approach, the analyst may ask what special attributes, such as physical requirements, sensory and perceptual requirements, intellectual functioning, specific knowledge and skills, are needed to perform this job. Using this approach, an analysis of a clerk's job may show that perceptual accuracy is necessary to complete the task of checking long lists of numbers for correctness.

One job analysis method is not necessarily more correct than the other. In practice, both approaches or combinations of both are involved. A skilled analyst will attempt to use the best approach for the situation at hand. In general, the more researchers know about a specific job, the more likely their hypotheses and ideas about selection measures will have predictive utility for that job. Therefore, researchers will choose the method of analysis they believe will yield the most useful information about a job.

Selecting the Measurement Method   Once we have identified the important job activities and necessary characteristics of personnel to adequately perform a job, we are ready to consider the approach we will use in selection. There are a host of methods available, including paper-and-pencil tests, job or work sample tests, interviews, and biographical data questionnaires, to name only a few. The specific nature of the job (such as tasks performed, level of responsibility), the skill of the individual(s) responsible for administering, scoring, and interpreting selection measures, the number and types of applicants making application (such as level of reading and writing skills, presence of physical handicaps), the costs of testing, and the resources (such as time and dollars) available for test development are just some of the variables that will impact on the selection of a measurement medium. If large numbers of applicants are making application for the job, paper and-pencil measures will be carefully considered. If applicant appearance (both physical and interpersonal) is critical, then some form of a behavioral exercise might be proposed. If manipulative skills appear to be critical to job success, then tests involving the manipulation of a physical apparatus may be necessary to measure respondents' motor responses. The method chosen will ultimately depend on the job and organizational context in which the job is performed.

Exhibit 3.5 presents an example of a checklist that was used to identify selection methods to be developed for selecting industrial electricians. The listing under "Job Requirements" consists of elements of the job identified through a job analysis that were found to be critical to the job success of a company's industrial electricians. The requirements are the knowledge, skills, and individual attributes that a newly hired electrician must have upon entry into the job. The listing under "Selection Method" represents the possible means by which the essential job requirements can be assessed. After studying the job and the organization, the selection researcher decided that certain methods would be suitable for assessing some requirements while other measures would be appropriate for other job requirements. The suitable methods for specific job requirements are indicated by a check mark. For example, it was decided that a paper-and-pencil test was most suitable for determining applicants' knowledge of the principles of electrical wiring, whereas a work sample test was chosen to determine applicants' ability to solder electrical connections. Chapters 10–17 discuss predictor and criterion measures in detail and give you more insight into choosing appropriate instruments.

Developing Specifications for the Selection Measure   After a job has been analyzed and some tentative methods considered for assessing the important aspects

EXHIBIT 3.5	CHECKLIST USED TO MATCH SELECTION METHODS WITH JOB REQUIREMENTS FOR THE JOB OF INDUSTRIAL ELECTRICIAN

Selection Method

Job Requirements	Work sample test	Paper-and-pencil test	Selection interview	Biographical data form	Reference check	Application form
1. Knowledge of Principles of electrical writing		✓				
2. Ability to solder electrical connections	✓					
3. Ability to troubleshoot electrical wiring problems using a voltmeter	✓					
4. Care and repair of electrical equipment		✓				
⋮				⋮		
N. Previous work experience in hazardous work environments			✓		✓	✓

of the job, the selection researcher probably has some vague mental picture of what each method may be like. In this step, the researcher attempts to clarify the nature and details of each selection measure by developing specifications for their construction. For each measure considered, the specifications developed should include the following:

1. The functions the measure is intended to serve,

2. Operational definitions of each variable to be measured,

3. The number and examples of each type of item, question, etc., to be included in the measure,

4. The nature of the population for which the measure is to be designed,

5. The time limits for completing the measure, and

6. The statistical procedures to be used in selecting and editing items, questions, etc., on the measure.[22]

Referring again to our electrician's job, we can see how job content might be translated into the specifications for a paper-and-pencil test used to measure what an industrial electrician needs to know to perform the job. In preparing the test, the first step is to examine the principal content of the job by preparing a topical outline. From discussions with incumbents and supervisors as well as additional job analysis information, the job of industrial electrician is broken down into several components as shown in Exhibit 3.6. Although the outline is informative, it is not immediately clear what test items could be prepared on each of these topics. The outline in Exhibit 3.7 takes us a step further by showing what a worker needs to know to perform the principal components of the job listed in Exhibit 3.6. Breaking down what a worker needs to know in an outline similar to that in Exhibit 3.7 makes it easier to prepare appropriate questions. Finally, in Exhibit 3.8, the two topical outlines are merged. The chart shown helps us to specify the test item budget, that is, the specific number of items to be prepared for measuring the components of the job. Theoretically, at least one item could be developed for each cell in the chart shown in Exhibit 3.8. Our test, however, is only a *sampling* of behavior; we cannot ask all possible questions covering all possible elements of information. By using the chart in collaboration with knowledgeable and competent personnel involved with the job, we can specify a reasonable number of test items for each cell chosen to be included in the test. Test items may now be constructed in proportion to the number identified in the cells of the chart.

Constructing the Preliminary Form of the Measure   Now that the specifications for a measure have been determined, we are ready to prepare an initial version of our measure. The items, questions, and so on, chosen to compose the contents of the preliminary form should be developed in concert with the specifications laid out in the previous step.

Administering the Preliminary Form   Following development, the initial form should be pilot-tested. The measure should be administered to a sample of people from the same population for which the measure is being developed. In order to provide data suitable for analyzing the contents of the measure, the measure should be given to a rather sizable sample. For example, if a test is being developed where item analyses are to be performed, a sample of at least 100, preferably several hundred, will be needed.

Preparing the Revised Form   Based on the data collected in the previous step, analyses are performed on the preliminary data. The objective is to revise the proposed measure by correcting any weakness and deficiencies noted. For example, if a test is being developed, item analyses are used to choose the content of the test so that it will discriminate between those who know and those who do not know the information covered.

Determining Reliability and Validity of the Measure   At this point, we have a revised measure that we hypothesize will predict some aspect(s) of job success. Thus we are ready to conduct reliability and validity studies to test our hypoth-

| EXHIBIT 3.6 | OUTLINE OF MAJOR COMPONENTS OF THE INDUSTRIAL ELECTRICIAN'S JOB |

I. **Using Electrical Equipment**
   A. Motors
   B. Fixtures, switches, junction boxes
   C. Appliances (refrigerators, air conditioners, fans)
   D. Communication devices (intercom, telephone)
II. **Using Electrical Instruments**
   A. Ohmmeter
   B. Voltmeter
   C. Ammeter
   D. RPM meter
   E. Oscilloscope
III. **Working with Hand and Power Tools**
   A. Drills (1/2″ and 1/4″)
   B. Socket wrenches
   C. Soldering iron
   D. Wire cutters
   E . Screwdrivers
IV. **Using Electrical Components and Materials**
   A. Coaxial cable
   B. Electrical wiring (#6 to #22)
   C. Solder

| EXHIBIT 3.7 | WHAT AN INDUSTRIAL ELECTRICIAN NEEDS TO KNOW TO PERFORM THE JOB |

I. **Technical Skills**
   A. Reading schematic drawings
   B. Calculating electrical units of measurement
   C. Understanding fundamental operations
   D. Knowledge of principles of electricity
II. **Knowledge of Trade Terms**
   A. Electrical components
   B. Electrical wiring
   C. Tools
III. **Knowledge of Care and Use of Tools**
   A. Selection for appropriate tasks
   B. Correct procedures for use
   C. Care and maintenance
   D. Purchasing tools
IV. **Safety Information**
   A. Prevention of injury to self
   B. Prevention of injury to others
V. **Information About Electrical Supplies**
   A. Specifications for choosing supplies
   B. Purchasing supplies

EXHIBIT 3.8	FORM USED TO DETERMINE THE ITEM BUDGET FOR THE INDUSTRIAL ELECTRICIAN TEST

	Topic	Technical Skills	Knowledge of Trade Terms	Knowledge of Care and Use of Tools	Safety Information	Information About Electrical Supplies	TOTAL ITEMS
Electrical Equipment	Motors						
	Fixtures, switches, junction boxes						
	Appliances						
	Communication devices						
Electrical Instruments	Ohmmeter						
	Voltmeter						
	Ammeter						
	RPM meter						
Tools	Oscilloscope						
	Drills						
	Socket wrenches						
	Soldering iron						
	Wire cutters						
	Screwdrivers						
Electrical Components	Coaxial cable						
	Electrical wiring						
	Solder						

The header "Information" spans the columns: Technical Skills, Knowledge of Trade Terms, Knowledge of Care and Use of Tools, Safety Information, Information About Electrical Supplies.

esis. We examine in the next two chapters how reliability and validation research may be conducted. Essentially, we want to answer these questions: "Are the scores on our selection measure dependable for selection decision making purposes?" and "Is the selection measure predictive of job success?"

Implementing the Selection Measure After we have obtained the necessary reliability and validity evidence, we can then implement our measure. Cut-off or passing scores will need to be developed. Norms or standards for interpreting how various groups (in terms of gender, ethnicity, level of education, etc.) score on the measure may also be needed to help interpret the results. Once implemented, we will continue to monitor the performance of the selection measure to ensure that it is performing the function for which it is intended.

As you can see, there is a great deal of technical work involved in the development of a selection measure. Shortcuts are seldom warranted and, in fact, are to be discouraged. In addition, there are significant costs associated with the development of selection measures. The technical ramifications and the associated costs in developing selection measures are two principal reasons why selection researchers frequently use suitable, existing measures rather than developing their own.

Interpreting Scores on Selection Measures
Using Norms

If you took a test, had it scored, and then were told that you made a 69, how would you feel? Probably not very good! But a moment after receiving your score, you would probably ask how this score compared to what others made. Your question underscores one of the basic principles of interpreting the results of selection measurement procedures. That is, in order to interpret the results of measurement intelligently we need two essential kinds of information: (a) information on how others scored on the measure and (b) information on the validity of the measure.[23]

Let's return to your test score of 69 for a moment. Suppose you were told that the top score was 73. All of a sudden you might feel a lot better than you felt a few moments ago. However, you are also told that everyone else who took the test scored 73. Now how do you feel? Without information on how relevant others scored, any score is practically meaningless. In order to attach any meaning to a score, we need to compare it to the scores of others who are similar in terms of characteristics such as age, level of education, type of job applied for, gender, and ethnicity. Thus a score may take on different meanings depending upon how it stands relative to the scores of others in particular groups. In a group, such as one based on age, a score of 69 may be high. In a group such as one based on level of education, the score may be very low. Our interpretation will depend on the score's relative standing in these other groups.

These scores of relevant others in groups that we use for score interpretation are called *norms*. They are used to show how well an individual performs with respect to a specified group of people. For example, standardized norms reported in test manuals are designed to rank-order examinees from high to low on the attribute that is being assessed. The purpose is to determine how much of the measured attribute a person has in relation to others on whom the same test information is available. This group of persons on whom test score information is available and used for comparison purposes is referred o as a *normative sample* or *standardization* group. The *Wonderlic Personnel Test*, for instance, reports norms based on groups defined by the following variables: age of applicant, educational attainment, gender, position applied for, type of industry, and geographical region.

Normative data can be useful in understanding and evaluating scores on selection measures. However, there are several points that should be kept in mind when using norms to interpret scores. First, the norm group selected should be *relevant* for the purpose it is being used. Norms will be meaningless or even misleading if they are not based upon groups with whom it is sensible to compare individuals being considered for employment. For example, suppose individuals applying for the job of an experienced electrician took the *Purdue Test for Electricians.* Let's assume that normative sample data were available for trade school graduates who had taken the test as well as the employer's experienced electricians. If the company is trying to hire experienced electricians, the relevant norm group would be the company's experienced electricians rather than the norm group representing trade school graduates. Clearly, the former is more relevant to company needs for experienced personnel. If the norm group consisting of inexperienced personnel had been used, very misleading results, perhaps some with serious consequences, could have occurred. There can be many norm groups reported in selection manuals. Care must be exercised to ensure the appropriate group is chosen when interpreting scores on measures.

Second, rather than using norms based on national data, an employer should accumulate and use *local* norms. A local norm is one based upon selection measures administered to individuals making application for employment with a particular employer. Initially, when a test is implemented, appropriate norms published in a test manual may have to be used, but local norms should be developed as soon as 100 or more scores in a particular group have been accumulated. Passing test scores should then be established on the basis of these local data rather than just taken from published manuals.[24]

A third point to consider is that norms are *transitory.* That is, they are specific to the point in time when they were collected. Norms may, and probably do, change over time. If the attribute being assessed is not likely to change, then older norms are likely to be more or less relevant. However, the more likely the attribute may change over time, the more current the normative data should be. For example, individuals tend to score higher on general mental ability tests than test takers of 10 to 20 years ago. Thus, an individual's mental ability test scores would appear higher using older norms than if current norms were used.

There is no prescribed period of time for publishers of selection measures to collect new normative data. Some may collect such information every four or five years; others may collect normative data every ten years. The point is that norms which appear to be dated should be interpreted very cautiously. Where feasible, normative data should be continuously collected by the user of selection measures.

Norms are not always necessary in HR selection. For example, if five of the best performers on a test must be hired or if it is known that persons with scores of 70 or better on the test make suitable employees, then a norm is not necessary in employment decision making. One can simply use the individuals' test scores. On the other hand, if one finds that the applicants' median selection test scores are significantly below that of a norm group, then the recruitment practices of the firm should be examined. They may not be attracting the best job applicants; norm data would help in analyzing this situation.

In using normative information, we rely on statistical methods to aid our interpretation of what a test score means. There are a two basic methods we use frequently for expressing and interpreting test scores with respect to norms. These are percentiles and standard scores.

Using Percentiles

The most frequently used statistic in reporting normative data is the *percentile*. Since the purpose of a norm is to show relative standing in a group, percentile scores are derived to show *the percentage of persons in a norm group who fall below a given score on a measure*. Thus, if an individual makes a 75 on a test and this score corresponds to the 50th percentile, then that individual would have scored better than 50 percent of the people in a particular group who took the test. A percentile score is not a percentage score. A percentage score is like a raw or obtained score. For instance, if 1 out of 200 people taking a 100-item test correctly answered 50 questions, his or her score would be 50, or 50 percent correct. But is this score high or low? By using percentiles, we can compare that score with the other 199 test takers' scores to make that determination. Thus 50 percent correct may correspond to a percentile score ranging from 0 to 100 depending on the others' test performance.

In general, the higher the percentile score, the better a person's performance relative to others in the normative sample. Scores above the 50th percentile indicate above-average performance; scores below this percentile represent below-average performance. Exhibit 3.9 illustrates how normative percentile data are typically reported in test manuals.

Percentile scores are very useful in interpreting test scores; however, they are subject to misuse. Charles Lawshe and Michael Balma point out there is a tendency for some users to want to interpret these percentile scores as if they were on a ratio scale.[25] Thus if Susan Shadow, an applicant for a job, scores 5 percentile points higher on a selection test than Jack Nackis, another job applicant, some may want to conclude that Susan is 5 percent better than Jack for the job. However, such use of percentile scores cannot be made for at least two reasons.

First, a difference of five percentile points may not indicate a real difference in people; the difference may be nothing but chance resulting from unreliability of the test. (In the next chapter, you will see how the standard error of measurement can be used to make such a determination.) Second, percentile scores are based on an *ordinal* scale of measurement, not a ratio scale. Thus, we can make greater than or less than statements in comparing scores, but we cannot say how much higher or how much lower one percentile score is from another. For instance, a percentile score of 60 is not twice as good as a percentile score of 30.

There is another limitation of percentile scores that should also be noted. Because percentile scores are on an ordinal scale, they cannot be legitimately added, subtracted, divided, or multiplied. Statistical manipulations are not possible with percentiles. For this and other reasons, test scores are also frequently expressed as *standard* scores (one example of standard scores is entered as a "z" score shown in Exhibit 3.9).

EXHIBIT 3.9	HYPOTHETICAL ILLUSTRATION OF HOW PERCENTILE NORMS ARE FREQUENTLY REPORTED IN TEST MANUALS

Test Raw Score	z Score	Percentile
50	3.0	99.9
45	2.0	97.7
40	1.0	84.1
35	0.0	50.0
30	−1.0	16.0
25	−2.0	2.0
20	−3.0	1.0

Using Standard Scores

There are many different types of standard scores that may be reported in manuals accompanying commercially available tests to be used in selection. Some of the more common ones are z, T, and stanine scores. We will not go into all of the statistical details of these standard scores, but we do need to comment about their role in interpreting scores on selection measures.

In general, standard scores represent adjustments to raw scores so it is possible to determine the proportion of individuals who fall at various standard score levels. These scales indicate, in common measurement units, how far above or below the mean score any raw score is. By common measurement unit, we mean these scores are on a scale so that score differences have equal intervals and, therefore, can be added, subtracted, multiplied, and divided. Let's look at a few types of standard scores.

One of the most common standard scores is the z score. In computing z scores, the formula is

$$z = \frac{(X - M)}{SD}$$

where

z = the standard score
X = an individual's raw or obtained score
M = the mean of the normative group's raw scores
SD = the standard deviation of the normative group's raw scores

Using this formula, z scores can be obtained for all individuals on whom test score data are available. The computations result in scores that range from -4.0 to +4.0 and are directly interpretable in terms of their distance from the normative group mean in standard deviation units. For example, a person with a z score of 1.0 is 1 standard deviation above the group mean; a person with a z score of −1.5 is 1 1/2 standard deviations below the group mean.

In order to avoid negative numbers, T scores are often used. These scores

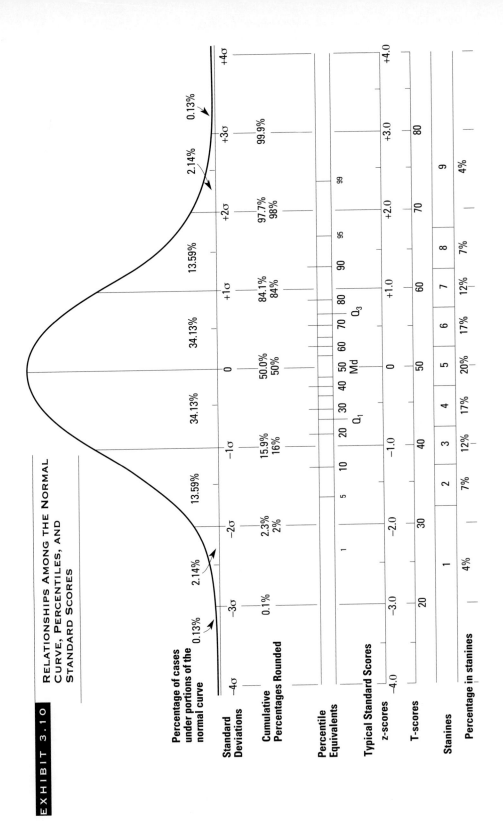

EXHIBIT 3.10 RELATIONSHIPS AMONG THE NORMAL CURVE, PERCENTILES, AND STANDARD SCORES

Percentage of cases under portions of the normal curve

0.13% 2.14% 13.59% 34.13% 34.13% 13.59% 2.14% 0.13%

Standard Deviations
−4σ −3σ −2σ −1σ 0 +1σ +2σ +3σ +4σ

Cumulative Percentages Rounded
0.1% 2.3% 15.9% 50.0% 84.1% 97.7% 99.9%
         2%   16%   50%   84%   98%

Percentile Equivalents
1   5   10 20 30 40 50 60 70 80   90   95   99
                     Q₁   Md   Q₃

Typical Standard Scores

z-scores
−4.0 −3.0 −2.0 −1.0 0 +1.0 +2.0 +3.0 +4.0

T-scores
20   30   40   50   60   70   80

Stanines
1   2   3   4   5   6   7   8   9

Percentage in stanines
4% 7% 12% 17% 20% 17% 12% 7% 4%

are similar to z scores, but they are adjusted so that all individuals' T scores are positive. One common form of T scores has a mean of 50 and a standard deviation of 10. To compute such a T score, we simply compute the z score and then use the following formula: $T = 10 z + 50$. Thus a person's z score of 1.0 is equivalent to a T score of 60.

Stanine scores are another form of standard scores. In this case, a single number ranging from 1 to 9 is used to represent individuals' normative score performance. Stanines are computed by rank-ordering scores from lowest to highest. The 4 percent with the lowest scores get a stanine score of 1, the next 7 percent get a stanine of 2, and so on. The higher the stanine score, the better the performance on a selection measure.

As you might expect, there is an interrelationship among percentiles and the various standard scores we have mentioned. Exhibit 3.10 depicts the relationships among these scores. The figure shows a normal distribution of scores made on a test. Under the normal curve are various standard scores expressed as percentiles, z scores, T scores, and stanines. As you see can, the mean score of this distribution corresponds to the 50th percentile, a z score of 0, a T score of 50, and a stanine of 5. An individual who scores 1 standard deviation above the mean would have a percentile score of 85, a z score of 1, and so forth. Many other comparisons are also possible by using Figure 3 .10.

The biggest problem with the use of standard scores is that they are subject to misinterpretation. For this reason, percentiles are the most common metric presented by publishers of selection measures.

Although normative data are helpful in interpreting scores on selection measures, what we really want to know is how well a selection measure predicts future job performance. Norms do not tell us what a score means in terms of important job behaviors or criteria of job performance. Sometimes, users will assume that a relationship exists between selection measures and these criteria, but without reliability and validity evidence, we do not know if this assumption is warranted. In the next two chapters, we will review methods for determining the reliability of selection measures as well as methods for examining the link between predictors and job success.

References

[1] Jum C. Nunnally, *Introduction to Psychological Measurement* (New York: McGraw-Hill, 1970), p. 7.

[2] Fred N. Kerlinger, *Foundations of Behavioral Research* (New York: Holt, Rinehart, and Winston, 1973), p. 432.

[3] Edwin E. Ghiselli, *Theory of Psychological Measurement* (New York: McGraw-Hill, 1964), pp. 9–35.

[4] The "mean" is the average score of a group of persons on a variable such as a test. The "standard deviation" is a number that represents the spread of scores for a group of persons around the group's average score on a variable. As the standard deviation increases, the spread or differences among individuals' scores becomes larger. "Correlations" show the degree of relationship between variables. Chapter 5 gives a more thorough description of correlational procedures used in selection research.

[5] See Kerlinger, *Foundations of Behavioral Research*, pp. 438-441; J. P. Guilford, *Psychometric Theory* (New York: McGraw-Hill, 1954), pp. 15-16.

[6]Wayne Cascio, *Applied Psychology in Personnel Management,* 3d ed. (Reston, Va.: Reston, 1987), p. 128.

[7]Frank J. Landy and Donald A. Trumbo, *Psychology of Work Behavior* (Homewood, Ill.: Dorsey Press, 1985), pp 80; 91.

[8]Charles H. Lawshe and Michael J. Balma, *Principles of Personnel Testing* (New York: McGrawHill, 1966), pp. 35-42.

[9]Robert Guion, *Personnel Testing* (New York: McGraw-Hill, 1965), p. 91.

[10]Bureau of National Affairs, *ASPA-BNA Survey No. 45—Employee Selection Procedures* (Washington, D.C.: Bureau of National Affairs, May 5, 1983), pp. 1-12 and Bureau of National Affairs, *Recruiting and Selection Procedures* (Washington, D.C.: Bureau of National Affairs, May 1988), pp. 17-24.

[11]*Personnel Management: Policies and Practices—Report No. 22* (Englewood Cliffs, NJ.: Prentice-Hall, April 2, 1975). See also Carlyn J. Monahan and Paul M. Muchinsky, "Three Decades of Personnel Selection Research: A State-of-the-Art Analysis and Evaluation," *Journal of Occupational Psychology* 56 (1983): 215-225; Richard H. Lent, Herbert A. Aurbach, and Lowell S. Levin, "Research Design and Validity Assessment," *Personnel Psychology* 24 (1971): 247-274; Richard H. Lent, Herbert A. Aurbach, and Lowell S. Levin, "Predictors, Criteria, and Significant Results," *Personnel Psychology* 24 (1971); 519–533.

[12]Jack J. Kramer and Jane Close Conoley, *Eleventh Mental Measurements Yearbook* (Lincoln: Buros Institute of Mental Measurements, University of Nebraska Press, 1989). Also, see Jack J. Kramer and *Supplement to the Tenth Mental Measurements Yearbook* (Lincoln: Buros Institute of Mental Measurements, University of Nebraska Press, 1990).

[13]American Psychological Association, *Standards for Educational and Psychological Testing* (Washington, D.C.: American Psychological Association, 1985).

[14]Geraldine Scholl and Ronald Schnur, *Measures of Psychological, Vocational, and Educational Functioning in the Blind and Visually Handicapped* (New York: American Foundation for the Blind, 1976).

[15]Andrew L Comrey, Thomas E. Backer, and Edward M. Glaser, *A Sourcebook for Mental Health Measures* (Los Angeles: Human Interaction Research Institute, 1973).

[16]Ki-Taek Chun, Sidney Cobb, and John R. P. French" *Measures for Psychological Assessment* (Ann Arbor,: Institute for Social Research, University of Michigan, 1976).

[17]Raymond B. Cattell and Francis W. Warburton, *Objective Personality and Motivation Tests* (Urbana: University of Illinois Press, 1967).

[18]Armand Lauffer, *Assessment Tools for Practitioners, Managers, and Trainers* (Beverly Hills, Calif.: Sage Publications, 1982).

[19]Carole A. Beere, *Women and Women's Issues: A Handbook of Tests and Measures* (San Francisco: Jossey-Bass, 1979).

[20]Oscar Buros, *The Seventh Mental Measurements Yearbook* (Highland Park, NJ.: Gryphon Press, 1972), p. xxvii.

[21]In several places throughout the book, we suggest that a consultant may be necessary to perform certain tasks or to accomplish specific selection objectives. Ideally, these tasks and objectives could be accomplished *within* the organization. However, access to needed organizational resources is not always possible. External consultants may be required. When should outside advice be sought? Basically, whether a selection consultant is or is not used depends on the answer to the following question: *Does the organization have the expertise, time, and other resources to adequately solve the selection problem?* If the answer is "no," then a consultant is necessary.

Assuming a selection consultant is needed, we might ask "What qualities should be sought in a consultant?" Many criteria can be listed, but, *at a minimum,* a selection consultant should:

1. hold a Ph.D. in industrial/organizational psychology with training in psychological measurement, statistics, and selection-related content areas, such as, job analysis, test construction, performance evaluation;

2. have conducted selection, test validation, and job analysis research projects in other organizations; and

3. provide references from client organizations where selection research projects have been completed.

In addition to these criteria, a selection consultant will likely have published books or selection oriented articles in the industrial-organizational psychology and personnel management literature. Additional criteria for choosing a selection consultant can be found in Professional Affairs Committee of Division 14, *Guidelines for Choosing Consultants for Psychological Selection Validation research and Implementation* (Washington, D.C.: American Psychological association, 1983).

Other factors are also important in choosing a consultant. For a discussion of these considerations and the roles and values of a consultant, see Achilles A. Armenakis and Henry B. Burdg, "Consultation Research: Contributions to Practice and Directions for Improvement," *Journal of Management* 14 (1988): 339-365.

[22]Robert L. Thorndike, *Personnel Selection* (New York: John Wiley, 1949), p. 50.

[23]Cascio, *Applied Psychology in Personnel Management*, p. 142.

[24]Harold G. Seashore and James H. Ricks, *Norms Must Be Relevant* (Test Service Bulletin No. 39) (New York: The Psychological Corporation, May 1950), p. 19.

[25]Lawshe and Balma, *Principles of Personnel Testing*, p. 75.

4

Reliability of Selection Measures

What Is Meant by Reliability

The use of physiological tests by physicians is a common practice in the United States. One such test, the measurement of blood cholesterol, has been recognized as one of the most important. Too much cholesterol in the blood leads to deposits in the arteries that reduce blood flow to the heart. Because of its importance to their health, Americans are routinely encouraged to have their blood tested and to know their cholesterol level. Over 100 million cholesterol tests at a cost of over a billion dollars were administered in 1987.[1]

The dependability of the results produced by cholesterol tests, however, has recently come into question. Some have alleged that much of the data produced by the tests contain error and can produce inaccurate and misleading information. A physicians' group decided to investigate the problem. The group asked 5,000 of the nation's top laboratories to run cholesterol tests on identical samples of blood with a known cholesterol level of 262.6 milligrams per deciliter. The results showed widely differing reports—ranging from 101 to 524; over half of the tests were judged unacceptable.[2]

These data show that a test many view as essential produced results which, in many cases, were not dependable or reliable. Because of the lack of dependability of the test results, people undergoing the test may face serious consequences. For example, persons falsely testing low may forgo dietary changes or the use of cholesterol-reducing drugs their physicians could have prescribed. Those testing falsely high may suffer unnecessary anxiety, unpleasant side effects from the drugs, as well as the expense of unnecessary drug therapy.

The measures we use in HR selection do not have the same physiological implications as do tests used in medicine. However, as in our cholesterol testing example, we have similar concerns regarding the dependability of measures commonly used in selection decision making. That is, we want to be sure we have measures that will produce dependable, consistent, and accurate results when we use them. If we are going to be using data to make predictions concerning the selection of people, we need to be sure that these decisions are based upon data that are reliable and accurate. We do not want to use measures that give one type of information at one time and on another occasion produce a completely different set of results. Obviously, we need accurate data to identify the best people available. We need accurate information for moral and legal reasons as well. Let's look at another example involving the dependability of information, but in this case, in the context of selection.

Taylor Spottswood, HR manager at Datasources, Inc., had just finished scoring a computer programming aptitude test that had been administered to ten individuals making application for a job as a computer programmer. Since it was around 5 P.M. and he had some errands to run, he decided to carry the tests home and review them that night. While on his way home, Taylor stopped by a store to pick up some office supplies. Without thinking, Taylor inadvertently left his briefcase containing the ten tests on the front seat of his car. When he returned, the briefcase was missing. After filing a report with the police, Taylor went home, wondering what he was going to do. The next day, Taylor decided that all he could do was locate the applicants and have them return again for testing. After a day of calling and explaining the lost test scores, arrangements were made for the ten applicants to come in and retake the programming aptitude test. Two days later all ten applicants arrived and, once again, took the same test. Wouldn't you know it though; the day after readministering the tests, Taylor received a visit from the police with his briefcase and its contents intact. Taylor removed the ten tests and set them beside the stack of ten tests just taken. He muttered to himself, "What a waste of time." Out of curiosity, Taylor scored the new set of exams just to see how the applicants had done on the retest. He carefully recorded the two sets of scores. His recorded results are shown in Exhibit 4.1.

After reviewing the data, Taylor thought, "What a confusing set of results!" The scores on the original tests had changed, and changed rather dramatically. Taylor pondered the results for a moment. He had expected the applicants' test scores to be the same from one testing to the next. They were not. Each of the ten persons had a different score for the two tests. "Now why did that happen? Which of the two sets of scores represents these applicants' programming aptitudes?" he asked himself.

The situation we've just described is similar to that represented by our cholesterol testing illustration. Taylor, too, needs dependable, consistent data for selection decision making. Yet, from our selection example, we can see that his test scores are different for no apparent reason. Thus it appears he does not have the consistent, dependable data he needs. These characteristics of data we have mentioned, that is, *consistency*, *dependability*, and *stability*, are all meant when we refer to the concept of *reliability*.

A Definition of Reliability

Reliability is a characteristic of scores on selection measures that is necessary for effective HR selection. In our example, the computer programming aptitude test was apparently an unreliable measure, and it is this unreliability that may have contributed to the large differences in test scores that Taylor found.

| EXHIBIT 4.1 | SUMMARY OF HYPOTHETICAL TEST AND RETEST RESULTS FOR TEN APPLICANTS TAKING THE PROGRAMMING APTITUDE TEST |

Applicant	First Test	Second Test
J. S. Simon	35	47
S. B. Green	57	69
G. T Johnson	39	49
C. A. Snyder	68	50
J. A. Fukai	74	69
K. W. Mossholder	68	65
C. A. Cronenberg	54	38
A. A. Armenakis	71	78
J. R. Parrish	41	54
K. R. Davis	44	59

There are a host of definitions that have been given for the term *reliability*. In our discussion, we will touch upon several of these. But, for now, we want to consider a fundamental definition of the concept. In the context of HR selection, when we refer to reliability, we simply mean *the degree of dependability, consistency, or stability of scores on a measure (either predictors, criteria, or other variables) used in selection research.* In general, reliability of a measure is determined by the degree of consistency between two sets of scores on the measure. Thus, in our earlier selection example, we would have expected the programming aptitude test to have yielded very similar results from one testing period to the next *if* the test produced reliable data. Since similar results were not obtained, we would probably conclude there were errors of measurement with the test. Thus a careful study of the reliability of the test should be made.

Errors of Measurement

It is important to keep in mind that reliability deals with *errors of measurement*. In this sense, when a measure is perfectly reliable, it is free of errors. Relative to measures of psychological characteristics, measures of physical attributes frequently have high degrees of measurement reliability. Unfortunately, many of our selection measures that are designed to assess important job-related characteristics such as knowledge, skills, and abilities do not have the same preciseness of measurement as measures of physical characteristics. By examining Exhibit 4.2, you can see that reliability tends to be higher for the physical characteristics at the top of the figure than for the psychological attributes at the bottom. This is not to say that our measurement reliability of important selection characteristics is poor. But because selection measures do not have perfect reliability, they contain some degree of measurement error. In general, the greater the amount of measurement error, the lower the reliability of a selection measure; the less the error, the higher the reliability will be. Thus if errors of measurement can be

EXHIBIT 4.2

RELATIVE RELIABILITY OF MEASUREMENT OF VARIOUS HUMAN ATTRIBUTES

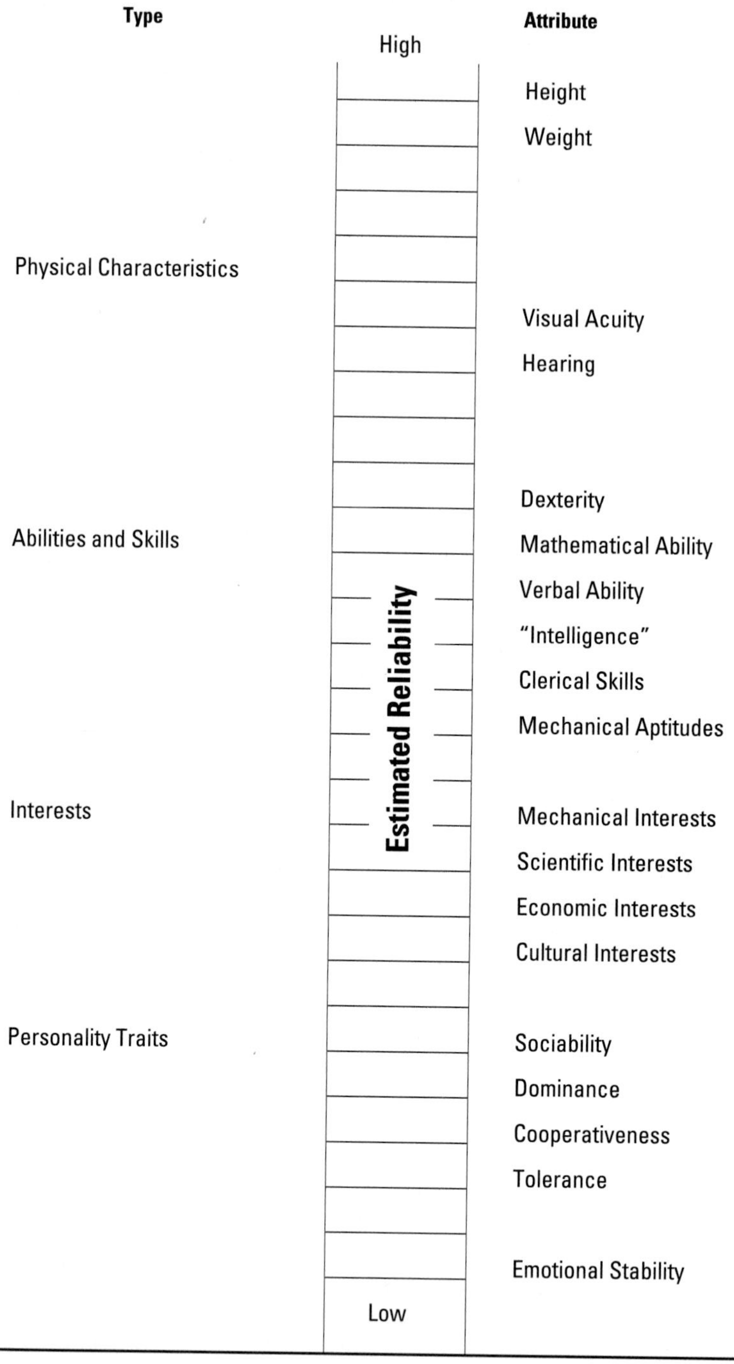

Type	Estimated Reliability	Attribute
	High	
		Height
		Weight
Physical Characteristics		
		Visual Acuity
		Hearing
		Dexterity
Abilities and Skills		Mathematical Ability
		Verbal Ability
		"Intelligence"
		Clerical Skills
		Mechanical Aptitudes
Interests		Mechanical Interests
		Scientific Interests
		Economic Interests
		Cultural Interests
Personality Traits		Sociability
		Dominance
		Cooperativeness
		Tolerance
		Emotional Stability
	Low	

SOURCE: Based on Lewis E. Albright, J.R. Glennon, and Wallace J. Smith, *The Use of Psychological Tests in Industry* (Cleveland: Howard Allen, 1963), p. 40.

assessed, a measure's reliability can be determined. What, then, are "errors of measurement"?

As we have seen, when we use selection devices such as tests, we obtain numerical scores on the measures. These scores serve as a basis for selection decision making. Since we are using scores as a basis for our decisions, we want to know the "true" scores of applicants for each characteristic being measured. For example, if we administer a mathematics ability test, we want to know the "true" math ability of each testee. But unless our measure is perfectly reliable, we will encounter some difficulties in knowing these true scores. In fact, we may get mathematics ability scores for individuals that are quite different from their true abilities. Let's see why.

The score obtained on a measure, that is the *obtained* score, consists of two parts: a *true* component and an *error* component. Thus, the components of any obtained score (X) can be summarized by the following equation:

$$X_{obtained} = X_{true} + X_{error}$$

where

$X_{obtained}$ = obtained score for a person on a measure,

X_{true} = true score for a person on the measure, i.e., actual amount of the attribute measured that a person really possesses, and

X_{error} = error score for a person on the measure, i.e., amount that a person's score was influenced by factors present at the time of measurement.

This notion of a score being composed of true and error parts is a basic axiom of measurement theory.[3]

True Score   The true score is really an ideal conception. It is the score individuals would obtain if external and internal conditions to a measure were perfect. For example, in our mathematics ability test, an ideal or true score would be one where the following conditions existed:

1.   Individuals answered correctly the same percentage of problems on the test that they would have if *all possible* problems had been given, and

2.   Individuals answered correctly the problems they actually knew without being affected by any external factors, such as lighting or temperature of the room in which the testing took place, their emotional state, or their physical health.

Another way of thinking about a true score is to imagine that an individual takes a test measuring a specific ability many different times. With each testing, his scores will differ somewhat; after a large number of testings, the scores will take the form of a normal distribution. The differences in scores are treated as if due to errors of measurement. But the average of all test scores best approximates his true ability. Therefore, we might think of a true score as being *the mean or average score made by an individual on many different administrations of a measure.*

This idealized situation does not exist. The notion of a true score, however, helps to define the idea that there is a specific score that would be obtained *if* measurement conditions were perfect. Because a true score can never be measured exactly, the obtained score is used to estimate the true score.

Error Score   A second part of the obtained score is the error score. This score represents *errors measurement.* Errors of measurement are *those factors that affect obtained scores but are not related to the characteristic, trait, or attribute being measured.*[4] These factors are present at the time of measurement and distort respondents' scores either over or under what they would have been on another measurement occasion. There can be many reasons why individuals' scores may differ from one measurement occasion to the next. Fatigue, anxiety, a loud noise occurring during testing that produces different effects on individuals' responses to selection measures are only a few of the factors that may explain differences in individuals' scores over different measurement occasions.

Exhibit 4.3 shows the relationship between reliability and errors of measurement for three levels of reliability of a selection measure. Hypothetical obtained and true scores are given for each of the reliability levels. Errors of measurement are shown by the shaded area of each bar. With *decreasing* errors of measurement, reliability of the measure *increases.* Notice that with increasing reliability, more precise estimates of an individual's true score on the measure can be made. That is, there is not as much error present. For example, suppose an individual's true score on the measure is 50. For a measure that has low reliability, a wide discrepancy between the obtained scores (40 to 60) and the true score (50) is possible. In contrast, in a measure with high reliability, the possible obtained scores (45 to 55) yield a closer estimate of the true score (50).

How much error exists in a selection measure is an important attribute of the measure. If scores on a selection measure contain too much error, we should be concerned, as we cannot have much confidence in a selection device if excessive error is present. If a measure is just composed of error, then a score on that measure cannot reflect a score on the attribute thought to be assessed by the measure. Thus if we are using a test that claims to measure general mental ability but the reported reliability is so low that the test scores are only composed of error, then our "intelligence test" cannot possibly measure mental ability. With excessive error, a selection measure will not be useful. If there is little error present, the measure *may* be applicable in selection. (The next chapter discusses other characteristics of a measure that make it effective.)

Where do these errors come from? There can be several different sources. The importance of any particular one will depend on the nature of the measure itself (i.e., a paper-and-pencil measure, a behavior, the degree of standardization), what is being measured (i.e., an ability, personality trait, an attitude, etc.), the situation in which the measure is being used, and the method of estimating reliability. Table 4.1 summarizes some of the more common sources of error that contribute to the unreliability of a selection measure.[5] As you examine the

EXHIBIT 4.3

RELATIONSHIP BETWEEN ERRORS OF MEASUREMENT AND RELIABILITY OF A SELECTION MEASURE FOR HYPOTHETICAL OBTAINED AND TRUE SCORES

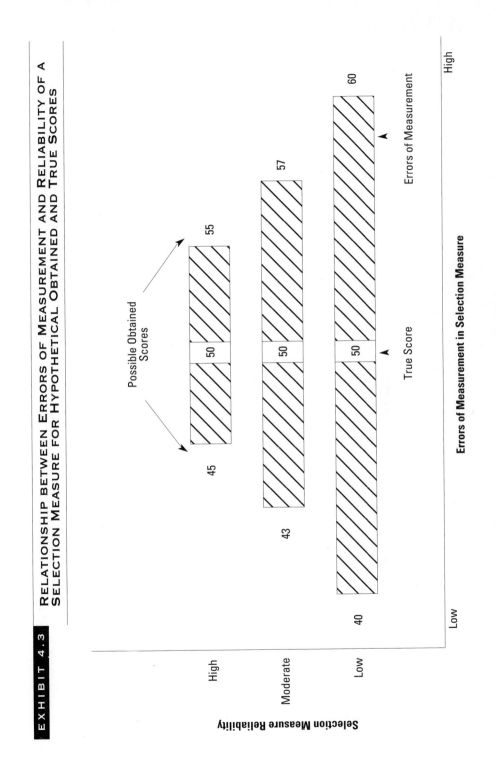

TABLE 4.1	EXAMPLES OF SOURCES OF ERRORS OF MEASUREMENT CONTRIBUTING TO UNRELIABILITY IN HUMAN RESOURCE SELECTION MEASURES	
Source of Error	**Conditions Under Which an Error May Occur**	**Example of Error**
Individual responding to a selection measure	Where an individual's physical and mental health, motivation, mood, level of stress, understanding of instructions, etc., affect how the individual responds to a selection measure.	A supervisor does not think top management really uses her performance ratings of her subordinates. Thus, when giving ratings, she completes the performance evaluation forms as soon as possible with little thought given to individuals' actual job performance.
Individual administering a selection measure	Where the administrator of a selection measure affects the responses of the individual completing the measure.	Two employment interviewers interview the same job applicants using the same interview questions. One interviewer frequently smiles and nods approvingly during the interview; the other does not.
Individual scoring a selection measure	Where judgment and subjectivity on the part of the scorer of a selection measure play a role in scoring.	An individual scores the responses of individuals to a personality inventory. Precise rules for scoring the responses are not specified.
Physical conditions under which a selection measure is administered	Where heating, cooling, lighting, noise, etc., affect how an individual responds to a selection measure.	While taking a test, respondents are interrupted by a power failure that affects the cooling and lighting in the room.

NOTE: By use of the term *selection measure*, we mean both predictors and criteria.

table, keep in mind that these errors can affect predictors, such as tests, as well as criteria, such as performance evaluations.

An important objective in developing and using selection measures is to reduce errors of measurement as much as possible. By reducing these errors, individual differences in scores on selection measures will more likely be due to true differences rather than chance (or error) differences among individuals. Reliable measures that are useful in HR selection will control or minimize the presence of these errors of measurement. Because errors are controlled, reliable measures give us more confidence in making decisions such as the suitability of one job applicant over another. Selection decisions based on reliable measures will also be fairer for the applicants involved.

Methods of Estimating Reliability

Reliability is generally determined by examining the relationship between two sets of measures measuring the same thing.[6] Where the two sets of measures yield *similar* scores, reliability will be *raised*. If scores from the measures tend to be *dissimilar*, reliability will be *lowered*. Referring again to our earlier example involving Taylor Spottswood, HR manager of Datasources, we saw that he had two sets of programming aptitude test scores. In Taylor's case, the two sets of test scores were different from each other. Because the two sets of scores were different, they suggested that the stability of measurement of programming aptitude was low.

Where scores are generally consistent for people across two sets of measures, reliability of a measure will be enhanced. For example, if a person's math ability score remains the same for two different administrations of a test, it will add to the reliability of the test. However, if factors (such as fatigue) cause *differential changes* in people across both sets of measures, the factors will contribute to *unreliability*. These factors are then considered as sources of errors of measurement because they are chance factors influencing responses to a measure.

Since reliability theory is only an idealized concept of what does or does not contribute to reliability, we cannot measure reliability per se. We can only *estimate* it. Thus we should not think of *the* reliability of a measure, but rather an *estimate* of reliability. We will see that alternative procedures can be used to provide different estimates of reliability. One of the principal ways in which these procedures differ is in terms of how they treat the various factors (see Table 4.1) that may alter measurements of people. Some procedures will consider some of these factors to be error while others will not. Obviously, you might ask; "Which method should be used?" There is not one best way. The choice will depend on each specific situation for which a reliability estimate is desired.

Statistical procedures are commonly used to calculate what are called "reliability coefficients." Oftentimes, techniques involving the *Pearson product-moment correlation coefficient* are utilized to derive reliability coefficients. We do not go into the statistical details of the correlation coefficient here; those are discussed in the next chapter. But we describe briefly how the coefficient is obtained. Specifics concerning the interpretation of the reliability coefficient are given in the next section.

A reliability coefficient is simply an index of relationship. It summarizes the relation between two sets of measures for which a reliability estimate is being made. The calculated index varies from .00 to 1.00. In calculating reliability estimates, the correlation coefficient obtained is regarded as a direct measure of the reliability estimate. The *higher* the index or coefficient, the less the measurement error, and the *higher* the reliability estimate. Conversely, as the coefficient approaches .00, errors of measurement increase and reliability correspondingly decreases. Of course, we want to employ selection measures having high reliability coefficients. With high reliability, we can be more confident that a particular measure is giving a dependable picture of individuals' true scores for whatever the attribute being measured.

There are many methods of estimating reliability. We discuss four principal ones most often employed or reported in selection research studies: (a) test-retest, (b) parallel or equivalent forms, (c) internal consistency, and (d) interrater reliability estimates. As Milton Blum and James Naylor point out, an important characteristic that differentiates among these procedures is what each method considers to be errors of measurement.[7] One method may treat a factor as error while another may treat the same factor as meaningful information. The method chosen will depend upon what factors a researcher may want to treat as error as well as which of the following questions are to be addressed by reliability procedures.

1. How dependably can people be assessed with a measure at a given moment?

2. How dependably will data collected by a measure today be representative of the same people at a future time?

3. How accurately will scores on a measure represent the true ability of people on the trait being sampled by a measure?

4. When individuals are being rated by more than one rater, to what degree do raters' evaluations vary from one rater to another? Or, to what extent are the scores for individuals due to the raters rather than to the individuals' behavior or other characteristics being rated?

As you examine these questions, you can see that each one considers reliability to be the degree of consistency between two or more measurements of the same thing.

Test-Retest Reliability Estimates

One obvious way for assessing the reliability of scores obtained on a selection measure is to administer the measure twice and then correlate the two sets of scores using the Pearson product-moment correlation coefficient. This method is referred to as *test-retest reliability*. It is called test-retest reliability because the *same* measure is used to collect data from the *same* respondents at two *different* points in time. Because a correlation coefficient is calculated between the two sets of scores over time, the obtained reliability coefficient represents a coefficient of stability. Thus the coefficient indicates how similarly the same group of respondents score on the same measure over two time periods.

As an example of test-retest reliability estimation, suppose we wanted to determine the reliability of our mathematics ability test mentioned earlier. First, we administer the test to a representative group of individuals. After a period of time, say eight weeks, we readminister and score the same test for the same individuals. In order to estimate test-retest reliability, we simply correlate the two sets of scores (test scores at time 1 correlated with scores at time 2) using the Pearson product-moment correlation.

Exhibit 4.4 illustrates the basic design for test-retest reliability determination. The exhibit also shows the effect on the reliability coefficient when the relative positions of individuals change from one testing to the next. (Of course, we would use more than the five persons listed in the exhibit for estimating reliability; we are showing these individuals' scores simply for illustration purposes.)

EXHIBIT 4.4	ILLUSTRATION OF THE DESIGN FOR ESTIMATING TEST-RETEST RELIABILITY

	Test Scores Time 1 (t1)		Test Scores Time 2 (t2)					
Job Applicant	Time 1 t1	Rank t1	Case A t2$_a$	t1-t2$_a$	Rank t2$_a$	Case B t2$_b$	t1-t2$_b$	Rank t2$_b$
J. S. Friedman	96	1	90	−6	1	66	−30	2
J. A. Fukai	87	2	89	2	2	52	−35	3
B. Y. Woodward	80	3	75	−5	3	51	−29	4
T. A. Hinata	70	4	73	3	4	82	12	1
A. C. Zimiski	56	5	66	10	5	50	−6	5

NOTE: Test-retest reliability for Time 1-Time 2 (Case A) = .94; test-retest reliability for Time 1- Time 2 (Case B) = .07.

Time 1 in the exhibit shows the five individuals' scores on the mathematics ability test for the initial administration of the test. At a later date, Time 2, the test is readministered to the same individuals. Exhibit 4.4 shows two possible outcomes (Case A and Case B) that could result from this retesting. (Only one retest is needed to compute reliability.) Case A presents one possible set of scores for the individuals. Notice in Case A two points. First, there has been some slight change in scores from Time 1 to Time 2 testing. J. S. Friedman's original test score of 96, for instance, fell to 90 upon retesting, a loss of 6 points. Some of the other applicants' scores also fell slightly while others slightly increased. Second, the *rank ordering* of the applicants' scores remained the same from one testing to the next. Friedman's score was the highest on the original test and even though it fell upon retesting, his score was still the best for the group. The others' rank ordering of scores also remained the same across the two testings. Because of the relatively small changes in applicants' absolute test scores and the identical ranks of these scores over time, a high reliability coefficient would be expected. A test-retest reliability coefficient computed between the Time 1 scores and the Time 2 (Case A) scores is .94. This estimate confirms our expectation. It represents a high test-retest reliability coefficient with little error present. Reduced errors of measurement increase the generalizability of individuals' mathematics ability as measured by the initial testing.

Now look at Case B. When you compare this set of retest scores with those originally obtained at Time 1, you can see rather large *differential* rates of change among the individuals' scores. (Some individuals' scores have changed more than others. Compare, for example, Fukai's 35-point test score change with Zimiski's 6-point change.) These differential rates of change have also altered the individuals' relative rank orderings in the two sets of scores. Due to these differential test score and rank-order changes between Time 1 and Time 2 (Case B), the test-retest reliability is very low, only .07. This coefficient suggests a great deal of error in measurement. The obtained scores on the test represent very little of the mathematics ability of those taking the test.

The higher the test-retest reliability coefficient, the greater the true score and the less error that is present. If reliability were equal to 1.00, no error would exist in the scores; true scores would be perfectly represented by the obtained scores. A coefficient this high would imply that scores on the measure are not subject to changes in the respondents or the conditions of administration. If reliability were equal to .00, a test-retest reliability coefficient this low would suggest that obtained scores on the test are nothing more than error.

Any factor that differentially affects individuals' responses during one measurement occasion and not on the other creates errors of measurement and lowers reliability. As we saw in Table 4.1, there are many sources of error that can change scores over time, and hence, lower test-retest reliability. Some of these errors will be associated with differences within individuals occurring from day to day (such as illness on one day of testing) while others will be associated with administration of a measure from one time to the next (such as distracting noises occurring during an administration). Further, there are two additional factors that may also affect test-retest reliability. These factors are (a) *memory* and (b) *learning*.

Recall that earlier we said *any* factor that causes scores within a group to change differentially over time will decrease test-retest reliability. Similarly, *any* factor that causes scores to remain the same over time will increase the reliability estimate. If all respondents on a selection measure remember their previous answers to an initial administration of a measure and then on the retest respond according to their memory, the reliability coefficient will increase. How much it will increase will depend upon how well they remember their previous answers.

The effect of memory, however, will be to make the reliability coefficient artificially high—an *overestimate* of the true reliability of scores obtained on the measure. Rather than reflecting stability of a measure's scores over time, a test-retest reliability coefficient may tend to reflect the consistency of respondents' memories. In general, when considering reliability we are not interested in measuring the stability of respondents' memories. But we are interested in evaluating the stability of scores produced by the measure.

One way of lessening the impact of memory on test-retest reliability coefficients is to increase the time interval between the two administrations. As the length of time increases, respondents are less likely to recall their responses. Thus, with increasing time intervals, test-retest reliability coefficients will generally decrease.

You can probably see that there could be many different test-retest reliability estimates depending upon when the two administrations take place. Theoretically speaking, the number of estimates could be infinite. How long a period should be used? There is no one best interval, but probably from several weeks up to six months is reasonable depending upon the measure and the specific situation.

Although a lengthy interval between two administrations would appear to be a viable alternative for countering the effects of memory, too long a period opens up another source of error—*learning*. If respondents between the two time intervals of testing learn or change in such a way that their responses to a measure are different on the second administration of a measure than they were on the first, then test-retest reliability will be lowered. For instance, if respondents recall items asked on an initial administration of a test and then learn answers so their responses are different on the second administration, learning will have changed their scores. Or, in another instance, respondents may have been exposed to information (such as a training program) that will cause them to alter their answers the second time a test is administered. Whatever the source, when individual differences in learning take place so that responses are differentially affected, reliability will be lowered.

Notice that because of learning, we may have a selection measure with scores that appear to be unstable over time. Yet, their unreliability is not really due to the errors of measurement we have been discussing. In fact, systematic, but different rates of change among respondents through learning may account for what would appear to be unreliability. Nevertheless, actual calculation of a test-retest reliability coefficient will treat such changes as error, thus contributing to unreliability. Therefore, with a long time interval between administrations of a measure, test-retest reliability may *underestimate* reliability because learning could have caused scores to change.

In addition, selection measures that involve traits of personality, attitudes, or interests are usually not considered to be static but in a state of change. Here again, it may be inappropriate to use test-retest reliability with measures of these attributes because any changes found will be treated as error. In contrast, reliability of measures involving attributes such as mental ability that is relatively stable over time may be suitably estimated with test-retest reliability.

Given some of the potential problems with test-retest reliability, when should it be used? There are no hard and fast rules, but some general guidelines can be offered. These guidelines include the following:

1. Test-retest reliability is appropriate when the length of time between the two administrations is long enough to offset the effects of memory or practice.[8]

2. When there is little reason to believe that memory will affect responses to a measure, test-retest reliability may be employed. A situation where memory may have minimal effects may be one where (a) there is a large number of items on the measure, (b) the items are too complex to remember (for example, items involving detailed drawings, complex shapes, or detailed questions), and (c) retesting occurs after at least eight weeks.[9]

3. When it can be confidently determined that nothing has occurred between the two testings that will affect responses, test-retest can be used.

4. When information is available on only a single item or measure, test-retest reliability is appropriate.

Robert Guion further notes that the method is also useful for certain types of measures such as those involving sensory discrimination and psychomotor abilities.[10] However, he cautions that careful consideration should be given before using the procedure with performance rating data. (As we indicated earlier, performance ratings are frequently used as criterion measures.) Many different factors can influence the stability of ratings. Changes in performance or day-to-day incidents can occur within relatively brief periods and may affect the stability of rating data. Then, too, there is the question of whether the technique is measuring the stability of ratees' performance or stability of raters' ratings.

If *stability* of measurement over time is of interest, test-retest reliability is a suitable method to use. However, if the reliability coefficient is low, we will not know if the low coefficient is because of low reliability or the lack of stability in the attribute being measured. If, on the other hand, our interest is in the dependability with which scores are provided by a measure at one point in time, then other reliability procedures, for example internal consistency, are needed.

Parallel or Equivalent Forms Reliability Estimates

In order to control the effects of memory on test-retest reliability (which can produce an overestimate of reliability), one strategy is to use, not the same measure twice, but equivalent versions of the measure. Each version of the measure has different items, but the questions assess the same attribute being measured in precisely the same way. One form of the measure would be administered to respondents followed by a second administration of the other form. Like our test-retest procedure, a Pearson correlation would be computed between the two sets of scores (Form A correlated with Form B scores) to develop a reliability estimate. Estimates computed in this manner are referred to as *parallel or equivalent forms reliability* estimates. The reliability coefficient itself is often called a *coefficient of equivalence* because it represents the consistency with which an attribute is measured from one version of a measure to another. As the coefficient approaches 1.00, the *set* of measures is viewed as equivalent or the same for the attribute measured.

To have a parallel forms reliability estimate, at least two equal versions of a measure must exist. Looking again at the math ability test that we referred to earlier, we can review the basic requirements of equivalent forms of a measure. The basic process in developing parallel forms is outlined in Exhibit 4.5.

Initially, a universe of possible math ability items is identified. Items that represent the specific topics and types of math abilities important to us compose what is called the "universe of possible math items." This universe of math ability item content is also referred to as the "content domain" of the test. Selected items are then administered to a large sample of individuals representative of those to whom the math ability test will be given. Individuals' responses are used to identify the difficulty of the items and to be sure the items are measuring the same math ability construct. Next, the items are rank-ordered according to their difficulty and randomly assigned in pairs to form two samples of items. Sample 1 items compose Form A of our math ability test; Sample 2 items make up Form B. If our defining and sampling of math ability item content has been correctly conducted, we should have two equivalent forms of our math ability test. Among the various statistical criteria used to define form equivalency are the following:

1. The forms should contain the same number and type of items.

2. Each form should have the same level of difficulty.

3. Averages and standard deviations of the scores obtained by respondents to the forms should be the same.

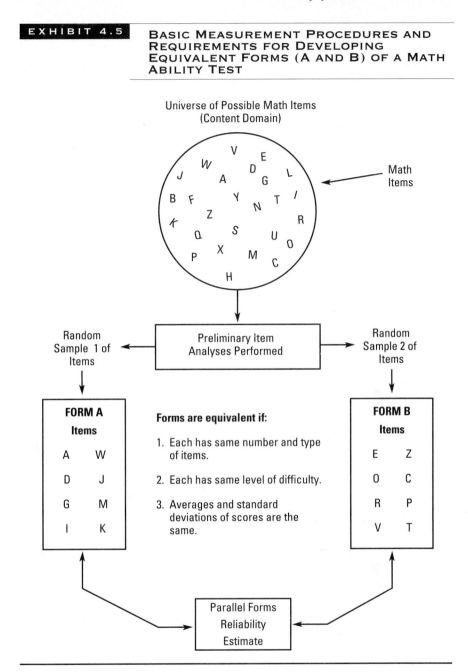

EXHIBIT 4.5

BASIC MEASUREMENT PROCEDURES AND REQUIREMENTS FOR DEVELOPING EQUIVALENT FORMS (A AND B) OF A MATH ABILITY TEST

Universe of Possible Math Items
(Content Domain)

Math Items

Random Sample 1 of Items

Preliminary Item Analyses Performed

Random Sample 2 of Items

FORM A

Items

A	W
D	J
G	M
I	K

Forms are equivalent if:

1. Each has same number and type of items.

2. Each has same level of difficulty.

3. Averages and standard deviations of scores are the same.

FORM B

Items

E	Z
0	C
R	P
V	T

Parallel Forms Reliability Estimate

Once created, one form is administered after the other form has been given. The time interval between the two administrations can be brief, within a day or so, or long, for instance, two weeks. In this manner, a reliability estimate can be obtained rather quickly without concern for the effects of memory on responses. Depending on the time interval between the two administrations, there can be many parallel forms reliability estimates.

In practice, equivalency of forms is not easy to achieve. Chance or random effects of the ways in which samples of items are selected can produce item differences in the forms. As a consequence, the forms will be different, thus curtailing reliability. For example, item differences on the two forms of our math ability test could result in one form being more difficult than the other. Form-to-form differences will cause individuals to have changes in their scores from one administration to the next, and reliability of test scores will be lowered. Since it is very difficult to meet all of the criteria of equivalent forms, some writers use the term *alternate forms* to refer to forms that approximate but do not meet the criteria of parallel forms.[11]

For some selection measures, such as math, spelling, and vocabulary tests, it is possible to obtain reasonably equivalent forms. Equivalent forms of these and other ability measures are commercially available. Use of equivalent forms in ability testing is often used to prevent individuals from improving their scores on a second testing and to lessen the possibility that test content will be shared with others. However, the construction of equivalent forms of a biographical data or personality inventory would require considerable effort, time, skills, and other resources.

Because genuine or true equivalent forms are difficult to obtain and because differences may exist from one administration to another, reliability coefficients computed between parallel forms tend to be conservative estimates. Yet, where equivalent forms can be obtained, this estimate of reliability is almost always preferable to test-retest reliability. If a high parallel forms reliability estimate is obtained, the coefficient suggests that individuals' scores on the measure would be very similar if they had taken an equivalent test on a different occasion.

So far, we have discussed reliability in the context of *two* administrations of a measure. But what if we want to control the effects of memory on responses and do not have the time to wait for memory to be diminished before administering a retest? Or what if an equivalent form of a selection measure does not exist? There are options available to handle those situations where retests or equivalent forms are not feasible.

Internal Consistency Reliability Estimates

Guion has concluded that one important characteristic of a reliable measure is that the various parts of a total measure should be so interrelated that they can be interpreted as measuring the same thing. An index of a measure's similarity of content is an *internal consistency reliability* estimate. Basically, an internal consistency reliability estimate shows *the extent to which all parts of a measure (for example, items or questions) are similar in what they measure.*[12] Thus a selection measure is internally consistent or homogeneous when individuals' responses or performance on one part of the measure are related to their responses on other parts. For example, if we have 5 simple addition items on a test (for example, $12 + 23 = ?$), individuals who can answer correctly one of the items can probably answer correctly the remaining 4. Those who cannot answer one will likely be unable to answer correctly the others. If this assumption is true, then our 5-item test is internally consistent or homogeneous because individuals' performance on the test items are related. Sometimes writers refer to a test that measures one attribute, such as our 5-item addition test, as *unidimensional*. A measure that assesses multiple attributes, such as addition, subtraction, multiplication, and division, is referred to as *multidimensional*. Performance on one component is not necessarily related to performance on another. An internal consistency reliability estimate indicates the degree of homogeneity (that is, similarity) of measurement by all parts of a measure.

When a measure is created to assess a specific concept, such as mathematics ability, the items chosen to measure that concept really represent only a portion of all possible items that could have been selected. If the sample of selected items truly assesses the same concept, then respondents should answer these items in the same way. What must be determined for the items chosen is whether respondents answer the sample of items similarly. Internal consistency reliability shows the extent to which the data are free from error due to the ways the items were phrased, interpreted by respondents, and so on.

To test the internal consistency hypothesis, the idea is to examine the relationship between similar parts of a measure. The internal consistency hypothesis can be tested by simply correlating individuals' scores on these similar parts. A high estimate suggests that respondents' answers to one part are similar to their responses on other parts of the measure; hence, the measure is internally consistent. Like our other methods for estimating reliability, internal consistency reliability is applicable to many different types of selection measures, including predictors and criteria.

Internal consistency estimates tend to be among the most popular reliability procedures used. In general, the following three procedures are applied most often: (a) split-half reliability, (b) Kuder-Richardson reliability, and (c) Cronbach's coefficient alpha (α) reliability.

Split-Half Reliability Estimates   One of the internal consistency options is referred to as *split-half* or *subdivided test reliability* estimates. Split-half reliability involves a *single* administration of a selection measure. Then, for *reliability calculation purposes*, the measure is divided or split into two halves so that scores for each part can be obtained for each individual. To assess split-half reliability, the first problem is how to split the measure to obtain the most comparable halves. The most common method for creating these two halves of a measure is to score all *even*-numbered items as a "test" and all *odd*-numbered items as a "test." When split in this manner, the distribution of the items into the two test parts approximates a random assignment of items. Then, as in our previous estimates, the Pearson correlation is used to determine the extent of relation between the two test part scores. The resulting f correlation coefficient is the reliability estimate.[13] Strictly speaking, a split-half reliability estimate is not a pure measure of internal consistency.[14] Like the parallel forms reliability coefficient, the obtained coefficient primarily represents a coefficient of equivalence. Thus, the coefficient tends to show similarity of responses from one form to an equivalent one.

Exhibit 4.6 illustrates how two parts of a measure may be developed and split-half reliability determined. However, the example shown is a bit different from some of our earlier illustrations. Previously, we employed predictors in our examples, but in Exhibit 4.6 we are using a criterion measure.

EXHIBIT 4.6   REPRESENTATION OF ODD-EVEN (DAY) SPLIT-HALF RELIABILITY COMPUTED FOR A JOB PERFORMANCE CRITERION MEASURE

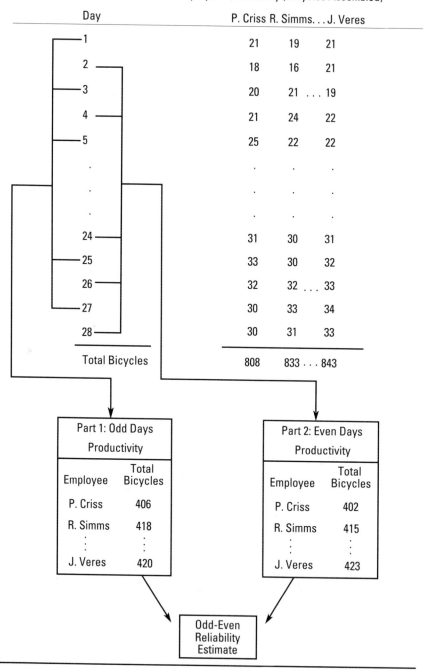

As we specified earlier in the chapter, reliability estimates are important for *all* variables being studied.

Let's assume that we wanted to know the reliability of an employee productivity measure that was serving as a criterion in a selection research study involving bicycle assemblers. Basically, the measure is the total number of bicycles assembled by each employee during a 28-day period. For purposes of brevity, we have shown in Exhibit 4.6 the total number of bicycles assembled by employees during an abbreviated 28-day period.

Once we have complete data for our employees on each of the 28 days, we can subdivide our measure into two parts. The odd-numbered days (day 1, 3, 5, . . . , 25, 27) and the associated production for each employee compose Part 1 while the even-numbered days (day 2, 4, . . . , 24, 26, 28) and their associated employee productivity data are assigned to Part 2. Total scores or total productivity is obtained for each part by summing the respective daily production rates. Next, a correlation is computed between the employees' production rates (Part 1 correlated with Part 2) to obtain a reliability estimate of the employee productivity measure (total bicycles assembled). This same procedure could be applied to a predictor, such as a test, as well. Rather than having odd- and even-numbered days, odd- and even-numbered items on the measure would be used. Identical procedures as outlined in Exhibit 4.6 would then be applied.

The obtained reliability coefficient developed on the two halves of a measure is not a very precise estimate. Other things being equal, reliability increases with increasing length of a measure. Our split-half reliability estimate, however, is based on a correlation between scores on only *half* of the measure; thus it *underestimates* actual reliability. The length of the measure was reduced when we split it into two halves, an odd-numbered and even-numbered part. Therefore, a correction is needed to determine the reliability of the full or complete measure. A special formula, the Spearman-Brown prophecy formula, is used to make the correction.[15] Essentially, the formula shows what the reliability estimate would have been if the correlation had been based on the full rather than the part measures.

The Spearman-Brown formula used to correct a split-half reliability coefficient is as follows:

$$r_{ttc} = \frac{n r_{12}}{1 + (n - 1)r_{12}}$$

where

r_{ttc} = the corrected split-half reliability coefficient for the total selection measure,

n = number of times the test is increased in length, and

r_{12} = the correlation between parts 1 and 2 of the selection measure.

For instance, let's examine the *corrected* split-half reliability of the criterion measure of bicycle assembler productivity. Part 1 of the productivity measure consisted of total bicycles assembled on all odd days of the month while Part 2 was total bicycles assembled on all even days. Assume that the correlation between Parts 1 and 2 was .80. This correlation is the reliability coefficient for *half* the criterion measure (bicycles assembled). By applying the Spearman-Brown formula, the corrected reliability for the *total* criterion measure (bicycles assembled) is as follows:

$$r_{ttc} = \frac{2(.80)}{1 + (2-1).80}$$

With the corrected reliability estimate of .89, we have a more precise estimate of the reliability of the total criterion measure.

Because it is computed from a one-time only administration of a measure, split-half reliability does not detect any of the errors of measurement that can occur over time, such as changes in individual respondents or changes in administration of a measure. Therefore, this procedure will tend to result in a liberal or inflated estimate of reliability.

This method of reliability estimation is *not* appropriate for any measure that has a time limit associated with its completion. In many cases, for example, timed tests have rather easy questions, and scores are a function of how many items are completed. If questions are very simple, then individuals are likely to get correct nearly all that are attempted. As a result, individuals are likely to differ only in terms of how many questions they complete. Odd and even scores will be very similar up until the point that time has expired because most items will be answered correctly. Beyond that point, responses will also be very similar because they were not answered. As a consequence, a split-half reliability estimate computed on a test with a time limit will be spuriously high and meaningless.

Kuder-Richardson Reliability Estimates   There are many different ways to divide a measure in order to compute a split-half reliability estimate. Because the *Kuder-Richardson reliability* procedure takes the *average* of the reliability coefficients that would result from *all* possible ways of subdividing a measure, it helps solve the problem of how best to divide a measure for calculating reliability. (There are several different types of Kuder-Richardson formulas. The most popular and the one on which this discussion is based is called *K-R 20* because it is the twentieth formula in a series of reliability formulas discussed by George Kuder and Marion Richardson.[16]) It, too, involves the single administration of a measure. The procedure is used for determining the consistency of respondents' answers to any measure that has items scored in only two (dichotomous) categories, for example, questions on a verbal achievement test that are scored as either "right" (=1) or "wrong" (=0). Whereas the split-half method examines consistency of response between parts or halves of a measure, the Kuder-Richardson method assesses *interitem* consistency of responses. The resulting coefficient estimates *the average of the reliability coefficients that would result from all possible ways of subdividing a test*.[17] Because it represents an average of all possible splits, Kuder-Richardson reliability estimates are usually lower than those obtained from split-half estimates.

In general, the more similar or homogeneous the content of a measure, the more likely respondents' answers across the items will be similar. As the content of a selection measure becomes more similar, Kuder-Richardson reliability coefficients will increase. Thus, large reliability coefficients will reflect high interitem consistency and, therefore, high homogeneity or similarity of content. A high coefficient suggests that items on the measure hang together and have a common theme. For example, if one arithmetic ability test contains only items dealing with division while another arithmetic test contains items dealing with division, multiplication, addition, and subtraction, the first test will demonstrate more interitem consistency than the latter one.[18] The first test addresses only one aspect of arithmetic ability while the other test four. In addition, scores on the first test will be less ambiguous than scores on the second test. For instance, on the first test a score of 20 can only be arrived at by some knowledge of division. However, for the second test, a score of 20 could be arrived at in a variety of ways. Various combinations of items correct for each of the four arithmetic operations could result in a score of 20. Thus our understanding of what a score represents on the first test will be clearer than for the second test.

In order to compute K-R 20, several pieces of information are needed on the test results for a group of individuals. As long as we can determine (a) how the group performed on each item of the test as well as (b) each individual's total test score, the coefficient can be computed. Data such as those shown in Exhibit 4.7 are what is needed to compute K-R 20. The formula for computing K-R 20 is as follows:

$$r_{tt} = \frac{k}{k-1} \left(\frac{\sum p_i(1-p_i)}{\sigma_y^2} \right)$$

where

k = number of items on the test,

p_i = proportion of examinees getting each item (*i*) correct,

$1 - p_i$ = proportion of examinees getting each item (*i*) *in*correct, and

σ_y^2 = variance of examinees' total test scores.

Cronbach's Coefficient Alpha (α) Reliability Estimates K-R 20 is a suitable approach for estimating internal consistency reliability when the items on the measure are scored with only two categories. Sometimes, however, items or questions on selection measures are not scored as a dichotomy. Instead, a continuum or range of response options representing an interval scale is given for an item. In Exhibit 3.4, for instance, we presented an example of an employee performance appraisal rating form for which total scores on the form could be used as a criterion in a selection research study. Returning again to the form, suppose that overall job performance is obtained by summing the 5 items on the rating form. If we want to determine how well those items, when combined, reflect an overall picture of job performance, we need a method to estimate the internal consistency of these 5 combined items. Kuder-Richardson reliability would not be appropriate since each item on the rating form involves more than two response categories on an interval scale. In those cases in which we are interested

EXHIBIT 4.7		AN EXAMPLE OF DATA USED IN COMPUTING K-R 20 RELIABILITY COEFFICIENT							
			Test Items						Test Score
Testee	1	2	3	4	5	6	7	8	
Wiley Boyles	1	1	1	1	1	1	1	1	8
Stan Harris	0	0	0	1	1	1	0	1	4
Bill Alsup	1	0	1	1	1	0	1	1	6
Sidney Craft	0	0	0	0	0	0	1	1	2
David Speed	1	0	1	1	0	0	0	0	3
Dwight Norris	1	0	0	1	1	1	1	0	5
Number Correctly Answering Item	4	1	3	5	4	3	4	4	

NOTE: 0 = incorrect response; 1 = correct response.

in knowing the internal consistency of responses to a measure but in which responses are based on an interval scale, we have to use another technique. In these situations, Cronbach's *coefficient alpha* (α) can be employed and the result interpreted like K-R 20 reliability.[19] Thus it, too, represents an average reliability coefficient computed from all possible split-half reliabilities. Put another way, it represents the average correlation of each item with every other item on a measure. Coefficient alpha also enables us to determine *how well the items being combined or added together are measuring the same thing.* We can answer questions such as the following: "To what degree do items on the measure seem to be measuring the same attribute?" or "How well do items on a measure hang together?" When the items are measuring the same attribute, then it is expected that individuals' responses across these items should be highly consistent, that is, a high coefficient alpha. If coefficient alpha reliability is unacceptably low, then the items on the selection measure may be assessing more than one characteristic.

Let's consider in more detail another example of the use of coefficient alpha. Exhibit 4.8 shows the results of two sets (Case 1 and Case 2) of employment interviewers' ratings of 8 interviewees. After asking a series of questions, the interviewers rated the job applicants on four rating scale items. The four rating scales concerned the extent to which interviewees had socialized and worked with others. Ratings were made using the following scale: 1 = None, 2 = Little, 3 = Some, 4 = Much, and 5 = Very Much. The purpose of the ratings was to identify job applicants who had the ability to work well with others as members of a team.

Case 1 illustrates the ratings for one set of 8 interviewees, persons A through H. For each individual in Case 1, read down the columns and examine the ratings given to the four items. For example, applicant A received ratings of 4, 5, 5, and 4. Notice that although there were differences *among* the interviewees in the ratings received, the four ratings given to any one interviewee were quite similar. That is, individuals in Case 1 who received high ratings on one item tended to receive high ratings on the other items. A similar pattern is found for those rated low on any one of the scales.

EXHIBIT 4.8

AN EXAMPLE OF INTERVIEWER RATING DATA IN COMPUTING COEFFICIENT ALPHA (α) RELIABILITY

Rating Scale Items Used by Interviewers to Rate Interviewee Ability to Work with Others	Case 1 Interviewees								Case 2 Interviewees							
	A	B	C	D	E	F	G	H	I	J	K	L	M	N	O	P
1. Positive relations with coworkers	4	1	4	2	4	3	5	2	1	4	4	5	3	2	1	2
2. Preference to work with others	5	1	4	2	4	4	5	2	2	3	1	4	3	3	1	5
3. Participation in social activities	5	1	4	2	5	3	5	3	4	1	3	3	4	4	3	4
4. Involvement in community, religious, and athletic activities	4	1	5	3	5	2	5	3	2	5	5	2	1	5	3	3
Total Rating of Interviewee Ability to Work with Others	18	4	17	9	18	12	20	10	9	13	13	14	11	14	8	14

NOTE: The rating scale used by employment interviewers to rate the extent of interviewees' ability to work with others was as follows: 1 = None, 2 = Little, 3 = Some, 4 = Much, and 5 = Very Much. Case 1 coefficient alpha reliability = .83; Case 2 coefficient alpha reliability = .40.

Case 2 is different. As you read down the columns of data for applicants I through P, you can see there is no apparent pattern in the ratings. That is, an individual may be rated high on one item (such as, interviewee I on item 3) yet rated low on another (item 1). This same, almost random pattern of ratings is true for the remaining applicants as well.

In order to check the internal consistency reliability of the ratings, coefficient alpha reliability was computed for both Cases 1 and 2. Because the item ratings tend to go together in Case 1, there is the indication that whatever is being measured is being measured consistently. The computed coefficient alpha reliability of .83 confirms our conclusion that the item ratings tend to hang together and measure the same construct. (We may not be sure just exactly what that construct is. That is a question to be answered by a validation study.) As you probably expected, coefficient alpha reliability of the ratings in Case 2 is low, only .40. A coefficient this low suggests that the ratings are unreliable and do not assess one common attribute. Thus our total rating score does not reflect an overall assessment of an interviewee's ability to work as members of a team. The rating scale data used in Case 2 need to be improved (for example, through interviewer training or more clearly defining the rating scale items) prior to consideration of their use.

The formula for computing coefficient alpha is conceptually similar to that of K-R 20. The only information needed is (a) individuals' total scores and (b) their responses to each item or question on the measure. The following formula summarizes the computation of coefficient alpha:

$$\alpha = \frac{k}{k-1}\left(1 - \frac{\Sigma\sigma_i^2}{\sigma_y^2}\right)$$

where

k = number of items on the selection measure,
σ_i^2 = variance of respondents' scores on each item (i) on the measure, and
σ_y^2 = variance of respondents' total scores on the measure.

A more convenient computational formula for coefficient alpha is

$$\alpha = \frac{k}{k-1}\left(1 - \frac{n\Sigma i^2 - \Sigma T^2}{n\Sigma X^2 - (\Sigma X)^2}\right)$$

where

k = number of items,
n = number of persons on whom data are available,
Σ_i^2 = sum of the squared individual scores,
ΣT^2 = sum of the squares of the k item total scores,
ΣX^2 = sum of the squares of the n person total scores, and
ΣX = sum of the n person total scores.

Data such as those shown in Exhibit 4.8 can be used with this formula to compute coefficient alpha reliability.

The computation of K-R 20 and coefficient alpha are two of the most commonly reported reliability procedures in the HR selection literature today. At a minimum, users as well as developers of selection measures should routinely compute and report these reliability estimates.

Interrater Reliability Estimates

Many of the measures employed in HR selection are *objective* measures, such as a multiple-choice ability test. An objective measure is one that does not require judgment when it is scored. That is, in scoring objective measures either manually or by computer, a specific scoring key is used; individual judgment does not play a role in scoring. When *subjective* measures, such as those involving ratings, are implemented, however, subjective judgment plays an important role in scoring. Scoring depends not only on what is being rated, such as the behavior of a person, but also on the characteristics of the rater, such as the rater's biases and opinions. These two sources of scoring information contribute to errors of measurement. Rating jobs by job analysts, rating subordinates' job performance by supervisors, rating interviewees' performance in a selection interview by interviewers, and judging applicants' performance on a behavioral-based measure, such as answering a telephone in a simulated emergency call, are examples of applications of measures that involve degrees of judgment in scoring.

Because the individual biases of raters, interviewers, observers, judges, and analysts can affect the scoring of subjective measures, multiple raters are often utilized. Multiple raters are employed usually for two principal reasons: (a) to help counter any individual rater biases and (b) to assess the degree of objectivity present among raters. However, when multiple raters are used, an important problem is determining if scores vary significantly among the raters. The determination of consistency among raters has been termed *interrater reliability.*[20] (Other terms that have been used to describe interrater reliability are *interobserver* and *interjudge* reliability.)

Interrater reliability estimates test the hypothesis that ratings are determined by characteristics of the rater (for example, the rater's biases that contribute to errors of measurement) rather than by what is being rated. Differences among raters may result from any of several reasons. For instance,

1. Raters interpreting rating rules or standards differently in making their ratings, and

2. Raters not interpreting rating rules consistently or not perceiving whatever is being rated (e.g., jobs, people, etc.) well enough to make their ratings.

Differences in raters' judgments are considered to be a source of error. The purpose of calculating interrater reliability is to determine if raters are consistent in their judgments. If raters differ significantly in their ratings, it is impossible to determine the true score of the attribute being rated. The rating data will be contaminated with the idiosyncratic interpretations of what is being rated by each particular rater, and the rating data, therefore, are considered unreliable.

The computation of interrater reliability can involve any of a number of statistical procedures. Most of these procedures tend to fall into one of the three following categories: (a) interrater agreement, (b) interclass correlation, and (c) intraclass correlation. (A similar system of categorizing interrater reliability methods as applied to job analysis data has been developed by Edwin Cornelius.[21])

Interrater Agreement   In some rating situations, a reliability coefficient for raters is not computed, rather rater agreement is determined. For instance, two job analysts may be observing an employee performing her job. The analysts are asked to observe the individual's task activities and then indicate whether or not specific job behaviors are performed. Rater agreement, indices are often used in such rating situations. Percentage of rater agreement, Kendall's coefficient of concordance (*W*),[22] and Cohen's kappa (*k*)[23] are three of the most popular indices for estimating interrater agreement. Unfortunately, as Ronald Berk points out, some of the interrater agreement indices are not good estimators of rating reliability.[24] For example, when the behavior being examined occurs at a very high or very low frequency, indices such as percentage of rater agreement and the coefficient of concordance may produce a spuriously high indication of agreement between raters. This is because they fail to take into consideration the degree of rater agreement due to chance. In addition, interrater agreement indices are generally restricted to nominal or categorical data that reduces their application flexibility. Furthermore, some of the indices are not directly related to the traditional conception of reliability; each tends to offer its own distinctive description of the rating process.

  Although interrater agreement indices have their limitations, they are still widely employed in selection research. Percentage of rater agreement is probably the most often reported estimate. When this index is used, Keith Miller recommends that minimum acceptable agreement for a new measure should be 80 percent and for an established one, 90 percent.[25]

Interclass Correlation   *Inter*class correlations are employed when two raters are making judgments about a series of targets or objects being rated (such as interviewees, jobs, subordinates). Most often, these judgments are based on an interval rating scale. The Pearson product-moment correlation (*r*) and Cohen's weighted kappa (*k*)[26] are the two procedures most commonly reported as an interclass correlation. Essentially, the interclass correlation shows the amount of error between two raters. Berk suggests that an interclass correlation should be .90 or higher.[27] When the coefficient is less than .90, more specific operational criteria for making the ratings or training the raters in how to apply the rating criteria may be needed to enhance interrater reliability.

Intraclass Correlation   When three or more raters have made ratings on one or more targets, *intra*class correlations can be made. Intraclass correlation shows the average relationship among raters for all targets being rated. Exhibit 4.9 illustrates the basic research design of a study where an intraclass correlation can be computed. (If only two raters were involved, the figure would depict the typical design for an interclass correlation.) In this example, each of three employment interviewers interviewed a group of job applicants. After interviewing the applicants, each interviewer made a rating of each applicant's performance in the

EXHIBIT 4.9	EXAMPLE OF A RESEARCH DESIGN FOR COMPUTING INTRACLASS CORRELATION TO ASSESS INTERRATER RELIABILITY OF EMPLOYMENT INTERVIEWERS

	Interviewer		
Interviewee	1	2	3
A. J. Mitra	9	8	8
N. E. Harris	5	6	5
R. C. Davis	4	3	2
•	•	•	•
•	•	•	•
•	•	•	•
T. M. Zuckerman	7	6	7

NOTE: The numbers represent hypothetical ratings of interviewees given by each interviewer.

interview. Intraclass correlation can be used to determine how much of the differences in interviewees' ratings are due to their true differences in interview performance and how much is due to errors of measurement. Two types of reliability information on the raters are typically obtained with the intraclass correlation. These are (a) the average reliability for one rater and (b) the average reliability for all raters making ratings. Benjamin Winer has outlined the basic model and process for computing intraclass correlations. He has also shown how the procedure can be used with ordinal as well as dichotomous rating data.[28]

Finally, Ronald Berk[29] and Lawrence James and his associates[30] have extended the concept of intraclass correlation to other situations for which the computation of interrater reliability is important. Their procedures permit assessing interrater reliability for ratings of one or more targets on one or more rating characteristics by a group of raters.

Table 4.2 provides a descriptive summary of the methods we have discussed for estimating the reliability of selection measures. In addition to the questions addressed by each method, the table presents information on the assumptions as well as procedural aspects of the methods.

Interpreting Reliability Coefficients

The chief purpose behind the use of measures in HR selection research is to permit us to arrive at sound judgments concerning people to whom these measures are applied. For these judgments to have any value, they must be based on dependable data. When data are not dependable, any decisions based on this information are of dubious worth. Thus one goal of selection managers is to utilize measures that will provide dependable information.

Reliability analyses help us to determine the dependability of data we will use in selection decision making. Through reliability we can estimate the amount of error included in scores on any measure we choose to study. Knowing reliability, we can estimate how precisely or loosely a score for a measure can be interpreted. But how do we go about interpreting a reliability coefficient?

TABLE 4.2

DESCRIPTIVE SUMMARY OF MAJOR METHODS FOR ESTIMATING RELIABILITY OF SELECTION MEASURES

Reliability Method	Question Addressed	Number of Forms	Number of Administrations	Description	Assumptions	Sources of Error That Lower Reliability
Test-Retest	Are the scores on a measure consistent over time?	1	2	One version of a measure is given to same respondents during two sessions with a time interval in between.	• Respondents do not let answers on first administration affect those on second administration. • Respondents do not "change" (for example, through learning) from one administration to the other.	• Any changes in respondents and differences in answers for test and retest due to changes occurring over time.
Parallel Forms (immediate administration)	Are the two forms of a measure equivalent?	2	1 or 2	Two versions of a measure are given to same respondents during one session.	• The two forms are parallel. • Respondents do not let completion of first version affect completion of second.	• Any differences in similarity of content between the two forms
Parallel Forms (long-term administration)	Is the attribute assessed by a measure stable over time? Are the two forms of a measure equivalent?	2	2	Two versions of a measure are given to same respondents during two sessions with a time interval in between.	• The two forms are parallel. • Respondents do not let completion of first version affect completion of second. • Respondents do not "change" (for example, through learning) from one administration to the other.	• Any differences in similarity of content between the two forms.

Split-Half (Odd-Even)	Are respondents' answers on one half (odd items) of a measure similar to answers given on the other half (even items)?	1	One version of a measure is given to respondents during one session.	• Splitting a measure into two halves produces two equivalent halves. • Measure is not speeded (answers are not based on a time limit).	• Any differences in similarity of item content in one half of the measure versus the other half.
Kuder-Richardson and Coefficient Alpha	To what degree do items on the measure seem to be measuring the same attribute? How well do items on a measure hang together?	1	One version of a measure is given to respondents during one session.	• Only one attribute is measured. • Measure is not speeded (answers are not based on a time limit). • K-R 20 is suitable for dichotomous items. • Coefficient alpha is suitable for items on a continuum.	• Any differences in similarity of item content • More than one attribute, concept, or characteristic assessed by a measure.
Interrater (Interobserver/Interjudge)	To what degree do raters agree in their ratings?	1	One version of a measure is given to two or more raters during one session.	• Raters are equal or interchangeable. • Raters base their ratings on what is rated; extraneous factors do not influence ratings.	• Any biases of the raters that influence the ratings are given. • Raters are not knowledgeable of what to rate and how to make ratings.

What exactly does a coefficient mean? How high or low must a coefficient be for a particular measure to be used? These are but a few of the questions that can be asked in interpreting a reliability coefficient. Next we examine some of the issues that bear on the interpretation of reliability.

What Does a Reliability Coefficient Mean?

As we said earlier, calculation of reliability estimates results in an index or a coefficient ranging from .00 to 1.00. A variety of symbols are used to indicate reliability; typically, reliability is represented by an r followed by two identical subscripts. For example, the following would be the reliability symbols for the four measures of X, Y, 1, and 2: r_{xx}, r_{yy}, r_{11}, and r_{22}. (The symbol r followed by identical subscripts implies that a measure is correlated with itself.)

After the symbol, a numerical coefficient is reported. Again, the values will range from .00 indicating no reliability (a measure composed entirely of error) to 1.00 or perfect reliability (no error present in the measure). Without going through too many of the technical details, let's see what the coefficient means. Harold Gulliksen has shown that the reliability coefficient is equivalent to the squared correlation between true and obtained scores for a measure and can be directly interpreted as the coefficient of determination.[31] Or,

$$r_{xx} = r^2_{tx}$$

where

    r_{xx} = reliability coefficient,
    r^2_{tx} = squared correlation between true and obtained scores,
    x = obtained scores, and
    t = true scores.

Therefore, the reliability coefficient can be interpreted as *the extent (in percentage terms) to which individual differences in scores on a measure are due to "true" differences in the attribute measured and the extent to which they are due to chance errors.* For example, if we have a test called "X," and the reliability of Test X equals .90 (that is, r_{xx} = .90), then 90 percent of the differences in test scores is due to true variance and only 10 percent due to error. The reliability coefficient provides an indication of the proportion (%) of total differences in scores that is attributable to true differences rather than error.

The reliability coefficient summarizes the dependability of a measure for a *group* of individuals. It does not indicate which individuals within the group are or are not providing reliable data. When we examine a reliability coefficient, we should understand that the estimate refers to the scores of a group of individuals on a specific measuring device and not to a specific person. Thus it is quite possible to have a reliable selection measure as indicated by a high reliability estimate; but one or more people within the group may provide responses to the measure that contain considerable error. Unreliable performance by a respondent on a reliable measure is possible, but reliable performance on an unreliable measure is impossible.

In sum, when examining any particular reliability coefficient, consider that it is

- specific to the reliability estimation method and group on which it was calculated,

- a necessary but not a sufficient condition for validity,

- based on responses from a group of individuals,

- expressed by degree, and

- determined ultimately by judgment.[32]

How High Should a Reliability Coefficient Be?

This question has been asked many times. Different opinions exist. Unfortunately, there is no clear-cut, generally agreed upon value that can be given above which reliability is acceptable and below which it is unacceptable. Obviously, we want the coefficient to be as high as possible; however, how low a coefficient can be and still be used will depend on the purpose for which the measure is to be used. The following principle generally applies: *The more critical the decision to be made, the greater the need for precision of the measure on which the decision will be based, and the higher the required reliability coefficient.*[33]

In the practice of HR selection, employment decisions are based on predictors such as test scores. From the perspective of job applicants, highly reliable predictors are a necessity. In many selection situations, there are more applicants than job openings available. Competition can be keen for the available openings. Thus a difference of a few points in some applicants' scores can determine whether they do or do not get hired. Any measurement error in a predictor could seriously affect, in a negative and unfair way, some applicants' employment possibilities. You might be asking, but isn't it possible this same measurement error could produce higher scores for some applicants than might be expected, thus helping them obtain employment? Yes, it is possible for some scores to be inflated through error; here again, these scores could be unfair to the applicants "benefited" by errors of measurement. Because of misleading scores, organizations may be hiring such individuals and placing them in job situations they may not be able to handle. Job requirements may be too high relative to their true abilities. Although they may get the job, they may not be able to cope with it, leading to frustration and dissatisfaction for both employee and employer.

From the perspective of the organization attempting to hire executives or other key personnel (whose decisions may affect the success of the entire organization), reliable evidence of applicants' qualifications is also a necessity. The cost of being wrong in the assessment of key managerial personnel can be very high. Imprecise predictors can have long-term consequences for an organization. Dependable predictors are essential for accurately evaluating these key personnel.

But what about criteria? Isn't it just as important that criterion measures be reliable too? Of course, criterion measures, such as employees' performance appraisal ratings, should be reliable. However, *in the context of personnel selection,* their reliability need not be as high as that of predictors for them to be useful.[34] When predictors are used, they are generally employed to make individual decisions, for example, "How does one applicant's score compare with another?" or "Did the applicant make a passing score?" When scores are used for making decisions about individuals, it is critical that the measure used to produce these scores be a highly reliable one.

In contrast, criterion data are often employed to examine attributes that may be related to job performance. Employment decisions about individuals are not made with criteria; therefore, reliability coefficients need not be as high. However, as we see in the next chapter, it will not be possible to show empirical validity of a predictor if the criterion with which it is being correlated is not reliable.

Several writers have offered some rough guidelines regarding desirable magnitudes of reliability coefficients for selection measures. On the whole, their thoughts are directed toward predictors rather than criteria or other variables that might be present in selection situations. Jum Nunnally has suggested that in applied settings when important decisions are being made with respect to test scores, a reliability coefficient of .90 is the absolute minimum that should be accepted.[35] Lewis Aiken[36] as well as Elliot Weiner and Barbara Stewart[37] think that if a procedure is being used to compare one individual with another, a reliability of .85 or higher is necessary. Their suggested reliability coefficient is somewhat lower than Truman Kelly's recommended minimum of .94 to evaluate the level of individual accomplishment.[38] All in all, when predictors are being used in HR selection practice, we generally feel that a reliability coefficient no lower than .85 (and preferably .90 or higher) should be the absolute minimum in most selection situations. However, our conclusion needs to be tempered somewhat, since a number of factors can influence the size of an obtained reliability coefficient. Through the impact of factors, such as the range of talent in the respondent group for the attribute being assessed, it is possible for a reliability coefficient lower than .85 to be fully as good as one substantially higher. (For further information on this point, see the following sections on factors influencing the reliability of a measure and the standard error of measurement.) Reliability is specific to the group on which it is calculated. It can be higher in one situation than another because of situational circumstances that may or may not affect the preciseness (reliability) of measurement. To clarify how these can influence reliability in a context involving selection measures, let's briefly examine several of these factors.

Factors Influencing the Reliability of a Measure

As we have discussed, a reliability coefficient is an estimate. Many factors can have an effect on the actual magnitude of a coefficient. Here, we mention seven important factors that can affect estimated reliability: (a) method of estimating reliability, (b) individual differences among respondents, (c) length of a measure, (d) test question difficulty, (e) homogeneity of a measure's content, (f) response format, and (g) administration of a measure.

Method of Estimating Reliability   We have seen that different procedures for computing reliability treat errors of measurement in different ways. One result is that different reliability estimates will be obtained on a measure simply from the choice of procedure used to calculate the estimate. Some methods will tend to give more liberal (upper-bound or higher) estimates while others will tend to be more conservative (lower-bound or lower) in their estimates of the true reliability of a measure. Therefore, it is important for any individual evaluating a particular selection procedure to know which procedure was used and to know what methods tend to give liberal and conservative estimates.

Exhibit 4.10 presents a very rough characterization of relative reliability in terms of whether methods tend to give upper- or lower-bound estimates of a measure's true reliability, *other things equal*. We discuss a few of these "other things"—factors that can affect reliability—in this section. It is important to emphasize that the hierarchy in Exhibit 4.10 is based on general results reported for selected measures. In any one specific situation, it is possible that the rank order of methods may vary; a method characterized as usually providing lower-bound reliability may in fact give a higher estimate than one generally ranked above it.

Parallel forms reliability usually provides a lower estimate than other techniques because of changes occurring over time and differences from one form or version of a measure to another. These changes contribute to errors of measurement. If a test is measuring more than one attribute, Kuder-Richardson or coefficient alpha reliability will underestimate true reliability; if a measure has a time limit, reliability will be overestimated by the procedure. Because of memory, test-retest reliability will likely be high, but as the time interval between administrations lengthens, memory will have less impact and estimated reliability will fall. The effect on reliability of lengthening the time interval between administrations will be similar for parallel forms reliability as well.

Frank Womer has suggested several informal guidelines for judging the acceptability of reliability coefficients estimated by various methods for any measure in general.[39] For internal consistency reliability (odd-even split, Kuder-Richardson, and coefficient alpha), he feels that one should be skeptical of reliability coefficients lower than .85. For parallel forms reliability, estimates can be somewhat lower, say around .80, and still be acceptable. Of course, these guidelines are one person's opinion. Some may think they are too stringent and others that they are not stringent enough.

Individual Differences Among Respondents   Another factor influencing a reliability estimate is the range of individual differences or variability among respondents on the attribute measured. If the range or differences in scores on the attribute measured by a selection device is large, the device can more reliably distinguish among people. Generally speaking, the greater the variability or standard deviation of scores on the characteristic measured, the higher the reliability of the measure of that characteristic.

In part, this finding is based on the conception of reliability and its calculation by means of a correlation coefficient. Change or variation *within* a person, such as changing a response from one administration to another, detracts from

EXHIBIT 4.10 ROUGH CHARACTERIZATION OF RELIABILITY METHODS IN TERMS OF GENERALLY PROVIDING UPPER- OR LOWER-BOUND ESTIMATES

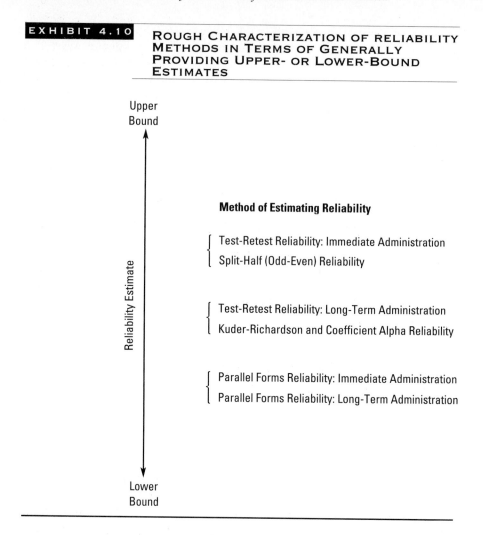

Upper Bound

Reliability Estimate

Method of Estimating Reliability

{ Test-Retest Reliability: Immediate Administration
{ Split-Half (Odd-Even) Reliability

{ Test-Retest Reliability: Long-Term Administration
{ Kuder-Richardson and Coefficient Alpha Reliability

{ Parallel Forms Reliability: Immediate Administration
{ Parallel Forms Reliability: Long-Term Administration

Lower Bound

reliability; we have already discussed this issue as errors of measurement. On the other hand, differences *among* people are considered to be true differences. Such true variation contributes to reliability. Therefore, if variability or individual differences increase *among* respondents (true) while variation *within* individuals (error) remains the same, reliability will increase. Range of ability in the group of individuals being assessed is not something that can usually be controlled or manipulated. However, it should be kept in mind when reviewing reliability coefficients. A reliability coefficient of .75 for a predictor might be acceptable in a very homogeneous group of people but unacceptable in a very heterogeneous group. Because individual differences can vary a great deal for various groups such as those based on educational level or age, it is imperative for a user of selection measures to review reliability data for relevant groups of respondents. Developers and publishers of commercially available predictors should report, at a minimum, separate reliability coefficients and predictor standard deviations for such respondent groups.

Length of a Measure   In general, as the length of a measure increases, its reliability will also increase. One way of thinking about this relationship is to look out of a window for a second or two and then try to describe in detail what you saw. As you increase the number of times you look out of the window in one- to two-second intervals, you will probably find that the accuracy and details of your description increase. Thus with increasing measurement, that is, observation out of the window, your description begins to approximate the true situation outside the window. A similar effect occurs when a selection measure is lengthened. Only a sample of possible items is used on a given measure. If all possible questions could be used, a person's score on the measure would very closely approximate his or her true score. Thus as we add more and more relevant items to our measure, we get a more precise and reliable assessment of the individual's true score on the attribute measured. Exhibit 4.11 illustrates the link between selection measure length, probability of measuring the true score, and test reliability. Initially, we have a universe of all possible test items. As we select test items from the universe and double the test length from 5, 10, 20, . . . , 80 items, we see that the probability of measuring the true score increases. Using the Spearman-Brown prophecy formula we discussed earlier, we can see that reliability also increases, from .20 for a 5-item test to .80 for an 80-item test. If we were to continue these calculations, we would see that the reliability of an unreliable short test increases rapidly as similar test items are added. However, these improvements in reliability begin to diminish after a point with increasing test length.

A variation of the Spearman-Brown formula mentioned earlier and shown here can be used to determine how much a measure must be lengthened to obtain a desired reliability:

$$n = \frac{r_{ttd}\,(1 - r_{tt})}{r_{tt}\,(1 - r_{ttd})}$$

where

> n = number of times a measure must be lengthened,
> r_{ttd} = desired level of reliability *after* the measure is lengthened, and
> r_{tt} = reliability of the test *before* the measure is lengthened.

Suppose, for instance, the reliability of a 10-item test is .75. It is desired that the reliability should be .90. Substitution in the formula shows that to obtain the desired level of reliability, the test must be three times as long or 30 items.

Test-Question Difficulty   When an employment test, such as an ability test, contains questions that are scored as either "right" or "wrong," the difficulty of the questions will affect the differences among job applicants' test scores. If the items are very difficult or very easy, differences among individuals' scores will be reduced because many will have roughly the same test score, either very low or very high.

As an example, refer to Exhibit 4.12. Suppose we administered a single test question to a group of 10 applicants. We have two groups of applicants: those

EXHIBIT 4.11   RELATION BETWEEN TEST LENGTH, PROBABILITY OF MEASURING THE TRUE SCORE, AND TEST RELIABILITY

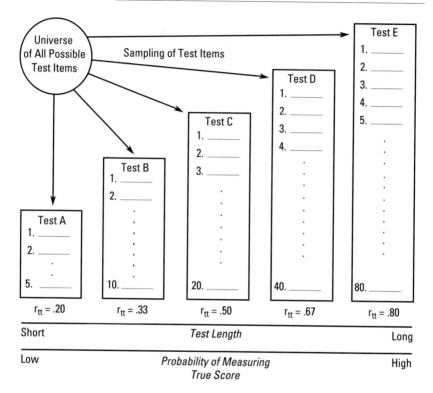

who got the question correct and those who missed it. In Case 1, only one person (10 percent of the applicants) gets the question correct. We can discriminate between that one individual and any one of the remaining 9 who missed it, a total of 9 comparisons or discriminations ($1 \times 9 = 9$ discriminations). We can also make the same number of discriminations if 9 get it correct and only one misses the question ($9 \times 1 = 9$ discriminations).

However, if in Case 2, 5 (50 percent of the applicants) get the question correct and 5 miss it, we can make significantly more discriminations. In this case, we can make 25 discriminations (5×5 discriminations) between pairs of individuals from the two groups. We learned earlier that increasing variability in scores increases reliability. Therefore, because variability or variance in scores increases with greater numbers of discriminations, reliability of a selection test is enhanced.

Test questions of moderate difficulty (where roughly half or 50 percent of the testees get a question correct) will spread out the test scores. Because there is a greater range in individual scores, finer distinctions among testees can be made. Test questions of moderate difficulty permit these finer distinctions, and tests that contain many items of moderate difficulty will tend to be more reliable than those tests with many items that are either very difficult or very easy.

EXHIBIT 4.12	ILLUSTRATION OF THE RELATION BETWEEN TEST QUESTION DIFFICULTY AND TEST DISCRIMINABILITY

Case 1: Item Difficulty = .10 (10% Get Test Question Correct)

Testees Who Got Question:

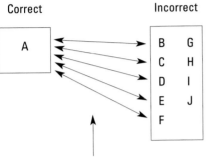

Correct   Incorrect   Number of Discriminations:

A   B   G   C   H   D   I   E   J   F

=   9 discriminations can be made between the 1 (A) who got the item correct and the 9 (B–J) who missed it.

Discriminations

Case 2: Item Difficulty = .50 (50% Get Test Question Correct)

Testees Who Got Question:

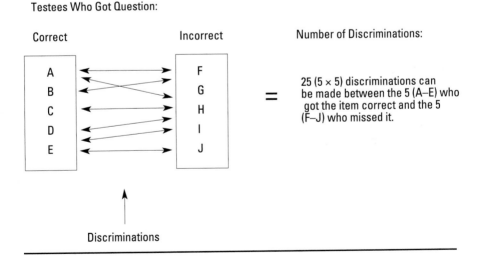

Correct   Incorrect   Number of Discriminations:

A   F   B   G   C   H   D   I   E   J

=   25 (5 × 5) discriminations can be made between the 5 (A–E) who got the item correct and the 5 (F–J) who missed it.

Discriminations

Homogeneity of a Measure's Content In our discussion of Kuder-Richardson and coefficient alpha reliability, we noted that both of these internal consistency methods represent the *average* correlation among all items on a measure. To the extent that items on a measure do not relate to all other items on the same measure, internal consistency reliability will fall. Thus internal consistency reliability can be enhanced in several ways. First, new items can be added to a measure that are comparable in quality and measure the same construct as the original items that compose the measure. Second, items on the measure that do not correlate with each other or the total score on the measure can be eliminated. Either of these steps will enhance the homogeneity of a measure's content and, therefore, increase internal consistency reliability.

Response Format   Any factor that systematically contributes to differences among individuals' scores on a measure will enhance the reliability of the measure. One factor that will contribute to these differences is the response format for recording answers to a selection measure. As the number of response options or categories on a measure increases, reliability will also increase. Suppose interviewers are using a 10-item rating form to judge the suitability of interviewees for a job. Answers to the 10 items are summed to obtain an overall employment suitability score for each interviewee. If each item has only two rating options (for example, 1 = unsuitable; 2 = suitable), then the only possible total scores are from 10 to 20. However, if five rating options are given for each of the 10 items, then possible scores can range from 10 to 50. Finer distinctions among interviewees can potentially be made with the latter scale. This scale can produce a greater spread in interviewees' employment suitability scores thus enhancing reliability. Up to a point, reliability can be enhanced by increasing the number of possible scores that a selection measure can have. For instance, research has shown that the reliability of rating scales can be improved by offering from five to nine rating categories.[40]

Administration of a Measure   As we have noted, various factors we have called errors of measurement can have a bearing on the reliability of a measure. For example, emotional and physical states of respondents, lack of rapport with the administrator of a measure, unpleasant conditions (e.g., too noisy or too cold) in which a measure is administered, and inadequate knowledge of how to respond to a measure can contribute to errors of measurement. Where errors of measurement are present, reliability will be lowered.

Standard Error of Measurement

We have just seen that reliability coefficients are useful for describing the general stability or homogeneity of a measure. The coefficient gives us some degree of assurance of the dependability of *most* repondents' scores on a measure. However, the various methods of computing reliabilities that we have discussed do not give us an idea of the error to be expected in a particular *individual's* score on the measure. Reliability is a group-based statistic.

In order to obtain an estimate of the error for an individual, we can use another statistic called the standard error of measurement. The statistic is simply a number in the same measurement units as the measure for which it is being calculated. The higher the standard error, the more error present in the measure, and the lower its reliability. Thus, the standard error of measurement is not another approach to estimating reliability; it is just another way of expressing it. The formula for calculating the standard error is as follows:

$$\sigma_{meas} = \sigma_x \sqrt{1 - r_{xx}}$$

where

σ_{meas} = the standard error of measurement for measure X,
σ_x = the standard deviation of obtained scores on measure X, and
r_{xx} = the reliability of measure X.

For example, let's assume that the mathematics ability test that we referred to earlier has a reliability of .90 and a standard deviation of 10. The standard error of measurement for a mathematics ability score on this test would be calculated as follows:

$$10 \sqrt{1 - .90} = 10\sqrt{.10} = .10(.316) = 3.16.$$

To illustrate how the standard error of measurement can be applied, let's look at an example. Suppose we had an applicant come into our employment office, take our math ability test, and make a score of 50. We could use the standard error to estimate the degree his or her test score would vary if he or she were retested with the test on another day. By adding and subtracting the standard error from the math test score (50 ± 3.16), we would obtain a range of math ability scores (46.84 to 53.16). One possible interpretation of this range might be that the chances are two to one that the applicant's true math ability lies somewhere between 46.8 and 53.2. Alternatively, we could say if he or she were given the test 100 times, we would expect that roughly two-thirds (68 percent) of the time the math ability scores would fall within the range of 46.8 to 53.2.

The standard error of measurement possesses several useful application characteristics. First, the measure is useful in that it forces us to think of scores on a measure not as exact points but as an approximation represented by a band or range of scores. Because selection measure scores contain error, an individual's score on a measure is only one of a variety of possible scores the individual could have obtained.

Second, the standard error of measurement can aid decision making in which only one individual is involved. For instance, suppose a passing or cutoff score on a test was set for a nuclear power facility operator's job. The job itself involves operations that could drastically affect the safety of both workers and citizens. If an individual applicant scores within 2 points of the passing score and the standard error of measurement for the test is 4 points, there is a very good chance that the employment decision will be in error. For this reason, the employer may only consider those applicants that score a minimum of one standard error of measurement above the passing score.

Importantly, the standard error of measurement can also be used to determine whether scores for individuals differ significantly from one another. For instance, imagine that we had two job applicants who had taken our math ability test. Jacob Farrar scored 50; Alicia Tatum scored 47. Can we conclude that Jacob is the better applicant solely in terms of math ability as measured by the one test score? The standard error of measurement can help us decide. If our standard error is 3.16 and the difference between our two applicants' scores is 3, then it is entirely possible that the difference in scores is due to chance. On retesting, Alicia may score higher than Jacob.

This same principle also applies to a measure administered to a large group of individuals. If we administer and score a test for 50 job applicants, we can rank the applicants on the basis of their test scores from high to low. If the standard error of measurement is large relative to the differences among these scores (standard deviation), then our rank order is likely to change if the applicants are retested. In general, the higher the standard error, the more susceptible our rank order of test scores is subject to change upon retesting. As you can see, with a large standard error, it may simply be due to chance that one individual scored higher than a group of others. Without an error index, we may assume these differences are meaningful and make employment decisions on the basis of these differences. With this index, however, we are in a better position to determine who really scored significantly higher or lower on a measure.

With respect to interpreting differences in individuals' scores, Lewis Aiken has offered the following guidelines:

1.   The difference between two individuals' scores should not be considered significant unless the difference is at least twice the standard error of measurement of the measure.

2.   The difference between scores of the same individual on two different measures should be greater than twice the standard error of measurement of either measure before the difference should be treated as significant.[41]

Another use of the standard error of measurement is in establishing how confident we may be in scores obtained from different groups of respondents. For example, suppose we had administered a test to 100 male and 100 female job applicants. For the male applicants, reliability for the test was .85 (standard deviation = 26); for the female applicants, it was .70 (standard deviation = 10). On the face of reliability information alone, it would appear that we might have more confidence in individual scores obtained for men than in those for women. However, when we use the reliability data *and* standard deviation information to compute the standard error, we find that the standard error of measurement for men is 10.1, and for women it is 5.5. Therefore, we should have greater confidence in a female applicant's test score than we should in a male applicant's score. This example highlights an important conclusion: *Without considering the variability of the group on the attribute measured (the standard deviation), reliability information alone will not permit us to compare relative confidence in scores for individuals in different groups.* Because the standard error is not affected by group variability, the statistic can enable us to make this important comparison.

In using the standard error of measurement, we have implicitly made an important assumption. That is, a score on a measure is equally accurate for the complete range of scores. However, it is possible that a test may be more accurate for one range of scores than for another. For example, our math ability test may be a more accurate predictor for individuals scoring low in math ability than for those scoring high. Yet, even where this assumption may be violated, the standard error measurement offers many advantages as an overall estimate of error.[42]

The standard error of measurement is a statistic you will likely come across in reading and studying various commercially available predictors (in particular, tests) to be used in selection. It is one of the most popular measures used in reporting test results since it serves as a corrective for the tendency to place undue weight on one measurement. The measure has become so popular that the College Board includes information on the standard error of measurement and its interpretation in results sent to takers of the Scholastic Aptitude Test (SAT) for college admissions.[43]

Because of its importance, the statistic should be routinely reported with each reliability coefficient computed for a measure. In practice, if you want to make a cursory comparison of the reliability of different measures, the reliability coefficient can be used. However, to obtain a complete picture of the dependability of information produced by a measure and to help interpret individual scores on the measure, the standard error of measurement is essential.

Evaluating Reliability Coefficients

From our discussion of reliability, you probably recognize that there are many issues to be considered in evaluating reliability coefficients. We have noted throughout our discussion that the estimation of reliability of selection measures is one essential requirement in appropriately applying these measures. Some users may believe that commercially available measures will provide all requisite information and the determination and assessment of reliability data will not be necessary. Past experience with some commercially available measures suggests otherwise. The Buros Institute of Mental Measurements conducted a review of over 1,000 commercially available tests published in *The Eighth Mental Measurements Yearbook*. Their results on the availability of reliability information were not encouraging. For the tests listed, they found that

- over 22 percent were without any reliability information,

- 7 percent had neither reliability nor validity data,

- 9 percent had no reliability data for certain subtests or forms, and

- 28 percent did not report any normative data.[44]

These facts suggest that one should not assume reliability information will be provided just because a user purchases a test from an apparently reputable test publisher. Any user should carefully search for and insist on reliability information on selection measures.

Assuming such information can be found, the next step is to systematically evaluate the reported data. To facilitate the evaluation of reliability data, we have summarized, in question form, some of the issues to be considered. These questions are listed in Table 4.3. All of the questions have been addressed in this

| TABLE 4.3 | QUESTIONS TO CONSIDER IN EVALUATING RELIABILITY COEFFICIENTS |

Question

1. Does the coefficient reflect the precision of a measure by indicating how well items hang together in measuring an attribute?

2. Does the coefficient reflect the constancy or stability of an attribute as assessed by a specific measure over time?
   A. Is the interval between test and retest so short that memory could have an effect?

   B. Is the interval between test and retest so long that learning or other changes in respondents could have occurred?
   C. Is the coefficient based on parallel forms of a measure administered over time?

   D. Is a test-retest coefficient computed for a measure that can be expected to change because of the nature of the attribute being measured?

3. Do scores on the measure for which the coefficient is computed depend on how quickly respondents can respond to the measure? Is a time limit involved?

4. Is the coefficient based on respondents like those for whom a measure is being considered?

5. Is the coefficient based on a large enough number of people that confidence can be placed on the magnitude of the coefficient?

6. Is information provided on the range of ability for the attribute measured of the group on which the coefficient is based?

7. Is a standard error of measurement provided for the reliability coefficient?

Once these questions have been addressed, then a user may ask:

8. Is the coefficient high enough to warrant use of the measure?

Comment

If interest is in determining the degree to which items on a measure are assessing the same content, an internal consistency estimate is appropriate.

If stability of performance is of interest, some form of test-retest reliability should be reported.
Depending on the situation, the interval should not be shorter than several weeks.

Depending on the situation, the interval should not be longer than six months; a typical interval is six to eight weeks.
If so, are data available to indicate that the forms are indeed parallel?

Some measures can be expected to change over time because of their nature. Examples might include performance ratings and attitudinal measures.

If a time limit for completing a measure is involved, the coefficient should not be based on an internal consistency estimate.

A coefficient is more meaningful if it is based on a group like the one to which the measure will be administered. For example, if a measure is going to be given to job applicants, a coefficient should be available for similar job applicants.

The larger the sample size on which the coefficient is based, the more dependable the estimate of reliability. A sample size of at least 100, and preferably 200, is desired.

Standard deviations and ranges of scores should he given for each group on which a coefficient is reported.

An index of the standard error of measurement should be given for each coefficient.

The more important the selection decision to be based on a specific measure, the higher the required reliability coefficient.

SOURCE: Questions 3, 4, 5, and 7 are based in part on Alexander G. Wesman, *Reliability and Confidence* (Test Service Bulletin No. 44) (New York: The Psychological Corporation, May 1952), p.7.

chapter. When examining reliability coefficients of selection measures, this checklist can serve as a useful means for reviewing the major considerations involved in reliability interpretation.

Reliability: A Concluding Comment

In this chapter, we have discussed the concept of reliability of measurement and reviewed various approaches to its determination. Although the assessment and interpretation of reliability can be a complex one, it nevertheless is a fundamental element to the proper use of HR selection measures. As we see in Chapter 5, the validity of a measure depends on its reliability; the interpretation of the meaning of a score on a selection measure, or its validity, cannot be made if the measure is not reliable.

In addition, we have seen that a selection measure being used as a predictor must also be highly reliable for making accurate assessments and decisions about individuals seeking employment. Where inaccurate information is used in employment decision making, the possibility for employment practices that unfairly discriminate against certain groups (women, older workers, the disabled, and ethnic minorities) increases. Knowledge of reliability information and other associated statistics such as the standard error of measurement aid in determining the possibility of bias in selection. With respect to the role of reliability and bias in testing, Arthur Jensen has concluded that

> Unreliability and instability of test scores are the most fundamental forms of test bias. Most people think of bias only as unfair discrimination that favors or disfavors members of particular groups. But, unreliability and instability of measurement are sources of individual bias that involve all persons on whom tests are used, regardless of their group membership. Also, when tests are used for selection, unreliability and instability contribute to group biases in selection and rejection, even when the tests are completely fair and unbiased in all other respects.[45]

References

[1] Walt Bogdanich, "Inaccuracy in Testing Cholesterol Hampers War on Heart Disease," *Wall Street Journal*, February 3, 1987, pp. 1–2.

[2] Bogdanich, "Inaccuracy in Testing Cholesterol Hampers War on Heart Disease," p. 1.

[3] Our treatment of reliability is based on *classical* reliability theory. Other developments have offered alternative approaches to the study of reliability theory (see, for example, Lee J. Cronbach, Goldine C. Gleser, Harinder Nanda, and Nageswari Rajaratnam, *The Dependability of Behavioral Measurements: Theory of Generalizability for Scores and Profiles* (New York: Wiley, 1972); however, for the beginning student, our approach will suffice.

[4] Our discussion of "errors of measurement" primarily assumes that these errors occur at random. Robert M. Guion (*Personnel Testing*, New York: McGraw-Hill, 1965, pp. 28–29) distinguishes between random and constant errors. Constant errors appear consistently with repeated measurement whereas random errors affect different

measurements to different degrees. Constant errors can be of two types. First, there are constant errors due to the measurement instrument, such as scoring a test with an incorrect answer key. Second, there are constant errors due to the measurement situation, such as an individual who consistently scores 20 points too low each time he takes a test due to his test anxiety.

[5] Howard B. Lyman, *Test Scores and What They Mean* (Englewood Cliffs, N J.: Prentice-Hall, 1986).

[6] Guion, *Personnel Testing*, p. 37.

[7] Milton Blum and James Naylor, *Industrial Psychology: Its Social and Theoretical Foundations* (New York: Harper & Row, 1968), p. 41.

[8] Wayne Cascio, *Applied Psychology in Personnel Management*, 4th ed. (Reston, Va.: Reston, 1991), p. 136.

[9] Jum C. Nunnally, *Introduction to Psychological Measurement* (New York: McGraw-Hill, 1970), p. 123.

[10] Guion, *Personnel Testing*, p. 40.

[11] Mary J. Allen and Wendy M. Yen, *Introduction to Measurement Theory* (Monterey, Calif: Brooks/Cole, 1979), p. 77.

[12] Guion, *Personnel Testing*, p. 42.

[13] In practice, the coefficient needs to be "corrected" by use of the Spearman-Brown prophecy formula. The application of this formula is discussed later in this section.

[14] Guion, *Personnel Testing*, p. 42.

[15] David Magnusson, *Test Theory* (Reading, Mass.: Addison-Wesley, 1966), pp. 73–74.

[16] George F. Kuder and Marion W. Richardson, "The Theory of the Estimation of Test Reliability," *Psychometrika* 2 (1937): 151–160.

[17] Anne Anastasi, *Psychological Testing* (New York: Macmillan. 1976), p. 116.

[18] Anastasi, *Psychological Testing*, p. 116.

[19] Lee J. Cronbach, "Coefficient Alpha and the Internal Structure of Tests," *Psychometrika* 16 (1951): 297-334.

[20] For a discussion of interrater reliability issues in the context of collecting personnel selection data (such as, job analysis data) through observation methods, see Mark J. Martinko, "Observing the Work," in *The Job Analysis Handbook for Business, Industry, and Government*, ed. Sidney Gael (New York: Wiley, 1987), pp. 419-431 and Sandra K. Mitchell, "Interobserver Agreement, Reliability, and Generalizability of Data Collected in Observational Studies," *Psychological Bulletin* 86 (1979): 376-390.

[21] Edwin T. Cornelius, "Analyzing Job Analysis Data," in *The Job Analysis Handbook for Business, Industry, and Government*, ed. Sidney Gael (New York: Wiley, 1987), pp. 353-368.

[22] Maurice G. Kendall and Alan Stuart, *The Advanced Theory of Statistics*, 4th ed. (London: Griffin, 1977).

[23] Jacob Cohen, "A Coefficient of Agreement for Nominal Scales," *Educational and Psychological Measurement* 32 (1972): 37-46.

[24] Ronald Berk, "Generalizability of Behavioral Observations: A Clarification of Interobserver Agreement and Interobserver Reliability," *American Journal of Mental Deficiency* 83 (1979): 460-472.

[25] Keith Miller, *Principles of Everyday Behavior*, 2d ed. (Monterey, Calif.: Brooks/Cole, 1980). See also, Donald P. Hartmann, "Considerations in the Choice of Interobserver Reliability Estimates," *Journal of Applied Behavior Analysis* 10 (1977): 103-116.

[26] Jacob Cohen, "Weighted Kappa: Nominal Scale Agreement with Provision for Scaled Disagreement of Partial Credit," *Psychological Bulletin* 70 (1968): 213-230.

[27] Ronald Berk, "Minimum Competency Testing: Status and Potential," in *The Future of Testing*, ed. Barbara S. Plake and Joseph C. Witt (Hillsdale, N.J.: Erlbaum, 1986), pp. 123-124.

[28] Benjamin J. Winer, *Statistical Principles in Experimental Design*, 2d ed. (New York: McGraw-Hill, 1971), pp. 283-305.

[29] Berk, "Generalizability of Behavioral Observations: A Clarification of Interobservel Agreement and Interobserver Reliability."

[30] Lawrence R. James, Robert G. Demaree, and Gerrit Wolf, "Estimating Within-Group Interrater Reliability with and without Response Bias," *Journal of Applied Psychology* 69 (1984): 85-98. Cf. Frank L. Schmidt and John E. Hunter, "Interater Reliability Coefficients Cannot Be Computed When Only One Stimulus is Rated," *Journal of Applied Psychology* 74 (1989): 368–370.

[31] Harold Gulliksen, *Theory of Mental Tests* (New York: John Wiley, 1950).

[32] Berk, "Minimum Competency Testing: Status and Potential," p. 121.

[33] Alexander G. Wesman, *Reliability and Confidence*, Test Service Bulletin No. 44 (New York: The Psychological Corporation, May 1952), p. 3.

[34] Guion, *Personnel Testing*, p. 47

[35] Jum C. Nunnally, *Psychometric Theory* (New York: McGraw-Hill, 1967), p. 226.

[36] Lewis R. Aiken, *Psychological Testing and Assessment*, 2d ed. (Boston: Allyn & Bacon, 1988), p. 100.

[37] Elliot A. Weiner and Barbara J. Stewart, *Assessing Individuals* (Boston: Little, Brown, 1984), p. 69.

[38] Truman Kelly, *Interpretation of Educational Measurements* (Yonkers, N.Y.: World Book, 1927).

[39] Frank B. Womer, *Basic Concepts in Testing* (Boston: Houghton Mifflin, 1968), p. 41.

[40] Paul E. Spector, *Summated Rating Scale Construction* (Newbury Park, Sage, 1992), p. 21.

[41] Aiken, *Psychological Testing and Assessment*, p. 61.

[42] Nunnally, *Psychometric Theory*, p. 203.

[43] Anne Anastasi, "Mental Measurement: Some Emerging Trends," in *The Ninth Mental Measurements Yearbook*, ed. James V. Mitchell (Lincoln : Buros Institute of Mental Measurements, University of Nebraska—Lincoln, 1985), pp. xxiii-xxix.

[44] James V. Mitchell, "Testing and the Oscar Buros Lament: From Knowledge to Implementation to Use," in *Social and Technical Issues in Testing*, ed. Barbara S. Plake (Hillsdale, NJ.: Erlbaum, 1984), pp. 114–115.

[45] Arthur Jensen, *Bias in Mental Testing* (New York: Macmillan, 1980), p. 259.

5

more needed on Utility
"   "   Binning & Barrett

Validity of Selection Measures

An Overview of Validity

In the last chapter, we pointed out that one important characteristic we need to have in any test, interview, or other selection measure we may use is *reliability*. So far, we have examined in some detail various issues regarding the reliability of measures. Here, we focus on the topic of *validity*, its relation to reliability, and the principal analytic strategies available for determining the validity of measures. Validity represents the most important characteristic of measures used in HR selection. It shows what is assessed by selection measures and determines the kinds of conclusions we can draw from data produced by such measures.[1]

Validity: A Definition

When we are concerned with the judgments or inferences we can make from scores on a selection measure, then we are interested in its *validity*. In this sense, validity refers to *the degree to which available evidence supports inferences made from scores on selection measures.*

One way to illustrate the process of inference making is to think of a common measure that many of us often make—a simple handshake. Think of the last time you met someone for the first time and shook that person's hand. How did their hand feel? Cold? Clammy? Rough? Firm grip? "Dead-fish" grip?

Did you make attributions about that person? For example, if the person's hand was rough, did you conclude *"He must do physical labor."* If it was clammy and cold, did you think *"He must be anxious or nervous."* If you received a "dead-fish" grip, did you deduce *"He must not be assertive."* Well, if you had these or similar feelings, then you drew inferences from a measure. Our next question should be, Is there evidence to support the inferences we have drawn? We study validity to collect evidence on the inferences we can make from our measures.

In the context of selection, we want to know how well a predictor (such as a test) is related to criteria important to us. If a predictor is correlated with job-relevant criteria, then we can draw inferences from scores on the measure about individuals' future job performance in terms of these criteria. For example, if we have an ability test that is related to job performance, then scores on the test can be used to infer a job candidate's ability to perform the job in question. Because test scores are related to job performance, we can be assured that, on the average, applicants who score high on the test will do well on the job.

Historically, people have tended to think of *the* validity of a measurement device. Actually, it is not the measure itself or the content of the measure (such as test items) that are valid; it is the inferences that can be made from scores on the measure. There is not just one validity; there can be many. The number will depend on the number of *inferences* to be made for the criteria available. Validity is not an inherent property of a selection measure but is a relationship between the selection measure and some aspect of the job. In some cases, validity may be expressed quantitatively or in other cases, judgmentally. Whatever the form, there may be many different validities for any one measure. These validities will simply depend on those criteria found or judged to be related to the measure and the inferences to be drawn from these relations.

The process that we go through in discovering what and how well a device measures is called *validation.* The results of this process represent evidence that tells us what types of inferences may be made from scores obtained on the measurement device. For instance, let's suppose that a manager believes that a master's degree is essential for satisfactory performance in a job involving technical sales. The manager is inferring that possession of the degree leads to adequate job performance while absence of the degree results in unacceptable job performance. In validating the use of the educational credential as a selection standard, the manager attempts to verify the inference that the degree is a useful predictor of future job success. The manager is not validating the educational selection standard per se, but rather the inferences made from it. Therefore, there can be many validities related to the standard.[2] Thus validation involves the research processes we go through in testing the appropriateness of our inferences.

The Relation Between Reliability and Validity

When we discussed the concept of reliability, we used terms such as *dependability, consistency,* and *precision* of measurement. Although these are important characteristics of any measurement device, it is possible to have a measure that is very reliable but does not measure what we want. For example, imagine we have a device that will measure job applicants' eye color in a very precise and dependable manner. Now, suppose we use the device to try and predict applicants' job performance. Subsequent research, however, shows that color of applicants' eyes has no relation with how well they perform their jobs. Thus our results show that our highly reliable measure is quite worthless for meeting our objective of predicting subsequent job performance. As you can see, the question of *what* is being measured by a device is as critical as the question of *how dependable* is the measure.

Rather than existing as two distinct concepts, reliability and validity go hand in hand. Let's see how they are interrelated. With respect to our eye color measure, we may have a highly reliable tool that has no validity in human resource selection. However, we *cannot* have high validity if we do not have high reliability. If a measure cannot correlate with itself, then we should not expect it to correlate with some criterion external to the measure. High reliability is a necessary but not a sufficient condition for high validity.

Statisticians have also demonstrated the intimate quantitative interrelationship between validity and reliability.[3] The validity of a measure such as a test will depend on its reliability as well as the reliability of the criterion with which it is correlated. Stated quantitatively, the relationship between validity and reliability is

$$r_{xy} = \sqrt{r_{xx}\, r_{yy}},$$

where

r_{xy} = correlation between measure X and criterion Y (the validity coefficient),
r_{xx} = reliability coefficient of measure X, and
r_{yy} = reliability coefficient of criterion Y.

For example, if the reliability of a test (X) is .81 and the reliability of the criterion (Y) is .60, then *maximum possible* validity of the test is .70, that is,

$$r_{xy} = \sqrt{(.81)(.60)}.$$

As you can tell from the formula, if reliability of *either* test X or criterion Y were lower, maximum possible validity would be lower as well. If either our test or criterion were completely unreliable (i.e., = .00), then the two variables would be unrelated, and validity would be zero. (We discuss the meaning of a validity coefficient later in this chapter.) Thus reliability or unreliability limits possible validity. To enhance maximum possible validity, reliability should be as high as possible for our predictors *and* our criteria.

Types of Validity Strategies

A *validation study* provides the evidence for determining the inferences that can be made from scores on a selection measure. Most often, such a study is carried out to determine the accuracy of judgments made from scores on a predictor about important job behaviors as represented by a criterion. There are a number of different strategies for obtaining this evidence to see if these inferences are accurate and can be supported. For our purposes, we discuss three strategies that have been used for validating measures employed in human resource selection: (a) *criterion-related* validity consisting of both concurrent and predictive validity, (b) *content* validity, and (c) *construct* validity. While the organization of our discussion may imply the three approaches are separate and distinct, it is important to recognize that the three are quite interrelated and cannot be logically separated. Criterion-related and content validity help to lay the foundation for determining construct validity. Ultimately, when the results of these strategies for any particular selection measure are taken together as a whole, they form the evidence for determining what is really being measured.

Criterion-Related Validity Strategies

Inferences about performance on some criterion from scores on a predictor, such as an ability test, are best examined through the use of a criterion-related validation study. Two approaches have typically been undertaken when conducting a criterion-related study, (a) a *concurrent* and (b) a *predictive* validation study. In some respects these approaches are very similar. That is, information is collected on a predictor and a criterion and statistical procedures are used to test for a relation between the two sources of data. Results from these procedures answer the question, Can valid inferences about job performance be made from our predictor? Although there are a number of similarities between concurrent and predictive strategies, we have chosen to separate our discussion in order to highlight their unique characteristics.

Concurrent Validity

In a concurrent validation strategy, sometimes referred to as the "present-employee method," information is obtained on both a predictor and a criterion for a *current* group of employees. Because predictor and criterion data are collected roughly at the same time, this approach has been labeled "concurrent validity." Once the two sets of data (predictor and criterion information) have been collected, they are statistically correlated. The validity of the inference to be drawn from the measure is signified by a statistically significant relationship (usually determined by a correlation coefficient) found between the predictor and measure of job success or criterion.

An Example As an example of a concurrent validation study, let's imagine we want to determine if some ability tests might be valid predictors of successful job performance of industrial electricians working in a firm. First, a thorough analysis of the job of industrial electrician is undertaken. Drawing on job analysis methods and techniques such as those described in Chapters 8 and 9, we attempt to uncover the critical tasks, elements, or functions actually performed on the job. From these identified tasks, we then infer the requisite knowledge, skills, abilities (KSAs), and other characteristics required for successful job performance. Exhibit 5.1 summarizes three hypothetical tasks and several relevant KSAs that were found to be important in our industrial electrician's job. (Keep in mind, we are providing only some example tasks and KSAs; there could be more in an actual job setting.) Two of the KSAs were found to be critical in performing the three job tasks: (a) Knowledge of Electrical Equipment and (b) Ability to Design/Modify Mechanical Equipment for New Applications. A third KSA, Ability to Follow Oral Directions, was judged to be of less importance in successfully performing the job and was not used as a basis for choosing our selection tests.

After the requisite KSAs have been identified, the next step is to select or develop those tests that appear to measure the relevant attributes found necessary for job success. As shown in Exhibit 5.1, three commercially available tests were chosen as experimental predictors of electricians' job success. These three tests were (a) *Bennett Mechanical Comprehension Test* (Form AA), (b) *Purdue Test*

EXHIBIT 5.1

SELECTION OF EXPERIMENTAL ABILITY TESTS TO PREDICT IMPORTANT KSAs FOR THE JOB OF INDUSTRIAL ELECTRICIAN

	Linking of KSAs to Critical Job Tasks (10 = High Relation; 1 = Low Relation)			
		KSAs		
Critical Job tasks	1. Knowledge of Electrical Equipment	2. Ability to Design-Modify Mechanical Equipment for New Applications	•••	8. Ability to Follow Oral Directions
1. Maintains and repairs lighting circuits and electrical equipment such as motors and hand tools	9.7	3.4	•••	1.5
• • •	• • •	• • •		• • •
5. Installs equipment according to written specifications and working drawings	9.5	3.3	•••	2.2
• • •	• • •	• • •		• • •
10. Independently constructs basic electrical/mechanical devices	7.2	9.4	•••	2.2

	Does Test Appear Suitable for Assessing KSA?			
Selected Tests	KSA 1	KSA 2	•••	KSA 8
A. Bennett Mechanical Comprehension Test (Form AA)	No	Yes	•••	N.A.
B. Purdue Test for Electricians	Yes	No	•••	N.A.
C. Purdue "Can You Read A Working Drawing?" Test	Yes	Yes	•••	N.A.

NOTE: The numbers shown are mean ratings given by subject matter experts used in the anaysis of the industrial electrician's job. High ratings indicate that a particular KSA is relevant to the successful performance of a critical job task. "Yes" indicates that a test appears to be useful in assessing a particular KSA. "N.A." indicates that a test was not applicable to a particular KSA.

for Electricians, and (c) *Purdue "Can You Read a Working Drawing?" Test.* How were these three tests selected? The tests were chosen based on our knowledge of what KSAs were required on the job and our knowledge of those existing tests that seemed to tap these KSAs. As we explain in Chapter 9, usually this process of inferring what devices might be used to measure the derived KSAs involves some form of subjective judgment. Expert advice can play an important role in choosing the most appropriate measures. For this reason, experienced selection consultants are often employed in choosing and developing selection measures.

Next, our three tests are administered to industrial electricians currently working in the firm. They are told their participation is voluntary; the tests are being given for research purposes only; and their test scores will not affect how they are evaluated or their employment with the company.

Shortly after, or while the tests are being administered, another step in the validation process is undertaken. In this step, criterion information representing measures of electricians' job performance is collected. As with our predictors, the criterion measures are developed based on the job analysis results. Performance appraisal ratings or more objective measures such as accident rates or errors in equipment repair might serve as criteria. Whatever the criteria, it is essential that the measures chosen be relevant indicators of performance as identified by the job analysis.

At this point, both predictor and criterion data have been collected. As depicted in Exhibit 5.2, the final step is to analyze the results using statistical procedures. A common practice is to statistically correlate (using the Pearson product-moment correlation coefficient) the sets of predictor and criterion data. Tests are considered to be valid predictors of performance if statistically significant relationships with criteria exist. If one or more of our tryout tests is found to be significantly correlated with a criterion, we will give serious consideration to incorporating the measure(s) in our selection program. In summary, Table 5.1 outlines the basic steps taken in a concurrent validation study.

Strengths and Weaknesses   If it can be assumed that the necessary requirements for conducting an empirical concurrent validation study are met, there is a positive argument for using this method. With a concurrent validity approach, an investigator has almost immediate information on the usefulness of a selection device. However, there are three factors that can affect the usefulness of a concurrent validation study: (a) differences in job tenure or length of employment of the employees who participate in the study, (b) the representativeness (or unrepresentativeness) of present *employees* to job *applicants,* and (c) the motivation of employees to participate in the study.

If job experience is related to performance on the job, then any predictor/criterion relationship *may* be affected by an irrelevant variable—job tenure. Since most people learn as they perform their jobs, it is entirely feasible that job experience may indeed influence their scores on either a predictor or criterion measure.

Second, if a concurrent validation study is being undertaken for a selection measure, another problem may arise. We want to use the predictor or selection device whose validity is based on current *employees* to predict subsequent job

EXHIBIT 5.2

REPRESENTATION OF RELATING PREDICTOR SCORES WITH CRITERION DATA TO TEST FOR VALIDITY

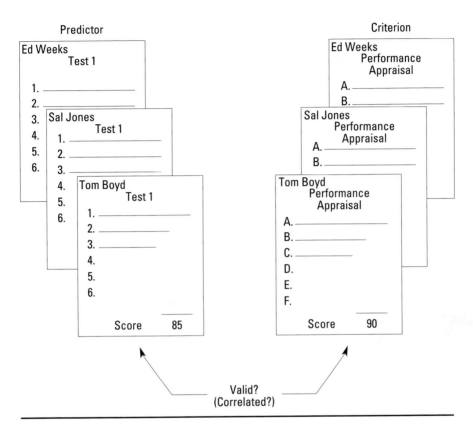

TABLE 5.1

SUMMARY OF MAJOR STEPS UNDERTAKEN IN CONDUCTING CONCURRENT AND PREDICTIVE VALIDATION STUDIES

Concurrent Validation
1. Conduct analyses of the job.
2. Determine relevant KSAs and other characteristics required to perform the job successfully.
3. Choose the experimental predictors of these KSAs.
4. Select criteria of job success.
5. Administer predictors to current employees and collect criterion data.
6. Analyze predictor and criterion data relationships.

Predictive Validation
1. Conduct analyses of the job.
2. Determine relevant KSAs and other characteristics required to perform the job successfully.
3. Choose the experimental predictors of these KSAs.
4. Select criteria of job success.
5. Administer predictors to job applicants and file results.
6. After passage of a suitable period of time, collect criterion data.
7. Analyze predictor and criterion data relationships.

success of job *applicants*. If applicants are characteristically different from job incumbents (for example, younger, with less job experience, less education), then the generalizability of the results of our study based on incumbents may not apply to applicants. Because of employee turnover or dismissal, our current employee group may be highly select and not at all representative of applicants.

Finally, since we are basing our study on employees who have a job rather than applicants who do not, our participants may not have a high level of motivation to properly respond to our experimental selection measure. As a consequence, our concurrent validation study *may* be significantly limited.

Predictive Validity

Rather than collecting predictor and criterion data at one point in time (like our concurrent validity approach), predictive validity involves the collection of data *over* time. In the context of HR selection, job *applicants* rather than job incumbents are used as the source of data. For this reason, it is sometimes known as the "future-employee" or "follow-up" method. The basic steps are also summarized in Table 5.1.

An Example   To illustrate the predictive validation method, let's return to the industrial electrician example. The steps involving job analysis, choice of criteria, and the selection of tests we want to try out are identical to those under the concurrent validation approach. The really significant difference between the two methods occurs at the step—*test administration*. Here, our tests are administered to job *applicants* rather than current employees. Once administered, the measures are then filed and applicants employed on the basis of other available selection data (such as other tests, interviews, etc.). Answers to our experimental measures are *not* used in making selection decisions. After our electrician applicants have been selected, trained, placed in their jobs, and have had time to learn their jobs adequately (perhaps as long as six months or more), criterion data representing job success are collected on the applicants. Then, after criterion data have been assembled, the two sets of scores (scores on our experimental predictors and criterion) are statistically correlated and examined for any possible relationships.

Strengths and Weaknesses   There are several important differences between predictive and concurrent validity. Under predictive validity, there is a time interval between the collection of predictor and criterion data. Applicants rather than incumbents serve as the data source and, as such, may have a higher, more realistic level of motivation when they complete the predictor measure. Differences between these individuals and subsequent applicants with respect to job tenure are not a problem with the predictive approach since the same level of job experience applies to both. Under the predictive validity method, the inference tested or question answered is, Can the predictor predict future behavior as measured by criterion data?

Because of the inference tested by predictive validity, the method is appropriate for measures used in HR selection. The method addresses itself to the basic selection issue as it normally occurs in the employment context, that is, how well will job applicants *be able* to perform on the job. The biggest weakness, of course, with the predictive validity model is the time interval required to determine the validity of the measure being examined. If relatively few people a month are being hired by an organization, it may take a number of months to obtain a sufficient sample size to conduct a predictive validity study. Moreover, it can be very difficult to explain to managers the importance of filing selection measure information *before* using the data for HR selection purposes.

From our discussion of concurrent and predictive validity strategies, it may seem there is only one way in which each of these validity designs may be carried out. In practice, however, there may be several different ways for conducting concurrent and predictive validity studies. Robert Guion and C. J. Cranny, for instance, have summarized five variations in which a predictive study might be conducted.[4] These are illustrated in Exhibit 5.3. In a similar fashion, different versions of the concurrent validity strategy also exist. These different ways of conducting a criterion-related validity study serve to show that in practice, a variety of approaches might be used.

At times a particular criterion-related design employed might not fit neatly into our categories of predictive and concurrent validity. For instance, suppose a personnel manager hypothesizes that college grade point average (GPA) is related to job performance of sales personnel. GPA was *not* used in making hiring decisions but is only available for *current employees*. To test her hypothesis, she correlates GPA with first-year sales and finds a relationship between the two variables. Is this a predictive validity study (it was *not* really done with applicants)? Is this a concurrent validity strategy (the data were gathered over time)? As you can see, our study design has elements of both predictive and concurrent validity strategies; it does not fall cleanly into either category. Whatever the design employed, the critical issue is not so much the criterion-related validity category to which it belongs. As we have seen, some designs such as that of our college grades and sales performance example may be difficult to classify. Rather the real question to be answered is, "What inferences will the design of a criterion-related validity study permit?"[5]

Concurrent Versus Predictive Validity Strategies

It has generally been assumed that a predictive validation design is superior to a concurrent one. Because of the problems we mentioned earlier in our discussion of the concurrent design, predictive designs have been thought to provide a better estimate of validity. Evidence provided by several investigators has indicated otherwise. For example, a review of 99 published criterion-related validity studies showed a greater number of validation studies based on a concurrent validation design than a predictive one.[6] Minimal differences were found, however, in the validation results of the two types of designs. Another review of validity estimates of ability tests also revealed no significant differences in validity estimates derived from the two designs.[7] Results from these two studies suggest that a concurrent validation approach may be just as viable as a predictive validation one.

EXHIBIT 5.3	EXAMPLES OF DIFFERENT PREDICTIVE VALIDITY DESIGNS

Type of Predictive Validity Design	Description of Procedure
1. Follow-up—Random Selection	Applicants are tested and selection is random; predictor scores are correlated with subsequently collected criterion data.
2. Follow-up—Present System	Applicants are tested and selection is based on whatever selection procedures are already in use; predictor scores are correlated with subsequently collected criterion data.
3. Select by Predictor	Applicants are tested and selected on the basis of their predictor scores; predictor scores are correlated with subsequently collected criterion data.
4. Hire and Then Test	Applicants are hired and placed on the payroll; they are subsequently tested (e.g., during a training period), and predictor scores are correlated with criteria collected at a later time.
5. Shelf Research	Applicants are hired and their personnel records contain references to test scores or other information that might serve as predictors. At a later date, criterion data are collected. The records are searched for information that might have been used and validated had it occurred to anyone earlier to do so.

SOURCE: Based on Robert M. Guion and C. J. Cranny, "A Note on Concurrent and Predictive Validity Designs: A Critical Reanalysis," *Journal of Applied Psychology* 67 (1982): 240 and Frank J. Landy, *Psychology of Work Behavior* (Homewood, Ill.: Dorsey Press, 1985), p. 65.

Requirements for a Criterion-Related Validation Study

Just because a criterion-related validation study is desired does not mean that such a study can be conducted. It must first be feasible. And, to be feasible, certain minimum requirements must be met. In the case of a validation study, "a poor study is not better than none."[8]

At least four requirements are necessary before a criterion-related study should be attempted. These include the following:

1. *The job should be reasonably stable and not in a period of change or transition.* Otherwise, the results of a study based on a situation at one point in time may not apply to the new situation.

2. *A relevant, reliable criterion that is free from contamination must be available or feasible to develop.*

3. *It must be possible to base the validation study on a sample of people and jobs that is representative of people and jobs to which the results will be generalized.*

4. *A large enough sample of people on whom both predictor and criterion data have been collected must be available.* Large samples (over several hundred) are frequently required in order to identify a predictor-criterion relationship if one really exists. With small samples, it may be mistakenly concluded that a predictor is not valid when in fact it is. The probability of finding that a predictor is significantly related to a criterion when it is truly valid is lower with small sample sizes than with larger ones.[9]

Content Validity Strategy

Within the last ten years or so, content validation has been receiving increasing attention by practitioners involved in selection. Because of this increased interest, we spend some time reviewing this method.

Basically, a selection measure has content validity when it can be shown that its content (items, questions, etc.) representatively samples the content of the job for which the measure will be used.[10] "Content of the job" is composed of those job behaviors that are necessary for effective job performance. The behaviors that compose the content of the job to be assessed are referred to as the *job content domain. For a measure to possess content validity, it must be representative of the job content domain.* This requirement is true for both predictors and criteria. But, in addition to job behaviors, selection measures (in particular, predictors such as paper-and-pencil tests) should also be representative of the KSAs necessary for performing these behaviors. If we want to infer the extent to which a job applicant possesses a skill or knowledge that is necessary to perform a job at the present time (present job competence), then a content validity strategy is appropriate.[11]

Content validity differs from predictive and concurrent validity in two important ways. First, the prime emphasis in content validity is on the *construction* of a *new* measure rather than the validation of an *existing* one. The procedures employed are designed to help ensure that the measure being constructed representatively samples what is to be measured, such as the KSAs required on a job. Second, the method principally involves the role of expert judgment in determining the validity of a measure rather than the application of quantitative techniques. *Judgments* are used to describe the degree to which the content of a selection measure represents what is being assessed. For this reason, content validity has been called a form of "descriptive" validity.[12] With its emphasis on *description*, content validity contrasts with concurrent and predictive validities, where the emphasis is on statistical *prediction*.

Sometimes, *face* validity is confused with the concept of *content* validity. Whereas content validity deals with the representative sampling of the content domain of a job by a selection measure, face validity concerns the *appearance* of whether a measure is measuring what is intended. A selection test has face validity if it appears to job applicants taking the test that it is related to the job. However, just because a test appears to have face validity does not mean it has content or criterion-related validity—it may or may not. Hence face validity is not a form of validity in a technical sense. But face validity can be important. If a test appears to test takers to be related to the job, then they are likely to have a more positive attitude toward the organization and its selection procedures. Positive attitudes toward selection measures may yield very positive benefits for an organization. For example, applicants who believe selection procedures are face valid indicators of their ability to perform a job may be more motivated to perform their best on these procedures. Also, if rejected for a job, applicants may perceive the selection procedures to be less biased than if measures without face validity were used. In this situation, rejected applicants from protected groups may be less likely to file a discrimination charge against an organization that uses face valid selection measures than an organization that does not. From this perspective, face validity may be thought of as a "comfort factor." Since some job candidates and some managers may be very resistant to the use of selection measures such as tests, they need to "feel" that a measure is fair and appropriate. Face validity of a measure helps to provide this comfort factor.

Drawing on some earlier writings, Benjamin Schneider and Neal Schmitt have outlined some key elements for implementing a content validity strategy.[13] We summarize the major aspects of several of these:

1. *Conduct of a Comprehensive Job Analysis*—Job analysis is the heart of any validation study. In particular, job analysis is the essential ingredient in the successful conduct of a content validation study. The results of a job analysis serve to define the job content domain; by matching the job domain to the content of the selection procedure, content validity is established.

    A number of court cases have affirmed the necessity for analyzing the content and nature of the job for which a selection procedure is used.[14] For example, the Supreme Court ruled in *Albemarle Paper Co. v. Moody* that job analysis must play an integral role in any validation study.[15] With respect to content validation studies per se, the *Uniform Guidelines* specify that a job analysis should result in the following products:

    A. A description of the tasks performed on the job
    B. Measures of the criticality and/or importance of the tasks
    C. A specification of KSAs required to perform these critical tasks
    D. Measures of the criticality and/or importance of KSAs, which include
        (1) an operational definition of each KSA
        (2) a description of the relationship between each KSA and each job task
        (3) a description of the complexity/difficulty of obtaining each KSA
        (4) an indication of whether each KSA is necessary for successful performance on the job[16]

    Each important job task identified in the job analysis will likely require at least some degree of a KSA for successful task performance. Here, the KSAs required to perform these tasks are specified. Most often, these KSAs are identified by working with subject matter experts who have considerable knowledge of the job and the necessary KSAs needed to perform it. This step typically involves subjective judgment on the part of participants in identifying the important KSAs. Because inferences are involved, the emphasis in this step is on defining *specific* KSAs for *specific* job tasks. By focusing on specific definitions of tasks and KSAs, the judgments involved in determining what KSAs are needed to perform which tasks are less likely to be subject to human error.

2. *Selection of Experts Participating in a Content Validity Study*—As we have noted, the application of content validity requires the use of expert judgment. Usually, these judgments are obtained from job incumbents and/or supervisors serving as subject matter experts. Subject matter experts are individuals who can provide accurate judgments about the tasks performed on the job, the KSAs necessary for performing these tasks, and any other information useful for developing selection measure content. Because of their importance, it is essential that these judges be carefully selected and trained in how to serve as a judge. Chapter 7 describes in more detail the characteristics important for these judges to possess.

3. *Specification of Selection Measure Content*—Once the job tasks and KSAs have been appropriately identified, the items, questions, or other content to compose the selection measure are specified. This phase of content validation is often referred to as *domain sampling*. That is, the items, questions, or other content are chosen to constitute the selection measure so they represent the behaviors or KSAs found important for job performance. The content included is in proportion to the relative importance of the job behaviors or KSAs found important for job performance. Subject matter experts who are knowledgeable of the job in question review the content of the measure and judge its suitability for the job. Final determination of selection measure content depends on these experts' judgments.

To aid the review of selection measure content, such as a multiple-choice test or structured interview, Richard Barrett has proposed the Content Validation Form (CVF).[17] Basically, the form consists of 18 questions that serve as a guide or audit for analyzing the appropriateness of selection measure content in a content validation study. Individuals knowledgeable of the job (for example, incumbents) working with a test development specialist record their evaluations and the rationale behind them for each part of the test being reviewed. The questions on the CVF are organized into three test review areas. The CVF review areas and a sample question from each are as follows:

A. **Test as a Whole:**
   (1) Have applicants had access to education, training, or experience necessary to prepare them to take the test?
   [ ] Yes
   [ ] No, test performance depends on education that is not available to some applicants
   [ ] No, some applicants have not had the opportunity for relevant experience

B. **Item-by-Item Analysis:**
    (2) Is the knowledge required to answer the question required of the incumbent to perform the work?
    [ ] Yes
    [ ] No, used by higher level
    [ ] No, used by lower level
    [ ] No, information available from reference
    [ ] No, not relevant to work performance

C. **Symptoms of Questionable Tests:**
    (3) Can competent practitioners pass the test?
    [ ] Yes
    [ ] No, too high a passing score
    [ ] No, information never learned
    [ ] No, information, once learned, forgotten through disuse

In developing a predictor (for example, a selection interview, multiple-choice test) to be used in selection, one key issue is the fidelity or comparability between the format and content of the predictor and the performance domain of the job in which the predictor will be used. Two types of predictor–job performance fidelity must be addressed (a) physical fidelity and (b) psychological fidelity. Physical fidelity concerns the match between how a worker actually behaves on the job and how an applicant for that job is asked to behave on the predictor used in selection. For example, a driving test for truck driver applicants that requires driving activities an incumbent truck driver must actually perform, such as backing up a truck to a loading dock, has physical fidelity. A typing test requiring applicants to use a word processor to type actual business correspondence that is prepared by current employees using the same word processor also has physical fidelity.

Psychological fidelity occurs when the same knowledge, skills, and abilities required to perform the job successfully are also required on the predictor. For example, a patrol police officer may have to deal with hostile and angry citizens. Asking police officer job applicants to write a statement describing how they would handle a hostile individual is not likely to have psychological fidelity. KSAs different from those required on the job, such as the ability to express one's self in writing, may be called for by the written statement. On the other hand, psychological fidelity might be found in a role-playing simulation in which police patrol applicants might interact with an actor playing the role of an angry citizen.[18]

In general, when physical and psychological fidelity of the selection predictor mirrors the performance domain of the job, content validity is enhanced. Such a measure is psychologically similar because similar behaviors as well as knowledge, skills, and abilities required for incumbent performance are asked of applicants.

4. *Assessment of Selection Measure and Job Content Relevance*—Another important element in content validation is determining the relevance of the

selection measure content for assessing the content of the job. Charles Lawshe has proposed a quantitative procedure called the *Content Validity Ratio* (CVR) for making this determination.[19] Basically, the CVR is an index computed on a panel (job incumbents and supervisors) of experts' ratings of the degree of overlap between the content of a selection measure and the content of the job. Each panel member is presented the contents of a selection measure and asked to make ratings of these contents. For example, items on a job-knowledge test are given to the panel members. Members judge each test item by indicating whether the KSA measured by the item is (a) *essential*, (b) *useful but not essential*, or (c) *not necessary for job performance*. These judgments are used in the following formula to produce a CVR for each item on the test:

$$\text{CVR} = \frac{n_e - N/2}{N/2},$$

where n_e is the number of judges rating the test item as essential and N is the total number of judges on the rating panel. The computed CVR can range from 1.00 (all judges rate an item essential) to .00 (half of the judges rate it essential) to –1.00 (none of the judges rate it essential). Because it is possible a CVR could have occurred by chance, it is tested for statistical significance using tables presented by Lawshe. Statistically significant items would suggest correspondence with the job. Nonsignificant items in which most of the judges do not rate "essential" can be eliminated from the test. By averaging the CVR item indexes, a Content Validity Index (CVI) for the test as a whole can be also derived. The CVI indicates the extent to which the panelists believe the overall ability to perform on the test overlaps with the ability to perform on the job. Hence the index serves as a representation of overall selection measure and job content overlap.

Once a measure is developed, it should exhibit high internal consistency reliability (for example, K-R 20, coefficient alpha). When feasible, an internal consistency reliability estimate should be computed. A high internal consistency reliability estimate shows that each part of the measure (such as test items) reflects the same attribute. Performance on one part is associated with performance on every other part as well as the measure as a whole.

Some Examples of Content Validation

Since the content validity approach can have wide applicability in the selection of individuals for jobs requiring generally accepted KSAs (such as reading ability, knowledge of mathematics, ability to read drawings, etc.), we examine some examples of content validation to illustrate the method.

Lyle Schoenfeldt and his colleagues were interested in developing an industrial reading test for entry-level personnel of a large chemical corporation. Job analysis was used to determine *what* materials entry-level personnel needed to be able to read upon job entry as well as the *importance* of these materials to job performance. These analyses showed that entry-level employees read four basic types of materials: (a) safety (signs, work rules, safety manuals), (b) operating procedures (instruction bulletins, checklists), (c) day-to-day operations (log books, labels, schedules), and (d) other (memos, work agreements, application materials). The safety and operating procedures materials were judged most important, as they accounted for roughly 80 percent of the materials read while performing the job. The test was then constructed so that approximately 80 percent of the test items reflected these two types of materials. The test itself was developed from the content of *actual* materials current employees had to read upon job entry.[20]

In a hypothetical example, imagine we want to build content valid measures for use in selecting typist-clerks in an office setting. Again, based on the job analysis procedures discussed previously, it is found that incumbents need specific KSAs to perform specific tasks. From the example tasks and KSAs shown in Exhibit 5.4, two specific job performance domains are identified that we want to be able to predict: (a) typing performance and (b) calculating performance. For our measures to have content validity, we need to build them in such a way that their content representatively samples the content of each of these domains. Where should the measures' contents come from? For the contents to be most representative, they should be derived from what incumbents actually do on the job. For example, we might develop a performance measure that would ask an applicant to format an actual business letter in a specific style and then type it within a prescribed period of time. Similarly, we might ask applicants to use a ten-key adding machine to compute and check some actual, reported business expenses. Further, in computing scores, the measures might be weighted so that each reflects its relative importance in performing the job. In our example, typing correspondence accounts for approximately 75 percent of the job while 15 percent involves calculating expense claims. (The remaining 10 percent consists of other tasks.) Thus our typing measure should be weighted 75 percent to reflect its relative importance to calculating. As you can tell from our example task statements, KSAs, and measures, we are attempting to develop selection measures whose content representatively maps the actual content of the job itself. To the extent we are successful, content validity of the measures can be supported.

Job incumbents and supervisors serving as subject matter experts play an important role in establishing the content validity of our measures. These experts are used to identify the important tasks performed on the job and the relevant KSAs needed to perform these tasks successfully. Also, as we saw earlier through the computation of the content validity ratio, they may also serve in judging the appropriateness of content for the measures. (The role of subject matter experts in conducting job analyses is discussed in Chapter 8.) All of these judgments taken in sum represent the foundation for determining the content validity of the selection measures being developed for our typist-clerk position.

EXHIBIT 5.4

EXAMPLE TASKS, KSAS, AND SELECTION MEASURES FOR ASSESSING KSAS OF TYPIST-CLERKS

Example KSAs of Typist-Clerks	Example Job Tasks of Typist-Clerks				Selection Measures of KSAs
	1. Types and proofreads business correspondence, reports, and proposals upon written instruction	• • •	5. Checks and computes travel claims and expenses using a ten-key adding machine		
1. Skill in typing reports and correspondence at a minimum of 50 words per minute	✔				Speed typing test of business correspondence
2. Ability to read at 12th grade reading level	✔				Reading test involving reports, correspondence, and proposals at 11th grade reading level
3. Knowledge of business letter styles used in typing business correspondence	✔				Formatting and typing test of business correspondence
4. Knowledge of arithmetic at 10th grade level including addition, subtraction, division, and multiplication			✔		Arithmetic test requiring arithmetic calculations on business expense data using ten-key adding machine
⋮	⋮		⋮		⋮
9. Ability to operate a ten-key adding machine			✔		Arithmetic test requiring arithmetic calculations on business expense data using ten-key adding machine
Percentage (%) of time performed	75%	• • •	15%		

NOTE: A check mark indicates that a KSA is required to perform a specific job task. Selection measures of KSAs are those developed to assess particular KSAs.

Inappropriateness of Content Validation

As we have seen, content validity provides evidence that a selection measure representatively samples the universe of job content. This evidence is based principally on expert judgment. As long as a selection measure assesses *observable* job behaviors, for example, a driving test used to measure a truck driver applicant's ability to drive a truck, the inferential leap in judging between what a selection device measures and the content of the job is likely to be rather small. However, the more abstract the nature of a job and the KSAs necessary to perform it (for example, the skill of a manager to provide leadership, the possession of emotional stability), the greater the inferential leap required in judging the link between the content of the job and the content of a selection measure. Where inferential leaps are large, error is more likely to be present. Therefore, it is much more difficult to accurately establish content validity for those jobs characterized by more abstract functions and KSAs than for jobs whose functions and KSAs are more observable.

What is central to the concept of content validity is that the selection measure appropriately samples the domain of job content. Whenever there is a difference in the specific content of the measure and the KSAs required to perform the tasks of a job, then an inferential leap or judgment is necessary for determining if the measure appropriately samples the job. Exhibit 5.5 descriptively summarizes the inference points required in establishing the content validity of a measure. The first inference point **(1)** is from the job itself to the tasks identified as composing it. Where careful and thorough job analysis techniques focusing on job tasks are used, the judgments necessary for determining whether the tasks accurately represent the job will probably have minimal error. The next inference point **(2)** is from the tasks of the job to identified KSAs required for successful job performance. Here again, complete, thorough job analyses can minimize possible error.

The final inference point **(3)** is most critical. It is at this point that final judgments regarding content validity of the selection measure are made. Here we are most concerned with the psychological fidelity between the measure and the job performance domain. Specifically, to make the inferential leap supporting content validity, we must address three important issues that contribute to psychological fidelity:

1. Does successful performance on the selection measure require the same KSAs needed for successful job performance?

2. Is the mode used for assessing test performance the same as that required for job or task performance?

3. Are KSAs *not* required on the job present in our predictor?[21]

If we can deal with these issues successfully, our inferential leaps can be kept small. As long as the inferential leaps are acceptably small, that is, the selection measure is composed of content that clearly resembles important job tasks and KSAs, arguments for content validity inferences are plausible. For jobs involving

EXHIBIT 5.5

DEPICTION OF THE INFERENCE POINTS
FROM JOB CONTENT TO SELECTION
MEASURE CONTENT IN CONTENT
VALIDATION

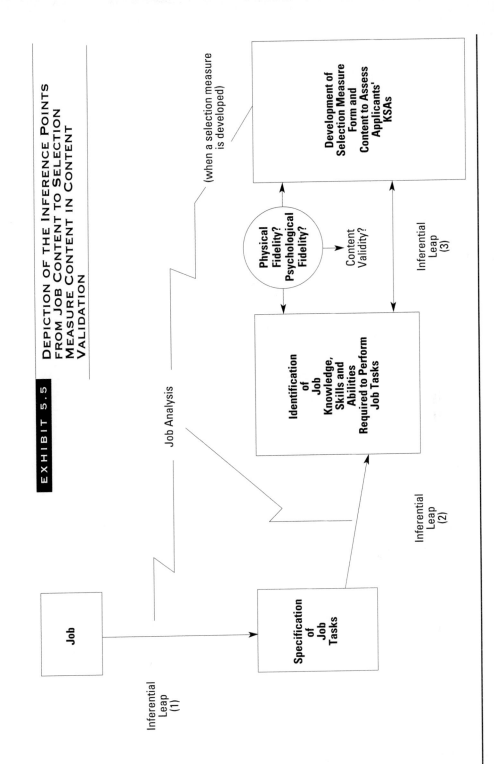

activities and processes that are *directly observable* (such as for the job of a typist), only *small inferences* may be required in judging the relation between what is done on the job, the KSAs necessary to do the job, and the KSAs assessed by the selection measure. For jobs whose activities and work processes are *less visible* and more abstract (such as those of an executive), greater inferences must be made between job activities, applicant requirements for successful performance, and selection measure content. In general, the greater the inferential leaps being made in a content validity study, the more likely errors will be made, and the more difficult it will be to establish content validity. At this point, other validation strategies will be needed, such as criterion-related approaches.

The *Uniform Guidelines* recognize the limits of content validation and specify some situations where content validation alone is not appropriate; other validation methods have to be used. These situations include the following:

1. When mental processes, psychological constructs, or personality traits (such as judgment, integrity, dependability, motivation) are not directly observable but inferred from the selection device[22]

2. When the selection procedure involves KSAs an employee is expected to learn on the job[23]

3. When the content of the selection device does not resemble a work behavior; when the setting and administration of the selection procedure does not resemble the work setting[24]

From our discussion, it should be evident that, as a validation method, content validity differs from criterion-related techniques in the following ways: (a) in content validity, the focus is on the selection measure itself, while in the others, the focus is on an external variable, (b) criterion-related validity is narrowly based on a specific set of data, whereas content validity is based on a broader base of data and inference, and (c) a statement of criterion-related validity is couched in terms of precise quantitative indices (prediction) while content validity is generally characterized using broader, more judgmental descriptors (description).[25]

Because content validation emphasizes judgmental rather than statistical techniques for assessing the link between the selection standard and indicators of job success, some writers question its use. Their main criticism is that content validity is primarily concerned with inferences about the *construction* of content of the selection procedure rather than with predictor scores. Thus, since validity of selection standards concerns the accuracy of inferences from predictors, some have argued, that which is "content validity" is not really validity at all.[26]

Content Versus Criterion-Related Validation: Some Requirements

So far, we have discussed several approaches to validation. The choice of a validation strategy implies that certain requirements must first be evaluated and met. Each of the validation strategies discussed to this point has a particular set of requirements. These requirements must be met for a specific strategy to be viable.

A review of these requirements serves as a means for determining the feasibility of a particular validation methodology. We have prepared a summary of requirements in which HR selection issues are in question. Drawing principally from the *Uniform Guidelines*, the *Principles*,[27] and other sources in the literature, the major feasibility requirements for conducting criterion-related (concurrent and predictive) and content validation methods have been summarized. These requirements are listed in Table 5.2. The requirements shown are not meant to be exhaustive,

| TABLE 5.2 | BASIC CONSIDERATIONS FOR DETERMINING THE FEASIBILITY OF CRITERION-RELATED AND CONTENT VALIDATION STRATEGIES |

Criterion-Related Validation[a]

1. Must be able to assume the job is reasonably stable and not undergoing change or evolution.
2. Must be able to obtain a relevant, reliable, and uncontaminated measure of job performance (that is, a criterion).
3. Should be based as much as possible on a sample that is representative of the people and jobs to which the results are to be generalized.
4. Should have adequate statistical power in order to identify a predictor-criterion relationship if one exists. To do so, must have:
   a. adequate sample size;
   b. variance or individual differences in scores on the selection measure and criterion.
5. Must be able to obtain a complete analysis of each of the jobs for which the validation study is being conducted. Used to justify the predictors and criteria being studied.
6. Must be able to make the inference that performance on the selection measure can predict future job performance.
7. Must have ample resources in terms of time, staff, and money.

Content Validation

1. Must be able to obtain a complete, documented analysis of each of the jobs for which the validation study is being conducted. Used to identify the content domain of the job under study.
2. Applicable when a selection device purports to measure existing job skills, knowledge, or behavior. Inference is that content of the selection device measures content of the job.
3. Although not necessarily required, should be able to show that a criterion-related methodology is not feasible.
4. Inferential leap from content of the selection device to job content should be a small one.
5. Most likely to be viewed as suitable when skills and knowledge for doing a job are being measured.
6. Not suitable when abstract mental processes, constructs, or traits are being measured or inferred.
7. Most likely will not provide sufficient validation evidence when applicants are being ranked.
8. A substantial amount of the critical job behaviors and KSAs should be represented in the selection measure.

---

[a]Criterion-related validity includes both concurrent and predictive validity.

SOURCES: Society of Industrial and Organizational Psychology, *Principles for the Validation and Use of Personnel Selection Procedures*, 3d ed. (College Park, Md.: Author, 1987), pp. 7–8; Equal Employment Opportunity Commission, Civil Service Commission, Department of Labor, and Department of Justice, *Adoption of Four Agencies of Uniform Guidelines on Employee Selection Procedures*, 43 Federal Register 38,295, 38,300–38,301, 38,303 (Aug. 25, 1989); Robert M. Guion, *Personnel Testing* (New York: McGraw-Hill, 1965).

only illustrations of major considerations when HR selection is involved. Also, the requirements serve as considerations for deciding the feasibility of a particular validation approach; they are *not* complete technical requirements.

Construct Validity Strategy

The last validation strategy we mention is construct validity. When psychologists use the term *construct*, they are generally referring to the postulated concept, attribute, characteristic, or quality thought to be assessed by a measure or an indicant. When a measure is used in selection research, it is believed that the measure assesses "something." That "something" is the construct.[28] Thus terms such as *intelligence, sociability,* and *clerical ability* are all theoretical abstractions called constructs. But their indicants (such as a clerical ability test) are operational, concrete measures of these constructs.

For example, suppose we have a test called the General Mental Ability Test. The test is *thought* to serve as an indicant of general intelligence. As we review it, we may believe that the construct of intelligence is being assessed by the test. For example, we look at the test's content and see items involving topics such as verbal analogies, mathematical problem solving, or scrambled sentences. But does this indicant really assess the construct of intelligence? We hypothesize that it does, but does it? Construct validation tests our hypothesis. In this sense, construct validation is a research process involving the collection of evidence used to test hypotheses about relationships between measures and their constructs.

Let's take a simple example to illustrate an approach to construct validation of a hypothetical measure called the Teamwork Inventory, or TI. Currently, many manufacturing organizations maintain that the ability of employees to work effectively as members of a work team is a critical requirement in manufacturing jobs. Let's assume that we have analyzed such a manufacturing job and found that the performance dimension *Working as a Team Member* (a construct) is important to successful performance. The *Ability to Work with Others* (another construct) is hypothesized to be an important ability in performing this job dimension. As we look at our two constructs, we develop indicants that could be used to assess them. For instance, supervisors' ratings are used as an indicant of the construct *Working as a Team Member* while a paper-and-pencil test, the Teamwork Inventory (TI), is developed to assess the construct *Ability to Work with Others*. Our particular interest is a construct validation study of the TI.

Exhibit 5.6 shows the hypothesized links between the constructs and their indicants.[29] Construct validation is an accumulation of evidence that supports the links among the various indicants and constructs. In our current example and from the perspective of personnel selection, we are ultimately interested in the link between the TI indicant and *Working as a Team Member* construct (link **5**). Evidence of this link can come from several sources. One source might be a criterion-related validation study between the TI and supervisory ratings of performing as a team member (link **1**). Content validation studies might also provide additional evidence (links **2** and **3**). However, other forms of evidence can also be accumulated to determine if our TI test assesses the construct of *Ability to Work with Others*.

EXHIBIT 5.6	A HYPOTHETICAL EXAMPLE OF CONSTRUCT VALIDATION OF THE LINK BETWEEN THE ABILITY TO WORK WITH OTHERS (CONSTRUCT) AND THE TEAMWORK INVENTORY (INDICANT)

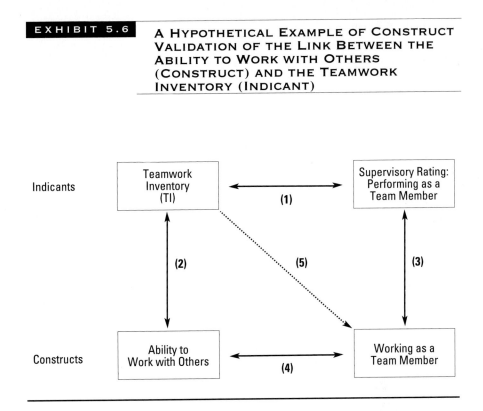

Literature reviews might suggest the characteristics of individuals who work effectively on teams. We might hypothesize, for instance, that such individuals would be extroverted, have a high need for affiliation, would have played/participated extensively in group activities such as team sports while growing up, and would have belonged to a number of social organizations. Measures of these variables such as personality inventories and biographical data questionnaires would be administered along with the TI to current employees. If our hypothesized associations are found, we have another piece of evidence regarding the construct validity of the TI.

We might design another study in which the TI and other selection measures are given to job applicants. Employees are hired without knowledge of TI scores and placed in work teams. Six months or so later, we ask team members to rate how well individuals fit within their assigned team and collect absenteeism data. Earlier, we hypothesized that individuals possessing the ability to work on a team would show less absenteeism from the work group and be rated by their peers as an effective team member. If we find that employees who scored high on the TI had less absenteeism and were rated more effective than individuals scoring low on the TI, we have more evidence of construct validity.

Additionally, studies investigating the relation between the TI and professionally developed measures of our hypothesized teamwork construct could be conducted. Positive relationships would be expected. Experiments might also be designed to determine if high scoring individuals on the TI behave in ways predictably different from those scoring low. If our anticipated results are found, we have even more evidence of TI construct validity. As you can see, we have suggested a variety of procedures that could be adopted to test our hypothesis that the Teamwork Inventory effectively measures the ability to work with others.

Our example highlights the major steps for implementing a construct validation study as follows:

1. The construct must be carefully defined and hypotheses formed concerning the relationships between the construct and other variables.

2. A measure hypothesized to assess the construct is developed.

3. Studies testing the hypothesized relationships (formed in step 1) between the constructed measure and other, relevant variables are conducted.[30]

Since construct validation may be conducted when no available measure exists, the "thing" or "construct" being validated requires a number of measurement operations. Results of studies such as the following are particularly helpful in construct validation:

1. Intercorrelations among the measure's parts should show if the parts cluster into one or more groupings. The nature of these groupings should be consistent with how the construct is defined.

2. Parts of the measure belonging to the same grouping should be internally consistent or reliable.

3. Different measures assessing the same construct as our developed measure should be related with the developed measure. Measures assessing different constructs that are not hypothesized to be related to the construct of interest should be unrelated.

4. Content validity studies should show how experts have judged the manner in which parts of the measure were developed and their sampling of the job content domain.[31]

You can probably see from our illustration that construct validity is a process of accumulating empirical evidence of what a selection measure measures. The more evidence we collect, the more assurance we have in our judgments that a measure is really doing what was intended. As such, construct validation represents a much broader definition of validity than we might find in a single criterion-related or content validation study. Through accumulated evidence (that may come from other validation strategies, literature reviews, controlled experiments, etc.), we can answer what and how well a selection measure assesses what it measures. At this point construct validation is still a developing issue.[32] There is not complete, uniform agreement on the exact methods the strategy entails. Future clarification of the strategy will also clarify its application.

Empirical Considerations in Criterion-Related Validity Strategies

Even if we have conducted content validation studies on a selection measure, at some point, we will probably want to answer two important questions:

1. Is there a relationship between applicants' responses to our selection measure and their performance on the job?

2. If so, is the relationship strong enough to warrant the measure's use in employment decision making?

Questions such as these imply the need for statistical or empirical methods for determining validity, that is, criterion-related validity. Because of their importance, we review some of the empirical methods and issues most commonly encountered in conducting criterion-related validation research.

Correlation

Computing Validity Coefficients   One of the most frequent terms you will see in reading selection research studies is the term *validity coefficient*. Basically speaking, a validity coefficient is simply an index that summarizes the degree of relationship between a predictor and criterion. Where does the validity coefficient come from? What does it mean? To answer these questions, let's refer to an example. Consider for a moment that a predictive validity study is being conducted. We want to know if a mechanical ability test is useful in predicting the job performance of operative workers. During a one-week employment period, we administered the test to 50 job applicants. No employment decisions were based on the test scores. Six months later, we can identify 20 individuals who were hired and are sill employed.[33] (In practice, we would want to have more than just 20 people in our validation study. Ideally, we would have at least several hundred people on whom both predictor and criterion data are available. Because of space considerations, we have used a small sample to *illustrate* the data in the accompanying tables and exhibits.) As a measure of job performance, we ask their supervisor to judge their performance using a performance appraisal rating form. Total scores on the appraisal form are calculated, and they represent employee job performance. Thus for each employee we have a pair of scores: (a) scores on the mechanical ability test and (b) their six-month performance appraisal scores. These example data are shown in Table 5.3.

A scattergram or scatterplot is initially made of data like those in Table 5.3 for visual inspection of any possible relationships between predictor and criterion variables. An example scattergram of our data is shown in Exhibit 5.7. Each point in the graph represents a plot of the *pair* of scores for a single employee. For instance, employee Q has a test score of 79 and a performance rating of 91. Although a scattergram is useful for estimating the existence and direction of a relationship, it really does not help us specify the *degree* of relationship between our selection measure and job performance. For this purpose, a more precise approach is to calculate an index that will summarize the degree of any relationship that

TABLE 5.3		

HYPOTHETICAL TEST SCORE AND JOB PERFORMANCE RATING DATA COLLECTED ON 20 OPERATIVE EMPLOYEES

Employee ID	Mechanical Ability Test Score	Job Performance Rating
A	86	74
B	97	91
C	51	67
D	41	31
E	60	52
F	70	70
G	73	74
H	79	59
I	46	44
J	67	61
K	71	52
L	88	75
M	81	92
N	40	22
O	53	74
P	77	74
Q	79	91
R	84	83
S	91	91
T	90	72

NOTE: **Mechanical Ability Test Score** = Number of items correct on a 100-item test taken at time of employment. **Job Performance Rating** = Supervisory rating given after six months' employment, where 1 = poor performance and 100 = outstanding performance.

might exist. Most often, the Pearson product-moment or simple correlation coefficient (r) is used to provide that index. The correlation coefficient, or in the context of personnel selection the "validity coefficient," summarizes the relationship between our predictor and criterion. Often, the validity coefficient is represented as r_{xy} where r represents the degree of relationship between X (the predictor) and Y (the criterion). Other types of correlation coefficients (such as phi and biserial) may serve as validity coefficients, but the Pearson is the most common.

There are two important elements of a validity coefficient: (a) its sign and (b) its magnitude. The sign (either + or –) indicates the *direction* of a relationship; its magnitude indicates the *strength* of association between a predictor and criterion. The coefficient itself can range from –1.00 to .00 to +1.00. As the coefficient approaches +1.00, there is a *positive* relationship between performance on a selection measure and a criterion. That is, high scores on a predictor are associated with high scores on a criterion and low scores on the predictor are related with low criterion scores. As the coefficient moves toward –1.00, however, there is a *negative* or inverse relation between scores on the predictor and criterion. But, as the index moves toward .00, then any relationship between the two variables

EXHIBIT 5.7	HYPOTHETICAL SCATTERGRAM OF MECHANICAL ABILITY TEST SCORES AND JOB PERFORMANCE RATINGS FOR 20 OPERATIVE WORKERS

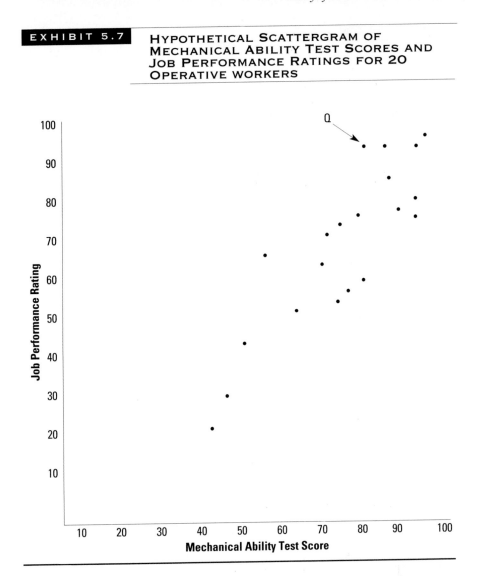

decreases. When the validity coefficient is not statistically significant or is equal to .00, then no relationship exists between a predictor and criterion. *If a validity coefficient is not statistically significant, then the selection measure is not a valid predictor of a criterion.* These predictor/criterion relations are summarized in Exhibit 5.8.

Using simple correlation, suppose we find that the validity coefficient for our example data in Exhibit 5.7 is .80. Next, after consulting the appropriate statistical table (usually found in psychological measurement or statistics books), we test the coefficient to see if there is a true or statistically significant relationship between our test and job performance or if the correlation arose simply because of chance. Our significance test will help us determine the probability that the relationship identified for our *sample* of 20 job applicants can be expected to be found only by chance in the *population* of job applicants from which our sample

EXHIBIT 5.8	DESCRIPTION OF POSSIBLE PREDICTOR/CRITERION RELATIONSHIPS OF A VALIDITY COEFFICIENT

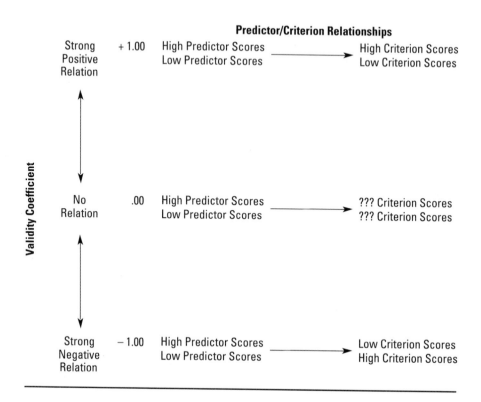

Predictor/Criterion Relationships

Strong Positive Relation	+ 1.00	High Predictor Scores Low Predictor Scores	→ High Criterion Scores Low Criterion Scores
No Relation	.00	High Predictor Scores Low Predictor Scores	→ ??? Criterion Scores ??? Criterion Scores
Strong Negative Relation	− 1.00	High Predictor Scores Low Predictor Scores	→ Low Criterion Scores High Criterion Scores

Validity Coefficient

came. Usually, if the probability is equal to or less than .05, it is concluded that there is a statistically significant relationship between a predictor and criterion. That is, a true relationship exists between the predictor and criterion for the population of job applicants. In our example, assume we find that our validity coefficient of .80 is statistically significant (usually written as "$r = .80, p \leq .05$"). A significant result suggests that if we conducted our study in the same manner 100 times, in 95 of these we would find a similar relation between our predictor and criterion. In only five cases, we would not. Thus we are reasonably confident that the relation did not arise because of chance, and a dependable relationship exists. We can now conclude that our test is valid for predicting job performance.

Interpreting Validity Coefficients   Once we have found a statistically significant validity coefficient, we might well ask, "What precisely does the coefficient mean?" There are several approaches we can take to answer this question.

   When we look at the distribution of our criterion scores shown in Table 5.3, one fact is evident. Some employees perform better than others; some do very well, others not so well. If our predictor is useful, it should help in explaining some of these differences in performance. By squaring the validity coefficient (r^2_{xy}), we can obtain an index that indicates our test's ability to account for these individual performance differences. This index, called the *coefficient of determination, represents the percentage of variance in the criterion that can be explained by variance associated with the predictor.* In our case, the coefficient of determination is .64 ($.80^2$), indicating that 64 percent of the differences (or variance) in individuals' job performance can be explained by their differences in test scores. Relatively speaking, our validity coefficient of .80 (or coefficient of determination of .64) for this sample of 20 employees is high. Only on relatively infrequent occasions do validity coefficients, especially for a single predictor, much exceed .50; a more common size of coefficient is in the range of .30 to .50. Thus coefficients of determination for many validity coefficients will range from roughly .10 to .25.

Another index that has been reported in older validation research studies is the *index of forecasting efficiency.*[34] The index shows the percentage improvement in selection by using a valid predictor as opposed to a non-valid one. It is computed from the formula

$$\text{Forecasting Efficiency} = 1 - \sqrt{1 - r^2_{xy}} \, ,$$

where r_{xy} = the validity coefficient. For instance, if a test has a validity of .50, the index of forecasting efficiency would indicate that the valid test performs roughly 13 percent better than a nonvalid test.

In addition to the coefficient of determination and the index of forecasting efficiency, *expectancy tables* and *charts* can be used. Since expectancy tables are frequently employed as an aid in interpreting prediction, we save our discussion of them for the next session.

Finally, *utility analysis* can also be used. Its computation is far more complex than the methods we just described. Yet, it offers, perhaps, the ultimate interpretation of a valid predictor and its impact in a selection program for managers in an organization. By translating the usefulness of a validity coefficient into dollars, utility analysis adds an economic interpretation to the meaning of a validity coefficient. Because of its current importance in the field of HR selection, we devote a later section of this chapter to a discussion of utility analysis.

Prediction

A statistically significant validity coefficient is helpful in showing that for a *group* of persons a test is related to job success. However, the coefficient itself does not help us in predicting the job success of *individuals.* Yet the prediction of an individual's likelihood of job success is precisely what an employment manager wants. For individual prediction purposes, we can turn to the use of linear regression and expectancy charts to aid us in selection decision making. These should only be developed for those predictors that have proven to have a statistically significant relationship with the criterion. In using these methods, a practitioner is simply taking predictor information, such as test scores, and predicting individuals' job success, such as rated job performance, from this information. For each method, one key assumption is that we are utilizing information collected on a past or present group of employees and making predictions for a *future* group of employees.

Linear Regression   Basically, linear regression involves the determination of how changes in criterion scores are functionally related to changes in predictor scores. A regression equation is developed that mathematically describes the functional relationship between the predictor and criterion. Once the regression equation is known, criterion scores can then be predicted from predictor information. In general, there are two common types of linear regression you are likely to come across: *simple* and *multiple* regression.

Simple Regression   In simple regression, there is only one predictor and one criterion. To illustrate, let's refer back to Exhibit 5.7 that depicted the relationship between mechanical ability test scores and job performance ratings for 20 operative workers. In Exhibit 5.9, we show the same scattergram except that we have also fitted a special line to the plotted scores. This line is called the *regression line*. It summarizes the relationship between the test and the job performance ratings. The line has been fitted statistically so that it is at a minimum distance from each of the data points in the figure. Thus the regression line represents the line of "best fit."

   In addition to depicting the fit of the regression line graphically, we can also describe it mathematically in the form of an equation called the *regression* or *prediction equation*. This equation takes the form of the algebraic expression for a straight line, that is,

$$\hat{Y} = a + bX,$$

where

   $\hat{Y}$ = predicted score of the criterion variable,
   a = intercept value of the regression line,
   b = slope of the regression line or regression weight, and
   X = score on the predictor variable.

   The data points around the regression line and validity coefficient are closely related. The validity coefficient represents how well the regression line fits the data. As the validity coefficient approaches + or – 1.00, the data points move closer to the line. If a validity coefficient equals + or – 1.00, then the data points will fall exactly on the regression line itself, and prediction will be perfect. However, as the coefficient moves away from + or – 1.00 (toward .00), the points will be distributed farther from the regression line, and more error will exist in our predictions.

   To illustrate the role of the regression line and regression equation in prediction, let's look further at our example. The regression line in Exhibit 5.9 is represented by the equation $\hat{Y} = 3.02 + .91(X)$ where $\hat{Y}$ is predicted job performance (our criterion) and X is a score on our mechanical ability test administered to applicants for the operative job. The intercept (3.02) is the value where the

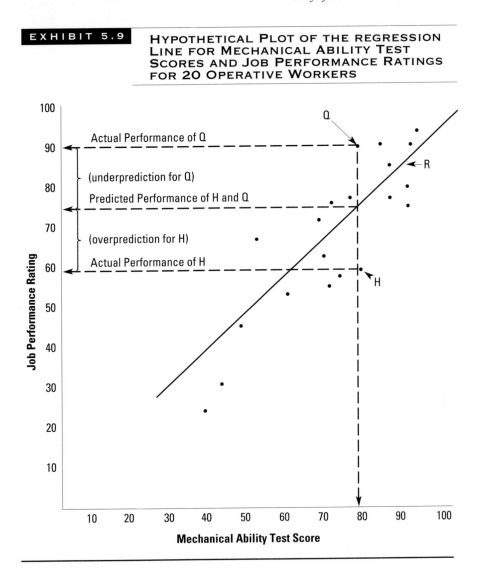

EXHIBIT 5.9 HYPOTHETICAL PLOT OF THE REGRESSION LINE FOR MECHANICAL ABILITY TEST SCORES AND JOB PERFORMANCE RATINGS FOR 20 OPERATIVE WORKERS

regression line crosses the *Y*-axis. It represents an applicant's predicted job performance if his or her test score were zero. Finally, the slope of the line is represented by .91. The slope is often called a *regression weight* or *regression coefficient* because it is multiplied times the score on the predictor (our mechanical ability test). The slope or regression weight represents the amount of change in the criterion variable per one unit change in the predictor. Thus for every one unit increase in applicants' test scores, we would expect a .91 increase in job performance. A positive validity coefficient indicates a positive slope of the regression line (see Exhibit 5.9) and, hence, a positive regression weight. A negative validity coefficient means a negative slope and negative regression weight.

Once we have our regression line, we can use it to predict our criterion scores. For example, if an applicant applying for our operative job is given the test, we would locate the score on the X-axis, move upward to the regression line, and then move across to the Y-axis to find his or her predicted job performance score. As you can see in Exhibit 5.9, individual R who has a test score of 84 is predicted to have a job performance rating of approximately 80. Since individual R actually has a performance rating of 83, our prediction is close. As there is not a perfect 1.00 correlation between the test and job performance, there will be some error in prediction. For instance, persons H and Q both scored 79 on the test, but notice our predictions have error. For person H, we would *overpredict* performance. With a test score of 79, performance is predicted to be 73, but it is actually only 59. Conversely, for person Q, performance would be *underpredicted*. With the same test score (79), predicted performance is 73 but actual performance is 91. Even though errors in prediction are made and even though some may appear rather large, they will be smaller for the *group* of persons than if the predictor information and regression line is not used and only random guesses (for example, with an invalid predictor) are made.

Rather than using the regression line, we can use our regression equation to predict job performance. By substituting a person's test score for X in our regression equation, multiplying the test score times the regression coefficient (.91), and then adding it to the constant value (3.02), we can derive a predicted job performance score. Thus for our test score of 86, we would predict subsequent rated job performance to be equal to 81. Our calculation would be as follows:

$$\hat{Y} = 3.02 + .91(X)$$

$$\hat{Y} = 3.02 + .91(86)$$

$$\hat{Y} = 3.02 + 78.26$$

$$\hat{Y} = 81.28 \text{ or } 81.$$

As we saw in our preceding example, because our test is not perfectly related to job performance, we will have some error in our predictions. Only if all of our data points fall precisely on the regression line (r_{xy} = + or – 1.00) will error not be present. In making employment decisions, we must take this degree of error into account. The *standard error of estimate* is a useful index for summarizing the degree of error in prediction.[35] It is determined from the following equation:

$$sd_{y \cdot x} = sd_y \sqrt{1 - r^2_{xy}},$$

where

$sd_{y \cdot x}$ = standard error of estimate,
sd_y = standard deviation of criterion scores Y, and
r_{xy} = validity coefficient for predictor X and criterion Y.

The standard error of estimate can be interpreted as the standard deviation of the errors made in predicting a criterion from a selection measure. It is expected that, on the average, 68 percent of *actual* criterion scores will fall within

±1 standard error of *predicted* criterion scores, and 95 percent of actual criterion scores will fall within ±1.96 standard errors of predicted criterion scores. For example, assume the standard deviation of our job performance ratings is 7.5. Also, assume that the validity of our test designed to predict these ratings is .80. The standard error of estimate would be computed as follows:

$$sd_{y \cdot x} = 7.5\sqrt{1 - .80^2}$$

$$sd_{y \cdot x} = 7.5\sqrt{.36}$$

$$sd_{y \cdot x} = 4.50.$$

Assume that a person scores 86 on the test. Using the regression equation we discussed in the previous section, we calculate that all persons scoring 86 on the test would be predicted to have a job performance rating of 81. Notice that we have a *predicted* level of job success, but how confident can we be that individuals' *actual* job success will approximate the predicted level? The standard error of estimate can help us. Basically, it enables us to establish a range of predicted criterion scores within which we would expect a percentage of actual criterion scores to fall. For applicants with a predicted performance rating of 81, we would expect, on the average, 68 percent of them to have *actual* performance ratings between 77 and 86 (81 ± 4.50). For this same performance level, we would also expect 95 percent of the applicants' actual job performance ratings to fall between 72 and 90 [81 ± (1.96 × 4.50)].

Multiple Regression   In addition to simple regression, *multiple* regression can also be used to predict criterion scores for job applicants. Whereas the simple regression model assumes only *one* predictor, multiple regression assumes *two or more* predictors are being used to predict a criterion. If the additional predictors explain more of the individual differences among job applicants' job performance than would have been explained by a single predictor alone, our ability to predict a criterion will be enhanced. As our ability to predict improves (that is, validity increases), fewer errors will be made in prediction of applicants' subsequent job performance.

The general model for multiple regression is as follows:

$$\hat{Y} = a + b_1 X_1 + b_2 X_2 + \cdots + b_n X_n,$$

where

$\hat{Y}$ = predicted criterion scores,
a = intercept value of the regression line,
b_1, b_2, b_n = regression weights for predictors X_1, X_2, and X_n, and
X_1, X_2, X_n = scores on predictors X_1, X_2, and X_n.

If, for example, we had administered the mechanical ability test and a biographical data questionnaire and if these two predictors are related to our job performance measure, we could derive a multiple regression equation just as we did with simple regression. However, in this case, our equation would have two regression weights rather than one. Suppose our multiple regression equation looked as follows:

$$\hat{Y} = 3.18 + .77X_1 + .53X_2,$$

where

$\hat{Y}$ = predicted criterion scores (job performance measure),
3.18 = intercept value of the regression line (a),
.77 = regression weight of the mechanical ability test,
.53 = regression weight of the biographical data questionnaire,
X_1 = score on the mechanical ability test, and
X_2 = score on the biographical data questionnaire.

In order to obtain a predicted job performance score, we would simply substitute an individual's two predictor scores in the equation, multiply the two scores times their regression weights, sum the products, and add the intercept value to obtain predicted performance. For instance, suppose an individual scored 84 on the mechanical ability test and 30 on the biographical data questionnaire. The predicted job performance score would be obtained as follows:

$$\hat{Y} = 3.18 + .77(84) + .53(30),$$

$$\hat{Y} = 3.18 + 64.68 + 15.90,$$

$$\hat{Y} = 83.76 \text{ or } 84$$

The multiple regression approach has also been called a compensatory model. It is called compensatory because different combinations of predictor scores can be combined to yield the same predicted criterion score. Thus if an applicant were to do rather poorly on one measure, he or she could compensate for this low score by performing better on the other measure. Examples of compensatory selection models include those frequently used as a basis for making admission decisions in some professional graduate schools.

Cross-Validation   Whenever simple or multiple regression equations are used, they are developed to optimally predict the criterion for an existing group of persons. But when the equations are applied to a new group, the predictive accuracy of the equations will most always fall. This "shrinkage" in predictive accuracy is because the new group is not identical to the one on which the equations were developed. Because of the possibility of error, it is important that the equations be tested for shrinkage *prior* to their implementation in selection decision making. This checkout process is called *cross-validation*. There are two general methods of cross-validation: (a) *empirical* and (b) *formula* estimation. With *empirical* cross-validation, there are several approaches that can be taken. In general, a regression equation developed on one sample of individuals is applied to another sample of persons. If the regression equation developed on one sample can predict scores in the other sample, then the regression equation is "cross-validated." One common procedure of empirical cross-validation involves the following steps:

1. A group of persons on whom predictor and criterion data are available is *randomly* divided into two groups.

2. A regression equation is developed on one of the groups (called the "weighting group").

3. Next, the equation developed on the weighting group is used to predict the criterion for the other group (called the "holdout group").

4. Predicted criterion scores are obtained for each individual in the holdout group.

5. For persons in the holdout group, *predicted* criterion scores are then correlated with their *actual* criterion scores. A high, statistically significant correlation coefficient indicates that the regression equation is useful for individuals other than those on whom the equation was developed.

As an alternative to empirical cross-validation, *formula* cross-validation can be used. Under this procedure, only one sample of persons is used. Special formulas are employed to predict the amount of shrinkage that would occur if a regression equation were applied to a similar sample of persons. With knowledge of (a) the number of predictors, (b) the original multiple correlation coefficient, and (c) the number of people on which the original multiple correlation was based, the *predicted* multiple correlation coefficient can be derived. This predicted multiple correlation coefficient estimates the coefficient that would be obtained if the predictors were administered to a new but similar sample of persons and the multiple correlation statistically computed. The obvious advantage to these formulas is that a new sample of persons does not have to be taken. Philippe Cattin has summarized these formulas and the circumstances in which they are appropriate.[36] In addition Kevin Murphy has provided additional evidence on the accuracy of such formulas.[37] In general, he has concluded that formula cross-validation is more efficient, simpler to use, and no less accurate than empirical cross-validation.

Whatever the approach, cross-validation is *essential*. It should be routinely implemented whenever regression equations are used in prediction.

Expectancy Tables and Charts   An expectancy *table* is simply a table of numbers which shows the probability that a person with a particular predictor score will achieve a defined level of success. An expectancy *chart* presents essentially the same data except that it provides a visual summarization of the relationship between a predictor and criterion.[38] As we suggested earlier, expectancy tables and charts are useful for communicating the meaning of a validity coefficient. In addition, they are helpful as an aid in predicting the probability of success of job applicants. As outlined by Charles Lawshe and Michael Balma, the construction of expectancy tables and charts is basically a five-step process:

1. Individuals on whom criterion data are available are divided into two groups, Superior Performers and Others. Roughly, half of the individuals are in each group.

2. For each predictor score, frequencies of the number of employees in the Superior and Other groups are determined.

3. The predictor score distribution is divided into fifths.

4. The number and percentage of individuals in the Superior group and Other group are determined.

5. An expectancy chart that depicts these percentages is then prepared.[39]

To illustrate the development of an expectancy table and chart, let's go through a brief example. First, let's assume that we have the test scores from 65 machinists who took the Machinist Aptitude Test, as well as their most recent performance appraisal ratings. For our purposes, assume we have determined that individuals with a performance rating of 9 or more are Superior performers while those with scores of 8 or less are classified in the Other group. A Pearson product-moment correlation between the sets of test scores and appraisal data for our 65 machinists indicates there is a statistically significant validity coefficient of .45 between the test scores and performance ratings. Exhibit 5.10 shows the scattergram of the test scores plotted against the performance ratings. The horizontal lines represent roughly equal fifths of the distribution of predictor scores. Table 5.4 is the expectancy table developed from the plotted data. Basically, it shows the chances out of 100 of an individual's being rated superior on the job, given a range of Machinist Aptitude Test scores. For example, persons scoring between 30 and 34 have roughly an 85 percent chance of being rated superior while those scoring between 1 and 6 have only a 33 percent chance. The individual expectancy chart, Exhibit 5.11 summarizes these same results in a graphic fashion.

As you can see in Exhibits 5.11 and 5.12, there are two types of expectancy charts: (a) *individual* and (b) *institutional*. The *individual* chart shows the probability that a person will achieve a particular level of performance given his or her score on the test. Thus the individual chart permits individual prediction.

The *institutional* chart indicates what will happen within an organization if all applicants above a particular *minimum* score are hired. For example, in our study of machinists, 77 percent of the applicants with a minimum score of 23 on the Machinist Aptitude Test will be superior; 64 percent of those with a minimum score of 7 will be rated superior. By using the institutional chart, one can estimate what will happen in the organization if various passing or cutoff scores are used for a selection measure.

EXHIBIT 5.10	HYPOTHETICAL SCATTERGRAM OF SCORES BY 65 MACHINISTS ON THE MACHINIST APTITUDE TEST PLOTTED AGAINST JOB PERFORMANCE RATING

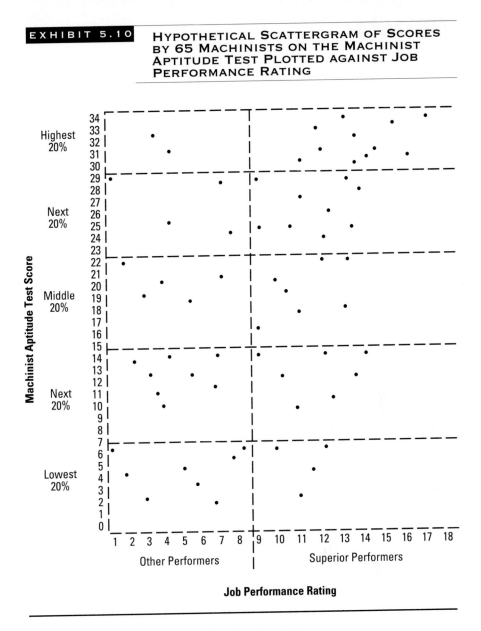

Factors Affecting the Size of Validity Coefficients

Robert Guion has pointed out that the size of a validity coefficient is dependent on a variety of factors.[40] Any number of factors may have an effect, but four seem to be predominant in determining the magnitude of a validity coefficient.

Reliability of Criterion and Predictor Earlier we described the intimate interrelationship between reliability and validity. The point is that to the extent a predictor or criterion has error, it will be unreliable. The more error present,

TABLE 5.4				

PERCENTAGE OF MACHINISTS RATED AS SUPERIOR FOR VARIOUS MACHINIST APTITUDE TEST SCORE RATINGS

Machinist Aptitude Test Score Range	Other Performers	Superior Performers	Total	% Superior Performers
Top 20%:				
30–34	2	11	13	85
Next 20%:				
23–29	4	9	13	69
Middle 20%:				
15–22	5	7	12	58
Next 20%:				
7–14	8	7	15	47
Low 20%				
1–6	8	4	12	33
Total	27	38	65	

EXHIBIT 5.11		

HYPOTHETICAL INDIVIDUAL EXPECTANCY CHART SHOWING CHANCES IN 100 OF BEING RATED SUPERIOR ON THE JOB OF MACHINIST FOR VARIOUS TEST SCORE RANGES ON THE MACHINIST APTITUDE TEST

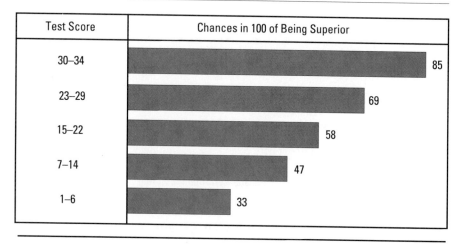

Test Score	Chances in 100 of Being Superior
30–34	85
23–29	69
15–22	58
7–14	47
1–6	33

the more unreliable these variables will be. *Any unreliability in* either *the criterion or predictor will lower the correlation or validity coefficient computed between the two.* If *both* predictor and criterion variables have measurement error, error is compounded and the validity coefficient will be lowered even further. Because of the negative effect of lowered reliability on validity, we should strive for high reliability of *both* the predictor and criterion to get an accurate assessment of what true validity may be.

EXHIBIT 5.12	HYPOTHETICAL INSTITUTIONAL EXPECTANCY CHART SHOWING PERCENTAGE OF PERSONS ABOVE VARIOUS MINIMUM SCORE CATEGORIES ON MACHINIST APTITUDE TEST WHO CAN BE EXPECTED TO BE CONSIDERED SUPERIOR IN THE JOB OF MACHINIST

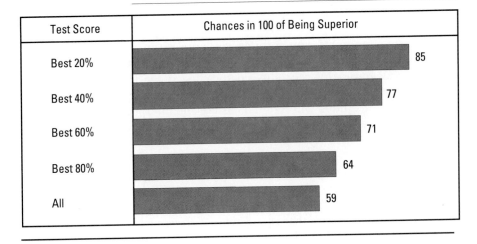

Test Score	Chances in 100 of Being Superior
Best 20%	85
Best 40%	77
Best 60%	71
Best 80%	64
All	59

If the validity coefficient is restricted or attenuated by unreliability of the predictor or criterion, it is possible to make statistical adjustments to see what validity would be if the variables had perfect reliability. This adjustment is referred to as *correction for attenuation.* Although unreliability in predictor scores can be corrected, in HR selection applications we have to use predictor data as they normally exist. Selection decisions are made with the actual predictor information collected. Thus correction for attenuation in predictor scores is not made typically. On the other hand, correction for unreliability in criterion data is made in selection using the following formula:

$$\hat{r}_{xy} = \frac{r_{xy}}{\sqrt{r_{yy}}}$$

where

$\hat{r}_{xy}$ = (corrected) validity coefficient of the predictor if the criterion were measured without error,

r_{xy} = correlation between the predictor and criterion (that is, the validity coefficient), and

r_{yy} = reliability coefficient of the criterion.[41]

For example, assume the validity of a test is .35 and reliability of the criterion is .49. Substituting in the formula shows that with a perfectly reliable criterion, the correlation between the test and criterion would be .50, a respectable validity coefficient.

Correction for attenuation can be used to evaluate a predictor when we have a criterion that may be highly relevant for our use but has low reliability. In this situation, we will have a clearer picture of the true value of the predictor. Correction can also suggest if the search for another predictor may be worthwhile. For instance, if our original validity coefficient is very low, say .20, but correction shows it to be high, say .70 or higher, a search for better predictors of our criterion will likely be fruitless. Also, we may have avoided throwing out a valuable predictor.

In using the correction formula, accurate estimates of reliability are essential. From our discussion of reliability, we saw that many factors can affect the magnitude of reliability coefficients. If the formula is used with *under*estimates of true criterion reliability, misleading *over*estimates of corrected predictor validity will result. Thus use and interpret the results of reliability correction formulas with caution when accurate estimates of reliability are unknown.

Restriction of Range　One of the important assumptions in calculating a validity coefficient is that there is variance among individuals' scores on the criterion and predictor. By variance, we simply mean that people have different scores on these measures, that is, individual differences. When we calculate a validity coefficient, we are asking, Do these predictor and criterion score differences vary or move together? That is, are systematic differences among people on the criterion associated with their differences on the predictor? If there is little variance or range in individuals' scores for one or both variables, then the magnitude of the validity coefficient will be lowered. Smaller differences on predictor or criterion scores means that it will be more difficult for the predictor to identify differences among people as measured by the criterion. Thus lowered validity will occur.

Restriction in range is the term used to describe situations in which variance in scores on selection measures has been reduced. In selection practice, there are a number of circumstances in which range restriction can occur. For instance, in a predictive validation study, suppose an employer uses the test being validated (or other devices correlated with the test) as the basis for selection decision making. Later, when individuals' test scores are correlated with their criterion scores, the validity coefficient will be curtailed. Range restriction occurs because individuals scoring low on the test were not hired. Their test scores could not be used in computing the validity coefficient because criterion data were unavailable.

In addition, criterion scores may also be restricted. Restriction of criterion scores may occur because turnover, transfer, or termination of employees has taken place prior to the collection of criterion data.

From our examples, you can see that restriction of scores can happen for either predictor, criterion, or both variables. Any form of restriction will lower computed validity. What we need to know is what validity would be if restriction had not occurred. Fortunately, a number of formulas have been developed to make the necessary statistical corrections in selection practice.[42] For example, the formula for estimating the true validity when restriction of range has occurred on a predictor is

$$\hat{r}_{xy} = \frac{r_{xy_r}\left(\dfrac{SD_u}{SD_r}\right)}{\sqrt{1-(r_{xy_r})+(r_{xy_r})^2\left[\dfrac{(SD_u)^2}{(SD_r)^2}\right]}},$$

where

$\hat{r}_{xy}$ = estimated validity if restriction had not occurred,

r_{xy_r} = validity coefficient computed on restricted scores,

SD_u = standard deviation of predictor scores from unrestricted group, and

SD_r = standard deviation of predictor scores from restricted group.

As an example, assume the standard deviation (a measure of individual differences) of applicants' scores on a test was 10. After making selection decisions using the test, the standard deviation of applicants' scores who were hired is 2. The validity coefficient computed for those hired is .20. Using the formula, we can estimate the test's validity if all individuals had been hired, and there was no restriction in the range of test scores. That is,

$$r_{xy} = \frac{(.20)\dfrac{10}{2}}{\sqrt{1-(.20)^2 +(.20)^2\left[(10)^2 /(2)^2\right]}} = \frac{1.00}{1.40} = .71.$$

The estimated validity of .71 is considerably higher than our original validity of .20. Thus range restriction had considerable effect. Table 5.5 illustrates the effect of various levels of range restriction for three hypothetical validity coefficients (.20, .50, and .80) found for a group having restricted predictor scores. Entries in the table were computed from the formula. These entries show estimated validity coefficients under various range restriction conditions. Where range restriction is low (that is, standard deviation of unrestricted predictor scores approximates that of restricted scores), computed validity is very close to estimated validity. But where range restriction is high (see, for example, 10/2 in Table 5.5), estimated validity on unrestricted scores differs substantially from validity computed on restricted scores.

Criterion Contamination   If scores on a criterion are influenced by variables other than the predictor, then criterion scores may be contaminated. The effect of contamination is to alter the magnitude of the validity coefficient. For instance, one criterion frequently used in validation studies is a performance evaluation rating. We may want to know if performance on a selection measure is associated with performance on the job. However, performance ratings are sometimes subject to being contaminated or biased by extraneous variables such as gender and ethnicity of ratees or raters or by the job tenure of persons being

| TABLE 5.5 | HYPOTHETICAL DATA ILLUSTRATING THE EFFECT OF RESTRICTION OF RANGE IN PREDICTOR SCORES ON TEST VALIDITY |

		Predictor Validity Using Restricted Predictor Scores		
	SD_u/SD_r	.20	.50	.80
	High 10/2	.71	.94	.99
Restriction in Range	10/4	.45	.82	.96
of Predictor Scores	10/6	.32	.69	.91
	10/8	.25	.55	.85
	Low 10/10	.20	.50	.80

NOTE: SD_u/SD_r = Standard deviation of unrestricted predictor scores/standard deivation of restricted predictor scores. Entries in the cells of the table represent estimated validity coefficients for various levels of range restriction in predictor scores.

rated. If criterion ratings are influenced by variables that have nothing to do with actual job performance, then our obtained validity coefficient will be affected. In some cases, the validity coefficient will be spuriously high; in others, spuriously low. Moreover, it is not always possible to know in advance the direction of these effects.

Consider another example. One of the authors was recently engaged in a validation study of a selection measure for bank proof machine operators. A proof machine is used by operators to encode magnetic numbers on the bottom of checks so they can be processed by a computer. The bank kept meticulous records of the number of checks processed by operators for specific time periods. Thus it appeared that a sound behavioral measure of performance was available that could be used as a criterion in the validation study. However, further analysis showed that even though the proof machines looked the same externally, some of the machines had different internal components. These different components permitted faster check processing. Our apparently "good" criterion measure was contaminated. Rather than solely measuring differences in operators' performance, the productivity measure was also tapping differences in equipment. Without proper adjustments, the measure would be useless as a criterion.

Another classic example of criterion contamination is when "total dollar sales" is being used as a criterion in a validation study of tests designed to measure traveling salespersons' selling ability. Suppose there are differences in the types of geographical territories sales personnel must work. Some territories contain long-term customers so that all the salesperson has to do is take an order. In other, less mature territories, sales are much more difficult to achieve. A salesperson must really be able to sell in order to make a sale. Without some adjustment in the total dollar sales measure, criterion contamination will be present. Sales performance differences, as measured by total dollar sales, will be due more to territory assignment than to selling ability. The result will be a misleading validation study.

When contaminating effects are known, they should be controlled either by statistical procedures such as partial correlation, by the research design of the validation study itself (for example, including only those employees in a validation study that have the same length of employment), or by adjustments to criterion data such as the computation of ratios. Again, the reason for controlling contaminating variables is to obtain a more accurate reading of the true relationship between a predictor and a criterion.

Violation of Statistical Assumptions   Among others, one important assumption of a Pearson correlation is that there is a *linear*, or straight-line relationship between a predictor and a criterion. If the relationship is nonlinear, the validity coefficient will give an underestimate of the true relationship between the two variables. For example, in Exhibit 5.13, four scattergrams summarizing various relations between a selection measure and criterion are shown. Case 1 shows a situation in which there is a linear or straight-line relationship. A Pearson correlation coefficient would be appropriate for representing the relationship. However, the other three cases show nonlinear associations; in these, the Pearson would be inappropriate. In Case 4, for instance, if a Pearson correlation were calculated on these data, the correlation would be equal to .00. Yet, we can see that there is a relationship. Low as well as high test performance is associated with high criterion scores. We know that a relation exists in Case 4, but our Pearson statistic will not detect it; other analyses are called for. If we had simply computed the correlation without studying the scattergram, we could have drawn an incorrect conclusion. Prior to computing a validity coefficient, a scattergram should *always* be plotted and studied for the possibility of nonlinear association.

Utility Analysis

Picture yourself for a moment as a HR manager at a large manufacturing plant. Suppose you are looking at the results of a test validation study that shows a statistically significant validity coefficient of .50 for a test developed to predict the job performance of production workers in the plant. Obviously, you are excited about the results, since they suggest that the test can be used as an effective screening tool for production workers. Tomorrow, you will be meeting with the executive staff of the plant, and you have been asked to summarize the results and implications of the validation study. As you consider who will be at the meeting and what you are going to say, it becomes painfully obvious that the individuals in attendance (vice president of operations, vice president of accounting, etc.) are simply not going to understand the meaning of a validity coefficient. Thus, you find yourself thinking, "What can I say so they will understand what this validity coefficient means?"

The situation we have just described is not that unusual. Frequently, those of us working in the field of HR selection find ourselves in situations where it is very difficult to translate our research findings into practical terms understood by top management. This problem is particularly compounded when validation studies are being conducted and communicated. Few top-level managers outside of HR management understand what a validity coefficient is much less what it means. Yet, we have to find a common terminology to communicate this meaning if we are going to compete with other departments in our organization for

EXHIBIT 5.13 APPROPRIATENESS OF PEARSON *r* FOR VARIOUS SELECTION MEASURE–CRITERION RELATIONSHIPS

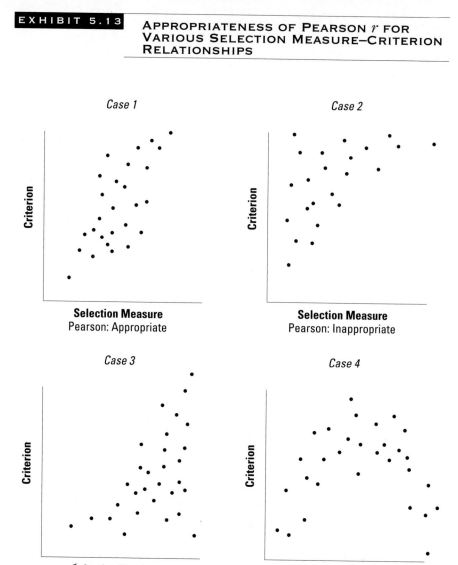

Case 1
Criterion
Selection Measure
Pearson: Appropriate

Case 2
Criterion
Selection Measure
Pearson: Inappropriate

Case 3
Criterion
Selection Measure
Pearson: Inappropriate

Case 4
Criterion
Selection Measure
Pearson: Inappropriate

scarce resources. It is also important that we find a means to translate our research findings into concepts and terms that management can understand and deal with if we hope to see the results of our work implemented.

As you think about a common terminology that will be understood by most managers, you will probably conclude that a dollar-and-cents terminology is a practical option for communicating results. Thus if we can translate the results of our validation work into economic dollar-and-cents terms, we will probably receive the attention and understanding we want from other managers.

A Definition of Utility Analysis   The concept of *utility analysis* can be used to translate the results of a validation study into dollar-payoff terms that can be understood by managers. Utility analysis summarizes the overall usefulness of a selection measure or selection system. *Using dollar-and-cents terms, it shows the degree to which use of a selection measure improves the quality of individuals selected over what would have happened if the measure had not been used.*[43]

Some Preliminary Work on Utility   Although the validity coefficient, coefficient of determination, and index of forecasting efficiency have been used for many years with selection measures, these statistical procedures do not define the utility of valid selection measures. None of these statistics relate to the economic value of a selection measure or recognize that a measure's usefulness depends on the nature of the situation in which it is employed.[44] Early work by H. C. Taylor and J. T. Russell is often recognized as the initial step in the development of utility analysis.[45] They suggested that the percentage of employees who will be identified as successful following the use of a valid test will depend on three factors:

1. *Validity Coefficient*—The correlation of the test with a criterion.

2. *Selection Ratio*—The ratio of the number of persons hired to the number of applicants available. (The smaller the ratio, the more favorable for the organization, since it can be more selective in who is selected.)

3. *Base Rate*—The percentage of employees successful on the job *without* use of the test. (A low base rate suggests that with the current selection system, there is difficulty in identifying satisfactory workers. Use of a valid test should improve the identification of satisfactory employees.)

Taylor and Russell produced a series of tables that showed the utility of a test (that is, the increase in the percentage of successful employees selected following the use of a valid test) varied substantially depending on the test's validity, the selection ratio, and the base rate. Thus, by means of the Taylor-Russell model, it was demonstrated that a test could be useful even when the validity coefficient was low.

Subsequent years led to additional, more complex utility models, such as those by James Naylor and Lester Shine,[46] Hubert Brogden,[47] and Lee Cronbach and Goldine Gleser.[48] These models refined the concept of utility and led to its translation in terms of dollar payoffs. In particular, the Brogden and Cronbach and Gleser models laid the foundation for most utility models in use today. They proposed the evaluation of the use of a valid test in terms of dollar payoffs. That philosophy underlies much of utility analysis as applied currently in the field of personnel selection.

An Example Application of Utility Analysis   To fully describe an example application of utility analysis would be much too involved for our purposes here. However, we have adapted an example outlined by Richard Arvey and Robert Faley to briefly illustrate its use.[49]

Frank Schmidt and his associates[50] applied a utility model to examine the expected net gain in dollars obtained by using a valid test for selection as compared to random selection or another predictor that was not valid. Their utility model was as follows:

$$\text{Expected Gain (\$)} = N_s r_{xy} SD_y z_x - N_t c,$$

where

r_{xy} = validity coefficient of the selection measure,
SD_y = standard deviation of job performance in dollars,
z_x = average test score of those selected in z-score form,
c = cost of testing per job applicant,
N_t = number of applicants tested, and
N_s = number of applicants selected.

Suppose we have conducted a concurrent validation study of a test and found a validity coefficient of .50. Of every 100 applicants that apply for the job under study, 10 are hired; thus the selection ratio is .10, or 10 percent. Assuming that individuals are hired on the basis of their test scores, and the top 10 percent is hired, the average test score in standardized z-score form is 1.29. The standard deviation in dollars for job performance is assessed at $5,000 per year. Standard deviation in dollars represents individuals' contributions to productivity for the organization. An individual who is one standard deviation above the mean on job performance is worth $5,000 more to the organization than an individual with average job performance. Finally, suppose that the cost of purchasing, administering, scoring, and filing the test is $20 per applicant. When these values are substituted in the equation the result is

$$\text{Expected Gain (\$)} = 10(.50)(\$5,000)(1.29) - 100(20)$$

$$= \$30,250.$$

Use of the valid test (versus random selection or a nonvalid predictor) for one year to select workers would yield the organization an expected net gain in productivity worth $30,250 for every 10 employees hired. *Gain per worker selected* can be derived by dividing the expected gain by 10, that is, the number of workers selected. Thus the gain per worker selected per year would be $3,025.

With the expected gain equation, it is possible to examine the effects of the equation's components on test utility. By systematically varying these components, impacts on expected gain can be seen. For example, increased testing costs, lowered validity, or an increased selection ratio will lower utility.

In a published account of an actual utility analysis, Frank Schmidt and John Hunter examined the dollar payoff of using a valid test (the Programmer Aptitude Test) in selecting computer programmers employed by the federal government.[51] Results of their analyses showed that under the most conservative selection conditions, an estimated productivity increase for one year's use of the test was $5.6 million. Other researchers have also translated selection procedure utility into dollar payoffs.[52]

It is important to recognize that utility analysis is a developing concept. A number of utility analysis equations incorporating additional elements (for example, job tenure and recruitment) are currently being proposed.[53] In addition, some debate has developed and research is continuing on the methods for deriving suitable standard deviation of job performance measures (SD_y).[54] Some of these methods involve cost accounting approaches[55] while others involve subject matter experts making ratings of performance.[56] These data are then used for computing standard deviations of performance.

As you recall, we began this discussion by noting that a means was needed for translating the value of a valid test into dollar-and-cents terms that could be understood by practicing managers. Utility analysis is one means for dealing with this need. But, in addition, utility analysis might be used to address other needs as well. For instance, rising costs of personnel programs, including personnel selection, will place more and more demands on HR management directors for accountability. Here again, utility analysis would appear to have a very bright future for meeting this challenge as well.

Broader Perspectives of Validity

Concurrent, predictive, content, and construct validity are generally recognized as being the principal strategies employed in validation studies. However, other approaches have been offered that take a broader perspective of validity. Rather than studying predictor and criterion data collected on employees in *one* job and in *one* organization, these methods attempt to incorporate information obtained on jobs and incumbents across a *number* of situations. These methods are called *synthetic validity* and *validity generalization*.

Synthetic Validity

One of the real dilemmas in conducting criterion-related validation research is the need for having a large number of people on whom both predictor and criterion data are available. Because of the statistical procedures commonly employed, substantial amounts of data are required in order to detect any dependable relationships that might exist between predictors and criteria, that is, criterion-related validity. Except for relatively few lower-level or operative types of jobs, many organizations may not have jobs that have large numbers of applicants or incumbents on whom validation research can be conducted. Small organizations have rather obvious problems in terms of numbers of people available for participation. In addition, since many upper-level jobs are becoming more specialized, limiting even further the number of research participants available, the opportunities for conducting criterion-related validation studies on such jobs may also be very limited. As Robert Guion points out, when a small organization of 50 or so people may be hiring only one or two people a year, ordinary empirical validation cannot be performed.[57] Thus, according to Guion, the organization has three options: (a) to use tests or other measures without validation, (b) to rely on subjective judgments of whom to hire, or (c) not use any selection measures at all. If a firm wants to use tests, some form of validation is essential. To use tests without supporting validity evidence is to ask for problems. Yet, if only small sample sizes are available, what can an organization do?

As one means for dealing with the problem of small validation sample sizes, *synthetic validity* has been suggested.[58] Basically, synthetic validity is an approach that involves the following:

1.   Conducting job analyses for a number of different jobs,

2.   Identifying dimensions of work common to the jobs for all jobs analyzed, and

3.   Validating selection measures for the common job dimensions by using employees on these jobs.

As a simple example, suppose an organization wants to validate some tests for three different jobs. After using a job analysis questionnaire, it is found that even though the job titles are different, some of the jobs require identical types of tasks. Exhibit 5.14 illustrates three jobs and the task dimensions that are common to each. As you can see, the three jobs and their number of incumbents are as follows: (a) Typist (n = 60), (b) Clerk (n = 50), and (c) Receptionist (n = 40). Three example job dimensions characterizing these jobs include (a) *Following Directions,* (b) *Typing,* and (c) *Dealing with the Public.* The Xs in the matrix represent the job dimensions common to each job. For instance, *Following Directions* and *Typing* characterize the job of Typist while *Typing* and *Dealing with the Public* are most descriptive of the Receptionist job.

In the lower half of Exhibit 5.14, the measures that were developed or chosen from commercially available ones to assess each of the job dimensions are listed. For example, the Oral Directions Test was selected to determine if it could predict the job dimension, *Following Directions.* Criterion measures (such as performance ratings) are developed for each job dimension. Jobs sharing a common dimension are combined for validating the selection measure. For instance, for the job dimension *Following Directions,* the Typist and Clerk jobs are combined (combined sample size = 110); for the job dimension *Typing,* the Typist and Receptionist jobs are grouped together (combined sample size = 100); and, finally, for the job dimension *Dealing with the Public,* the jobs of Clerk and Receptionist are combined (combined sample size = 90). Notice that by combining jobs that require the same work activity, we are able to increase our sample sizes substantially over those we would have had if only one job had been used. We can collapse jobs together because we are studying a common work activity. In this sense, validity is "synthetic"; we are not creating validity per se, but rather creating a situation that will permit a better estimate of validity. The major advantage is that selection measures are validated across several jobs in an organization rather than for only one job.

Once the jobs have been combined on common job dimensions, criterion measures (such as performance ratings) have been collected on each employee

EXHIBIT 5.14	ILLUSTRATION OF TEST VALIDATION USING SYNTHETIC VALIDITY

Job	Number of Employees	Job Dimension		
		Following Directions I	Typing II	Dealing with the Public III
Typist	60	X	X	
Clerk	50	X		X
Receptionist	40		X	X
Total employees in combined jobs		110	100	90

	Job Dimension		
	I	II	III
Oral Directions Test	**		
Typing Test		**	
Public Relations Test			**
Total number of employees available for test validation	110	100	90

NOTE: X represents job dimensions characteristic of a job. Jobs sharing an X for the same dimension require the same job function. ** indicates the selection measure chosen for predicting success on a particular job dimension.

performing the job dimensions, and selection measures have been administered, test and criterion data are then correlated. Statistically significant relationships indicate a valid selection measure. As you can see, rather than validating a measure for a whole job, we have broken jobs down into component job dimensions and validated our selection measures against these specific components. Because our sample sizes are larger than they would have been for any one job, we can more appropriately perform a criterion-related validation study.

For the small firm with jobs in which there are a number of incumbents, synthetic validity may offer one solution to the thorny problem of small sample size. The principal assumption in employing a synthetic validity approach is that our analyses of jobs will identify job dimensions common to those jobs studied. For lower-level, clerical, or operative types of jobs, it seems that synthetic validity may be a viable option. However, the applicability of the method to higher-level positions, where work functions may be more diverse and more difficult to measure, is still open to question.

For the small organization, building a database sufficiently large enough to conduct an empirical validation study is a particularly difficult problem. Possible options include (a) combining similar jobs or components of jobs across different organizations such as in a cooperative validation study, (b) combining similar jobs or components of jobs within and across organizations, and (c) accumulating data over time. Using experts to judge the relationship between selection system and job content is another possibility.[59]

As compared to large organizations, the types of evidence available for showing job relatedness are often quite different in small organizations. Rational judgment is likely to play a far more important role in validity studies within small organizations than large ones. In such cases, the more evidence, even judgmental evidence, we can collect on job relatedness, the better.

Validity Generalization

A Brief Overview   With respect to the validation of tests, one key assumption that has developed over the years is that the validity of a test is specific to the job or situation where the validation study was completed. This assumption has come to be known as the "situational specificity hypothesis" in selection procedure validation.

In the late 1960s and early 1970s, some classic studies were published by Edwin Ghiselli, among others, that suggested confirmation of this hypothesis. Ghiselli, for example, collected data on literally hundreds of test validation studies that reported the relationships among a number of predictors and two groups of criteria: job proficiency and training criteria.[60] Examination of his results showed considerable differences or variation in the validity coefficients across studies even when similar tests were used to predict the criteria for practically identical jobs. Results of Ghiselli and others' work seemed to support the situational specificity hypothesis: Test validity is specific to the job situation. Supporters of the hypothesis believed that validity differences were attributed to dissimilarities in the nature of the specific employment situation or job in which a study was conducted, for example, the nature of the criteria used, the nature of the organization, or the insensitivity of a job analysis to identify "real" job differences. Thus the recommendation from many selection researchers was that a separate validation study should be conducted for a selection measure when it is to be used in a different organization, a different job, or for a different group of employees.

In the late 1970s, the situational specificity hypothesis began to be challenged. Frank Schmidt, John Hunter, and their colleagues amassed and presented an impressive amount of evidence that cast considerable doubt on the validity of the situational hypothesis.[61] Results from their analyses of validation studies involving cognitive ability tests led them to conclude that test validity does, in fact, generalize across situations. They argued that much of the differences found in a test's validity for similar jobs and criteria across different validation studies are *not* due to situational specificity but rather to statistical artifacts and measurement deficiencies in the validation studies themselves. Schmidt and Hunter hypothesized that these artifacts that accounted for the differences among the validity coefficients reported in validation studies were due to the following factors:

1.   Differences in criterion reliability,

2.   Differences in test reliability,

3. Differences in the restriction of range of scores,

4. The use of small sample sizes,

5. The amount and kind of criterion contamination and deficiency,

6. Computational and typographical errors, and

7. Slight differences among tests thought to be measuring the same attributes or constructs.[62]

Through a series of studies, Schmidt, Hunter, and their colleagues conducted a number of investigations called *validity generalization* studies. Their objective was to determine if these hypothesized artifacts explained differences found among validity coefficients computed for specific cognitive ability tests used in very similar jobs. If the artifacts were found to explain a large portion of the differences among the validity coefficients, then the situational specificity hypothesis would be disconfirmed. Such a result would suggest that with appropriate evidence, the validity of a test is generalizable from one situation to another that is very similar (that is, similar in terms of the same type of test and job on which the validity evidence had been accumulated). Conversely, if only a small portion of the differences in validity coefficients were explained by the artifacts, it would indicate that test validity is situation specific. That is, rather than being generalizable from one situation to another, test validity information must be collected in each new setting in which a test is used.

Validity Generalization Methods Several articles have outlined the details of the methodology used by Schmidt, Hunter, and their associates for testing the situational hypothesis.[63] Basically, their methodology corrected for the effects of the first four artifacts just listed; the remaining three could not be corrected with the available data. Their major steps were as follows:

1. Obtain a large number of published and unpublished validation studies.

2. Compute the average validity coefficient for these studies.

3. Calculate the variance of differences among these validity coefficients.

4. Subtract from the amount of these differences, the variance due to the effects of small sample size.

5. Correct the average validity coefficient and the variance for errors that are due to other artifacts (that is, differences in criterion reliability, test reliability, and restriction in the range of scores).

6. Compare the corrected variance to the average validity coefficient to determine the variation in study results.

7. If the differences among the validity coefficients are very small, then validity coefficient differences are concluded to be due to the artifacts and not to the nature of the situation. Therefore, validity is generalizable across situations.

Schmidt, Hunter, and their associates have generally concluded that the situational specificity hypothesis cannot be supported. They have argued that separate validity studies are not needed for each job. They suggest that validity generalization exists. Thus from Schmidt and Hunter's investigations, validity generalization may be defined as follows: *validity generalization involves evidence that validity information accumulated on a selection measure in a series of studies can be applied in a new setting involving the same or very similar jobs.* (We have more to say in Chapter 13 about validity generalization as it applies to ability tests.) Thus where adequate validity generalization evidence for a test is available, the results can be generalized to settings having very similar jobs. A separate validation study for each job is not needed.

Early validity generalization work by Schmidt and Hunter focused on the generalizability of cognitive ability paper-and-pencil tests. More recent work has suggested that validity generalization extends beyond mental ability testing. Validity generalizability has also been reported to exist for predictors such as biographical data,[64] personality inventories,[65] and assessment centers.[66] Current work continues with other predictors.

The findings of Schmidt, Hunter, and their colleagues have not gone without challenge.[67] Some of the criticisms concern the statistical and methodological procedures used to derive validity generalization. Other criticisms deal with the criteria used for defining the existence of validity generalization.

Schmidt and his colleagues conclude that such criticisms are concerned more with fine-tuning the method of validity generalization and do not detract significantly from its overall methodology and conclusions.[68] Some independent evidence seems to support their contention. The National Research Council Committee on the General Aptitude Test Battery of the U.S. Employment Service reviewed the statistical and measurement procedures of validity generalization and generally concluded they were scientifically sound.[69]

The work of Schmidt, Hunter, and their associates has important implications for the future of validation research in HR selection. The numerous validity generalization studies available suggest that the validity of a test is more generalizable across *similar* situations and *similar jobs* than has been previously thought. This conclusion should not be interpreted to mean that a test that is valid in one job will be valid for any other job. However, sufficient validity information on one job may be generalizable to other, very similar jobs. Ultimately, if validity generalization evidence for a test is available, a validation study may not have to be carried out. Instead, it may be possible to use previous validation research to support the validity of the test.

Validity Generalization Requirements   In order to use validity generalization evidence, the following conditions must be met:

1. The selection measure to be used in the new employment setting must assess the same knowledge, skill, ability, trait, or construct, or be a representative example of the measure used in the validity generalization study.

2. The job in the new employment setting must be similar to the same job or group of jobs included in the validity generalization study. If these conditions can be met, then there is evidence of test validity in the new employment setting.[70]

To meet these conditions, specific supporting information is needed. This information includes the following:

1. Validity generalization evidence consisting of studies summarizing a selection measure's validity for similar jobs in other settings.

2. Data showing the similarity between jobs for which the validity evidence is reported and the job in the new employment setting (an analysis of the job in the new employment setting is mandatory); and

3. Data showing the similarity between the selection measures in other studies composing the validity evidence and those measures to be used in the new employment setting.[71]

If validity generalization of predictors continues to be found, and *if* it is accepted by the courts and society in general, validity generalization evidence will play an extremely important role in future validation efforts. If we can assume its existence (and there is mounting evidence we can), an obvious advantage to the use of validity generalization is that the time and resource savings as compared to traditional criterion-related test validation research could be considerable. In addition, our fundamental understanding of what factors contribute to job performance and success may also be enhanced.

However, Schmidt and his colleagues appear pessimistic about the future of validity generalization in the United States.[72] Although the U.S. Supreme Court's 1989 decision in *Wards Cove Packing Co. v. Atonio* could encourage the use of validity generalization by employers, the Department of Labor announced an intention to suspend its validity generalization-based testing program for two years. The government's choices were to continue to adjust test scores to eliminate differences among whites, blacks, and Hispanics and be criticized for reverse discrimination or drop the score adjustments and be attacked for adverse impact. Schmidt et al. believe that passage of the 1991 civil rights bill may, in fact, all but eliminate the transportability of tests and validity generalization. They feel the bill may place an even heavier burden of test validation requirements on employers than the 1971 *Griggs v. Duke Power Co.* standards. As a consequence, local validation studies for each job in each company may be required. Job performance may be the only acceptable criterion; turnover, absenteeism, accident rates, and other criterion measures would not be considered sufficient.

Validity generalization results may not constitute a legal defense in employment discrimination lawsuits.[73]

So what is the future for validity generalization? At this point, it is tough to say. Further research on the validity generalization model, future versions of federal and professional guidelines on employee selection and test validation, future decisions in employment discrimination cases, and passage of federal laws will inform us when, or if, validity generalization has matured and been accepted as a viable validation strategy.

References

[1] Society for Industrial and Organizational Psychology, *Principles for the Validation and Use of Personnel Selection Procedures*, 3d ed. (College Park, MD.: Author, 1987), p. 4.

[2] Charles H. Lawshe, "Inferences from Personnel Tests and Their Validity," *Journal of Applied Psychology* 70 (1985): 237–238; Marvin D. Dunnette and Walter C. Borman, *Annual Review of Psychology* 30 (1979): 477–525. For an example of a published validation study, see John D. Arnold, John M. Rauschenberger, Wendy G. Soubel, and Robert M. Guion, "Validation and Utility of a Strength Test for Selecting Steelworkers," *Journal of Applied Psychology* 67 (1982): 588–604.

[3] Edwin E. Ghiselli, John P. Campbell, and Sheldon Zedeck, *Measurement Theory for the Behavioral Sciences* (San Francisco: Freeman, 1981).

[4] Robert M. Guion and C. J. Cranny, "A Note on Concurrent and Predictive Validity Designs: A Critical Reanalysis," *Journal of Applied Psychology* 67 (1982): 239–244.

[5] Frank J. Landy, *Psychology of Work Behavior* (Homewood, Ill.: Dorsey Press, 1985), p. 65.

[6] Neal Schmitt, Richard Z. Gooding, Raymond A. Noe, and Michael Kirsch, "Meta-analyses of Validity Studies Published between 1964 and 1982 and the Investigation of Study Characteristics," *Personnel Psychology* 37 (1984): 407–422.

[7] Gerald V. Barrett, James S. Phillips, and Ralph A. Alexander, "Concurrent and Predictive Validity Designs: A Critical Reanalysis," *Journal of Applied Psychology* 66 (1981): 1–6.

[8] Society for Industrial and Organizational Psychology, *Principles for the Validation and Use of Personnel Selection Procedures*, p. 7.

[9] Ibid.

[10] Ibid., pp. 18–19. An interesting example of the content validity of a biographical data questionnaire developed to predict test performance of electrician job applicants can be found in Ronald D. Pannone, "Predicting Test Performance: A Content Valid Approach to Screening Applicants," *Personnel Psychology* 37 (1984): 507–514.

[11] Lawshe, "Inferences from Personnel Tests and Their Validity," p. 237.

[12] Charles Lawshe has shown that a form of quantitative analysis may be applied in content validity—See Charles H. Lawshe, "A Quantitative Approach to Content Validity," *Personnel Psychology* 28 (1975): 563–575. For an example of a study using Lawshe's quantitative content validity approach, see Michael K. Distefano, Margaret W. Pryer, and Robert C. Erffmeyer, "Application of Content Validity Methods to the Development of a Job-Related Performance Rating Criterion," *Personnel Psychology* 36 (1983): 621–632.

[13] Benjamin Schneider and Neal Schmitt, *Staffing Organizations* (Glenview, Ill.: Scott, Foresman, 1986).

[14] Kleiman and Faley, "Assessing Content Validity: Standards Set by the Court," *Personnel Psychology* 31 (1978); 701–713.

[15] *Albemarle Paper Company v. Moody*, 422 U.S. 405 (1975).

[16] Equal Employment Opportunity Commission, Civil Service Commission, Department of Labor, and Department of Justice, *Adoption of Four Agencies of Uniform Guidelines on Employee Selection Procedures*, 43 *Federal Register* 38, 305 (Aug. 25, 1978).

[17] Richard S. Barrett, "Content Validation Form," *Public Personnel Management* 21 (1992): 41–52.
[18] Irwin L. Goldstein, Sheldon Zedeck, and Benjamin Schneider, "An Exploration of the Job Analysis-Content Validity Process," in *Personnel Selection in Organizations*, eds. Neal Schmitt and Walter C. Borman (San Francisco: Jossey-Bass, 1993), pp. 7–10.
[19] Lawshe, "A Quantitative Approach to Content Validity."
[20] Lyle F. Schoenfeldt, Barbara B. Schoenfeldt, Stanley R. Acker, and Michael R. Perlson, "Content Validity Revisited: The Development of a Content-Oriented Test of Industrial Reading," *Journal of Applied Psychology* 61 (1976): 581–588.
[21] Goldstein, Zedeck, and Schneider, *Personnel Selection in Organizatinos.*
[22] Equal Employment Opportunity Commission et al., Adoption of Four Agencies of *Uniform Guidelines on Employee Selection Procedures*, p. 38, 303.
[23] Ibid., p. 38, 302.
[24] Ibid.
[25] Robert M. Guion, "Recruiting, Selection, and Job Placement," in *Handbook of Industrial and Organizational Psychology*, ed. Marvin D. Dunnette (Chicago: Rand McNally, 1974), p. 786.
[26] Mary L. Tenopyr, "Content-Construct Confusion," *Personnel Psychology* 30 (1977): 47–54. See also Robert M. Guion, "Content Validity—the Source of My Discontent," *Personnel Psychology* 1 (1977): 1–10; Robert M. Guion, "Content Validity: Three Years of Talk—What's the Action?" *Public Personnel Management* 6 (1977): 407–414; and Robert M. Guion, " 'Content Validity' in Moderation," *Personnel Psychology* 31 (1978): 205–213.
[27] Society for Industrial and Organizational Psychology, *Principles for the Validation and Use of Selection Procedures.*
[28] Robert M. Guion, *Personnel Testing* (New York: McGraw-Hill, 1965), p. 128.
[29] Based on John F. Binning and Gerald V. Barrett, "Validity of Personnel Decisions: A Conceptual Analysis of the Inferential and Evidential Bases," *Journal of Applied Psychology* 74 (1989): 478–494.
[30] W. Bruce Walsh and Nancy E. Betz, *Tests and Assessment* (Englewood Cliffs, N.J.: Prentice Hall, 1990), p. 67.
[31] Ghiselli, Cambell, and Zedeck, *Measurement Theory for the Behavioral Sciences*, pp. 284–287.
[32] Paul R. Sackett and Richard D. Arvey, "Selection in Small *N* Settings," in *Personnel Selection in Organizations*, eds. Neal Schmitt and Walter C. Borman (San Francisco: Jossey-Bass, 1993), pp. 431–432.
[33] In some employment settings, an organization may not have as many applicants or employ as many persons as given in our example. Thus empirical validity may not be technically feasible. Under such circumstances, other approaches to validity such as content validity, validity generalization, and synthetic validity may need to be considered.
[34] Clark L. Hull, *Aptitude Testing* (Yonkers, N.Y.: World Book, 1928).
[35] Ghiselli, Cambell, and Zedeck, *Measurement Theory for the Behavioral Sciences*, p. 145.
[36] Philippe Cattin, "Estimation of the Predictive Power of a Regression Model," *Journal of Applied Psychology* 65 (1980): 407–414.
[37] Kevin R. Murphy, "Cost-Benefit Considerations in Choosing among Cross-Validation Methods," *Personnel Psychology* 37 (1984): 15–22.
[38] Charles H. Lawshe and Michael J. Balma, *Principles of Personnel Testing* (New York: McGraw-Hill, 1966), p. 301.
[39] Ibid., pp. 306–308.
[40] Guion, *Personnel Testing*, pp. 141–144.
[41] J. P. Guilford, *Psychometric Methods* (New York: McGraw-Hill, 1954), pp. 400–401.
[42] Robert L. Thorndike, *Applied Psychometrics* (Boston: Houghton Mifflin, 1982). C. A. Olson and B. E. Becker, "A Proposed Technique for the Treatment of Restriction of Range in Selection Validation," *Psychological Bulletin* 93 (1983): 137–148.
[43] Milton L. Blum and James C. Naylor, *Industrial Psychology: Its Theoretical and Social Foundations* (New York: Harper & Row, 1968); Wayne F. Cascio, *Costing Human*

Resources: The Financial Impact of Behavior in Organizations (Boston: Kent, 1982), p. 130.

[44] Schneider and Schmitt, *Staffing Organizations*, p. 264.

[45] H. C. Taylor and J. T. Russell, "The Relationship of Validity Coefficients to the Practical Effectiveness of Tests in Selection," *Journal of Applied Psychology* 23 (1939): 565–578.

[46] James C. Naylor and Lester C. Shine, "A Table for Determining the Increase in Mean Criterion Score Obtained by Using a Selection Device," *Journal of Industrial Psychology* 3 (1965): 33–42.

[47] Hubert E. Brogden, "On the Interpretation of the Correlation Coefficient as a Measure of Predictive Efficiency," *Journal of Educational Psychology* 37 (1946): 64–76.

[48] Lee J. Cronbach and Goldine C. Gleser, *Psychological Tests and Personnel Decisions* (Urbana: University of Illinois Press, 1965).

[49] Richard D. Arvey and Robert H. Faley, *Fairness in Selecting Employees*, 2d ed. (Reading, Mass.: Addison-Wesley, 1988), pp. 44–45.

[50] Frank L. Schmidt, John E. Hunter, Robert C. McKenzie, and Tressie W. Muldrow, "Impact of Valid Selection Procedures on Work-Force Productivity," *Journal of Applied Psychology* 64 (1979): 609–626.

[51] Ibid.

[52] See, for example, Wayne F. Cascio and Val Silbey, "Utility of the Assessment Center as a Selection Device," *Journal of Applied Psychology* 64 (1979): 107–118; John E. Hunter and Ronda F. Hunter, "The Validity and Utility of Alternative Predictors of Job Performance," *Psychological Bulletin* 96 (1984): 72–98; Frank L. Schmidt, John E. Hunter, A. N. Outerbridge, and Marvin H. Trattner, "The Economic Impact of Job Selection Methods on Size, Productivity, and Payroll Costs of the Federal Work Force: An Empirically Based Demonstration," *Personnel Psychology* 39 (1986): 1–29.

[53] John W. Boudreau, *Utility Analysis: A Review and Agenda for Future Research*, in *Advances in Personnel Selection and Assessment*, eds. M. Smith and I. Robertson (London: Wiley, in press).

[54] Michael J. Burke and James T. Frederick, "Two Modified Procedures for Estimating Standard Deviations in Utility Analysis," *Journal of Applied Psychology* 71 (1986): 334–339 and Jack E. Edwards, James T. Frederick, and Michael J. Burke, "Efficacy of Modified CREPID SDy's on the Basis of Archival Organizational Data," *Journal of Applied Psychology* 73 (1988): 529–535.

[55] Olen L. Greer and Wayne Cascio, "Is Cost Accounting the Answer? Comparison of Two Behaviorally Based Methods for Estimating the Standard Deviation of Job Performance in Dollars with a Cost-Accounting Approach," *Journal of Applied Psychology* 72 (1987): 588–595.

[56] Schmidt, Hunter, McKenzie, and Muldrow, "Impact of Valid Selection Procedures on Work-Force Productivity."

[57] Guion, *Personnel Testing*, p. 169.

[58] Robert M. Guion, "Synthetic Validity in a Small Company: A Demonstration," *Personnel Psychology* 18 (1965): 49–63; Kevin W. Mossholder and Richard D. Arvey, "Synthetic Validity: A Conceptual and Comparative Review," *Journal of Applied Psychology* 69 (1984): 322–333.

[59] Sackett and Arvey, *Personnel Selection in Organizations*, pp. 423–425; 445.

[60] Edwin E. Ghiselli, *The Validity of Occupational Aptitude Tests* (New York: Wiley, 1966) and Edwin E. Ghiselli, "The Validity of Aptitude Tests in Personnel Selection," *Personnel Psychology* 26 (1973): 461–477.

[61] See, for example, Frank E. Schmidt and John E. Hunter, "Development of a General Solution to the Problem of Validity Generalization," *Journal of Applied Psychology* 62 (1977): 529–540; Frank L. Schmidt, John E. Hunter, and Kenneth Pearlman, "Task Differences as Moderators of Aptitude Test Validity in Selection: A Red Herring," *Journal of Applied Psychology* 66 (1981): 166–185; Frank L. Schmidt, John E. Hunter, Kenneth Pearlman, and Guy S. Shane, "Further Tests of Schmidt-Hunter Bayesian Validity Generalization Procedure," *Personnel Psychology* 37 (1984): 317–326; and

Frank L. Schmidt, Benjamin P. Ocasio, Joseph M. Hillery, and John E. Hunter, "Further Within-Setting Empirical Tests of the Situational Specificity Hypothesis in Personnel Selection," *Personnel Psychology* 38 (1985): 509–524.

[62] The formulas used to correct for the first four artifacts can be found in Schmidt, Hunter, Pearlman, and Shane, "Further Tests of the Schmidt-Hunter Bayesian Validity Generalization Procedure."

[63] Ibid.

[64] Frank L. Schmidt and H. R. Rothstein, "Application of Validity Generalization Methods of Meta-Analysis to Biographical Data Scales Used in Employment Selection," in *Advances in Biodata Research*, eds. M. D. Mumford and G. S. Stokes (Palo Alto, Calif.: Consulting Psychologists Press, in press).

[65] M. R. Barrick and M. K. Mount, "The Big Five Personality Dimensions and Job Performance: A Meta Analysis," *Personnel Psychology* 41 (1991): 1–26.

[66] Neal Schmitt, J. R. Schneider, and J. R. Cohen, "Factors Affecting Validity of a Regionally Administered Assessment Center," *Personnel Pyscology* 43 (1991): 1–12.

[67] See, for example, H. G. Osburn, John C. Callender, Jack M. Greener, and Steven Ashworth, "Statistical Power of Tests of the Situational Specificity Hypothesis in Validity Generalization Studies: A Cautionary Note," *Journal of Applied Psychology* 68 (1983): 115–122; Jen A. Algera, Paul G. W. Jansen, Robert A. Roe, and Pieter Vijn, "Validity Generalization: Some Critical Remarks on the Schmidt-Hunter Procedure," *Journal of Occupational Psychology* 57 (1984): 197–210; John C. Callender and H. G. Osburn, "Another View of Progress in Validity Generalization: Reply to Schmidt, Hunter, and Pearlman," *Journal of Applied Psychology* 67 (1982): 846–852; Larry James, Richard Demaree, and Stanley Mulaik, "A Note of Validity Generalization Procedures," *Journal of Applied Psychology* 71 (1986): 440–450; and Edward Kemery, Kevin Mossholder, and Larry Roth, "The Power of the Schmidt and Hunter Additive Model of Validity Generalization," *Journal of Applied Psychology* 72 (1987): 30–37.

[68] Frank L. Schmidt, Deniz S. Ones, and John E. Hunter, in "Personnel Selection," *Annual Review of Psychology* (Stanford; Annual Reviews, 1992), p. 631.

[69] J. A. Hartigan and A. K. Wigdor, *Fairness in Employment Testing: Validity Generalization, Minority Issues, and the General Aptitude Test Battery* (Washington, D.C.: National Academy Press, 1989).

[70] Society for Industrial and Organizational Psychology, *Principles for the Validation and Use of Selection Procedures*, p. 28.

[71] For a study illustrating the classification of jobs in the context of validity generalization, see Edwin T. Cornelius, Frank L. Schmidt, and Theodore J. Carron, "Job Classification Approaches and the Implementation of Validity Generalization Results," *Personnel Psychology* 37 (1984): 247–260.

[72] Schmidt, et al., "Personnel Selection," pp. 628; 631; 650–651.

[73] Ibid., pp. 661–662.

6

Strategies for Selection Decision-Making*

Roger selects about a hundred employees each year for various positions at the plant. He is proud of his skill in selection and boasts that he can pick applicants who will be successful with near perfect accuracy. However, an examination of employee records reveals a different story. The turnover rate of good employees is quite high, many employees employed by Roger turned out to be poor performers and were later terminated, and one applicant who Roger rejected was hired by a competitor and is now their most productive manager. What went wrong with the selection process and why is Roger so overconfident about his hiring prowess?

The mystery is even more perplexing because Roger's company uses validated selection devices in its hiring process. In fact, they hired consultants to help them design their current selection system, which is considered state-of-the-art and capable of withstanding legal challenges. Applicant data are carefully collected and documented throughout each phase of the selection process.

In an interview with Roger, the flaws of the selection process emerged. Investigators discovered that although Roger systematically collects a variety of information about each applicant using valid selection devices, he makes his final select/reject decisions by gut feel, or intuition. He sizes up applicants using the collected data and then compares them to his own mental image of a good employee.

There are two primary reasons for the low quality of Roger's selection decisions as well as his overconfidence in his own decision making. First, although Roger uses data collected from valid selection instruments, he combines the information from these various sources unsystematically. In fact, unbeknownst to him, Roger is inconsistent in his many selection decisions. Second, Roger is unaware of his true hits and misses as a decision maker because he does not keep records of his own decision making, and the company does not audit his selection decisions periodically. Together, these practices lead to suboptimal selection decision making for both Roger and his organization.

*This chapter was written by Mark Lengnick-Hall.

How can selection decision making be improved? To begin, we need to focus on selection decision making as much as we do on developing and administering valid selection devices. By following sound and systematic decision-making procedures along with feedback on decision outcomes, Roger and other managers can improve their effectiveness. We begin by describing characteristics of selection decisions. Then we outline and assess different methods for combining predictive information. Next we list five systematic decision-making procedures that can improve selection decision making. We conclude the chapter with practical advice for making selection decisions.

Characteristics of Selection Decisions

Selection decisions come in two basic varieties: simple and complex. Simple selection decisions involve one position with several applicants. Applicants are assessed on the KSAs important to job success. The applicant who most closely approximates the requirements of the job is selected. Complex selection decisions are those involving several applicants and several positions. Here the decision is not only whom to select but which job to place them on.

In either case, simple or complex, the INFORMATION PROCESSING DEMANDS = [NUMBER OF APPLICANTS] × [AMOUNT OF SELECTION DATA COLLECTED], and these demands can become great when there are many applicants and many types of selection data are collected on each one. When time and other costs are factored into the decision, even relatively simple selection decisions can become costly. Imagine a situation that occurred in Duluth, Minnesota, a few years ago when 10,000 applicants applied for 300 operator positions at a paper mill. The paperwork alone must have been staggering!

Managers, supervisors, and others who hire employees have several decision options. They can decide to select (the decision could also be to promote or to train) an applicant, or they can reject the applicant from further consideration. Another alternative is to defer the decision and gather more information. This may be done, for example, after all applicants for a position have been interviewed, but no clear choice emerges. Additionally, a decision maker may decide to select an applicant on probation. If the employee does not meet expectations during the probationary period, the relationship is terminated. Whatever option is chosen may result in either desirable or undesirable outcomes for the organization.

Ideally, selection decisions would result in desired outcomes, that is, employing those who succeed in the job and rejecting those who would not succeed in the job. However, even under the best circumstances, mistakes will be made. Two types of selection decision mistakes are false positives (or erroneous acceptances) and false negatives (erroneous rejections). A *false positive error* occurs when the applicant passes through all of the selection phases, is employed, but proves unsuccessful on the job. This error is costly and sometimes disastrous depending on the nature of the job. Additionally, it may be difficult to terminate some false positives, adding further to the organization's costs. Many organizations use a probationary period (e.g., six weeks for nonexempt employees or six months for exempt employees) to reduce the long-term consequences of false positive errors.

False negative errors are equally problematic. These errors occur when an applicant is rejected but would have been successful on the job. The applicant might have been rejected at any phase of the selection process. While this error is harder to detect than a false positive error, it can be equally damaging to the organization. An applicant for a key job (e.g., design engineer) rejected at one organization may prove costly if she develops a new marketable product for a competitor. Likewise, a minority applicant inappropriately rejected for a position may successfully challenge the incorrect decision in a costly EEO lawsuit.

Decision makers cannot avoid selection errors entirely, but they can take precautions to minimize them. By following systematic procedures like those we discuss next, the probability of making correct decisions is higher than if seat-of-the-pants decision-making procedures are the norm. But before we describe some specific strategies for making selection decisions, let's see why systematic decision-making procedures are preferred.

Methods for Collecting and Combining Predictive Information

Predictive information can be collected and combined using a number of methods. We describe eight strategies based on whether the information was collected either mechanically or judgmentally and whether the information was combined for decision making either mechanically or judgmentally[1] (see Table 6.1).

The term *mechanical* refers to whether the data were either collected or combined without human judgment. Data that are more objective, such as test scores collected for selection decisions, would fall into this category. In addition, selection decisions based on data combined by a formula would be considered mechanical. *Judgmental* refers to data that are either collected or combined using human judgment. Data that are more subjective, such as ratings based on an

TABLE 6.1	STRATEGIES FOR COLLECTING AND COMBINING PREDICTIVE DATA	
Mode of Data Collection	**Mode of Data Combination**	
	Judgmental	*Mechanical*
Judgmental	Pure Judgment	Trait Ratings
Mechanical	Profile Interpretation	Pure Statistical
Both	Judgmental Composite	Mechanical Composite
Either/Both	Judgmental Synthesis	Mechanical Synthesis

SOURCE: Bernard M. Bass and Gerald V. Barrett, *People, Work, and Organizations*, 2d ed. (Boston: Allyn & Bacon, 1981), p. 392.

interview, would fit in this category. In addition, selection decisions based on data combined into an overall impression would be considered judgmental.

Pure judgment is a strategy in which judgmental data are collected and combined by judgment for decision making. No objective data (e.g., tests) are collected. The decision maker forms an overall judgment of the predicted success of the applicant. The overall judgment may be based on some traits and/or standards in the mind of the decision maker (e.g., beliefs about what it takes to make a good employee on the job) for making the judgment, but these criteria are usually not made explicitly. The decision maker's role is to both collect the information and make a decision about the applicant. For example, a receptionist is selected based on a judgment of performance in the interview. No ratings are made. The decision maker uses gut feel to make the decision. The decision is based on implicit traits of good secretaries the manager has employed in the past.

A *trait rating* strategy is one in which judgmental data are collected, but they are combined mechanically. The decision maker makes judgmental ratings of the applicants based on interviews, application blanks, and so on. Ratings are then entered into a formula, and an overall score is computed for each applicant. The decision maker's role is to collect the information (i.e., the ratings), but the decision is based on the results of the mechanically calculated predictions. For example, applicants for a sales representative job are assessed in several interviews. Judgmental ratings are entered into a formula and an overall score is computed across the interviews. The highest scoring applicant receives the job offer.

Profile interpretation is a strategy in which data are collected mechanically but combined judgmentally. The decision maker reviews all of the objectively collected data (from tests and other measures obtained on the applicant) and then makes an overall judgment of the applicant's suitability for the job. For example, a manager of a telemarketing firm selects telephone operators in another location based on biographical data, tests scores, and so on, received in the mail or by fax. The data are combined judgmentally into an overall impression of whether the applicants would make successful operators.

A *pure statistical* strategy involves collecting data mechanically and combining it mechanically. For example, an applicant applies for an administrative assistant job by responding to application and biographical-data questions via a computer terminal. The data collected are then combined by a formula calculated on the computer. The selection supervisor receives a printout that lists applicants in the order of their overall combined scores.

A *judgmental composite* strategy is one in which both judgmental and mechanical data are collected and then combined judgmentally. This is probably the most commonly used method and the one used by Roger in the example at the beginning of the chapter. The decision maker combines all of the information about an applicant and makes an overall judgment about the applicant's likely success on the job. For example, a test (mechanical) and interview (judgmental) information are collected on auto mechanic applicants. The selection manager looks at all of the information and makes an overall judgment of whether or not to employ the applicant, but uses no formula or other means to calculate an overall score.

A *mechanical composite* is a strategy that collects both judgmental and mechanical data and then combines them mechanically. Test scores, biographical-data scores, interview ratings, and recommendations are combined using a formula that predicts job success. For example, assessment centers used for managerial promotion decisions typically use a mechanical composite strategy for making decisions about who to promote.

A *judgmental synthesis* approach is one in which all information (both mechanical and judgmental data) is first mechanically combined into a prediction about the applicant's likely success. Then this prediction is judged in the context of other information about the applicant. For example, engineering applicants are scored on the basis of tests and biographical-data. A panel of interviewers then discusses the applicants' characteristics and make its decisions about who to hire on the basis of both their predicted success (from the formula) along with the judgment of the interviewers on how well the applicants will fit in the organization.

A *mechanical synthesis* is a strategy that first combines subjectively all information (both mechanical and judgmental) into a prediction about the applicant's likely success. This prediction is then mechanically combined with other information (e.g., test scores) to create an overall score for each applicant. For example, test scores and interview information are reviewed by the work team. The members of the work team make their individual predictions of the likely success of each applicant. These predictions are then entered with other information into a formula to predict the applicant's likely success on the job.

Which Method Is Best?

One review examined 45 studies in which 75 comparisons were made regarding the relative efficiency (superior, equal, or inferior in prediction) of two or more of the eight methods of collecting and combining the information just described. It found that the statistical, mechanical composite, and mechanical synthesis methods were always either equal or superior to the other methods. These results have been replicated in numerous other studies.[2]

Why does a mechanical combination of data yield better results than a judgmental combination? Bernard Bass and Gerald Barrett[3] suggest four reasons for the superiority of mechanical over judgmental methods for making selection decisions. First, the accuracy of prediction may depend on the proper weighting of predictors regardless of which approach is used. Since it is almost impossible to judge what weights are appropriate with any degree of precision, even mechanical approaches that use equal weightings are more likely to make better decisions. Second, as data on additional applicants are added to already available data, more accurate models can be created statistically. This makes it possible to improve the decision-making model continuously and adapt it to changing conditions in the environment. Decision makers relying solely on judgment have cognitive limits in their ability to improve their prediction models. In fact, many decision makers rely on a judgmental model developed early in life and never change, thus leading to increasing rather than decreasing selection errors. In our opening example, Roger may have developed his model of the good employee in the early 1960s, and he continues to adhere to it into the 1990s. Third, decision makers relying on judgment can only do as well as a statistical model and then only if they have been thorough, objective, and systematic in both collecting and combining the information. Since many managers and supervisors make selection decisions only sporadically, it is less likely they will be thorough, objective, and systematic in collecting and combining the information. Consequently, their decisions will not even equal those of a statistical model. Fourth, decision makers are more likely to add considerable error if they are allowed to combine judgmentally both subjective data (e.g., interview assessments) along with objective data (e.g., test scores). Their implicit theories (derived from past experience as well as other sources) of good applicants may bias their evaluations and ultimately decisions to select or reject an applicant. Furthermore, their inconsistency across decisions can have numerous causes: time pressures to make a decision, a bad day at the office, or even comparisons to the most recently selected. Statistical models will make an allowance for such error and reduce the impact of individual biases on decision outcomes.

Implications for Decision Makers

It is clear from our discussion that a statistical combination of various information sources is better than a judgmental combination for making selection decisions. While gut feel, or intuitive decisions, probably give the decision maker a feeling of control over the process and confidence in his or her judgment, it is usually not warranted by the quality of decision outcomes.

The judgment of the decision maker can and should play an important part in data gathering (e.g., interview assessments), but it should not play a major role in *combining* the various sources of information into a prediction about success. A mechanical formula/statistical model that is systematically derived and systematically applied is the best way to make accurate hiring decisions. When judgmental data are collected (e.g., interview assessments), it is better to convert those assessments to a rating and then enter that data into a statistical formula that combines the various data to make a prediction of job success.

While there is ample evidence supporting the use of mechanical approaches for making selection decisions, both managers and applicants continue to resist their use. Often managers resist change, and may feel threatened if asked to use formulas for making selection decisions rather than their own simple judgment. Since the role of the manager shifts to providing input rather than making judgmental decisions, some selling may be necessary to convince them that superior decisions will result from following such systematic procedures.[4]

Applicants are also likely to resist the use of statistical models for making selection decisions. Rene Dawes[5] describes a young woman who was overheard complaining that she had been rejected from a graduate program without even an interview. She did not believe the decision makers could possibly know what she was like using a mechanical procedure for combining data and making selection decisions. As we can see from this example, it may be necessary to convince applicants as well as managers that these procedures are the most appropriate to use.

Five Alternative Selection Decision-Making Models

The following five selection decision-making models conform to the prescription of creating mechanical models for combining predictive information. However, these models make no assumptions about how the data are collected (they can be collected through either mechanical or judgmental means). Each of these models focuses on systematic procedures for combining predictive information. In addition, each of these models makes implicit assumptions about the nature of job performance and the relative importance of multiple predictors.

To make these models easier to understand, let's look at an example that shows how decisions are made using each approach. Table 6.2 presents the data for the example. This job involves handling patient records, customer billing, insurance filing, and filing patient records. Four tests and a structured interview are used to obtain predictor information on applicants. The math test requires computing answers to problems involving addition, subtraction, multiplication, and division. Scores can range from 0 to 15. The filing test requires applicants to separate a deck of index cards into two decks (one by name and the other by number) and then sort them (alphabetically for the name stack and numerically for the number stack). Scores can range from 0 to 30. The spelling test requires applicants to circle the correctly spelled word in each pair of words provided. Scores can range from 0 to 65. The accuracy test requires applicants to compare simulated patient charts with simulated printouts of patient records and identify errors. Scores can range from 0 to 15. The structured interview is scored numerically with 5 representing an excellent

| **TABLE 6.2** | PATIENT ACCOUNT REPRESENTATIVE TEST AND APPLICANT DATA |

	Test Data				
	Math Test	Filing Test	Spelling Test	Accuracy Test	Structured Inteview
Maximum Possible Score	15	30	65	15	25
Regression Weights*	1	.8	.9	.7	.5
Cutoff Scores	7	22	50	6	10
Maximum Score	12	26	50	10	18

* The regression equation is $y = x_1 + .8x_2 + .9x_3 + .7x_4 + .5x_5$.

	Applicant Test Scores				
Applicant	Math Test	Filing Test	Spelling Test	Accuracy Test	Structured Inteview
Amanda	6	30	55	15	25
Dave	14	21	63	10	11
Carl	9	29	60	8	12
Rebecca	15	22	50	5	24
Cyndy	8	23	55	14	13

answer, 3 an average answer, and 1 a poor answer. Scores can range from 0 to 25, with higher scores meaning better applicant performance.

Alternative One: Multiple Regression

We discussed multiple regression in Chapter 5. As you recall, in this model you measure each applicant on each predictor and then enter the applicants' predictor scores into an equation that weights each score in order to arrive at a total score (e.g., predicted job performance). Regression weights are determined by each predictor's influence in determining criterion performance. Using this model, it is possible for two applicants with different individual predictor scores to have identical overall predicted scores. For example, in a two predictor case ($Y = B_1X_1 + B_2X_2$) where the regression weight for the first predictor $B_1 = 2$ and the regression weight for the second predictor $B_2 = 1$ you could have the following: applicant A ($X_1 = 50, X_2 = 0$), applicant B ($X_1 = 0, X_2 = 100$), applicant C ($X_1 = 10, X_2 = 80$), and all three applicants would have equivalent predicted scores of 100.

The multiple regression model makes two basic assumptions: (a) the predictors are linearly related to the criterion, and (b) since the predicted score is a function of the sum of the weighted predictor scores, the predictors are additive and can compensate for one another (i.e., possession of a lot of one of the predictors [KSA] compensates for having only a little of another predictor). In fact, as we see in the example, you could possess none of a particular KSA and still receive a high overall score if you possessed a substantial amount of another important KSA!

There are several advantages to the multiple regression approach. It minimizes errors in prediction and combines the predictors optimally to yield the most efficient estimate of criterion status. Furthermore, it is a very flexible method. It can be modified to handle nominal data, nonlinear relationships, and both linear and nonlinear interactions.[6] Regression equations can be constructed for each of a number of jobs using either the same predictors weighted differently or different predictors. The decision maker then has three options: (a) if selecting for a single job, then the person with the highest predicted score can be selected; if selecting for two or more jobs, the decision maker has the following additional options: (b) place each person on the job for which the predicted score is the highest, or (c) place each person on that job where his or her predicted score is farthest above the minimum score necessary to be considered satisfactory.[7]

The multiple regression approach has disadvantages as well. Besides making the assumption that scoring high on one KSA can compensate for scoring low on another KSA without a minimum level required for each predictor, there are statistical issues that are sometimes difficult to resolve. For example, when relatively small samples are used to determine regression weights, the weights may not be stable from one sample to the next.[8] Moreover, the multiple regression approach requires assessing all applicants on all predictors, which can be costly with a large applicant pool.

The multiple regression approach is most appropriate to use when a tradeoff among predictor scores does not affect overall job performance. In addition, it is best used when the sample size for constructing the regression equation is large enough to minimize some of the statistical problems just noted. However, as the size of the applicant pool increases the costs of selection become much larger.

In the example in Table 6.2, the regression equation is provided. Overall scores indicating the predicted success for each applicant are first calculated by entering the individual predictor scores into the equation. Once the overall scores have been calculated, then the applicants can be rank-ordered based on their overall predicted scores. Ordering the applicants based on their overall predicted scores would result in the following ranking: (1) Amanda [predicted score = 102.5], (2) Dave [predicted score = 100], (3) Carl [predicted score = 97.8], (4) Rebecca [predicted score = 93.1], and (5) Cyndy [predicted score = 92.2].

Alternative Two: Multiple Cutoffs

In this model, you measure each applicant on each predictor. Applicants are rejected if any of their predictor scores fall below the minimum cutoffs.

This model makes two important assumptions about job performance: (a) there is a nonlinear relationship among the predictors and the criterion—that is, a minimum amount of each important KSA is necessary for successful performance of a job (the applicant must score above each minimum cutoff to be considered for the job), and (b) predictors are not additive or compensatory. Any lack or deficiency in one KSA cannot be compensated for by having a great deal of some other KSA (an applicant cannot have "0" on any single predictor).

The advantages of this model are that it narrows the applicant pool to a smaller subset of candidates who are all minimally qualified for the job. In addition, it is conceptually simple and easy to explain to managers.[9]

There are two major disadvantages to using this approach to selection decision making. First, like the multiple regression approach, it requires assessing all applicants using all predictors. Therefore, with a large applicant pool, the selection costs may be large. Second, the multiple cutoff approach only identifies those applicants that are minimally qualified for the job. There is no clear-cut way to determine how to order those applicants who pass the cutoffs.

A multiple cutoff approach is probably most useful when physical abilities are essential for job performance. For example, eyesight, color vision, and strength are required for such jobs as police, fire, and heavy manufacturing work.[10] A multiple cutoff decision-making approach would be appropriate for these kinds of jobs.

In the example in Table 6.2, the cutoff scores for each predictor are provided. Carl and Cyndy pass the cutoffs; Amanda, Dave, and Rebecca do not. There is no easy way to choose between the two acceptable applicants. A random choice (e.g., a coin toss) would perhaps be the fairest method.

Alternative Three: Multiple Hurdle

In this model, each applicant must meet the minimum cutoff for each predictor before going to the next predictor. That is, to remain in the viable applicant pool, each applicant must pass each predictor sequentially. Failure to pass a cut-off at any stage in the selection process results in the applicant being dropped from further consideration. An alternative procedure that accomplishes the same results is to calculate a composite multiple regression for each applicant at each successive hurdle. Whenever the probability of success for an applicant drops below some arbitrary value, the applicant is rejected.

In a variation of the multiple hurdle approach, called the *double-stage strat-egy*,[11] two cutoff scores are set, C1 and C2 (see Exhibit 6.1). Those whose scores fall above C2 are accepted unconditionally, and those whose scores fall below C1 are rejected terminally. Applicants whose scores fall between C1 and C2 are accepted provisionally, with a final decision made based on additional testing. This approach has been shown to be equal or superior to all other strategies at all degrees of selectivity.[12]

In the multiple hurdle approach, like the multiple cutoff method, it is assumed there is a minimum level of each KSA necessary for performance on the job. It is not possible for a high level of one KSA to compensate for a low level of another KSA without negatively affecting job performance. Thus the assump-tions of the multiple hurdle approach are identical to those of the multiple cut-off approach. The only distinction between the two is in the procedure for gathering predictor information. In the multiple cutoff approach the procedure is nonsequential, whereas in the hurdle approach the procedure is sequential.

The multiple hurdle approach has the same advantages as the multiple cut-off approach. In addition, it is less costly than the multiple cutoff approach, since the applicant pool becomes smaller at each stage of the selection process. More expensive selection devices can be used at later stages of the selection process on only those applicants that are likely to be hired.

The major disadvantage of this approach relates to establishing validity for each predictor. Since each stage in the selection process reduces the applicant pool to only those on the high end of the ability distribution, restriction of range is a likely problem. As in concurrent validation strategies, this means the

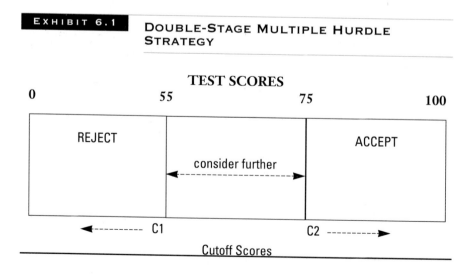

EXHIBIT 6.1   DOUBLE-STAGE MULTIPLE HURDLE STRATEGY

TEST SCORES

| 0 | 55 | 75 | 100 |

REJECT

consider further

ACCEPT

C1   C2

Cutoff Scores

obtained validity coefficients may be underestimated. An additional disadvantage to this approach is the increased time necessary to implement it.

The multiple hurdle approach is most appropriate in situations where subsequent training is long, complex, and expensive.[13] It is also a useful decision-making approach when there is an essential KSA necessary for job performance that cannot be compensated for by the possession of higher levels of other KSAs. For example, typing for a clerical job is an essential skill. Better than average filing skills cannot compensate for the inability to type. There is no reason to further evaluate applicants who cannot pass the typing test. The multiple hurdle approach is also appropriate when there is a large applicant pool, and some of the selection procedures are expensive to administer. For example, when hiring for an information systems manager job you may use a written test as the first hurdle to narrow the applicant pool before administering more expensive assessment devices later to a smaller pool of applicants.

In the example in Table 6.2, the cutoffs for each predictor are provided. Assume the predictors are administered sequentially in the following order: math test, filing test, spelling test, accuracy test, and structured interview. Amanda would be eliminated from the applicant pool after the math test. Dave would be eliminated after the filing test. Rebecca would be eliminated after the accuracy test. Carl and Cyndy would pass all hurdles and thus be equally acceptable for the job.

Alternative Four: Combination Method

In this model, you measure each applicant on each predictor. An applicant with any predictor score below a minimum cutoff is rejected. Thus the combination method is identical to the multiple cutoff procedure to this point. Next, use multiple regression to calculate overall scores for all applicants who pass the cutoffs. Then the applicants who remain can be rank-ordered based on their overall scores calculated by the regression equation. This part of the procedure is identical to the multiple regression approach. Consequently, the combination method is a hybrid of the multiple cutoff and multiple regression approaches.

The combination method has two major assumptions. The more restrictive assumption is derived from the multiple cutoff approach. That is, a minimal level of each KSA is necessary to perform the job. After that level has been reached, more of one KSA can compensate for less of another KSA in predicting overall success of the applicants. This assumption is derived from the multiple regression approach.

The combination method has the advantages of the multiple cutoff approach. But rather than merely identifying a pool of acceptable candidates, which is what you get when using the multiple cutoff approach, the combination approach additionally provides you with a way to select among acceptable applicants.

The major disadvantage of the combination method is that it is more costly than the multiple hurdle approach, since all applicants are screened on all predictors. Consequently, you do not get the savings in cost afforded by the multiple hurdle approach's of reducing the applicant pool.

The combination method is most appropriate to use when the assumption of multiple cutoffs is reasonable and in addition more of one KSA can compensate for another above the minimum cutoffs. It is also more appropriate to use this approach when the size of the applicant pool is not too large and the cost of administering the selection instruments does not vary greatly among instruments.

In the example in Table 6.2, the cutoffs for each predictor are provided. Carl and Cyndy pass all of the cutoffs; Amanda, Dave, and Rebecca do not. Overall scores indicating the predicted success for each applicant that passes all cutoffs are then calculated by entering the individual predictor scores into the equation. Once the overall scores have been calculated, the applicants can be rank-ordered based on their overall predicted scores. Ordering the applicants based on their overall predicted scores would result in the following ranking: (1) Carl [predicted score = 97.8] and (2) Cyndy [predicted score = 92.2].

Alternative Five: Profile Matching

In this model you first measure current successful employees on the job across several predictors. Then you average their scores on each predictor to obtain an overall profile of scores necessary for successful job performance. Next you measure applicants on each predictor and compare their score profiles to the ideal profile. Applicants' profiles that are most similar to the ideal profile are then employed. Profiles can differ in terms of (a) level—the mean score of the person over the variables in the profile, (b) dispersion—how widely scores in a profile diverge from the average level, and (c) shape—the ups and downs in the profile.[14]

There are two methods for defining profile similarity.[15] In the D^2 method, you calculate the differences between the applicant's score and the ideal profile on each predictor, square the differences, and sum them. The larger the differences, the poorer the match. Here is the formula for calculating D^2:

$$D^2 = \sum (X_{ij} - X_{sj})^2$$

$\sum_{k} D^2$ = the degree to which the profile of the applicant matched the "ideal" profile

X_{ij} = score of person i on trait j

X_{sj} = score of ideal profile on trait j

A second method for determining profile similarity requires calculating the correlation between the applicants' scores on the predictors with the scores on the predictors for the "ideal" profile. The higher the correlation, the better the match. There are high scores where the ideal is high and low scores where the ideal is low.

Jum Nunnally[16] recommends the D^2 approach because it considers profile level, dispersion, and shape whereas the correlation approach only considers profile shape. Selection decisions can be made in one of two ways:[17] (a) Select those people whose profile points tend to be the highest (i.e., their average profile score is used). This is equivalent to using a multiple regression selection model where each profile trait has an equal regression weight (low profile scores on one trait can be compensated for by high profile scores on another trait), or (b) Select those people who have profiles with the highest average profile score and whose points all lie above their corresponding "ideal" profile counterparts. This is equivalent to a combination of the multiple cutoff (the ideal profile scores become the minimum cutoffs) and multiple regression approach (higher on some traits can compensate for lower scores on others).

This model assumes that the composite profile of successful employees is significantly different from the composite profile of unsatisfactory employees. Milton Blum and James Naylor[18] point out that this assumption should be established empirically.

The major advantage of this approach is that it does not require setting arbitrary cutoff scores for decision making. Furthermore, it makes it possible to rank-order applicants based on their similarity to the ideal profile.

The major disadvantages of this approach include the requirement of establishing significant group differences on important KSAs before selecting applicants. There is likely a restriction of range problem in establishing group differences on current employees. In addition, ideal profiles are sample specific and should be checked periodically, much like weighted application blanks. Moreover, this method assumes one best profile when in fact there may be several profiles that are equally predictive of success, but not captured by this decision-making model.

Perhaps the most serious critique of this model was articulated by Frank Landy and Don Trumbo.[19] They argue that information about the validity of the predictors is often ignored in profile matching models, a critical oversight. For example, assume that out of 7 predictors, the successful group is above average on predictors 3, 5, and 6, about average on predictors 2 and 4, and below average on predictors 1 and 7. If each of the 7 predictors has predictive validity, then predictors 3, 5, and 6 would have positive validity coefficients, predictors 1 and 7 negative coefficients, and predictors 2 and 4 curvilinear coefficients (average scores predictive of success, but low and high scores predictive of something less than success). If the average score values are taken as characterizing the population from which the successfuls are a subsample, then the failures must have values on the opposite side of the mean. But when the successfuls are average, they could deviate from the population only if the failures were high and low, but not average on that trait. Landy and Trumbo conclude that because of this information about the validity of the elements in the profile (which are not usually presented), the multiple regression approach should be preferred over profile matching.

This decision-making approach is appropriate to use when there is a clearly best type of employee for the job (i.e., one best profile for job success). When this assumption is unreasonable, the multiple regression approach offers an alternative, since it allows for more than one configuration of KSAs to be predictive of job success.

In the example in Table 6.2, the average scores for each predictor (i.e., the ideal profile) are provided. Calculating the D^2 for each applicant results in rank-ordering them as follows: (1) Rebecca [$D^2 = 86$], (2) Cyndy [$D^2 = 91$], (3) Amanda [$D^2 = 151$], (4) Carl [$D^2 = 158$], and (5) Dave [$D^2 = 247$]. The correlation method would result in rank-ordering the applicants as follows: (1) Carl [r = .992], (2) Cyndy [r = .975], (3) Dave [r = .966], (4) Amanda [r = .965], and (5) Rebecca [r = .960]. Note that when the correlation method is used there is practically no difference among the applicants. Each of them has a profile that is highly correlated with the ideal profile.

Setting Cutoff Scores

In three of the selection decision-making models just described (multiple cutoff, multiple hurdle, and combination) it is necessary to establish cutoff scores. This section describes methods for setting cutoff scores in both the simple case with one predictor and in the more complex case with multiple predictors. Cutoff scores can be established based on (a) judgments of the difficulty of test/predictor items or (b) the performance of persons whose ability to perform some task is known.[20]

Single Predictor Case

Two relatively simple methods can be used to set cutoff scores when you have a single predictor. *Thorndike's "predicted yield" method*[21] requires obtaining the following information for establishing a cutoff score (a) the number of positions available during some future time period, (b) the number of applicants to be expected during that time period, (c) the expected distribution of the applicants' predictor scores. The cutoff score is then determined based on the percentage of applicants that need to be hired in order to fill the positions. For example, if you need 20 machinists and you expect 250 people to apply for the jobs, then your selection ratio will be .08 (20/250). Since 92 percent of the applicants will be rejected, the cutoff score should be set at the 92d percentile on the local norms (norms based on the company's past experience) plus or minus one standard error of measurement.

In the *expectancy chart method*[22] you use the same analytical procedure as in the Thorndike method to determine the expected selection ratio. Once you have determined the expected percentage of applicants that will be rejected, you identify the score associated with that percentile plus or minus one standard error of measurement.

Multiple Predictor Case

When you have more than one predictor, it becomes necessary to establish cutoffs for each predictor (as in the multiple cutoff, the multiple hurdle, or the combination methods). The methods we discuss here are based on setting cutoff scores for tests; however, they can be adapted to other selection devices as well. For example, Neal Schmitt and Richard Klimoski describe how the Angoff method was adapted to setting cutoff scores for an in-basket examination.[23]

The *Ebel method*[24] is based on an analysis of the difficulty of test items. First, experts rate all test items on the following basis: (a) difficulty (hard, medium, easy), and (b) relevance to job performance (essential, important, acceptable, and questionable). This rating produces 12 categories of items. For each of the categories of items, judges are then asked what percentage of the items a borderline test taker would be able to answer correctly. The judges are asked the following question: "If a borderline test taker had to answer a large number of questions like these, what percentage would he or she answer correctly?" The cutoff score is calculated by multiplying the percentage of items correct times the number of questions in each category and then summing the products across all of the separate categories. See Table 6.3 for an example of this method.

TABLE 6.3   **THE EBEL METHOD FOR SETTING CUTOFF SCORES**

	Easy		Medium		Hard	
	Questions	**% Correct**	**Questions**	**% Correct**	**Questions**	**% Correct**
Relevance to Job Performance						
Essential	22, 17, 10, 5, 2	90	12, 19	80	11, 15, 25	70
Important	1, 8, 23, 30	85	16, 26, 27, 29	70	4, 24	65
Acceptable	3, 6, 13	80	14, 21	65	18	55
Questionable	7	60	21, 32	50	none	—

(Header above the three pairs: **Difficulty of Test Items**)

Category	% Correct	Number of Questions	Expected Score for Category
Essential			
easy	90	5	.90 × 5 = 4.5
medium	80	2	.80 × 2 = 1.6
hard	70	3	.70 × 3 = 2.1
Important			
easy	85	4	.85 × 4 = 3.4
medium	70	4	.70 × 4 = 2.8
hard	65	2	.65 × 2 = 1.3
Acceptable			
easy	80	3	.80 × 3 = 2.4
medium	65	2	.65 × 2 = 1.3
hard	55	1	.55 × 1 = .55
Questionable			
easy	.60	1	.60 × 1 = .60
medium	.50	2	.50 × 2 = 1.0
hard	0	0	0
	Sum (Expected Total Score)		21.55

In the *Angoff method*[25] judges are also used to establish the cutoff scores. As William Angoff describes it, ". . . the judges would think of a number of minimally acceptable persons, instead of only one such person, and would estimate the proportion of minimally acceptable persons who would answer each item correctly. The sum of these probabilities, or proportions, would then represent the minimally acceptable score." See Table 6.4 for an example of this procedure.

A modification of this procedure, described as the *modified Angoff method*, reduces the score calculated by the Angoff method by one, two, or three standard errors of measurement. This adjustment has been accepted in numerous court cases.[26]

Neal Schmitt and Richard Klimoski propose a variation of the Angoff method.[27] Their variation was applied to a 25-item in-basket examination used as part of a promotional procedure in a governmental organization. Each of the 25 items was scored on a 4-point scale with 4 an indication of a superior answer and 1 judged as a clearly inferior response. Expert judges (job incumbents) were asked to review the in-basket items and provide responses to the following question for each item: "Consider a *minimally competent applicant* for a middle-level manager's

TABLE 6.4	THE ANGOFF METHOD FOR SETTING CUTOFF SCORES

Question Number	Proportion Answering Correctly
1	.90
2	.55
3	.70
4	.80
5	.85
6	.60
7	.55
8	.75
9	.95
10	.60
11	.75
12	.60
13	.55
14	.80
15	.70
16	.70
17	.70
18	.75
19	.65
20	.55
	Sum = 14.0

Unmodified Cutoff Score	14.0
Modified Cutoff Score (with 1 SEM = 2.1)[†]	11.9

[†]SEM = Standard Error of Measurement.

position in state government. This is not an outstanding candidate or even an average applicant, but one that could perform tests at a *minimally* satisfactory level. Now look at each item and the scoring instructions for that item. What percentage of these *minimally competent* applicants would receive a score of 4 on these items? What percentage would receive a score of 3? Of 2? Of 1?" For example, one judge might evaluate an item as follows: 4 = 0 percent, 3 = 30 percent, 2 = 60 percent, and 1 = 10 percent. This judge indicates that most (60 percent) of the minimally competent applicants can write a response to this in-basket item that would receive a score of 2. Average scores of judges for each item would be calculated. Then these averages would be totaled across all items to determine the cutoff score. This method would also be useful for other selection instruments, such as determining cutoff scores for structured interviews.

The *contrasting groups method* uses a judgment of the test takers rather than the items as the basis for determining cutoff scores.[28] (This method is also described in Chapter 11.) The first step is to divide test takers (usually job incumbents) into qualified and unqualified groups based on judgments of their knowledge and skills. The next step is to calculate the percentage of test takers who are qualified and unqualified at each test score. The cutoff score is chosen at that point where the proportion of qualified test takers is equal to the proportion of unqualified test takers. This assumes that rejecting unqualified candidates is as important as accepting qualified candidates. If you wish to minimize either false positive or false negative errors, then the cutoff score can be moved either up or down.

Legal and Psychometric Issues

Little guidance on setting cutoff scores is given in the two principal documents referred to for legal and psychometric selection standards. The *Uniform Guidelines on Employee Selection Procedures*[29] states the following about cutoff scores:

> Where cutoff scores are used, they should normally be set so as to be reasonable and consistent with normal expectations of acceptable proficiency within the work force. Where applicants are ranked on the basis of properly validated selection procedures and those applicants scoring below a higher cutoff score than appropriate in light of such expectations have little or no chance of being selected for employment, the higher cutoff score may be more appropriate, but the degree of adverse impact should be considered.

The *Principles for the Validation and Use of Personnel Selection Procedures*[30] states the following regarding cutoff scores: "Cutoff or other critical scores may be set as high or as low as the purposes of the organization require, if they are based on valid predictors."

In a review of the legal and psychometric literature on cutoff scores, Wayne Cascio and colleagues[31] offered the following guidelines:

- It is unrealistic to expect a single best method of setting cutoff scores for all situations.

- Begin with a job analysis that identifies relative levels of proficiency on critical knowledge, skills, abilities, and other characteristics.

- The validity and job relatedness of the assessment procedure are critical considerations.

- How a test is used (criterion- or norm-referenced) affects the selection and meaning of a cutoff score.

- When possible, data on actual performance should be considered carefully.

- Set cutoff scores high enough to ensure that minimum standards of job performance are met.

- Cutoff scores should be consistent with normal expectations of proficiency within the work force.

Ranking versus Banding for Making Selection Decisions

In deciding which applicants to hire, you have a choice of two basic approaches. You can (a) rank-order the applicants based on their overall scores and select from the top down, or (b) group applicants based on a range of scores and select any applicant in the qualified range. Each of these procedures is discussed next.

Rank-ordering applicants by their selection scores assumes that a person with a higher score will perform better on the job than a person with a lower score. There is some controversy over whether it is appropriate to use rank ordering when content validation has been used as the strategy for validating the selection procedure.[32] The *Uniform Guidelines* state that tests validated by content validation strategies should only use minimum cutoffs and not rank ordering for selection decisions. However, the evidence for a linear relationship between ability and performance is so overwhelming that unless there is convincing evidence of a nonlinear relationship between predictor and criterion, selecting the highest scoring person is always the best approach. The *Principles for the Validation and Use of Selection Procedures*[33] supports this position and states that ". . . selecting from the top scorers on down is almost always the most beneficial procedure from the standpoint of the organization if there is an appropriate amount of variance in the predictor."

One issue related to rank ordering is its potentially negative effect on adverse impact. This has been dealt with among state employment services that use the GATB (General Aptitude Test Battery) for job referrals. Since blacks and Hispanics tend to have slightly lower average scores than whites on such tests, using a rank-order approach with top-down selection may select a disproportionately larger number of whites than blacks or Hispanics. In order to prevent adverse impact resulting from the use of this test, many state employment agencies have practiced race norming. *Race norming* or *within-group scoring* is a procedure whereby applicants are ranked on their test scores within their racial groups.[34]

For example, whites would be rank-ordered on their test scores in comparison to other whites. Blacks would be rank-ordered on their test scores in comparison to other blacks, Hispanics in comparison to other Hispanics, and so on. Selection decisions would be made by taking the top "X" percentile from each group. This procedure was developed in order to gain some of the benefits of rank-order decision making without creating additional adverse impact. The average quality of hires would be greatest with a rank-order procedure applied across all groups; however rank ordering within groups allows for achieving the highest average quality while still pursuing affirmative action goals.

The Civil Rights Act (CRA) of 1991 made race norming a prohibited practice.[35] In fact, the CRA prohibits the adjustment of scores, the use of different cutoff scores, or the alteration of results of employment-related tests on the basis of ethnicity, religion, gender, or national origin. One alternative to race norming that should be permissible is banding, or establishing ranges of equivalent scores, where the test does not predict differential success within the band.

Banding assumes that all applicants who score within a range of scores are equally likely to succeed on the job. It assumes that an individual's score may not precisely represent his or her job performance potential. Consistent with classical test theory, banding takes into account the concept of the standard error of measurement. Bands (or score ranges) can be established in a number of ways: (a) using a specific percentage of the examinee group in a band, (b) using proportions of examinees in bands that would approximate a normal distribution of scores, (c) using specific intervals of raw scores, or (d) using the standard error of measurement. The particular method chosen is not important as long as bands can be rationally differentiated from each other.

Two methods for establishing bands have been accepted by the courts: (a) the standard error of measurement method, and (b) the standard error of differences method. In the *standard error of measurement method* you begin by calculating the standard error of measurement for the test or predictor. Then you multiply the standard error of measurement by 2 and subtract the product from a score. This results in a range of scores that are basically equivalent 95 percent of the time. For example, assume that the standard error of measurement (SEM) is equal to 2.98. Multiplying 2.98 by 2 gives you a product of 5.96. If the top score is 95, subtracting 5.96 results in a score of 89.04. Thus scores between 89.04 and 95 are not significantly different.

In the *standard error of differences method* you also begin by calculating the standard error of measurement. Then you multiply it by the square root of 2. This number is then multiplied by 2 to determine the range of scores where you can be 95 percent sure that the difference is real. For example, assume that the SEM = 2.98. The standard error of differences (SED) calculation is $2(2.98 \times \sqrt{2}) = 8.43$. If the top score is 95, subtracting 8.43 results in a score of 86.57. Scores

EXHIBIT 6.2   **FIXED VERSUS SLIDING BANDS FOR COMPARING TEST SCORES**

Fixed Band

95
88   88   88
87
85
84   84   84   84

82
80   80

79
78   78   78   78
77   77

Sliding Band

95
88   88   88
87
85
84   84   84   84

82

80   80

79

78   78   78   78
77   77

Note: Test scores *within* a band are not considered to be significantly different. Test scores in *different* bands are considered to be significantly different.

between 86.57 and 95 are not significantly different. Note that the SED method results in a slightly larger band width than the SEM method.

Bands can be established as either fixed or sliding. See Exhibit 6.2. *Fixed bands* use the top score attained as the starting point. The top score minus the range of score values (standard error of measurement times 2) constitutes the band. Individuals within this band can be selected in any order. If more individuals must be selected than are in the first band, a second band must be created. The highest remaining score is now the basis for determining the band of score values using the same procedure.

In Exhibit 6.2, the first fixed band is created by taking the top score (95) and subtracting the band width (2.98 × 2 = 5.96). This results in a band range from 89.04 to 95. One applicant is within the first band. After that applicant has been selected, the second band is created by subtracting the band width (5.96) from 89.03 (the next highest score after selecting all applicants in the first band). This results in a band range from 83.07 to 89.03. Nine applicants are within the second band and any one of them can be selected. After all of the applicants in the second band have been selected, the third band is created by subtracting the band width from 83.06. This results in a band range from 79.10 to 83.06.

With *sliding bands*, each selection decision is based on those applicants that are still available for selection. You start with the highest scorer to determine the band range, as in the previous procedure. However, it is not necessary to select everybody in the band before the next band is created. Only the top scorer needs to be selected for the band to change. Once the top scorer is selected, then the next highest score is used to establish the new band. Thus the band slides down each time the top scorer is selected. This provides a larger number of applicants to select from and makes it possible to select some of the applicants who have lower scores and would not be available using the fixed band method.

In Exhibit 6.2, the first sliding band is created by taking the top score (95) and subtracting the band width (5.96). This results in a band range from 89.04 to 95. After the top scorer (the applicant with the 95) has been selected, the second band is created by subtracting the band width from the next highest remaining score (88). This results in a band range from 82.04 to 88. After the three applicants with the highest score (88) have been selected, then the band can be changed again. This time, the band width (5.96) is subtracted from the next highest remaining score (87) resulting in a band range from 81.04 to 87. Consequently, the band slides downward including more applicants each time the highest scoring applicant(s) are selected.

Using either the fixed or the sliding band approach makes it possible to reduce adverse impact, since all applicants within the band are considered equal. This may make it possible to choose a larger number of minorities than would be feasible in a situation where they do not make the very top scores. It is unclear whether using banding to identify equally qualified individuals and then choosing on the basis of ethnicity or gender within the band will withstand legal challenge. The CRA's mixed motive clause[36] indicates than an employer violates the law when the complaining party can demonstrate that race, sex, color, religion, or national origin was a motivating factor in the employment decision. Thus affirmative action programs that go beyond outreach or extra recruitment efforts and include preferential selection may be contested under this provision. It may, therefore, be prudent to use the banding procedures to identify equally qualified candidates and then use a random procedure for selecting from among those included in the band. Banding increases the likelihood that a minority would have the opportunity to be selected. Then, random selection from within the band would ensure that the final decision was not "motivated" by ethnicity or gender.

A Practical Approach to Making Selection Decisions

There are several issues to consider when choosing among selection decision-making procedures: (a) Should the procedure be sequential (e.g., multiple hurdle) or nonsequential (e.g., multiple regression or multiple cutoff)? (b) Should the decision be compensatory (e.g., multiple regression) or noncompensatory (e.g., multiple cutoff, multiple hurdle, or profile matching)? (c) Should the decision be based on ranking applicants or should it be based on banding acceptable applicants?

In making the choice among decision-making options you should begin by assessing the job and the nature of job performance. What determines success on the job? What factors contribute to success and how are they related? After you have answered these questions, the next issues to consider include (a) the number of applicants expected, (b) the cost of selection devices used, and (c) the amount of time you can devote to the selection decision.

Once you have decided on a selection decision-making strategy, you must implement it systematically in order to reap the potential benefits. Furthermore, the results of numerous studies of decision making are clear: *If you can develop and use an objective linear model, you can improve your decision making.* Many selection decisions meet the criteria[37] necessary for building such a model: (a) the same decision is made repeatedly (normal turnover requires hiring for the same position numerous times), (b) data on the outcomes of past decisions are available (applicants are hired and their performance can be tracked over time), and (c) you have good reason to expect the future will resemble the past (many jobs change very little, if at all, over time). When these models are built using sound validation strategies as discussed in this book, powerful decision aids become available to decision makers.

In many cases, however, it is not possible to build objective linear models because of the sporadic nature of selection and the small number of applicants employed. This is especially true for many small businesses. Furthermore, for owners and managers of small businesses, selection is but one of many important activities competing for their time. What can decision makers in this situation do to improve their selection decisions?

Suppose a small business owner needs to employ an assistant.[38] First, she specifies what tasks this assistant will be asked to perform and the standards of performance that the assistant will be judged against. Next, she thinks of activities she could ask an applicant to do during the interview and selection process that are similar to if not exactly what the assistant would do on the job. After identifying some job-related activities the applicants could be asked to do, the owner next thinks about what weights should be attached to each of the activities used for selection. While these weights are subjective, and not based on an empirical analysis of previous hires, they are at least made explicit before the selection process begins. By using some simplified rating process to assess each applicant on each selection activity, the owner then has a systematic procedure for collecting data on applicants and ensuring that applicants are evaluated on the same criteria. Once the applicants have been processed in this manner, the final selection decision can then be based on a "subjective linear model."[39] By multiplying the weights attached to each selection activity times the rating she gave each applicant, and then summing these products, an overall score can be calculated for each applicant that yields a systematically derived judgment of the applicant's likely success on the job.

An even better subjective decision-making procedure than the one just described uses a technique called bootstrapping.[40] *Bootstrapping* is based on the assumption that while people can often make sound judgments, they are not typically able to articulate how they made those judgments. Using this technique requires having the decision maker make judgments on a series of cases (e.g., selection decision judgments based on a number of applicant files). Then, through regression analysis, the weights the decision maker used to arrive at a particular ranking can be inferred. The regression analysis shows how much weight, on average, the decision maker has put on each of the underlying factors. As J. Edward Russo and Paul Schoemaker describe it, "In bootstrapping, you seek to build a model of an expert using his or her own intuitive predictions, and then use that model to *outperform* the expert on new cases."[41] This method works because when you ask a person to make a prediction, "you get wisdom mixed in with random noise." Judgments based on intuition suffer greatly from random noise caused by an array of factors ranging from fatigue and boredom to stress and anxiety. Bootstrapping produces a standard procedure for decision making that eliminates the random noise while retaining the "core wisdom." Consequently, by using bootstrapping, the decision will be made in the same way today, tomorrow, next week, and next year. Numerous studies support the finding that bootstrapped models consistently do better at predictions than simple intuitive judgments. This leads us to the fascinating conclusion that models of our own subjective decision-making processes can be built that outperform us! Nevertheless, when an objective model can be constructed, it still outperforms both bootstrapped models and simple intuition. Therefore, it is always best to use an objective model whenever possible.

One last issue we must address when discussing a practical approach to making selection decisions is procedural fairness. Whether you use a systematic objective model of decision making or a simple intuitive approach, it is critical that the procedures be perceived as fair. In selection, the term *face validity* is used to describe selection practices that applicants believe to be reasonable (e.g., using a mechanical ability test for a machinist job would likely seem reasonable to an applicant applying for the job). But in addition to selection instruments having face validity, decision-making procedures, too, must be seen as fair.

One factor that seems to affect whether or not decision-making procedures are viewed as fair is how well they are justified.[42] This seems especially important for dealing with applicants who are rejected during the selection process. Rejected applicants will accept their rejection better if they believe they were treated justly, had a fair chance to obtain the job, and that someone better qualified received the job. Objective decision-making models built on solid evidence should be easier to justify to applicants than intuitive models that cannot be clearly articulated. However, regardless of which approach is used, ensuring procedural fairness should be a major consideration when developing selection procedures.

Auditing Selection Decisions: Learning from Your Successes and Failures

The only way you can improve your selection decision making is to learn from what you have done in the past. This dictum applies at both the organizational level and at the individual level. At the organizational level, validation studies can help improve overall organizational selection decision making by identifying scientifically those factors that predict job success and eliminating those factors that do not predict job success. Using validation strategies to merely comply with legal requirements is a gross underutilization of this powerful technology. Organizations that routinely validate their selection practices set the context for good decisions to occur. Organizations that do not routinely validate their selection practices create a decision-making context that may or may not lead to desirable outcomes.

At the individual level, most managers do not think about their success and failure rate at making selection decisions. This is not surprising, since numerous selection decisions may be made over many years. Yet it is surprising that managers are not held as accountable for their selection decisions as they are for other decisions, such as capital equipment purchases. Aren't a high number of bad selection decisions as damaging to an organization as the purchase of an unreliable piece of machinery? Several bad selection decisions can lead to lower productivity, high separation and replacement costs, as well as potentially damaging litigation. So how can managers be held accountable for their selection decisions as well as learn from their successes and failures?

The decision-making literature suggests that a simple box-score tally of successes and failures can improve decision making over time.[43] Decision makers learn from their feedback that either supports or disconfirms their predictive models. This simple procedure may not have prevented Roger (remember him from the beginning of the chapter?) from making selection errors, but it would certainly have reduced his overconfidence in his decision-making ability! Furthermore, if these individual decision audits are made throughout the organization, both good and bad decision makers can be identified for either reinforcement or remedial training.

Conclusions

Even the best designed selection systems will not produce good selection decisions unless good selection decision-making procedures are used as well. To ensure that an organization maximizes the effectiveness of its selection system, the following prescriptions should be followed: (a) Use valid selection devices, (b) Encourage managers and others who make selection decisions to participate in the data-gathering process (e.g., interview ratings, etc.), but dissuade them from making selection decisions based on gut feel or intuition, (c) Train managers and others who make decisions to make systematic and consistent selection decisions (preferably using one of the approaches described in this chapter) and to keep track of their own hits (correct decisions) and misses (incorrect decisions), and (d) Periodically audit selection decisions throughout the organization to identify areas for improvement. These prescriptions do not guarantee that you will always make correct decisions, but they do tilt the odds in your favor!

References

[1] Jack Sawyer, "Measurement and Prediction, Clinical and Statistical," *Psychological Bulletin* 66 (1966): 178–200.

[2] For a review, see Benjamin Kleinmutz, "Why We Still Use Our Heads Instead of Formulas: Toward an Integrative Approach," *Psychological Bulletin* 107 (1990): 296–310.

[3] Bernard M. Bass and Gerald V. Barrett, *People, Work, and Organizations*, 2d ed. (Boston: Allyn & Bacon, 1981), 397–398.

[4] In the book by J. Edward Russo and Paul J. H. Schoemaker, *Decision Traps* (New York: Simon & Schuster, 1989), the authors provide several compelling strategies for convincing people to adopt mechanical approaches for combining predictive information.

[5] Max Bazerman, *Judgment in Managerial Decision Making* (New York: Wiley, 1990), 175.

[6] Wayne F. Cascio, *Applied Psychology in Personnel Management*, 4th ed. (Englewood Cliffs, N.J.: Prentice Hall, 1991), 286.

[7] Milton L. Blum and James C. Naylor, *Industrial Psychology: Its Theoretical and Social Foundations* (New York: Harper & Row, 1969), 68–69.

[8] See Wayne F. Cascio, E. R. Valenzi, and Val Silbey, "Validation and Statistical Power: Implications for Applied Research," *Journal of Applied Psychology* 63 (1978): 589–595 and Wayne F. Cascio, E. R. Valenzi, and Val Silbey, "More on Validation and Statistical Power," *Journal of Applied Psychology* 65 (1980): 135–138.

[9] Cynthia D. Fisher, Lyle F. Schoenfeldt, and James B. Shaw, *Human Resource Management* (Boston: Houghton Mifflin, 1990), 231.

[10] Neal W. Schmitt and Richard J. Klimoski, *Research Methods in Human Resources Management* (Cincinnati: South-Western, 1991), 302.

[11] Cascio, *Applied Psychology in Personnel Management*, 289.

[12] Lee J. Cronbach and Goldine C. Gleser, *Psychological Tests and Personnel Decisions*, 2d ed. (Urbana: University of Illinois Press, 1965).

[13] Richard R. Reilly and W. R. Manese, "The Validation of a Minicourse for Telephone Company Switching Technicians, *Personnel Psychology* 32 (1979): 83–90.

[14] Jum C. Nunnally, *Psychometric Theory*, 2d ed. (New York: McGraw-Hill, 1978) 438–440.

[15] Blum and Naylor, *Industrial Psychology: Its Theoretical and Social Foundations*, 73–74.

[16] Nunnally, *Psychometric Theory*, 438–440.

[17] Blum and Naylor, *Industrial Psychology: Its Theoretical and Social Foundations*, 75.

[18] Blum and Naylor, *Industrial Psychology: Its Theoretical and Social Foundations*, 72–73.

[19] This example is from their book, Frank J. Landy and Don A. Trumbo, *Psychology of Work Behavior* (Homewood, Ill.: Dorsey Press, 1980), 174–175.

[20] Schmitt and Klimoski, *Research Methods in Human Resources Management*, 302.

[21] Robert L. Thorndike, *Personnel Selection: Test and Measurement Techniques* (New York: Wiley, 1949).

[22] Cascio, *Applied Psychology in Personnel Management*, 288.

[23] Schmitt and Klimoski, *Research Methods in Human Resources Management*, 303.

[24] Robert L. Ebel, *Essentials of Educational Measurement* (Englewood Cliffs, N.J.: Prentice-Hall, 1972).

[25] William H. Angoff, "Scales, Norms, and Equivalent Scores," in *Educational Measurement*, ed. Robert L. Thorndike (Washington, D.C.: American Council on Education, 1971), 508–600.

[26] Richard E. Biddle, "How to Set Cutoff Scores for Knowledge Tests Used in Promotion, Training, Certification, and Licensing," *Public Personnel Management* 22 (1993): 63–80.

[27] Schmitt and Klimoski, *Research Methods in Human Resources Management*, 303.

[28] The contrasting groups method is described in detail in the discussion of setting cut-off scores for weighted application blanks. See George W. England, *Development and Use of Weighted Application Blanks* (Minneapolis: Industrial Relations Center, University of Minnesota, 1971).

[29] Equal Employment Opportunity Commission, Civil Service Commission, Department of Labor, and Department of Justice, *Adoption of Four Agencies of Uniform Guidelines on Employee Selection Procedures*, 43 Federal Register 38, 290–38, 315 (Aug. 25, 1978).

[30] Society for Industrial and Organizational Psychology, *Principles for the Validation and Use of Personnel Selection Procedures*, 3d ed. (College Park, Md. Author, 1987), 32.

[31] Wayne F. Cascio, Ralph A. Alexander, and Gerald V. Barrett, "Setting Cutoff Scores: Legal, Psychometric, and Professional Issues and Guidelines," *Personnel Psychology* 41 (1989): 1–24.

[32] Schmitt and Klimoski, *Research Methods in Human Resources Management*, 301.

[33] Society for Industrial and Organizational Psychology, *Principles for the Validation and Use of Personnel Selection Procedures*, 32.

[34] For an excellent discussion of these issues regarding the General Aptitude Test Battery, see John A. Hartigan and Alexandra K. Wigdor, *Fairness in Employment Testing: Validity Generalization, Minority Issues, and the General Aptitude Test Battery* (Washington, D.C.: National Academy Press, 1989).

[35] Lawrence Z. Lorber, "The Civil Rights Act of 1991," in *Legal Report* (Washington, D.C.: Society for Human Resource Management, Spring 1992), 1–4.

[36] Lorber, 1–4.

[37] Russo and Schoemaker, *Decision Traps*, 138.

[38] This procedure is similar to one described in Benjamin Schneider and Neal Schmitt, *Staffing Organizations* (Glenview, Ill.: Scott, Foresmann, 1986), 416.

[39] Russo and Schoemaker, *Decision Traps*, 131–134.

[40] Ibid., 134–137.

[41] Ibid., 135.

[42] See, for example, R. J. Bies and D. L. Shapiro, "Voice and Justification: Their Influence on Procedural Fairness Judgments," *Academy of Management Journal* 31 (1988): 676–685.

[43] Kleinmutz, 296–310.

III

Job Analysis in Human Resource Selection

In selecting personnel to fill job vacancies, managers are ultimately faced with some important questions that must be addressed. These questions include the following: What tasks are new employees required to perform? What knowledge, skills, and abilities (that is, employee or job specifications) must new employees possess to perform these tasks effectively? If certain specifications are used, is it then possible to develop selection instruments such as tests or employment interviews that could be used in making selection decisions? For any job under study, what factors or measures exist that represent job success? These are but a few of the questions that confront managers involved in human resource selection. Answers are not always obvious and seldom easy. Yet, whatever the issue in human resource selection, there is one managerial tool that can and should be used first in addressing selection considerations—*job analysis*.

This section provides an overview of the job analysis process in the context of HR selection. Our objectives are fourfold:

1. To explore the role of job analysis,

2. To describe various techniques used in collecting job information,

3. To examine how job information can be used to identify employee specifications (such as knowledge, skills, and abilities or KSAs) necessary for successful job performance, and

4. To examine how these specifications can be translated into the content of selection measures including predictors (such as tests, employment interviews, and application forms) as well as criterion measures (such as performance appraisal rating forms and objective measures of productivity).

7

Preparing for Job Analysis: An Overview

Role of Job Analysis in HR Selection

A Definition and Model

There are probably as many definitions of job analysis as there are writings on the topic. For our purposes though, when we refer to *job analysis*, we simply mean *a purposeful, systematic process for collecting information on the important work-related aspects of a job.* Some possible types of work-related information to be collected might include the following:

1. Work activities—what a worker does; how, why, and when these activities are conducted,

2. Tools and equipment used in performing work activities,

3. Context of the work environment, such as work schedule or physical working conditions, and

4. Requirements of personnel performing the job, such as knowledge, skills, abilities, or other personal characteristics, like physical characteristics, interests, or personality.[1]

The information obtained from a job analysis has been found to serve a wide variety of purposes.[2] For example, over 40 years ago Joseph Zerga identified more than 20 uses of job analysis data.[3] More recently, job analysis data have been used in areas such as compensation, training, and performance appraisal among many others. Of particular interest here is the application to HR selection.

Broadly speaking in the context of HR selection, job analysis data are frequently used to:

1. Identify employee specifications (KSAs) necessary for success on a job,

2. Develop predictors or measures of job applicants used to screen them and forecast who is likely to be a successful employee on a job, and

3. Develop criteria or standards of performance that employees must meet in order to be considered successful on a job.

By examining factors such as the tasks performed on a job as well as the KSAs needed to perform these tasks, an idea of what job behaviors ought to be measured by predictors and criteria used in employment screening can be obtained. As an example, consider the job of a bank teller. An analysis of a teller's job might identify a number of tasks that are critical to successful job performance. Examination of these tasks as well as the KSAs needed to perform them might reveal a number of important findings. For instance, a job analysis may reveal that balancing receipts and disbursements of cash, performing arithmetic operations on numbers involving dollars and cents, and entering transaction information into a computer are critical teller tasks. Conversely, selling certificates of deposit and savings bonds, opening savings accounts, and handling transactions involving the payoff of customer loans are less critical tasks performed by a teller. Further analysis of such job information may indicate that one important criterion of successful teller performance is the dollar balance of a teller's receipts and disbursements for a workday. That is, a teller should not take in more (an "overage") or fewer (a "shortage") dollars than he or she has disbursed. An examination of the KSAs associated with a teller's balancing receipts and disbursements might show the ability to add, subtract, multiply, and divide numbers involving decimals is *one* important requirement. Therefore, in searching for a predictor of teller success, attention would be given to locating or developing one that provides information on a teller's capability to perform arithmetic operations on monetary numbers.

When predictors and criteria are developed based on the results of a job analysis, a selection system that is job-related can be developed. As we suggested in earlier chapters, by using a job-related selection system we are in a much better position to predict who can and who cannot adequately perform a job. In addition, with a job-related selection system, we are far more likely to have an employment system that will be viewed by job applicants as well as the courts as being a "fair" one.

Exhibit 7.1 outlines a general framework for the application of a job analysis in the context of HR selection. Initially, an analysis of a job is conducted using any of a number of available techniques. We have mentioned that, most often, information on the critical job tasks, duties, or work behaviors performed on the job will be identified initially. The identification of these critical job tasks is used to produce two important products: (a) criterion measures such as performance appraisals or productivity assessments and (b) predictor measures such as tests,

EXHIBIT 7.1 ROLE OF JOB ANALYSIS IN HUMAN RESOURCE SELECTION

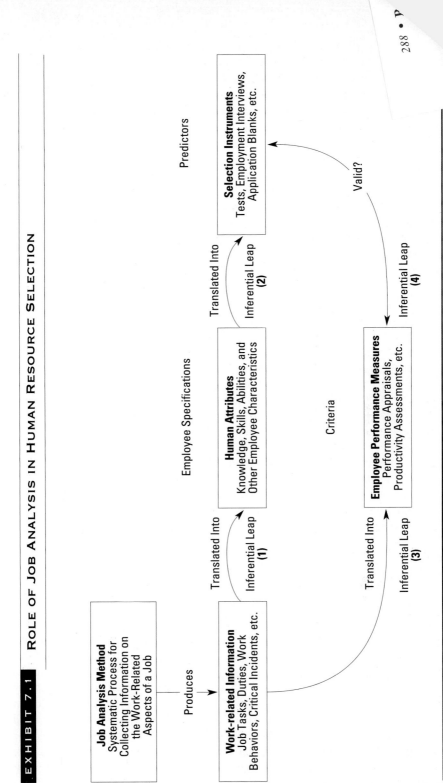

application forms, or employment interviews. Oftentimes, criterion measures are developed or identified directly from job task information. However, the development of predictors typically requires some intermediate steps. For example, from job task information, employee specifications (that is, the KSAs and other personal characteristics) that are needed to perform the critical job tasks are specified. Usually this step involves the judgment of job experts (such as supervisors or key job incumbents) to estimate the necessary employee specifications. Once employee specifications have been identified, it is possible to develop measures of these employee requirements; these are the measures that will serve as employee screening tools.

Assuming that predictor and job performance measures are derived from a job analysis, it is expected that job applicants' performance on the predictors will be related to their performance on the job (as represented by the criterion measures). As we learned in previous chapters, a validation study tests this hypothesized relationship. What is important here is the recognition that it is the job analysis process which is the foundation of the effectiveness of any HR selection system. Where job analysis is incomplete, inaccurate, or simply not conducted, a selection system may be nothing more than a game of chance—a game that employer, employee, and job applicants alike may lose.

Growth in Job Analysis

Richard Uhrbrock provided perhaps the first published history of job analysis in his writings on the topic in the early 1920s.[4] Some 60 years after Uhrbrock's work first appeared, Jai Ghorpade and Thomas Atchinson reexamined some of the historical development of job analysis. As described by Ghorpade and Atchinson, job analysis has had an interesting though, at times, erratic history. From the turn of the century through the 1940s, there was widespread enthusiasm for the use of job analysis. The management literature in the 1950s and 1960s did not devote as much attention to the field as previously, but practitioners were busy applying job analysis methods to problems of recruitment and placement.[5] For instance, in 1969 a national survey of 681 firms employing job analysis reported that over 90 percent used the information in recruiting and placing personnel.[6] There are not comparable data on current practices, but the literature shows a significant increase in attention given to job analysis, beginning in the 1970s.[7] This attention has focused on the use of job analysis not only in the basic personnel areas of recruitment, placement, training, and compensation but in selection as well. At least three interrelated reasons account for this renewed interest. First, there has been the realization that jobs are not static entities; that is, the nature of jobs may change for any number of reasons, such as technological advancements, seasonal variations, or the initiatives of an incumbent.[8] Thus, as managers have recognized the importance of job information in HR decision making, there has been an accompanying recognition of the need for up-to-date information on the jobs themselves. In addition to the need for current, accurate job data, two other factors have influenced the role of job analysis in selection. Federal guidelines on employee selection procedures (such as the *Uniform Guidelines* mentioned in Chapter 2) have had a significant effect.[9]

These guidelines have generally required that job analyses be performed as part of the development, application, and validation of selection devices. We say more in the next section about these guidelines, but needless to say, they have elevated the importance of job analysis.

Similarly, court cases involving employment discrimination in selection have underlined the significance of job analysis.[10] We discuss selected cases in the section that follows. Generally speaking, rulings in various cases have held that job analysis must play an integral role in any research which attempts to show a correlation between job performance and a selection measure.

Legal Issues in Job Analysis

In recent years, job analysis has become a focal point in the legal context of HR selection. The principal source for this development can be traced to the passage of Title VII of the 1964 Civil Rights Act. As we discussed in Chapter 2, Title VII makes it illegal for an organization to refuse to select an individual or to discriminate against a person with respect to compensation, terms, conditions, or privileges of employment because of the person's race, sex, color, religion, or national origin. Since many Title VII cases have concerned the role of discrimination in selection for employment, job analysis has emerged as critical to the prosecution or defense of a discrimination case. Thus job analysis and its associated methodologies have become intertwined with the law. Within this legal vein, two developments have amplified the importance of job analysis in selection research: (a) the adoption of the *Uniform Guidelines on Employee Selection Procedures* by the federal government and (b) litigation involving discrimination in selection, arising under Title VII as well as the Fifth and Fourteenth Amendments to the U.S. Constitution.

Court Cases Involving Job Analysis Although a number of cases involving job analysis have been heard in the courts, two early Supreme Court cases are particularly important. Perhaps the seminal one with respect to job analysis is *Griggs v. Duke Power Co.*, which we discussed in Chapter 2.[11] Even though the term *job analysis* is not mentioned per se, *Griggs* gave the legal impetus to job analysis. The case implies that an important legal requirement in a selection device validation program is an analysis of the job for which the device is used.

As we have mentioned, in *Griggs*, Duke Power was employing a written test and a high school diploma as requirements for entry into a supervisory position. The Court noted that these selection standards were used "without meaningful study of their relationship to job-performance ability. Rather, a vice-president of the company testified, the requirements were instituted on the company's judgment that they generally would improve the overall quality of the work force."[12] Thus the Court ruled that "What Congress has commanded is that any test used must measure the person *for the job* [emphasis added] and not the person in the abstract."[13] The implication behind the ruling in *Griggs* is that for employers to attempt to meet this job-relatedness standard, they must first examine the job. Measurement of the job is accomplished through job analysis.

Similarly, *Albemarle Paper Co. v. Moody* is especially important.[14] In *Albemarle*, the Court, for the first time, expressly criticized the lack of a job analysis in a validation study. It was noted by the Court that "no attempt was made to analyze the jobs in terms of the particular skills they might require."[15] As with *Griggs*, the Court again gave weight to the use of job analysis.

Albemarle is noteworthy for its support of job analysis. Like *Griggs*, its predecessor, *Albemarle* was a Supreme Court case. Plaintiffs as well as lower courts look for guidance from rulings of the Supreme Court. Thus it can be expected that the insistence on a job analysis in selection cases will encourage other courts to look for the presence (or lack) of a job analysis.

This case is also significant for a second reason. The Court supported the *EEOC Guidelines on Employee Selection Procedures*,[16] which required the undertaking of a job analysis in a validation study. As we see in the next section, the Court's endorsement of these guidelines, as well as the subsequently issued *Uniform Guidelines*, has emphasized the role of job analysis in HR selection.

There are numerous court cases that could be cited in addition to *Griggs* and *Albemarle*. On the whole, decisions and remedies in these cases emphasize the importance of job analysis. An examination of these cases would be helpful in isolating the standards used by the courts in evaluating job analysis in validation research. In this light, Duane Thompson and Toni Thompson reviewed 26 selected federal court cases to determine the criteria the courts used in assessing job analyses conducted in the development and validation of tests. Their review produced a set of job analysis characteristics, which they suggest are capable of withstanding legal scrutiny. Although these characteristics may vary depending on issues such as type of job analysis, type of validation strategy, and purpose of the analysis, the standards serve as a useful guide for understanding the judicial view. The legal standards identified by Thompson and Thompson are as follows:

1. Job analysis must be performed and must be for the job for which the selection instrument is to be utilized.

2. Analysis of the job should be in writing.

3. Job analyst(s) should describe in detail the procedures used.

4. Job data should be collected from a variety of current sources and by knowledgeable job analyst(s).

5. Sample size should be large and representative of the jobs for which the device will be used.

6. Tasks, duties, and activities should be included in the analysis.

7. The most important tasks should be represented in the selection device.

8. Competency levels of job performance for entry-level jobs should be specified.

9. KSAs should be specified, particularly if a content validation model is followed.[17]

Federal Guidelines on Employee Selection During the period from 1966 to 1978, various sets of federal regulations on employee selection were issued.[18] The Equal Employment Opportunity Commission (EEOC), the Office of Federal Contract Compliance (OFCC), the Civil Service Commission (currently the U.S. Office of Personnel Management), and the Department of Justice offered guidelines for employers to follow in their selection procedures. Although some employees may have treated these guidelines as nothing more than a guide, the *Albemarle* case enhanced their role. As noted earlier, the Court gave deference to the EEOC guidelines, at least to the portion that discussed job analysis. The impact of the Court's opinion has been to make it mandatory for selection managers to be intimately familiar with their content.

Current federal regulations noted in the *Uniform Guidelines* supersede previous regulations and represent a joint agreement among the EEOC, Department of Justice, Department of Labor, and Civil Service Commission (now the U.S. Office of Personnel Management). Given the substantial weight accorded to the *Uniform Guidelines* in recent court cases, it can be expected that the courts will continue to give emphasis to the importance of job analysis.

Many of the legal issues surrounding job analysis have concerned the necessity for employing these methods when developing and implementing a selection program. Since the early 1980s, however, another set of legal questions has arisen concerning the actual application of job analysis procedures. Because most of these methods involve some degree of human judgment, cases have been appearing in the courts in which technical aspects of job analysis implementation are involved. In many instances, the issue has been to determine if the inferences made from job analysis data based largely on human judgments have discriminatory impact on protected classes of job applicants. Returning again to Exhibit 7.1, it shows four points where judgment may be involved in the use of job analysis information in personnel selection. These judgments are referred to in the literature as "inferential leaps." For instance, at inference point 1 in Exhibit 7.1, the KSAs and other personal characteristics are inferred from the job tasks performed on a job. Because humans are involved in the process of inferring human attributes from work-related information, there is the possibility of error. The greater the role of human judgment, the larger the inferential leap, and, therefore, the greater the opportunity for discriminatory impact. In particular, inference points 1 and 2 represent areas where much equal opportunity litigation has centered when job analysis issues are in question.

Of course, the extent of inferential leaps to be made in any one job analysis application will depend on the particular situation. Factors such as the validation strategy being used (for example, content versus criterion), the type of job (for example, hourly versus managerial), and the attribute being assessed (for example, a physical skill versus a personality trait) affect the degree of inferential leaps made.

Summary

Although it would be convenient, it is simply impossible to specify one clear, suitable, standard means for meeting *all* the technical and legal considerations of a job analysis. Situations, problems, and technical issues are so varied that proper conduct of a job analysis is a complex, resource-consuming process. There is no one standard way. As Paul Sparks, former personnel research coordinator of Exxon, has stated, "I, for one, find it very difficult to find an agreed-upon professional standard in the area of job analysis. . . . We're due for a lot more research, a lot more litigation, and a lot more court decisions before we have a standard."[19]

Nevertheless, absence of an agreed-upon standard should not be viewed as a basis of minimizing the legal role of job analysis. At the third Annual Conference on EEO Compliance/Human Resources Utilization, Donald Schwartz, EEOC personnel research psychologist, noted that, from a legal viewpoint, the government looks first to see if a job analysis has been undertaken in a validation study. He went on to say, "In my opinion, the absence of a job analysis is fatal to a validity study in a court challenge, and will continue to be fatal to a validity study regardless of what the professional standards say."[20] According to Schwartz, the legal requirements transcend the professional standards. The government as well as the courts look for adequacy in a job analysis. "The courts have since the earliest decisions in this area strongly emphasized the need for an adequate job analysis in support of the use of a test or other questioned procedure. . . . Job analyses which do not provide the necessary information do not support a claim of validity regardless of how much information they provide."[21]

So far, we have seen that job analysis plays both technical and legal roles in the development of a HR selection system. The next section focuses on the implementation of a job analysis in the context of selection.

Implementation of a Job Analysis

Implementation of a job analysis involves a sequence of activities and decision points. Even though these activities may vary depending on their purpose, there are at least seven major decision points typically involved in job analysis for HR selection purposes: (a) organizing for a job analysis, (b) choosing jobs to be studied, (c) reviewing the relevant literature, (d) selecting job agents, (e) collecting job information, (f) identifying job or employee specifications, and (g) incorporating employee specifications in selection devices. Successful job analysis research involves careful planning with respect to each of these tasks. In the remaining portions of this chapter, we concentrate on the first *four* decision points of the job analysis process. Chapter 8 focuses on the fifth decision point, the methods of collecting job information. The final chapter in this part, Chapter 9, deals with the last two decision points, that is, how job analysis results are used to identify employee specifications and how selection measures are developed from these specifications.

Organizing for a Job Analysis

We have discussed some of the technical and legal issues that must be given consideration in conducting a job analysis. But, once it has been decided to undertake a job analysis, the next question is how should the effort be organized? In answering this question, there are three basic organizational issues to be addressed: (a) who should perform the job analysis; (b) how should the project be managed; and (c) what resources will be needed to conduct the project.

Who Should Perform the Job Analysis? The application of a job analysis for the purpose of developing an HR selection system must conform to a number of scientific and legal requirements. Because of these requirements, professionally trained and experienced job analysts are necessary to conduct and, possibly, defend in court the methods used. In some situations, individuals employed within an organization will have the necessary training and skills to perform a job analysis. However, it should be kept in mind that job analysis requirements for selection program development or for validation research may be quite different from a job analysis conducted for purposes such as job evaluation or training program development. Errors in job analysis, particularly for HR selection applications, can be very costly. Thus, because of the special requirements in HR selection, many organizations will probably need a consultant to conduct the work. In many cases, the individuals responsible for the job analysis will be the same ones responsible for developing and conducting the selection research program.

Since a job analysis lays the foundation for an HR selection program, a thorough, systematic process should be used when evaluating prospective consultants to conduct a job analysis or other aspects of the selection program. These steps might include (a) sending out a request for proposals to consulting firms and academic consultants; (b) asking for an on-site visit by prospective consultants; (c) requiring the submission of a formal proposal that outlines the client's objectives, research steps to be taken, project costs, deliverables, and the credentials of the consulting staff; and (d) selecting among prospective consultants.[22]

How Should the Project Be Managed? Regardless of whether a job analysis project is conducted by personnel within an organization or by outside consultants, an administrative organization will be necessary to coordinate the job analysis activities. The individuals responsible for the coordination efforts will depend on a number of factors including the scope of the work, the complexity of the specific job analysis methods used, the resources allocated to the project, and whether the project is conducted by staff members in the organization or by outside consultants. Usually, ultimate responsibility for job analysis rests with top management, the operating managers, and the human resources department. Unless top management and line managers provide the necessary support, it will be difficult for the project to succeed.[23]

Like most organizational projects, political issues in an organization can have a significant impact on the success of a job analysis study. Seldom is there a "good" time to conduct such a study. Some operating managers see a job analysis as an interference in their operations, a distraction to their employees, or a cause for lost productivity.[24] Employees serving as participants in the study may be resistant to the study as well. If participation takes them away from their jobs and their pay is tied to productivity, employees are not going to be too excited about participating. If employees believe that the analysis may raise their work standards or lower their job security, resistance will be encountered.

Job analyses and their associated validation studies are oftentimes conducted in organizations where employment discrimination is common and where litigation may have limited hirings and promotions for years. This situation is particularly true in public employment settings. In such an atmosphere, gaining support of all affected individuals and groups is crucial to success of the project.[25] For these reasons, it is necessary that certain steps be taken to address potential problems before they arise. Michael Carrell and Frank Kuzmits, for example, recommend the formation of a job analysis coordinating committee. Under a committee structure, individual representation would be from the major departments housing the jobs to be studied. Committee representation would permit members to discuss with their department the nature of the process and to reassure employees who feel threatened.[26]

In addition, meetings between participants and representatives of the job analysis staff should also be held. These meetings should

1. introduce the job analysis staff, describe what a job analysis is, and tell participants why they are needed;

2. explain why a job analysis is being conducted;

3. explain what information is needed;

4. establish an open, nonthreatening climate for gathering job information; and

5. answer questions about the project's purpose, methods, and results.[27]

The key purpose of these meetings is to give participants the opportunity to express their feelings and raise questions about the project. Participants may hold very negative attitudes. When they exist, these feelings must be addressed and defused as much as possible prior to beginning job analysis work.

It is imperative that clear lines of authority and responsibility be established for the manager of the project. Clarity of authority helps make possible coordination of many diverse activities. A single individual should be charged with responsibilities for coordination of the job analysis in addition to other activities such as selection device development or validation. Ideally, this individual would be knowledgeable about job analysis methods, selection systems, validation strategies, statistical procedures, and so forth. Realistically, the individual may not have this expertise. If such skills are not available within the organization, the core person must have the resources and authority for hiring an appropriate consultant.

The job analysis coordinator may be required to perform a wide array of duties. These would probably include the following:

1. Serve as a channel of communication to and from top management;

2. Assess the technical capabilities of the internal staff;

3. Recruit and transfer additional personnel to the project, such as clerical help (for editing, data coding, data entry), technical consultants, and data collectors;

4. Make work assignments and monitor progress;

5. Plan and schedule the job analysis and related activities;

6. Design training and orientation sessions for staff;

7. Supervise the selection of jobs and job agents;

8. Prepare and revise job analysis materials;

9. Supervise data analyses; and

10. Meet with and counsel employees to alleviate any perceived threats from job analysis (for example, layoffs, higher work standards, lower pay rates).[28]

What Resources Will Be Needed to Conduct the Project? Several different types of resources will be needed to complete a job analysis successfully. Most of these fall into one of the following four resource categories: (a) a job analysis staff, (b) computer resources, (c) time, and (d) monetary support.

Whether internal staff members or an outside consulting firm is used, a job analysis staff will probably need to be composed of the following positions:

1. Clerk/Typists—Individuals who are responsible for clerical activities such as typing correspondence, typing data collection measures, logging and filing data collection measures, coding and entering data for computer analysis.

2. Job Analysts—Individuals who are responsible for collecting the necessary job information.

3. Project Staff Members—Individuals who may collect job information but are also responsible for analyzing job data.

4. Project Manager—A single individual responsible for planning, organizing, and coordinating the job analysis effort.[29]

A second necessity is computer resources. Job analysis projects often involve the collection of large amounts of information from a number of individuals working in a variety of jobs or positions. The accompanying mass of data resulting from such projects requires the use of statistical procedures for summarizing the results. Microcomputers or large mainframe computers and appropriate software packages are necessary for analyzing such data. Thus when a job analysis project is being planned, access to a computer, computer time, and software are mandatory.

Time itself is another resource many managers fail to consider when conducting a job analysis. Obviously, how much time the project requires will depend on many variables such as the number and capabilities of the staff, the specific job analysis procedures employed, the number of jobs analyzed, whether internal staff or outside consultants are employed, and the commitment of the organization to the project. Regardless of the number of variables, there are a series of steps that must be planned and for which appropriate time estimates must be made. These steps include the following:

1. Planning the project;

2. Gaining necessary approvals from managers;

3. Organizing data collection efforts and conducting staff meetings;

4. Training staff members in job analysis methodology;

5. Collecting job data;

6. Editing and coding job information;

7. Entering collected job data into a computer;

8. Analyzing job data;

9. Interpreting the results of the analysis;

10. Writing up the results of the analysis; and

11. Applying the results in the HR selection program.

Monetary support is a final major resource that will affect the success of any job analysis project. When planning a job analysis project, some of the major factors requiring financial support that should be estimated are salaries and benefits of the project staff; office supplies; travel; data processing; acquisition and scoring of data collection measures (if a commercially available job analysis system is being implemented); development and preparation of data collection measures (if a job analysis system is being tailored to an organization's specific needs);

postage and telephone; report preparation; project implementation; and the fees for any consultants used on the project.

Organizing and managing a job analysis is not an easy assignment. It cannot be conducted by just any available person. Some writers believe otherwise, but we recommend that care be exercised in assigning the responsibilities for a job analysis. Erich Prien succinctly summarizes this point:

> Although job analysis is an essential feature of almost every activity engaged in by industrial-organizational psychologists, the subject is treated in textbooks in a manner which suggests that any fool can do it and thus it is a task which can be delegated to the lowest level technician. This is quite contradictory to the position taken by Otis (1953) in explicating and defending the practice, and is clearly at variance with the statements in the EEOC Selection Guidelines (however vague these statements may be) admonishing the researcher to do a *thorough* job analysis in test selection and in criterion development. Job analysis for these purposes is not accomplished by rummaging around in an organization; it is accomplished by applying highly systematic and precise methods.[30]

Choosing the Jobs to Be Studied

Once a job analysis staff has been assembled, the next issue to be addressed is the choice of job(s) on which an analysis will be made. The answer is not as obvious as it sounds. Most organizations conducting selection research are going to have limited resources that can be devoted to the project. Thus an organization will be forced to choose among many job possibilities on which analyses need to be made. A number of criteria might be employed for choosing the initial jobs for research. Some recommended criteria are discussed here.

Representativeness of the Job   Based on this standard, a job chosen as part of the study would be one that closely resembles other jobs within the organization. If we assume that correspondence between the content of a selected job and a specific selection device is high, then it might be reasoned that other jobs resembling the job chosen for the study might also correspond to the selection device. Therefore, validity generalization from one job to relevant others might be argued. It would seem that such a procedure would help to eliminate the time- and resource-consuming tasks of analyzing every job under consideration. This is not likely, however. Before such an inference can be made, it must be *documented* that jobs are indeed similar. Documentation is provided through job analysis. Given this requirement, it is difficult to conceive of significant benefits accruing to an organization relying *solely* on this criterion for choosing jobs.

Criticality of the Job   In some organizations, such as social or health services organizations, certain jobs may be so critical that the mental or physical well-being of the clients depends on them. They may be at greater risk due to an inappropriate selection standard than may other groups, for example, employees or job applicants. Therefore, those jobs posing possible physical or psychological harm to clients would seem to be a reasonable place to begin. If it can be assumed that the use of a device in selection decisions is not likely to harm eventual clients, one could claim this not to be a suitable criterion for choosing a job for study. Conversely, if it is thought that the use of such a standard could lead to negative impacts on clients, then the degree of client vulnerability that is characteristic of particular jobs would be a very relevant consideration.

Number of Applicants for the Job   From the perspective of employment discrimination, the number of applicants for a specific job is an important factor. If a selection device is not valid, the greatest impact would be on those jobs having the largest number of applicants. (Quite often, these are jobs with the greatest number of incumbents.) In order to protect an organization from this possibility, initial job analysis studies might be directed toward those jobs in which a discrimination charge is most likely. With this criterion, it is assumed that the greater the number of applicants for a specific job, the greater the probability of a discrimination charge by an aggrieved applicant.

Stability/Obsolescence of Job Content   As content (in terms of actual tasks or KSAs required for task performance) of jobs changes, it becomes necessary periodically to reexamine the job content. Therefore, another important criterion is the frequency of and extent to which job content is modified. Jobs that change often require more frequent checks on content. Conversely, jobs whose content remains stable over time do not require frequent checks once a thorough job analysis has been made.

Evidence of Adverse Impact in Selection   As we discussed in Chapter 2, adverse impact occurs when there is "a substantially different rate of selection in hiring . . . which works to the disadvantage of members of a race, sex, or ethnic group."[31] When adverse impact has taken place, the *Uniform Guidelines* specify that the employer must be able to demonstrate that the selection standard is related to job performance. To be in compliance, an organization would want to initiate a job analysis study for those jobs where adverse impact has occurred.

Entry-Level Jobs in an Organization   The *Uniform Guidelines* are directed principally toward entry-level jobs in any organization to which the guidelines apply.[32] Entry-level jobs are those positions in an organization that new employees enter having once passed the selection standards. The selection measures used for such jobs are of particular interest, since it is those measures that determine who does and who does not get employed. Jobs requiring minimum performance on a selection device for entry by new employees would be the relevant ones for consideration.

Jobs Serving as Links to Higher-Level Jobs   Often, certain entry-level jobs serve as *gatekeepers* or *links* to other, higher-level jobs in an organization's career sequence. Thus promotion to jobs providing more status, greater authority, or more pay may only occur when an individual has acquired experience in a specific job. When promotion rates from such linking jobs are low, these jobs become possible candidates for study.

Evidence of Performance Deficiencies Jobs characterized by performance deficiencies (such as low productivity, high turnover) call attention to the question of relevance (validity) of the selection devices used as qualifications for employment. Although the standards for job entry may not be the sole reason for inadequate performance, they certainly merit examination as to their validity. Organizations may want to select those jobs in which performance is inadequate because there is an implication that the selection standard may not be associated with job performance. Reexamination of the standard would begin by an analysis of the job.

Jobs That Are Physically Demanding Jobs characterized by the performance of many physical activities is another possibility when considering the Americans with Disabilities Act (ADA). These jobs may be open to complaints of discrimination or to requests for accommodation. Therefore, it may be beneficial to choose such jobs for analysis. The job analysis should include the determination of essential job functions, development of selection procedures, and determination of when accommodations can be made in testing (for example, administering a written test orally when reading or writing is not an essential aspect of the job).

There is not one exclusive criterion that every organization should use in choosing specific jobs for job analysis. Organizational characteristics such as geographical location, size, resources, structure, policies, and practices will impinge on the choices available. In practice, it will probably be found that several of the criteria just described will need to be applied simultaneously in choosing jobs for analysis. Depending on the perspectives of the organization, however, different criteria may emerge. For example, from a legal point of view, the following types of jobs should be emphasized:

1. Jobs showing adverse impact in selection,

2. Jobs serving as entry-level positions in an organization, and

3. Jobs having a large number of applicants.

From the perspective of the client of special human services organizations, jobs that may affect the psychological or physical well-being of the client should be chosen. Finally, from the standpoint of operations management, the following options should be considered:

1. Jobs with performance deficiencies,

2. Jobs whose content has changed, and

3. Jobs serving as links to higher-level positions.

Obviously, these various criteria present the problem of where to begin. Remember that the requirements of the particular organization will determine the options chosen. However, *at a minimum,* two types of jobs should always be considered first: (a) entry-level jobs and (b) jobs where adverse impact has occurred in hiring.

Caution should be exercised in the job choices made. In particular, careful attention should be given when using job titles to make the decision. Since titles may be associated with pay classifications that cluster jobs into a general pay class, they may mask task differences. For example, Richard Thorton and Michael Rosenfeld's analysis of the job of employment service interviewer revealed that a number of these people actually worked as claims examiners. Furthermore, in an additional analysis, they found 26 different jobs in an analysis of the job title "Police Sergeant."[33] Consultation with knowledgeable job experts (for example, experienced incumbents or supervisors) can help to clarify the jobs under consideration.

Reviewing the Relevant Literature

After a job has been selected for analysis, the next task is to conduct a review of job analysis literature for the job in question. The goal of the review should be to determine the data collection methods used by others, their analyses, problems, and results. A review of related literature can have the following benefits:

1. It can show how previous investigators have conducted their analyses and enable the researcher to evaluate various approaches for conducting the analysis.

2. It can serve to identify potential problems as well as associated methods and techniques for treating these problems should they develop.

3. It can help to locate additional sources of data not considered by the analyst.

4. It can serve as a means for comparing the results of the present job analysis with those of similar studies.[34]

5. It can suggest the task activities performed on a job and the KSAs as well as other employee characteristics needed to perform the tasks.

A variety of sources of information within the organization may be available. Initially, organization charts and existing job descriptions should be reviewed. Organization charts can show how a given job relates to other jobs in the company. Job descriptions, if they exist, serve as an orientation point for understanding major tasks and responsibilities of the job. Some caution should be taken in the acceptance of these descriptions, however. In many cases, they may not accurately or adequately capture the nature of a job. For example, changes in job activities that may have naturally occurred over time or that are due to technological advancements may make a job description out of date. Preliminary interviews with informed incumbents or supervisors can be used as a check.

In addition to information within an organization, literature sources outside the organization should also be explored. Use of external sources should certainly include the *Dictionary of Occupational Titles (DOT)*[35] as well as other publications. Because of the widespread use of the *DOT*, we spend some time reviewing this job information source.

Dictionary of Occupational Titles (DOT)   During the 1930s Depression, Congress created the United States Employment Service to aid workers in finding suitable employment and to aid employers in identifying suitable employees. As a component of the Employment Service, the Occupational Analysis Program was a group organized with the responsibility of producing job information that would aid the placement of job seekers in employing organizations. One product of their work was the publication of a dictionary of occupational information referred to as the *Dictionary of Occupational Titles*, or *DOT*.

Since publication of the first edition in 1939, four editions of the *DOT* have been published. The fourth edition, published in 1977 and revised in 1991, is the current version. This volume provides information on over 12,000 occupations and an additional 16,000 related occupational titles. As defined in the *DOT*, an "occupation" is simply a description of a group of individual jobs whose tasks are essentially the same. For instance, the example job of bank teller we referred to earlier in the chapter is simple called "Teller" in the *DOT*. The definitions reported are the results of analyses of jobs performed in organizations around the country. Because of the diversity of data collected, the data reported on an occupation in the *DOT* is a composite of information. Thus it is possible that an occupation may vary from one job situation to another on certain characteristics.

Each occupation in the *DOT* is identified by a unique nine-digit code; these digits are assigned based on the nature of the tasks performed. For example, the code number of the occupation Teller is 211.362-018. The first digit assigns an occupation to one of nine broad categories, for example, "Professional, Technical, or Managerial" (0 or 1). In the Teller example, the "2" corresponds to the designation "Clerical and Sales" (2).

The first and second digits in combination are more specific definitions of the occupational categories. There are 83 divisions that group occupations on the basis of the general types of skills and knowledge required; activities performed; machines, tools, and equipment used; and products produced. Thus the number "21" for Teller represents "Computing and Account-Recording Occupations." When the third digit is added to the first two, for example, "211," the 83 divisions are further subdivided into 564 occupational groups. Each group is defined by a three-digit code. The code "211," for example, represents "Cashiers and Tellers." In sum, the first three digits of the code represent increasing specificity of the nature of work performed in an occupation, such as:

Occupational Code	Category	Increasing Specificity
2	Clerical and Sales	
21	Computing and Account-Recording	↓
211	Cashiers and Tellers	

The second, or middle set of three digits are the worker functions ratings of the tasks performed in the occupation. The numbers describe the complexity with which incumbents perform their work in relation to data, people, and things. Basically, the fourth, fifth, and sixth digits represent job analysts' ratings of the complexity of tasks performed. Although the complete individual rating scales are too long to reproduce here (see our discussion of Functional Job Analysis (FJA) in the Appendix to Chapter 8), *higher* numbers on the scales represent *simpler* tasks while *lower* numbers represent more *complex* tasks performed. In brief the rating scales (without their definitions) are as follows:[36]

	DATA (4th Digit)	PEOPLE (5th Digit)	THINGS (6th Digit)
High Complexity	0 Synthesizing	0 Mentoring	0 Setting Up
	1 Coordinating	1 Negotiating	1 Precision Working
↓	2 Analyzing	2 Instructing	2 Operating-Controlling
	3 Compiling	2 Supervising	3 Driving-Operating
	4 Computing	4 Diverting	4 Manipulating
	5 Copying	5 Persuading	5 Tending
	6 Comparing	6 Speaking-Signaling	6 Feeding-Offbearing
		7 Serving	7 Handling
Low Complexity		8 Taking Instructions-Helping	

From the fourth, fifth, and sixth digits in our Teller occupation example (that is, "362"), the following general description of teller job activities can be obtained:

DATA

Compiling: Gathering, collating, or classifying information.

PEOPLE

Speaking-Signaling: Talking with and/or signaling people to convey or exchange information. Includes giving assignments to helpers or assistants.

THINGS

Operating-Controlling: Starting, stopping, controlling, and adjusting the progress of machines or equipment.

The final three numbers of the occupational code do not carry substantive meaning as the first six do. They are simply used to differentiate an occupation from others, and they facilitate record-keeping needs of the Employment Service.

In addition to job-related information summarized by the *DOT* occupational code, narrative descriptions are also provided. Exhibit 7.2 illustrates the *DOT's* description of the occupation Teller. You should note that the exhibit also illustrates the various components of the *DOT's* occupational definitions. Each *DOT* description typically has these parts; they are defined as follows:[37]

1. **Occupational Code**—A 9-digit number that classifies each occupation.

2. **Occupational Title**—The title of the occupation (shown in bold capital letters) that is used in the majority of the occupations in which it was found.

3. **Industry Designation**—A classification of the occupation into an occupational group to differentiate between occupations with the same title but different work activities. The information can be used to determine the (a) location of the occupation (for example, financial), (b) types of duties associated with the occupation (for example, education), (c) any products manufactured (for example, textiles), (d) processes used (for example, petroleum refining), and (e) any raw materials used (for example, stonework).

4. **Alternate Titles**—Other names or titles of the occupation that are used less frequently than the occupation title. These titles are synonyms for the occupational title given initially.

5. **Body of the Definition**—A narrative description of an occupation's principal activities that consists of three main parts:

   a. **Lead Statement**—The first sentence that summarizes the entire occupation in terms of activities, objectives of the activities, tools and equipment used, products made or services rendered, equipment used, instructions followed, or judgments made. The statement is followed by a colon (:).

   b. **Task Element Statements**—Specific tasks the worker performs in order to meet the objectives summarized in the lead statement. The task statements begin with an action verb.

   c. **"May" Items**—Descriptions of task activities that are performed by workers in the occupation in some organizations but not in others. Each task statement begins with the word "May."

6. **Undefined Related Titles**—When applicable, undefined related titles are given at the end of the occupational definition, preceded by a phrase, such as "May be designated according to. . . ."

7. **Definition Trailer**—Selected characteristics and other profile data of the occupation are given in all-capital letters at the end of the complete

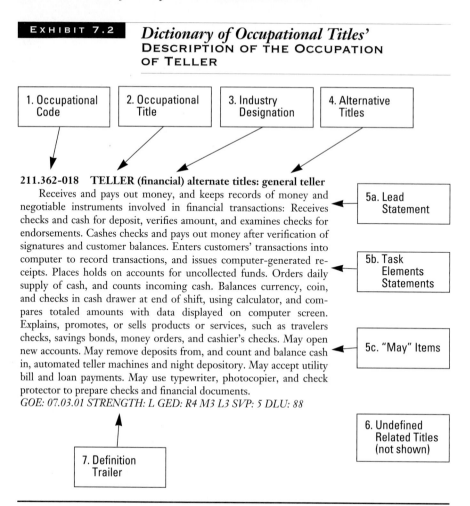

EXHIBIT 7.2

Dictionary of Occupational Titles'
DESCRIPTION OF THE OCCUPATION
OF TELLER

| 1. Occupational Code | 2. Occupational Title | 3. Industry Designation | 4. Alternative Titles |

211.362-018 TELLER (financial) alternate titles: general teller
Receives and pays out money, and keeps records of money and negotiable instruments involved in financial transactions: Receives checks and cash for deposit, verifies amount, and examines checks for endorsements. Cashes checks and pays out money after verification of signatures and customer balances. Enters customers' transactions into computer to record transactions, and issues computer-generated receipts. Places holds on accounts for uncollected funds. Orders daily supply of cash, and counts incoming cash. Balances currency, coin, and checks in cash drawer at end of shift, using calculator, and compares totaled amounts with data displayed on computer screen. Explains, promotes, or sells products or services, such as travelers checks, savings bonds, money orders, and cashier's checks. May open new accounts. May remove deposits from, and count and balance cash in, automated teller machines and night depository. May accept utility bill and loan payments. May use typewriter, photocopier, and check protector to prepare checks and financial documents.
GOE: 07.03.01 STRENGTH: L GED: R4 M3 L3 SVP: 5 DLU: 88

5a. Lead Statement

5b. Task Elements Statements

5c. "May" Items

6. Undefined Related Titles (not shown)

7. Definition Trailer

SOURCE: U.S. Department of Labor, *Dictionary of Occupational Titles* (Washington, D.C.: U.S. Government Printing Office, 1991), p. 183.

definition. This information is new for the 1991 revision of the *DOT*. The trailer contains the following selected occupational analysis characteristics:

a. **Guide for Occupational Exploration (GOE) Code**—Additional information about the interests, aptitudes, entry-level preparation and other traits required for successful performance in the occupation are given. The GOE code classifies jobs at three levels of consideration using a six-digit code:

   (1) *Interest areas*—All jobs are clustered into one of 12 groupings based on common interests. These groupings are identified with the first two digits of the six-digit code. Examples of these occupational clusterings are: 01 = Artistic, 02 = Scientific, 03 = Plants-Animals, 04 = Protective, . . . , 12 = Physical Performing.

(2) *Work groups*—Each occupation is further classified into one of 66 work groups using the second set of two digits. Occupations that require the most education, training, and experience are in the first group; those requiring the least are listed in the last group. An example of work groups under the Interest Area-Business Detail (07) would be 01 = Administrative Detail, 02 = Mathematical Detail, 03 = Financial Detail, . . . , 07 = Clerical Handling.

(3) *Subgroups*—The 66 work groups are next subdivided into 348 subgroups of occupations, using the third two-digit code, reflecting even more homogeneous interests and aptitudes requirements. For example, under Clerical Handling (07), there are the following subgroups: 01 = Filing, 02 = Sorting and Distribution, and 03 = General Clerical Work.

The GOE description for Teller is 07.03.01 (Business Detail, Financial Detail, Paying and Receiving).

b. **Strength Rating (Physical Demands)**—This code reflects the estimated overall strength requirements of the job expressed by one of five terms: Sedentary Work (S), Light Work (L), Medium Work (M), Heavy Work (H), and Very Heavy Work (VH). An example of Medium Work in which the Strength Factor is expressed is as follows:

> *Medium Work*—Exerting 20 to 50 pounds of force occasionally, and/or 10 to 25 pounds of force frequently, and/or 10 to 20 pounds of force constantly to move objects.

c. **General Education Development (GED)**—This factor is a rating of those aspects of education (formal and informal) required for satisfactory job performance. It is composed of three divisions: (a) Reasoning Development, (b) Mathematical Development, and (c) Language Development. Each of these three divisions involves a numerical rating from 1 to 6. The higher the rating, the greater the required general education development. Abbreviated definitions of the rating scale are:

	Reasoning Development	*Mathematical Development*	*Language Development*
High Education Development ↑	6 = Using abstract concepts, symbols, (e.g., formulas), and scientific theories	6 = Using advanced calculus, modern algebra, or statistics	6 = Creating literature or techical reports, or teaching or supervising those who do
	⋮	⋮	⋮
Low Education Development ↓	1 = Following 1- or 2-step instructions. Dealing with problems that fit simple rules	1 = Adding, subtracting, making change, or measuring	1 = Reading up to 2,500 words, printing simple sentences, or speaking using normal correct order

d. **Specific Vocational Preparation (SVP)**—This rating is the amount of time required by a typical worker to learn the techniques, acquire information, and develop the capability for average performance on the job. The higher the rating, the greater the length of required preparation.

Listed here are examples of the ratings used to define the levels of time of specific vocational preparation needed:

	Level		Time
High	9	=	Over 10 years
Vocational	8	=	Over 4 years up to and including 10 years
Preparation	7	=	Over 2 years up to and including 4 years
↕	6	=	Over 1 year up to and including 2 years
	5	=	Over 6 months up to and including 1 year
	4	=	Over 3 months up to and including 6 months
Low	3	=	Over 1 month up to and including 3 months
Vocational	2	=	Anything beyond short demonstration up to and including 1 month
Preparation	1	=	Short demonstration only

e. **Date of Last Update (DLU)**—The final element is an indication of the last year in which information describing an occupation was collected. A DLU of "88" would mean that the occupation was last studied by an analyst in 1988.

When job analyses were performed for the occupations contained in the *DOT*, information on worker attributes considered necessary for individuals working in a particular occupation was also collected. Each of the occupations was scored on the following types of worker attributes:

1. *Training time*—The amount of educational development and vocational preparation required of a worker for average job performance.

2. *Aptitudes*—The abilities required of a worker in order to learn how to perform job tasks.

3. *Temperaments*—The personal traits of a worker that are useful in adjusting to a job.

4. *Interests and preferences*—The preferences of a worker for performing various activities related to job performance.

5. *Physical demands*—The physical requirements needed by a worker to perform a job.

6. *Environmental conditions*—The physical working conditions in which a job is performed.[38]

Unfortunately, the complete set of worker attribute data was not published in earlier editions (prior to 1991) of the *DOT*. Some of the attribute information can be found in a companion publication to the *DOT* titled *Selected Characteristics of Occupations Defined in the Dictionary of Occupational Titles*.[39] This publication provides rating data on *DOT* jobs for the following worker attributes: (a) *training time* (including necessary levels of mathematical and language abilities as well as specific vocational preparation), (b) *physical demand characteristics*, and (c) *environmental conditions*. To use the manual, all that is needed is the *DOT* occupational code for the job in question. Once the job code is located in the manual, the attribute ratings can simply be referenced for identifying important employee characteristics. (In Exhibit 7.2, which shows the *DOT* Teller occupation description, note that some of this information is now included in the Definition Trailer.)

Worker attribute information is particularly important in personnel selection. It is these attributes, usually expressed through KSAs, that we use as a basis for selecting or developing predictors to be used in selection. As we have seen, the *DOT* and related publications provide some useful information on worker attributes. Another source of potentially beneficial worker attribute information that should be consulted is *The Enhanced Guide for Occupational Exploration*.[40] Using data from the Department of Labor, the Census Bureau, and other governmental and private sources, a database of information was assembled on 2,500 of the most common jobs in the United States. In addition to *DOT* information and other job-related data, the sourcebook provides worker attribute details in the following areas:

1. **Academic Codes**—The code consists of two components:

    a. *Ed*—The educational degree or certification typically required for entry into the occupation.

    b. *Eng*—The extent to which jobs require knowledge of and proficiency in the use of the English language.

2. **Aptitudes Code**—The extent to which incumbents should possess the following aptitudes: general learning ability, verbal ability, numerical aptitude, spatial ability, form perception, clerical perception, motor coordination, finger dexterity, manual dexterity, and eye-hand-foot coordination.

3. **Temperaments Code**—The adaptability or trait requirements of workers in the occupation, for example, directing or supervising others, influencing or persuading others, working with people.

4. **Stress-Related Code**—The presence of stress in an occupation based on the existence of one or more of the following factors in the job: using emotional control, tolerating repetition, accepting responsibility, and sustaining attention.

5. **Physical Requirements**—The job requirements as they relate to the following physical demands: vision; hearing (including talking and hearing); lifting; walking or other mobility; climbing or balancing; stooping, kneeling, crouching, or crawling; handling; and fingering, feeling, or reaching.

6. **Work Environment Code**—The physical conditions in which the work of the occupation is performed. These include work location (inside or outside), extremes of cold, extremes of heat, wet or humid conditions, noise or vibration, hazards, and fumes, odors, or dust.

Both the *Selected Characteristics of Occupations Defined in the Dictionary of Occupational Titles* and *The Enhanced Guide for Occupational Exploration* can be used to form hypotheses regarding attributes that might be needed in an occupation. Exhibit 7.3 summarizes selected worker attributes identified for the occupation of Teller using these sources.

At this point, you might be wondering "If the *DOT* provides all of this job information, why do an analysis of specific jobs in a particular organization? Why not simply look up the job in the *DOT* and use that information as the job analysis?" There are several reasons why we would not want to rely solely on the *DOT* for job analysis information. For one, job titles alone do not always accurately describe job content. Even though jobs in different organizations may have identical titles, the actual job activities may be quite different. By applying one common description to all jobs with the same title, important job content may be overlooked. Second, jobs change. The content of jobs at one point in time may be completely different several years later.

Third, the *DOT* data alone will not meet the necessary requirements of a job analysis for HR selection purposes. We summarized earlier the legal standards for an acceptable job analysis that were identified by Thompson and Thompson.[41] When applying these standards as criteria for conducting a job analysis, we can easily see that *DOT* data alone will not suffice. Other job analysis steps must be taken.

Finally, while the compilation and production of the *DOT* represents the most complete and comprehensive description of occupations in the United States to date, the data themselves are not free from problems. A number of investigators have been critical of the *DOT* data.[42] Some of these criticisms have included questionable reliability and validity of the worker function and attribute ratings,[43] the relatively small number of job analyses conducted for each occupational title (almost two-thirds of the occupations in the latest edition of the *DOT* were based on the analysis of fewer than three jobs), and many of the job analyses used do not meet the standards for a complete job analysis.[44]

Even though there are problems with the *DOT*, it is still a source that should be reviewed. When used in the context of HR selection, it can help us form hypotheses about job content and the necessary employee attributes for job performance. These hypotheses can provide direction to the actual job analysis and the development of suitable selection measures.

EXHIBIT 7.3	SUMMARY OF WORKER ATTRIBUTES IDENTIFIED FOR THE JOB OF TELLER

	Worker Attributes
Physical Demands[a]	• Involves light work
	• Requires lifting of 20 pounds maximum
	• Requires walking or standing to a significant degree or when it involves sitting most of the time, involves a degree of pushing and pulling of arm or leg controls
	• Requires reaching, handling, fingering, and feeling
	• Requires talking and hearing spoken words
	• Requires normal vision (with or without correction)
	• Requires normal hearing
Environmental Conditions[b]	• Involves inside work where there is protection from weather conditions but not necessarily temperature changes
Reasoning Development[c]	• Apply principles of rational system to solve practical problems and deal with a variety of variables where there is limited standardization
	• Interpret instructions in written or oral form
Mathematical Development[c]	• Compute discount, interest, profit, and loss; commission markups, and selling price; ratio and proportions, and percentages
Language Development[c]	• Read at rate of 190–215 words per minute. Read adventure stories, look up unfamiliar words in a dictionary
	• Write compound and complex sentences, using cursive style, proper punctuation

(continued)

| EXHIBIT 7.3 | (CONTINUED) |

Language Development (*cont.*)[c]

- Speak clearly with correct pronunciation, using present, perfect, and future tenses

High Aptitudes

- Requires general learning ability
- Requires numerical aptitude
- Requires clerical perception
- Requires motor coordination
- Requires finger dexterity

Temperaments[d]

- Involves working with people
- Involves doing repetitive work
- Involves doing precise work to close tolerances

Stress[e]

- Requires ability to maintain emotional control of feelings
- Requires ability to tolerate repetition

SOURCES: U.S. Department of Labor, *Selected Characteristics of Occupations Defined in the Dictionary of Occupational Titles* (Washington, D.C.: U.S. Government Printing Office, 1981), pp. 225, 465–473, and Marilyn Maze and Donald Mayall, *The Enhanced Guide for Occupational Exploration* (Indianapolis: JIST Works, 1991).

[a] Physical requirements and capacities a worker must have to meet physical demands of the job.

[b] Physical surroundings of a worker in a job.

[c] Those aspects of education that contribute to the acquisition of skills but do not have a specific vocational objective.

[d] Adaptability requirements of the worker.

[e] Amount of time required to learn the techniques, acquire information, and develop the facility needed for average job performance.

Other Literature Sources Other sources of materials in a literature review might include professional associations, labor unions and contracts, training and educational materials produced by the organization, professional publications (such as *Personnel Psychology, Journal of Occupational and Organizational Psychology, Public Personnel Management, Journal of Applied Psychology*), and previous job analyses or studies. Again, the purpose of this search is not to replace the proposed job analysis but to provide a frame of reference for comparing results with the proposed study. Knowledge gleaned from these sources should enhance the quality of job-related research and the development of selection measures.

The next two issues, selecting job agents and choosing a method for collecting job information, are really interrelated. Decisions made in one area necessarily affect those made in the other. However, in order to better clarify important aspects of each, we discuss these decision points separately. In the remaining portion of this chapter, the emphasis is on issues involved in choosing job agents. The following chapter addresses the methods used in collecting job information.

Selecting Job Agents

Job information can be collected by a variety of means ranging from mechanical means, such as videotaping equipment, to human observers. Most often people serve as *job agents*. Job agents are *individuals who are responsible for collecting and providing information about jobs.* In general, there are three classes of agents that can be employed to collect job data: (a) job analysts, (b) job incumbents, and (c) job supervisors.[45] Each type has its own particular characteristics, advantages, and disadvantages. We now focus our attention on unique aspects of each.

Job Analysts   Job analysts are individuals specially trained to collect and analyze job information systematically. Analysts generally have received formal training in one or more methods of job analysis, although, more often than not, they use interviews or observational methods to collect their data. Individuals serving as analysts may be employed within or from outside an organization requiring job analysis. When internal analysts are used, they frequently work as staff specialists out of personnel or industrial engineering offices. External analysts are typically private consultants. These individuals generally are hired under contract to analyze jobs for a specific purpose, for example, compensation, training, or selection.

The chief advantage when trained capable analysts are used is that an organization is purchasing the services of skilled individuals to perform their jobs. Because of their training, it might be expected (though little research is available) that resulting analyses would generally be more objective, valid, and reliable than comparable ones completed by less formally prepared agents.[46]

With respect to consultants, an issue that typically arises is when should an outside consultant be hired to perform a job analysis rather than doing the analysis using resources within the organization. There are no specific definitive answers, since that will depend on the particular situation. The key issue is: Are appropriately qualified people available within the organization who can perform the job analysis and other activities necessary to meet the requirements for a sound selection system? For most organizations, the answer is "no." Nevertheless, for those who want to think about the option, consider the following guidelines:

1. If a job analysis is being performed as a onetime activity, then use of a consultant may be more cost effective than trying to develop the capabilities to conduct the analysis using internal resources.

2. Costs of performing a job analysis using internal resources are likely to be underestimated. Fees for using a consultant with an agreed-upon scope of work are likely to be more predictable than those for conducting a job analysis with internal resources.

3. A do-it-yourself approach to job analysis can prove to be a valuable learning experience for staff members who are not knowledgeable in job analysis methods. However, slower project progress, lesser quality of work, reduced defensibility of the work, and an increased potential for catastrophe should be anticipated.

4. Internal staff members performing a job analysis are likely to have less credibility than outside consultants.

5. For purposes such as selection measure development and validation, job analysis must conform to legal and technical standards; thus the consequences of error can be very high. Because of these rigorous legal and technical standards, professionally trained personnel will be required to perform a job analysis. These personnel are more likely to be available outside of the organization than within it.[47]

Even if the internal staff has the requisite skills for conducting a job analysis, there are some additional issues to consider in choosing between an outside consultant or the internal staff. If the number of jobs to be analyzed is small, consultants may provide useful, relatively economical data. However, when the number of jobs is large, the amount of time and associated expense required for good coverage may be prohibitive.

In addition to the number of jobs to be studied, other factors that will affect the choice of a consultant as a job analyst include (a) *location of the jobs*—if widely dispersed, there will be greater expense in travel, time, and associated costs; (b) *complexity of the jobs*—the less observable and more diverse the tasks, the greater is the need for a skilled agent; and (c) *receptiveness of job incumbents to external analysts*—if incumbents feel threatened by external analysts (for example, they fear increased productivity standards, layoffs, or termination), the potential costs to the organization (such as lowered productivity) will be greater. This is not a comprehensive list, but it provides a range of factors that should be evaluated in deciding whether to use a job analyst.

If external job analysts are going to be used, they may be solicited from a variety of sources ranging from private consulting firms to university professors to branches of offices in state and federal governments. Certification of training (such as completion of specialized job analysis training programs) may be available from some analysts. However, training is no guarantee of quality. Examples of previous work in job analyses *associated with employee selection*, recommendations from previous organizational clients, and acceptance of the analyst's work in a court case involving HR selection are some of the best screening tools for selecting job analysts.

Job Incumbents The second type of agent is the job incumbent or employee. Generally speaking, employees working in a job should be in the best position to describe it. Furthermore, they can describe what is *actually* done rather than what *should be* done.

When using this type of agent, several issues have to be taken into consideration. First, employees may not be interested in reporting on their jobs. Emphasis on the importance of job analysis and use of incentives may be needed to gain the desired level of involvement. Second, employees are generally not prepared to participate in job analysis. Training may be required. Unless training is available, the project may be restricted to using only some of the easiest (not necessarily the most applicable) methods of collecting job data. An additional concern among some investigators is that employees may inflate their jobs.[48] If employees perceive it to be beneficial (such as having their jobs appear to be overly complex to improve their pay classification), they may overstate the exact nature of what they do. In addition, by having incumbents participate in a job analysis, some political gains might be made in terms of gaining employee acceptance of organizational changes made on the basis of the job analysis results. This advantage may be particularly true when organizational functions and practices other than selection are based on job analysis results.

Use of incumbents is not without its problems. Yet there are some possible benefits. As noted earlier, employees are in the best position to provide complete, accurate data on their jobs. Usually large numbers of employees are available, thus providing multiple assessments of the same job. When a large number of jobs are to be analyzed, the use of incumbents may be the most efficient option as a job data source.

Incumbents serving as job respondents should be selected carefully. Research on characteristics of good agents has not been plentiful, but some desirable traits can be hypothesized. The first requirement is that participation of an employee in job analysis should be voluntary. Where motivation and interest are low, quality of participation is likely to be low. Also, given the method of collecting job information (for example, interviews, questionnaires), employees should possess appropriate oral communicating, reading, and/or writing skills.

Incumbents should have been on their jobs a minimum of six months. This minimum standard may vary depending on the nature of the job in question. The role of minimum job tenure is to ensure that persons chosen will have been on their jobs long enough to give complete and accurate information about the job. Similarly, a maximum period of tenure may also be desirable. Since some job analysis methods require respondents to characterize tasks of newly hired employees, workers with high seniority in a specific job may have difficulty with this requirement. Long-tenured employees may be unable to recall accurately what a job was like when they were hired. Then, too, tasks that were required when these employees were first employed may have changed. A maximum period of job tenure, like a minimum period, will vary from one job to the next. But avoiding workers with too short or too long periods of service can help to eliminate some potentially critical job analysis problems.[49] After setting maximum and minimum tenure levels, inclusion of incumbents in the job analysis representative of the tenure range should be considered. Frank Landy and Joseph Vasey found that incumbent experience in a police job had an influence on how incumbents rated job tasks. They concluded that tenured individuals performed different tasks because seniority enabled them to choose their assignments.[50]

A final comment should be made about selecting a sample of incumbents. When jobs that have a small number of incumbents who meet our selection criteria are analyzed, it may be necessary to use all available persons. Conversely, when jobs have a large number of incumbents, a sample can be drawn. The specific sampling strategy may vary depending on the nature of the organization (for example, size, geographical dispersion) and type of job. In general, a form of stratified random sampling would be most appropriate. Under this sampling strategy, the sample is classified according to designated incumbent characteristics or strata (such as gender, ethnicity, tenure, and factors related to the job or organization such as location or shift). Then, individuals are randomly drawn from these classifications. The idea behind the method is to choose a random sample of job agents that best represents the incumbent population being studied. If there are very small numbers of ethnic minorities and women, it may be necessary to oversample them. In this way, a large enough sample would be available to reflect their views adequately.

Given the legal considerations involved in HR selection, sampling strata based on gender and ethnicity should definitely be employed. Sampling based on major individual difference variables, like gender and ethnicity, as well as other incumbent characteristics thought to be linked to quality of data obtained would be most defensible if a discrimination charge arises.

Sampling of incumbents will likely be necessary for most organizations when incumbents are used as data sources. However, some organizations have chosen to survey the entire population of employees in a job. For example, the U.S. Air Force has attempted to collect data from all incumbents in a job. Information is then deleted from individual raters if it does not approximate the average ratings of the group. With this type of analysis, the measure of job activity is the average of most, if not all, incumbents' judgments.[51]

Job Supervisors Supervisors can also serve as job agents. Since they supervise incumbents performing the job under study, they should be in a position to provide objective data on jobs. Supervisory assessments assume, of course, that supervisors have worked closely with incumbents and have complete information about employees' jobs. Paul Sparks has suggested that supervisors know relatively well what employees do and should be able to make *relative* judgments about job activities. However, there appears to be a tendency for supervisors to characterize subordinates' work in terms of what *should be* done rather than what is *actually* done.[52]

Since only a few supervisors may be needed to supervise a number of jobs, supervisors will likely be widely dispersed. Thus reliance on a large number of supervisors for job data may substantially increase project costs. Problems like inaccessibility have discouraged the use of supervisors in job analysis research. However, even where supervisors do not serve as the principal information source, they can serve as a means for cross-checking or verifying job data collected elsewhere.

Characteristics thought to be useful in choosing incumbents as job agents similarly apply to supervisors. Factors such as willingness to participate, possession of oral communicating, reading, and/or writing skills, knowledge of the job being studied, and minimum and maximum tenure in a specific job should be important considerations.

Research on Job Agents Attention has been given by researchers to various issues in job analysis. Unfortunately, little job agent research appears to have been directed toward problems such as the accuracy of agents, differences among agents in rating jobs, characteristics of effective agents, and the validity and reliability of job data produced by various types of agents. Thus it is difficult to specify firm, consistent findings that can guide the selection of agents. Some limited data, however, are available.

A few investigations have tested the accuracy of estimated versus actual time spent on different aspects of jobs. On the whole, moderate to high relationships have been found between the incumbents' estimated time and the actual time spent on their job activities. Higher relationships between the time estimated and the time actually spent have generally existed for observable work activities than for more subjective activities such as planning.[53]

Several investigations have been conducted for the purpose of comparing the responses of job incumbents with supervisors' responses in a job analysis. Charles Lawshe[54] and Herbert Meyer[55] tested for differences between foremen and their supervisors in their perceptions of the foreman's job. They found large differences between the supervisors and foremen regarding how foremen spent their time in various job functions. Meyer also reported relatively high disagreement between foremen and general foremen concerning the foreman's job responsibilities. Disagreement between supervisors and their subordinates was also found by A. P. O'Reilly in terms of the tasks performed and the level of skills and knowledge required to perform them.[56] In contrast to these studies, Joe Hazel, Joseph Madden, and Raymond Christal investigated supervisor-subordinate similarity in perception of general job duties versus specific job tasks. Higher supervisor-subordinate agreement was noted for the ratings of general job duties than for specific tasks.[57]

A series of other investigations have explored further differences among agents serving as sources of job information. Jack Smith and Milton Hakel compared the responses among five groups of agents to a standardized job analysis questionnaire (the Position Analysis Questionnaire or PAQ). The five groups of job agents were (a) supervisors, (b) incumbents, (c) analysts, (d) college students who knew nothing about the jobs being rated, and (e) college students who knew nothing about the jobs but were given job specifications. Smith and Hakel reported higher evaluations of questionnaire items that were most socially desirable by incumbents and supervisors. In addition, they found high correlations among the five groups in their questionnaire responses.[58] The surprising finding that college students who knew nothing more than the title of a job could produce results consistently similar to supervisors, incumbents, and analysts was addressed in later studies. Edwin Cornelius, Angelo Denisi, and Allyn Blencoe[59] concluded that Smith and Hakel's reported differences among job agents was really due to some methodological problems. A later study by Robert Harvey and Susana Lozada-Larsen also rejected the idea that naive job agents with only limited information about a job other than the job title could provide job ratings as good as those of job agents with extensive information. Expert job agents were more accurate in their ratings of jobs than agents with very limited job information.[60]

A few studies have sought to examine the relationship between agent characteristics and their ratings of jobs. Kenneth Wexley and Stanley Silverman[61] and Patrick Conley and Paul Sackett[62] found that incumbents' level of job performance was not associated with their ratings of job tasks or of worker characteristics necessary to perform the jobs. However, Wayman Mullins and Wilson Kimbrough reported an association between performance level and job analysis outcomes.[63]

If incumbent demographic characteristics are found to be related to the quality of job data provided in a job analysis, these characteristics could be used for screening incumbents participating in the analysis. When demographic characteristics of job agents have been studied, some low to moderate relationships between such characteristics and agents' ratings of jobs have been indicated. For the most part, however, research on job agent characteristics and job analysis results has produced a patchwork quality of findings. Sometimes relationships are found, and, at other times, they are not. We simply do not have a complete understanding as to why. The results cited here are representative of the findings from studies investigating links between job agent characteristics and job analysis results.

Richard Arvey and his colleagues reported gender differences in agents' ratings with females giving lower ratings to the job rated than males.[64] However, without knowledge of what the job was really like, it is impossible to determine if the women were too lenient or men too strict in their ratings. Additionally, Neal Schmitt and Scott Cohen found that women reported more activities that occurred within the organization whereas men reported more activities related to financial and budgetary matters and interacting with groups of individuals outside of the organization. The gender differences, however, were not great.[65]

Frank Landy and Joseph Vasey noted that ethnicity was not associated with job analysis results.[66] John Veres and his coworkers identified racial differences in a job analysis of clerical workers. They concluded that such differences would lead to different definitions of the job content domain.[67] Similarly, Neal Schmitt and Scott Cohen found that ratings of time spent were more variable for minority members as a function of their level of involvement in group tasks.[68] When minority members were responsible for group tasks, their time spent ratings were consistent for all levels of involvement. Yet the racial differences observed in ratings were rather minor.

Edwin Cornelius and Keith Lyness showed that years of education was positively associated with the quality of job analysis data produced.[69] In contrast, two studies concluded that years of education was uncorrelated with the quality of job analysis data.[70] Cornelius and Lyness,[71] Mullins and Kimbrough,[72] and Schmitt and Cohen[73] all found that job tenure was independent of the quality of job analysis data given. Alternatively, Landy and Vasey[74] concluded that tenure affected job analysis results. Finally, Samuel Green and Thomas Stutzman reported low to moderate positive correlations between organizational tenure and years of education with various indices developed for selecting incumbents to respond to a task analysis inventory.[75]

We might ask what these results tell us in terms of the differences among job agents in performing a job analysis and the quality of data they collect. Definitive answers to these questions, which specify how a job agent should be used, simply cannot be made. Our present research base on agents' performance is not developed to the degree we would like. On the other hand, these results, as well as recommendations from researchers working in the area of job analysis, can give us some *broad* guidelines to follow. As long as it is remembered that these are general suggestions, not answers, they may be useful to us in choosing and using job agents. Guidelines and conclusions drawn from the research cited earlier as well as from a review by Edwin Cornelius[76] include the following:

1. Incumbents can provide accurate estimates of the actual time spent in performing specific job tasks.

2. Supervisors and incumbents are likely to disagree in ratings of specific job tasks performed. Agreement is likely to be higher when broader job duties are rated.

3. Supervisors who directly supervise the job being analyzed seem to be most helpful in providing KSA information; incumbents seem best at providing task information.

4. Expert job agents with extensive information about a job provide better quality job rating data than agents with limited job information.

5. The relations between incumbent job performance, education, gender, and ethnicity and job analysis results are somewhat equivocal. In some situations, relationships are found; in others, they are not. When relationships are found, they tend to be rather low.

6. Supervisors and incumbents, as opposed to job analysts, may have a tendency to inflate ratings of their jobs when the purpose of the job analysis involves making decisions about issues that are highly desirable (for example, wage and salary decisions).

7. From a legal perspective, the sample of job incumbents to be used as agents should be selected to represent the incumbent population in terms of gender and ethnicity as well as other characteristics thought to be important.

8. Our last guideline requires a comment. Rather than using demographic characteristics as predictors of agents' quality of job analysis ratings, it

may be possible to develop a more direct measure or index of the quality of the ratings given. For example, Samuel Green and Thomas Stutzman have suggested that a "carelessness index" be included as part of a structured job analysis questionnaire.[77] A carelessness index is composed of tasks that are known *not* to be performed by an incumbent population. These tasks are placed randomly among tasks on the questionnaire that are known to be performed. Respondents are asked to read all tasks and make judgments about them. Those respondents who indicate they perform tasks known not to be performed would be judged as providing inaccurate data and, thus, would be eliminated from the job analysis. Green and Stutzman's carelessness index would seem to offer some promise for identifying suitable incumbents serving as job agents.

In order to carry out job analysis activities, one must choose which of the actual methods to use. Our next chapter reviews the major options to consider when selecting among these methods.

References

[1] Ernest J. McCormick, "Job and Task Analysis," in *Handbook of Industrial and Organizational Psychology*, ed. Marvin Dunnette (Chicago: Rand McNally, 1976), pp. 652–653.

[2] Wayne Cascio, *Applied Psychology in Personnel Management*, (Reston, Va.: Reston, 1991).

[3] Joseph E. Zerga, "Job Analysis, A Resumé and Bibliography," *Journal of Applied Psychology* 27 (1943): 249–267.

[4] Richard S. Uhrbrock, "The History of Job Analysis," *Administration* 3 (1922): 164–168.

[5] Jai Ghorpade and Thomas J. Atchinson, "The Concept of Job Analysis: A Review and Some Suggestions," *Public Personnel Management* 9 (June 1980): 134. For a review of the job analysis literature through 1970, see Erich P. Prien and William W. Ronan, "Job Analysis: A Review of Research Findings," *Personnel Psychology* 24 (1971): 371–396. For historical accounts of job analysis, see Ernest S. Primoff and Sidney A. Fine, "A History of Job Analysis," in *The Job Analysis Handbook for Business, Industry, and Government*, ed. Sidney Gael (New York: Wiley, 1988), pp. 14–29 and Jimmy L. Mitchell, "History of Job Analysis in Military Organizations," in *The Job Analysis Handbook for Business, Industry, and Government*, ed. Sidney Gael (New York: Wiley, 1988), pp. 30–36.

[6] Jean J. Jones and Thomas DeCotiis, "Job Analysis: National Survey Findings," *Personnel Journal* 48 (October 1969): 805–806.

[7] Thomasine Rendero, "Consensus," *Personnel* 58 (January–February 1981): 4–12.

[8] Marvin D. Dunnette, *Personnel Selection and Placement* (Belmont, Calif.: Wadsworth, 1966).

[9] Donald W. Myers, "The Impact of a Selected Provision in the Federal Guidelines on Job Analysis and Training," *Personnel Administrator* 26 (July 1981): 41–45; D. Patrick Lacy, "EEO Implications of Job Analysis," *Employee Relations Law Journal* 4 (Spring 1979): 525–526; Paul Sparks, "Legal Basis for Job Analysis," in *The Job Analysis Handbook for Business, Industry, and Government*, ed. Sidney Gael (New York: Wiley, 1988), pp. 37–47.

[10] Duane E. Thompson and Toni A. Thompson, "Court Standards for Job Analysis in Test Validation," *Personnel Psychology* 35 (1982): 872–873; see also Clement J. Berwitz, *The Job Analysis Approach to Affirmative Action* (New York: Wiley, 1975).

11 *Griggs v. Duke Co.*, 401 U.S. 424, 436 (1971).

12 Ibid.

13 Ibid.

14 *Albemarle Paper Co. v. Moody*, 422 U.S. 405 (1975).

15 Ibid.

16 Equal Employment Opportunity Commission, *Guidelines on Employee Selection Procedures*, 35 Federal Register 12,333-12,336 (1970).

17 Thompson and Thompson, "Court Standards for Job Analysis in Test Validation," pp. 872–873.

18 Equal Employment Opportunity Commission, Civil Service Commission, Department of Labor, and Department of Justice, *Adoption of Four Agencies of Uniform Guidelines on Employee Selection Procedures*, 43 Federal Register 38,290-38,315 (Aug. 25, 1978), referred to in the text as the *Uniform Guidelines;* Equal Employment Opportunity Commission, Office of Personnel Management, Department of Treasury, *Adoption of Questions and Answers to Clarify and Provide a Common Interpretation of the Uniform Guidelines on Employee Selection Procedures*, 44 Federal Register 11,996-12,009 (1979); Equal Employment Opportunity Commission, *Guidelines on Employee Selection Procedures*, 41 Federal Register 51,984-51,986 (1976).

19 Bureau of National Affairs, "Professional, Legal Requirements of Job Analysis Explored at Chicago Conference," *Daily Labor Report*, May 30, 1980, pp. A-1–A-8.

20 Ibid., p. A-5.

21 Ibid. For additional perspectives on legal issues in job analysis, see Stephen E. Bemis, Ann Holt Belenky, and Dee Ann Soder, *Job Analysis: An Effective Management Tool* (Washington, D.C.: Bureau of National Affairs, 1983): pp. 126–128 and Sparks, "Legal Basis for Job Analysis."

22 David M. Van De Voort and Beverly K. Stalder, "Organizing for Job Analysis," in *The Job Analysis Handbook for Business, Industry, and Government*, ed. Sidney Gael (New York: Wiley, 1988), pp. 320–323.

23 Randall S. Schuler, *Personnel and Human Resources Management* (St. Paul, Minn.: West, 1981), p. 96.

24 Milton D. Hakel, Beverly K. Stalder, and David M. Van De Voort, "Obtaining and Maintaining Acceptance of Job Analysis," in *The Job Analysis Handbook for Business, Industry, and Government*, ed. Sidney Gael (New York: Wiley, 1988), p. 330.

25 Irwin L. Goldstein, Sheldon Zedeck, and Benjamin Schneider, "An Exploration of the Job Analysis—Content Validity Process," in *Personnel Selection in Organizations*, eds. Neal Schmitt and Walter Borman (San Francisco: Jossey-Bass, 1993), pp. 3–34.

26 Michael R. Carrell and Frank E. Kuzmits, *Personnel: Management of Human Resources* (Columbus, Ohio: Merrill, 1982), pp. 75–76.

27 Hakel, Stalder, and Van De Voort, "Obtaining and Maintaining Acceptance of Job Analysis," pp. 331–332.

28 Robert J. Teare and Hubert S. Feild, *The National Classification Validation Study: A Synthesis Report on the Analysis of Jobs* (Silver Spring, Md.: National Association of Social Workers, 1984), pp. 11–13.

29 Van De Voort and Stalder, "Organizing for Job Analysis," pp. 323–324.

30 Erich P. Prien, "Development of a Clerical Description Questionnaire," *Personnel Psychology* 18 (1977): 167.

31 Equal Employment Opportunity Commission et al., *Adoption of Four Agencies of Uniform Guidelines on Employee Selection Procedures*, p. 38,307.

32 Ibid., pp. 38,296-38,297.

33 Richard F. Thorton and Michael Rosenfeld, *The Design and Evaluation of Job Analysis Procedures Conducted for the Purpose of Developing Content Valid Occupational Assessment Measures* (Princeton, N.J.: Center for Occupational and Professional Assessment, Educational Testing Service, 1980), p. 13.

34 Ibid., p. 7.

35 U.S. Department of Labor, Employment and Training Administration, *Dictionary of*

Occupational Titles, 4th ed. (Washington, D.C.: U.S. Government Printing Office, 1991). See also a supplement to the *DOT*, U.S. Department of Labor, Employment and Training Administration, *Dictionary of Occupational Titles Fourth Edition Supplement* (Washington, D.C.: U.S. Government Printing Office, 1972).

[36] U.S. Department of Labor, Employment and Training Administration, *Dictionary of Occupational Titles*, pp. xix.

[37] Ibid., pp. xvii–xxiii; 1009–1024.

[38] Ann R. Miller, Donald J. Treiman, Pamela S. Cain, and Patricia A. Roos, *Work, Jobs, and Occupations: A Critical Review of the Dictionary of Occupational Titles* (Washington, D.C.: National Academy Press, 1980) p. 29.

[39] U.S. Department of Labor, Employment and Training Administration, *Selected Characteristics of Occupations Defined in the Dictionary of Occupational Titles* (Washington, D.C.: U.S. Government Printing Office, 1981). See also U.S. Department of Labor, Employment and Training Administration, *Guide for Occupational Exploration* (Washington, D.C.: U.S. Government Printing Office, 1979).

[40] Marilyn Maze and Donald Mayall, *The Enhanced Guide for Occupational Exploration* (Indianapolis: JIST Works, 1991).

[41] Thompson and Thompson, "Court Standards for Job Analysis in Test Validation."

[42] Miller, Treiman, Cain, and Roos, *Work, Jobs, and Occupations: A Critical Review of the Dictionary of Occupational Titles.*

[43] Pamela S. Cain and Bert Green, "Reliability of Ratings Available from the *Dictionary of Occupational Titles*," *Journal of Applied Psychology* 68 (1983): 155–165. Paul Geyer, John Hice, John Hawk, Ronald Boese, and Yevonne Brannon ("Reliabilities of Ratings Available from the Dictionary of Occupational Titles," *Personnel Psychology* 42 (1989): 547–560) using standard *DOT* job analysis procedures found that the majority of 70 *DOT* rating scales produced reliabilities exceeding .80, and 25 scales yielded reliability estimates between .90 and .98.

[44] John S. Lawrence, "Occupational Information: Status and Sources," in *The Job Analysis Handbook for Business, Industry, and Government*, ed. Sidney Gael (New York: Wiley, 1988), p. 379.

[45] Ernest J. McCormick, "Job Information: Its Development and Applications," in *ASPA Handbook of Personnel and Industrial Relations*, ed. Dale Yoder and Herbert G. Heneman (Washington, D.C.: BNA, 1979), pp. 4–43. Sources of bias in job analysis have been studied by Richard D. Arvey, Greg A. Davis, Sherry L. McGowen, and Robert L. Dipboye, "Potential Sources of Bias in Job Analytic Processes," *Academy of Management Journal* 25 (1982): 621–629; Erich P. Prien and S. D. Saleh, "A Study of Bias in Job Analysis," *Journal of Industrial Psychology* 1 (1963): 113–117; Llewellyn W. Wiley and William S. Jenkins, "Method of Measuring Bias in Raters Who Estimate Job Qualifications," *Journal of Industrial Psychology* 1 (1963): 16–22.

[46] One study found increased reliability and accuracy for trained analysts when using the Job Components Inventory, but no differences in reliability or accuracy using trained or untrained analysts using the PAQ. Michael A. Surrette, Michael G. Aamodt, and Daniel L. Johnson, "Effects of Analyst Training and Amount of Available Job Related Information on Job Analysis Ratings," *Journal of Business and Psychology* 4 (1990): 134–451.

[47] Van De Voort and Stalder, "Organizing for Job Analysis," pp. 315–317.

[48] Ernest J. McCormick, *Job Analysis* (New York: AMACON, 1979).

[49] In contrast to our suggestion that a minimum length of time on a job may be important in choosing incumbents to participate in a job analysis, three studies found no relationship between job tenure and quality of job analysis data produced. (See Edwin T. Cornelius and Keith S. Lyness, "A Comparison of Holistic and Decomposed Judgment Strategies in Job Analysis by Job Incumbents," *Journal of Applied Psychology* 65 (1980): 155–163; Wayman C. Mullins and Wilson W. Kimbrough, "Group Composition as a Determinant of Job Analysis Outcomes," *Journal of Applied Psychology* 73 (1988): 657–664; Neal Schmitt and Scott A. Cohen,

"Internal Analysis of Task Ratings by Job Incumbents," *Journal of Applied Psychology* 74 (1989): 96–104). Another found only a moderate relationship. (See Samuel B. Green and Thomas Stutzman, "An Evaluation of Methods to Select Respondents to Structured Job Analysis Questionnaires," *Personnel Psychology* 39 (1986): 543–564).

[50] Frank J. Landy and Joseph Vasey, "Job Analysis: The Composition of SME Samples," *Personnel Psychology* 44 (1991): 27–50.

[51] In most applications, the mean is the preferred descriptive statistic for representing job analysis ratings.

[52] Paul Sparks, "Job Analysis," in *Personnel Management*, ed. Kenneth Rowland and Gerald Ferris (Boston: Allyn & Bacon, 1981). See also Paul Sparks, *Job Analysis under the New Uniform Guidelines* (Houston, Tex.: Personnel Research, Exxon Corporation, August 1979).

[53] Stephen J. Carroll and William H. Taylor, "Validity of Estimates by Clerical Personnel of Job Time Proportions," *Journal of Applied Psychology* 53 (1969): 164–166; John R. Hinrichs, "Communications Activity of Industrial Research Personnel," *Personnel Psychology* 17 (1964): 193–204.

[54] Charles H. Lawshe, *Psychology of Industrial Relations* (New York: McGraw-Hill, 1953).

[55] Herbert H. Meyer, "Comparison of Foreman and General Foreman Conceptions of the Foreman's Job Responsibility," *Personnel Psychology* 12 (1959): 445–452.

[56] A. P. O'Reilly, "Skill Requirements: Supervisor-Subordinate Conflict," *Personnel Psychology* 26 (1973): 75–80.

[57] Joe T. Hazel, Joseph M. Madden, and Raymond E. Christal, "Agreement between Worker-Supervisor Descriptions of the Worker's Job," *Journal of Industrial Psychology* 2 (1964): 71–79.

[58] Jack E. Smith and Milton D. Hakel, "Convergence Among Data Sources, Response Bias, and Reliability and Validity of a Structured Job Analysis Questionnaire," *Personnel Psychology* 32 (1979) 677–692.

[59] Edwin T. Cornelius, Angelo S. Denisi, and Allyn G. Blencoe, "Expert and Naive Raters Using the PAQ: Does it Matter?" *Personnel Psychology* 37 (1984): 453–464.

[60] Robert J. Harvey and Susana R. Lozada-Larsen, "Influence of Amount of Job Descriptive Information on Job Analysis Rating Accuracy," *Journal of Applied Psychology* 73 (1988): 457–461.

[61] Kenneth N. Wexley and Stanley B. Silverman, "An Examination of Differences between Managerial Effectiveness and Response Patterns on a Structured Job Analysis Questionnaire," *Journal of Applied Psychology* 63 (1978): 646–649.

[62] Patrick R. Conley and Paul R. Sackett, "Effects of Using High- versus Low-Performing Job Incumbents as Sources of Job Analysis Information," *Journal of Applied Psychology* 72 (1987): 434–437.

[63] Wayman C. Mullins and Wilson W. Kimbrough, "Group Composition as a Determinant of Job Analysis Outcomes," *Journal of Applied Psychology* 73 (1988): 657–664.

[64] Richard D. Arvey, Emily M. Passino, and John W. Lounsbury, "Job Analysis Results as Influenced by Sex of Incumbent and Sex of Analyst," *Journal of Applied Psychology* 62 (1977): 411–416.

[65] Neal Schmitt and Scott A. Cohen, "Internal Analyses of Task Ratings by Job Incumbents,: *Journal of Applied Psychology* 74 (1989): 96–104.

[66] Landy and Vasey, "Job Analysis: The Composition of SME Samples."

[67] John G. Veres, Samuel B. Green, and Wiley R. Boyles, "Racial Differences on Job Analysis Questionnaires: An Empirical Study," *Public Personnel Management* 20 (1991): 135–144.

[68] Schmitt and Cohen, "Internal Analyses of Task Ratings by Job Incumbents."

[69] Cornelius and Lyness, "A Comparison of Holistic and Decomposed Judgment Strategies in Job Analyses by Job Incumbents."

[70] Landy and Vasey, "Job Analysis: The Composition of SME Samples" and Wayman C. Mullins and Wilson W. Kimbrough, "Group Composition as a Determinant of Job Analysis Outcomes."

[71] Cornelius and Lyness, "A Comparison of Holistic and Decomposed Judgment Strategies in Job Analyses by Job Incumbents."

[72] Mullins and Kimbrough, "Group Composition as a Determinant of Job Analysis Outcomes."

[73] Schmitt and Cohen, "Internal Analyses of Task Ratings by Job Incumbents."

[74] Landy and Vasey, "Job Analysis: The Composition of SME Samples."

[75] Green and Stutzman, "An Evaluation of Methods to Select Respondents to Structured Job Analysis Questionnaires."

[76] Edwin T. Cornelius, "Practical Findings from Job Analysis Research," in *The Job Analysis Handbook for Business, Industry, and Government,* ed. Sidney Gael (New York: Wiley, 1988), pp. 48–68.

[77] Green and Stutzman, "An Evaluation of Methods to Select Respondents to Structured Job Analysis Questionnaires." See also Samuel B. Green and John G. Veres, "Evaluation of an Index to Detect Inaccurate Respondents to a Task Analysis Inventory," Department of Psychology, Auburn University, Auburn, Alabama, 1988.

8

Applying Job Analysis Techniques

In Chapter 7, we outlined four of seven major decisions points involved in job analysis for HR selection purposes. These four steps included (a) organizing for a job analysis, (b) choosing jobs to be studied, (c) reviewing the relevant literature, and (d) selecting job agents. At step five, we are ready to begin the actual collection of information about jobs that is important for developing a useful selection system. In this chapter and its appendix, we are concerned with some of the various techniques available for collecting job information. We focus on those methods often used for HR selection applications. These methods are not the only ones currently being used; however, the ones we discuss provide an overview of the wide array of methods available.

Collecting Job Information

Earlier we said that one principal role of job analysis in HR selection is to assess job content so that knowledge, skills, abilities (KSAs) and other requisite employee specifications can be identified. It is these employee specifications that we want to translate into selection measures such as tests, interviews, and the like. Assuming our selection measures are valid, they, in turn, may be used for selection decision-making purposes. The process of developing valid selection measures that assess employee specifications requires several points where judgment or inferences must be made. Exhibit 8.1 summarizes these inferential points.

At the first inference point, data collected from a job analysis are used to infer KSAs and other relevant employee specifications. A second inference point is then reached concerning the content of selection measures that reflect these identified specifications. An important goal is to minimize the chance of error at each inference point. Our resulting specifications will be useful only to the extent that our inferences are accurate and complete. If our inferences are wrong, our selection measures will be useless for predicting successful job performance.

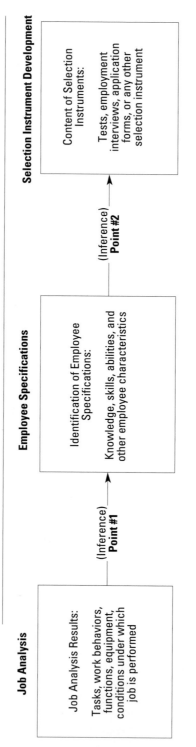

Job Analysis

Job Analysis Results:

Tasks, work behaviors, functions, equipment, conditions under which job is performed

(Inference)
Point #1

Employee Specifications

Identification of Employee Specifications:

Knowledge, skills, abilities, and other employee characteristics

(Inference)
Point #2

Selection Instrument Development

Content of Selection Instruments:

Tests, employment interviews, application forms, or any other selection instrument

Obviously, the process depends on the data derived initially from the job analysis. If these data are incomplete, inaccurate, or otherwise faulty, subsequent judgments based on these data will be incorrect. In the end, we will have an inappropriate, invalid, perhaps illegal selection device. Thus we must be very careful in our choice of methods for collecting job information.

At this point, we should note that many of the methods we review and discuss tend to focus on the tasks performed by job incumbents. Other researchers in the field of HR selection do not necessarily agree about using these detailed job-task approaches for all HR selection applications. In particular, writers in the area of validity generalization tend to support more holistic methods of job analysis.[1] Their argument is that task-oriented job analysis is not of much value for selection when measures of employee ability and aptitudes are concerned. On the other hand, when noncognitive attributes of applicants are being assessed or content validation strategies are being used with job knowledge or work sample tests, task-oriented job analysis is needed.[2]

A Categorization of Job Analysis Methods

Various systems have been used to classify methods for collecting job information. Dichotomies such as qualitative versus quantitative, structured versus unstructured, subjective versus objective have been proposed for categorizing the various techniques. For our purposes, the distinction between *work-oriented* and *worker-oriented* methods seems most useful.[3] As we see in the next chapter, each of these types of methods has important implications for the ways in which employee specifications are derived from job analysis data.

Work-oriented job analysis deals with a description of the various tasks performed on a job. Emphasis is generally on what is accomplished by the worker, such as "Records customer complaints in customer complaint file."[4] The product of these methods is the description and characterization (in terms of ratings such as frequency, importance, and difficulty) of tasks or job duties. From these task descriptions, employee specifications are then inferred. The basis for all work-oriented job analysis techniques is the *task* and for this reason, these techniques tend to be job specific.

Whereas work-oriented methods tend to focus on specific job tasks, *worker-oriented job analysis examines broad human behaviors involved in work activities.* The focus is not on specific tasks; rather, general aspects of jobs that describe the perceptual, interpersonal, sensory, mental, and physical activities is the prime concern.[5] Because of their broad focus, worker-oriented methods are generic in nature and can be applied to a wide spectrum of jobs.

Although we have suggested using work versus worker orientation as a basis for classifying job analysis methods, the distinction is not always clear. Some techniques, such as the job analysis interview, can elicit both types of information. In addition, one approach is not necessarily better than the other. The decision of which to use will depend on many factors, for example the purpose of the analysis, its cost, and the availability of trained personnel. Both forms are legally acceptable (assuming they are appropriately applied), so particular circumstances will determine which approach to use.

A Survey of Job Analysis Methods

We divide our review of specific job analysis methods into two parts. The first part, presented in this chapter, covers the following three job analysis methods: (a) the job analysis interview, (b) the job analysis questionnaire, and (c) the Position Analysis Questionnaire (PAQ). The second part, found in the appendix to this chapter, focuses on the following additional techniques: (a) Critical-Incidents Technique, (b) Fleishman Job Analysis Survey (F-JAS), (c) Functional Job Analysis (FJA), and (d) Job Element Method (JEM).

In both sections, we describe each technique, its application, and its advantages and disadvantages. We do not advocate one particular technique to the exclusion of others. There are many methods available to the user; our omission of a specific one should not be interpreted as a condemnation of it. We concentrate in this book on those methods that seem to be most popular in HR selection practice. A total of seven job analysis methods are reviewed. With the exception of the job analysis interview, job analysis questionnaire, and critical-incidents technique all represent specific job analysis systems and involve particular data collection/analysis procedures. As all of these systems depend on either a questionnaire or an interview for collecting information, we begin with a description of these general methods (interviews and questionnaires) and then move to one specific method, the Position Analysis Questionnaire.

The Job Analysis Interview

Description

The interview is one of the most frequently used methods of job analysis, capable of meeting a wide array of purposes.[6] Essentially, a job analysis interview consists of a trained analyst asking questions of supervisors or incumbents about the duties and responsibilities; KSAs required; equipment; and/or conditions of employment for a job or class of jobs.

Job analysis data collected through interviews are typically obtained through group or individual interviews with incumbents or supervisors. A key assumption of the method is that participants are thoroughly familiar with the job being studied. Large groups of incumbents may be used when it is certain that all incumbents are performing the same major activities. Supervisory groups are sometimes employed in order to verify incumbent information and to provide information unavailable to employees in the job. In other cases, supervisors are used because supervisors may feel less threatened than incumbents in discussing incumbents' job activities with a stranger, or they may be better able to comment on the necessary employee characteristics required to perform these activities successfully.

A job analysis interview may be structured or unstructured. For selection purposes, a structured interview in which specific questions are asked and means are available for recording answers to these questions, such as rating scales or interview answer forms, is essential. An unstructured interview consists of a job analyst collecting information about a job without a specific list of questions developed prior to the interview. Based on our earlier discussion in Chapter 7 of the technical and legal issues involved in job analysis, a structured interview is much more likely than an unstructured one to provide the kind of job analysis data that can be used effectively in selection applications. Therefore, when we speak of a job analysis interview, we are referring to one that is structured.

In the context of HR selection, a job analysis interview is typically performed for one or more of the following reasons:

1. To collect job information, for example, information on job tasks, that will serve as a basis for developing other job analysis measures, such as a job analysis questionnaire

2. To serve as a means for clarifying or verifying information collected previously through other job analysis methods

3. To serve as a method, perhaps as one of several used, for collecting relevant job data for developing a selection system

Considerations on Applicability

The interview can be applied to a variety of jobs from those with activities that are basically physical in nature, such as a laborer's, to those with activities that are primarily mental, such as a manager's. When used with knowledgeable respondents, the interview makes it possible to identify activities that may go unobserved or occur over long time periods.

An important step toward its effective application is in the planning of the interview itself. Plans should be formulated so that objectives of the interview are clear (for example, identifying and rating job tasks); who is going to be interviewed is known (for example, incumbents with six or more months of job experience); the questions and means for recording answers to them are clearly specified (for example, an interview schedule listing the questions and forms for recording responses); and who will conduct the interviews is identified (for example, consultants, staff members, etc.).

We discussed in Chapter 7 the types of job agents and their role in providing job analysis data. Our discussion in that chapter applies also to planning a job analysis interview. But what about the questions to be asked? There are numerous approaches that could be taken in phrasing and posing questions in an interview. No one method is suitable for all cases. Exhibit 8.2 presents a shortened sample job interview schedule for use with a single job incumbent that asks for job data in a wide variety of areas. The schedule shown illustrates only some of the types of questions that might be asked. Supplementary forms would also be used with the schedule to systematically record incumbents' responses to the questions.

An Example

An approach adopted by the U.S. Office of Personnel Management (formerly the U.S. Civil Service Commission) is one possibility when a job analysis interview is going to be used.[7] This approach can be applied when the interview is the principal method for collecting job analysis data.

EXHIBIT 8.2	**AN EXAMPLE OF A TYPICAL JOB ANALYSIS INTERVIEW SCHEDULE (ABBREVIATED) FOR USE WITH AN INCUMBENT**

Name of Employee _____   Payroll Title _____

Job Analyst _____   Department _____

Date _____   Work Location _____

Important Job Tasks
1. Describe your job in terms of what you do.
2. How do you do it? Do you use special tools, equipment, or other sources of aid? If so, list the names of the principal tools, equipment, or sources of aid you use.
3. Of the major tasks in your job, how much time does it take to do each one? How often do you perform each task in a day, week, or month?

Knowledge, Skills, and Abilities Required
What does it take to perform each task in terms of the following:
1. Knowledge required
   a. What subject matter areas are covered by each task?
   b. What facts or principles must you have an acquaintance with or understand in these subject matter areas?
   c. Describe the level, degree, and breadth of knowledge required in these areas or subjects.
2. Skills required
   a. What activities must you perform with ease and precision?
   b. What are the manual skills that are required to operate machines, vehicles, equipment, or to use tools?
3. Abilities required
   a. What is the nature and level of language ability, written or oral, required of you on the job? Are there complex oral or written ideas involved in performing the task, or simple instructional materials?
   b. What mathematical ability must you have?
   c. What reasoning or problem-solving ability must you have?
   d. What instructions must you follow? Are they simple, detailed, involved, abstract?
   e. What interpersonal abilities are required? What supervisory or managing abilities are required?
   f. What physical abilities such as strength, coordination, visual acuity must you have?

Physical Activities
Describe the frequency and degree to which you are engaged in such activities as pulling, pushing, throwing, carrying, kneeling, sitting, running, crawling, reaching, climbing.

Environmental Conditions
Describe the frequency and degree to which you will encounter working conditions such as these: cramped quarters, moving objects, vibration, inadequate ventilation.

EXHIBIT 8.2   (CONTINUED)

Typical Working Incidents

Describe the frequency and degree to which you are doing the following:

    a. Working in situations involving the interpretation of feelings, ideas, or facts in terms of personal viewpoint.

    b. Influencing people in their opinions, attitudes, or judgments about ideas or things.

    c. Working with people beyond giving and receiving instructions.

    d. Performing repetitive work, or continuously performing the same work.

    e. Performing under stress when confronted with emergency, critical, unusual, or dangerous situations; or in situations in which work speed and sustained attention are make-and-break aspects of the job.

    f. Performing a variety of duties often changing from one task to another of a different nature without loss of efficiency or composure.

    g. Working under hazardous conditions that may result in violence, loss of bodily members, burns, bruises, cuts, impairment of senses, collapse, fractures, electric shock.

Records and Reports

What records or reports do you prepare as part of your job?

Source of Job Information

What is the principal source for instructions you receive on how to do your job (for example, oral directions or written specifications)?

Supervisory Responsibilities

1. How many employees are directly under your supervision?
2. Do you have full authority to assign work; correct and discipline; recommend pay increases, transfers, promotions, and discharge for these employees?

Other

Are there any additional elements about your job that would help me better understand what you do? If so, please describe them.

    The key initial step in characterizing a job with this interview procedure is the identification of critical job tasks. Once identified, each task is described in terms of factors such as KSAs required for task performance as well as environmental conditions surrounding task performance. Because of the importance of the task to the interview method, it may be helpful to review how job tasks are analyzed and structured with this method. After all, it is the task statement from which worker specifications are ultimately developed.

    Task statements are written so that each shows:

1. What the worker does, by using a specific action verb that introduces the task statement

2. To whom or what he or she does it, by stating the object of the verb

3.   What is produced, by expressing the expected output of the action

4.   What materials, tools, procedures, or equipment are used[8]

Using these task characteristics, let's see how they are applied in an actual inter-view context to develop appropriate task statements.

Suppose, for example, an analyst is reviewing the job of welfare eligibility examiner in a human services agency. Assume further that background and supplementary data have been obtained from the incumbent. The interviewer asks the respondent to describe his or her job in terms of what is done, how, for what purpose, and using what equipment or tools. The interviewee then describes the job as follows:

> I interview applicants for food stamps—ask the applicants all the pertinent questions that will help to determine their eligibility. For example, are they working part time, receiving other assistance, etc.
>
> To carry out the job I have to interpret regulations, policies, and actually make decisions about eligibility. Some applicants are referred to other assistance units. Some applicants need detailed explanations of policies at a level they can understand, to avoid their reacting unpleasantly over a decision. They also get advice about their appeal rights from me. I visit homes to evaluate a client's circumstances and make determinations. I verify what the client has said on the application: household composition, shelter arrangements, income, etc. This helps me determine whether the food stamp costs have been correctly or incorrectly determined.
>
> At times, I work in outreach centers and homes of applicants to make determinations. I make personal appearances at high schools, colleges, and civic organizations to outline and explain the food stamp program.[9]

Following these comments, the analyst then uses the task statement criteria listed earlier to produce task statements representing important task activities. Table 8.1 summarizes the classification of content for one important task. Once classified, the content is rewritten to produce an easy-to-read, understandable statement. The goal of the rewriting process is to produce task statements that can be understood by persons unfamiliar with the job. For example, the task content classified in Table 8.1 could be rewritten as follows:

1.   Asks client questions, listens, and records answers on standard eligibility form, using knowledge of interviewing techniques and eligibility criteria in order to gather information from which client's eligibility for food stamps can be determined.[10]

If the analyst follows through with the process just described, 6 to 12 important task statements are typically identified. From the interview response given earlier, additional tasks might include the following:

TABLE 8.1	CLASSIFICATION OF INTERVIEW CONTENT TO DEVELOP A TASK STATEMENT		
Performs What Action? (Verb)	**To Whom or What? (Object of Verb)**	**To Produce What? (Expected Output)**	**Using What Tools, Equipment, Work Aids, Processes?**
Asks Questions, Listens, Records Answers	To/of Applicant on Eligibility Form	In Order to Determine Eligibility	Eligibility Form Eligibility Criteria in Manual Interviewing Techniques

SOURCE: U.S. Civil Service Commission, *Job Analysis: Developing and Documenting Data* (Washington, D.C.: U.S. Government Printing Office, 1973), p. 6.

2. Determines eligibility of applicant in order to complete client's application for food stamps using regulatory policies as a guide.

3. Decides on and describes other agencies available for client to contact in order to assist and refer client to appropriate community resources using worker's knowledge of resources available and knowledge of client's needs.

4. Explains policies and regulations appropriate to applicant's case in order to inform applicants of their status with regard to agency's regulations and policies.

5. Evaluates information gained from home visit, interview, and observation in order to decide if home conditions are consistent with original application, using original application and agency's housing standards as guide.

6. Meets with, talks to, answers questions, and discusses with members of high schools, colleges, and civic organizations in order to outline and explain food stamp program using knowledge and experience of food stamp program.[11]

After the important job tasks have been stated, the analyst then characterizes each statement in terms of frequency of performance; KSAs required; physical activities required; environmental conditions; and other factors thought to be important to task performance. Questions such as those in the sample interview schedule shown in Exhibit 8.2 can be used to make these determinations for each task. An illustration may help to clarify the task characterization process. For the moment, let's reexamine the second task identified in the study of welfare eligibility examiner. The task was stated as follows: "Determines eligibility of applicant in order to complete client's application for food stamps using regulatory policies as a guide." The description of the task using the interview schedule might be made as shown in Exhibit 8.3. In addition to those characteristics

EXHIBIT 8.3	CHARACTERIZATION OF A SELECTED JOB TASK: THE JOB OF WELFARE ELIGIBILITY EXAMINER

Task 2:

Determines eligibility of applicant in order to complete client's application for food stamps using regulatory policies as a guide.

Task Characterization

Knowledge Required:

1. Knowledge of contents and meaning of items on standard application form
2. Knowledge of Social-Health Services food stamp regulatory policies
3. Knowledge of statutes relating to Social-Health Services food stamp program

Skills Required:

None

Abilities Required:

1. Ability to read and understand complex instructions such as regulatory policies
2. Ability to read and understand a variety of procedural instructions, written and oral, and convert these to proper actions
3. Ability to use simple arithmetic—addition and subtraction
4. Ability to translate requirements into language appropriate to laypersons

Physical Activities:

Sedentary

Environmental Conditions:

None

Typical Working Incidents:

Working with people beyond giving and receiving instructions

Interest Areas:

1. Communication of data
2. Business contact with people
3. Working for the presumed good of people

SOURCE: U.S. Civil Service Commission, *Job Analysis: Developing and Documenting Data* (Washington, D.C.: U.S. Government Printing Office, 1973), pp. 13–14.

illustrated in the exhibit, additional task data such as ratings of task importance or frequency of task performance may also be obtained. These ratings may be made by use of rating scales by the job incumbent to further describe the job task. (We discuss such scales later in the chapter.) This same process is then carried out for each task statement. In the end, we should have a clearer picture of the demands, activities, and conditions of employment of the job being studied.

Guidelines for Use

At the conclusion of the interview, the analyst attempts to verify the data collected. Verification may be obtained by reviewing the job analysis results with the immediate supervisor(s) of the incumbent(s) interviewed.

The success of the interview as a job analysis technique depends, to a large extent, on the skill of the interviewer. A successful interviewer must possess several important skills such as the ability to listen, put individuals at ease, probe and prompt for answers from reluctant interviewees, and control the direction of an interview—all vital to a successful job analysis.[12] With such skills, an interviewer may be able to tease out job information that may go undetected by other forms of analysis. To enhance the likelihood of success in using the technique, certain guidelines should be followed. Some suggestions for improving the chance of success in using the interview are given in Exhibit 8.4.

Limitations of the Job Analysis Interview

The job analysis interview is certainly one option for collecting job data. However, it has its limitations. The interview often suffers from a lack of standardization and has limited possibilities for covering large numbers of respondents. If thorough documentation is not collected as the interview is conducted, important legal requirements of job analysis information are likely to go unmet. The skills and procedures used by the individual analyst principally determine the utility of the interview.

In addition, there are other limitations. Unless group interviews can be conducted, the technique requires a great deal of time and may not be cost efficient if many jobs need to be studied. Depending on the interviewee and the type of job being reviewed, an interviewer may literally be required to track through an entire job in specific detail. Such a process is not only expensive but may require a highly skilled interviewer to identify the needed content.

Another major problem is that the technique may be plagued with distortion of information. Wayne Cascio has noted that if interviewees believe it to be beneficial (for example, leading to an increase in wages), they may exaggerate their activities and responsibilities to reflect a more complex job.[13] It can be quite difficult to identify distorted job information. Verification from the supervisor or other incumbents can be used as a check. However, comparisons across subjective data are difficult and expensive to make.

In general, a job analysis interview should not be relied on as the sole method when the analysis is being conducted for selection purposes. When employed as a supplementary source, however, interview data can be helpful. For

EXHIBIT 8.4	GUIDELINES FOR CONDUCTING A JOB ANALYSIS INTERVIEW

Opening the Interview

1. Put the worker at ease by learning his (or her) name in advance, introducing yourself, and discussing general and pleasant topics long enough to establish rapport. Be at ease.
2. Make the purpose of the interview clear by explaining why the interview was scheduled, what is expected to be accomplished, and how the worker's cooperation will help in the production of tools for use in personnel selection.
3. Encourage the worker to talk by always being courteous and showing a sincere interest in what he (or she) says.

Steering the Interview

1. Help the worker to think and talk according to the logical sequence of the duties performed. If duties are not performed in a regular order, ask the worker to describe the duties in a functional manner by taking the most important activity first, the second most important next, and so forth. Request the worker to describe the infrequent duties of his (or her) job, ones that are not part of his (or her) regular activities, such as the occasional setup of a machine, occasional repairs, or infrequent reports.
2. Allow the worker sufficient time to answer each question and to formulate an answer. He (or she) should be asked only one question at a time.
3. Phrase questions carefully, so that the answers will be more than 'yes' or 'no.'
4. Avoid the use of leading questions.
5. Conduct the interview in plain, easily understood language.
6. Control the interview with respect to the economic use of time and adherence to subject matter. For example, when the interviewee strays from the subject, a good technique for bringing him (or her) back to the point is to summarize the data collected up to that point.
7. Conduct the interview with consideration for any nervousness or lack of ease on the part of the worker.

Closing the Interview

1. Summarize the information obtained from the worker, indicating the major duties performed and the details concerning each of the duties.
2. Close the interview on a friendly note.

Miscellaneous Do's and Don'ts for Interviews

1. Do not take issue with the worker's statements.
2. Do not show any partiality to grievances or conflicts concerning the employer-employee relations.
3. Do not show any interest in the wage classification of the job.
4. Do not talk down to the worker.
5. Do not permit yourself to be influenced by your personal likes and dislikes.
6. Be impersonal. Do not be critical or attempt to suggest any changes or improvements in the organization or methods of work.
7. Talk to the worker only with permission of her or his supervisor.
8. Verify job data, especially technical or trade terminology, with the supervisor or department head.
9. Verify completed job analysis interview with the proper official.

SOURCE: Based on U.S. Department of Labor, Manpower Administration, *Handbook for Analyzing Jobs* (Washington, D.C.: U.S. Government Printing Office, 1972), pp. 12–13.

example, interviews can be used to identify content for other job analysis methods, such as developing task analysis inventories, or for clarifying responses to other methods.[14]

The Job Analysis Questionnaire

Description

The job analysis questionnaire has been proposed as one way to handle some of the problems of the job analysis interview. This method consists of a printed questionnaire distributed to respondents who are asked to make some form of judgment about job information presented on the questionnaire. Job information, such as activities or tasks; tools and equipment used to perform the job; working conditions in which the job is performed; and the KSAs or other characteristics needed by incumbents to perform the job successfully, is listed on the questionnaire. Respondents often use some form of a rating scale to indicate the degree to which various aspects of job information listed on the questionnaire apply to their jobs.

There are numerous forms of job analysis questionnaires, but they all tend to fall into one of two classes: (a) *prefabricated* or existing questionnaires or (b) *tailored* questionnaires developed for a specific purpose or a specific job. Prefabricated questionnaires are usually generic measures developed for use with a variety of jobs. These inventories consist of a preestablished set of items describing some aspects of a job that respondents (for example, job incumbents, supervisors, observers) judge using a rating scale. Frequently, the aspects of jobs that respondents are asked to rate deal with job activities or functions performed. Because these questionnaires are already developed, many are designed to be taken "off-the-shelf" and applied by a knowledgeable user. Some examples of prefabricated job analysis questionnaires that are amenable for use in HR selection applications are as follows:

1. *Common Metric Questionnaire*[15]

2. *Professional and Managerial Position Questionnaire*[16]

3. *Executive Position Description Questionnaire*[17]

4. *Management Position Description Questionnaire*[18]

5. *Managerial and Professional Job Functions Inventory*[19]

6. *Position Analysis Questionnaire*[20]

7. *Threshold Traits Analysis System*[21]

In contrast to existing job analysis inventories that may apply to several or even many jobs, tailored job analysis questionnaires are typically prepared by an organization (or its consultants) for application to a *specific* job. Like prefabricated instruments, these questionnaires also include tasks or other aspects of jobs to be rated by a respondent. Because the focus of tailored questionnaires is usually on one job, the aspects of the job listed on the questionnaire tend to be more specific than those given on an existing measure.

Since we will discuss one prefabricated measure (the Position Analysis Questionnaire) later in this chapter, we turn our attention now toward the most popular type of tailored job analysis questionnaire employed in HR selection: the task analysis inventory.

The Task Analysis Inventory

A task analysis inventory is a questionnaire principally composed of a listing of tasks (100 or more tasks is not unusual) for which respondents make some form of judgment. Usually these judgments are ratings given by respondents using a task rating scale, such as frequency of task performance.

Because many different tasks may exist in any job, this type of job analysis questionnaire is typically directed toward only one job or a class of very similar jobs. Most often, the inventory is intended for use by incumbents. Nevertheless, supervisors and observers can complete it assuming they are knowledgeable about the job being studied.

Historically, the method has been widely used in military settings, in particular by the U.S. Air Force.[22] Investigators such as Raymond Christal, Joseph Madden, Joseph Morsh, and their associates at the Human Resources Laboratory at Lackland Air Force Base, Texas, are largely responsible for much of our knowledge about task inventories. Although the origin of task inventories may be traced to the military, their use for selection purposes by both public and private employers has grown substantially. One important reason for the increasing use of these inventories is that many employers have adopted a content validation strategy for selection measures for which the inventories are particularly helpful.

The Nature of Task Inventories   A task inventory often contains three major categories of information (a) background information on respondents, (b) a listing of the job tasks with associated rating scales, and (c) other or miscellaneous information. Information on respondents such as name, gender, ethnicity, tenure on the job being rated, tenure with the employing organization, job location, and title of the job being rated should be included on the task inventory. Identifying information is useful should the need arise to contact respondents (for example, for clarifying responses), and demographic information is valuable for performing analyses such as comparing how different types of respondents view the job being rated. In addition, respondent information can be important in dealing with any legal questions that may arise about a job analysis. For example, it may be necessary to show that respondents to the task inventory are representative of minority or other protected groups on the job or that the respondents have the necessary qualifications to serve as job analysis agents.

The second part of a task analysis inventory includes the job tasks and their rating scales. Exhibit 8.5 presents a condensed example of this portion of a task analysis inventory.

EXHIBIT 8.5	A CONDENSED EXAMPLE OF A TASK ANALYSIS INVENTORY FOR THE JOB OF PERSONNEL ANALYST

Directions: We are interested in knowing more about your job. Below is listed a number of tasks you may perform on your job. Using the rating scales given below, rate each task as to (a) how *frequently* you perform it and (b) how *important* it is for newly hired workers in a job like yours to be able to perform this task when they first begin work. Read each task and then place your rating in the two spaces to the right of each task.

Frequency of Performance	Importance for Newly Hired Employees
1 = Not Performed at All	1 = Not Performed at All
2 = Seldom	2 = Somewhat Important
3 = Occasionally	3 = Moderately Important
4 = Frequently	4 = Very Important
5 = Almost All of the Time	5 = Extremely Important

Job Tasks	Frequency of Performance	Importance for Newly Hired
1. Prepare job descriptions for secretarial jobs.	[ ]	[ ]
2. Check file folders for disposition of medical and dental records.	[ ]	[ ]
3. Initiate requests for identification cards from terminated personnel.	[ ]	[ ]
4. Describe company policies to newly hired employees.	[ ]	[ ]
5. Write computer programs in BASIC to analyze personnel absenteeism and turnover data.	[ ]	[ ]
⋮	⋮	⋮
105. Plan and develop training programs for newly hired clerical personnel.	[ ]	[ ]

The inventory shown is one used to analyze various tasks associated with the job of personnel analyst. Since most inventories are similar to the one exhibited, we use it to point out two important characteristics: (a) the *phrasing of tasks* to be rated and (b) the use of *rating scales* for judging the tasks.

First, we see that the item being judged is a *task*. If we compare the phrasing of the tasks shown in Exhibit 8.5 with those developed by the Office of Personnel Management interview procedure discussed earlier for the job of welfare eligibility examiner, we find that the two sets of tasks differ. From our comparison, we see that the task statements developed previously appear to be more complex. Tasks that were identified under the interview procedure described what was done as well as the results of those actions. Work aids, materials, methods, and other requirements of a job incumbent were noted. In contrast, in our task inventory example the tasks are not as fully developed. As Frank Sistrunk and Philip Smith have noted, most task statements are concerned with *what* gets done. Tasks, as listed in questionnaires, usually give no information on the situation surrounding the activity. On the other hand, tasks developed by other job analysis methods (for example, the Office of Personnel Management interview, Functional Job Analysis) usually provide information on what, how, and why.[23]

Another important characteristic of any task inventory is the *rating scale used* by the respondent to judge the given tasks. A rating scale provides a continuum or range of options (most often consisting of five to seven steps) that respondents can use to express their perceptions of a task. Numbers are employed to define degrees of respondents' views. For example, *Relative Time Spent on Task Performance* is an often used task rating measure.[24] A common form of such a scale is as follows:

Relative to the time you spend on other tasks on the job, how much time do you spend on this job task?

0 = This task is not performed

1 = Much below average

2 = Below average

3 = Slightly below average

4 = About average

5 = Slightly above average

6 = Above average

7 = Much above average

The illustration here is just one way of phrasing the rating measure for time spent on task performance. Many other forms are possible and could be used. Regardless of the scale, the objective of a rating scale is to identify the *degree* to which a task is perceived to possess a rated characteristic.

Quite often, respondents use more than one rating scale to assess job tasks. The scales chosen depend on any number of issues, such as the number of tasks to be rated, the time available, the capabilities of incumbents (for example, educational level, reading ability), the complexity of the job (the more complex, the more scales needed to assess the job adequately), and the purpose of the task analysis. With respect to purpose, if the analysis is being performed as part of a validation study, specific rating scales will be needed. For example, in a content validation study, the following task rating categories should be considered:

1. Frequency of task performance,

2. Task importance or criticality,

3. Task difficulty, and

4. Whether the task can be learned on the job relatively quickly.[25]

The third portion of the task inventory may focus on parts of the job, other than tasks, that also account for job performance. For instance, this last section is sometimes used to assess the physical working conditions of the job (for example, degree of heating and cooling; amount of lifting, standing, sitting, walking, etc.; degree of job stress; equipment and tools used in performing the job).

Development of Task Inventories Because most task inventories are aimed toward a specific job, they may have to be developed by the user. This process is time consuming and often expensive. Access to previous inventories or analyses of the job in question as well as use of technical experts in job analysis and questionnaire development are important determinants of the cost and success of the method. For those organizations committed to the development and administration of a task inventory, Ernest McCormick has summarized the major steps.[26] Similarly, Joseph Morsh and Wayne Archer have offered a series of guidelines to be followed in preparing task statements.[27] Some of the major steps and guidelines are listed in Table 8.2. Basically, development of a task inventory should be carried out in a sequential fashion such as that outlined. There is no one best way. However, suggestions like those noted increase the chances that the resulting questionnaire will meet the objectives for which it is intended.

Once developed, the inventory is ready for application. In discussing various aspects of administering task inventories, Raymond Christal and Johnny Weissmuller make several useful suggestions. First, they recommend that respondents' names and other identifying information be collected. Several reasons for using identifying information are that it (a) helps ensure high-quality information, (b) is necessary if follow-up studies are going to be conducted, and (c) is useful when combined with personnel file data (such as scores on selection measures and demographic characteristics). Second, they advocate administration to large numbers of incumbents, since data reliability is improved. Finally, optical scanning sheets are recommended to minimize time, cost, and errors in coding and data entry.[28]

Application of Task Analysis in Selection A task analysis inventory is used to define the most important tasks or activities that compose incumbents' jobs. It is this core group of job tasks that serves as the basis for inferring the KSAs and other characteristics needed to perform the job successfully. Since most jobs we are interested in studying may be reasonably complex, lists of task statements and

TABLE 8.2 **SUMMARY OF STEPS AND GUIDELINES FOR DEVELOPING TASK ANALYSIS INVENTORIES**

Sequential Steps for Developing Content of Task Inventories

1. Technical manuals, previous job analyses, and other job-related reports are reviewed for possible task-item content.
2. Technical job experts (consultants, selected incumbents/supervisors) prepare lists of tasks known to be performed.
3. Interviews are held with job incumbents and supervisors to identify additional tasks.
4. Tasks identified are reviewed for duplication, edited, and incorporated into an initial version of the inventory. Tasks are developed subject to task-writing guidelines.
5. First draft is prepared and submitted to a panel of experts (or incumbents and/or supervisors) for review.
6. Panel of reviewers adds, deletes, or modifies tasks for developing another draft of the inventory.
7. Steps 5 and 6 are repeated, using the same or similar panel, until an acceptable draft has been developed.
8. Task inventory is then pilot tested on a sample of respondents to whom the final version will be given.
9. Appropriate modifications are made as needed.
10. Steps 8 and 9 are repeated until a final, acceptable version is developed.

Guidelines for Writing Task Statements

When task statements are identified, they should:
1. Characterize activities, not skills or knowledge.
2. Have an identifiable beginning and ending.
3. Represent activities performed by an individual worker, not activities performed by different individuals.
4. Have an identifiable output or consequence.
5. Avoid extremes in phrasing activities; statements should not be too broad or too specific.
6. Be developed by full-time inventory writers (preferably); supervisors/incumbents should serve as technical advisers.

When task statements are written, they should:
1. Mean the same thing to all respondents.
2. Be stated so that the rating scale to be used makes sense.
3. Be stated so that the incumbent is understood to be the subject of the statement. The pronoun "I" should be implied. For example "(I) number all card boxes."
4. Be stated so that an action verb is in the present tense.
5. Have an object of the action verb.
6. Use terms that are specific, familiar, and unambiguous.

SOURCES: Based on Ernest J. McCormick, "Job Information: Its Development and Applications," *ASPA Handbook of Personnel and Industrial Relations,* ed. Dale Yoder and Herbert G. Heneman (Washington, D.C.: BNA, 1979), p. 4–66; Joseph E. Morsh and Wayne B. Archer, *Procedural Guide for Conducting Occupational Surveys in the United States Air Force* (PRL-TR-67-11, AD-664 036) (Lackland Air Force Base, Tex.: Personnel Research Laboratory, Aerospace Medical Division, 1967), pp. 8–11.

accompanying rating scales are one of the principal means used in assessing job tasks. Once the task rating data have been collected, subsequent statistical analyses of the ratings are used to isolate the most important or most critical aspects of the job.

Any of several statistical techniques can be applied to the rating data to identify important job tasks.[29] In many cases, these techniques may involve the calculation of simple descriptive statistics (such as means, standard deviations, and percentages) and the application of decision rules to define critical job tasks. For instance, let's look at a simple example. Assume for a moment that we have given a comprehensive task analysis inventory to a large sample of bank clerks. Among other judgments, the clerks were asked to use a seven-point rating scale (1 = Of No Importance to 7 = Of Major Importance) to judge each task. Analyses of the data were conducted and descriptive information obtained. We will use two of the numerous tasks listed to illustrate our point. Exhibit 8.6 shows the two example tasks and some associated descriptive statistics computed on the task ratings.

In deciding which tasks should be classified as important to the job, some *minimum* statistical criteria are chosen that a task must meet to be considered critical. As a possibility, we could set the following (in this example, arbitrary) cutoff points:

1. A task must receive a mean rating of 4.00 or higher (the higher the mean, the more important the task).

2. A task rating must have a standard deviation of 1.00 or lower (the lower the standard deviation, the greater the degree of agreement among employees in their task ratings).

3. Most (75 percent of more) employees must perform the task.

Using these standards, Task 9 would be chosen and Task 67 omitted (see Exhibit 8.6). The task "Use basic arithmetic to add, subtract, divide, and multiply monetary figures with decimals" would be added to other tasks that meet our evaluation criteria. These tasks would be deemed the most important ones that compose the job. Inferences concerning the content of selection measures would be based on the pool of tasks derived from application of these criteria to the task ratings.

Sometimes several rating scales are employed by raters when judging job tasks. That is, employees are asked to judge job tasks on several different criteria, such as frequency of task performance, importance of the task, and difficulty of the task. When multiple rating scales have been used, some researchers have simply arithmetically combined all of the rating scores for each task.[30] As in our previous example, the results of these arithmetic procedures are used to determine task importance.

Whatever the analyses used, the most important tasks are the basis on which inferences regarding the content of our selection measures rests. The major idea behind the application of task analysis inventories is to define *important* job content. That determination can serve as the source of statements about requisite

EXHIBIT 8.6	EXAMPLE TASK STATEMENTS AND ASSOCIATED DESCRIPTIVE STATISTICS USED IN IDENTIFYING IMPORTANT JOB TASKS		
Task Statement	**Mean Importance**[a]	**Standard Deviation**	**% Employees Performing Task**
9. Use basic arithmetic to add, subtract, divide, and multiply monetary figures with decimals.	6.74	0.68	99.2
67. Recommend to customers investment account options for investing savings.	1.21	1.56	8.9

[a]The ratings of task importance were made using a rating scale ranging from 1= Of No Importance to 7 = Of Major Importance.

worker specifications and development or selection of devices for choosing among job applicants. In addition, the defined job content can also serve as one basis for applying specific validation models such as content validity.

Advantages and Disadvantages of Task Analysis   Any job analysis technique will have its own unique assets and limitations; task analysis is no different. On the positive side, task inventories offer an efficient means for collecting data from large numbers of incumbents in geographically dispersed locations. Additionally, task inventories lend themselves to quantifying job analysis data. Quantitative data are invaluable in analyzing jobs and determining core job components.

Yet Wayne Cascio has pointed out some important problems with these inventories. Development of task inventories can be time consuming and expensive. Motivation problems often become significant when inventories are long or complex. Ambiguities and questions that arise during administration of the inventory may not be addressed; whereas in a method like the interview, problems can be resolved as they come up. As these difficulties become magnified, one can expect the respondents to become less cooperative, with a concomitant decline in the quality of data collected.[31]

Yes, there are problems with task inventories. But when properly developed, administered, and analyzed, they offer a viable option for collecting job information.

In comparison to job analysis interview and questionnaire methods that can be adapted to a variety of uses, a number of specialized job analysis systems are available. In general, these systems advocate particular procedures, analyses, or forms for collecting job information. Most often, these systems are copyrighted and are available only from commercial vendors, consulting firms, or the developers themselves. Special training in application of these various systems is sometimes required. As with job analysis materials, formal preparation in the use of a particular technique is often available from vendors or special consultants.

Developments in many of these systems have made them particularly promising for HR selection applications. The remainder of this chapter concentrates on one of these popular job analysis systems: the Position Analysis Questionnaire, or PAQ. The appendix at the end of this chapter contains descriptions of several other job analysis systems.

The Position Analysis Questionnaire (PAQ)

Of all job analysis methods we review, perhaps none has the research base and breadth of application of the Position Analysis Questionnaire (PAQ).[32] Roughly 25 years of research have established the PAQ as one of the leading off-the-shelf, or prefabricated, measures of jobs currently available. Primarily, the PAQ was developed to produce a means for analyzing a wide spectrum of jobs. Because the questionnaire is worker oriented, that is, it focuses on generalized worker behaviors describing how a job is done, the PAQ can be used for many types of jobs. Because of its prominence in the field of job analysis, we look closely at the nature and use of this questionnaire.

Description   The PAQ is a standardized, structured job analysis questionnaire containing 195 items, or *elements*. Of this total, 187 items concern work activities and work situations, seven relate to compensation issues, and the final item deals with the exempt or nonexempt status of the position being analyzed. These elements are *not* task statements. Rather, they represent *general work behaviors, work conditions, or job characteristics*. An analyst must decide if each of the items applies to the job under study. If it does, then a rating scale is used to indicate the degree to which that item applies to the job. Because of the generic wording of the job items appearing on the PAQ, the questionnaire is applicable to many jobs in the public and private sectors.

Items on the PAQ are organized into six basic divisions or sections. These divisions and a definition are as follows:

1. *Information Input*—Where and how a worker gets information needed to perform the job.

2. *Mental Processes*—The reasoning, decision making, planning, and information processing activities that are involved in performing the job.

3. *Work Output*—The physical activities, tools, and devices used by the worker to perform the job.

4. *Relationships with Other Persons*—The relationships with other people that are required in performing the job.

5. *Job Context*—The physical and social context where the work is performed.

EXHIBIT 8.7	AN EXAMPLE OF ITEMS FROM THE POSITION ANALYSIS QUESTIONNAIRE (PAQ)

3 WORK OUTPUT
3.1 Use of Devices and Equipment
3.1.1 Hand-held Tools or Instruments

Consider in this category those devices which are used to move or modify workpieces, materials, products, or objects. Do not consider measuring devices here.

Code Important to This Job (1)
N Does not apply
1 Very Minor
2 Low
3 Average
4 High
5 Extreme

Manually powered

50 _____ Precision tools/instruments (that is, tools or instruments powered by the user to perform very accurate or precise operations, for example, the use of engraver's tools, watchmaker's tools, surgical instruments, etc.)

51 _____ Nonprecision tools/instruments (tools or instruments powered by the user to perform operations not requiring great accuracy or precision, for example, hammers, wrenches, trowels, knives, scissors, chisels, putty knives, strainers, hand grease guns, etc. Do not include long-handled tools here.)

52 _____ Long handled tools (hoes, rakes, shovels, picks, axes, brooms, mops, etc.)

53 _____ Handling devices/tools (tongs, ladles, dippers, forceps etc., used for moving or handling objects and materials; do not include here protective gear such as asbestos gloves, etc.)

Powered (manually controlled or directed devices using an energy source such as electricity, compressed air, fuel, hydraulic fluid, etc., in which the component part which accomplishes the modification is hand-held, such as dentist drills, welding equipment, etc., as well as devices small enough to be entirely hand-held)

54 _____ Precision tools/instruments (hand-held powered tools or instruments used to perform operations requiring great accuracy or precision, such as small dentist drills, or laboratory equipment used for especially accurate or fine work)

55 _____ Nonprecision tools/instruments (hand-held, energy powered tools or instruments used to perform operations not requiring great accuracy or precision, for example, ordinary power saws, large sanders, clippers, hedge trimmers, etc., and related devices such as electric soldering irons, spray guns or nozzles, welding equipment, etc.)

SOURCE: Ernest J. McCormick, P. R. Jeanneret, and Robert C. Mecham, *Position Analysis Questionnaire*, © 1969 by Purdue Research Foundation, West Lafayette, Ind. 47907. Reprinted with permission.

6. *Other Job Characteristics*—The activities, conditions, and characteristics other than those already described that are relevant to the job.[33]

One example of several PAQ items dealing with *Work Output* activities is shown in Exhibit 8.7.

Rating scales are used in the PAQ for determining the extent to which the 194 items are relevant to the job under study. Six different types of scales are used:

1. *Extent of Use*—The degree to which an item is used by the worker.

2. *Amount of Time*—The proportion of time spent doing something.

3. *Importance to This Job*—The importance of an activity specified by the item in performing the job.

4. *Possibility of Occurrence*—The degree to which there is a possibility of physical hazards on the job.

5. *Applicability*—Whether an item applies to the job or not.

6. *Special Code*—Special rating scales that are used with a particular item on the PAQ.[34]

On the whole, each of the rating scales consists of six categories. For example, the scale "Importance to This Job" is composed of the following rating points:

N(0) = Does Not Apply
1 = Very Minor
2 = Low
3 = Average
4 = High
5 = Extreme

Raters using the PAQ can also use midpoint ratings (that is, .5) between the whole-number scale points to make even finer judgments for jobs being analyzed.[35]

The PAQ has served a variety of purposes. For the most part, the instrument has been used for (a) predicting aptitude requirements for jobs, (b) evaluating jobs and setting compensation rates, and (c) classifying jobs. Recently, the measure has been applied to other uses as well, such as grouping jobs into families, developing personnel evaluation systems, predicting stress associated with various jobs, and as an element in developing career planning systems.

Application Actual application of the PAQ can be thought of as a four-step sequence of activities. Although the specific steps may vary somewhat from one administration to the next, the sequence described here explains most PAQ application activities.[36]

1. Selecting and Training Agencies to Analyze Jobs Various options are available for choosing agents to collect PAQ data. Either one or a combination of three groups of individuals are likely to be used from inside the organization to provide job information. These groups consist of (a) trained job analysts, (b) job incumbents, and (c) job supervisors. Job analysts will probably be the best prepared to use the PAQ. If job incumbents or supervisors are utilized, they should be individuals who know the job being studied (having, for example, six months or more of job experience) and have high reading and verbal skills. (Interviewing *and* observational skills may also be required). Most often, these incumbents are likely to be white-collar rather than operative or blue-collar personnel. Furthermore, when incumbents are being used as analysts, it is recommended that there be a group session with a discussion leader knowledgeable of the content and administration of the PAQ who can interpret the PAQ items in terms related to the job studied. Where possible, at least three incumbents, working independently but with a PAQ-experienced leader, are recommended for completing the PAQ for each job title. Where large numbers of incumbents exist for a job title, a 10 to 20 percent sample of incumbents should be chosen.[37] The use of multiple analysts permits an examination of interanalyst (interrater) reliability, that is, the extent to which analysts agree in their analyses of a job.

2. Selecting Persons to Provide Job Information   This step in the collection of PAQ data is obviously related to the first. Once the type of analyst has been chosen, individuals who will provide job information must be identified. These persons are usually incumbents who have sufficient experience to know the job. Supervisors can also be employed, assuming they have had relevant and recent experience on the job in question. Whoever the persons used, great care should be exercised in their selection. The chosen individuals will literally determine the quality and value of the data obtained.

3. Analyzing the Jobs Selected   The PAQ can be completed by an analyst observing the job or by interviewing selected incumbents or supervisors. It may also be completed by an incumbent or supervisor serving as a respondent. (When this approach is used, a PAQ-experienced individual is highly recommended to help them complete the questionnaire.) The particular method chosen (interview, observation, self-report questionnaire) will depend to a large degree on the type of agent selected for data collection.

Since the PAQ was developed to analyze a wide variety of jobs, some items will necessarily apply to some jobs and not to others. Thus, even though the questionnaire appears long, by design only one-third to one-half of the items will be answered for most jobs. Time requirements for PAQ completion may range from less than one hour for a trained analyst up to four hours for analyses involving interviews or group PAQ administration sessions. Typical times for PAQ completion are two to four hours per job title.

4. Analyzing PAQ Data   Because empirical data are collected with the PAQ, a wide variety of analyses are available. These can range form simple tabulations to more complex analyses. For example, one analysis that is useful in HR selection is to determine the basic nature of a job in terms of the dimensions of work activity measured by the PAQ. Several studies have found that the PAQ measures 32 specific and 13 overall dimensions of jobs.[38] Operational definitions of these dimensions are listed in Exhibit 8.8. It is possible to score any job analyzed in terms of these dimensions. Once scored, a profile of job content can be created and used to characterize the job analyzed. Thus the PAQ makes it possible to depict a job quantitatively in terms of the job dimension scores. And, as we discuss in Chapter 9, these dimension scores can then be employed to provide a direct estimation of worker aptitude requirements of jobs. Tests and other selection measures to assess these important worker aptitudes can then be developed or chosen.

Whatever analyses are chosen, special arrangements for analysis will more than likely have to be made. A computer program for on-site scoring can be

| EXHIBIT 8.8 | OPERATIONAL DEFINITIONS OF THE JOB DIMENSIONS OF THE POSITION ANALYSIS QUESTIONNAIRE (PAQ) |

Specific Dimensions

Division 1: Information Input

1. Interpreting what is sensed
2. Using various sources of information
3. Watching devices/materials for information
4. Evaluating/judging what is sensed
5. Being aware of environmental conditions
6. Using various senses

Division 2: Mental Processes

7. Making decisions
8. Processing information

Division 3: Work Output

9. Using machines/tools/equipment
10. Performing activities requiring general body movements
11. Controlling machines/processes
12. Performing skilled/technical activities
13. Performing controlled manual/related activities
14. Using miscellaneous equipment/devices
15. Performing handling/related manual activities
16. General physical coordination

Division 4: Relationships with Other Persons

17. Communicating judgments/related information
18. Engaging in general personal contacts
19. Performing supervisory/coordination/related activities
20. Exchanging job-related information
21. Public/related personal contacts

Division 5: Job Context

22. Being in a stressful/unpleasant environment
23. Engaging in personally demanding situations
24. Being in hazardous job situations

Division 6: Other Job Characteristics

25. Working nontypical vs. day schedule
26. Working in businesslike situations
27. Wearing optional vs. specified apparel
28. Being paid on a variable vs. salary basis
29. Working on a regular vs. irregular schedule
30. Working under job-demanding circumstances
31. Performing structured vs. unstructured work
32. Being alert to changing conditions

Overall Dimensions

33. Having decision, communicating, and general responsibilities
34. Operating machines/equipment
35. Performing clerical/related activities

(continued)

EXHIBIT 8.8	(CONTINUED)

Overall Dimensions (*continued*)

36. Performing technical/related activities
37. Performing service/related activities
38. Working regular day vs. other work schedules
39. Performing routine/repetitive activities
40. Being aware of work environment
41. Engaging in physical activities
42. Supervising/coordinating other personnel
43. Public/customer/related contacts
44. Working in an unpleasant/hazardous/demanding/environment
45. Having a nontypical schedule/optional apparel style

SOURCE: Ernest J. McCormick, Robert C. Mecham, and P. R. Jeanneret, *Position Analysis Questionnaire Technical Manual (System II)* (Logan, Utah: PAQ Services, 1977), pp. 7–9. Used with permission.

purchased or arrangements for scoring can be made through PAQ Services, Inc. of Logan, Utah, a firm organized to distribute the PAQ and to conduct computer analyses and research on the method.

Advantages and Disadvantages   Wayne Cascio has noted two important concerns with the PAQ. First, the reading level required by the instrument is that of a college graduate. Therefore, the questionnaire should not be used with analysts having reading skills below the college level. Second, the PAQ scores the basic work behaviors (elements) rather than the specific tasks of a job. As a consequence, scoring similarities in jobs may mask actual task differences. For instance, Cascio cites a study by Arvey and Begalla who found that a police officer's job profile is quite similar to a housewife's because of the trouble-shooting and emergency-handling orientation common to both jobs.[39]

Because the PAQ does not focus on task activities, there are some purposes of job analysis that cannot be adequately served by the PAQ alone. For instance, job descriptions should characterize a job in terms of the specific activities performed. Since the PAQ does not cover actual task activities, other methods of job analysis would be required in order to develop job descriptions.

These disadvantages are certainly limitations on the use of the PAQ. Yet the method has some clear assets. The PAQ provides a *standardized* means for collecting quantitative job data across a wide spectrum of jobs. Standardization helps to ensure that different jobs are assessed in a similar fashion. Because quantitative, standardized information is collected, comparisons across many jobs can be made.

The PAQ has also been found to provide reliable and valid job data. The method is one of the few we have that has extensive reliability and validity data reported. Finally, estimation of worker requirements necessary for jobs can be obtained from the PAQ. This particular information can help to suggest the employee specifications that are so necessary in establishing a viable HR selection program.

Supplementary Methods for Collecting Job Information

The job analysis methods discussed in this chapter and its appendix offer a variety of ways for collecting and analyzing job information. In addition to these methods, several other procedures are also available for retrieving job analysis data. For the most part, these methods are merely supplementary ways for collecting job data. They are concerned with the analysis and use of job information. Nevertheless, some users may find them helpful in particular situations.

Technical conferences[40] are one possibility. These conferences are simply group interview sessions, designed to identify the characteristics of a specific job, conducted between a job analyst and knowledgeable supervisors or incumbents. *Worker diaries*[41] are another option. Here, job incumbents record their daily job activities using some form of log or diary. The *Critical-Incidents Technique*[42] approach (see Appendix 8A) involves the development of a series of statements, based on direct observation or memory, describing incidents of good and poor job performance. Critical incidents can provide very valuable information about important components of the job. These components can serve as a basis for developing descriptive information about a job, such as the content of a task inventory or a job performance evaluation form. *Work participation* can also be used to obtain job information in some limited contexts. With this procedure, the job analyst performs the job. Thus first-hand information is obtained about what characteristics and tasks compose the job. Only relatively simple jobs typically lend themselves to application of the work participation method. Finally, for jobs comprising principally physical activities, *direct observation*[43] can be an appropriate method. This particular technique is usually used in conjunction with one or more of the other methods discussed in the chapter or the appendix.

Collection of Job Information:
A Comparison of Methods

In the context of HR selection, the *Uniform Guidelines* state that all HR selection techniques should be demonstrated to be job related. One of the critical components of this demonstration is a systematic review of information about the job for which a selection method is to be used. As far as a particular job analysis method is concerned, the *Uniform Guidelines* leave open to choice the specific techniques that may be applied. The *Uniform Guidelines* specify that "any method of job analysis may be used if it provides the information required for the specific validation strategy."[44] Although this guide appears to be a flexible one, a potential user may be in a quandary in deciding among the various analysis methods. Unfortunately, little empirical research is available on the superiority of one method over another. As Edwin Cornelius, Theodore Carron, and Marianne Collins conclude, only a small amount of research has been conducted that compares the utility of various approaches.[45] Since some of these studies may have important implications for those using job analysis in HR selection, we review several of them briefly.

Edward Levine, Ronald Ash, and Nell Bennett have completed the most comprehensive comparative investigation to date on selected job analysis methods. Sixty-four public sector personnel specialists were asked to analyze four job classifications (Accountant 1, Accountant 2, Mental Health Worker, Mental Health Technician) using four methods of job analysis (*Critical-Incidents Technique*, task analysis, PAQ, and the Job Element Method, or JEM). (Each of these methods is discussed in the chapter or its appendix.) In addition to conducting the actual job analyses, the participants were asked (a) to rate each job analysis method in terms of selected attitudinal criteria such as difficulty of use, clarity of results, utility for content validation purposes, adequacy for developing performance measures, and (b) to develop a selection test or examination plan based on the job analysis results. A number of important findings were reported. With respect to users' attitudes toward the methods, the PAQ was judged less favorably than the other methods. Much of the negative attitudes concerning the PAQ seemed to be due to its non-job-specific language and difficult reading level. Further, the critical incidents method was favored by study participants for providing relevant information for developing performance measures. The JEM was viewed more positively than other methods as being appropriate for highlighting specific job components and for establishing content validity. In actual conduct of job analyses, the PAQ was the least expensive; critical incidents was the most expensive method. On the other hand, the four methods did not differ substantially in terms of time and costs for developing selection test examination plans.[46]

In a related study, Levine, Bennett, and Ash surveyed 106 personnel specialists employed in state and local governments concerning their attitudes toward job analysis methods. The JEM and task analysis were employed by more respondents and viewed more positively than critical incidents or the PAQ. However, none of the methods was thought to completely satisfy the requirements for job analysis information in selection.[47]

Edward Levine, Ronald Ash, Hardy Hall, and Frank Sistrunk sought to determine how job analysts viewed the practicality of a variety of job analysis methods. A questionnaire survey of 93 job analysts (respondents were about equally distributed across colleges and universities, state and local governments, private businesses, and private consulting firms) resulted in several important method differences. The PAQ consistently received the highest ratings in terms of standardization, off-the-shelf availability, and reliability; critical incidents and the JEM were among the lowest rated. Additionally, the PAQ was judged to require the least amount of respondent time to complete.[48]

Finally, George Hollenbeck and Walter Borman compared the results of two job analysis methods for the job of stockbroker at a national brokerage firm. One of these methods consisted of a task analysis questionnaire administered to 581 brokers. The other approach was the critical incidents method in which 300 critical performance behaviors were collected from 26 representatively selected managers of stockbrokers. Comparative examination of the two sets of job data showed some similarities. However, to a large extent, the results produced were different. These method discrepancies led Hollenbeck and Borman to conclude that different methods may be suitable for different selection purposes. For example, they suggested that a task inventory is probably most appropriate for defining the important elements of performance (sometimes referred to as the "performance domain") in a job. Once the performance domain is defined, selection tests can be developed to resemble important task statements from the inventory. If the content of the tests has been mapped from the content of the job, the task analysis approach could be useful in supporting the content validity of a test. They also suggested that critical incidents might be more valuable for establishing the personal attributes (KSAs) that account for success or failure on the job. Thus this method might be most useful for defining the content of measures to be used in selection.[49]

Potential Usefulness of Methods

Although some users may wonder which job analysis method is best for HR selection purposes, the answer is not as straightforward as one would like. For one thing, our research base delimiting the usefulness of various approaches is far from complete. Many of our judgments about job analysis methods rest more on opinion than on fact. Second, any overall assessment must account for a variety of considerations (such as cost, ease of use, and validation strategy) in making an evaluation. Some methods are appropriate in light of some criteria; others are more useful given other considerations. Even though an overall assessment may not be feasible, we can evaluate, in a limited way, selected job analysis methods in terms of specific factors that are important for HR selection. We offer such appraisal here.

Gary Brumback, Tania Romashko, Clifford Hahn, and Edwin Fleishman have proposed a series of criteria that should be considered in judging the potential usefulness of methods for collecting job information.[50] We have taken most of their considerations plus an additional one suggested by Frank Sistrunk and Philip Smith (cost of applying a method)[51] and one of our own (utility in developing selection measures) and evaluated each of the methods reviewed in the chapter and its appendix. Our evaluations are summarized in Table 8.3 and are discussed here. Before reviewing our evaluations, note that our assessments are based principally on subjective judgments. As we have noted, little objective data are available for assessing many of these techniques; the ratings shown come from our own as well as others' opinions. So, in studying the table, you should be aware that different users may hold different views about these methods. Regardless of the ratings given, the criteria provide some critical considerations that should be reviewed by any user contemplating adoption of a specific technique for personnel selection.

1. **Currently Operational:** *Has the method been tested and refined so it is now operational and ready for use?* Each of the methods reviewed in this chapter and its appendix has been tested and can be adopted for use. However, the fact that these methods are available should not be interpreted to mean they are equally suitable for every user or selection purpose.

2. **Off-the-Shelf Availability:** *Is the data collection instrument to be used ready-made or must it first be designed and constructed?* Only one method, the PAQ, can be considered ready for application without requiring further

TABLE 8.3 SUMMARY EVALUATION OF SEVEN JOB ANALYSIS METHODS

Evaluation Factor	Interview	Task Analysis Inventory	Position Analysis Questionnaire (PAQ)	Critical-Incident Techniques	Fleishman Job Analysis Survey (F-JAS)	Functional Job Analysis (FJA)	Job Element Method (JEM)
1. *Currently Operational?*	Yes	Yes	Yes	Yes	Yes	Yes	Yes
2. *Off-the-Shelf Availability?*	No	No	Yes	No	In-Part	In-Part	In-Part
3. *Occupational Versatility?*	High	Moderate/High	High	High	High	High	High
4. *Standardization?*	No	Yes	Yes	No	Yes	No	No
5. *User/Respondent Acceptability?*	High	Moderate/High	Low/Moderate	Moderate	Moderate/High	High	Moderate
6. *Required Amount of Job Analyst Training?*	Moderate	Low	Moderate	Low/Moderate	Low	High	Moderate/High
7. *Sample Size?*	Small	Large	Small	Small	Small/Moderate	Small	Small
8. *Suitability for Content Validity?*	Low	High	Low	Low	Moderate	Moderate	Low
9. *Suitability for Criterion-Related Validity?*	Low/Moderate	High	High	Low/Moderate	High	High	High
10. *Reliability?*	Unknown	High	High	Unknown	High	High	Unknown
11. *Utility in Developing Selection Measures*	Low	Moderate	Moderate	Low/Moderate	Moderate	Moderate	Moderate/High
12. *Cost?*	Moderate/High	Moderate/High	Low/Moderate	Moderate/High	Low/Moderate	Moderate/High	Low/Moderate

SOURCE: Based, in part, on Gary B. Brumback, Tania Romashko, Clifford P. Hahn, and Edwin A. Fleishman, *Model Procedures for Job Analysis, Text Development and Validation* (Washington, D.C.: American Institutes for Research, 1974), pp. 102–107.

research. Methods such as F-JAS, FJA, or JEM are, in part, ready for use, but additional developments are necessary. These developments consist of specifying the tasks or job elements required in a specific job. Existing rating scales are then applied to the identified tasks or elements. Methods like the task inventory require the development of task content as well as associated rating scales for characterizing these tasks. Although it may appear that off-the-shelf measures are preferable, some writers (for example, Brumback et al.) have suggested that methods involving the determination of specific task content are more appropriate for selection purposes than those having ready-made content.[52] Thus, in some situations, methods utilizing tailored measures *may* be more desirable than those incorporating preexisting measures.

3. **Occupational Versatility:** *To what extent can the method be applied to a wide variety of jobs?* All of these techniques can be applied to a wide variety of jobs. However, those that focus principally on tasks may be limited to jobs where it is easy to describe task content. For instance, in jobs such as managerial ones, it may be difficult to completely describe their content using typical task statements. In such jobs, activities such as planning are not easily described by task statements. Therefore, task-based questionnaires may not be as occupationally versatile as methods like the PAQ that deal with broader worker functions.

4. **Standardization:** *Are the procedures used with the method so structured that data collected from different sources at different times can be compared?* Methods that use small groups of analysts in collecting job information may not have the capability of producing comparable data. For example, when different panels of subject matter experts are used to develop employee specifications for a job, such as with the JEM, different lists of specifications may be developed by the different panels.[53] In contrast, because the PAQ and F-JAS require job analysts to use a structured procedure for rating a specified list of work behaviors or KSAs, they are the most standardized of the methods reviewed.

5. **User/Respondent Acceptability:** *To what extent is the method including the various aspects of its application acceptable to respondents and users of the method?* Most of the job analysis methods are at least minimally acceptable. However, it seems task-based methods create problems for some respondents because of their length. In order to complete many of the data collection devices used in these methods, respondents are sometimes required to spend rather lengthy, tedious periods of time completing the appropriate materials. Most respondents would prefer briefer, easier types of measures. Levine, Ash, and Bennett's research showed the PAQ as receiving some of the most unfavorable ratings by users among the four methods studied.[54] Other investigators have drawn different conclusions.[55] Given its basic nature, the PAQ will probably elicit the greatest diversity of opinion of any of the methods reviewed.

6. **Required Amount of Job Analyst Training:** *How much training must a job analyst receive in order to apply the method correctly?* FJA appears to require the highest level of training. The reason is that JFA places a premium on the identification and correct preparation of task statements. In order to apply FJA correctly, training is mandatory not only in task development but in applying FJA rating scales to the specified tasks.

   Methods like JEM can also require moderate levels of job analyst preparation. Since this method employs a specific sequence of activities to be performed, an analyst should be thoroughly familiar with the steps required for application. Also, this method involves group application; thus an analyst must also be prepared to direct group meetings and conduct group job analyses.

7. **Sample Size:** *How many respondents or sources of information are required to produce dependable job analysis data?* More than any other technique, the PAQ recommends the fewest number of respondents, typically as few as three or four per job title. The JEM is also efficient in this respect, requiring approximately six to eight participants. These methods contrast with those such as the task inventory that may involve hundreds of respondents. The questions facing users of methods like the PAQ and JEM are how reliable are these few judge? and how generalizable are the results? Unless job agents are carefully selected, statistical, and possibly, legal challenges may be difficult to meet.

8. **Suitability for Content Validity:** *Will the method support the requirements for establishing content validity of a selection measure?* In content validity, a selection measure is supported by showing that it representatively samples significant aspects of a job. Since the PAQ and JEM procedures place such little emphasis on specific job tasks, we feel that users should be very cautious when applying these techniques in content validation research. Modifications to the JEM procedure have been made in order to make it more suitable for content validation research.[56] Also, with respect to the JEM and its use in content validation research, other writers take exception to our concerns.[57] Unless the job interview focuses specifically on task data, it alone should not be relied on either. As we saw in Chapter 5, content validation requires that specific information be collected about tasks on a job. Some job analysis interviews, as well as the PAQ and JEM, may not meet this requirement.

9. **Suitability for Criterion-Related Validity:** *Will the method support the requirements for establishing criterion-related validity of a selection measure?* In criterion-related validity, a selection procedure is supported by establishing a statistical relationship between scores on a selection measure and a measure of job performance. In general, most of the methods are useful in identifying content of selection measures and criteria of job performance that can be used in a criterion-related validation study.

10. **Reliability:** *Will the method provide consistent, dependable results?* Most of our methods can yield reliable job data. For some, such as the interview, sufficient research has not been conducted to verify their ability to provide consistent, reliable data. In contrast, the F-JAS and PAQ have established procedures for determining the extent to which analysts agree in their job assessments.

11. **Utility in Developing Selection Measures:** *How useful is a procedure in developing selection measures for a particular job?* Ideally, job analysis methods suggest the content of selection devices, such as items or questions to be used on a test. The methods should permit specification of the explicit rationale for developing selection measures. In addition, acceptable job analysis methods should also serve as a source for ideas and content of criterion measures, such as rating scales, to be used in a validation study. Most of the methods can be used to meet these needs. One of the methods (JEM) has established procedures that systematically take an analyst through the analysis of a job to the development of selection measures. This specific procedure is likely to be most helpful in translating job content into job specifications and specifications into selection measures.

12. **Cost:** *What is the estimated cost of the method? (Cost includes cost of materials, necessary training, consulting assistance, salary of job analysts, and clerical support.)* In terms of total dollar expenditures, the PAQ and F-JAS are probably the least expensive of the methods. JEM can also be relatively inexpensive; however, panels of job experts have to be convened at least on several occasions. Thus indirect costs associated with taking key personnel from their jobs for extended periods must be considered. Task inventories can be rather expensive to develop, apply, and analyze. Because task inventories must be tailored to a job, costs will increase accordingly. Generally speaking, the more tailored the approach, the greater the associated costs.

Use of Multiple Job Analysis Methods

In this chapter and its appendix, we review a series of job analysis methods and offer a set of evaluation criteria for determining how suitable each may be for HR selection purposes. No one method will be completely appropriate for every selection situation.

For some users, a review of methods may show that one job analysis approach will not be sufficient in the context of HR selection. Instead, multiple methods of job analysis may be needed. A survey by Edward Levine and his associates of 93 experienced job analysts' attitudes toward using multiple job analysis methods showed support of a multiple-method approach. In their survey, they found that of 93 respondents, 80 preferred a combination of methods, 9 preferred a single approach, and 4 were not sure.[58] In addition, Gary Brumback and his colleagues note that job analysis is still a relatively imprecise endeavor, and the results of any one method should be corroborated by the results of another. Therefore, they recommend that whatever the job, whatever the measure, whatever the validation strategy to be used, a multimethod approach is preferable to reliance on a single method. From their view, the costs involved in using multiple methods are more than offset by the advantages of their use. They conclude, "In this period of 'legislated employment,' this risk of having what may be an otherwise valid qualification requirement overturned is certainly not worth the modest cost of an independent verification of the job analysis results."[59] In general, we agree with their comments. Yet we should also keep in mind that we may be faced with the problem of developing a means to reconcile any differences we may find in the results produced by two or more job analysis methods. If these differences cannot be reconciled, then job analysis results may be open to both technical and legal challenges.

Analysis of Jobs That Do Not Exist: Strategic Job Analysis Method

We have mentioned throughout our discussion that selection procedures must be based on a job analysis. We have discussed at length the use of methods to analyze jobs as they are *currently* being performed. But suppose you are in a situation where a job does not yet exist or is about to undergo a drastic change, for example, through organizational restructuring? How do you do a job analysis for a job about to change? How do you conduct an analysis when a job does not exist but is being created? In these cases, selection procedures must be able to distinguish between individuals who can and who cannot perform the job as it *will* be performed in the future.

Conducting a job analysis of "future jobs" in our hypothetical situation is a problem. One option for handling current jobs that will be changed in the future is what Benjamin Schneider and Andrea Konz refer to as "strategic job analysis."[60] The purpose of their approach is to define the tasks and KSAs thought to be needed for a job as it is predicted to exist in the future. In essence, the method consists of the following steps:

1. An analysis of the job is made to identify current tasks and KSAs.

2. Subject matter experts (for example, job incumbents, supervisors, managers) knowledgeable of the job are assembled in a workshop to discuss how future issues (for example, technological change) are likely to impact the job.

3. Information on expected future tasks and KSAs is collected from individuals knowledgeable about these expected job changes.

4. Differences between present and future judgments about the job are identified to isolate those tasks and KSAs where greatest change is anticipated. It is this task and KSA information that serves as the basis for selecting incumbents in a job that does not currently exist.

Obviously, a key component of the entire process is the subject matter expert who is asked to predict future job change. If a current job is being changed, incumbents, supervisors, managers, and other experts are asked to forecast changes in job activities and KSAs. If a job is being created rather than a current one modified, a more creative approach to selecting experts to make future job task and KSA predictions will be needed. Individuals within the organization who can envision what the job will be like should be selected. In addition, others who may be outside of the organization but have specific technical knowledge about the needed changes should be considered. For example, persons in the organization familiar with corporate strategy and technological change might be helpful. Supervisors and incumbents of jobs that have tasks similar to those predicted for the new one can also participate. If the new job entails running a new piece of equipment, a technical representative of the manufacturer may provide useful information regarding the tasks and worker requirements necessary for effectively running the machine.

The process of strategic job analysis has many yet-to-be resolved issues. For example, what is the validity of experts' future job predictions? What experts are most helpful and accurate in forecasting changes? What is the best way for workshops to be conducted and job analyses applied to collect the data needed? Will this approach be accepted if challenged in the courts? These questions are but a few of the unanswered issues that remain. Nevertheless, given the rapid technological changes that many organizations are experiencing, strategic job analysis or a similar approach is likely to become a necessity. At this point, the details of application wait to be refined. Clearly, more research on methods for identifying employee specifications of future jobs is an important need.

References

[1] See, for example, Frank L. Schmidt, John Hunter, and Kenneth Pearlman, "Test Differences as Moderators of Aptitude Test Validity in Selection: A Red Herring," *Journal of Applied Psychology 66* (1981): 166–185.

[2] Frank L. Schmidt, Deniz S. Ones, and John E. Hunter, "Personnel Selection," in *Annual Review of Psychology* (Stanford, Calif.: Annual Reviews, 1992), p. 655.

[3] Some writers include a third category of job analysis methods, *attribute-oriented* methods. Methods in this category attempt to assess the worker attributes (for example, KSAs) needed to perform a job. Another classification scheme is Robert J. Harvey's taxonomy of job analysis methods. Basically, his taxonomy clusters job analysis methods into nine groupings based on the metric used for rating jobs and their behavioral specificity. See Robert J. Harvey, "Job Analysis," in *Handbook of Industrial and Organizational Psychology*, ed. Marvin D. Dennette (Palo Alto, Calif.: Consulting Psychologists Press, 1990), p. 85.

[4] Ernest J. McCormick, "Job Information: Its Development and Applications," in *ASPA Handbook of Personnel and Instutrial Relations*, ed. Dale Yoder and Herbert G. Heneman (Washington, D.C.: BNA, 1979), p. 4–41.

[5] Ibid. For an analytic comparison of the phrasing of work- and worker-oriented questionnaire content, see John C. Allen, "Multidimensional Analysis of Worker-Oriented and Job-Oriented Verbs," *Journal of Applied Psychology 53* (1969): 73–79.

[6] Thomasine Rendero, "Consensus," *Personnel 58* (January–February 1981): 4–12.

[7] U.S. Civil Service Commission, *Job Analysis: Developing and Documenting Data* (Washington, D.C.: U.S. Civil Service Commission, Bureau of Intergovernmental Personnel Programs, 1973).

[8] Ibid., p. 5.

[9] Ibid., pp. 11–12.

[10] Ibid., p. 6.

[11] Ibid., p. 12.

[12] Sidney Gael, "Interviews, Questionnaires, and Checklists," in *The Job Analysis Handbook for Business, Industry, and Government,* ed. Sidney Gael (New York: Wiley, 1988), pp. 394–402.

[13] Wayne Cascio, *Applied Psychology in Personnel Management* (Reston, Va.: Reston, 1982), p. 59.

[14] Gael, "Interviews, Questionnaires, and Checklists," p. 392.

[15] Robert J. Harvey, *CMQ A Job Analysis System: Directions for Administering the CMQ* (San Antonio, Tex.: The Psychological Corporation, 1992).

[16] Ernest J. McCormick and P. Richard Jeanneret, "Position Analysis Questionnaire (PAQ)," in *The Job Analysis Handbook for Business, Industry, and Government,* ed. Sidney Gael (New York: Wiley, 1988), p. 840.

[17] John K. Hemphill, *Dimensions of Executive Positions* (Columbus, Ohio: Bureau of Business Research, The Ohio State University, Research Monograph No. 98, 1960).

[18] Ronald C. Page, "Management Position Description Questionnaire," in *The Job Analysis Handbook for Business, Industry, and Government,* ed. Sidney Gael (New York: Wiley, 1988), pp. 860–879.

[19] Melany E. Baehr, "The Managerial and Professional Job Functions Inventory (formerly the Work Elements Inventory)," in *The Job Analysis Handbook for Business, Industry, and Government,* ed. Sidney Gael (New York: Wiley, 1988), pp. 1072–1085.

[20] McCormick and Jeanneret, "Position Analysis Questionnaire (PAQ)," pp. 825–842.

[21] Felix M. Lopez, "Threshold Traits Analysis System," in *The Job Analysis Handbook for Business, Industry, and Government,* ed. Sidney Gael (New York: Wiley, 1988), pp. 880–901.

[22] Jimmy L. Mitchell, "History of Job Analysis in Military Organizations," in *The Job Analysis Handbook for Business, Industry, and Government,* ed. Sidney Gael (New York: Wiley, 1988), p. 30–36. See also Ernest S. Primoff and Sidney A. Fine, "A History of Job Analysis," in *The Job Analysis Handbook for Business, Industry, and Government,* pp. 14–29.

[23] Frank Sistrunk and Philip L. Smith, *Critiques of Job Analysis Methods,* Vol. 2 (Washington, D.C.: Office of Criminal Justice Education and Training, Law Enforcement Assistance Administration, Grant Number 78-CD-AX-0003, 1980).

[24] This scale is typical of the relative scales used in job analysis in the military. For example, see Raymond E. Christal and Johnny J. Weissmuller, "Job-Task Inventory Analysis," in *The Job Analysis Handbook for Business, Industry, and Government,* ed. Sidney Gael (New York: Wiley, 1988), pp. 1040–1041.

[25] Duane E. Thompson and Toni A. Thompson, "Court Standards for Job Analysis in Test Validation," *Personnel Psychology* 35 (1982): 872–873 and Edward L. Levine, James N. Thomas, and Frank Sistrunk, "Selecting a Job Analysis Approach," in *The Job Analysis Handbook for Business, Industry, and Government,* ed. Sidney Gael (New York: Wiley, 1988), p. 345. Redundancy in task ratings can be an issue when considering rating scales to be used. See Lee Friedman, "Degree of Redundancy Between Time, Importance, and Frequency Task Ratings," *Journal of Applied Psychology* 75 (1990): 748–752.

[26] McCormick, "Job Information: Its Development and Applications," pp. 4-66–4-67.

[27] Joseph E. Morsh and Wayne B. Archer, *Procedural Guide for Conducting Occupational Surveys in the United States Air Force* (PRL-TR-67-11, AD-664 036) (Lackland Air Force Base, Tex.: Personnel Research Laboratory, Aerospace Medical Division, 1967), pp. 8–11.

[28] Christal and Weismuller, "Job-Task Inventory Analysis," pp. 1036–1050.

[29] For a review of statistical techniques that can be used in analyzing job analysis data, see Edwin T. Cornelius III, "Analyzing Job Analysis Data," in *The Job Analysis Handbook for Business, Industry, and Government,* ed. Sidney Gael (New York: Wiley, 1988), pp. 353–368.

[30] Wayne Cascio and Robert Ramos, "Development and Application of a New Method

for Assessing Job Performance in Behavioral/Economic Terms," *Journal of Applied Psychology* 71 (1986): 20–28. See also Patrick Conley and Paul Sackett, "Effects of Using High- versus Low-Performing Job Incumbents as Sources of Job Analysis Information," *Journal of Applied Psychology* 72 (1987): 434–437 for an example of the application of empirical criteria for defining important job tasks.

31 Cascio, *Applied Psychology in Personnel Management*, p. 59. For a different view of using a task inventory-based system of job analysis labeled the "Work Performance Survey System (WPSS)," see Sidney Gael, *Job Analysis* (San Francisco: Jossey-Bass, 1983).

32 Ernest J. McCormick, P. Richard Jeanneret, and Robert C. Mecham, "A Study of Characteristics and Job Dimensions as Based on the Position Analysis Questionnaire (PAQ)," *Journal of Applied Psychology* 56 (1972): 347–368.

33 Ibid., p. 349.

34 PAQ Services, Inc., *Job Analysis Manual for the Position Analysis Questionnaire (PAQ) (System II)* (Logan, Utah: PAQ Services, 1977), pp. 2–3.

35 McCormick and Jeanneret, "Position Analysis Questionnaire (PAQ)," p. 830.

36 PAQ Services, Inc., *Job Analysis Manual for the Position Analysis Questionnaire (PAQ)*, pp. 7–14.

37 McCormick and Jeanneret, "Position Analysis Questionnaire (PAQ)," pp. 834–835.

38 Ernest J. McCormick, Robert C. Mecham, and P. Richard Jeanneret, *Technical Manual for the Position Analysis Questionnaire (PAQ) (System II)* (Logan, Utah: PAQ Services, 1977), pp. 7–9.

39 Cascio, *Applied Psychology in Personnel Management*, p. 62.

40 Sidney Gael, "Subject Matter Expert Conferences," in *The Job Analysis Handbook for Business, Industry, and Government*, ed. Sidney Gael (New York: Wiley, 1988), p. 432–445.

41 Louis J. Freda and John J. Senkewica, "Worker Diaries," in *The Job Analysis Handbook for Business, Industry, and Government*, ed. Sidney Gael (New York: Wiley, 1988), pp. 446–452.

42 David A. Bownas and H. John Bernardin, "Critical Incident Technique," in *The Job Analysis Handbook for Business, Industry, and Government*, ed. Sidney Gael (New York: Wiley, 1988), pp. 1120–1137.

43 Mark J. Martinko, "Observing the Work," in *The Job Analysis Handbook for Business, Industry, and Government*, ed. Sidney Gael (New York: Wiley, 1988), pp. 419–431.

44 Equal Employment Opportunity Commission, Civil Service Commission, Department of Labor, and Department of Justice, *Adoption of Four Agencies of Uniform Guidelines on Employee Selection Procedures*, 43 Federal Register 38,300 (Aug. 25, 1978).

45 Edwin T. Cornelius, Theodore J. Carron, and Marianne N. Collins, "Job Analysis Models and Job Classification," *Personnel Psychology* 32 (1979): 693–708.

46 Edward L. Levine, Ronald A. Ash, and Nell Bennett, "Exploratory Comparative Study of Four Job Analysis Methods," *Journal of Applied Psychology* 65 (1980):524–535.

47 Edward L. Levine, Nell Bennett, and Ronald A. Ash, "Evaluation and Use of Four Job Analysis Methods for Personnel Selection," *Public Personnel Management* 8 (January–February 1979): 146–151.

48 Edward L. Levine, Ronald A. Ash, Hardy L. Hall, and Frank Sistrunk, "Evaluation of Job Analysis Methods by Experienced Job Analysts," *Academy of Management Journal* 26 (1983): 339–347.

49 George P. Hollenbeck and Walter C. Borman, "Two Analyses in Search of a Job: The Implications of Different Analysis Approaches," paper presented at the 84th annual convention of the American Psychological Association, Washington, D.C., August 1976.

50 Gary B. Brumback, Tania Romashko, Clifford P. Hahn, and Edwin A. Fleishman, *Model Procedures for Job Analysis, Test Development, and Validation* (Washington, D.C.: American Institutes for Research, 1974), pp. 102–108.

51 Sistrunk and Smith, *Critiques of Job Analysis Methods*, Vol. 2, pp. 16–17.

[52] Brumback et al., *Model Procedures for Job Analysis, Test Development, and Validation*, p. 103.

[53] Ibid.

[54] Levine, Ash, and Bennett, "Exploratory Comparative Study of Four Job Analysis Methods," pp. 528–529.

[55] McCormick, Mecham, and Jeanneret, *Technical Manual for the Position Analysis Questionnaire (PAQ) (System II)*, pp. 3–4.

[56] Ernest S. Primoff, Cynthia L. Clark, and James R. Caplan, *How to Prepare and Conduct Job Element Examinations: Supplement* (Washington, D.C.: Office of Personnel Research and Development, 1982), p. 18.

[57] Ernest S. Primoff and Lorraine Eyde, "Job Element Analysis," in *The Job Analysis Handbook for Business, Industry, and Government*, ed. Sidney Gael (New York: Wiley, 1988), p. 821.

[58] Levine et al., "Evaluation of Job Analysis Methods by Experienced Job Analysts," p. 9. For an application of a multimethod appraoch, see Ronald A. Ash, "Job Elements for Task Clusters: Arguments for Using Multi-Methodological Approaches to Job Analysis and a Demonstration of Their Utility," *Public Personnel Management* 11 (Spring 1982), pp. 80–90.

[59] Brumback et al., *Model Procedures for Job Analysis, Test Development, and Validation*, p. 101.

[60] Benjamin and Andrea Konz, "Strategic Job Analysis," *Human Resource Management* 28 (1989): 51–63.

Some Additional Job Analysis Techniques

In this appendix to Chapter 8, we briefly describe four job analysis techniques. There are additional procedures that can be used in developing a selection program; the ones included here will give you an appreciation of the diversity of options available. The techniques summarized are as follows:

1. Critical-Incidents Technique,

2. Fleishman Job Analysis Survey (F-JAS),

3. Functional Job Analysis (FJA), and

4. Job Element Method (JEM).

Our discussion is necessarily brief. For those of you who are interested in the specifics involved in applying these methods, the references cited at the end of this appendix give a detailed discussion of their use.

Critical-Incidents Technique

Description

The Critical-Incidents Technique was originally developed to gather information to determine training needs and develop performance appraisal forms.[1] The process is designed to generate a list of especially good and poor (critical) examples of performance that job incumbents exhibit (incidents). The object of the Critical-Incidents Technique is to gather information regarding specific behaviors that actually have been observed, not judgmental or trait-oriented descriptions of performance. These behaviors are then grouped into job dimensions. The final list of job dimensions and respective critical incidents provides a great deal of qualitative information about a job and the behaviors associated with job success or failure.

Because the basic elements of information collected are job behaviors rather than personal traits, it is a work-oriented procedure. Each critical incident consists of (a) a description of a situation, (b) the effective or ineffective behavior performed by a job incumbent, and (c) the consequences of that behavior. The result of the Critical-Incidents Technique is a list of events where employees performed tasks poorly or exceptionally well. A representative sample of all job tasks may not be in the list, but the range of incidents provides information from which performance dimensions and worker specifications can be inferred.

Application

The Critical-Incidents Technique can be used for a variety of selection purposes. For the purposes of this appendix, we examine the use of the technique to generate a list of job-related behaviors from which inferences are based regarding worker specifications. Critical incidents are also useful in determining how to measure these worker specifications in a way that is consistent with what actually occurs on the job. The steps for implementing the method include the following.

1. **Selecting the Method for Critical-Incidents Collection** Critical incidents can be gathered from job experts in (a) a group setting, (b) individual interviews, or (c) by administering a questionnaire. Each of these three options have advantages and disadvantages. The most efficient method of gathering critical incidents is by working with a group of job experts. Each job expert in the group is asked to write as many critical incidents as he or she can. This approach entails less time for the analysts, and job experts may help jog each other's memories and subsequently generate a greater number of critical incidents. There are times when it is not possible to gather the information in a group setting. For example, job experts may not be very skilled at writing. In this case, individual interviews would be conducted and incidents recorded as the job expert remembers them. Individual interviews may also be used when the information is confidential or embarrassing in nature and should not be discussed in a group. Also, if the job experts are managers or executives, it may be difficult for them to find a common time to meet as a group. The final method, the questionnaire, should only be used with individuals who are very skilled at expressing themselves in writing and are excited about participating in the process. Otherwise, the resulting critical incidents obtained may be insufficient in content and/or number.[2] Regardless of the means chosen to interact with job experts, the procedure for collecting critical incidents remains relatively constant.

2. **Selecting a Panel of Job Experts** The Critical-Incidents Technique is frequently applied by a job analyst working with subject matter experts. With this particular procedure, it is important to think carefully about the job experts chosen to participate in the process. Job incumbents, subordinates, and supervisors are likely to provide very different types of information. Individuals should be chosen who have had the opportunity to observe others' performance on the job. Normally, this would include supervisors and job incumbents who have been in the position for a long period of time (four to five years).[3]

3. **Generating Critical Incidents** Use of a structured format for generating critical incidents statements is best. A structured format should be used whether a questionnaire or interview is being conducted.

    Job experts are asked to think back and to recall actions workers have taken while performing the job that illustrate unusually effective or ineffective performance. Then, job experts write statements describing effective and ineffective performance that meet the following four characteristics of a good written critical incident:

a. It is specific (a single behavior),
b. It focuses on observable behaviors that have been, or could be, exhibited on the job,
c. It briefly describes the context in which the behavior occurred, and
d. It indicates the consequences of the behavior.[4]

A resulting critical incident should be detailed enough to convey the same image of performance to at least two individuals who are knowledgeable about the job. The following is an example of a critical incident for a supervisory job:

> Nontoxic waste was being picked up by a disposal company. The order ticket was in error and read that the waste was toxic and to be disposed in a manner only suitable for nontoxic waste. The supervisor signed the disposal order without taking time to read it. As a consequence, EPA fined the company $5,000 for improper disposal of waste.

In this incident, there is only one critical behavior exhibited by the supervisor: signing the disposal ticket without reading it. It is an observable behavior that could be exhibited on the job. How many times have you watched someone sign a document without reading it? It is also phrased in behavioral terms, not in reference to any personal traits of the supervisor (for example, careless, lacks attention to detail, hasty, trusting). There is enough detail for the reader to understand the situation, and the consequences of this behavior are clear.

4. **Defining Job Dimensions**   Job dimensions are determined by analyzing the content of the critical incidents and identifying common themes among the incidents. One way to do this is to write each critical incident on a separate card. Then these cards are sorted by a judge into piles representing common themes. The sorting continues until all of the incidents are in piles, and all piles are of a reasonable size. (Piles that are too big may be representative of more than one theme, and those with only one or two incidents may not really be a theme.) Once the incidents have been sorted by theme, each theme is given a label that names the dimension. To help establish confidence in clustering incidents into dimensions, other job analysts or experts are asked to re-sort the incidents into the dimensions. If there is not agreement about the dimension to which a critical incident belongs, it is prudent to drop that critical incident.

Advantages and Disadvantages

The Critical-Incidents Technique clearly results in a great deal of interesting, specific, job-related information. Further, this information is behavioral in nature, not trait based. Thus worker behaviors are documented, and these can be translated into specific job tasks. In addition, the described behaviors are "critical" incidents, so the information most likely represents important aspects of the job. On the other hand, it is not clear that the incidents reported represent the full scope of the job.[5] Consequently, dimensions based on these critical incidents may not be representative of the entire job. Further, the dimensions may not be stable, given that they are the product of the analysts' judgments. The process is also labor intensive, and the results are very situation specific. Considerable effort will be required for each new endeavor, since it is doubtful that the information can be transferred from one setting to another.

Fleishman Job Analysis Survey (F-JAS)

Description

The F-JAS was developed by Edwin Fleishman to help identify worker specifications for a job, job dimension, or task. Thus it is a worker-oriented approach to be applied once job duties have been identified.

The F-JAS consists of behaviorally anchored rating scales for 52 abilities. Each of the abilities is classified into one of four general ability categories including (a) cognitive, (b) psychomotor, (c) physical, and (d) sensory/perceptual. Job experts are asked to determine the level of each ability required to perform the job. In addition to the 52 ability scales, research is being conducted on several other scales. Information is currently being collected on the following research dimensions: (a) interactive/social and (b) knowledge/skill scales. The research scale for interactive/social abilities includes 9 items, and the scale for knowledge/skills is comprised of 11 items.[6]

Application

In applying the F-JAS, several steps are involved that include the following:

1. Determining Level of Analysis First, a decision must be made as to whether abilities are to be inferred for the job as a whole, a specific job dimension, or for specific job tasks. Because we are interested in using the F-JAS to provide information for HR selection purposes, it would likely be most appropriate to use the method at the task level. The *Uniform Guidelines* require that job analysis evidence shows that an identified ability is tied to the job task requiring that specific ability. This requirement is particularly important when a content validation study is being conducted.[7]

2. Selecting Job Agents Anyone who is knowledgeable of the job, including incumbents, supervisors, and job analysts, can complete the survey. Fleishman suggests administering the survey to 20 to 30 raters to maximize reliability of the job analysis rating data.

3. Rating Ability Levels for Each Task Only tasks that are important to the job should be used in developing or choosing selection measures. Therefore, some means, such as a task analysis inventory, must be used to identify those important tasks to be rated.[8]

It may not be necessary to use all of the F-JAS ability rating scales. Rating each of the abilities for each important job task will be very time consuming and produce a large amount of rating data. There may be some abilities that clearly are not required for the position. If this is the case, job experts can be exempted from rating those abilities not related to the job. The exempted abilities are then indicated as such on the F-JAS computerized rating form. However, care should be taken in making this decision. Job experts should only be exempted from rating abilities when there is a good reason to do so. If there is any question whether the ability is required for the job, then the ability should be rated by job experts for each job task.[9]

Job agents make their ratings by specifying the "level" of each ability required for each task. Each of the abilities has a 7-point rating scale with behavioral anchors defined from a variety of jobs. The job expert compares the level of the ability needed to perform each task with the level described by the anchors. The required ability level most comparable to that described in the rating scale is then assigned to the task. If, for example, clerical workers were rating the ability *Near Vision* for the task of editing documents using a word processor on a computer, the job expert would compare the level of the ability required for editing to the behavioral anchors on the scale. Exhibit 8A.1 illustrates some of the rating scale points used to judge the ability, *Near Vision*.[10] The job expert would study these behavioral anchors. A clerical worker probably does not need to see close objects to the level required to read the fine print of a legal journal. He or she probably needs a higher level of near vision than that required to read dials on the dashboard of a car, however, since editors must read the document closely. In a car, only a glance is needed to read the dials of a dashboard. Thus the clerical worker needs near vision at a level between those two anchors, so a rating of 4 would be given.

4. Analyzing Results For each task, the mean rating across all raters for each ability is computed. The result for each task is a profile of ability levels required for task performance.

5. Selecting Tests Selecting tests is beyond the scope of determining worker requirements and ability specifications. However, Fleishman has published the *Handbook of Human Abilities* to accompany the F-JAS that lists measures for each of the abilities composing the survey.[11] The *Handbook* can be a useful source, particularly if a criterion validation strategy is possible.

Advantages and Disadvantages

Much research has gone into identifying the concise list of abilities and behavioral anchors represented in the F-JAS scales. The method is straightforward and easy to adopt. It would seem to be a viable option for identifying worker specifications following a task analysis. In particular, when a criterion-related validation study is being conducted, the F-JAS may very well be suitable for suggesting possible predictors to be used in selection. However, the method may not be as appropriate when using a content validation strategy.

Functional Job Analysis (FJA)

Description

Over 35 years ago, Sidney Fine and his associates recognized that one of the problems in studying work is the impreciseness of language used in describing

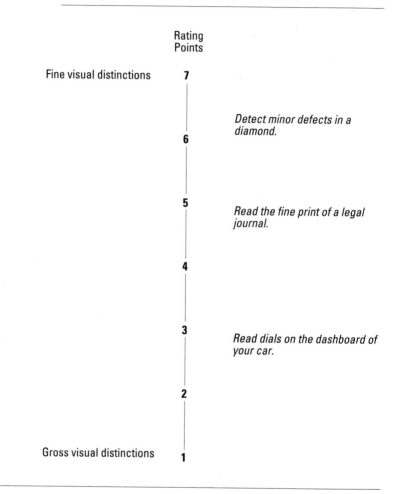

EXHIBIT 8A.1	RATING SCALE POINTS IN FLEISHMAN'S JOB ANALYSIS SURVEY (F–JAS) USED TO RATE THE ABILITY *"Near Vision"*

Rating
Points

Fine visual distinctions   **7**

     6   *Detect minor defects in a diamond.*

     5   *Read the fine print of a legal journal.*

     4

     3   *Read dials on the dashboard of your car.*

     2

Gross visual distinctions   **1**

SOURCE: Based, in part, on Edwin A. Fleishman, *Rating Scale Booklet F-JAS Fleishman Job Analysis Survey* (Palo, Alto, CA: Consulting Psychologist Press, 1992).

jobs. As a consequence, efforts were undertaken to begin work on a system for accurately defining and measuring workers' job activities. The system that emerged was labeled Functional Job Analysis (FJA). The method probably represents the most thorough procedure for applying a standardized, controlled language for describing and measuring the tasks performed on a job by a worker.

Two types of task information are obtained from FJA: (a) *what a worker does*, that is, the procedures and processes engaged in by a worker as a task is performed and (b) *how a task is performed* in context of the physical, mental, and interpersonal involvement of the worker with the task.[12] These types of information are used to clarify both what a worker does and the results of those job behaviors.

Before describing some specifics of FJA, let's look at the method from a broad view. The key ingredient in analyzing a job is proper development of task statements. Once identified, these tasks are then rated by a job analyst or employees serving as subject matter experts (or SMEs) using special sets of rating scales. The ratings provided serve as a basis for inferring worker specifications required for task performance.

When using FJA, judgments about jobs are based on at least two premises:[13]

1. *All jobs require workers to deal, in some degree, with People (clients, customers, coworkers, etc.), Data (information or ideas), and Things (machines or equipment).* Thus workers' job activities can be represented by task statements in relation to People, Data, and Things. Specific tasks require different levels of involvement with these three areas. For example, tasks characterized principally by relation to Things require a worker to draw on physical resources (strength, coordination, etc.). When a task focuses on Data, the worker is required to use mental resources (knowledge, memory, etc.). When a task demands involvement with People, interpersonal resources (courtesy, empathy, tact, etc.) are needed.

2. *The tasks a worker performs in relation to People, Data, and Things can be measured by rating scales.* Rating scales permit an analyst to describe empirically a task in terms of its relation to People, Data, Things, and other characteristics by using a standardized format and language. Based on the task statement and the ratings given to the task, employee specifications are developed.

Application

FJA is frequently applied by an analyst working with job incumbents, either individually or in groups. The objective is to describe what a worker does in performing the job and *not* what gets done. Take the job of bus driver for instance. As Sidney Fine and Wretha Wiley point out, FJA emphasizes what the bus driver does. That is, he or she performs a series of sequenced tasks in driving the bus and collecting fares. Emphasis is not given to what gets accomplished, that is, passengers being carried by a bus operated by a driver.[14]

As we suggested earlier, application of FJA involves a number of activities. There is not just one way to apply FJA. In some cases, a job analyst may observe and interview individual workers in studying a job. Based on results of these observations and interviews, the analyst makes ratings of the tasks performed on the job. In another type of application, groups of workers serving as subject matter experts (or SMEs) are convened; they are asked to identify job tasks and make judgments about these tasks in terms of several criteria. Listed here is a series of steps that outlines one general form of FJA application.[15] In specific applications, some of these steps may be omitted; other steps may be substituted or modified.

1. **Organizing Job Incumbents to Analyze the Job**   Incumbents who are knowledgeable of the job being studied (SMEs) are assembled in a session to rate the job. The purpose of this initial session is to explain their role in conducting a job analysis.

2. **Specifying Job Outputs**   In the next step, the SMEs are asked to specify the outputs they produce on their job. Questions such as, "What have you been employed to produce?" or "What are the results of your work?" are posed to the SMEs.[16] Basically, this step is a catalyst for the SMEs to begin thinking about the next step—the identification of job tasks used to produce these outputs.

3. **Identifying Job Tasks**   The fundamental unit of work under study is the task. A task represents "a fundamental, stable work element consisting of a behavior and a result."[17]

    Preparation of good task statements is the most critical step in applying FJA. Much time, care, effort, and expertise must be given to precisely wording a task statement to reflect a job activity. Such explicit task statements are needed to enhance the validity of inferences to be drawn about employee specifications. Thus it is assumed that the more explicit and precise a task statement, the more accurate the inferences drawn about these specifications. Since the wording of a task statement is so crucial, we review how these statements are constructed.

    Based on information collected from observation of the job or interviews with incumbents, task statements are written so they answer the following questions:

    a.   *Who* performs the task?

    b.   What *action* is performed?

    c.   What immediate *result* is accomplished?

    d.   What *tools*, equipment, or work aids are used?

    e.   What *instructions* (prescribed or discretionary) are followed?[18]

    Table 8A.1 illustrates how a task statement for the job of intake social worker may be decomposed and written to meet the just described criteria. This same process is applied until a suitable list of task statements has been developed.

    The next three phases of applying FJA are used to measure the complexity of the tasks defined in step 3. To do so, task ratings are made using the following rating scales: (a) *Worker Functions Scales*, (b) *Scale of Worker Instructions*, and (c) *Scales of General Educational Development*.

4. **Measuring Worker Functions**   The *Worker Functions Scales* consist of separate ratings of People, Data, and Things. The scales themselves are

TABLE 8A.1 AN EXAMPLE TASK STATEMENT PREPARED UNDER FUNCTIONAL JOB ANALYSIS (FJA) FOR THE JOB OF INTAKE SOCIAL WORKER

Complete Task Statement: Asks client questions, listens to responses, and writes answers on standard intake form, exercising leeway as to sequence of questions, in order to record basic identifying information.

Criteria:	1. Who? (subject)	2. Performs what action?	3. To accomplish what?	4. With what tools?	5. Upon what instructions?
Guideline:	Subject of the statement is understood to be the "worker."	Use a specific action verb.	Purpose of the action performed should be stated so that its relation to objectives is clear and performance standards can be set.	Should identify the tangible instruments used by a worker in performing a task.	Should reflect the nature and source of instructions the worker receives in terms of that specified and that left to the worker's discretion.
Example:	No subject.	*Asks* client questions, *writes* answers, *listens* to responses.	To establish a client information system that enables workers to locate clients quickly and efficiently.	Forms, pens.	Prescribed: Following standard intake form. Discretionary: Exercising some leeway as to sequence of questions.

SOURCE: Based on Sidney A. Fine and Wretha W. Wiley, *An Introduction to Functional Job Analysis* (Kalamazoo, Mich.: W. E. Upjohn Institute for Employment Research, 1971), pp. 10–12.

too long to reproduce each one here, but the Data scale is shown in Exhibit 8A.2 to provide an illustration. The Data rating scale consists of six rating points or levels and eight functional areas (Comparing, Copying, Computing, etc.). The levels range from simple (Comparing) to complex (Synthesizing) functions. In applying the Data scale, for instance, a job analyst (or SME) carefully reads a task statement. Definitions of each of the eight functions on the scale are studied, and the level is chosen that best describes the data orientation of the task statement. The level selected reflects the extent to which a worker is required to be involved with information, ideas, facts, and statistics in performing a task. Involvement may range from simple recognition through degrees of arranging, modifying, or even reconceptualizing data.[19] Although the specific content varies, the People and Things rating scales are similar in format and application.

The three Data, People, and Things scales provide two ways of assessing task requirements. These ways include (a) task *level* and (b) task *orientation*. Level shows the *relative complexity* of a task as compared to other tasks. In obtaining a score for level, an analyst (or SME) studies a task and then selects the function on a scale that is most appropriate for the task examined. The numerical score for level is the number corresponding to the particular function chosen. For example, suppose the Data scale is being used in evaluating a task. If *Compiling* (level = 3B) is chosen, the task involves a higher level of functioning than that required for *Copying* (level = 2) but a lower level of functioning than *Analyzing* data (level = 4).

The *Orientation* measure indicates the *relative involvement* of a worker with Data, People, and Things as a task is performed. The measure involves assigning a percentage (usually in units of 5 percent or 10 percent) to each of the three functions scored for a task. The sum of the three orientation scores equals 100 percent. The higher the percentage assigned to a function (that is, People, Data, Things), the greater the degree of emphasis of that function in the task rated.[20]

In summary, level and orientation measures represent the worker's mental, physical, and interpersonal involvement with a task. Level is determined by choosing three functions, one each from the Data, People, and Things scales. Orientation measures are derived by weighting (%) and three functions for each task to show the relative emphasis on the functions. Applications of level and orientation measures yield results similar to the following example task for the intake social worker's job.[21]

Example Task: Asks client questions, listens to responses, and writes answers on standard intake form, exercising leeway as to sequence of questions, in order to record basic identifying information.

Area	Function	Level	Orientation (%)
Data	Copying	2	50
People	Exchanging Information	2	40
Things	Handling	1A	10

| EXHIBIT 8A.2 | DATA FUNCTION SCALE (CONDENSED) USED WITH FUNCTIONAL JOB ANALYSIS (FJA) |

Level	Definition

Comparing

1   Selects, sorts, or arranges data, people, or things, judging whether their readily observable functional, structural, or compositional characteristics are similar to or different from prescribed standards, e.g., checks oil level, tire pressure, worn cables; observes hand signal of worker indicating movement of load.

Copying

2   Transcribes, enters, and/or posts data, following a schema or plan to assemble or make things and using a variety of work aids. Transfers information mentally from plans, diagrams, instructions, to workplace or work site.

Computing

3A   Performs arithmetic operations and makes reports and/or carries out a prescribed action in relation to them. Interprets mathematical data on plans, specifications, diagrams, or blueprints.

Compiling

3B   Gathers, collates, or classifies information about data, people, or things, following a schema or system but using discretion in application.

Analyzing

4   Examines and evaluates data (about things, data, or people) with reference to the criteria, standards, and/or requirements of a particular discipline, art, technique, or craft to determine interaction effects (consequences) and to consider alternatives.

Innovating

5A   Modifies, alters, and/or adapts existing designs, procedures, or methods to meet unique specifications, unusual conditions, or specific standards of effectiveness within the overall framework of operating theories, principles, and/or organizational contexts.

Coordinating

5B   Decides time, place, and sequence of operations of a process, system, or organization, and/or the need for revision of goals, policies (boundary conditions), or procedures on the basis of analysis of data and of performance review of pertinent objectives and requirements. Includes overseeing and/or executing decisions and/or reporting on events.

Synthesizing

6   *Takes off in new directions* on the basis of personal intuitions, feelings, and ideas (with or without regard for tradition, experience, and existing parameters) *to conceive new approaches* to or statements of problems and the development of system, operational, or aesthetic "solutions" or "resolutions" of them, typically outside of existing theoretical, stylistic, or organizational context.

NOTE: The arabic numbers assigned to definitions represent the successive levels of this ordinal scale. The A and B definitions are variations on the same level. There is no ordinal difference between A and B definitions on a given level.

SOURCE: Sidney A. Fine Associates, Washington, D.C., 1985. Adapted with permission.

In this example, 50 percent of the worker's involvement in the task is at the *Copying* level (writing answers on a standard intake form). But the worker is also involved interpersonally with people (40 percent) by *Exchanging Information* (talking with people to obtain information). Also, the worker is required to use physical resources in *Handling* papers and pens (10 percent).

5. **Measuring Worker Instructions**   In addition to characterizing tasks in terms of Things, Data, and People, FJA also provides for measuring the degree of *prescription* and *discretion* in task performance. *Prescribed* aspects of tasks represent those areas in which the worker has no control over what is done. *Discretionary* components involve those aspects of tasks in which the worker must decide on the execution of tasks. In order to assess the degree of prescription/discretion, the *Scale of Worker Instructions* is used. It is similar in format and application to the *Worker Functions Scales*, in which lower levels represent high task *prescription* and higher levels represent high task *discretion*. When prescription is high, task performance requires little or no judgment; where discretion is high, mental effort is required in performing the task.[22]

The *Scale of Worker Instructions* is an eight-point rating scale. Examples of five rating levels are illustrated in Exhibit 8A.3.

6. **Measuring Worker Qualifications**   The final set of rating scales is specifically directed toward the problem of determining selected worker qualifications. The *Scales of General Education Development* (GED) serve as a means for determining basic educational skills needed to perform a task. Thus the GED scales assess a specific task's demands on a worker's reasoning, mathematical, and language development. The following measures compose the GED scales:

   a. *Reasoning Development Scale*—concerns the problem-solving and decision-making demands of a task.

   b. *Mathematical Development Scale*—focuses on the mathematical operations ranging from counting to higher mathematics required by a task.

   c. *Language Development Scale*—relates to the demands of a task to deal with oral and written materials, covering from simple to complex sources of information.[23]

Exhibit 8A.4 summarizes three levels of each of the GED scales. Their application is identical to that discussed previously for other FJA ratings. Scores are obtained by choosing the level on a scale that best meets the task characteristics under review. The results of the GED scales, when coupled with results of other ratings, provide the basic information needed for developing selected employee specifications.

7. **Identifying Employee Specifications**   At this point in FJA application, the actions and end results of a job have been noted. The analyst next

| EXHIBIT 8A.3 | SCALE OF WORKER INSTRUCTIONS (CONDENSED) USED WITH FUNCTIONAL JOB ANALYSIS (FJA) |

Level   Definition

1   Inputs, outputs, tools, equipment, and procedures are all specified. Almost everything the worker needs to know is contained in the assignment. The worker is supposed to turn out a specified amount of work or a standard number of units per hour or day.

2   Inputs, outputs, tools, and equipment are all specified, but the worker has some leeway in the procedures and methods used to get the job done. Almost all the information needed is in the assignment instructions. Production is measured on a daily or weekly basis.

3   Inputs and outputs are specified, but the worker has considerable freedom as to procedures and timing, including the use of tools and/or equipment. The worker may have to refer to several standard sources for information (handbooks, catalogs, wall charts). Time to complete a particular product or service is specified, but this varies up to several hours.

•   •
•   •
•   •

7   There is some question as to what the need or problem really is or what directions should be pursued in dealing with it. In order to define the problem, to control and explore the behavior of the variables, and to formulate possible outputs and their performance characteristics, the worker must consult largely unspecified sources of information and devise investigations, surveys, or data analysis studies.

8   Information and/or direction comes to the worker in terms of needs (tactical, organizational, strategic, financial). Worker must call for staff reports and recommendations concerning methods of dealing with them. He or she coordinates both organizational and technical data in order to make decisions and determinations regarding courses of action (outputs) for major sections (divisions, groups) of the organization.

SOURCE: Sidney A. Fine Associates, Washington, D.C., 1985. Adapted with permission.

attempts to identify the KSAs or other employee characteristics needed to perform the job tasks. In identifying KSAs, SMEs might be asked the following questions:

> What does it take for you to produce satisfactory results when you perform your job tasks? In answering this question, think of yourself as the supervisor of this work and needing to hire new staff. What will you be looking for in your new workers? When you mention a characteristic, connect it to a specific task.[24]

(Sidney Fine refers to these "specifications" as "performance standards."[25] To keep the terminology consistent with our discussion of job analysis in this chapter, we use the term *specifications* to refer to these performance standards.)

8. **Administering a Job Task Questionnaire** This last step is an optional one. When desired, the tasks that have been identified either through observation and/or interview with SMEs can be included in a questionnaire. Other incumbents on the job who were not part of the original task development process can be surveyed and asked to make ratings of the tasks in terms of criteria such as frequency, criticality, and importance of task performance.

Advantages and Disadvantages

Clearly, FJA represents a comprehensive quantitative procedure for analyzing jobs. The methods and standardized language that are employed help to ensure a systematic approach to job analysis. Further, the rating scales used with the method appear to provide reliable task analysis data.[26] On the other hand, FJA's assets have some associated costs. The method is somewhat laborious and time consuming. Special training is mandatory in order to apply FJA effectively—training that can be expensive.

Job Element Method (JEM)
Description

Whereas many of the methods of job analysis we have examined begin with identification of tasks or basic work functions, the *Job Element Method* (JEM) developed by Ernest Primoff has a different orientation.[27] Basically, it is a worker-oriented process designed to identify the characteristics of superior workers on a job. Supervisors and/or incumbents develop a list of these characteristics and then rate them in such a way that the characteristics essential to superior performers are delineated. These qualities are what Primoff calls *job elements*. Job elements include a wide variety of characteristics that describe superior performers on a job. These elements consist of worker characteristics such as the following:

A knowledge, such as knowledge of accounting principles; a skill, such as skill with woodworking tools; an ability, such as ability to manage a program; a willingness, such as willingness to do simple tasks repetitively; an interest, such as interest in learning new techniques; or a personal characteristic, such as reliability or dependability.[28]

Once identified, the elements are translated into more specific employee characteristics called *subelements*. For example, the element *Ability to Make Electrical Calculations* may have been identified for the job of industrial electrician. Subelements for this element might be:

EXHIBIT 8A.4	REASONING, MATHEMATICAL, AND LANGUAGE DEVELOPMENT SCALES (CONDENSED) USED WITH FUNCTIONAL JOB ANALYSIS (FJA)

Reasoning Development Scale

Level	Definition
1	• Have the commonsense understanding to carry out simple one- or two-step instructions in the context of highly standardized situations. • Recognize unacceptable variations from the standard and take emergency action to reject inputs or stop operations.
2	• Have the commonsense understanding to carry out detailed but uninvolved instructions where the work involves a *few* concrete/specific variables in or from standard/typical situations.
• • •	• • •
6	• Have knowledge of a field of study of the highest abstractive order (e.g., mathematics, physics, chemistry, logic, philosophy, art criticism). • Deal with nonverbal symbols in formulas, equations, or graphs. • Understand the most difficult classes of concepts. • Deal with a large number of variables and determine a specific course of action (e.g., research, production) on the basis of need.

Mathematical Development Scale

Level	Definition
1	• Counting to simple addition and subtraction; reading, copying, and/or recording of figures.
2	• Use arithmetic to add, subtract, multiply, and divide whole numbers. Reading scales and gauges as in powered equipment where readings and signals are indicative of conditions and actions to be taken.
• • •	• • •
5	• Have knowledge of advanced mathematical and statistical techniques such as differential and integral calculus, factor analysis, and probability determination. • Work with a wide variety of theoretical mathematical concepts. • Make original applications of mathematical procedures, as in empirical and differential equations.

(continued)

EXHIBIT 8A.4	(CONTINUED)

Level	Language Development Scale Definition
1	• Cannot read or write but can follow simple oral, *pointing-out* instructions. • Sign name and understand ordinary, routine agreements when explained, such as those relevant to leasing a house; employment (hours, wages, etc.); procuring a driver's license. • Read lists, addresses, safety warnings.
2	• Read short sentences, simple concrete vocabulary; words that avoid complex Latin derivations. • Converse with service personnel (waiters, ushers, cashiers). • Copy written records precisely without error. • Keep taxi driver's trip record or service maintenance record.
• • •	• • •
6	• Report, write, or edit articles for technical and scientific journals or journals of advanced literary criticism (e.g., *Journal of Educational Sociology, Science, Physical Review, Daedalus*).

SOURCE: Sidney A. Fine Associates, Washington, D.C., 1985. Adapted with permission.

Element:	1.	*Ability to make electrical calculations*
Subelements:	a.	Determining the voltage across a resistor in a series circuit
	b.	Computing power in a circuit for given levels of voltage and amperage

Content of selection devices such as tests are developed based on these elements and subelements.

In comparison to the other job analysis techniques we have discussed, the JEM approach differs in an important way. Rather than focusing on job tasks or worker functions per se, the JEM is aimed toward *directly* identifying those employee characteristics that should be assessed by selection measures. Thus, from this perspective, we view the JEM more as a means for developing worker specifications and their measures than strictly a means for collecting information about the important work-related aspects of a job.

Application

The JEM involves several important phases that carry a user through the job element identification—selection device development process. The job element identification, or job analysis, side of the method involves several major steps.[29]

1. **Selecting a Panel of Raters** On the whole, success of the JEM depends on judgments provided by a panel of experts. However, in contrast to some techniques, it does not use a group of analysts working independently. The group or panel chosen typically consists of about six incum-

bents or supervisors working as raters or subject matter experts (SMEs). Individuals used are those who know the requirements of a job and can recognize characteristics of superior performers.

2. **Developing Job Elements and Subelements**   After a panel of experts has been assembled, the next step is to develop a comprehensive list of job elements and subelements. Panel members are told they have been brought together to identify KSAs and other characteristics that are needed by workers to perform the job under study. Questions such as "If you had to pick out one person to get a special bonus for outstanding work, what might you look for?"[30] are asked in order to stimulate panelists in generating job elements. After an exhaustive list of elements has been produced, the SMEs are asked to list specific subelements for each element.

3. **Rating Job Elements and Subelements**   The third phase of the JEM process involves each panel member independently rating the elements and subelements identified in the previous step. The goal is to identify the critical characteristics of workers, that is, the elements and subelements that are essential for successful performance on the job.

   SMEs evaluate the importance of each element and subelement by rating them according to the following four scales of worker characteristics:

   a. The degree to which *barely acceptable workers* have the element or subelement (2 = All Have, 1 = Some Have, 0 = Almost None Have)

   b. The importance of the element or subelement in *identifying superior workers* (2 = Very Important, 1 = Valuable, 0 = Does Not Differentiate)

   c. The extent to which *trouble would be likely if the element or subelement were ignored* in selecting workers (2 = Much Trouble, 1 = Some Trouble, 0 = Safe to Ignore)

   d. By requiring applicants to have an element or subelement, the *practicality* of expecting applicants to have the characteristic and then using the characteristic to fill job openings (2 = Fill All Openings, 1 = Fill Some Openings, 0 = Fill No Openings)

All of the ratings are made on a special type of form called the "Job Element Blank."[31]

4. **Analyzing JEM Data**   Once the ratings have been made, quantitative scores are computed for each of the elements and subelements. These are developed from specific scoring formulas that incorporate the ratings made on the Job Element Blank using the four rating criteria just described. Decisions as to which elements and subelements should be

included in a selection measure are based on the computed scores. Specific minimum scores are used to define the appropriate elements and subelements.[32]

5. **Amplifying Subelement Definitions** Now that the subelements have been identified and chosen for inclusion in selection measures, the SMEs are asked to furnish work examples of each subelement. The goal is to be as specific as possible in defining a KSA or some other characteristic that reflects the nature of the subelement. Because these work examples will be used to define the content and nature of the selection measure operationally, it is important that they reflect specific aspects of the job. For this reason, other job analysis techniques are often used to develop work examples that amplify and clarify the nature of these subelements.

Ernest Primoff, Cynthia Clark, and James Caplan, for example, recommend the use of Sidney Fine's Functional Job Analysis (FJA) approach to develop and characterize work examples in the form of job tasks.[33] Results of the Job Element Method are incorporated with the key aspects of Functional Job Analysis. Job tasks are tied to specific subelements that serve as work examples for these subelements.

At the conclusion of these steps, several products are obtained. A list of the important elements of the job has been developed; a list of the worker characteristics (subelements) that reflect these elements has been given; and job tasks that illustrate work examples have been tied to these worker characteristics. These products ultimately serve as the basis for developing the content of selection measures.

Advantages and Disadvantages

When carried throughout the Job Analysis → Test Development → Test Validation process, the JEM offers a unique alternative for identifying important employee specifications and constructing measures for them. However, Gary Brumback and his associates have found that the method is "almost too unwieldy and unstructured . . . in the initial stage of soliciting preliminary job elements for subject matter experts."[34] In addition, Frank Sistrunk and Philip Smith point to logistical problems in simply assembling a panel of experts. They note that when using high-level personnel, the schedules of participants are not likely to mesh, making it difficult to organize panel members. In addition, taking key members away from their jobs for the necessary amount of time may create some organizational problems, particularly for small organizations.[35]

The JEM has also been criticized for ignoring the specification of job tasks. It has been alleged that the absence of task data makes it difficult to show that an element is job-related if it cannot be demonstrated that the element is necessary to do a specific task. As a result, the JEM may not be the best job analysis method to use for some types of validation studies (such as content validation). However, recent modifications in the JEM have attempted to address this criticism.[36]

The JEM has approximately a 25-year history; it has been widely used in the public sector to develop selection measures in various trades and labor occupations. With some of its newer modifications, it holds promise as another method for identifying employee specifications to be incorporated into selection devices.

References for the Appendix

[1] John C. Flanagan, "The Critical Incident Technique," *Psychological Bulletin* 51 (1954): 327–358.

[2] David A. Bownas and H. John Bernardin, "Critical Incident Technique," in *The Job Analysis Handbook for Business, Industry, and Government*, ed. Sidney Gael (New York: Wiley, 1988), pp. 1120–1137.

[3] Ibid.

[4] Ibid., p. 1121.

[5] Ibid.

[6] Edwin A. Fleishman and Maureen E. Reilly, *Administrator's Guide F-JAS: Fleishman Job Analysis Survey* (Palo Alto, Calif.: Consulting Psychologists Press, 1992).

[7] Equal Employment Opportunity Commission, Civil Service Commission, Department of Labor, and Department of Justice, *Adoption of Four Agencies of Uniform Guidelines on Employee Selection Procedures*, 43 Federal Register 38290-38315 (Aug. 25, 1978).

[8] Edwin A. Fleishman and Maureen E. Reilly, *Administrator's Guide F-JAS: Fleishman Job Analysis Survey* (Palo Alto, Calif.: Consulting Psychologists Press, 1992).

[9] Ibid.

[10] Edwin A. Fleishman, *Rating Scale Booklet F-JAS: Fleishman Job Analysis Survey* (Palo Alto, Calif.: Consulting Psychologists Press, 1992).

[11] Edwin A. Fleishman, *Handbook of Human Abilities* (Palo Alto, Calif.: Consulting Psychologists Press, 1992).

[12] Sidney A. Fine and Wretha W. Wiley, *An Introduction to Functional Job Analysis: A Scaling of Selected Tasks from the Social Welfare Field* (Kalamazoo, Mich.: W. E. Upjohn Institute for Employment Research, 1977), pp. 9–10.

[13] Ibid., pp. 13–17.

[14] Ibid., p. 12.

[15] For another listing of steps describing the application of FJA, see Sidney A. Fine, "Functional Job Analysis," in *The Job Analysis Handbook for Business, Industry, and Government*, ed. Sidney Gael (New York: Wiley, 1988), pp. 1019–1035.

[16] Ibid., p. 1027.

[17] Howard C. Colson, Sidney A. Fine, David C. Myers, and Margaret C. Jennings, "The Use of Functional Job Analysis in Establishing Performance Standards for Heavy Equipment Operators," *Personnel Psychology* 34 (1981): 352.

[18] Fine and Wiley, *An Introduction to Functional Job Analysis: A Scaling of Selected Tasks from the Social Welfare Field*, pp. 10–12.

[19] Ibid., p. 15.

[20] Ibid., p. 16.

[21] Ibid., p. 17.

[22] Ibid., pp. 20–21.

[23] Ibid., pp. 27–30.

[24] Fine, "Functional Job Analysis," p. 1027.

[25] Ibid.

[26] Sidney A. Fine, A. M. Holt, and M. F. Hutchinson, *Functional Job Analysis: How to Standardize Task Statements* (Kalamazoo, Mich.: W. E. Upjohn Institute for Employment Research, 1974).

[27] Ernest S. Primoff, *How to Prepare and Conduct Job Element Examinations* (Washington, D.C.: Personnel Research and Development Center, U.S. Civil Service Commission, TS-75-1, 1975). See also Ernest S. Primoff, Cynthia L. Clark, and James R. Caplan, *How to Prepare and Conduct Job Element Examinations: Supplement* (Washington, D.C.: Office of Personnel Management, Office of Personnel Research and Development, 1982).

[28] Ibid., p. 2.

[29] Ernest S. Primoff and Lorraine Dittrich Eyde, "Job Element Analysis," in *The Job Analysis Handbook for Business, Industry, and Government,* ed. Sidney Gael (New York: Wiley, 1988), pp. 807–824.

[30] Ibid., p. 809.

[31] Ibid., p. 810.

[32] Ibid., p. 813.

[33] Primoff, Clark, and Caplan, *How to Prepare and Conduct Job Element Examinations: Supplement,* pp. 5–6.

[34] Gary B. Brumback, Tania Romashko, Clifford P. Hahn, and Edwin A. Fleishman, *Model Procedures for Job Analysis, Test Development and Validation* (Washington, D.C.: American Institutes for Research, 1974), p. 19.

[35] Frank Sistrunk and Philip L. Smith, *Critiques of Job Analysis Methods* (Washington, D.C.: Office of Criminal Justice Education and Training, Law Enforcement Assistance Administration, Vol. 2, Grant Number 78-CD-AX-0003, 1980).

[36] Primoff, Clark, and Caplan, *How to Prepare an d Conduct Job Element Examinations: Supplement.*

9

Incorporating Job Analysis Results in Selection Measures

To this point, we have examined several aspects of job analysis. We have looked at the issues involved in preparing for a job analysis: organizing a job analysis, choosing the jobs to be studied, reviewing the relevant literature, and selecting the job agents. Further, we have explored in some detail the actual application of job analysis in terms of collecting job information through various job analysis methods. But by this time you may be wondering, How do we actually use our collected data for developing or choosing selection measures? Recall for a moment Exhibit 8.1, discussed in Chapter 8. In that figure, we showed that job analysis results are used to determine the relevant knowledge, skills, abilities (KSAs) or other employee specifications needed for effective performance on the job. Once identified, these specifications, in turn, serve as the basis for *constructing* (such as in developing questions for an employment interview schedule) or *choosing* (such as in selecting a previously developed ability test) the needed selection measures. In this chapter, we study the last two elements of Exhibit 8.1, that is, (a) the determination of KSAs and other personal characteristics from job analysis data (identification of employee specifications) and (b) the incorporation of employee specifications in our selection instruments (determination of selection measure content). These two elements are the key steps in implementing job analysis results for HR selection purposes.

Identification of Employee Specifications

In our earlier discussion of Exhibit 8.1, we noted that judgments or inferences on the part of job analysts play an important role in identifying employee specifications. However, the resulting specifications will be useful only to the extent that the inferences are accurate and complete. If the inferences are wrong, the selection measures will not be useful for predicting job performance. In addition, given current federal laws and executive orders, inappropriate selection measures may produce a situation that is ripe for charges of adverse impact against certain applicant groups or one in which new employees are unqualified for the job for which they were employed. Both situations are unfair to employers and employees alike. The probability of situations such as these arising can be minimized by taking appropriate steps to ensure, as much as possible, that the inferences are correct. Fortunately, several approaches have been developed for dealing with the problem of systematically inferring employee specifications from job analysis data. In this section, we address the inference problem by describing a few of these methods.

We plan to review two different approaches to determining employee specifications from job analysis data. Each of the two approaches chosen for inferring employee specifications offers a different perspective from the other. The first approach to be examined is derived from *task analysis;* the other is based on the *Position Analysis Questionnaire.* Both represent frequently used job analysis methods. As we have seen, a task analysis inventory typically involves using a questionnaire composed of a large number of statements describing specific tasks or activities performed on a job. Respondents use rating scales (such as task importance or task frequency) to describe each task presented. Generally speaking, task analysis is specific to one job.

The Position Analysis Questionnaire, or PAQ, is the second job analysis method to be addressed. In Chapter 8, we noted that the PAQ is basically a standardized commercially-available job analysis questionnaire that assesses general human behaviors involved in work. Rating scales are used to describe the extent to which any one of numerous behaviors characterize a specific job. Because the PAQ focuses on general human behaviors, it can be applied to a wide array of jobs.

These two approaches were chosen for specific reasons. The task analysis approach was picked because task data are oftentimes gathered and frequently recommended for identifying or developing tests to be used for selection.[1] The PAQ was selected because it offers a unique means for deriving and measuring job attributes for use in selection.[2] It is representative of structured questionnaires that use a predetermined set of items to study a variety of jobs. When taken together, the two approaches present an interesting contrast of methods for identifying employee specifications.

Before addressing these methods, we need to make a few general comments. First, as there are numerous job analysis methods other than those we have reviewed, there are also other job analysis/employee specifications approaches that could be offered. For example, Frank Landy[3] has illustrated how the tasks of a patrol police officer's job can be analyzed in terms of Edwin Fleishman's taxonomy of human abilities.[4] The identified abilities required to perform the tasks on a job serve as the basis for choosing the type of selection predictor to use (for example, a paper-and-pencil test or an interview) as well as the specific content of the measure (for example, test items requiring deductive reasoning).

The two methods described in this chapter represent a fairly diverse group of methods. Thus they serve more as examples of the range of possible approaches than as final answers. Second, each one involves the use of judgment on the part of users. Even though judgment is involved, the approaches are designed to lead *systematically* from an analysis of the job to identification of employee specifications to determination of selection measure content. Finally, remember that whatever the approach, it is employed for two reasons: (a) to enhance the likelihood of choosing appropriate employee specifications and, in turn, valid selection instruments and (b) to meet certain legal requirements as mandated by the *Uniform Guidelines*. Depending on the situation at hand, some approaches may be more appropriate than others.

Determination of Employee Specifications: The Task Analysis Approach

The various approaches to the development of KSAs and other employee specifications from the results of a task analysis generally follow similar procedures. In this sense, these approaches represent a traditional method of establishing job requirements.[5] Although there are unique aspects associated with any one employee specifications development method based on tasks, most methods incorporate the following sequential steps:

1. Identifying and rating job tasks,

2. Specifying KSAs necessary for successful job performance,

3. Rating the importance of identified KSAs,

4. Identifying other employee specifications necessary for job performance,

5. Linking KSAs and other employee specifications to job tasks, and

6. Developing the content areas of selection measures.

The goal of these six steps is the development of a systematic selection plan and content sources for constructing and/or choosing appropriate HR selection instruments. We now describe how each of these steps may be applied to accomplish this goal.

1. Identifying and Rating Job Tasks The first step under the task analysis approach is the specification of job tasks. This step is crucial because it serves as the basis from which KSAs are developed and selection measures are chosen or constructed. A number of different approaches we have mentioned can be used. For example, group interviews with subject matter experts in conjunction with task-based questionnaires is a common approach for developing task statements and collecting task data. Because of the importance of task data, the proper development of task statements is critical. Thus rules, such as those we discussed in Chapter 8 for developing task statements, are important for generating the type of task information we need. In sum, appropriate task statements (a) begin with an action verb and (b) describe **what** the worker does, **how** the worker does it, to **whom** or **what,** and **why** the worker does it. The following example portrays an incorrect and a corrected task statement:

Incorrect: *"Assists with the inspection of construction projects."*
Comment: First, the *What* is ambiguous and gives no real information as to the action. Second, neither the *Why* nor the *How* questions have been answered.

What   *To Whom/What*
Corrected: "Inspects/construction operations (erosion control, Portland cement concrete paving, asphaltic concrete paving, painting, fencing, sign placement)/in order to

Why
ensure compliance with construction specifications/by

How
comparing visual observations with construction specifications and plans, and verbal instructions; with daily review by the supervisor."[6]

Whatever the task-oriented job analysis method used to generate task statements, results from the application of one or more of these methods serves as input to this step.

Once we have task data, we attempt to isolate the most important tasks performed on a specific job. For example, when comprehensive task inventories are used, it is necessary to identify only those tasks most critical to the job. Typically, we would use job agents' ratings of the tasks to make this determination. In our earlier discussion of task analysis inventories, we described how tasks are frequently rated on a variety of rating scales, such as frequency of performance, criticality, and consequence of error, to name a few. As we saw in Chapter 8, we can employ these ratings to isolate a job's most important or most critical aspects. There, we saw that one possible tack is to use statistical indices (averages, standard deviations, frequencies) created from the rating scales and decision rules applied to these indices to define important tasks. For example, we may require that all important tasks receive a minimum average rating on one or more of our rating scales. Tasks whose average ratings exceed our cutoff score are then selected. Or, we may choose only those tasks rated in the upper quartile (top 25 percent) of all task ratings given. Any one or more of several criteria can be used. The important point is that a standard is employed so that it is possible to objectively justify the selection of important job tasks.

Whatever the analyses used, the "most important" tasks are the basis on which inferences regarding selection instrument content rests (see Inference Point #2, Exhibit 8.1). The major idea behind the application of task analysis inventories is to define important job content. As illustrated in Exhibit 8.1, that determination serves as a guideline for defining requisite employee specifications and developing selection instruments for choosing among job applicants.

When work-oriented methods like FJA are used, it may not be necessary to choose a subset of important job tasks. Usually, such methods deal with significantly fewer tasks than those appearing on a task inventory. All tasks identified may represent important job duties; therefore, it may not be necessary to go through a task selection process.

2. Specifying KSAs Necessary for Successful Job Performance   Once critical job tasks have been identified, we are ready to specify the KSAs required for successful performance of these tasks. The remaining steps are applied only to those tasks deemed to be critical to the job. We cannot overemphasize the importance of producing accurate, complete KSA statements. As we will see, correct phrasing of the statements is *absolutely essential* to developing useful selection instruments. In general, the guideline for developing sound KSA statements is that it should indicate **what** the KSA is, to **what effect** or the **context** it operates, and the **level or degree of accuracy** it is used.[7] Several stages are necessary in appropriately specifying these KSAs.

Selection of a KSA Rating Panel   The first stage is to select a panel of job experts who can identify important KSAs. Such a panel may be composed of those who participated in a job's prior task analysis (Step 1) or formed from a new group of individuals. Listed here are several considerations that should be used in forming the KSA rating panel:[8]

1. *A panel of job experts (at least 10 to 20) is preferable over only one or two individuals.* Emphasis, however, should not be given exclusively to *numbers* of experts; we are more interested in the *quality* of their job knowledge and participation. If their assessments and inferences regarding KSAs are incorrect, resulting selection instruments will necessarily suffer.

2. *Characteristics we should seek in job agents (described earlier in Chapter 8) are also relevant in choosing the KSA rating panel.* These characteristics include the following: (a) participation should be voluntary, (b) incumbents should have performed adequately on the job in question, and (c) participants should have served on the job at least six months. In addition, women and minority group members should be represented on the panel.

Preparation of KSA Panelists   Whatever the data collection methodology, some form of orientation and training of KSA panelists will be needed. Panel members will likely require explanations as to what is meant by KSAs, why KSAs are important, and what their roles are to be in identifying and rating KSAs.

Collection of KSA data can take a variety of forms. Survey questionnaires completed independently by panelists can be used. Alternatively, group meetings of panel members can be convened, discussions held, and listings made of KSAs by panelists working independently within groups.

In specifying KSAs, panelists basically review the tasks identified from the job analysis and ask, "What knowledge, skills, or abilities are needed to perform each of these job tasks successfully?" Although the KSAs may not be written at the same level of specificity as task statements, several guides should be followed in their preparation. Again, the significance of the appropriate phrasing of the KSA statements is to facilitate making inferences concerning employee specifications for a job. Criteria that should be considered include the following:

1. *Panelists should have a clear understanding of what is meant by "knowledge," "skills," and "abilities."* Definitions of these terms can vary, but for our use the following definitions are appropriate:

   Knowledge: A body of information, usually of a factual or procedural nature that makes for successful performance of a task.[9]

   Skill: An individual's level of proficiency or competency in performing a specific task.[10] Level of competency is typically expressed in numerical terms.

   Ability: A more general, enduring trait or capability an individual possesses at the time when he or she first begins to perform a task.[11]

   Frequently, some analysts have difficulty in distinguishing between skills and abilities.[12] For purposes of preparing KSA statements, it is not absolutely essential that a statement is correctly classified as a skill or an ability. In fact, some job analysis systems ignore the specification of abilities altogether and simply focus on knowledge and skills. What is important for us is the statement itself; the statement, not its classification, serves as the basis for inferring selection instrument content.

2. *Statements should be written so they show the kind of knowledge, skill, or ability and the degree or level of each that is needed for successful task performance.* For example, in describing "typing skill," it should be specified if the typing skill requires typing tables of data composed of complex numbers within a specified time period, typing letters at a self-paced rate, or typing handwritten manuscripts at the rate of 40 words per minute.[13]

3. *Statements should be written so they specify the highest level that is required for the job.* For example, if statistical skills involving the calculation of correlation coefficients are needed to perform a task, there is no need to list an ability to count or a knowledge of basic mathematics as other KSAs. These would have been covered in the statistical skill statement.[14]

4. *Specific statements are preferable to broad, general ones that lack clarity as to what actual KSAs are required.* In preparing a statement it may be necessary to probe with job experts the exact nature, degree, breadth, and precision of a stated KSA. If, for instance, a statement such as "Knowledge of Mathematics" is offered, it may be necessary to ask "What kind?," "To what extent?," "To solve what types of problems?" Use of probing questions should permit the development of more complete and useful statements of what specifications are needed to perform a job.

5. *Although it may be possible to prepare a long list of KSAs for many jobs, emphasis should be given to identifying those that determine "successful" performance on*

the job. That is, KSAs rated as most important to job success by KSA-rating panelists should be emphasized.

6. *In preparing knowledge statements, adjective modifiers (for example, "thorough," "some") relative to the degree or extent of knowledge required should not be used.* Here are some examples of appropriate knowledge statements: "Knowledge of typing procedures for use with *Wordperfect* 6.0 word processing program on an IBM personal computer including setting margins, tabulating, automatic centering, making corrections, and storing files." "Knowledge of statistical principles, calculation on a programmable calculator, and interpretation of partial, simple, and multiple correlation coefficients."

7. *In preparing ability statements, adjective modifiers of level or extent of the ability required should not be used.* Vague adverbs implying some level of performance (for example, "rapidly," "effectively") should not be used to modify the action of the statement.[15] Ability statements should avoid confusing the action of the ability with the result of that action. For instance, look at this statement: "Ability to maintain accurate clerical accounting records." The results of the action "Maintain accurate accounting records" is treated as the action itself. The statement would be better written like this: "Ability to log accounting transactions in order to maintain accurate and up-to-date accounting records."

After all KSAs have been suggested, it is quite possible some statements will require editing. When editing is needed, the objective should be to specify important content in as much detail as possible and give examples where appropriate. Several illustrations of KSAs developed in previous job analysis studies follow:

Knowledge:
"Knowledge of building materials including the uses, storage, and preparation of materials such as aluminum siding, masonite, concrete block, and gypsum board."

"Knowledge of the development, scoring, and application of employee performance appraisal techniques such as behaviorally anchored rating scales, management-by-objectives, graphic rating scales, and mixed standard scales."

Skills:
"Skill in using a bank proof machine to process 50 checks per minute without error."

"Skill in typing business correspondence at 50 words per minute without error."

Abilities:
"Ability to testify orally as an expert witness in an employment discrimination lawsuit."

"Ability to use basic arithmetic to calculate flow of current through an electrical circuit."

With respect to abilities, a special comment is needed. Rather than developing abilities tailored to a specific job, predetermined abilities can also be rated using the Fleishman Job Analysis Survey (F-JAS) developed by Edwin Fleishman and his associates. (see Appendix 8A for a more complete description of the F-JAS.)[16] The F-JAS consists of rating scales designed to be used by an analyst in judging the extent to which each of 52 abilities (for example, Oral Comprehension, Perceptual Speed, Reaction Time) is required to perform a job or task. (An additional 20 research rating scales concerning interactive and social skills as well as specific knowledges, for example, electrical/electronic, mechanical, are presently under development.) Each ability is measured by a 7-point rating scale, with example behaviors describing various ability levels. The abilities appraised cluster into four categories: (a) mental abilities, (b) physical abilities, (c) abilities that require some action to be taken when specific sensory cues are present, and (d) abilities having to do with perceived incoming sensory information.

At the present time, application of the scales for selection purposes has been somewhat limited. Nevertheless, the measures hold future promise as a means for systematically measuring abilities across a wide spectrum of jobs.

Potential Problems in KSA Determination   The development and specification of KSA statements is not always as straightforward a task as we have presented it to be. Several different problems may occur. For example, if the KSA panelists serving as subject matter experts (SMEs) are not properly trained, they may produce very broad, undefined KSA statements that are relatively useless in developing a measure. KSA statements such as "Ability to Work under Stress" are not very helpful in understanding exactly what is required to be successful on the job. Such KSAs are very likely to be developed when SMEs simply want to take a job task and add words to it such as "Knowledge of," "Ability to," or "Skill at" in defining KSAs. For instance, the task of handling customer complaints becomes "Ability to Handle Customer Complaints." Not only is the KSA undefined and of little use in developing a predictor, but this process assumes a unique KSA for each job task. Realistically, a particular KSA may underlie many job tasks.[17]

3. Rating the Importance of Identified KSAs   For selection instruments to be useful, they should reflect the importance of different KSAs required for a specific job. That is, those KSAs that are most important for a job should account for more selection instrument content than less important ones. Determination of KSA importance is usually made by job experts giving ratings to the listed KSAs. Although KSAs can be judged on any number of factors, in general, there are three principal ways of viewing KSA importance to a job:

1. KSA importance in performing the job as a whole,

2. KSA importance for job applicants to have upon entry or when first hired, and

3. KSA importance in differentiating among applicants, that is, KSA importance in ranking candidates from good to poor versus KSAs considered as indicators of who should and should not be employed.[18]

Methods of Judging KSA Importance The methods used in rating KSA importance are similar to those used in assessing the importance of job tasks. That is, some form of survey questionnaire consisting of a listing of KSA statements and relevant rating scales is used by respondents (KSA panel members) in judging KSA importance. Actual questionnaire formats including rating scales can vary from one application to the next. However, most rating scales employed resemble one or more of the following examples:

A. How important is this KSA for acceptable job performance:
   0. Of No Importance
   1. Moderately Important
   2. Very Important
   3. Critical

B. Must a newly hired employee possess this KSA?
   1. Yes
   2. No

C. To what degree does this KSA distinguish between superior and adequate performance of newly hired employees?
   0. Not At All
   1. Moderately
   2. Considerably
   3. To a Great Degree

David Lewin has cautioned that unless certain criteria are considered in choosing KSAs for selection measures, it is possible to obtain a distorted picture of the actual importance of employee specifications. Therefore, he has recommended that all KSAs be evaluated on at least the following criteria:

1. *The percentage of an applicant population that can be expected to have a sufficient amount of a KSA to successfully perform the job.* The smaller the percentage of the available labor pool possessing the KSA, the more important it is to measure the KSA. However, if the KSA is learned on the job, it should not be assessed.

2. *The degree to which an employee with more of a KSA will be a better employee than one with less of the characteristic.* To the extent that more of a KSA is viewed as leading to better job performance, the more important is the KSA.

3. *The extent to which serious consequences could occur if a KSA is not examined.* If serious effects could occur, then more importance should be given.[19]

Example of KSA Importance Rating In order to get a better appreciation of the nature and application of a questionnaire utilizing such scales, an example may be helpful. The U.S. Office of Personnel Management has developed an experimental method for obtaining job expert judgments on the importance of KSAs.[20] Basically, its application resembles the methods we have described earlier. That is, a survey questionnaire is distributed to a panel of experts who make judgments regarding identified KSAs. Application of the questionnaire is designed to enable an analyst to determine (a) the degree to which differences in KSAs among employees are related to differences in performance effectiveness, (b) those KSAs required when beginning a job, and (c) the extent to which it is practical for applicants in the labor pool to possess necessary KSAs.[21]

4. Identifying Other Employee Specifications Necessary for Job Performance   Other than KSAs, jobs may require that applicants possess certain personal specifications which are necessary for adequate performance. Such specifications typically include the following types (a) physical requirements, (b) licensure/certification requirements, and (c) other/miscellaneous requirements.[22]

Physical Requirements   Physical requirements are those qualifications workers must possess in order to physically perform their jobs. These requirements may involve a number of physical abilities requiring specific levels of hearing, seeing, speaking, or lifting, to name a few. For example, the ability to lift and carry a specific amount of weight must be set for firefighters. Or, minimum levels of corrected visual acuity could be used in choosing nuclear plant operators who must visually monitor dials and meters at a distance. Operative or physically demanding jobs are likely to require more physical abilities for adequate performance than are managerial positions. Thus when setting employee specifications for operative positions, physical ability qualifications should routinely be considered. Care, however, should be taken to be sure that any specified physical abilities are essential to the job. Careful review will help to ensure compliance with the Americans with Disabilities Act (ADA).

The relevance of physical qualifications can be assessed in either of two ways: (a) listing and rating physical abilities required for a job or (b) rating a preestablished set of physical abilities. Where a listing and rating of physical abilities is concerned, the same methods described for generating and rating KSAs can be used. Emphasis is placed on developing observable and measurable statements descriptive of physical job requirements. Examples of such statements include:

"See well enough to read a voltmeter dial from a distance of five feet"

"Be strong enough to carry a 180 pound dead weight down a 50-foot ladder."

"Hear well enough to carry on a telephone conversation without electronic amplification."

Once listed, these characteristics can be rated using appropriate scales like those utilized in judging KSAs. For example, ratings of physical abilities might be based on variables such as importance or criticality to performance. Analyses can then be made of the ratings to determine those physical abilities most important for a job. Selection measures comprising important physical abilities can next be developed or chosen.

Rather than developing a rating scale of physical requirements, existing measures, such as Edwin Fleishman's *Physical Abilities* scales, can be employed.[23] The *Physical Abilities* scales are designed to examine the extent to which a job requires various physical abilities to perform it. The scales are a subset of Fleishman's *Job Analysis Survey* (F-JAS) mentioned earlier in the chapter and the appendix to Chapter 8. Use of the *Physical Abilities* scales consists of an analyst making ratings of a job on nine rating scales, one for each of nine physical abilities (for example, Static Strength, Dynamic Flexibility, Stamina). Each rating scale has a set of definitions that includes examples of tasks representing differing amounts of an ability. The scales are first applied by an analyst observing a job or specific job task. Each scale is then studied, and the job or task is rated by assigning the most descriptive scale point value (1 to 7) to the job.

The *Physical Abilities* scales have been used in several different selection situations. For example, they have been used for identifying the physical requirements of jobs such as firefighter, sanitation worker, and police officer.[24] Importantly, the scales have been found to serve as a valuable foundation for determining which physical abilities are critical to a job. From such a foundation, a rationale is created for developing selection instruments for measuring these critical abilities.

Licensure/Certification Requirements The next set of specifications that may be legally necessary for job performance are special licensure or certification requirements. If these requirements are critical in performing a job, then they are important specifications that should be used in selection. Examples of licensure/certification requirements are a driver's license, a teaching certificate, and a first-class Federal Communications Commission (FCC) radiotelephone license. Since there may be a variety of such requirements. a particular questionnaire or form for determining these specifications is not provided. Instead, provision can be made on a survey questionnaire for a job analyst to list any important licensure or certification requirements. Like tasks and KSAs, these specifications can be rated on a scale to determine their importance in performing the job under study.

Other Necessary Requirements It is possible for requirements other than KSAs, licenses, or certificates to be critical to a job. More than likely, these requirements will be unique to a job; but, if they are critical to job success, they should be evaluated. Examples of these "other" requirements might be ownership of specific tools, equipment, or a vehicle. Some jobs may also require a willingness on the part of an applicant/incumbent to work under unusual conditions of employment, such as willingness to relocate every six months, to work overtime, to work specific shifts, to travel five days out of seven. Again, these requirements can be listed and rated in terms of their significance to job performance.

5. Linking KSAs and Other Employee Specifications to Job Tasks   It is critical to a job analysis that a clear relationship between KSAs and other employee specifications be established with the most important tasks performed on a job.[25] Therefore, provision must be made for showing that *each* identified KSA is tied to *at least* one important task for which it is required. Tying KSAs and other specifications to job tasks is important for several reasons. First, KSA → job task link information may be needed in the legal defense of a selection procedure. The *Uniform Guidelines* state that a relation be shown between each identified KSA and a work behavior. By typing these specifications to job tasks, evidence can be provided on how these specifications are required on a job. Second, specifications can improve the efficiency and effectiveness of selection instruments. If unnecessary specifications are included in selection instruments, not only are these measures wasteful of resources, but they may not identify the most qualified job applicants. By linking KSAs with important tasks, it is possible to check the appropriateness of selection specifications and associated selection instruments.

Methods of Establishing KSA → Job Task Links   Documentation of KSA → job task links can generally be accomplished in either of two ways: (a) by having job analysts list job tasks associated with each identified KSA or (b) by constructing a Job Task × KSA rating matrix and then having job analysts rate the degree to which a KSA is necessary to perform each task successfully.[26]

Some job analysis methods use a task-listing approach. An incumbent studies a knowledge or skill, reviews the stated job tasks, and then lists those duties that require each knowledge or skill. If a duty cannot be found to justify a particular knowledge or skill, then that specification is removed as an important consideration in developing selection instruments.

The second method of linking KSAs and job tasks consists of pairing every KSA with every task. Job or subject matter experts judge the link between the various KSA → task pairs by using a rating scale. Any number of scales can be used. One form used by Irwin Goldstein and his colleagues is:[27]

2 = Essential   This knowledge or ability is essential to the performance of this task. Without this knowledge or ability, you would not be able to perform this task.

1 = Helpful   This knowledge or ability is helpful in performing this task. This task could be performed without this knowledge or ability, although it would be more difficult or time consuming.

0 = Not Relevant   This knowledge or ability is not needed to perform this task. Having this knowledge or ability would make no difference in the performance of this task.

Another scale is one based on an importance rating, where 0 = Not at All Important to 4 = Extremely Important. Table 9.1 shows the results of a partial

TABLE 9.1	MEAN RATINGS OF KSA IMPORTANCE TO TASK PERFORMANCE FOR THE JOB OF HR SELECTION ANALYST

Knowledge, Skills, Abilities (KSAs)

Job Tasks	Knowledge of Record-Keeping Procedures	Knowledge of Psychometrics	Knowledge of Applied Statistics	Knowledge of Test Validation Requirements	Knowledge of Development of Task Inventories	Ability to Give Oral Testimony in Court Hearings	• • •	Skill in Using Computerized Data Analysis Packages (e.g., SPSS)
1. Computes adverse impact statistics for selection measures	1.9	1.5	3.7	2.0	0.9	0.0		3.8
2. Constructs written tests for use in HR selection	3.1	4.0	3.5	3.0	2.7	0.0	• • •	1.7
3. Conducts job analyses on entry-level clerical jobs	3.3	3.0	2.9	3.7	3.9	0.0		2.1
4. Develops affirmative action plans and programs and monitors impact	2.4	1.2	0.7	1.2	0.8	1.0		1.3
				•				•
	•			•				•
	•			•				•
N. Maintains job applicant applications and selection test records	3.8	0.0	0.5	0.3	0.0	0.0	• • •	0.0

NOTE: The task and KSA statements have been abbreviated to conserve space. KSA by task ratings were made using the following scale:

How important is this KSA in performing this task?

0 = Not at all important
1 = Somewhat important
2 = Important
3 = Very important
4 = Extremely important

Job Task × KSA rating matrix for selected tasks and KSAs for the job of HR selection analyst. Only a portion of the tasks and KSAs are noted, but they serve to illustrate how the ratings are made. The numbers in the cells represent average ratings given by a group of panelists to the importance of KSAs. Greater importance of a KSA is shown with higher mean ratings. As can be seen, some KSAs are important for several tasks while others are critical to the performance of only one.

Licensure/certification and other characteristics that may be treated as employee specifications should also be tied to job tasks. When these specifications are used, they can be judged along with KSAs. However, in certain situations, it may not be meaningful to tie a specification to a job task. In those cases, reasons justifying their criticality should be listed. For example, if it is specified that a suitable applicant for a radio technician job should hold a first-class FCC radiotelephone license, it should be noted that this specification is required by federal law. The idea behind this documentation is to provide evidence that the specification is indeed required to perform a job.

Whatever the method chosen (listing or rating), the linking of KSAs, licensure/certification, and other specifications to job tasks is a critical step in job analysis. This linking step should not be taken lightly. The data obtained will ultimately help to justify the job analysis efforts and content of selection instruments. In addition, from the perspective of content validity, these links help to identify the tasks to be simulated by the selection measure. They provide job- and task-specific cues as to the design and content of selection measures that will have greatest fidelity with the job.

6. Developing the Content Areas of Selection Measures   So far, in developing appropriate employee specifications, we have studied the tasks performed on a job, the KSAs and other specifications needed for job performance, and the relationships between these specifications and job tasks. Our final step is to combine the task and KSA information in order to establish employee specifications to be covered in the selection instruments. Once established, selection instruments can be constructed or chosen to match these specifications. More is said about actually incorporating these specifications in selection instruments in the last section of the chapter. For now, however, we give attention to the development of content areas of the selection instruments. As we see, these areas are derived from the collected KSA information.

Important KSAs and Other Specifications   Table 9.2 presents a sample form for recording relevant KSA information. The form has been completed for the job we mentioned earlier, that is, HR selection analyst. Basically, the completed sheet summarizes the relevant task and KSA information collected about the job. It is this information that will be used in determining the content of the selection instruments. Let's see how each of the sections was prepared.

Column 1, "KSAs and Other Employee Specifications," lists all KSAs and other specifications identified by the panel of job experts. (The example KSAs have been abbreviated.) Of those noted, the KSAs and specifications most essential to successful job performance must be identified. The importance of these

TABLE 9.2	SUMMARY OF KSA TABULATIONS FOR DETERMINING CONTENT AREAS OF SELECTION INSTRUMENTS FOR THE JOB OF HR SELECTION ANALYST

	KSA Importance Criteria		
KSAs and Other Employee Specifications	**Mean Importance of KSA to Job Success**[a]	**Percentage Indicating a New Employee Should Possess This KSA**[b]	**Task Statement (Numbers) (and Mean Rating) for Which a KSA is Necessary**[c]
1. Knowledge of record-keeping procedures	1.6	50%	**2**(3.1), **3**(3.3), **4**(2.4),**N**(3.8)
2. Knowledge of psychometrics	3.0	100	**2**(4.0), **3**(3.0)
3. Knowledge of applied statistics	2.0	90	**1**(3.7), **2**(3.5), **3**(2.9)
4. Knowledge of test validation requirements	3.0	100	**1**(2.0), **2**(3.0), **3**(3.7)
5. Knowledge of development of task inventories	2.4	77	**2**(2.7), **3**(3.9)
6. Ability to give oral testimony in court hearings	1.1	30	None
•	•	•	•
•	•	•	•
•	•	•	•
N. Skill in using computerized data analysis packages (e.g., SPSS)	2.0	77	**1**(3.8), **3**(2.1)

NOTE: The KSA statements have been abbreviated in order to conserve space. KSA statements shown in bold are those selected for defining the content of selection measures.

[a] Important KSAs are those receiving a rating of 1.5 or higher on the following scale:
0 = Of No Importance
1 = Moderately Important
2 = Very Important
3 = Critical

[b] KSAs that should be possessed by newly hired employees are those chosen by 75% or more of the job analysts.

[c] Numbers *outside* of the parentheses are task statement numbers. Numbers *inside* the parentheses are average importance ratings of a KSA for that task's performance. The mean ratings are taken from Table 9.1.

specifications was assessed by two ratings: (a) KSA importance to successful job performance (from 0 = Of No Importance to 3 = Critical) and (b) necessity for a newly hired employee to possess a KSA (percentage of job experts indicating Yes or No). Other types of rating scales could have been used. What is critical is that we collect the judgments of experts on KSA importance and the necessity for new employees to possess these KSAs. Columns 2 and 3 present these data.

KSA Necessity for Task Performance   Column 4 of Table 9.2 draws on job task → KSA linking results shown earlier in Table 9.1. In Table 9.1, the job analysis panel's average ratings of KSA importance in performing each of the identified job tasks were presented. These ratings were based on a 5-point rating scale (where 0 = Not at All Important to 4 = Extremely Important). Now, suppose that any KSA with a 2.0 (= Important) or higher average rating for a particular task is judged as necessary for performance of that task. Column 4 in Table 9.2 summarizes those task statements (by number and mean importance rating) for which each KSA (noted in column 1) is important to task performance.

KSA Selections   At the conclusion of the summary analysis, those KSAs that should be included in the selection instruments can be identified. These KSAs will represent the content areas of our HR selection measures. Determination of these areas can be made by comparing the KSA ratings summarized on the rating form with preestablished rating criteria. For instance, in the example, the following rating criteria were used for defining important KSAs:

1.   A KSA must receive a mean importance to job success rating of 1.5 or higher (see column 2 in Table 9.2).

2.   The majority (75 percent or more) of job experts should agree that a KSA is necessary for a new employee to possess (see column 3).

3.   A KSA must be linked with an *important* job task for it to be considered. Application of this criterion has two requirements: (a) determination of important job tasks and (b) determination of KSAs tied to those important tasks. As we have seen, important job tasks can be identified in many different ways, such as those we discussed in our review of task analysis in Chapter 8. Once important job tasks have been identified, another determination has to be made. Here, KSAs important to job success must be identified. Usually, these determinations are made through ratings. In our example, for instance, KSAs important to job success were identified by those having an average importance to job success rating of 1.5 or higher. In column 2 of Table 9.2, we can see six KSAs met this criterion (KSA numbers 1, 2, 3, 4, 5, and N). Only one KSA (number 6) did not. Column 4 of Table 9.2 shows that each of the KSAs receiving an importance rating of 1.5 or higher was judged as necessary in performing at least one important job task. The KSA "Ability to Give Oral Testimony in Court" was not viewed as important to job success or necessary to the performance of any single job task.

TABLE 9.3	KSA CONTENT AREAS IDENTIFIED FOR MEASUREMENT BY SELECTION INSTRUMENTS FOR THE JOB OF HR SELECTION ANALYST

	Selection Instrument Content Area Criteria			
KSAs and Other Employee Specifications	Is This KSA an Important One?	Is This KSA Necessary for Newly Hired Employees to Possess?	Is This KSA Necessary for an Important Task?	Should This KSA Serve as a Selection Content Area?[a]
1. Knowledge of record-keeping procedures	Yes	No	Yes	No
2. **Knowledge of psychometrics**	Yes	Yes	Yes	**Yes**
3. **Knowledge of applied statistics**	Yes	Yes	Yes	**Yes**
4. **Knowledge of test validation requirements**	Yes	Yes	Yes	**Yes**
5. **Knowledge of development of task inventories**	Yes	Yes	Yes	**Yes**
6. Ability to give oral testimony in court hearings	No	No	No	No
•	•	•	•	•
•	•	•	•	•
•	•	•	•	•
N. **Skill in using computerized data analysis packages (e.g., SPSS)**	Yes	Yes	Yes	**Yes**

NOTE: The KSA statements have been abbreviated in order to conserve space.

[a] For a KSA to be chosen as a selection content area, each of the selection instrument content area criteria must be answered "Yes." These KSAs are identified in this column by a bold "**Yes**."

Content Areas of Selection Instruments Next, the KSAs that satisfy the rating criteria must be recorded. Content areas of the selection instruments are defined by those KSAs that meet *all* of the prescribed criteria. That is, (a) if a KSA is rated as important, (b) if it is believed new employees should possess the KSA upon job entry, *and* (c) if the KSA is linked to performance of an important job task, then it should be represented in the contents of the selection instruments.

Table 9.3 summarizes the final tabulations of the KSAs being evaluated. A review of this table shows that of the seven KSAs rated, five meet all of the rating criteria (that is, Knowledge of Psychometrics, Knowledge of Applied Statistics, Knowledge of Test Validation Requirements, Knowledge of Development of Task Inventories, and Skill in Using Computerized Data Analysis Packages (e.g., SPSS). Therefore, these five KSAs should be employed in defining the content of selection instruments for the job of HR selection analyst. Later, in the section of this chapter entitled "Incorporation of Employee Specifications in Selection Instruments," we look at how we might take these results and translate them into selection instruments such as tests, employment interviews, or application forms.

Determination of Employee Specifications: The PAQ Approach

Whereas the task analysis approach uses a panel of job experts to infer employee specifications, the Position Analysis Questionnaire (PAQ) takes a different tack. Under the PAQ approach, ratings of a job are made with the PAQ. Then, these ratings are compared with PAQ ratings of jobs in other organizations that are stored in the PAQ Services Inc. job databank. (The PAQ job databank consists of a national sample of PAQ ratings of 2200 jobs.[28]) Results of these job comparisons serve as the basis for defining employee specifications.

Several different types of information are useful in defining the requirements of a job. These types of information include (a) PAQ questionnaire items (or elements) and (b) PAQ job attribute data.[29]

PAQ Items as Employee Specifications

Individual items on the PAQ questionnaire can provide useful data for defining important employee specifications. When several raters are completing the PAQ for a job, average item ratings can be used to define the specifications.

An Example of PAQ Items as Employee Specifications   Let's look at an example of how PAQ items can be used to help set employee specifications. Suppose we are developing employee specifications for the job of senior shipping and receiving clerk. Initially, the job is analyzed by administration of the PAQ. As part of the analysis of the PAQ ratings, the 26 items that received the highest ratings in percentile terms are identified. Table 9.4 shows an abbreviated summary of the three PAQ items that received the highest ratings. From the table, it can be seen that the senior shipping and receiving job was rated higher than 99 percent of the 2200 jobs in the PAQ job databank on item 9 "Visual Sources of Job Information: Materials Not in Process." This score suggests that workers in the job obtain information from materials such as those being inspected or stored in a supply room or warehouse. Given the high rating assigned to the item, the ability to obtain job information by visually observing materials being inspected or stored appears to be important to the job.[30]

TABLE 9.4	SUMMARY OF THREE IMPORTANT PAQ ITEMS SERVING AS A BASIS OF EMPLOYEE SPECIFICATIONS FOR THE JOB OF SENIOR SHIPPING AND RECEIVING CLERK

PAQ Item Number	PAQ Item Name	Rating	Percentile
9.	*Visual Sources of Job Information: Materials Not in Process* Parts, materials, objects, etc. *not* in the process of being changed or modified that are sources of information when being inspected, handled, etc., such as items or materials in inventory, storage, etc.	5.0[a]	99
72.	*Transportation and Mobile Equipment: Powered Mobile Equipment* Operates movable vehicles not intended for highway use, for example, warehouse trucks, fork lifts, etc.	3.0[b]	98
132.	*Other Organizational Activities: Coordinates Activities* Coordinates, monitors, or organizes the activities of others to achieve certain objectives but does not have line management personnel, for example, legal adviser, administrative assistant, etc.	3.5[b]	96

SOURCE: Based on analyses obtained from PAQ Services Inc., Logan, Utah.

[a] Based on a rating scale where 1 = Nominal/Very Infrequent, 2 = Occasional, 3 = Moderate, 4 = Considerable, 5 = Very Substantial.

[b] Based on a rating scale where 1 = Very Minor, 2 = Low, 3 = Average, 4 = High, 5 = Extreme.

PAQ Job Attributes as Employee Specifications

A second type of PAQ employee specifications information is job attribute information. Under this approach, computerized analyses of *existing* data about worker qualifications are used to identify attributes associated with PAQ items. Once a job's important items have been identified, the associated attributes represent important employee specifications.

To better understand this method, we need to refer to some previous research on job attributes assessed by the PAQ. A list of 76 human attributes (49 of an "aptitudinal" nature and 27 of an "interest/temperament" nature) thought to be most relevant in HR selection was developed by Ernest McCormick and his colleagues.[31] Examples of these attributes are shown in Table 9.5. A sample

TABLE 9.5	SELECTED EXAMPLES OF 76 PAQ JOB ATTRIBUTES

Attributes of an Aptitude Nature

1. *Verbal Comprehension*—ability to understand the meaning of words and the ideas associated with them.
2. *Arithmetic Reasoning*—ability to reason abstractly using quantitative concepts and symbols.
3. *Perceptual Speed*—ability to make rapid discriminations of visual detail.
4. *Near Visual Acuity*—ability to perceive detail at normal reading distance.
5. *Manual Dexterity*—ability to manipulate things with the hands.
6. *Eye-Hand Coordination*—ability to coordinate hand movements with visual stimuli.
7. *Movement Detection*—ability to detect physical movement of objects and to judge their direction.
8. *Selective Attention*—ability to perform a task in the presence of distracting stimulation or under monotonous conditions without significant loss in efficiency.

Attributes of an Interest or Temperament Nature

1. *Working Alone*—working in physical isolation from others, although the activity may be integrated with that of others.
2. *Pressure of Time*—working in situations where time is a critical factor for successful performance.
3. *Working under Specific Instructions*—those that allow little or no room for independent action or judgment in working out job problems.
4. *Empathy*—seeing things from another person's point of view.
5. *Personal Risk*—risking of physical or mental illness or injury.
6. *Attainment of Set Standards*—attaining set limits, tolerances, or standards.
7. *Scientific/Technical Activities*—using technical methods for investigating natural phenomena using scientific procedures.
8. *Influencing People*—influencing opinions, attitudes, or judgments about ideas or things.

SOURCE: Based on Lloyd D. Marquardt and Ernest J. McCormick, *Component Analyses of the Attribute Data Based on the Position Analysis Questionnaire (PAQ)* (West Lafayette, Ind.: Occupational Research Center, Department of Psychological Sciences, Purdue University, 1973), pp. 34–38. Final report submitted to the Office of Naval Research, Arlington, Virginia.

of psychologists was asked to rate the relevance of each of these attributes to the items on the PAQ. (See Chapter 8 for a discussion of PAQ items.) From these ratings, a median rating for the relevance of each attribute for each PAQ item was obtained. The PAQ item–job attribute ratings permit some interesting descriptions. Once important PAQ items can be identified for a job, the attribute ratings represent a profile of the attributes or specifications necessary for performing the job successfully. But how can these attribute ratings be used to develop specifications for any particular job? The answer to this question lies with the administration of the PAQ itself. After PAQ ratings of a job are obtained, important PAQ items are specified. And, once the items characteristic of a job are known, it is simply a matter of identifying those attributes most relevant to performing these items. Thus these identified attributes serve as employee specifications to be used in HR selection.

An Example of PAQ Job Attributes Used as Employee Specifications We can also use the PAQ ratings of the senior shipping and receiving clerk job to illustrate the identification of job attributes to serve as employee specifications. Table 9.6 summarizes the results of the analyses of the PAQ data. This table shows only the two most important of a number of job attributes of an interest/temperament and the two most important of an aptitudinal nature that were identified from the PAQ data as being important in performing the critical aspects of the job. Referring to the table, the two most important attributes of an interest/temperament nature are (1) Working Under Specific Instructions and (2) Working with Tangible/Physical End Products. The two most important job attributes of an aptitudinal nature are (1) Depth Perception and (2) Mechanical Ability.

Beside each attribute in Table 9.6 is a percentile score. This score indicates the percentage of jobs (in the PAQ Services, Inc. databank) scoring lower on a specific job attribute than the job under investigation. For example, 78 percent of the jobs for which PAQ data are available scored lower than the job of senior shipping and receiving clerk on the attribute "Depth Perception." It appears "Depth

---

TABLE 9.6 SELECTED JOB ATTRIBUTE RATINGS OF AN INTEREST/TEMPERAMENT AND APTITUDINAL NATURE FOR THE JOB OF SENIOR SHIPPING AND RECEIVING CLERK

Attribute Number	Job Attribute	Percentile
	Attributes of an Interest/Temperament Nature:	
16.	*Working Under Specific Instructions* Working under conditions that allow little or no room for independent action or judgment in working out problems	80
21.	*Working with Tangible/Physical End Products* Working with material elements or parts that ultimately result in a physical product	76
	Attributes of an Aptitudinal Nature:	
48.	*Depth Perception* Ability to estimate depth of distances or objects (or to judge their physical relationships in space)	78
76.	*Mechanical Ability* Ability to determine the functional interrelationships of parts within a mechanical system	76

SOURCE: Based on analyses obtained from PAQ Services Inc., Logan, Utah.

Perception" is an important attribute for employees to have in performing the shipping and receiving clerk job. These attribute data will be used for identifying employee specifications from which selection instruments will be developed. More will be said about the choice of selection methods shortly; but keep in mind, judgments about selection methods are *not* eliminated. Inferences must still be made in choosing the specific instruments that will be used to measure the attributes identified as relevant to the job.

Obviously, the PAQ approach to deriving employee specifications is much easier, briefer, and less expensive than the task analysis approach outlined earlier. The essential requirement is the collection of valid and reliable PAQ data on the job under study. However, before sole reliance is placed on the PAQ method for developing selection instruments at least two issues must be resolved. First, the utility of this approach for developing appropriate selection instruments needs further investigation prior to widespread adoption. Second, certain legal questions that may arise regarding the development of employee specifications for a specific job (relative to many other jobs) need to be answered. For example, must each attribute be linked to specific job tasks? The PAQ does not provide such information. Irrespective of these issues, when a user decides to follow the approach, certain PAQ scoring arrangements must be made. As we mentioned earlier in our discussion of the PAQ in Chapter 8, necessary analyses can be coordinated through PAQ Services, Inc. of Logan, Utah, or, special software can be purchased for PAQ scoring on a microcomputer.

Incorporation of Employee Specifications in Selection Instruments

Now that we know what is required to perform a job (the employee specifications), how do we translate these specifications into selection instruments? The answer to this question can be very technical and detailed. The development of assessment methods requires the use of specially trained individuals such as industrial psychologists or test development specialists. Yet people working in HR management, like job analysts, can play an integral role in developing selection measures. The experience and information obtained during a job analysis is valuable for suggesting selection methods that reflect important KSAs and other employee specifications. To enhance the process of developing selection instruments, we need to look at several relevant considerations. It is the purpose of this section to indicate how identified KSAs can be incorporated into selection measures.

Development of a Selection Plan: The Task Analysis Approach

Before choosing selection instruments, it must be decided what the content of these instruments should be in order to assess important KSAs and other specifications as well as what type of instrument should be used to collect this information. This process of specifying content areas to measure KSAs as well as other worker requirements and choosing selection instruments to measure them is referred to as *developing a selection plan*. We can view the development of a selection plan as consisting of the following important phases:

1. Determining the relative importance of employee specifications, and

2. Choosing selection methods to measure these employee specifications.

Determining Relative Importance of Employee Specifications Previously, employee specifications such as KSAs important to a job were identified. For most jobs, however, it is unlikely that all specifications will be equally critical to job success. Some specifications will be more important than others, and it is these specifications that should play a more dominant role in determining the content and use of selection instruments. Before choosing tests or other selection devices, the relative importance of employee specifications that these measures are intended to assess must be determined.

Relative importance of employee specifications can be defined in a number of ways. For example, job experts might be administered a survey questionnaire to make relative determinations of KSA importance.[32] The questionnaire might consist of a listing of previously identified KSAs. Respondents could be asked to assign a relative importance weight, from 0 to 100 percent, to each KSA so that the sum of the weights totals 100 percent. The product of this process would be a relative weighting of the critical KSAs. Based on the example job of HR selection analyst, relative KSA importance weights might look as follows:

KSA	Mean Weight Assigned
1. Knowledge of psychometrics	25%
2. Knowledge of applied statistics	25%
3. Knowledge of test validation requirements	25%
4. Knowledge of development of task inventories	15%
• • •	• • •
N. Skill in using computerized data analysis packages (e.g., SPSS)	10%
Total Weight	100%

Rather than administering a separate questionnaire to define relative importance of KSAs, we could take another option. For instance, since we used a task analysis survey, we have already collected KSA and task importance information. We might assume that KSAs rated by SMEs as being more important for several job tasks should represent more selection measure content than KSAs judged as being less important for fewer tasks. Then we can simply multiply our *KSA importance* ratings by the *task importance* ratings for those tasks requiring the KSA. This calculation will yield points for each KSA. Relative weights can be determined by obtaining the proportion of each KSA's points for all total KSA points computed. The relative weight will indicate the extent of KSA coverage that should be present in the selection measure. By using a method such as this one, KSAs needed to perform a variety of important tasks will be represented in more selection measure content than KSAs used for only a few or less important tasks. Shortly, we will see the role these importance weights play in developing and choosing among predictors of job success.

Choosing Selection Methods to Measure Employee Specifications   A wide variety of means are available for assessing applicants. The remaining chapters discuss the nature and application of many of these methods. The choice of ways to assess relevant KSAs requires consideration of a number of factors. Inferences and judgments play an important role in deciding which means are best for measuring which specification. In considering the possible alternatives, a consultant, HR manager, or any personnel decision maker contemplating the choice of a selection measure should ask questions such as the following:[33]

1. *Have job applicants previously demonstrated successful performance of the tasks of the job?* If so, evaluation of past performance, such as thorough a biographical data questionnaire, may be appropriate.

2. *Can job applicants be observed performing the job or part of it? Is there a means for simulating the job in a test situation that is likely to require important behaviors as defined by the job? If so, is there a practical way of measuring performance?* When demonstration of successful performance is possible and measurable, a work sample test might seriously be considered.

3. *Would a written test be best for examining worker requirements in terms of eliciting desired reactions and practical scoring?* If "yes," a written test should be proposed.

4. *Would an opportunity for job applicants to express themselves orally through an interview cover job requirements that might go unassessed using other means?* In this case, a structured oral interview that can be objectively scored could be administered.

5. *Can the assessment method produce reliable and valid data for evaluating job applicants' possession of a KSA?* If not, the method should be dropped from consideration.

6. *Is it practical and within our resources to use a particular method for measuring a KSA?* If not, an alternative method may be considered.

John Campbell has illustrated how such a questioning approach might suggest alternative means for assessing the same KSA. For instance, suppose an ability such as "Ability to Relate Verbally to Persons of Varied Socioeconomic Levels" was found to be important for the job of social worker. Campbell notes that in studying this ability, several selection methods might be considered.

1. The applicant may have performed the same, or very similar, kinds of tasks in previous jobs. We could then try to find out how effective he or she was on that task in the past. . . .

2. If previous experience doesn't exist one might try to 'simulate' the task in some fashion. For example, one might contrive a role-playing situation and include as many of the real-life dynamics as possible. . . .

3. Several steps further removed from a direct sample of job behavior is the response of the applicant to open-ended questions when interviewed by members of the target group. [The interview] could pose hypothetical situations and focus on the content of the answers; or minority group interviewers could play the role of a hostile minority group member to see how the applicant handled the hostility. . . .

4. Some paper-and-pencil predictor could be used that poses a number of hypothetical situations for the applicant. . . .

5. One could use some test like Rokeach's Dogmatism Scale in the belief that it had something to do with how people relate to the problem of minority group members.[34]

Practical considerations will also play a role in choosing the type of selection measure to use. For example, if an organization has hundreds of applicants applying for a position such as that of a bank teller in a large urban bank, the possibility of using a multiple-choice paper-and-pencil test will be given very careful consideration because of its low cost and relative ease of administration to large groups of applicants.

An Example Selection Plan for the Job of HR Selection Analyst   Table 9.7 shows a selection plan for the example job of HR selection analyst. For illustration purposes, it is assumed only five KSAs are critical to this job. At the top of our plan, a variety of selection methods that could be used for this or any other job has been listed. You may be unfamiliar with some of these techniques; however, for our present purposes, complete understanding is not critical. We deal with many of these measures in subsequent chapters. What is important is understanding that we have chosen different methods to assess different KSAs. For purposes of illustration, we have purposely chosen a variety of methods to assess different KSAs. In practice, fewer methods would likely be used for any one job.

Let's study the example in more detail. With respect to the first two KSAs, "Knowledge of Psychometrics," and "Knowledge of Applied Statistics," we are dealing with specific bodies of information and knowledge in two related, technical fields. Because we are interested in the extent to which applicants possess knowledge of these technical areas, a written multiple-choice test is recommended. And, since the two content areas are judged to be equally important,

TABLE 9.7		

AN EXAMPLE SELECTION PLAN FOR THE JOB OF HR SELECTION ANALYST

KSAs to be Used in Selection	KSA Weight	Application Form	Biographical Data Questionnaire	Reference Check	Selection Interview	Work Sample Test	Assessment Center	Written Objective Test	Training and Experience Evaluation	Medical Examination	Other (specify)
1. Knowledge of psychometrics	25%							25%			
2. Knowledge of applied statistics	25							25			
3. Knowledge of test validation requirements	25	5%		5%	15%						
4. Knowledge of development of task inventories	15				10				5%		
N. Skill in using computerized data analysis packages (e.g., SPSS)	10	5				5%					
Total KSA Weight	100%	10%	0%	5%	25%	5%	0%	50%	5%	0%	0%

half of the exam should concentrate on psychometric issues, and the remainder should focus on applied statistics.

With respect to "Knowledge of Test Validation Requirements," we may be interested in applicants' knowledge and actual experiences with test validation matters. Three assessment methods are suggested. The application form could ask applicants for a list of previous experiences in test validation research. We may contact previous employers through reference checks to verify certain stated test validation capabilities. An oral interview could be used to let applicants describe in detail their experiences or, possibly, to respond to technical questions or situations concerning their knowledge of test validation research. Our selection method weights show that more emphasis should be placed on the interview than on the application form or reference check in appraising this KSA.

"Knowledge of Development of Task Inventories" could be assessed through a personal interview and a training and experience evaluation. In addition to questions about test validation, our selection interview should also incorporate questions involving applicants' knowledge about the development of task inventories. Training and experience evaluations should also play a role in the objective judgment of applicants' experiences with task inventories.

Finally, applicants' "Skill in Using Computerized Data Analysis Packages" should be evaluated. Relative to other KSAs, this skill plays a less critical role in accounting for job success as a selection analyst. An application form could ask for information on formal training, experience, or self-rated expertise with data analysis packages. Applicants would then be objectively scored on their skill in applying the packages to solve a realistic problem.

In addition to suggesting alternative methods for appraising job-relevant KSAs, a selection plan has an additional value. That is, the weights assigned to a selection method for each KSA are useful in determining the relative emphasis on the content areas of the measures. For instance, think back to the job of HR selection analyst. Let's say we decided we could use roughly 50 questions (because of time and cost considerations) to appraise the five important KSAs identified for the job. If 50 items represent the total number of items we can use, how do we determine the number of items employed to measure each KSA and the number included in each selection measure? We make these decisions by referring to the selection plan. Using the weights in the plan, we can see that half of the 50 items should be included in a written objective test. Of these 25 items (50 percent), roughly 12 should be devoted to measuring "Knowledge of Psychometrics" and the remainder directed toward "Knowledge of Applied Statistics." In contrast, approximately 25 percent of the 50 items should be allocated to an oral interview. Seven of these should concentrate on applicants' "Knowledge of Test Validation Requirements" and five on their "Knowledge of Development of Task Inventories."

As you look at our proposed selection plan, you may notice an interesting result. Our job analysis appears to have produced a selection program whose contents seem to reflect the major contents of the job. Selection measure/job content overlap is precisely what we want. The more we can ensure a match between content of our selection methods and demands of the job, the more confident we can be of the value of our selection program. Of course, we would not stop with a job analysis as final evidence of selection method usefulness; job analysis is really the first step. Where feasible, we would want to plan validation research studies to examine empirically how well our proposed measures actually predict successful job performance.

Development of a Selection Plan: The PAQ Approach

The PAQ approach offers a unique way of estimating job aptitude requirements to be used in HR selection. While drawing on a comprehensive analysis of a job by means of the PAQ, computerized statistical analyses are used to predict which types of paper-and-pencil tests may be most useful in selecting applicants for the job in question. The methods employed to identify the tests are somewhat complex and detailed. However, we can provide a general idea of what is done.

To convey the PAQ approach for developing selection instruments, we focus briefly on some previous research involving the PAQ.[35] Essentially, for a sample of 163 jobs, multiple correlations were developed between PAQ job dimensions (predictors) and nine worker aptitudes (criteria) as measured by the U.S. Employment Service's General Aptitude Test Battery (GATB). These nine aptitudes and a brief description of the tests used to measure them are as follows:

1. *Verbal Aptitude*—measured by a vocabulary test

2. *Numerical Aptitude*—measured by an arithmetic computation and reasoning test

3. *Spatial Aptitude*—measured by a test requiring the ability to visualize three-dimensional objects in three dimensions and the effects of moving the objects in these dimensions

4. *General Intelligence*—measured by the sum of the verbal, numerical, and spatial aptitudes

5. *Clerical Perception*—measured by a test involving the matching of names

6. *Form Perception*—measured by a test requiring the matching of tools and geometric forms

7. *Motor Coordination*—measured by a test requiring the placing of pencil marks in a set of squares

8. *Finger Dexterity*—measured by a test involving the assembly of washers and rivets

9. *Manual Dexterity*—measured by a test involving the movement of pegs on a board

The objectives of these analyses were twofold: (a) to determine how well the set of PAQ job dimensions predicted each of the nine aptitudes and (b) to develop prediction equations by which these aptitudes could be predicted from the PAQ job dimensions. On the whole, the job dimensions were strongly related to the aptitudes. Importantly, it was also possible to develop prediction equations for each GATB aptitude. Thus, for any new job, the PAQ could be applied, the job scored on the PAQ job dimensions, and the aptitudes important to job success identified. A user desiring selection measures for a job under study would choose measures (that is, GATB tests) of those aptitudes indicated as important for the job. Since the GATB tests are not available to private organizations, analyses similar to those outlined were conducted for 202 jobs on five aptitudes as measured by some commercially available tests.[36] Results similar to the GATB tests were found. These results suggest that the PAQ might be useful in identifying aptitudes for various jobs that are important for HR selection purposes.

Analyses of PAQ data to predict the best aptitudes for screening applicants for a job is an analysis option available through PAQ Services, Inc. Their vast databank of job information is used to identify these aptitudes. Once identified, those aptitudes suggested as important can be used as a basis for choosing (or developing) a test for use in selection.

Using an actual analysis, let's return to the job of senior shipping and receiving clerk. After analyzing the job by means of the PAQ, computerized analyses are used to score the job on relevant PAQ job dimensions. From these data, a series of GATB aptitude predictions are then developed; a portion of the actual results for the clerk's job are shown in Table 9.8. (We have presented only a portion of the most relevant information.)

In referring to the table, the "Mean Score" represents the predicted, average aptitude scores of incumbents working as a clerk. For each of these nine aptitudes, the data have been statistically adjusted so that the average score is equal to 100; roughly 50 percent of the working population would obtain a score of 100 or less. In general, the higher the mean score, the more important the aptitude to job performance.

"Predicted Validity Coefficient" in the table represents an estimate of the validity coefficient for each of the tests. These estimated validity coefficients are

TABLE 9.8   AN EXAMPLE OF PAQ ANALYSES USED IN DETERMINING APTITUDES IMPORTANT TO PERFORMANCE FOR THE JOB OF SENIOR SHIPPING AND RECEIVING CLERK

General Aptitude Tests (GATB)	Mean Score	Predicted Validity Coefficient	Probability of Use[a]	Predicted Low Score
General Intelligence	95.1	.19	.33	82.2
Verbal Aptitude	96.0	.10	.21	80.3
Numerical Aptitude	95.6	.18	.24	78.7
Spatial Aptitude	96.5	.19	.47<	79.3
Form Perception	97.0	.08	.36	82.9
Clerical Perception	98.3	.12	.34<	83.0
Motor Coordination	97.9	.15	.17	80.3
Finger Dexterity	91.2	.20	.21	73.3
Manual Dexterity	105.4	.16	.36<	85.6

SOURCE: Based on analyses obtained from PAQ Services, Inc., Logan, Utah.

[a] A < indicates an aptitude test that should be considered as a selection measure.

the validity that would be expected if a criterion-related validity study were conducted in which each GATB tests was used as a predictor and a generalized measure of job success (for example, supervisory ratings) was used as the criterion. The higher the predicted validity coefficient, the more likely the test (if used by itself) will be useful for selection decision making. Most of the predicted validity coefficients are low; however, Spatial Aptitude and Finger Dexterity are highest relative to the other aptitudes considered. Because many of the GATB tests are related with one another, it is not recommended to simply choose GATB tests that have the highest predicted validity coefficients. The next column of test information, "Probability of Use," provides more satisfactory information for choosing aptitude measures.

"Probability of Use" is a specially created index that indicates whether the U.S. Employment Service would be likely to use a particular aptitude test in developing a selection battery. The higher the score, the more likely a test would be incorporated. Tests with the highest estimates of use in selection are not necessarily those with the highest mean scores or predicted validity coefficients.[37] This is due to statistical reasons involving the interrelationships among the tests. High intercorrelations indicate that one test does not add very much to prediction over and above that which is predicted by the other test. When considering both the predicted validity coefficients and use in selection scores, Spatial Aptitude, Manual Dexterity, and Clerical Perception might be chosen for use.

Finally, the column "Predicted Low Score" shows potential cutoff or passing scores—at one standard deviation below the mean—to be used in selection. If the three passing scores specified by the tests had been used as the lowest scores for selecting applicants for the job of clerk, roughly one-third of the present employees would have been eliminated when they applied for employment.[38] Thus the "low score" gives a user some idea of the effect of possible passing/failing scores for the tests that might be used.

Another analytic option available from PAQ Services is the specification of commercially available tests that correspond to selected GATB aptitudes.[39] Exhibit 9.1 lists the commercial tests that match the aptitudes. Thus, once GATB aptitudes important for a job are identified, their commercial counterparts can be purchased and adopted for use. However, a note of caution should be given. The identified aptitudes should be treated as "hypotheses" of aptitudes thought to be important to performance on a job. Although the system may seem simple and straightforward, blind adoption of the results should be avoided, and caution in their interpretation should be exercised. For instance, Gary Brumback and his associates reported that the PAQ-GATB results were not helpful in identifying appropriate job aptitudes for the job of "fireman."[40] On the other hand, the PAQ option is appealing because it suggests that the PAQ can serve as the basis of the development of selection measures. Useful hypotheses regarding constructs or specific types of abilities (for example, numerical and verbal abilities) that are likely to be important to performance on a job can be developed. With these hypotheses in mind, predictions (based on GATB test scores) can be made about the specific types of tests to be chosen or developed for selection applications.

EXHIBIT 9.1	COMMERCIAL TESTS CORRESPONDING TO GENERAL APTITUDE TEST BATTERY (GATB) APTITUDES

GATB Aptitude	Commercial Test
General Intelligence	Wonderlic Personnel Test Adaptability Test Test of Learning Ability
Verbal Aptitude	Personnel Tests for Industry—Verbal Short Employment Tests—Verbal Employee Aptitude Survey—Verbal
Numerical Aptitude	Personnel Tests for Industry—Numerical Short Employment Tests—Numerical Employee Aptitude Survey—Numerical Arithmetic Index Flanagan Industrial Tests—Arithmetic Arithmetic Fundamentals Test
Spatial Aptitude	Revised Minnesota Paper Form Board Employee Aptitude Survey—Spatial Flanagan Industrial Tests—Assembly
Clerical Perception	Employee Aptitude Survey—Visual Speed and Accuracy Short Employment Tests—Clerical Minnesota Clerical Tests—Names

SOURCE: Based on Ernest J. McCormick, Robert Mecham, and P. R. Jeanneret, *Technical Manual for the Position Analysis Questionnaire (PAQ)* (Logan, Utah: PAQ Services, 1989), p. 53.

Other Approaches to the Identification of Employee Specifications

At the beginning of this chapter, we mentioned there are a number of approaches that might be used to identify the KSAs and other requirements of workers to perform their jobs successfully. We concentrated on only two of these (a) utilization of a task-based job analysis to identify critical job tasks and employment of SMEs to develop the requirements necessary to perform these tasks and (b) administration of the Position Analysis Questionnaire to specify the worker attributes needed for successful job performance. In this final section of the chapter, we highlight some additional methods that can also be adopted for developing employee specifications. Rather than developing tasks and then having individuals infer what worker characteristics are needed, these methods attempt to assess worker characteristics *directly*.

Job Element Method (JEM)   In the appendix to Chapter 8, we described the Job Element Method (JEM) approach to job analysis. As we mentioned, the philosophy behind the JEM is to impanel a group of SMEs and have them directly derive the elements and subelements (that is, KSAs and other personal characteristics) required of workers on the job. These elements and subelements serve as the basis for the content of predictors to be used in a HR selection system.

Skills and Attributes Inventory (SAI) Instead of having SMEs generate KSAs, Melany Baehr has developed a structured 96-item inventory that is designed for SMEs to rate the importance of an *existing* set of skills and abilities for job performance.[41] The inventory, called the Skills and Attributes Inventory, or SAI, is meant to be used for autonomous types of jobs for which direct supervision is infrequent. Although inferences are still involved with the use of the SAI (that is, estimating KSA importance), it is argued that by using a fixed set of KSAs, fewer inferences are needed on the part of SMEs (for example, stating precisely what are the KSAs required for the job). Use of a standardized set of attributes is also thought to reduce the chance that important attributes for a job are omitted.

Fleishman Job Analysis Survey (F-JAS) We described the F-JAS[42] in the appendix to Chapter 8; we do not repeat our description here. We simply mention it again for completeness of our discussion of KSA assessment methods. The F-JAS represents an important theoretically based method for assessing human abilities. It is one of the few such methods that is standardized and was developed from a theoretical framework of human abilities. Because of its significance, it is a direct KSA assessment method that is likely to see increased application in the future.

Threshold Traits Analysis (TTA) The final measure we mention is Felix Lopez's Threshold Traits Analysis (TTA).[43] The TTA is a questionnaire consisting of 33 worker traits (for example, Strength, Concentration, Oral Expression). It is completed by supervisors and/or incumbents serving as subject matter experts who rate the traits in terms of factors such as importance, uniqueness, relevancy, level, and practicality. As part of a larger system involving both worker job tasks and traits, the objective is to use the TTA along with other questionnaire measures to link specific worker traits with acceptable performance of important job tasks.

Conclusions

In the future, we expect measures that directly assess KSAs such as those just cited will be used more often to determine workers' job requirements. There are several reasons why direct KSA assessment procedures may be adopted. Some of these methods provide a more structured, standardized approach to the assessment of KSAs than those that rely simply on inferences by SMEs of KSAs from job tasks. Thus it might be hypothesized that direct KSA assessment methods offer a more complete, reliable evaluation of the KSAs necessary for job performance. Then too, for methods such as Fleishman's Job Analysis Survey that is tied to a theoretical taxonomy of human performance, we have a better understanding of the abilities that account for performance on a job.

Finally, by directly assessing important KSAs, one important inferential leap in the selection measure development process can be shortened. To the extent inferential leaps in the job analysis–selection measure development process can be minimized by use of comprehensive, standardized measures of worker requirements, it might be predicted that the likelihood of building more comprehensive, valid predictors of job performance will be enhanced.

To date, no such studies appear to exist which compare the effectiveness of the various methods that directly assess KSAs. Similarly, very few studies have apparently been conducted that contrast the direct KSA assessment approaches with those in which inferences are used to develop KSAs (for example, methods in which KSAs are inferred from job tasks). The few exceptions appear to be those studies conducted by Edward Levine and his colleagues.[44] Additional work is needed to determine if these methods can produce more effective predictors as well as a better understanding of the requirements for successful performance at work.

References

[1] Wayne F. Cascio, Applied Psychology in Personnel Management (Englewood Cliffs, N.J.: Prentice Hall, 1991).

[2] Edward L. Levine, Ronald A. Ash, and Nell Bennett, "Exploratory Comparative Study of Four Job Analysis Methods," *Journal of Applied Psychology* 65 (1980): 525.

[3] Frank J. Landy, "Selection Procedure Development and Usage," in *The Job Analysis Handbook for business, Industry, and Government*, ed. Sidney Gael (New York: Wiley, 1988), pp. 271–287.

[4] Edwin A. Fleishman and Marilyn K. Quaintance, *Taxonomies of Human Performance: The Description of Human Tasks* (Orlando, Academic Press, 1984).

[5] Gail M. Drauden, "Task Inventory Analysis in Industry and the Public Sector," in *The Job Analysis Handbook for business, Industry, and Government*, ed. Sidney Gael (New York: Wiley, 1988), pp. 1051–1071.

[6] Iowa Merit Employment Department, *Job Analysis Guidelines* (Des Moines: Iowa Merit Employment Department, 1974), p. 10.

[7] Irwin Goldstein, Benjamin Schneider, and Sheldon Zedeck, "An Exploration of the Job Analysis—Content Validity Process," in *Personnel Selection in Organizations*, eds. Neal Schmitt and Walter C. Borman (San Francisco: Jossey-Bass, 1993), pp. 3–34.

[8] U.S. Civil Service Commission, *Job Analysis for Improved Job-Related Selection* (Washington, D.C.: U.S. Civil Service Commission, Bureau of Intergovernmental Personnel Programs, 1976), pp. 1–2.

[9] Equal Employment Opportunity Commission, Civil Service Commission, Department of Labor, and Department of Justice, *Adoption of Four Agencies of Uniform Guidelines on Employee Selection Procedures*, 43 Federal Register 38,307–38,308 (Aug. 25, 1978); Edwin A. Fleishman, "Evaluating Physical Abilities Required by Jobs," *Personnel Administrator* 24 (June 1979): 83.

[10] Ibid.

[11] Ibid., See also Edwin A. Fleishman, "Evaluating Physical Abilities Required by Jobs," pp. 82–87.

[12] For an excellent discussion of the similarities and differences among knowledge, skills, abilities and other employee characteristics, see Robert J. Harvey, "Job Analysis," in *Handbook of Industrial and Organizational Psychology*, ed. Marvin D. Dunnette (Palo Alto, Calif.: Consulting Psychologists Press, 1990), pp. 75–79.

[13] Richard E. Biddle, *Brief GOJA: A Step-by-Step Job Analysis Instruction Booklet* (Sacramento, Calif.: Biddle and Associates, 1978), p. 27.

[14] Ibid., p. 28.

[15] Ibid.

[16] Edwin A. Fleishman, *Rating Scale Booklet F-JAS Fleishman Job Analysis Survey* (Palo Alto, Calif.: Consulting Psychologists Press, 1992).

[17] Landy, "Selection Procedure Development and Usage," p. 272.

[18] U.S. Civil Service Commission, *Job Analysis for Improved Job-Related Selection*, p. 23.

[19] David Lewin, "Cautions in Using Job Analysis Data for Test Planning," *Public Personnel Management* 5 (July–August 1976), 256.

[20] U.S. Civil Service Commission, *Job Analysis for Improved Job-Related Selection*, p. 24–30.

[21] Ibid., p. 27.

[22] Ibid.

[23] Edwin A. Fleishman, *Rating Scale Booklet F-JAS Fleishman Job Analysis Survey*.

[24] Ibid., p. 89. For a review of HR selection studies involving physical abilities in physically demanding jobs, see Michael A. Campion, "Personnel Selection for Physically Demanding Jobs: Review and Recommendations," *Personnel Psychology* 36 (1983): 527–550.

[25] U.S. Civil Service Commission, *Job Analysis for Improved Job-Related Selection*, p. 8; Equal Employment Opportunity Commission, et al., *Uniform Guidelines*, 43 Federal Register 38,302.

[26] Drauden, "Task Inventory Analysis in Industry and the Public Sector," pp. 1061–1064.

[27] Irwin Goldstein, Benjamin Schneider, and Sheldon Zedeck, "An Exploration of the Job Analysis–Content Validity Process." For a study of the reliability of skill-job task linkages, see Garry L. Hughes and Erich P. Prien, "Evaluation of Task and Job Skill Linkage Judgments Used to Develop Test Specifications," *Personnel Psychology* 42 (1989): 283–292.

[28] Robert C. Mecham, Ernest J. McCormick, and P. R. Jeanneret, *Position Analysis Questionnaire* Users Manual (System II) (Logan, Utah: PAQ Services, 1977), p. 37.

[29] P. Richard Jeanneret, "Computer Logic Chip Production Operators," in *The Job Analysis Handbook for Business, Industry, and Government*, ed. Sidney Gael (New York: Wiley, 1988), pp. 1335–1338. PAQ job dimensions can also be used in defining job requirements. They are not discussed here because requirements derived from PAQ elements tend to mirror those developed from PAQ dimensions.

[30] In addition to these items, another block of PAQ items is used to specify job requirements such as necessary job-related experience, time to learn the job, supervision received, and the number of nonsupervisory workers supervised. Results from these items are not presented in the current discussion.

[31] Lloyd D. Marquardt and Ernest J. McCormick, *Attribute Ratings and Profiles of the Job Elements of the Position Analysis Questionnaire* (PAQ) (West Lafayette, Ind.: Occupational Research Center, Purdue University, 1972); Robert C. Mecham and Ernest J. McCormick, *The Rated Attribute Requirements of Job Elements in the Position Analysis Questionnaire* (West Lafayette, Ind.: Occupational Research Center, Purdue University, 1969).

[32] Stephan J. Mussio and Mary K. Smith, *Content Validity: A Procedural Manual* (Chicago: International Personnel Management Association, 1973), pp. 24–27. For an alternative method of assessing KSAs, see Marvin D. Dunnette, Leatta M. Hough, and Rodney L. Rosse, "Task and Job Qualifications," *Human Resource Planning* 2 (1979): 37–51. In addition, other approaches to KSA determination are discussed in the last section of this chapter.

[33] U.S. Civil Service Commission, *Job Analysis for Improved Job-Related Selection*, pp. 10–11.

[34] John P. Campbell, "Comments on Content Validity: A Procedural Manual," unpublished report prepared for the Minneapolis Civil Service Commission as cited in Stephan J. Mussio and Mary K. Smith, *Content Validity: A Special Report* (Chicago: International Personnel Management Association, 1973): pp. 30–31.

[35] Ernest J. McCormick, Paul R. Jeanneret, and Robert C. Mecham, "A Study of Job Characteristics and Job Dimensions as Based on the Position Analysis Questionnaire (PAQ)," *Journal of Applied Psychology* 56 (1972): 347–368.

[36] Ernest J. McCormick, Angelo S. Denisi, and James B. Shaw, "Use of the Position Analysis Questionnaire for Establishing the Job Component Validity of Tests," *Journal of Applied Psychology* 64 (1979): 51–56. For an application of the PAQ in the context of HR selection, see J. Sparrow, J. Patrick, P. Spurgeon, and F. Barwell, "The Use of Job Component Analysis and Related Aptitudes in Personnel Selection," *Journal of Occupational Psychology* 55 (1982): 157–164 and J. Sparrow, "The Utility of the PAQ in Relating Job Behaviours to Traits," Journal of Occupational Psychology 62 (1989): 151–162.

[37] Ernest J. McCormick and P. Richard Jeanneret, "Position Analysis Questionnaire (PAQ)," in *The Job Analysis Handbook for Business, Industry, and Government*, ed. Sidney Gael (New York: Wiley, 1988), pp. 839.

[38] Additional information not shown in Table 9.8 is needed to determine the effects of the cutting scores; see Mecham, McCormick, and Jeanneret, *Position Analysis Questionnaire Users Manual* (System II), p. 40.

[39] PAQ Services, Inc., "GATB Employment Test Predictions Updated and Expanded," *PAQ Newsletter* (Logan, Utah: PAQ Services, March 1989), pp. 3–4.

[40] Gary B. Brumback, Tania Romashko, Clifford P. Hahn, and Edwin A. Fleishman, *Model Procedures for Job Analysis, Test Development, and Validation* (Washington, D.C.: American Institutes for Research, 1974), p. 17.

[41] Melany E. Baehr, *Skills and Attributes Inventory* (Park Ridge, Ill.: London House, 1971).

[42] Edwin A. Fleishman and Maureen E. Reilly, *Handbook of Human Abilities* (Palo Alto, Calif.: Consulting Psychologists Press, 1992).

[43] Felix M. Lopez, "Threshold Traits analysis System," in *The Job Analysis Handbook for Business, Industry, and Government*, ed. Sidney Gael (New York: Wiley, 1988), pp. 880–901.

[44] Levine et al., "Exploratory Comparative Study of Four Job Analysis Methods" and Edward L. Levine, Ronald A. Ash, Hardy Hall, and Frank Sistrunk, "Evaluation of Job Analysis Methods by Experienced Job Analysts," *Academy of Management Journal* 26 (1983): 339–348.

IV

Predictors of Job Performance

Predicting future events is a common part of our lives. We have all tried to guess the winner of a sporting event, who might ask us out, or what the questions on our next test may be. Some people, like fortune-tellers, meteorologists, stock brokers, and selection specialists also make prediction a large part of their jobs. They use some limited amount of currently available information to make judgments about future events. While all four of these occupations could use our help in improving the accuracy of their predictions, we are predicting that this section will be of more value to selection specialists than to the other three.

The information that the selection specialist uses to predict future job performance can be obtained from several different types of devices: application forms, interviews, tests, work simulations, and so on. Each of the chapters of this section treats a major type of device in detail. Our viewpoint is that if selection devices are properly developed, administered, scored, and interpreted, the information about applicants that is obtained and used in predicting job performance improves. As this happens, the success rate of prediction should also get better. For each of the chapters, the major objectives are as follows:

1. Describe the appropriate information about applicants that may be gathered by each type of selection instrument,

2. Point out the important measurement principles of each type of instrument, and

3. Present specific points about the proper development and use of each type of instrument.

10

Application Forms, Training and Experience Evaluations, and Reference Checks

Application Forms

Nature and Role of Application Forms in Selection

When applicants apply for a job in an organization, they are usually asked to complete an *application form* or *blank*. Practically all organizations utilize employment applications as a method for collecting pre-employment information to assess applicants' likelihood of success with an organization. Estimates show that over one billion application forms and résumés are screened each year by organizations in the United States.[1]

An application form typically consists of a series of questions designed to provide information on the general suitability of applicants for jobs to which they are applying. Questions are usually asked regarding applicants' educational background and previous job experiences as well as other areas that may be useful in judging candidates' ability to perform a job. The form itself may be brief and general or long and detailed. Whatever its exact nature, its principal purpose is to serve as a pre-employment screen regarding the future job success of job applicants. As such, it serves as a means for (a) deciding if applicants meet the minimum requirements of a position and (b) assessing and comparing the relative strengths and weaknesses of individuals making application.

When taken at face value, an application form may appear to be rather innocuous; it may seem to offer no real threat to any particular group of individuals. However, when used as a basis for selecting among job applicants, these forms can provide information that unfairly discriminates against some. For example, when application information that may be unrelated to a person's ability to perform a job (such as gender, ethnicity, age) is used to screen applicants, that application data can result in discriminatory selection practices.

Because application forms have been used to discriminate unfairly against protected groups, federal and state laws (such as Title VII of the 1964 Civil Rights Act and Fair Employment Practice statutes) have been passed to prevent discrimination by means of pre-employment inquiries. Further, the Equal Employment Opportunity Commission (EEOC) has adopted the view that application forms must conform to both the spirit and letter of Title VII. The EEOC's *Guide to Pre-Employment Inquiries* specifies the following:

> Employment application forms . . . have traditionally been instruments for eliminating, at an early stage, 'unsuited' or 'unqualified' persons from consideration for employment and often have been used in such a way as to restrict or deny employment opportunities for women and members of minority groups.[2]

Because of the widespread use of applications and the legal implications these forms hold for organizations, it is important that we look at some of the issues involved in the development and use of application forms.

Legal Implications of Application Forms

Some employers may think it desirable to obtain as much information as possible on the application form. With a lot of information available, it would seem easier to set up an initial screen for choosing among applicants. However, this "the more information, the better" mentality may create major problems for an employer. As we have said, federal and state laws affect the kinds of information that can be obtained on the application blank. Under these laws, it is generally assumed that *all* questions asked on an application form are used in making hiring decisions. Therefore, under a charge of discrimination, the burden of proof may be on the employer to demonstrate that *all* application questions are indeed fair and not discriminatory.

The law, according to EEOC pre-employment guidelines, cautions against questions on the application form that (a) disproportionately screen out minority group members or members of one sex, (b) do not predict successful performance on the job, or (c) cannot be justified in terms of business necessity.[3] In judging the suitability of a potential item, an employer should thoroughly review each question. The rating criteria listed in Table 10.1 are useful for examining the appropriateness of application form questions.

An employer has the right to establish and use job-related information for identifying the individuals qualified for a job. With respect to an employment application, an organization is free to ask almost any question it regards as important in selecting among job applicants. However, as we discussed in Chapter 2, if a complainant can show adverse impact resulting from selection practices, then the burden of proof is on the employer to demonstrate that the information provided by the application questions is not used in a discriminatory manner prohibited by law. Most often a complainant will argue that application items result in (a) *adverse impact* or (b) *disparate treatment*. Under *adverse impact*, members of a protected minority group may respond

TABLE 10.1	QUESTIONS TO BE ASKED IN EXAMINING APPROPRIATENESS OF APPLICATION FORM QUESTIONS

Yes	No	Question
[ ]	[ ]	1.Will answers to this question, if used in making a selection decision, have an adverse impact in screening out minorities and/or members of one sex (that is, disqualify a significantly larger percentage of members of one particular group than of others)?
[ ]	[ ]	2.Is this information really needed to judge an applicant's competence or qualifications for the job in question?
[ ]	[ ]	3.Does the question conflict with EEOC guidelines or recent court decisions?
[ ]	[ ]	4.Does the question conflict with the spirit and intent of the Civil Rights Act or federal and state statutes?
[ ]	[ ]	5.Does the question constitute an invasion of privacy?
[ ]	[ ]	6.Is there information available that could be used to show that responses to a question are associated with success or failure on a specific job?

SOURCE: Questions 1 and 2 are based on Equal Employment Opportunity Commission, *EEOC Guide to Pre-Employment Inquiries* (Washington, D.C.: Equal Employment Opportunity Commission, August 1981); questions 3 through 6 are based on Ernest C. Miller, "An EEO Examination of Employment Applications," *Personnel Administrator* 25 (March 1981): 68-69.

differently to a question than members of a majority group. For example, in response to the item "Do you own your home," whites may respond "yes" in greater proportion than blacks. If persons responding "no" are screened out of employment consideration, then the question will have an adverse impact on minority applicants. When *disparate treatment* is involved, different questions may be posed for different groups. For instance, it is disparate treatment if only women (not men) are asked "Do you have children under school age and, if so, what arrangements have you made concerning child care?"

In response, an employer has two basic options to show that application form items do not unfairly discriminate among applicants. An employer can either demonstrate (usually with statistics) that (a) the questions being challenged are predictive of job success or (b) the questions represent a bona fide occupational requirement. An item on an application form is justified as being a bona fide occupational requirement by showing "that it is necessary to the safe and efficient operation of the business, that it effectively carries out the purpose it is supposed to serve, and that there are no alternative policies or practices which would better or equally well serve the same purpose with less discriminatory impact."[4]

Selecting Application Form Content

For an organization to request information other than that necessary for initially judging applicants' qualifications to perform a job is to open itself to the possibility of a discrimination charge. Thus it is in the interest of an organization to carefully review the necessity of information requested on the application form.

What information is necessary? How does an organization decide if the information is in fact essential? Obviously, these are important question answers depend on the job for which an application form is going to be used. Using job analysis methods like those discussed in Chapter 8 we can identify items that could be useful in screening applicants for a job. However, job analysis alone will not completely resolve which items should be included on an application form. Once we have identified the possible questions to appear on the form, each one should also be reviewed for its fairness and usefulness.

In reviewing application form items, employers should first research the fair employment practice laws that may exist for their state. (Some states do not have laws regulating pre-employment inquiries. At the time of this writing, these include Alabama, Arkansas, Georgia, and Mississippi.) State fair employment practice laws determine the legal status of pre-employment inquiries, such as application form items, used by employers doing business within the state. One excellent source for review is *The Commerce Clearing House Employment Practice Guide*, Volume 3, State FEP Laws. A state-by-state review is important because what is legal in one state may be illegal in another. Twenty-two states have published lists of questions that are considered permissible or impermissible.[5] Furthermore, where state laws and regulations exist, the EEOC gives them more weight than federal standards, which are generally more permissive.

Using the rating criteria noted earlier in Table 10.1 and any state fair employment practice laws, employers should carefully review all items for their necessity and possible discriminatory impacts. For some questions under review (such as ethnicity), the answer may be obvious. For others, an appearance of discriminatory impact may not be so evident; yet, possible discriminatory effects may be present. Using principally the EEOC's *Guide to Pre-Employment Inquiries* as a basis, we review, some of the more frequently used content categories of application form items.[6] Although our review is not an exhaustive treatment of all possible types of items that could be used in each state, it does provide some guides to consider in preparing or revising an application form to be used in selection.

Name   Questions about the national origin, ancestry, or descent of an applicant's name should be avoided. Specific inquiries into the previous name of an applicant where a name has been changed in court or by marriage, or inquiries into the preferred title of an applicant such as Miss, Mrs., or Ms. should not be made.

Marital Status, Children, Child Care   Questions about marital status, pregnancy, and number and ages of children have been found to discriminate against women. It has also been found to be illegal to have different hiring policies for women and men with preschool children. Information on child care arrangements should not be asked solely of women.

Ethnicity   Items should not appear on the application form that request information concerning ethnicity. Similarly, items that could be construed as relating to an applicant's ethnicity (for example, hair and eye color) should not be asked unless they can be shown to be necessary requirements for the job.

Gender   More states expressly prohibit questions associated with applicant gender than any other topical area of the application.[7] As with questions related to ethnicity, questions involving an applicant's gender should also be avoided. These questions should only be used if shown to be a bona fide occupational requirement of the job.

Military Experience   Since minorities tend to have higher rates of undesirable discharges, general questions about an applicant's military service dates, type of discharge, and discipline received while in the service can prove to be discriminatory. However, questions that address specific skills or educational/training experiences acquired through military service that are relevant to the job may be posed.

Age   The Age Discrimination in Employment Act of 1967, as amended in 1986, prohibits discrimination in employment against people 40 years of age or older. An employer may ask for job applicants to give their ages on a job application, as long as the reason for asking their ages is not discriminatory. However, such pre-employment inquiries are carefully scrutinized by the EEOC and the courts for age discrimination. If an employer chooses to include a question on the application form that asks applicants' ages and if that information is not going to be applied in a discriminatory fashion, it should be noted on the application form that age information will not be used for a discriminatory purpose.[8] In general, any requirement or request that an applicant indicate his or her age (by directly stating, giving date of birth, or having to produce a birth certificate) will likely be viewed as deterring older applicants from applying for a job. Thus questions related to the specific age of an applicant usually should be avoided. On the other hand, statements can be made that hiring is subject to verification of minimum legal age or that, if hired, the applicant must furnish proof of age.

Work Availability on Holidays/Weekends   Many employers feel it is important to know if an applicant is available for work on weekends or holidays. However, the EEOC notes that employers have an obligation to accommodate the religious preferences of applicants. Therefore, the EEOC has concluded that pre-employment inquiries focusing on an applicant's availability may have an exclusionary effect on employment opportunities for some individuals holding certain religious beliefs. The EEOC states:

> Questions relating to availability for work on Friday evenings, Saturdays or holidays should not be asked unless the employer can show that the questions have not had an exclusionary effect on its . . . applicants who would need an accommodation for their religious practices, that

the questions are otherwise justified, and that there are no alternative procedures which would have a lesser exclusionary effect.[9]

It is permissible to inform the applicant of the organization's work schedule.

Height and Weight   Height or weight requirements are illegal if (a) they lead to a disproportionate number of minority members (such as Asian Americans) being screened out of a job, and (b) they are not related to job performance. In some cases where minimum height and weight requirements are used, higher proportions of white American males may be hired, since they tend to be larger on the average than women and some minority group members (for example, Asian-Americans). Questions regarding height and weight should only be asked if an employer can demonstrate minimum height/weight requirements are necessary for successful job performance.

Friends/Relatives Working for Employer   Information on friends or relatives working for an employer is often requested of applicants. However, if this information suggests a preference for the friends and relatives of present employees and the makeup of the work force is such that hiring of relatives and friends would reduce employment opportunities for women or minorities, then the information would be illegal. For example, if the racial and sexual composition of a job for which applications are being taken is principally white males, then questions on the application concerning friends or relatives currently employed might be viewed as discriminatory. The supposition would be that the question would be used to "screen in" individuals similar to those currently employed, that is, white males. (It should be noted that antinepotism policies of firms have generally been found to be legal.)

Sometimes, firms request information on the name of a relative to contact in case of an emergency. In some states, this information is not permissible. This type of information could be collected after employment.

Arrest/Conviction Records   Since some minority group members are arrested in higher proportion than their numbers in the population, the EEOC has ruled that arrest information has an unequal effect on the hiring of members of these groups. As a result, these minority group members have fewer employment opportunities and, therefore, arrest information is illegal. In developing an application form, an employer should omit any questions concerning arrest records.

Questions involving *conviction* records as opposed to arrest records have a different legal stance. An employer can give consideration to the relationship between an applicant's conviction for a crime and his or her suitability for a specific job. If conviction data are used, an employer should also collect and consider information on the number, recentness, and type of convictions of the applicant. Convictions cannot serve as an absolute bar to employment. The EEOC has also noted that if information on convictions is requested on the application form, the form should have a statement that a conviction record is not necessarily a bar to employment. Factors such as age at the time of the offense, rehabilitation, seriousness of the offense, and nature of the job and its relation to the nature of the conviction(s) should also be taken into consideration in judging the applicant. Some states require that denial of employment due to a prior conviction must be justified to the applicant in the form of a letter giving reasons for denial of employment.[10]

Citizenship   The EEOC *Guidelines on Discrimination Because of National Origin* specify that consideration of job applicants' citizenship *may* indicate discrimination on the basis of national origin.[11] The law protects both citizens and *noncitizens* with legal authorization to work in the United States from discrimination due to race, ethnicity, gender, religion, or national origin. Thus questions concerning citizenship *may* raise the possibility of charges of discrimination due to national origin. The Immigration Reform and Control Act of 1986 contains specific language regarding the employment of citizens, impending citizens, and legal aliens. The act has a bearing on the questions that can be asked on the application form concerning citizenship and the use of citizenship information in selection. In addition, questions on the application that involve citizenship status must be carefully worded in order to avoid discrimination due to national origin covered by the Civil Rights Act of 1964. An acceptable question is one such as "Can you, after employment, provide proof of your legal right to work in the United States?"

The categories described provide a summary of some of the major issues involved in developing various types of application form items. As we have stated, it is the questions themselves that determine the usefulness and legality of the application form. Of critical importance is the phrasing of the items that make up the questions on the form. A miscast question can undermine the usefulness and legality of the form and leave an organization vulnerable to a lawsuit.

Using the research of a number of writers, we have summarized in Table 10.2 some acceptable and unacceptable example application form questions based on some of the legal issues discussed earlier. In reviewing the table, several points should be kept in mind. First, an emphasis is placed on phrasing items to elicit information that is related to the specific job for which the application form is being used. Thus, as Ernest Miller suggests, simple rephrasing using appropriate job-related language can eliminate some "inappropriate" items. For example, a form could ask "Do you have any physical defects or impediments that might in any way hinder your ability to perform the job for which you have applied?" rather than "Do you have any physical defects?"[12] Second, an item that might be unacceptable in some situations could be acceptable in others. For example, an item may be usable if it can be shown that it provides information useful in predicting the success of a new employee on the job for which application is being made. Or, an item may provide information that represents a bona fide occupational requirement for a specific job. Further, the example items listed are not an exhaustive treatment of what should and should not be asked on the application form. The items shown are meant to be illustrative of what can be used. Thus the examples serve as a guide to planning, developing, and using application forms.

Since laws exist that affect the content of application forms, it might be assumed that most forms currently used by companies would comply with the

TABLE 10.2	EXAMPLES OF ACCEPTABLE AND UNACCEPTABLE QUESTIONS ASKED ON APPLICATION FORMS		
Subject of Question	**Acceptable Questions**	**Unacceptable Questions**	**Comments**
Name	"What is your name?" "Have you worked for this company under another name?" "Have you used a name (such as an assumed name or nickname) the company would need to know to check your previous work and educational records? If so, please explain."	"What was your maiden name?"	Questions about an applicant's name that may indicate marital status or national origin should be avoided.
Age	"Are you at least 18 years old?" "Upon employment, all employees must submit legal proof of age. Can you furnish proof of age?"	"What is your date of birth?" "What is your age?"	The Age Discrimination in Employment Act of 1967, and amended in 1986, prohibits discrimination against individuals 40 years of age and older. A request for age related data may discourage older workers from applying. Age data should only be collected when it can be shown to be a bona fide occupational requirement.
Race, Ethnicity, and Physical Characteristics	"After employment, a photograph must be taken of all	"What is your race?" "What is your	Information relative to physical characteristics may be associated with

TABLE 10.2 (CONTINUED)

Subject of Question	Acceptable Questions	Unacceptable Questions	Comments
Race, Ethnicity, and Physical Characteristics (continued)	employees. If employed, can you furnish a photograph?" "After employment, all employees are required to submit a physical description (eye, hair, height, and weight)." "Do you read, speak, or write a foreign language?"	height and weight?" "Would you please submit a photograph with your application for identification purposes?" "What is the color of your hair? Your eyes? "What language do you commonly use?" "How did you acquire your ability to read, write, or speak a foreign language?"	sexual or racial group membership. Thus, unless such information can be shown to be related to job performance, the information may be treated as discriminatory.
Religion	A statement may be made by the employer of the days, hours, and shifts worked.	"What is your religious faith?" "Does your religion keep you from working on weekends?"	Questions that determine applicants' availability have an exclusionary effect because of some people's religious practices. Questions should only be used if they can be shown not to have an exclusionary effect and are justified by business necessity.
Gender, Marital Status, and Family	"If you are a minor, please list the name and address of a parent or guardian." "Please provide the name, address,	"What is your sex? "Describe your current marital status." "List the number and ages of your children."	Direct *or* indirect questions about marital status, children, pregnancy, and childbearing plans frequently discriminate against women and may be a violation of Title VII.

(continued)

| TABLE 10.2 | (CONTINUED) | | |

Subject of Question	Acceptable Questions	Unacceptable Questions	Comments
Gender Marital Status, and Family (continued)	and telephone number of someone who should be con- tacted in case of an emergency."	"If you have children, please describe the provisions you have made for child care." "With whom do you reside?" "Do you have any dependents or relatives who should be contacted in case of an emergency?" "Do you prefer being referred to as Miss, Mrs., or Ms.?"	
Physical Health	"Do you have any physical condition or handicap that may limit your ability to perform the job for which you are applying? If so, please describe." "Are you willing to take a physical exam if the nature of the job for which you are applying requires one?"	"Do you have any physical disabilities, defects, or handicaps?" "How would you describe your general physical health?" "When was your last physical exam?"	A blanket policy excluding the handicapped is discriminatory. Where physical condition is a requirement for employment, employers should be able to document the business necessity for questions on the application form relating to physical condition.
Citizenship[a]	"If you are offered and accept a job, can you submit proof of your legal right to work in the U.S.?" "Do you have the	"Of what country are you a citizen?" "Please list your birthplace."	Consideration of an applicant's citizenship *may* constitute discrimination on the basis of national origin. The law protects citizens

[a] The Immigration Reform and Control Act of 1986 contains specific language regarding the employment of cit-izens, impending citizens, and legal aliens. The act has a bearing on the questions that can be asked on the appli-cation form concerning citizenship and the use of citizenship information in selection. In addition, questions on the application that involve citizenship status must be carefully worded in order to avoid discrimination due to national origin covered by the Civil Rights Act of 1964.

TABLE 10.2 (CONTINUED)

Subject of Question	Acceptable Questions	Unacceptable Questions	Comments
Citizenship[a] (continued)	legal right to live and work in the U.S.?"		*and* noncitizens with legal authorization to work in the U.S. from discrimination on the basis of sex, race, color, religion, or national origin.
Military Service	"Please list any specific educational or job experiences you may have acquired during military service that you believe would be useful on the job for which you are applying."	"Please list the dates and type of discharge you may have received from military service."	Minority service members have a higher percentage of undesirable military discharges. A policy of rejecting those with less than an honorable discharge may be discriminatory. This information may discourage minorities from applying for employment.
Arrest and Conviction Records	"Have you ever been convicted of a felony, or, during the last two years, of a misdemeanor which resulted in imprisonment? If so, what was the felony or misdemeanor? (A conviction will not necessarily disqualify you from the job for which you are applying. A conviction will be judged on its own merits with respect to time, circumstances, and seriousness.)"	"Have you ever been arrested?" "Have you ever been convicted of a criminal offense?"	Federal courts have held that a conviction for a felony or misdemeanor should not automatically exclude an applicant from employment. An employer can consider the relationship between a conviction and suitability for a job. When questions are used, there should be a statement that factors like age at time of offense, seriousness of

(continued)

TABLE 10.2 (CONTINUED)

Subject of Question	Acceptable Questions	Unacceptable Questions	Comments
Arrest and Conviction Records (continued)			violation, and rehabilitation will be considered.
Hobbies, Clubs, and Organizations	"Do you have any hobbies that are related to the job for which you are making application?" "Please list any clubs or organizations in which you are a member that relate to the job for which you are applying."	"Please list any hobbies you may have." "Please list all clubs or other organizations in which you are a member."	Applicant information on membership in clubs and organizations can be discriminatory. If membership is associated with the age, sex, race, or religion of the applicant, the data may be viewed as discriminatory. If questions on club/ organizational memberships are asked, a statement should be added that applicants may omit those organi- zations associated with age, race, sex, or religion.
Education	"Did you graduate from high school? From college?" "While in school, did you partici- pate in any activities or clubs which are related to the job for which you are applying?"	"When did you attend high school? College?" "In what extracurricular activities or clubs did you participate while in school?"	On the average, minority members tend to have lower levels of education than nonminority group members. Where educational requirements disqualify minority members at a higher rate than nonminority group members and it cannot be shown that the educational requirement is related to successful

| **TABLE 10.2** | (CONTINUED) | | |

Subject of Question	Acceptable Questions	Unacceptable Questions	Comments
Education (continued)			job performance, the courts have viewed educational requirements as discriminatory.
Credit Rating	None.	"Do you own your own car?" "Do you own or rent your residence?"	Use of credit rating questions tends to have an adverse impact on minority group applicants and has been found unlawful. Unless shown to be job-related, questions on car ownership, home ownership, length of residence, garnishment of wages, etc., may violate Title VII.

SOURCE: Based on Bureau of National Affairs, *BNA Handbook: Personnel Management* (Washington, D.C.: Bureau of National Affairs, 1983), pp. 201:231-201:240. Clifford M. Koen, "The Pre-Employment Inquiry Guide," *Personnel Journal* 59 (1980): 825-829; Debra D. Burrington, "A Review of State Government Employment Application Forms for Suspect Inquiries," *Public Personnel Management* 11 (1982): 55-60; Equal Employment Opportunity Commission, *Guide to Pre-Employment Inquiries* (Washington, D.C.: Equal Employment Opportunity Commission, 1981); Ernest C. Miller, "An EEO Examination of Employment Applications," *Personnel Administrator* 25 (1981): 63-70; Richard S. Lowell and Jay A. Deloach, "Equal Employment Opportunity: Are You Overlooking the Application Form?" *Personnel* 59 (1982):49-55; State of California, *Pre-Employment Inquiry Guidelines* (Sacramento, Calif: Department of Fair Employment and Housing, 1982).

law. However, several surveys suggest that numerous public and private employers still request information that could be viewed as inappropriate. (The term *inappropriate* does not mean that questions are illegal and cannot be asked. However, by their phrasing, the questions would be viewed by the courts in such a light as to make a user vulnerable to charges of discrimination if an investigation of unfair discrimination were conducted. Then, it would be up to each employer to justify use of these questions.)

Debra Burrington collected application forms from the state personnel office in each of the 50 states.[13] An analysis of the forms revealed that every form had at least one inappropriate inquiry; on the average, there were 7.7 such inquiries per application. Slightly less than half (42 percent) of the states had eight or more inappropriate items.

In a similar vein, Ernest Miller reviewed the applications of 151 randomly sampled *Fortune* 500 firms.[14] Only two used applications judged to be completely fair from an initial review. Almost 4 out of 10 firms' applications (38 percent) had more than 10 inappropriate inquiries. The following list shows four of the most frequent inappropriate questions and the percentage of firms for which the most inappropriate inquiries occurred:

1. Have you ever been arrested for a misdemeanor or felony? Describe. 64.7%

2. Dates attended grammar school? High school? 61.4%

3. What was your grade point average? Class standing? 59.5%

4. In what extracurricular activities did you participate? Clubs? Sports? 45.8%

Research by Richard Lowell and Jay Deloach substantiates Miller's findings regarding the frequency of inappropriate questions on the application.[15] Their review of application forms from 50 large well-known businesses showed 48 of the firms had at least one inappropriate item. The inappropriate items occurring in 25 percent or more of the forms reviewed clustered in the following categories: (a) military background, (b) education, (c) arrest records, (d) physical handicaps, and (e) age.

The results of these research studies illustrate rather impressively that many organizations' existing application forms may not fully comply with current equal employment opportunity law. Resources need to be directed toward reviewing and, where needed, revising these forms to ensure full compliance with the law while meeting an organization's selection needs.

Developing and Revising Application Forms

As we have seen, the questions asked on a job application form affect not only its effectiveness in selecting the best, most appropriate job applicants but may also result in a discrimination charge against the user or employer. Thus it is imperative that employers study carefully the development and/or revision of their application forms. In making this review, there are several points or strategies that should be considered. These points include the following:

1. *Because jobs are different, more than one application form will probably be needed* At the extreme, there could be one application form for each job. More realistically, however, one form will likely be used to cover a class or family of jobs, that is, jobs that require similar types of knowledge, skills, abilities, or tasks. For example, different versions of application forms may be used for job classes such as clerical/office personnel, sales personnel, operative workers, and managers.

2. *Job analysis data should serve as one basis for choosing employment application questions.* Although job analysis data are commonly used in developing other selection devices such as tests, few users consider these data in constructing their application forms. Not only should these analyses suggest useful items for the forms, but they should also serve as a basis for their legal justification.

3. *Every item proposed for inclusion should be reviewed using the item rating criteria listed in Table 10.1.* If a question (a) disqualifies a large percentage of members of protected groups, (b) appears not to be needed to judge an applicant's qualifications for a specific job, (c) has no evidence to show it is related to performance on the job, (d) could be viewed as an invasion of privacy, and/or (e) does not serve as a bona fide occupational requirement, then an employer should strongly consider excluding the question.[16] Be prepared to defend any questions used.

4. *Some jobs or classes of jobs may not require an in-depth applicant assessment by means of the application form. Therefore, if items are not needed or cannot be justified, then the questions should not be asked.* Only a brief form containing essential data might be used. Ernest Miller points out that this brief form might contain information such as (a) name, (b) address, (c) telephone number, (d) work experience, (e) level of education and training received, (f) skills possessed, and (g) social security number.[17] In general, the lower the organizational level of a job or job class, the shorter, less detailed the content of the application.

5. *Since application forms represent a selection device, they are subject to the Uniform Guidelines.* Because applications are covered by the *Uniform Guidelines*, employers must be able to show that items on the forms do not have discriminatory impact on protected groups or that the items are related to performance on the job. Adverse impact can be examined by using some of the methods we discussed in Chapter 2. In addition, the questions listed in Table 10.1 can also help to identify items that may be discriminatory.

    Validation of application form items is another option, but one not likely to be used by many employers. A study by the Bureau of National Affairs, for example, found that only about one out of ten firms reported they had conducted validation studies of application items.[18] As with job analysis, validation studies help to ensure that appropriate measures are used to predict job success, as well as to defend against a possible charge of unfair discrimination. We have more to say about the validation of employment applications when we discuss weighted application blanks in Chapter 11.

6. *The physical layout and format of the form should be thoroughly considered.* As a selection measure, the form should be reviewed for its attractiveness and ease of use by the applicant.

Because of various federal and state requirements, employers covered by these requirements need to collect and report demographic information (for example, gender, ethnicity, physical handicap) on their job applicants. Although it may appear efficient to simply collect the data on the application form, this strategy could lead to a discrimination charge. Descriptive data collected on a separate form or on a tear-off portion of the application form would be a more effective strategy. California's *Pre-Employment Inquiry Guidelines* provides an example for collecting and isolating demographic job applicant data from employment applications. The procedures mandated by the state are as follows:

1. The information must be set forth on a tear-off portion of the employment application or on a separate form.

2. The form should state the reason for requesting the information, how it is to be used, and that submitting the information is voluntary.

3. The form containing ethnic information shall be separated from the employment application as soon as that application is received by the employer and forwarded to the individual responsible for personnel research.

4. The forms shall be maintained in a separate file and the information shall not be made available to anyone involved in the hiring process.

5. The data shall be used to evaluate affirmative action recruitment efforts and to determine whether a protected class is adversely affected at any step in the selection process.

6. The data shall be kept to indicate final disposition on all job applicants.[19]

Whether employers follow procedures established by state laws or develop procedures on their own, they would be wise to adopt policies for handling demographic data on job applicants.

Accuracy of Application Form Data

Obviously, for application forms to be useful in selection, it is important that job applicants provide honest answers on the forms.[20] Some writers have argued that prospective employees may be more likely to respond honestly since their responses are given in their own handwriting. That is, they are personally accountable for their answers. On the other hand, an application form is a self-report selection measure. When people are competing for a job, self-report application data are susceptible to distortion; it is simply advantageous for an applicant to "look good." Falsification of application data can range from inflation of college grades to outright lies involving types of jobs held, companies worked for, or educational degrees earned. In addition, applicants may attempt to conceal gaps in their employment histories.

A common distortion seen by many HR managers involves reported college background. For applicants at some executive levels, misrepresentation of a specific degree such as the master of business administration (MBA) is a frequent practice. Walter Kiechel concludes that individuals who forge the MBA credential on their applications are typically individuals with little relevant job experience who completed their twenties just before the MBA became a highly prized degree, and who do not believe they can compete against those who have the degree.[21]

How prevalent is the practice of giving fraudulent data on job applications? There are not many studies that have explored the problem in detail. However, some limited investigations have addressed the issue. One survey of 223 corporate HR directors showed that roughly one-third believed falsifying employment or educational credentials was a common, growing problem.[22] The National Credential Verification Service of Minneapolis found that misrepresentation of academic and employment records occurred in almost one out of three of its investigations.[23]

Several empirical studies have identified the specific application items where distortion is most prevalent as well as their frequency of occurrence. James Mosel and Lee Cozan reported that accurate application data were found for job applicants applying for sales and office positions.[24] However, several studies have reported discrepancies in job application data. For instance, application data provided by 91 disabled applicants were compared with actual data. Of the 13 items studied, almost half (46 percent) of the items were distorted by over 20 percent of the applicants. These items and the prevalence of distortion by applicants were as follows: education (21 percent), pay on previous job (22 percent), job title of previous job (24 percent), length of employment (29 percent), age at disablement (33 percent), and receipt of assistance (55 percent).[25] In a similar study, Irwin Goldstein compared five application blank items with factual data for 111 persons applying for positions as nurse's aides. For the 111 previous employers, 15 percent indicated that an applicant had never worked for them. Also, there was a 25 percent disagreement for the item: "Reason(s) for leaving previous job." The two item categories for which discrepancies were greatest were duration of previous employment (57 percent) and previous salary earned (72 percent).[26]

If the data from these studies are applicable to other employment situations involving application forms, we can conclude that some distortion does take place. Most likely, distortion of these data is due to pressure on an applicant to obtain a desired job. Results also suggest applicants are most likely to distort those items believed to be related to whether a job offer will be made and the salary given. However, it should not be concluded that employment applications are worthless. Even though distortion is a problem, application forms can provide useful data for comparing and predicting the success of job applicants. Next, we see how the accuracy of application form data can be enhanced.

Enhancing Application Form Accuracy. As we have seen, accuracy of application form data can be a problem. Several steps can be taken to lessen the problems of applicant errors, distortion, and omission of data on the form. First, applicants should be told, preferably both verbally and in writing, that the information they give will affect their employability. Secondly, applicants should be informed that the data they provide will be thoroughly checked.[27] For example, a statement such as the following should be included on the form:

> All information you provide on this application will be checked. Driving, educational, employment, and any military records will be checked with appropriate individuals and groups such as local and state police, previous employers, previous schools attended, etc. Be sure and review your application to see that it is complete and that you did not omit any information.

The statement should be located and printed on the form so that it is easily seen and readable by applicants. Finally, applicants should be required to sign and date their application. A statement such as the following should be used:

> I certify that all statements and information I have given on this form are to the best of my knowledge complete and accurate.

Using Application Forms in HR Selection

An employment application represents only one means for evaluating job applicants' ability to perform a job. Certainly, other types of measures such as tests and interviews can also be used in conjunction with the application form. For the moment, however, we are concerned with *how* the application might be used in selection. Here, we briefly review several approaches for incorporating application data in hiring decisions.[28]

The alternatives for utilizing application data can range from those that are objective in their treatment of information to those that are more or less subjective. In addition, these approaches can be general or detailed. Although there is a variety of options available for handling application data, on the whole, the methods tend to fall into one of the following two categories: (a) weighted application blanks or (b) application form checklists and evaluations that are typically used to examine the training, education, and experience of job applicants.

Weighted Application Blanks   Under the weighted application blank (WAB) approach, an empirical scoring key is used to score applicants on their answers to an application form. A research study is conducted on application items, and responses are weighted so that they predict some aspect or measure of job success such as job tenure or productivity. Numerical scores are obtained for each applicant by summing the appropriate weights. The resulting scores are then used in making hiring decisions. We will discuss the development and use of weighted application blanks in more detail in the next chapter.

Application Form Checklists   There are many varieties of application form checklists. Because most of these emphasize assessing applicants' training, education, and experience, they are usually referred to as training and experience evaluations (or simply "T&E" evaluations). Because of the frequency of use and importance of training and experience evaluations, we treat T&E evaluations as another selection predictor.

Training and Experience (T&E) Evaluations
Nature and Role of T&E Evaluations in Selection

T&E evaluations are a way to rationally assess previous experience, training, and education information given by job applicants. The information is reported by the applicant on the application form itself or on a separate questionnaire completed along with the application. Whatever the form, applicants provide job-related information in areas such as their previous performance of specific tasks, prior training received, self-report ratings of the knowledge, skills, and abilities they possess, and past educational accomplishments. This information is then evaluated by a rater such as a HR selection specialist using a scoring plan. Scores from the evaluations can be used in a number of ways such as (a) the sole basis for simply deciding if an individual is or is not qualified, (b) a means for rank-ordering individuals from high to low based on a T&E score, (c) a basis for pre-screening applicants prior to administering more expensive, time-consuming predictors (for example, an interview), and (d) in combination with other predictors to make an employment decision. The objective of using the scores is to predict future job performance.

As we have mentioned, T&E evaluations are helpful in determining the minimum qualifications needed to perform a job. For instance, Lawrence Fogli has illustrate how an analysis of a supermarket cashier's job was used to develop a means where applicants rated their experience with such tasks.[29] Similarly, Marvin Dunnette, Leaetta Hough, and Rodney Rosse have also proposed a means for scoring how applicants' prior job experience, training, and academic performance are related to their ability to perform specific job tasks.[30]

Examples of T&E Evaluations To better understand T&E ratings, some examples may help. Our first example might be suitable when only a brief check of relevant portions of a job application for very minimal qualifications is needed. The second example T&E evaluation may be appropriate when a more thorough review of minimum qualifications is being made.

Exhibit 10.1 illustrates an example of a brief check. It is a checklist to be completed by a company HR specialist for applications submitted for the job of clerk/stenographer. The form is brief and simple, but it encourages the application reviewer to attend to those aspects of the application that are important for a successful clerk/stenographer. These aspects important to the job were identified in a previous job analysis. If an applicant meets each of the minimum qualifications listed, an employment decision may be made or additional testing offered. For example, if a candidate possesses all basic qualifications for the job, a filing or typing test might then be administered or an interview given.

EXHIBIT 10.1

BRIEF TRAINING AND EXPERIENCE EVALUATION USED FOR EVALUATING APPLICATIONS SUBMITTED FOR THE JOB OF CLERK/STENOGRAPHER

Name of Applicant: _____

Directions: Before beginning to complete this form, review the minimum qualifications for the job of Clerk/Stenographer listed below. Then, study each application form submitted for the job. After reviewing each application, indicate if the applicant possesses each minimum qualification. If an applicant meets the necessary requirements, check "Yes"; if not, then check "No." When there are job openings, applicants meeting all minimum qualifications will be invited in for additional consideration. After completing the checklist, please attach it to the application form and return the application to the personnel file.

Minimum Applicant Qualifications

Yes   No
☐   ☐   1. Maintained a filing system of letters, reports, documents, etc.
☐   ☐   2. Used an IBM personal computer and Wordperfect word processor to type letters and reports.
☐   ☐   3. Used a dictaphone in transcribing correspondence.

NOTE: This form is completed by a selection specialist.

A T&E evaluation like that in Exhibit 10.1 can be very helpful in making a quick, cursory screening of job applicants. In particular, it is useful in initial screening for those jobs in which large numbers of people are making application. When used in this context, the checklist can help to minimize unnecessary HR selection costs by ensuring that only suitable applicants receive further employment consideration. For example, if experience in using an IBM personal computer with WordPerfect word processing software to prepare letters and reports is a necessary requirement for performing the job of clerk/stenographer successfully, we might have on our checklist "Used an IBM personal computer and WordPerfect word processor to type letters and reports." An applicant must have at least this much relevant job experience, in addition to meeting other minimum qualifications, before being hired or asked to complete another selection measure such as a filing test. It is important to emphasize that the minimum qualifications listed on any pre-employment checklist should meet the criteria for establishing employee specifications that we discussed earlier in Chapters 8 and 9.

Exhibit 10.2 presents an example of a separate T&E evaluation form for the job of personnel research analyst. This form is representative of those training and experience assessment methods that are based on job tasks. Using a previous job analysis, tasks critical to the job were identified. We have listed only a few. For each of the important job tasks, applicants are asked to indicate their specific work experiences and/or any training received. With regard to work experience, for example, applicants might be asked to list dates of employment, previous employers, previous job titles, and supervisory responsibilities. Applicants might

EXHIBIT 10.2	AN EXAMPLE TRAINING AND EXPERIENCE EVALUATION FORM FOR THE JOB OF PERSONNEL RESEARCH ANALYST

Directions: Listed below are some important job tasks performed by a Personnel Research Analyst. Read each of the tasks. If you have had experience or training in performing a task, check the box marked "Yes." If you have not, then check the box marked "No." For the task(s) marked "Yes," please describe your experience and training you believe to be associated with each task. All of your responses are subject to review and verification.

Have you had experience or training with this task?

Task

Yes ☐ No ☐

1. **Computed and monitored applicant flow statistics for nonexempt job applicants using computerized statistical packages (for example, SPSS, SAS)**

Describe Your Relevant Experience:

Employer: _____ Title: _____
Dates of employment: From _____ To _____
Describe your experience with this task: _____
_____
_____

Describe Your Relevant Training:

Formal coursework and location: _____
_____
Training programs attended and location:
_____
On the job training: _____
_____

Name and address of person(s) who can verify this information:
_____
_____

Task

Yes ☐ No ☐

2. **Designed and conducted test validation studies for entry-level jobs.**

•
•
•

Task

•
•
•

Yes ☐ No ☐

3. **Supervised research assistants in collecting data for human resource studies.**

•
•
•

Task

•
•
•

Yes ☐ No ☐

4. **Trained personnel assistants in the use of personnel tests (for example, typing, basic math and verbal tests) for entry-level jobs.**

•
•
•

•
•
•

(continued)

EXHIBIT 10.2 (CONTINUED)

		Task
Yes ☐	No ☐	**5. Made oral presentations to line and/or upper-level managers on the results of personnel research studies.**

Describe Your Relevant Experience:
Employer: _____ Title: _____
Dates of employment: From _____ To _____
Describe your experience with this task: _____
_____
_____
_____

Describe Your Relevant Training:
Formal coursework and location: _____
_____
Training programs attended and location:
_____
On the job training: _____
_____

Name and address of person(s) who can verify this information:
_____
_____

NOTE: This form is completed by the job applicant.

also be asked to describe their educational background, specialized training, or specific skills acquired that might have prepared them to perform each of these tasks. In addition, applicants must provide names of persons who can be contacted to verify their self-reported information. Verification information helps to reduce inflated self-ratings of applicants' training and job experiences.

One of the products of the job analysis is the determination of what experience, education, and training are relevant for successful task performance.[31] For instance, for the task "Computed and monitored applicant flow statistics for nonexempt job applicants using computerized statistical packages (for example, SPSS, SAS)," we may require knowledge of college-level introductory psychological statistics and training in the use of SPSS, SAS, or equivalent computerized statistical packages. The reviewer of the T&E would simply study the applicants' reported experience, education, and training descriptions to determine if the minimum standards have been met. Each task would be reviewed in a similar manner, that is, comparing applicant descriptors with job task qualifications. These comparisons would be recorded using a summary form like that in Exhibit 10.3 Individuals who meet or exceed these minimum qualifications would be recommended for further consideration.

Assumptions of T&E Evaluations Ronald Ash and his colleagues note that use of T&E evaluations are based on several assumptions.[32] Some of these are listed here:

1. The written work experience and education information given by a job applicant is more accurate than when given by another means, for instance, in an interview. Previous research appears to support this assumption.

| EXHIBIT 10.3 | AN EXAMPLE RATING FORM FOR USE IN EVALUATING TRAINING AND EXPERIENCE OF APPLICANTS FOR THE JOB OF PERSONNEL RESEARCH ANALYST |

Directions: Read the minimum qualifications required to perform the job of Personnel Research Analyst. Then, compare these qualifications to the applicant's training and experience evaluations. If an applicant's qualifications meet or exceed the requirements for the job, check "Meets Requirements." If not, check "Does Not Meet Requirements."

Name of Applicant _____

Task	Minimum Qualifications	Applicant Rating
1. Computes and monitors applicant flow statistics for nonexempt job applicants using computerized statistical packages (for example, SPSS, SAS).	1. Has knowledge of college-level introductory psychological statistics course; normal coursework training or on-the-job training in use of SPSS, SAS or equivalent statistical packages.	☐ Meets Requirements ☐ Does Not Meet Requirements
2. Designs and conducts test validation studies for entry-level jobs.	2. Was responsible for conducting empirical validation studies or selection tests. Is knowledgeable of the content of the *Uniform Guidelines.*	☐ Meets Requirements ☐ Does Not Meet Requirements
3. Supervises research assistants in collecting data for personnel selection studies.	3. Directed or was primarily responsible for the work of others involving the collection of empirical data.	☐ Meets Requirements ☐ Does Not Meet Requirements
4. Trains personnel assistants in the use of personnel tests (for example, typing, basic math, and verbal tests) for entry-level jobs.	4. Had college-level course or training in testing and test administration.	☐ Meets Requirements ☐ Does Not Meet Requirements
5. Makes oral presentations to line and/or upper-level managers on the results of personnel research studies.	5. Made formal oral presentations of 15 to 30 minutes duration involving the presentation of quantitative data and results to a non-technical audience.	☐ Meets Requirements ☐ Does Not Meet Requirements

Based on the information shown, the applicant:

☐ Meets Requirements
☐ Does Not Meet Requirements for the job of Personnel Research Analyst.

Notes: _____   Rater: _____
_____
_____   Date: _____
_____
_____
_____

NOTE: This form is completed by a selection specialist.

2. T&E measures may work because they assess job-relevant abilities, skills, and motivation. The more individuals have been successful on past job-relevant tasks requiring these abilities and skills, the more they will be successful on similar tasks requiring these in the future. Also, the more experience and education aimed at a specific occupation, the greater the applicant's commitment and motivation to succeed in that occupation.

3. An applicant with more recent or longer training and experience is more qualified than one with older or shorter training and experience.

4. An applicant with progressive complexity in training and experience will be better qualified than one without this pattern.

5. Beyond a certain point, longer and more complex experience and training may result in less qualified applicants. Thus an individual who is overqualified for a position should receive a lower T&E score than one who is not overqualified.

6. T&E evaluation forms are, by nature, based on self-report information provided by applicants. It is assumed that applicants are truthful and accurate in their self-reports. The extent of information distortion may rest on external factors such as the local unemployment rate.

Methods of Collecting T&E Evaluation Information

There are many approaches to T&E evaluations. In general, most have in common the following characteristics: (a) a listing or description of tasks, KSAs, or other job-relevant content areas, (b) a means for applicants to describe, indicate, or rate the extent of their training or experience with these job content areas, and (c) a basis for evaluating or scoring applicants' self-reported training, experience, or education.

Abraham Flory, Edward Levine, Ronald Ash, Wayne Porter, and their associates have published excellent reviews of these methods.[33] We draw on their work to describe in the following sections some of the major methods in use.

Holistic Judgment   This particular method is not really a T&E evaluation as we have defined the term. Rather, it is an informal, unstructured approach that an individual takes when reviewing an application or T&E form. It merits a brief description because of the high frequency with which it is used. Essentially, an individual receives an application, résumé, or some other form on which training, experience, and education information are reported. The individual reviews the information and makes a broad, general judgment of the applicant's suitability. These judgments might be nothing more than "qualified" or "not qualified for this position." Judgments made are individualistic; that is, the standards used for evaluating T&E information exist in the mind of the individual evaluator. Thus they will vary from one evaluator to the next.[34]

As you can probably tell, an evaluator's judgments in the holistic approach are not formally recorded on a standardized form and scored; they are simply made by an individual after a cursory review of training and experience information. Because of its unstandardized nature and unknown reliability and validity, it should be avoided as an approach to T&E evaluations.

Point Method   Wayne Porter, Edward Levine, and Abraham Flory describe the point method as a T&E evaluation alternative often used in the public sector.[35] Essentially, this method consists of a preestablished rating system for crediting applicants' prior training, education, and experience considered relevant to the job. Points are assigned based on the recentness, amount of job experience, and amount of education received. Ideally, the specific points credited for job experience and education are determined through a job analysis.

Applicants meeting the minimum qualifications for the job are assigned a passing score of 70. For individuals who exceed the minimum qualifications, additional points are added to the score of 70 based on the length and recentness of experience (in months or years completed) or the amount (for example, in semester credit hours) of education received.

Exhibit 10.4 shows an example schedule for evaluating applicants and crediting their education and experience. In the first section, the minimum education and experience qualifications are listed for a specific position. Next, the sections crediting applicants' additional education and experience are shown. Notice that different point values are assigned depending on the level (A, B, or C) and amount of education received as well as the level and recentness of experience. A levels of education and experience are judged to be most directly relevant to the job; C levels are least relevant. Judgments about appropriate levels are predetermined by subject matter experts for the specific job in question. As you can see, more credit is given to A levels of education and experience than C levels. Also, more credit is given for more recent experience.

Analysts using the point method make their ratings and then sum the credited points assigned. In public sector jobs, these total scores are used solely or in addition to test information for ranking applicants on a merit system eligibility list.

It is important to recognize that the points credited for experience and education will vary from one job to the next. Exhibit 10.4 simply illustrates one scoring system. In fact, for some jobs, negative, or no credit may even be given because of the problem of overqualification for the position.

Although widely used, the point method has been criticized for its lack of validity and its specious precision in the manner in which points are assigned for experience and education. Another complaint against the method centers around its adverse impact against women, minorities, and younger applicants.[36] These are groups that have historically not had the same opportunities and time to attain the same level of experience and education that white males have had.

Grouping Method   The objective of the grouping approach is to divide applicants into groups that best represent each applicant's level of qualifications. The number of groups used will depend on the particular situation. More often than not, three or four groups are used:

| EXHIBIT 10.4 | AN EXAMPLE SCORING SYSTEM FOR THE POINT METHOD OF T & E EVALUATION |

Applicant Name: _____

Last Name   First Name   Middle Name

Position Applied For: _____

_____

Minimum Qualifications:

    Minimum Education: _____

    Minimum Experience: _____

_____

Additional Education Scoring:

	High School (year)		College (hours)				Graduate School (hours)			
	3	4	30	60	90	Degree	15	30	45	Degree
A Level	1	2	1.5	2	2.5	3.5	1	1.5	1.5	2.5
B Level	0	0	.5	1	1.5	2.5	.5	1	1	1

Additional Experience Scoring:

Year	'93	'92	'91	'90	'89	'88	'87	'86	'85	'84	'83	'82
A Level	3.5	3.5	3.5	2	2	2	2	1	1	1	1	1
B Level	2	2	2	1	1	1	1	.5	.5	.5	.5	.5
C Level	1	1	1	.5	.5	.5	.5	.3	.3	.3	.3	.3

Additional Education Score _____

Additional Experience Score _____

Rater: _____

Minimum Qualifications Score _____70.00

Date: _____

Total Score: _____

NOTE: This form is completed by a selection specialist.

High Group = involves applicants who are clearly suited and well qualified for the job
Middle Group = consists of applicants who do not fit either the high or low group
Low Group = has applicants who meet minimum qualifications but appear poorly suited for the job because of limited experience or training
Unqualified Group = consists of applicants who do not meet minimum qualifications

In classifying applicants to groups, training and experience information is considered simultaneously by a rater. Points are assigned to individuals based on their group membership. Thus all members of the high group may receive a score of 95; members in the middle group, a score of 85; and members of the low group, a score of 75. Individuals in the unqualified group receive 0 points and are rejected.

The combinations of training and experience chosen to define the groups should distinguish among the groups in terms of job success. Subject matter experts in job analysis are used to determine the combinations that best describe each group.

Because individuals in the same group receive the same score, ordinal ranking of applicants (as in the point method) does not occur. As Wayne Porter and others note, the grouping of applicants conforms better to the actual level of precision of T&E evaluations and measurement. That is, T&E evaluations are more like a blunt ax than a surgeon's scalpel in measurement precision.[37]

Exhibit 10.5 illustrates a scoring system using the grouping method for training and experience evaluation applied to the position of Accountant II. A T&E rater simply studies an applicant's application form or other means for

---

EXHIBIT 10.5   **AN EXAMPLE SCORING SYSTEM FOR THE GROUPING METHOD OF T&E EVALUATION**

Position: Accountant II

Group Score	Training and Experience Qualifications
95 =	Master of Science degree in accounting and one year experience in budget preparation, account auditing, and governmental accounting practice, **or** Bachelor of Science degree in accounting and three years' experience in budget preparation-account auditing, and governmental accounting practice.
85 =	Master of Science degree in accounting. **or** Bachelor of Science degree in accounting and two years' experience in governmental or general accounting practice.
75 =	Bachelor of Science degree in accounting and one year experience in governmental or general accounting practice.
0 =	Not Qualified; Minimum Qualifications = Bachelor of Science degree in accounting *and* at least one year experience in accounting practice.

NOTE: This form is used by a selection specialist.

recording training and experience information. Then, using the group definitions in Exhibit 10.5, the rater classifies the applicant to one of the groups listed. Points allocated to the group are then assigned to the applicant. Those points are the applicant's T&E score.

Behavioral Consistency Method   The behavioral consistency method is based on the following principles:

1.   Job applicants should be evaluated on the basis of behaviors that show differences between superior and minimally acceptable workers.

2.   These behaviors can be identified by using subject matter experts (SMEs) who have observed superior and marginal performance on the job.

3.   Information on applicants' past accomplishments with respect to these behaviors can be described by job applicants.

4.   Applicants' past accomplishments are predictive of their future behaviors.

5   Applicants' past accomplishments can be reliably rated by SMEs.[38]

The method requires job applicants to describe their past accomplishments in several job-related areas (usually five to seven) that have been judged to distinguish superior from marginal job performance. The description is a written narrative which includes examples of past achievements that applicants believe demonstrate their skills and abilities in each of these job-related areas. In writing their descriptions, applicants are asked to answer questions such as the following: What are examples of your past achievements that demonstrate the necessary abilities and skills to perform these job behaviors? What was the problem on which you worked? What did you do (in terms of an achievement) to solve the problem, and when did you do it? What percentage of credit do you claim for this achievement? What are the names and addresses of persons who can verify the achievement and credit you claim? Rating scales that describe levels of performance on job-related behaviors that distinguish superior from marginal job performance are used to evaluate applicants' written descriptions.

As an example of the behavioral consistency method consider the problem of graduate school admissions committees. Most graduate programs want students who can perform well. Obviously, there are academic grades, test scores such as those from the Graduate Record Examination, and faculty recommendations that can be used to predict performance. Assume we have a program and would like scores on a T&E measure to use with these measures in evaluating student applications.

After analyzing the "job" of graduate student, five behaviors are uncovered that are considered particularly important for graduate student applicants to have displayed in the past. Examples of these behaviors include thinking independently, conducting empirical research, and others. Let's take one of these behaviors, *conducting empirical research*, as an example.

Exhibit 10.6 gives an example of the behavioral consistency T&E method for describing an applicant's past accomplishments and activities in conducting

EXHIBIT 10.6 AN EXAMPLE OF THE BEHAVIORAL CONSISTENCY METHOD OF T&E EVALUATION

Job Behavior: Conducting Empirical Research

Concerns the conduct of research activities including designing a research study, collecting and analyzing data to test specific research hypotheses or answer research questions, and writing up research results in the form of a formal report.

For the behavior **Conducting Empirical Research** that is defined above, think about your past activities and accomplishments. Then write a narrative description of your activities and accomplishments in the space below. In your description, be sure and answer the following questions:

1. What specifically did you do? When did you do it?
2. Give examples of what you did that illustrate how you accomplished the above behavior.
3. What percentage of credit do you claim for your work in this area?

Description:

During my senior year (1993–94), I wrote a senior research thesis as a partial requirement for graduation with honors in psychology. I designed a research study to investigate the effects of interviewer race on interviewee performance in a structured interview. I personally designed the research study and conducted it in a metropolitan police department. White and African-American applicants for the job of patrol police officer were randomly assigned to white and African-American interviewers. After conducting an analysis of the patrol police job, a structured interview schedule was developed. The various interviewee-interviewer racial combinations were then compared in terms of their performance in the structured interview.

I consider the vast majority of the work (80%) to be my own. My major professor accounted for about 20% of the work. Her work consisted of helping to obtain site approval for the research, helping to design the study, and reviewing my work products.

Name and Address of an Individual Who Can Verify the Work You Described Above:

Name: Dr. Amy Prewett

Address: Department of Psychology

Pascal Univ. State College, ID

Phone: 607-555-0821

NOTE: This form is completed by the job applicant.

empirical research. The applicant wrote a description of his senior thesis research activities as being representative of the behavior *conducting empirical research.*

In Exhibit 10.7 a rating scale is shown that is used for evaluating the applicant's research description shown in Exhibit 10.6. Using the rating scale as a standard, the applicant was given a score of 6. Similar descriptions and ratings are made for the remaining four job-relevant graduate student behaviors. Scores on these behaviors are summed, and the total score represents the applicant's behavioral consistency score.

| EXHIBIT 10.7 | AN EXAMPLE RATING SCALE FOR SCORING THE BEHAVIORAL CONSISTENCY METHOD OF T&E EVALUATION |

Instructions for Scoring the Job Behavior: Conducting Empirical Research

Read the handwritten narrative the job applicant wrote describing activities and accomplishments in conducting empirical research. Then study the scale below. Choose the *one* score on the scale you believe that best represents or characterizes the applicant's narrative description of past empirical research work.

Empirical Research Behaviors

1 = Worked as a member of a student team. Helped design a study, collect and analyze data, and/or wrote a report describing the study and its results.

2 = Independently designed a study, collected and analyzed data, and/or wrote a report describing the study and its results. The study was conducted as a class requirement.

3 = Independently designed a study, collected and analyzed the data. The study was not an academic requirement.

4 = Worked as a research assistant for a professor. Helped with the collection and/or analysis of the data. The study was or will be submitted for presentation at an academic or professional meeting or will be submitted for journal publication.

5 = Was co-author or author of a paper that was submitted for presentation at an academic or professional meeting. The paper involved the collection and analysis of data.

6 = Wrote a research thesis as a graduation requirement that involved the collection of data, analysis of the data, and tests of research hypotheses or research questions.

7 = Was a co-author or author of a paper that was accepted for publication in a professional or academic journal. The paper involved the collection and analysis of data.

NOTE: This form is used by a selection specialist.

Leaetta Hough adapted the behavioral consistency approach to produce the "Accomplishment Record" method for selecting and promoting attorneys working in the federal government.[39] Over 300 attorneys working in a large federal agency described their major accomplishments illustrative of their competence in performing eight critical job behaviors (for example, planning and organizing, researching/investigating, and hard work/dedication). Raters were used to score their written descriptions by applying rating scales that described levels of competence in performing these eight job behaviors. Analysis of the Accomplishment Record showed it to be correlated with job performance (.25) and uncorrelated with other selection measures such as aptitude tests, academic performance, and so on. These results imply that the Accomplishment Record may be measuring a construct that is not assessed by traditional predictors of attorney job performance. Preliminary analyses also suggested that the method was fair for women, minorities, and white men.[40]

With its emphasis on job-related behaviors, the behavioral consistency approach to evaluating training and experience has some obvious advantages; however, it has limitations as well. One is that applicants must be able to communicate in writing. Second, because of the level of detail required in the descriptions as well as the mandatory verification, some prospective applicants may be discouraged from applying. Ronald Ash and Edward Levine, for instance, found that only slightly over half (56 percent) of their study participants chose to describe their achievements under the behavioral consistency method.[41] They also reported that in an earlier study by Frank Schmidt and his colleagues, only 20 percent of the study participants completed their descriptions.[42] Finally. the behavioral consistency method can be time consuming to develop, administer, and score.

Task-Based Method   Following a comprehensive analysis of the job for which a T&E method is desired, critical job tasks are identified. These critical job tasks serve as the basis for the task-based method. The tasks are listed on a form, and applicants are asked to rate each task listed. The rating may be nothing more than an indication of whether a task has or has not been performed before. An example of this form of task-based method was shown in Exhibit 10.2. Applicants may also be asked to rate task performance in terms of frequency, such as with a frequency rating scale (for example, 0 = Have Not Done to 5 = Have Done Every or Almost Every Workday), closeness of supervision received in task performance, or some other rating criterion. Furthermore, the applicant may be asked to list an individual who can verify their reported task performance. Verification is used to attempt to reduce the obvious inflation factor in such self-ratings. As another means for controlling inflation, some individuals have incorporated bogus tasks in the listings to try and identify applicants inflating their task ratings[43]

KSA-Based Method   The KSA-based method is quite similar to that of the task-based method. Rather than tasks, KSAs, such as specific computer programming skills or knowledge of the application and interpretation of specific statistical techniques, are listed on a questionnaire. Ratings such as whether a KSA is possessed or the level of a skill possessed can also be used. Verification through listings of previous jobs held, dates, and names of individuals are used to limit as much as possible the inflation factor in the ratings.

Reliability and Validity of T&E Evaluations

Reliability   As far as reliability is concerned, T&E evaluations tend to reflect rather high interrater reliability estimates. Ronald Ash and Edward Levine reported average interrater estimates in the .80s. The task-based method produced the highest reliability coefficient; the grouping method produced the lowest.[44] Frank Schmidt and his associates also reported interrater reliability estimates of T&E ratings in the .80s.[45]

Validity   Because T&E evaluation methods are based upon a job analysis, a number of studies have argued for content validity of the methods. Although limited in number, empirical validation studies have also appeared in the literature, and several of these are particularly important. From a review of studies, Frank Schmidt and his colleagues reported an average validity coefficient of T&E methods of .10.[46] John and Rhonda Hunter reanalyzed these studies, corrected the validity coefficient for unreliability of the supervisory ratings criterion, and found an average validity coefficient of .13 for the methods.[47]

Ronald Ash and Edward Levine compared four training and experience evaluation methods—the point, grouping, task-based, and behavioral consistency methods—in terms of reliability, validity, and time required for scoring.[48] In terms of validity, the grouping method exhibited the highest validity (.21 and .30) for two of three jobs under study. In terms of the average number of minutes required to score an application, the point and behavioral consistency approaches (taking 3.5 minutes each) required roughly twice as long as the task-based (1.8 minutes) and grouping (2.0 minutes) methods. Because of significantly higher validity and greater efficiency in scoring, Ash and Levine recommended that the grouping method be used for evaluating training and experience.

In the most comprehensive review to date, Michael McDaniel, Frank Schmidt, and John Hunter conducted a metaanalysis of the validity of four methods for rating training and experience.[49] (The grouping method was not reviewed in their study.) With overall job performance as the criterion, they examined a total of 132 validity coefficients based on over 12,000 observations. They found that the validity of training and experience ratings varied with the type of procedure used. The behavioral consistency method demonstrated the highest validity with a mean corrected validity coefficient of .45. Lower validities were found for the Illinois job element, point, and task methods with mean validities of .20, .15, and .11, respectively. Validity generalization was concluded to exist for the behavioral consistency and Illinois job element methods but not for the point and task-based approaches. However, Ronald Ash and associates have concluded that the point and task-based methods show useful validities for applicant groups having low levels of job experience (for example, three years or less).[50]

Recommendations for Using T&E Evaluations

Most applications of T&E evaluations have occurred in the public sector rather than the private sector. Based upon previous studies, there is evidence that suggests T&E evaluations tap job performance dimensions not assessed by other predictors.[51] By tying minimum job requirements to essential job tasks and KSAs through a well-developed T&E evaluation, minimum or preferred qualifications predictive of job performance can be set. In order to apply T&E evaluations effectively, the following guidelines are recommended:

1. Minimum amounts of training, experience, and education are among the most frequently used selection standards. Unless it can be justified, rather than use a selection standard such as a high school diploma as a minimum qualification, use T&E evaluations to set specific competencies job candidates should hold. These competencies may be expressed through job-

relevant KSAs applicants possess or prior performance of job-relevant tasks.

2. Employers using the holistic method of T&E evaluation should replace it with competency-based approaches such as the behavioral consistency, KSA-based and task-based self-assessment, and grouping methods.[52]

3. T&E evaluations are subject to the *Uniform Guidelines*. Like all selection devices, validation studies should be conducted on their job relatedness.

4. Although the typical validity coefficient may be relatively low, the available evidence is reasonably clear that some training and experience ratings are valid predictors of job performance. Nevertheless, Ash and Levine recommend that these procedures should only be used as rough screening procedures for positions where previous experience and training are necessary for job performance. For those entry-level jobs where only minimal levels of previous experience or training are required, they suggest that procedures, such as job-related tests, be considered instead.[53]

5. The utility of any good T&E evaluation system will depend on a thorough job analysis. One study has shown the importance of job analysis data when evaluating application blanks. When little job information was provided to application form reviewers, the degree of agreement among reviewers' assessments of applicants was likely to be low.[54] Seemingly, lack of job information contributes to greater reliance on non-job related information such as applicants' gender, ethnicity, and age.[55] Reliance on unstandardized evaluation forms and the absence of job information leads to reviewers' use of their own personal biases in evaluating T&E forms; hence, the result is low agreement among reviewers.

   Only through a job analysis can a user be assured that evaluations are made on information appropriate for use in selection. Job analysis methods, such as those discussed in earlier chapters or Edward Levine's B-JAM (Brief Job Analysis Method) job analysis method[56] that has a component of it tailored to T&E evaluation development, can be used.

6. Forms and procedures for collecting and scoring T&E evaluations should be standardized as much as possible.

7. Since T&E evaluations involve self-report data, some form of data verification, particularly data given by applicants who are going to be offered a job, should be made.

8. Where distortion of self-evaluation information is likely to be a problem, final hiring decisions based on other selection measures, such as ability, job knowledge, and performance tests, can minimize the inherent risks associated with T&E evaluations.

Reference Checks

Nature and Role of Reference Checks in Selection

Another technique that is sometimes used to select among job applicants is the checking of applicants' references or recommendations. This method involves an employer's collecting information about prospective job applicants from people who have had contact with the applicants. Information collected is used for the following purposes: (a) to *verify* information given by job applicants on other selection measures (such as application forms, employment interviews, or biographical data questionnaires), (b) to serve as a basis for predicting job success of job applicants,[57] and (c) to *uncover* background information (for example, a criminal record or unsafe driving record) on applicants that may not have been provided by applicants or identified by other selection procedures.

We saw in our earlier review of the accuracy of application form data that distortion can be a very real problem. Inaccurate information on self-reported prior employment, education, and acquired job skills have been given by job applicants to enhance their employability. Therefore, one principal purpose of a reference check is to verify what applicants have stated. When used in this manner, the method is only useful when it fails to confirm previous selection measure information given by applicants. Thus *reference checking serves more as a basis for negative selection, that is, detection of the unqualified, rather than identification of the qualified.*[58]

The second purpose of the reference check is to serve as a predictor of job success. Like application form data, a reference check used in this way assumes that past performance is a good predictor of future performance. While an application form may summarize what applicants say they did, a reference check is meant to assess how well *others* say the applicants did. It is presumed that information provided by others can be used to forecast how applicants will perform on the job in question.

Not only may applicants distort application information, but background information, such as a criminal record, may not be reported. Background information is often unreported by applicants when they believe it will affect their chances for employment. However, if unreported background information affects job performance or perhaps endangers the mental or physical well-being of coworkers, clients, or customers, a prospective employer may use reference checks for a third purpose—to identify applicants' job-relevant, but unreported background histories.

Reference checking is a common practice of many employers. It is one of the most popular pre-employment procedures for screening job candidates. Several surveys have documented that over 95 percent of the firms sampled said they engaged in checking references.[59] When information is collected, a significant number of organizations use the data for prediction rather than just for verification purposes. For example, a survey of 250 public and private organizations showed that over one-half utilized the method to obtain additional information about an applicant.[60] A more recent survey by the Bureau of National Affairs reported that 52 percent of 421 firms using reference checks employed the procedure to pass or fail job applicants.[61]

Types of Reference Data Collected

Generally speaking, four types of information are solicited through reference checks: (a) employment and educational background data, (b) appraisal of an applicant's character and personality, (c) estimates of an applicant's job performance abilities, and (d) willingness of the reference to rehire an applicant.[62] Also, with the passage of the Immigration Reform and Control Act of 1986, many employers now check to see that applicants are legally eligible to be employed in the United States.

Tables 10.3 and 10.4 illustrate the variety of employment and personal background information collected through reference checks by 245 employers participating in a nationwide survey by the Bureau of National Affairs.[63] Most (nine out of ten) firms checked information on applicants' work histories (for example, dates of most recent employment and reason for leaving most recent job). However, a significantly smaller number checked this same information for *all* position openings in their organizations. For instance, whereas 75 percent of the companies checked applicants' references, only 22 percent indicated they checked this same information for all openings in their companies (see Table 10.3).

Candidates' legal eligibility for employment was reviewed by the vast majority of firms (93 percent) and was checked for all position openings by 91 percent of the companies (see Table 10.4). Significantly fewer firms were inclined to check personal information on applicants as compared to work history data. These differences may be explained, in part, by the reference givers' unwillingness to comment on applicants' personal backgrounds for fear of being held legally accountable.

Methods of Collecting Reference Data

Reference information is usually collected in one of three ways: (a) in person, (b) by mail, or (c) by telephone.

TABLE 10.3	EMPLOYMENT INFORMATION CHECKED ON JOB APPLICANTS BY 245 COMPANIES	
Employment Information	**% of Companies Checking for *Any* Position**	**% of Companies Checking for *All* Positions**
Dates of most recent job	96%	75%
Reason for leaving most recent job	96	71
Information about jobs held prior to most recent job	94	59
Salary and position in most recent job	90	61
Professional references	75	22
Current supervisor's evaluation	73	35
Workers' compensation record	31	12

SOURCE: Adapted from the Bureau of National Affairs, Inc., *Recruiting and Selection Procedures* (PPF Survey No. 146) (Washington, D.C.: Bureau of National Affairs, May 1988), pp. 22-23.

| TABLE 10.4 | PERSONAL INFORMATION CHECKED ON JOB APPLICANTS BY 245 COMPANIES |

Personal Information	% of Companies Checking for *Any* Position	% of Companies Checking for *All* Positions
Legal eligibility for employment	93%	91%
Educational background	81	31
Personal references	64	17
Medical history	54	29
Driving record	53	6
Criminal record	49	12
Credit record	25	—a

[a]Data were not available.

SOURCE: Adapted from the Bureau of National Affairs, Inc., *Recruiting and Selection Procedures* (PPF Survey No. 146) (Washington, D.C.: Bureau of National Affairs, May 1988), pp. 23-24.

In-Person Checks   In-person checks involve personal contact with a reference giver. Most often, these contacts are part of background investigations and concern jobs in which an incumbent is a potential security or financial risk.

There is some indication that in-person contacts may uncover information not captured by written methods. Research by Howard Goheen and James Mosel showed that sensitive applicant characteristics, such as alcoholism and inadequate job performance, were revealed by in-person contacts that were not reported in a written questionnaire. In general, the investigators found little agreement between the two methods in the assessment of applicant characteristics.[64] However, because collecting reference information by means of in-person contacts is expensive and time consuming, it is not frequently used in most industrial selection programs. For example, the Bureau of National Affairs study we cited earlier showed that 13 percent of 245 employers used an outside investigator, and only 4 percent collected reference data in person.[65]

Mail Checks   Reference checks requested through the mail involve a written questionnaire or letter. With a questionnaire, references are usually asked to rate an applicant on a variety of traits or characteristics. When used in this manner, reference checks resemble traditional employee job performance ratings. Raters provide judgments of individual characteristics using some form of graduated rating scale. Space may also be provided for comments as well. Exhibit 10.8 presents one example of a typical reference questionnaire.

Reference checks collected through the mail can be a systematic, efficient means for collecting reference data. However, one of the biggest problems associated with mail questionnaires is their low return rate by reference givers. Mosel and Goheen reported a 56 percent return rate for over 4,700 reference questionnaires for 12 skilled occupations and a 64 percent return rate for over 16,000

EXHIBIT 10.8	EXAMPLE OF A MAIL QUESTIONNAIRE REFERENCE CHECK

Sales Applicant Reference Check

We are in the process of considering *James Ridley Parrish* (SS Number: *123-45-6789*) for a sales position in our firm. In considering him/her, it would be helpful if we could review your appraisal of his/her previous work with you. For your information, we have enclosed a statement signed by him/her authorizing us to contact you for information on his/her previous work experience with you. We would certainly appreciate it if you would provide us with your candid opinions of his/her employment. If you have any questions or comments you would care to make, please feel free to contact us at the number listed in the attached cover letter. At any rate, thank you for your consideration of our requests for the information requested below. As you answer the questions, please keep in mind that they should be answered in terms of your knowledge of his/her previous work with you.

1. When was he/she employed with your firm? From _____ 19____ to _____ 19____.

2. Was he/she under your direct supervision? ☐ Yes ☐ No

3. If not, what was your working relationship with him/her? _____

_____

4. How long have you had an opportunity to observe his/her job performance? _____

_____

5. What was his/her last job title with your firm? _____

6. Did he/she supervise any employees? ☐ Yes ☐ No. If so, how many? _____

7. What was his/her last gross income? $ _____ per year.

8. Why did he/she leave your company? _____

Below is a series of questions that deal with how he/she might perform at the job for which we are considering him/her. Read the question and then use the rating scale to indicate how you think he/she would perform based on your previous knowledge of his/her work.

9. For him/her to perform best, how closely should he/she be supervised?
   ☐ Needs no supervision
   ☐ Needs infrequent supervision
   ☐ Needs close, frequent supervision

10. How well does he/she react to working with details?
   ☐ Gets easily frustrated
   ☐ Can handle work that involves some details but works better without them
   ☐ Details in a job pose no problem at all

11. How well do you think he/she can handle complaints from customers?
   ☐ Would generally refuse to help resolve a customer complaint
   ☐ Would help resolve a complaint only if a customer insisted
   ☐ Would feel the customer is right and do everything possible to resolve a complaint

12. In what type of sales job do you think he/she would be best?
   ☐ Handling sales of walk-in customers
   ☐ Traveling to customer locations out-of-town to make sales

(continued)

EXHIBIT 10.8   (CONTINUED)

---

13. With respect to his/her work habits, check *all* of the characteristics below that describe his/her *best* work situation:
☐ Works best on a regular schedule
☐ Works best under pressure
☐ Works best only when in the mood
☐ Works best when there is a regular series of steps to follow for solving a problem

14. Do you know of anything that would indicate if he/she would be unfit or dangerous (for example, in working with customers or coworkers or in driving an automobile) in a position with our organization? ☐ Yes ☐ No. If yes," please explain. _____
_____

15. If you have any additional comments, please make them on the back of this form.

Your Name: _____

Your Title: _____

Address: _____

_____
          City   State   Zip

Company: _____

Telephone: _____

Thank you for your time and help The information you provided will be very useful as we review all application materials.

NOTE: This form is completed by the reference giver.

---

questionnaires for 22 professional and semiprofessional occupations.[66] One exception to these low return rates is in a study that reported receiving 85 percent of the reference check questionnaires mailed to previous employers of 147 clerical job applicants.[67] The return of mail reference checks can present a problem for employers. One means of encouraging the return of a mail check is to enclose a signed statement from the applicant authorizing a former employer to give the requested information and stating that the reference information will be kept confidential.

Letters of Reference   Another form of mail check is the letter of reference or recommendation. In this case, references write a letter evaluating a job applicant. Reference givers may be asked to address specific questions about an applicant or simply told to express any comments of their choice. Although there do not appear to be comparative data on the frequency of use, letters of reference are probably restricted to high-skill or professional jobs. When properly completed by a knowledgeable reference, letters may provide greater depth of information on an applicant than that obtained on a rating scale. However, since letters of recommendation usually come from writers suggested by a job applicant, negative comments are seldom given.

    Several investigations of the letter of reference have implied that the method may offer some predictive utility about an applicant. These studies suggest that even if only positive comments are given, it may still be possible to obtain some indication of the writer's true feelings.

Sherwood Peres and Robert Garcia compiled a list of 170 adjectives used in 625 letters of recommendation submitted for applicants of engineering jobs. Two hundred supervisors were asked to review the list of adjectives and to rate how well each one described their best and worst engineers. Analyses showed that there were five basic categories of adjectives used in the letters. These categories included adjectives dealing with applicants' (a) mental ability, (b) urbanity, (c) vigor, (d) dependability, and (e) cooperation. Adjectives dealing with mental ability were most related to job performance; adjectives dealing with cooperation and urbanity were least related to performance. Thus the researchers concluded that when reference givers do not believe an applicant is really qualified for a job, about the best they can say is that "Joe is a pretty nice guy." A seemingly positive letter of reference may actually be "damning with faint praise."[68]

Research by Albert Mehrabian[69] and by Arthur Wiens and associates[70] suggests that the number of words in a letter of reference may be a better indicator of a reference giver's attitude toward the person written about than the content itself. This body of research shows that a long letter is more indicative of a positive attitude than a short letter. This finding may be useful in those situations in which social constraints may inhibit a reference giver from expressing a negative attitude toward the person written about.

Even though there may be some positive aspects to letters of reference, there are some important disadvantages associated with them. Some of these disadvantages include the following:

1. Writers have the difficult task of organizing the letter.

2. Letter quality will depend on the effort expended by the writers and their ability to express their thoughts.

3. The same information will not be obtained on each applicant.

4. Areas or issues important to an organization may be omitted.

5. Scoring of the letter is subjective and based on the reader's interpretation.[71]

Yet the small possibility of negative information and the implications of such information justify for most users the continued collection of letters of recommendation.

Telephone Checks   Charles Pyron's survey of personnel managers in 60 firms showed that telephone contacts were used more frequently than written reference checks obtained through the mail. The Bureau of National Affairs survey confirmed this result. Over 90 percent of 245 employers said they used this method of collecting reference data.[72] A number of advantages attributed to the method probably account for its disproportionate use. These assets include the following:

1. Reference givers can be questioned and ambiguous comments clarified.

2. Information may be given orally that would not be given in writing.

3. The reference checking process can be speeded up.

4. It is easier to ensure that reference comments are being given by the person named rather than a clerk or secretary.

5. The way oral comments are given (for example, voice inflections, pauses) may be revealing of what a person really thinks.

6. A telephone reference check can yield a better reference return rate.

7. The personal nature of the telephone check contributes to greater responsiveness of the reference giver.[73]

In conducting the check, prepared questions may be asked or questions may be developed and posed by the reference taker during the interview. If an unstructured approach is used over the telephone, the utility of the data collected will be highly dependent on the skill and training of the telephone interviewer. Table 10.5 lists some questions frequently asked during a telephone reference check; these are *not* necessarily recommended questions.

Sources of Reference Data

A number of sources of reference information are available to employers. Each should be considered when conducting a reference check.

Former Employers As we have noted, former employers are an important source for verifying previous employment records and for evaluating an applicant' s previous work habits and performance. If available, data from former employers will more than likely be released through a personnel office. However, information from previous supervisors, when available, are particularly valuable.

Personal References Personal references supplied by the applicant is another source. As might be expected, most applicants will choose individuals as references because they believe they will receive a positive evaluation. If personal reference information is going to be requested, it should be checked. Through careful questioning, it may be possible to obtain useful information from the references. In particular, it is important to know how long and in what capacity the reference has known the applicant.

Investigative Agencies For several hundred dollars per applicant, there are numerous firms available who can conduct background checks on applicants. Background checks can focus on résumé and application information, credit

TABLE 10.5	SOME EXAMPLE QUESTIONS FREQUENTLY ASKED IN A TELEPHONE REFERENCE CHECK

1. Would you rehire the job applicant?
2. Why did the applicant leave your firm?
3. How long did the applicant work for your firm?
4. What is your general overall evaluation of the applicant?
5. What was the applicant's absenteeism record?
6. Does the applicant work well with others?
7. What were the applicant's responsibilities in order of importance?
8. What were the applicant's principal strengths, outstanding successes, and significant failures in his/her job activities?
9. How would you compare the applicant's performance to the performance of others with similar responsibilities?
10. How would you describe the applicant's success in training, developing, and motivating subordinates?
11. What does the applicant need to do for continued professional growth and development?
12. Were there any vehicle or personal injury type of accidents while the applicant was employed by you?
13. Do you know of anything that would indicate whether the applicant is unfit or dangerous for a position as _____.

SOURCE: Questions 1 through 7 are based on H. C. Pyron, "The Use and Misuse of Previous Employer References in Hiring," *Management of Personnel Quarterly* 9 (1970): 15-22; and questions 8 through 11 were based on Peter A. Rabinowitz, "Reference Auditing: An Essential Management Tool," *Personnel Administrator* 24 (1979): 37.

NOTE: The questions here are those that have frequently been used to collect information on job applicants. These questions are *not* being recommended. In general, any question may be asked, but the user should be sure that the information collected is related to the job for which the applicant is being considered before using the information in selection decision making.

ratings, police and driving records, personal reputation, lifestyle, and other information on the applicant. Many of these checks take the form of consumer reports, of which there are two basic types:[74]

1. *Consumer reports*—Any written or oral communication collected by an agency that concerns an individual's credit standing, character, general reputation, or personal characteristics that is used to establish an individual's eligibility for employment.

2. *Investigative consumer reports*—A consumer report or part of a consumer report that is based on personal interviews with an applicant's friends, neighbors, or acquaintances concerning an applicant.

If a job offer is not made to an applicant because of information included in a consumer report, the individual must be so informed. The employer is not required to reveal the contents of the report but must indicate the name and address of the consumer reporting agency making the report.[75]

Public Records In addition to the sources just listed, public records can also be searched. As with using any application information, an employer should take precautions before using such information. *The employer should be sure that the information solicited does not discriminate against a protected group and that it can be justified by the nature of the job for which applicant screening is being undertaken.* With this caution in mind, public records can be searched rather easily. Based on a review and discussion by Commerce Case Clearing House, these records include the following:[76]

1. *Criminal records*—In particular, before using these records, an employer should check to see if they are likely to discriminate against a protected group and if there is actual business necessity for using criminal record information. Jobs that have high degrees of public contact, have limited supervision, involve working at private residences or other businesses, involve personal care of others, such as children, or have direct access to others' personal belongings, valuables, or merchandise quite likely will require a search of such records. Assuming that such information is needed and can be used, there are two possible ways of collecting criminal record data. First, the employer can access the state's central criminal record repository. Each state has such a repository and, depending on state law, may be accessible by an employer. Second, criminal record data are available from individual counties. Whatever the source used, there are several points to keep in mind. Criminal record data may be inaccurate or incomplete. Thus if employment is not offered to an applicant because of his or her criminal record, employers covered by the Fair Credit Reporting Act must disclose to the applicant the name, address, and telephone number of the agency reporting the criminal record. The applicant must be given an opportunity to check the records. Criminal convictions cannot serve as an absolute bar to employment. Users of criminal record data should consider factors such as the nature and seriousness of the offense, the relation of the offense to the nature of the job sought, the individual's attempts at rehabilitation, and the length of time between the conviction and the employment decision.

2. *Driving records*—Driving record information can be obtained from the state department of motor vehicles. Information on traffic violations and other driving offenses, such as driving under the influence of alcohol or drugs, are available. In addition, the information can be used to check the name, birthdate, address, and physical description of an applicant. This information is useful for identifying falsified information given on the application form and confirming that an applicant is who he or she claims to be.

3. *Workers' compensation records*—These records are also usually available from a state agency. They show the types and number of claims that have been filed by an individual. The organization and completeness of the records can vary from one state to the next.

4. *Federal court records*—Civil and criminal federal court case information can be obtained by many employers through federal court records. Thus if it is known where an applicant has lived or worked, federal court records can be searched to identify any civil, criminal, or bankruptcy cases in which an individual has been involved. It should be noted that the Bankruptcy Act places limits on an employer's use of bankruptcy information in selection.

5. *Educational records*—We have pointed out the importance of checking educational records. Many universities and colleges, for example, will verify an individual's dates of attendance and any degrees held. Surveys have shown that a large percentage of colleges will provide the information over the telephone, and many will send an applicant's actual transcript when the proper requesting procedures are followed.

Usefulness of Reference Data

We have studied several aspects of the reference check including its role in selection, approaches to collecting reference data, and sources of reference data. The next question is, How valuable are these data in predicting the success of job applicants? Although there are not many empirical studies that have examined the effectiveness of the method, we present some limited results that are available on the type of reference giver and the reliability and validity of reference data.

Reference Giver   One essential element to having useful data is the reference giver. Unless the giver provides reliable and valid data on applicants, the information will not be helpful to selection decision making. For these data to be useful, individuals serving as references must meet four conditions: (a) they must have had a chance to observe the applicant in relevant situations, (b) they must be competent to make the evaluations requested, (c) they must want to give frank and honest assessments, and (d) they must be able to express themselves so their comments are understood as intended.[77]

Many different types of individuals, such as friends, relatives, college professors, teachers, immediate supervisors, coworkers, subordinates, and HR managers can serve as references. Because these individuals are likely to differ in areas such as the opportunity to observe the applicant, freedom from bias, and knowledge of the applicant, we would expect differences in the quality of their reference information. Several studies have evaluated the comparative value of information obtained from various groups. James Mosel and Howard Goheen examined the validity and leniency of ratings given by different reference groups. For 795 reference questionnaires collected on 400 employees in five jobs, they found supervisors and acquaintances provided reference data predictive of subsequent job performance, whereas personnel officers, coworkers, and relatives did not. In terms of rating leniency (that is, giving higher ratings than may be deserved) for 3,000 reference questionnaires on applicants for seven federal government jobs, friends and previous subordinates were most lenient; previous employers were least.[78]

Surveys of employers' opinions of the value of reference data given by specific reference groups have yielded similar results. A survey of commercial banks indicated that former employers' comments were most valuable.[79] Another study explored which previous employer groups were most helpful. The past supervisor, as opposed to the personnel department of the previous organization, was viewed as most beneficial.[80] Supervisors are usually in the best position to comment on applicants' work habits.

Reliability and Validity of Reference Data   In spite of the widespread use of reference checks, there is surprisingly little research evidence regarding their reliability and effectiveness in predicting applicants' subsequent job performance. Studies of reference data reliability have been rare. When reliability data have been reported, they have typically involved interrater (for example, among supervisors, acquaintances, and coworkers) reliability estimates of .40 or less. Although these estimates are low, they are not all that surprising. We might anticipate that different groups of raters might focus on different aspects of referees and judge them from different perspectives. These differences will contribute to different ratings and, thus, lower reliability.

Of the ten or so studies reporting validity data, their findings generally show that the relationships between reference ratings and measures of employee success (performance ratings and turnover) are low to moderate at best. For example, one review of seven studies of the validity of reference checks estimated an average validity coefficient of .14 for supervisory ratings and turnover criteria.[81]

John and Rhonda Hunter's meta-analysis of the validity of reference checks showed that validity ranged from a low of .16 for promotion criteria to a high of .26 for supervisor rating criteria.[82] Other predictors such as biographical data and ability tests generally fare far better in predicting job success than reference checks. Several factors apparently have some bearing on the utility of references in predicting job success. Conclusions regarding the impact of some of these factors include the following:

1.   References are likely to be more useful in predicting employee success when completed by an applicant's previous immediate supervisor.[83]

2.   Prediction is enhanced when (a) the reference giver on the previous job has had adequate time to observe the applicant, (b) the applicant is the same gender, ethnicity, and nationality as the supervisor on the pervious job.

3.   The old and new jobs are similar in content.[84]

You may wonder why reference checks do not perform better than they do in predicting applicants' subsequent performance. There are several possible explanations. First, the criteria or success measures with which reference checks have been statistically correlated have generally suffered from low reliability. As we saw in Chapters 4 and 5, when a criterion is characterized by unreliable information, we should not expect reference data to predict it statistically. Many of the criteria utilized in studies of the validity of reference data have had poor reliability. Supervisory ratings have frequently served as criteria, and these are notorious for their subjectivity and, sometimes, low reliability.

Another explanation for the apparent low value of reference measures is the narrow or restricted range of scores characteristic of many reference reports. Quite often, scores tend to be high with little negative information being given on an applicant. If all applicants generally receive the same high reference scores, then it is unreasonable to expect a reference check to predict how applicants will perform on a subsequent job. If we used only positive information, we would predict that all applicants would succeed. Yet we know that differences in job success will exist.

A third factor accounting for low validity of reference data is the problem of applicants' preselection of who will evaluate them.[85] Since applicants recognize that references may have a bearing on their employability, they are most likely to choose those who will have something positive to say about them. As we have noted, leniency is the rule rather than the exception. Preselection of references by applicants only exacerbates the restriction of range and inflation problems.

Other factors that we have already listed may also contribute to the effectiveness problem. Reference givers may not have had sufficient opportunity to observe the applicant on a job; they may not be competent; they may distort their ratings to help the applicant; and they may not be able to adequately communicate their evaluations.

Legal Issues Affecting the Use of Reference Checks

As with any HR selection measure, there are important legal concerns that an employer should consider when using reference checks for selection or providing reference data to another employer. Two broad categories of legal issues are particularly critical. The first of these comprises two matters: (a) the discriminatory impact reference checks may have against job applicants and (b) the defamation of job applicants' character through libel or slander.

The second category is one that is somewhat unique to reference checks. That issue involves complaints filed against employers for "negligent hiring" of employees. As we see in the following sections, the possibility of libel or slander suits *discourages* employers from providing reference information; the possibility of negligent hiring charges *encourages* the use of reference checks by prospective employers.

Discriminatory Impact and Defamation of Character   A few cases have appeared in the courts dealing with claims of discriminatory impact through reference checks. For example, in *Equal Employment Opportunity Commission v. National Academy of Sciences* (1976), a job applicant was refused employment on the basis of a poor reference by her previous supervisor. It was argued by the plaintiff that the reference check excluded a disproportionate number of blacks and was not related to performance on the job. Evidence presented by the defense led the court to conclude that there was no adverse impact, and that the reference check (through presentation of a validation study) was job-related.[86]

Defamation is another problem that can occur in reference checking, but it concerns the employer giving reference information as opposed to using the information for selection decision making. Although defamation is beyond our present concerns, it is an important problem for employers giving reference data and deserves a few comments.

From the perspective of providing reference information, defamation involves a written (libel) or oral (slander) false statement made by an employer about a previous employee that damages the individual's reputation.[87] For instance, in *Rutherford v. American Bank of Commerce* (1976), an individual brought a charge against her former employer because, in a letter of recommendation, the employer mentioned she had brought a sex discrimination charge against the firm. She was able to demonstrate that she could not obtain later employment because of the letter of recommendation. The court ruled on her behalf, saying that the employer illegally retaliated against her because she exercised her rights under Title VII.[88]

For defamation to occur, several elements must be present:

1. A written or oral defamatory statement must have been given.

2. There must be a false statement of fact. The employer must prove that the statement was made in good faith and was believed to be true.

3. Injury must have occurred to the referee, such as the inability of the referee to get another job because of the previous employer's statement.

4. The employer does *not* have absolute or qualified privilege. Under *absolute* privilege, an employer has immunity from defamation, such as in a legal proceeding. Under *qualified* privilege, an employer will not be held liable unless the information is knowingly false or malicious. Information that is judged to be truthful; based on facts; limited to the appropriate business purpose, that is, reference information; made on the proper occasion, and given to appropriate parties is likely to be judged as qualified privilege and, therefore, appropriate.[89]

Two additional cases help to illustrate further the impact of libel or slander in reference checking.

True v. Ladner (1986) is a case in which True, a public high school teacher, brought suit for libel and slander against Ladner, the school superintendent, based on Ladner's statements given during an inquiry by a prospective employer. Ladner characterized True as not being a good mathematics teacher, being more concerned with living up to his contract than going the extra mile as a teacher, and not being able to "turn students on" as a teacher. Although Ladner argued that these were his personal opinions and protected by his first amendment rights, the jury found from the evidence presented that Ladner's reference statements were given with "reckless disregard of their truth or falsity" and, therefore, libel and slander was committed against True. Under appeal, the jury's verdict was upheld by the Maine Supreme Judicial Court.[90]

In *Hall v. Buck* (1984), Buck, an insurance salesman, was fired by Hall & Co., Inc. Although he had a past history of high success in insurance sales, Buck was unable to find employment with several other insurance firms. Buck hired an investigator to find out the true reasons he was fired from Hall, Inc. Several employees of the firm made derogatory statements to the investigator about Buck. Testimony by one of Buck's prospective employers indicated that he did not make a job offer because a reference giver at Hall, Inc. said, among other comments, that he would not rehire Buck again. Evidence presented at the trial showed that the reference givers at Hall, Inc. made their statements based on secondhand information and that the statements made were not substantially true. Thus it was concluded that Hall, Inc. had committed slander and libel against Buck.[91]

The cases cited illustrate some legal ramifications for reference givers. However, reference users may also be in jeopardy even if adverse impact is not present. For example, Charles Pyron describes a hypothetical situation that could confront an employer using a reference check to screen applicants. He states, for instance, suppose an employer obtains letters of reference from previous supervisors who describe an applicant as a "trouble maker" and "real rebel." Using this information, the employer rejects the applicant. The applicant demands to know why, and, in response, the employer presents information obtained from the letters of reference. Pyron asks, "In short, the question is this: the two letters have, in a very real way, kept him from getting employment. Is he not entitled to sue the two supervisors for defamation of character? Might not he even be able to sue you, because you have, by your action, agreed with the judgment of the two supervisors?"[92]

The point in Pyron's example is that there is a tendency among some reference givers to go beyond necessity in describing people. Potential employers would be wise to recognize the signals of defamation and discount such reference data. Because of the *Uniform Guidelines*, Fair Credit Reporting Act (1971), Family Educational Rights and Privacy Act (1974), and some statutes included under state labor codes, there is a growing concern among employers about the legal implications of using reference checks in selection. Libel, slander, or defamation of an applicant's character are becoming very significant issues for some employers. As a consequence, some may believe that it is not permissible under the law to check references. *However, it is legal and even the duty of employers to check references.* They have the right to seek job-related reference information, to use such information in an appropriate manner in selection decision making, and to share appropriate information with individuals who have a legitimate need to know.[93]

Negligent Hiring   A charge of negligent hiring occurs when a third party such as a coworker, client, or customer of an organization files suit against an employer for injuries caused by an employee.[94] For example, suppose an exterminator for a pest control company who has come to inspect an apartment physically assaults a female resident. The victim in this incident might bring a negligent hiring suit against the pest control company. The focus of the plaintiff's charges in such a suit is that the employer knew or should have known that the employee causing the injuries was unfit for the job, and the employer's negligence in hiring the individual produced the plaintiff's injuries.

For an employer to be held liable in negligent hiring, five points must be covered:

1. An injury to a third party must be shown to be caused by an individual who is in the employment of a firm.

2. The employee must be shown to be unfit for the job that he or she holds.

3. It must be shown that the employer knew or should have known that the employee was unfit for the job.

4. The injury received by the third party must be a foreseeable outcome from hiring the unfit employee.

5. It must be shown that the injury is a reasonable and probable outcome of what the employer did or did not do in hiring the individual.[95]

Suits involving negligent hiring typically encompass the following types of issues: (a) those in which there was intentional employee misconduct such as a theft committed by an employee with a history of dishonesty, (b) those in which physical harm occurred such as an assault by an employee with a violent past, or (c) those in which an employee does not possess the skill or ability to perform a job task, an example being an inexperienced truck driver, and an individual is injured.[96] In judging employer negligence, the courts consider the steps an employer has taken to identify an unfit employee relative to the nature of the tasks performed by the employee. Reference checks along with background investigations are two types of pre-employment screens that many courts view as suitable for identifying potential problems.[97] Both of these screen are particularly appropriate for jobs that involve (a) access to other's residences, (b) little supervision, (c) public safety, and (d) work with individuals receiving personal care. For many jobs, documented reference checks alone can serve as important evidence in defending a negligent hiring suit?

As you read and think about reference checks you may be wondering: "Can't a company find itself in a catch-22 situation? That is, on the one hand, it may be important to obtain reference information prior to hiring, but on the other hand, past employers may not provide such information for fear of libel or slander suits by past employees. What then?" Certainly, there is concern among employers about the type of information released on past employees. For example, one writer makes the following recommendations about releasing reference information: (a) do not give out reference information over the telephone, (b) document all information that is released, (c) provide only specific, objective information, (d) obtain written consent from the employee prior to releasing reference information, and (e) do not answer a question involving an opinion of whether a previous employee would be rehired.[98]

Obviously, if many organizations follow these guidelines, it will be difficult for prospective employers to obtain much more than dates of employment and the last position held in the organization.

In order to encourage former employers to supply information on a past employee, Donald Myers recommends the following strategies:

1. Submit a written request for information on specific questions, (such as "Was the person ever disciplined or discharged for fighting?") that are relevant to making an employment decision.

2. Include a release form signed by the applicant stating that (a) the applicant has read and approves the information requested and (b) the applicant requests that the information be given.

If the previous employer refuses to provide such information, then

3. Call the person in charge of human resources and ask why the request was not honored.

4. Ask how a request should be made so it will be honored. If the previous employer still refuses to give the information, then

5. Inform the individual that failure to cooperate was being documented with date, time, and name of the person refusing the request.

6. Tell the individual that if the missing information is so relevant that the applicant will not be hired without it, the applicant will be told that the previous employer's refusal was the reason for the lack of an offer.[99]

From the perspective of negligent hiring suits, a key element is that written documentation shows that the employer *attempted* to collect background data on prospective employees. Even though necessary reference information may not be given by a past employer, a user of reference checks should carefully document what questions were asked and what information was obtained. From a legal point of view, the important question is, *Did the employer take reasonable steps and precautions to identify a problem employee, given the risks inherent in the tasks performed on the job?* Depending on the nature of these tasks, steps other than reference checks, such as providing comprehensive training, giving close supervision, and conducting an extensive background investigation, may be required.[100] However, for many jobs, verifying and checking references is considered an appropriate degree of care for identifying potential problem employees.

Recommended Steps for Using Reference Checks

From legal and practical perspectives, employers wanting to use reference checks should undertake several steps.

1. *Reference data are most properly used when the data involve job-related concerns.* Thus requested data should address KSAs or any other characteristics of the applicant that are necessary for successful job performance. Emphasis should be given to those characteristics that distinguish effective from

ineffective performance. How do we identify what KSAs or other characteristics are critical? As we discussed in earlier chapters, we make the determination from an analysis of the job for which we are selecting employees. If questions or ratings are restricted to those that can be demonstrated as being related to the job, then there should be no difficulties.

2. *Because we are tailoring the content of our reference check to the content of a specific job, we will likely need more than one general form for the various positions in an organization.* At the least, we will need a reference form for each cluster or family of jobs that require similar KSAs. Multiple forms obviously add multiple costs and additional work. But if we are going to obtain useful legal selection data and if we choose to use reference checks, multiple forms will probably be a necessity.[101]

3. *Reference checks are subject to the Uniform Guidelines.* Thus, as for any selection measure, we will need to monitor the fairness and validity of the reference check. If our reference checking system unfairly discriminates against protected groups or is not related to job success, we should change or eliminate our system. To do otherwise is not only legally foolish but jeopardizes our ability to choose competent employees.

4. *An objective (for example, a system that focuses on factual or behavioral data related to the applicant) rather than a subjective (such as trait ratings) reference checking system is less likely to be open to charges of discrimination.* Objective methods are more amenable to the development of scoring procedures and reliability and validity analyses. Such methods consist of those that focus on behaviors and have a specific scoring system. Objective approaches also help to ensure that the same information is obtained systematically on all applicants and that the information is used in the same manner. We should be certain that information that qualifies or disqualifies one, qualifies or disqualifies all. Written recommendations (such as a letter of reference) followed by a brief review often lead to subjective impressions and hunches that may not be valid.[102] If we use these measures in our selection program, we should be aware that subjective impressions and judgments are woefully inadequate.

5. *Applicants should be asked to give written permission to contact their references.* When actually contacting references, information should also be collected on how long that person has known an applicant and the position the person holds. This information can be useful for verifying responses or, if necessary, legally proving that the person contacted is in a position to provide the assessments being requested.

6. *Reference takers collecting information by telephone or in person should be trained in how to interview reference givers.* Preparation will be necessary in how to formulate questions and record responses systematically. Here again, an

objective approach to information collection will improve the quality of data ultimately collected.

7. *All reference check information should be recorded in writing.* If a legal suit is brought against an employer, reference data may serve as important evidence in defending against the suit. Documentation in writing is essential for the defense.

8. *If a job applicant provides references but reference information cannot be obtained, go back to the applicant for additional references.* Consider not hiring an applicant if complete reference information is not available. Hiring an applicant without such information can be very risky.

9. *Check all application form and résumé information.* In particular, focus on educational background (for example, schools attended, degrees earned, academic performance) and previous employment records (for example, dates of employment, job titles, duties performed). Gaps in information reported are red flags and signal a need for special attention. For instance, an individual may have recently spent time in jail for a crime directly related to the position to which he or she is applying.

10. A caveat on the use of negative information. Negative information received during a reference check frequently serves as a basis for rejecting an applicant. Caution is certainly advised in using *any* negative data as a basis for excluding applicants. *Before negative information is employed, we should (a) verify its accuracy with other sources, (b) be sure that disqualification on the basis of the information will distinguish between those who will fail and those who will succeed on the job, and (c) use the same information consistently for all applicants.*

As you read the literature on reference data, it is interesting to note an apparent pattern. Practitioner-oriented journals tend to view reference checks as playing an important role in HR selection. Apparently, the belief is that reference checks provide information not given by other measures. In contrast, articles in research-oriented journals generally regard reference checks as a relatively minor selection tool. Research studies that have investigated the utility of selection devices have typically concluded that references are not especially useful.[103] Although reference reports may not be as useful as other measures in predicting employee job success, they may be the *only* basis for detecting some information that would indicate unsatisfactory job performance. In this role, reference data will serve as a basis for identifying a relatively small portion of applicants who should not be considered further for a job. However, it may not be efficient to incorporate reference checks in selecting applicants for every job in an organization. The decision of whether to employ reference checks will vary across organizations and jobs. But we suggest that the higher the responsibility level associated with a particular position or the greater the risk posed by the position to customers, clients, and coworkers, the greater the need for a reference check.

References

[1] Edward L. Levine and Abraham Flory, "Evaluation of Job Applications: A Conceptual Framework," *Public Personnel Management* 4 (1975): 378-385.

[2] Equal Employment Opportunity Commission, *Guide to Pre-Employment Inquiries* (Washington, D.C.: Equal Employment Opportunity Commission, August 1981), p. 1.

[3] Ibid.

[4] Ibid.

[5] Philip Ash, "Law and Regulation of Preemployment Inquires," *Journal of Business and Psychology* 5 (1991): 291–308. See also Philip Ash, *The Legality of Preemployment Inquires* (Park Ridge, Ill.: London House, 1989). These sources contain excellent state-by-state reviews of laws and statutes which impact various items that might appear on application forms.

[6] Ibid. For some examples of application forms, see *BNA Handbook: Personnel Management, 1983* (Washington, D.C.: Bureau of National Affairs, 1983), pp. 201:906–201:927.

[7] Ash, "Law and Regulation of Preemployment Inquiries," p. 303.

[8] Michael B. Levin-Epstein, *Primer of Equal Employment Opportunity* (Washington, D.C.: Bureau of National Affairs, 1987).

[9] Ibid., p. 5.

[10] Ash, "Law and Regulation of Preemployment Inquiries," p. 299.

[11] Equal Employment Opportunity Commission, *Guidelines on Discrimination Because of National Origin*, 29 Code of Federal Regulations.

[12] Ernest C. Miller, "An EEO Examination of Employment Applications," *Personnel Administrator* 25 (March 1981): 63–70.

[13] Debra D. Burrington, "A Review of State Government Employment Application Forms for Suspect Inquiries," *Public Personnel Management* 11 (1982): 55–60.

[14] Miller, "An EEO Examination of Employment Applications," pp. 63–70.

[15] Richard S. Lowell and Jay A. Deloach, "Equal Employment Opportunity: Are You Overlooking the Application Form?" *Personnel* 59 (1982): 49–55.

[16] Miller, "An EEO Examination of Employment Applications," p. 66.

[17] Ibid.

[18] Bureau of National Affairs, *Selection Procedures and Personnel Records* (PPF Survey No. 114) (Washington, D.C.: The Bureau of National Affairs, September 1976).

[19] Department of Fair Employment and Housing, State of California, *Pre-Employment Inquiry Guidelines* (Sacramento, Calif.: Department of Fair Employment and Housing, May 1982).

[20] Wayne R. Porter and Edward L. Levine, "Improving Applicants' Performance in the Completion of Applications" *Public Personnel Management* 3 (1974): 314–317. For guidelines to applicants completing an application form, see Wayne R Porter, "The Job-Winning Application" (Tempe, Ariz.: Personnel Service Organization, 1976).

[21] Walter Kiechel, "Lies on the Resumé," *Fortune* 106 (August 23, 1982): 221–222, 224.

[22] Ibid., p. 221.

[23] Ibid.

[24] James N. Mosel and Lee W. Cozan, "The Accuracy of Application Blank Work Histories, "*Journal of Applied Psychology* 36 (1952): 365–369.

[25] David J. Weiss and Rene V. Dawis, "An Objective Validation of Factual Interview Data," *Journal of Applied Psychology* 44 (1960): 381–385.

[26] Irwin L. Goldstein, "The Application Blank: How Honest Are the Responses?" *Journal of Applied Psychology* 65 (1974): 491–494.

[27] Donald W. Myers, *Human Resources Management* (Chicago: Commerce Clearing House, 1992).

[28] Levine and Flory, "Evaluation of Job Applications: A Conceptual Framework," pp. 36–42.

[29] Lawrence Fogli, "Supermarket Cashier," in *The Job Analysis Handbook for Business, Industry, and Government*, ed. Sidney Gael (New York: Wiley, 1988), p. 1227.

[30]Marvin Dunnette, Leaetta Hough, and Rodney Rosse, "Task and Job Taxonomies as a Basis for Identifying Labor Supply Sources and Evaluating Employment Qualifications," *Human Resource Planning* 2 (1979): 48.

[31]Frank A. Malinowski, "Job Selection Using Task Analysis," *Personnel Journal* (April 1981): 288–291.

[32]Ronald Ash, James Johnson, Edward Levine, and Michael McDaniel, "Job Applicant Training and Work Experience Evaluation in Personnel Selection," in *Research in Personnel and Human Resource Management*, eds. Kenneth Rowland and Gerald Ferris (Greenwich, Conn: JAI Press, 1989), pp. 187–190.

[33]Wayne R. Porter, Edward L. Levine, and Abraham Flory, *Training and Experience Evaluation* (Tempe, Ariz.: Personnel Services Organization, 1976) and Ash, Johnson, Levine, and McDaniel, "Job Applicant Training and Work Experience Evaluation in Personnel Selection," pp. 199–209.

[34]Ash, Johnson, Levine, and McDaniel, "Job Applicant Training and Work Experience Evaluation in Personnel Selection," pp. 199–200.

[35]Porter, Levine, and Flory, "Training and Experience Evaluation," pp. 68–71.

[36]Ibid.

[37]Ibid., p. 4.

[38]Albert P. Maslow, *Staffing the Public Service* (Chelsea, Mich.: BookCrafters, 1983), p. 138.

[39]Leaetta M. Hough, "Development and Evaluation of the 'Accomplishment Record' Method of Selecting and Promoting Professionals," *Journal of Applied Psychology* 69 (1984): 135–146.

[40]Leaetta M. Hough, Margaret A. Keyes, and Marvin D. Dunnette, "An Evaluation of Three 'Alternative' Selection Procedures," *Personnel Psychology* 36 (1983) 261–276.

[41]Ash and Levine, "Job Applicant Training and Work Experience Evaluation: An Empirical Comparison of Four Methods," p. 575.

[42]Ibid.

[43]C. D. Anderson, J. L. Warner, and C. C. Spencer, "Inflation Bias in Self-Assessment Examinations: Implications for Valid Employee Selection," *Journal of Applied Psychology* 69 (1984): 574–580.

[44]Ronald A, Ash and Edward L. Levine, "Job Applicant Training and Work Experience Evaluation: An Empirical Comparison of Four Methods," *Journal of Applied Psychology* 70 (1985): 572–576.

[45]Frank Schmidt, J.R. Caplan, Stephen Bemis, R. Decuir, L. Dunn, and L. Antone, *The Behavioral Consistency Method of Unassembled Examining* (Washington, D.C.: U.S. Office of Personnel Management, Personnel Research and Development Center, 1979).

[46]Ibid.

[47]John Hunter and Rhonda Hunter, "The Validity and Utility of Alternative Predictors of Job Performance," *Psychological Bulletin* 96 (1984): 72–98.

[48]Ash and Levine, "Job Applicant Training and Work Experience Evaluation: An Empirical Comparison of Four Methods."

[49]Michael A. McDaniel, Frank L. Schmidt, and John E. Hunter, "A Meta-Analysis of the Validity of Methods for Rating Training and Experience in Personnel Selection," *Personnel Psychology* 41 (1988): 283–314.

[50]Ash, Johnson, Levine, and McDaniel, "Job Applicant Training and Work Experience Evaluation in Personnel Selection," p.220.

[51]Ibid. Hough, "Development and Evaluation of the 'Accomplishment Record' Method of Selecting and Promoting Professionals."

[52]Ibid., p. 220.

[53]Ash and Levine, "Job Applicant Training and Work Experience Evaluation: An Empirical Comparison of Four Methods," pp. 575–576.

[54]John A. Langdale and Joseph Weitz, "Estimating the Influence of Job Information on Interviewer Agreement," *Journal of Applied Psychology* 57 (1973): 23–27.

[55]Yoash Wiener and Mark L. Schneiderman, "Use of Job Information as a Criterion in Employment Decisions of Interviewers," *Journal of Applied Psychology* 59 (1974): 699–704.

[56]Edward Levine, *Everything You Always Wanted to Know About Job Analysis* (Tampa: Mariner, 1983).

[57]Alan N. Nash and Stephen J. Carroll, "A Hard Look at the Reference Check—Its Modest Worth Can Be Improved," *Business Horizons* 13 (1970): 43–49.

[58]Richard A Lilenthal, *The Use of Reference Checks for Selection* (Washington, D.C.: U.S. Office of Personnel Management, May 1980), p. 1.

[59]Ibid.

[60]George Beason and John A. Belt, "Verifying Applicants' Backgrounds," *Personnel Journal* 55 (1976): 345–348.

[61]Bureau of National Affairs, *Employee Selection Procedures* (ASPA-BNA Survey No. 45) (Washington, D. C.: The Bureau of National Affairs, May 5, 1983), p. 7.

[62]Wayne F. Cascio, *Applied Psychology in Personnel Management* (Englewood Cliffs, N.J.: Prentice Hall, 1987), pp. 255–256.

[63]Bureau of National Affairs, *Recruiting and Selection Procedures* (PPF Survey No. 146) (Washington, D.C.: Bureau of National Affairs, May 1988).

[64]Howard W. Goheen and James N. Mosel, "The Validity of the Employment Recommendation Questionnaire: II. Comparison with Field Investigations," *Personnel Psychology* 12 (1959): 297–301.

[65]Bureau of National Affairs, *Recruiting and Selection Procedures*, p. 24.

[66]James N. Mosel and Howard W. Goheen, "The Validity of the Employment Recommendation Questionnaire in Personnel Selection: I. Skilled Trades," *Personnel Psychology* 11 (1958): 481–490.

[67]Nash and Carroll, "A Hard Look at the Reference Check—Its Modest Worth Can Be Improved," pp. 43–49.

[68]Sherwood H. Peres and J. Robert Garcia, "Validity and Dimensions of Descriptive Adjectives Used in Reference Letters for Engineering Applicants," *Personnel Psychology* 15 (1962): 279–286.

[69]Albert Mehrabian, "Communication Length as an Index of Communicator Attitude," *Psychological Reports* 17 (1965): 519–522.

[70]Arthur N. Wiens, Russel H. Jackson, Thomas S. Manaugh, and Joseph D. Matarazzo, "Communication Length as an Index of Communicator Attitude: A Replication," *Journal of Applied Psychology* 53 (1969): 264–266.

[71]Lilenthal, *The Use of Reference Checks for Selection*, p. 3. See also, Stephen B. Knouse, "Letter of Recommendation: Specificity and Favorability of Information," *Personnel Psychology* 36 (1983): 331–342.

[72]Bureau of National Affairs, *Recruiting and Selection Procedures*, p. 24.

[73]H. Charles Pyron, "The Use and Misuse of Previous Employer References in Hiring," *Management of Personnel Quarterly* 9 (1970): 15–22; Lilenthal, *The Use of Reference Checks for Selection*, p. 2.

[74]Commerce Clearing House, *Privacy, Defamation and Reference Checks: Avoiding Employee Lawsuits* (Chicago: Commerce Clearing House, 1989), pp. 334–335.

[75]Ibid.

[76]Ibid., pp. 336–339.

[77]Milton Blum and James Naylor, *Industrial Psychology: Its Theoretical and Social Foundations* (New York: Harper & Row, 1968), p. 168.

[78]James N. Mosel and Howard W. Goheen, "The Employment Recommendation Questionnaire: III. Validity of Different Types of References," *Personnel Psychology* 12 (1959): 469–477.

[79]D. Dudley and W. French, "Personnel Reference Checking by Banks: Practice and Face Validity," *Business Review* (April 1964): 50–58.

[80]Pyron, "The Use and Misuse of Previous Employer References," pp. 15–22.

[81]For examples of these studies, see Mosel and Goheen, "The Validity of the Employment Recommendation Questionnaire in Personnel Selection: I. Skilled Trades," pp. 481–490; Goheen and Mosel, "The Validity of the Employment Recommendation Questionnaire: II. Comparison with Field Investigations"; Mosel and Goheen, "The Employment Recommendation Questionnaire: III. Validity of

Different Types of References"; Rufus C. Browning, "Validity of Reference Ratings from Previous Employers," *Personnel Psychology* 21 (1968): 389–393; Peres and Garcia, "Validity and Dimensions of Descriptive Adjectives Used in Reference Letters for Engineering Applicants," pp. 279–286.

[82]Hunter and Hunter, "Validity and Utility of Alternative Predictors of Job Performance."

[83]Mosel and Goheen, "The Employment Recommendation Questionnaire: III. Validity of Different Types of References," pp. 389–393.

[84]Stephen J. Carroll and Alan N. Nash, "Effectiveness of a Forced-Choice Reference Check," *Personnel Administration* 35 (1972): 42–46.

[85]Paul M. Muchinsky, "The Use of Reference Reports in Personnel Selection: A Review and Evaluation," *Journal of Occupational Psychology* 52 (1979): 287–297.

[86]*Equal Employment Opportunity Commission v. National Academy of Sciences*, 12 FEP 1690 (1976).

[87]Commerce Clearing House, *Privacy, Defamation and Reference Checks: Avoiding Employee Lawsuits*, p. 6.

[88]*Rutherford v. American Bank of Commerce*, 12 FEP 1184 (1976).

[89]Ann Marie Ryan and Marja Lasek, "Negligent Hiring and Defamation: Areas of Liability Related to Pre-Employment Inquires," *Personnel Psychology* 4 (1991): 307–313.

[90]*True v. Ladner*, 513 A. 2d 257 (1986).

[91]*Frank B. Hall & Co., Inc. v. Buck*, 678 S.W. 2d 612 (1984).

[92]Pyron, "The Use and Misuse of Previous Employer References," p.18.

[93]Cascio, *Applied Psychology in Personnel Management*, p. 256.

[94]James A. Branch, *Negligent Hiring Practice Manual* (New York: Wiley, 1988), p. 3.

[95]Ryan and Lasek, "Negligent Hiring and Defamation: Areas of Liability Related to Pre-Employment Inquires," pp. 294–301.

[96]Branch, "Negligent Hiring Practice Manual."

[97]Ibid., pp. 230–231.

[98]John D. Rice, "Privacy Legislation: Its Effect on Pre-Employment Reference Checking," *Personnel Administrator* 23 (1978): 46–51.

[99]Branch, *Negligent Hiring Practice Manual*, p. 223.

[100]Myers, *Human Resources Management*, p. 221.

[101]Lilenthal, *The Use of Reference Checks for Selection*, p. 6.

[102]Cascio, *Applied Psychology in Personnel Management*, pp. 255–256.

[103]Example practitioner articles that tend to view reference checks as making a positive contribution to HR selection include the following: Bruce D. Wonder and Kenneth S. Keleman, "Increasing the Value of Reference Checking," *Personnel Administrator* 29 (1984): 98–103; Peter A. Rabinowitz, "Reference Auditing: An Essential Management Tool," *Personnel Administrator* 24 (19 79): 34–38; Carol Sewell, "Pre-Employment Investigations: The Key to Security in Hiring," *Personnel Journal* 60 (1981): 82–85. In contrast, for research publications that have a less favorable view of reference checks, see James D. Baxter, Barbara Brock, Peter C. Hill, and Richard M. Rozell, "Letters of Recommendation: A Question of Value," *Journal of Applied Psychology* 66 (1981): 296–301; Muchinsky, "The Use of Reference Reports in Personnel Selection," p. 287–297.

11

Weighted Application Blanks and Biographical Data

Weighted Application Blanks

The Need for Systematic Scoring of Application Forms

As we have seen, application forms can provide much useful information about job applicants. Even though this information might be helpful in making selection decisions, a key issue facing any application reviewer is in deciding *what* application data are most beneficial in choosing successful job applicants. Where clear guides are not provided, selection decisions focusing on application information may be based on the personal biases, prejudices, and whims of each application reviewer. For example, in considering applicants for first-line supervisory jobs, some managers believe only applicants possessing a high school diploma should be hired. Others may not hold this view. But, in fact, is a minimum level of education mandatory for successful performance as a supervisor? Unless relationships between application data and job success are known, application information may be of limited help to managers involved in selection decisions. However, empirical scoring and statistical analyses performed on application data can be very helpful in isolating those specific factors predictive of job success. These analyses, in turn, can lead to a better understanding of application information and standardization in its use.

The Nature of Weighted Application Blanks

The *weighted application blank*, or WAB as it is sometimes called, is actually a technique for *scoring* application forms rather than a different personnel assessment tool. The procedure serves as a means for determining if individual items on an application form (such as previous job experience or years of education) distinguish between successful and unsuccessful employees Once identified, items related to employee job success are then weighted to reflect their degree of importance in differentiating good and poor performers. Applicants for a specific job are scored on these items, and predictions are made of applicants' probable job success. Total scores for all applicants are determined by summing the respective weights for the relevant application blank items. In this sense, the total score for a WAB is like that of any HR selection test. The score represents a measure of how well an applicant performs on items found to be predictive of job success. Cutoff or passing scores can then be set for comparison with total WAB scores in order to maximize the number of applicants who are predicted to be successful on the job.

The idea of the WAB has a long history. William Owens has traced the concept of a scorable application to an address made by Col. Thomas L. Peters of the Washington Life Insurance Company of Atlanta to the 1894 Chicago Underwriters' meeting.[1] Peters noted in his speech that one way to improve the selection of life insurance agents was "for managers to require all applicants to answer a list of standardized questions, such as the following: Present residence? Residences during the previous ten years? . . . Dependent or not dependent for support on own daily exertions? Amount of unencumbered real estate? Occupation during previous ten years? Previous experience in life insurance selling?"[2]

Although occasional articles on the application of WABs still appear in the professional literature, most attention was directed to the technique in the 1950s through the early 1970s. (George England lists over 100 studies on the WAB appearing during this period.)[3] In general, many of these studies found WABs to be very appropriate in selection. A number were particularly successful in predicting job tenure criteria for clerical[4] and sales[5] jobs. However, these are not the only types of jobs and measures of employee success for which WABs have been successful. WABs have also been successfully developed for jobs ranging from telephone operator[6] to production supervisor[7] to research scientist[8] to police officer.[9] Further, other applications suggest that WABs can serve as a basis for reducing various personnel costs such as those associated with employee turnover. For instance, use of a WAB in selecting clerical personnel for a county government was found to result in a potential savings of about $250,000 over a 25-month period.[10]

WABs may be particularly valuable in employment situations having the following characteristics:

1. Jobs in which a large number of employees are performing similar activities.

2. Jobs in which adequate personnel records are available on individual employees.

3. Jobs that require long and costly training programs.

4. Jobs in which the turnover rate is high.

5. Jobs in which there is a large number of applicants relative to position openings.

6. Jobs in which it is expensive to bring in applicants to the organization for interviewing and testing.[11]

Because of the potential applicability of the method to a variety of jobs, we summarize the major steps involved in applying the technique. The steps outlined are adapted from England's thorough treatment of the development of WABs. If you are interested, review his monograph, *Development and Use of Weighted Application Blanks.*[12]

Developing Weighted Application Blanks

At this point, we assume that an application form has been made up. Ideally, the items appearing on the application were developed from an analysis of the job. We further assume that the items have been screened for possible discriminatory impacts against protected groups (see Chapter 10). The objective now is to develop a scoring procedure for the application that will permit the prediction of applicants' job success. The eight steps that are typically involved in the development and application of a WAB are briefly described here.

1. Choosing the Criterion Perhaps the most critical step in the process is the choice of a measure of employee success or a criterion. It is this measure that a WAB is developed to predict; subsequent selection decisions are based on this measure. If measurement of the criterion is poor, then selection decisions based on a system designed to predict the measure will also be poor. Thus success of the entire development process will depend on the adequacy and accuracy of the criterion measure.

There are many different types of criteria that can be employed: (a) job tenure (or turnover), (b) absenteeism, (c) training program success, (d) rate of salary increase, (e) supervisory ratings, or (f) job performance. Criteria involving *behavioral* measures of performance such as job tenure, dollar sales, absenteeism, tardiness, compensation history, and job output are likely to provide more reliable data than subjective measures such as ratings. However, care should be taken to be sure that these behavioral measures provide reliable, uncontaminated, and meaningful assessments. In many cases, the most readily available criterion may not be the most useful.

Job tenure measures appear to be particularly amenable to prediction with WABs. As we suggested earlier, many, if not most, previously published studies have employed tenure as a criterion.

2. Identifying Criterion Groups Once a criterion has been chosen, it is necessary to form two criterion groupings of employees. A number of employees is assigned to each group, one representing a *high* criterion group (successful or desirable employees) and one representing a *low* criterion group (unsuccessful or undesirable employees). (Some writers recommend a minimum of 150 employees in each group.)[13]

For example, suppose we were attempting to develop a weighted application to predict job tenure of salesclerks at a large department store located in a large city. Through some preliminary research, we find that clerks who stay with the store 6 months or less are considered short-tenure employees; those who stay 12 months or more are considered long-term employees. (Employees with more than 6 months of job tenure but less than 12 months of tenure are excluded from the study.) After reviewing our employment files for the last 18 months, we identified 150 *short*-tenure and 150 *long*-tenure employees. Next, we need to further split each of our two criterion groups into *weighting* and *holdout* groups. Our groups should be formed such that a ratio of two employees are in each weighting group for every one employee in each holdout group. Thus, in the case of our present example, the product of this step will be a weighting and holdout group for our long-tenure clerks and a weighting and holdout group for our short-tenure clerks. Each of the two weighting groups will consist of approximately 100 employees, and the two holdout groups will be composed of about 50 employees. Exhibit 11.1 summarizes the formation of our groups.

Weighting groups serve as a basis for developing weights for application form items that differentiate between short- and long-tenure employees. Holdout groups are used to determine if the weights derived will hold up when applied to a sample of employees *not* included in the original development of the weights.

3. Selecting Application Blank Items   The items that will be used in developing the WAB will depend on the content and number of items on the application form itself. Based on our earlier discussion, the specific content of the form should be derived from a thorough analysis of the job for which a WAB is being developed.

England recommends that as many items as possible be used in initial analyses, since many will not differentiate among our successful and unsuccessful employee groups. The objective of this step is to propose items or variables derived from the actual application form that might be predictive of employee success. Many different types of items have been used in previous WAB studies. A number have been found to be predictive of various criteria such as tenure, absenteeism, and performance; some example items include: (a) size of hometown, (b) number of times moved in recent years, (c) length of residence at previous address, (d) years of education, (e) courses taken and preferred during high school, (f) type of previous jobs, (g) number of previous jobs, (h) tenure on previous jobs, (i) distance of residence from company, (j) source of reference to company, (k) reason for leaving last job, (l) length of time before available for employment, and (m) can current employer be contacted. Many other item examples could be cited. One point should be kept in mind when items are being proposed. The simplest and most apparent form of an item on the application may not be the most useful. It may be possible to develop several potential items from one question appearing on an application. For instance, if a question asks about individuals' previous jobs within a specified period, we may be able to develop items on the *number* as well as the *type* of jobs held. All forms of items should be included in the study.

EXHIBIT 11.1	EXAMPLE OF USE OF WEIGHTING AND HOLDOUT GROUPS IN DEVELOPING A WEIGHTED APPLICATION BLANK (WAB) TO PREDICT JOB TENURE OF SALESCLERKS

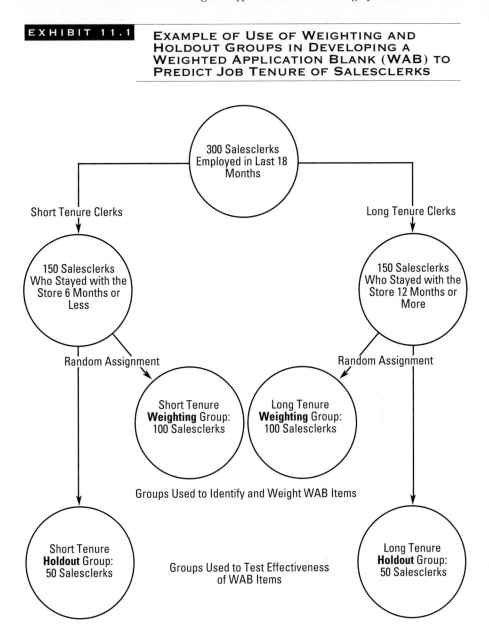

4. Specifying Item Response Categories For an application blank item to be useful in prediction, we have to know if certain responses are related to specific outcomes on our criterion of employee success. In order to test for any possible item response-criterion relationship, response categories must first be created for each of the WAB items. These categories serve as a way for scoring applicants' responses to our application blank items. For example, on an application blank for a life insurance salesperson, a question may ask "On how much life insurance do you personally pay premiums for yourself?" In order to score the item, we create response categories to measure the applicants' answers. For example, categories such as the following might be used to classify their answers:

A. None or less than $1,000 D. $50,00l to $75,000
B. $1,000 to $25,000 E. $75,001 to $100,000
C. $25,001 to $50,000 F. More than $100,000

Response categories are created for every item being examined as a possible predictor of the criterion. Next, we see how these categories are used.

5. Determining Item Weights   For an application blank item to be beneficial in predicting employee success, individuals in successful and unsuccessful weighting groups must differ in their responses to the item. Furthermore, the greater the response differences between the two groups, the more important an item is in predicting the criterion. Thus items should be given weights to reflect the degree of relationship with the criterion of employee success. These weights, in turn, will reflect an item's importance when future job applicants' WAB scores are determined.

To better understand this notion of weighting, let's return to our example of selecting salesclerks for a large department store. Recall in Step 2 we formed two weighting groups: (a) a short-term group consisting of 100 employees (who worked 6 months or less and quit) and (b) a long-term group composed of 100 employees (who worked 12 months or more). Among a number of items developed on the basis of a job analysis and appearing on the salesclerk application, there are two example items we want to review for their usefulness in predicting salesclerk turnover. These items are: "What is your level of education?" and "How many years of experience do you have in customer sales in a department store?" In Exhibit 11.2, we show the frequencies of the employees' answers to the response categories we developed for the two items. From examining the pattern of responses in the high- and low-tenure groups (see Columns 1 and 2), we can see what appears to be a relationship between the employees' responses to the questions and their tenure on the job. Specifically, high-tenure employees appear to have a high school diploma or equivalent and have experience in customer sales. To reflect these relationships, it is necessary to develop weights for scoring new salesclerk applicants' responses to the application questions. Column 3 shows the percentage differences in response categories between our high-and low-tenure weighting groups. The greater the positive difference, the more weight a category is given in scoring. Columns 4 and 5 represent weights that are derived from tables presented by England.[14] Notice the assigned weights in Column 5. These assigned weights represent scores for actual item responses to be summed when determining a total WAB score for future applicants. Hence, if applicants indicate they have a high school diploma or equivalent, they would receive 2 points. Applicants having less *or* more than a high school diploma or equivalent would receive 0 points. These item points would be combined with all other item responses found to be predictive of salesclerk job tenure (such as "More than 2 years of experience as a salesclerk" = 1). Based on these

| EXHIBIT 11.2 | THE DEVELOPMENT OF SCORING WEIGHTS FOR TWO APPLICATION BLANK ITEMS |

| | % Responding[a] | | | | |
	(1) High Tenure	(2) Low Tenure	(3) (1)–(2)[b]	(4) Net Weight[c]	(5) Scoring Weight[c]
Application Blank Item and Response Categories					
Level of education [d]:					
A. Less than high school diploma	5	5	0	0	0
B. High school diploma or General Equivalency Diploma (GED)	85	15	70	27	2
C. Some college	5	20	–15	–5	0
D. College diploma	5	60	–55	–17	0
Customer sales experience [e]					
A. None	3	70	–67	–25	0
B. 1 to 2 years	60	20	40	10	2
C. More than 2 years	37	10	27	6	1

[a] Based on 100 employees in each high- and low-tenure weighting group.

[b] Column 1 minus Column 2.

[c] Derived from tables presented in George W. England, *Development and Use of Weighted Application Blanks* (Minneapolis: Industrial Relations Center, University of Minnesota, 1971), pp. 27–28.

[d] Developed from the item: "What is your level of education?"

[e] Developed from the item: "How many years of experience do you have in customer sales in a department store?"

analyses, we would predict that the higher the total WAB score, the more likely an applicant would stay with the store for 12 or more months. However, before using these scoring weights, we must test their ability to predict tenure by applying them to an independent group of employees, that is, our holdout groups.

6. Applying Weights to Holdout Groups   Edward Cureton, among others, has argued that distorted results can be obtained when the usefulness of a test is evaluated for the same groups on whom the test was developed.[15] It can also be misleading to develop item weights for a WAB that differentiate between successful and unsuccessful groups and then evaluate the weights on these *same* groups.[16] *Application of WAB analyses are not recommended unless the weights can be evaluated on groups **different** from those used to develop the scoring weights.* It is *essential* that we check our scoring weights on a new applicant sample to be sure they are not due to chance. This process of checking our weights is referred to as *cross-validation.* Cross-validation is important since it helps to ensure that the weights did not occur simply because of chance.

One means for cross-validating these weights is to try out the weights on new applicants. This option is somewhat analogous to our predictive validation strategy discussed in Chapter 5. That is, new applicants complete the application form as well as other selection measures. Applicants are evaluated on the usual selection measures, but they are not scored using the WAB procedures. After a period of time for employees to have exhibited either job success or failure, we go back and score their initial applications using our weighting scheme. If the weighting system is useful, we should find that successful employees have significantly higher WAB scores than unsuccessful ones. If so, we can conclude that our WAB has value as a selection device. This evaluation strategy can be a good one to adopt; its main drawback, however, is the time we must wait to test the WAB.

Fortunately, we have another option. Recall that in Step 2 we created two holdout groups: a short-tenure group made up of 50 clerks (who worked 6 months or less and quit) and a long-tenure group made up of 50 clerks (who worked 12 months or more). These groups were held out from our initial development of the WAB scoring weights. Since we have designations of successful and unsuccessful clerks (that is, short- and long-tenure), our holdout groups can serve as a basis for trying out our scoring system. Thus our next step is simply to score individuals in both holdout groups on responses to the application form that were found to discriminate between our short- and long-tenure weighting groups.

7. Evaluating Holdout Groups' WAB Scores   At this point, all members of the holdout groups have received total WAB scores. A total WAB score is the sum of the assigned weights developed for those application form questions that differentiated among our initial weighting groups.

In order to see how well our scoring system separates our short- and long-tenure holdout groups, we can plot their total WAB scores. Example plots for the two holdout groups are shown in Exhibit 11.3. Total scores are shown on the bottom axis of each graph; each dot represents the total WAB score for one person.

By looking at the two graphs, we can see that scores for our high-tenure group are skewed toward high WAB total scores. Conversely, the low-tenure group is principally composed of lower WAB scores. These distributions help us test our expectation: if the WAB is successful, high-tenure employees should have higher WAB scores than low-tenure employees. Our plots tend to confirm this expectation.

8. Setting Cutoff Scores for Selection   In order to use the WAB in practical selection applications, we need to know what minimum or cutoff score should be used in selection decisions. The cutoff WAB score represents the point above which an applicant is selected or moved forward for further evaluation and below which an applicant is not. Our objective is to obtain a score that will optimally classify our holdout group members in the correct group (low- versus high-tenure). England provides computational details for deriving our optimum cutting score, but we can visually obtain a close approximation by inspecting our plots in Exhibit 11.3.[17] As you study the plots, draw a vertical line at the point where the overlap of the tails of the two distributions is the *least*. In Exhibit 11.3 that point occurs at a score of 10. Thus 10 is the WAB cutoff score that appears

EXHIBIT 11.3 DISTRIBUTIONS OF TOTAL WAB SCORES FOR SALESCLERKS IN HIGH- AND LOW-TENURE HOLDOUT GROUPS

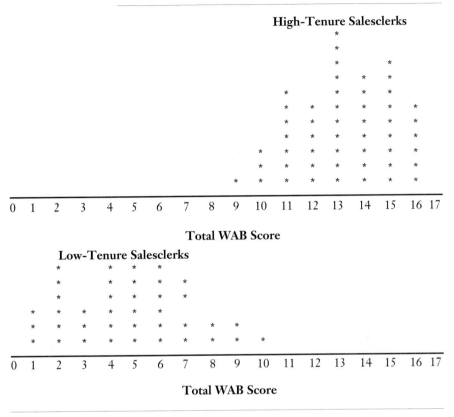

to optimally separate our two tenure groups. Notice that if we set a cutoff score higher than 10, say 12, we would reject all low-tenure job applicants; however, we would also reject some applicants who would have high tenure on the job. Similarly, a score set lower than 10, say 9, would accept all high-tenure job applicants but would raise the number of low-tenure applicants chosen. Ideally, the cutoff score we should use is that which rejects the maximum number of unsuccessful applicants and accepts the maximum number of successful ones. However, in applying cutoff scores, we cannot always employ the optimal score. External factors, such as labor market supply and demand, will affect our score settings. For example, when few applicants relative to job openings are available, we may have to lower our cutoff score to obtain the desired number of new employees. On the other hand, when we have a large number of applicants available, we can be more selective and, thus, set a higher cutoff score.

Using WABs in Human Resource Selection

Weighted application blanks can be used in at least two basic ways. They can be employed as (a) a preliminary screening device or (b) part of a battery of selection measures (including tests, interviews, etc.). As an initial screening tool, a WAB might be employed in those situations in which it is very expensive to further test or interview applicants or in which there is a very large number of applicants relative to positions available.[18] Applicants would first complete a WAB and, if successful, would then complete additional selection measures. Such a selection strategy could save considerable selection costs associated with test administration or recruitment (such as company visits by prospective employees). Application of the WAB would serve to trim the applicant pool to those for whom further investment of recruitment and selection resources would likely be beneficial. For example, research by Marilyn Quaintance showed that a WAB could be used to reduce selection costs by prescreening participants in a managerial assessment center. Application of the WAB indicated she could identify 83 percent of the participants who performed well in the assessment center and 62 percent who did not.[19]

A second strategy for utilizing a WAB is as an additional tool in a series of selection measures.[20] Rather than complete and successfully pass a WAB before taking other measures, applicants take the entire battery of measures. However, before adopting a WAB as part of a selection battery, one might ask whether a WAB is likely to improve prediction over other measures in the selection battery. England is careful to point out that WABs are typically developed on employee groups who were already hired using other selection measures. Nevertheless, since WABs frequently enhance the prediction of job success over that of other selection measures, it would appear that WABs can contribute something unique to the prediction of employee success. Thus, for some applications, WABs may prove to be a worthwhile addition to a group of selection predictors.

Assets of WABs   There are several benefits that a WAB has over traditional selection measures such as tests. First, it is not likely to be perceived as threatening to applicants. People applying for a job generally expect to fill out an application form for employment. Since there would appear to be no right or wrong answers, application forms may seem rather innocuous to an applicant. Second, if application information is something we are going to collect, WAB information is valuable if for no other reason than we do not have to pay extra for it.[21] Tests, interviews, and the like can have high direct costs associated with their purchase, development, administration, and scoring. When a measure requires a one-to-one relationship with an administrator, such as in a selection interview, direct costs can be quite high. Direct costs associated with a WAB are likely to be considerably lower. Finally, a WAB may assess important applicant characteristics that are not measured by tests or other selection measures. For example, in a classic study of the prediction of taxicab driver performance, Morris Viteles found that a WAB significantly distinguished successful from unsuccessful drivers. But what is most impressive about the WAB that was used is that seven application blank items significantly improved prediction over the company's selection tests of mental alertness and accident susceptibility. When cross-validated on 188 new drivers, the WAB would have rejected 60 percent of the poorest drivers but only 22 percent of the best; these results were obtained *after* use of the tests in driver selection.[22] Thus the WAB apparently was assessing important driver characteristics not measured by the tests.

Concerns in Using WABs   At first glance, it is easy to be impressed by the potential applicability of WABs to various selection situations. However, as with any technique, there are concerns that a potential user would be wise to consider prior to adoption. Some of these concerns have to do with assumptions of the method while others involve guidelines for use. Nevertheless, these are important considerations and should not be taken lightly. We list here some of the issues to be studied when designing and implementing a WAB within a selection program:

1. *No single WAB will apply to all jobs in a given organization or, perhaps, even the same job in different organizations.* Unique characteristics of a job will probably necessitate that a WAB be developed for that job or for a family of very similar jobs. Users should carefully review claims that a WAB can be developed for a wide cross section of jobs. In general, WABs should be tailored to the situation for which they are intended.

2. *When a WAB is developed, one assumption is that applicants who will be scored do not differ from the employees on whom the WAB was developed.* To the extent that applicant groups differ from employee groups on whom the WAB was developed (for example, in terms of ethnicity, gender, or other demographic characteristics, as well as life histories), scoring keys may not be useful in predicting applicant job success. In this sense, a WAB scoring key may produce an invalid selection measure.

3. *The measure of employee success (criterion) used in developing a WAB may change in importance over time.*[23] Therefore, if a new or different criterion emerges as important for prediction in selection, new WAB development procedures will need to be initiated. For example, if a WAB was developed to predict tenure, but accident rate became a more important criterion, a new WAB would have to be developed.

4. *Over time, the utility of a WAB in predicting employee success may diminish.* For example, Marvin Dunnette and his colleagues[24] as well as Paul Wernimont[25] found that the ability of a WAB to predict clerical employees' job tenure fell quite drastically within a five-year period. When a useful measure in selection is found, it is quite natural not to want to tamper with success. The tendency of some HR administrators is simply to continue to use the measure. This strategy could be a serious mistake with a WAB. Once developed and implemented, its usefulness in prediction should be reevaluated through cross-validation on new samples of employees hired in subsequent years. Reevaluation should occur every two to three years.

There are exceptions to this general concern of WAB decay over time. Steven Brown reported that the utility of a WAB held up for over a 38-year period despite labor market, economic, and job changes. Two principal reasons were the confidentiality of the scoring key and the large number of people on whom the system was developed.[26]

5. *Certain items on a WAB may violate state fair employment practice statutes or federal laws.* Although older WAB studies have found demographic characteristics of employees (such as age, gender, marital status, height, and weight) related to various employee success measures, many of these types of application blank items now violate a number of states' fair employment practice statutes. Users should be certain that items scored on a WAB do not violate these statutes or laws.

6. *Organizational changes can affect the applicability of a WAB.* Darrell Roach conducted a cross-validation study of a WAB over time to determine if changes in various organizational factors might affect the predictive power of a WAB. He found that changes in labor market conditions, increases in salary schedules, decentralization of the user company, and changes in personnel policies lowered the predictive power of the blank.[27] Since most organizations are likely to change in ways similar to those studied by Roach, periodic monitoring of WABs is again recommended.

Legal Considerations in Using WABs   Like tests and other selection measures, WABs are subject to the *Uniform Guidelines.* Users would be well advised to consider the legal implications of developing and using weighted application blanks in selection. It may be apparent from our description of the development of WABs that the method is basically an empirical procedure. Thus it is possible that application blank items which are weighted may bear no obvious or rational relationship to the job under study even though there may be a statistical relationship with employee success. A purely statistical relationship of application blank items with job success may not be a legally satisfactory explanation for using weights of nonjob-related items in a discriminatory manner.[28] As a case in point, Larry Pace and Lyle Schoenfeldt reviewed the application of a WAB by Richard Rosenbaum designed to predict employee theft.[29] Using procedures like those we have outlined, Rosenbaum found seven items to be predictive of employee theft in a mass merchandising company. These items included weight of 150 pounds or more, Detroit address, two or more previous jobs, does not wear eyeglasses, application carelessly prepared, at present address less than 13 years, and weight of less than 130 pounds. Pace and Schoenfeldt state that WAB procedures that weight items concerning gender, sex, race, religion, or national origin, or items that correlate with gender, ethnicity, religion, or national origin are potentially illegal if a protected group is adversely affected in employment. That is, if members of a minority group are hired less frequently than members of majority groups and if these decisions are based on items related to gender, ethnicity, or religion, then a WAB raises questions of illegality. As an example, they point out that Rosenbaum found applicants with Detroit addresses were more likely to have been caught stealing. They argue that since blacks may be more likely to live within the inner city, a location-of-residence item may adversely affect black applicants. (In contrast, Wayne Cascio presents an interesting application of how a WAB was developed to meet legal requirements. He found that a legally fair WAB could be developed and be useful in predicting the job tenure of minority and nonminority female clerks.[30]) Pace and Schoenfeldt recommend that job analysis be integrated into the development of weighted application blanks. We noted in the previous chapter that by tying application blank content to requisite job characteristics and demands, less potentially discriminatory and more rationally, legally defensible items can be developed. Unfortunately, many previous developers of application forms and users of WABs have not done this. As we specified earlier, we recommend that developers of applications and users of the WAB methodology begin with a thorough job analysis. The job analysis methods we have discussed can be helpful in developing both the application form and criteria the form is designed to predict.

Although numerous studies have documented the benefits in selection, the WAB is not widely used. For example, a survey by the Bureau of National Affairs of 437 companies' selection practices revealed that only 11 percent used a WAB in choosing new employees.[31] What reasons may explain this measure's limited use? The answer, quite likely, can be found in the following list:

1. Lack of familiarity with the technique,

2. Belief that a WAB is not useful in selection or will not improve prediction over other measures, and

3. Fear that use of the technique will open the company to charges of discrimination.

This chapter should have acquainted you with the possible benefits of weighted application blanks. We have seen that a WAB can be a useful selection tool; numerous studies testify that it can be especially beneficial in selecting sales, clerical, and secretarial workers. Further, there is some limited evidence to suggest that WABs may assess important characteristics of applicants not addressed by other selection devices.

Fear that use of a WAB may lead to charges of discrimination is not misguided. Although a WAB appears to hold promise for use in HR selection, the blind adoption of empirical procedures performed on questions haphazardly thrown together and called a "job application form" may lead to more problems than benefits. Sometimes, WAB analyses identify items that predict employee success empirically but are hard to explain rationally. Should these items create adverse impact against protected groups, users may have a difficult time defending their legality.

We think WABs can play a beneficial role in HR selection. However, we strongly recommend that any user contemplating installation of a WAB begin with a thorough analysis of the job in question. As we prescribed earlier in Chapter 10, the actual questions on the application form should be based on a job analysis. If the content of the application form can be tied to the results of a thorough job analysis, then the presence of items that are weighted, scored, and used in selection can be justified. Justification of a WAB can then be made both rationally *and* empirically.

Biographical Data

What Are Biographical Data?

A Definition of Biographical Information   Previous experience with WABs has provided compelling evidence that these measures are valuable for predicting several important aspects of job behavior. However, because application blanks tend to be short and nonsystematic in their coverage, many industrial psychologists have felt that the prediction and understanding of important job behaviors could be enhanced by a deeper study of applicants and their backgrounds. It has generally been assumed by these researchers that the best predictor of future behavior is past behavior. Thus if important past behaviors can be translated into a means suitable for measurement, an effective predictor can be developed.

William Owens has recounted the history of the development and use of biographical data in selection, and there is no need to retrace his comments here. It is sufficient to note that the origins of the use of biographical data in selection settings can be traced to several sources: (a) the successful experiences of selection researchers with weighted application blanks in the 1940s and 1950s, (b) the successful application of biographical data questionnaires in identifying military officer talent during World War II, and (c) the writings and research of advocates of biographical data such as Edwin Henry of Standard Oil (New Jersey) and William Owens of the University of Georgia.[32]

Although opinions differ as to exactly what should be called biographical data,[33] this information generally comprises those questions asked of applicants concerning their personal backgrounds and life experiences. Biographical information can be collected in several ways. Craig Russell, for example, used a system of structured interviews to gather biographical information on 66 candidates for general manager positions in a *Fortune* 500 firm. Interview questions focused on three background areas of each applicant: (a) accomplishments, disappointments, and what was learned from those experiences in college and positions held since entering the work force, (b) accomplishments, disappointments, and situational experiences in their current position relative to nine performance dimensions that had been identified for the general managers' job, and (c) career aspirations, prior formal developmental activities, self-perceptions, and how others were believed to perceive the applicant.[34]

In another application, Russell coded biographical information from life history essays written by cadets at the U.S. Naval Academy. The biographical information was found to predict leadership and academic performance of cadets at the academy.[35]

More commonly, however, biodata questions are presented in a self-report questionnaire. The questionnaire is usually in a standardized multiple-choice format that asks applicants to characterize themselves in terms of "demographic, experiential, or attitudinal variables presumed or demonstrated to be related to personality structure, personal adjustments, or success in social, educational, or occupational pursuits."[36] Thus biographical data questionnaire items may concern facts as well as "attitudes, feelings, and value judgments resulting from experiences."[37] The remainder of our discussion centers on the collection of biographical information through a questionnaire.

Various labels have been given to biographical data such as "autobiographical data, "personal or life history information," or "background data." We use the term *biodata;* whatever the name used, all refer to the same concept.

As is evident from our definition, a biodata questionnaire (frequently referred to as a "Biographical Information Blank," or BIB) can cover a variety of topics such as educational experiences, hobbies, family relations, use of leisure time, personal health, and early work experiences, to name only a few. Whereas a WAB generally focuses on limited, factual, verifiable information involving educational background, training, and work experience, a BIB, in contrast, may range over a broader spectrum of an individual's background, experiences, interests, attitudes, and values. Thus many of the items on a BIB may be more subjective than those on a WAB and may not be as easily verified, if at all. In terms of length, a BIB will typically be much longer than a WAB. For example, it is not unusual to find a BIB with a hundred items or more. A WAB, on the other hand, may involve only 10 to 15 items.

Types of Biodata Items   We have taken some time to explore the general nature of biodata as a selection measure. Now we examine some biodata item content. We can classify biodata item content into two groups: (a) the first based on the type of response options offered to a respondent (*response*-type) and (b) the second based on the specific behavioral content of the item itself (*behavior*-type).

Response-type classification refers to the kind of response scale a respondent is asked to use in answering biodata items.[38] Table 11.1 classifies some example biodata items into seven categories of response type.

The type of rating scale employed on a biodata questionnaire can significantly affect the subsequent scoring and analysis of the items. Most preferable (and the most common item format in biodata questionnaires) is a biodata item having an underlying continuum and requiring a single choice (see category 2 in Table 11.1). The continuum, single-choice form of item is most amenable to various kinds of statistical analyses; the other item types require special steps for scoring and analysis. At times, however, when constructing biodata questionnaires, it is not possible to put all items in the continuum, single-choice format; it may make more sense to use something different. In these instances, the other biodata item formats should be employed. Scoring (through dummy variable coding and treating each item option as a separate variable) and statistical provisions can be made to handle these variations.

Table 11.2 presents another taxonomy of biodata items. This particular classification categorizes biodata items in terms of behaviors to be judged by

TABLE 11.1   CLASSIFICATION OF EXAMPLE BIOGRAPHICAL DATA ITEMS BY RESPONSE TYPE

1. **Yes-No Response:**
   Are you satisfied with your life?
   a. Yes
   b. No
2. **Continuum, Single-Choice Response:**
   About how many fiction books have you read in the past year?
   a. None
   b. 1 or 2
   c. 3 or 4
   d. 5 or 6
   e. More than 6
3. **Noncontinuum, Single-Choice Response:**
   What was your marital status when you graduated from college?
   a. Married
   b. Single
   c. Divorced
   d. Separated
   e. Widowed
4. **Noncontinuum, Multiple-Choice Response:**
   Check each of the following activities you had participated in by the time you were 18.
   a. Shot a rifle
   b. Driven a car
   c. Worked on a full-time job
   d. Traveled alone over 500 miles from home
   e. Repaired an electrical appliance

5. **Continuum, Plus Escape Option:**
   When you were a teenager, how often did your father help you with your schoolwork?
   a. Very Often
   b Often
   c. Sometimes
   d. Seldom
   e. Never
   f. Father was not at home
6. **Noncontinuum, Plus Escape Option:**
   In what branch of the military did you serve?
   a Army
   b. Air Force
   c. Navy
   d. Marines
   e. Never served in the military
7. **Common Stem, Multiple Continuum:**
   In the last 5 years, how much have you enjoyed each of the following? (Use the rating scale of 1 to 4 shown below.)
   a. Reading books
   b. Watching TV
   c. Working on your job
   d. Traveling
   e. Outdoor recreation
      (1) Very much
      (2) Some
      (3) Very little
      (4) Not at all

SOURCE: Based on William A. Owens, "Background Data" in *Handbook of Industrial and Organizational Psychology*, ed. Marvin Dunnette (Chicago: Rand Mc-Nally, 1976), p. 613.

respondents.[39] By using this system, life history items can be classified along one or more of the following dimensions: (a) verifiable–unverifiable, (b) historical–futuristic, (c) actual behavior–hypothetical behavior, (d) memory–conjecture, (e) factual–interpretive, (f) specific–general, (g) response–response tendency, and (h) external event–internal event. Each of these dimensions represents a continuum. The categories are not mutually exclusive because it is possible for any single item to be characterized by more than one dimension. At any rate, the items listed provide some typical examples of those that appear in a biodata questionnaire.

Advantages of Biodata   Biodata can provide some unique advantages to the assessment of job applicants. These assets certainly argue for its consideration

TABLE 11.2	CLASSIFICATION OF EXAMPLE BIOGRAPHICAL DATA ITEMS BY BEHAVIORAL CONTENT

1. **Verifiable:**
Do you own a home?

   Unverifiable:
How much did you enjoy high school?

2. **Historical:**
How many jobs have you held in the past five years?

   Futuristic:
What job would you like to hold five years from now?

3. **Actual Behavior:**
Did you ever repair a broken radio so that it later worked?

   Hypothetical Behavior:
If you had your choice, what job would you like to hold now?

4. **Memory:**
How would you describe your life at home while growing up?

   Conjecture:
If you were to go through college again, what would you choose as a major?

5. **Factual:**
How many hours do you spend at work in a typical week?

   Interpretive:
If you could choose your supervisor, which characteristic would you want him or her to have?

6. **Specific:**
While growing up, did you collect coins?

   General:
While growing up, what activities did you enjoy most?

7. **Response:**
Which of the following illnesses have had?

   Response Tendency:
When you have a problem on your job, to whom do you turn for assistance?

8. **External Event:**
When you were a teenager, how much time did your father spend with you?

   Internal Event:
Which best describes your feelings when you last worked with a computer?

SOURCE: Based on James J. Asher, "The Biographical Item: Can It Be Improved?" *Personnel Psychology* 25 (1972): 252; and Wayne F. Cascio, *Applied Psychology in Personnel Management* (Englewood Cliffs, N.J.: Prentice-Hall, 1991), p.266.

and inclusion in our battery of selection devices. Some of these advantages are summarized as follows:

1. Biodata can serve as another means for collecting some of the information usually obtained in the selection interview with the advantages that an applicant is asked each question in the same way, and the answers are amenable to empirical scoring.

2. At least for verifiable information, the responses provided on a BIB tend to be very reliable and accurate.

3. Biodata items make it possible to achieve understanding of what makes for an effective employee rather than just simple prediction of employee success, as in a WAB. By studying the content of items related to measures of employee success, a great deal can be determined about what types of individuals stay on a job, are high producers, or are promoted through an

organization. This information may be useful to HR policymakers as well as selection managers.

4. Application of usual empirical scoring procedures generally ensures that only job-related questions are posed on a BIB. Although the procedures will not satisfy all legal requirements concerning fairness and avoidance of adverse impact, they provide an initial, important step toward meeting these needs.

5. Biodata has generally been shown to be as good of a selection measure as other methods; in many cases, the evidence suggests that biodata may be among the best in terms of predicting job success.[40]

Assumptions of Biodata   In using biographical data as a selection tool, we make several key assumptions. These assumptions are important, since they influence the quality and utility of the data we use in selection decision making. Therefore, when asking applicants to describe their past behaviors and their feelings about these behaviors, we assume the following:

1. *With the context reasonably constant, the best predictor of job applicants' future behavior is what they have done in the past.*[41] This assumption is really a basic axiom of psychological measurement, and the available evidence generally supports the assumption. For example, numerous studies have shown that the best predictor of college grade point average is high school grade point average. Sometimes only a few items of past behavior can be a predictor of important job behaviors. Edward Cureton, for instance, reported that the *single* item, "Did you ever build a model airplane that flew," contained in a BIB administered to prospective pilots during World War II, was almost as good a predictor of success in flight training as the *entire* Air Force test battery.[42] Apparently, individuals' previous work with airplanes reflected their interest and abilities to work with aircraft in the future. Similarly, four biodata items collected on a sample of almost 8,000 women and men were found to predict performance effectiveness in seven naval occupations.[43] Empirical evidence summarized by William Owens and Edwin Henry generally verify that biographical data serve as an outstanding predictor of criteria representing future employee behaviors.[44]

    The assumption that the best predictor of future behavior is past behavior does not mean that people will necessarily behave in the future as they have in the past. Instead, the assumption suggests that factors such as previous learning and heredity, as well as various resources, will make some behaviors more likely in new situations. An assessment of individuals' earlier behaviors and life experiences as well as the attitudes, values, and beliefs that individuals acquire from these situational exposures allow some predictions of their future behaviors.[45]

2. *The systematic measurement of applicants' past behavior and life experiences will provide an indirect measure of their motivational characteristics.* These charac-

teristics may be extremely difficult to measure with other forms of selection devices.[46] An assessment system based on biodata can serve as a basis for not only predicting but describing individuals. Such data can provide great amounts of information about individuals without requiring great amounts of time from them.[47]

3. Individuals will be less defensive in describing their previous behaviors than in discussing their motivations for these behaviors.[48] Where behaviors are public and have occurred, individuals may be less hesitant to report on these behaviors rather than why these behaviors have taken place. Thus, applicants may be more receptive to answering a biodata questionnaire than a personality inventory.

Developing Biodata Questionnaires

So far, we have defined biodata, examined some typical kinds of items appearing in a questionnaire, and looked at some of its assets and assumptions. It may seem to you that a biodata questionnaire merely consists of a lot of questions about job applicants' life histories. In part, that impression is true. We will probably use a questionnaire that is made up of a number of items. But a great deal of time, effort, and resources must be expended in deciding precisely *what* questions will be asked. It is the questionnaire item content that will determine in a large way the effectiveness of biodata as a selection measure. Since there is not likely to be a commercially available, off-the-shelf biodata questionnaire suitable for the numerous selection situations we may encounter, we will probably need to have our questionnaire tailor-made. Whether a questionnaire is developed by a user or by a consultant, users should be aware of the necessary steps to produce such a selection device. Thus, at this point, we review one procedure for developing a biodata questionnaire.

Steps in Construction   There are several steps involved in the development of a BIB. In practice, these steps apply to the development of almost any selection measure. Nevertheless, we summarize their application in constructing a BIB to be used in selection. Here are the steps:

1. Selecting a Job   Our starting point is the choice of a job for which we plan to use a BIB in selection. Biographical data questionnaires have been utilized in a wide variety of occupational settings. These applications have included jobs such as life insurance agents, executives, pharmaceutical scientists, and managers at various organizational levels.[49] From these titles, you can see that biodata questionnaires have been applied to jobs that are relatively high in responsibility. A BIB is not restricted to such jobs; it can be applied to lower-level jobs as well. However, because of the resource investment required to develop a BIB adequately, for some jobs there may not be a high enough return on investment to warrant development of the measure. For some lower-level jobs, a weighted application blank alone may suffice. That decision will differ from one selection situation to the next. Nevertheless, a potential user will first have to decide if a BIB is worthwhile for the job under consideration.

2. Analyzing the Job and Defining the Life History Domain Once we have identified the job, our next concern is to conduct a thorough analysis of the job (see Chapters 7, 8, and 9). One of several products of this analysis is particularly important in developing a biodata questionnaire. That product is the criterion or measure of job success/performance we are interested in predicting. As we have mentioned, there can be many different types of criteria, such as employee tenure or some objective measure of job performance. Our goal is to understand what antecedent behaviors and life experiences account for individuals' performance on our criterion. These antecedent behaviors and life experiences define the life history domain to be assessed by a biodata questionnaire. Biographical data items that reflect this domain will ultimately be developed and compose the questionnaire.

Job analysis is also important in BIB development because it helps to ensure a correspondence between contents of the biodata questionnaire and the job. With job information available, job-relevant background data can be developed.[50] Use of job-relevant biodata items may enhance the ability of a biodata questionnaire to predict relevant employee behaviors. Furthermore, by using biodata items that appear to be related rationally to the job, a biodata questionnaire will be more defensible in court in the event of a lawsuit. Then too, high job-BIB correspondence will certainly facilitate face validity of the measure. Face validity, in turn, can help to reduce the negative reactions of some job applicants toward biodata questionnaires.[51]

As we see in the next step of biodata questionnaire development, results of the job analysis can be used to develop hypotheses regarding the life history experiences that account for success on the job. Biodata items may then be written or selected from existing biodata inventories that assess the life history dimensions hypothesized as important to the job.

In addition to job analysis, other strategies can also be used to define the relevant life history domain.[52] For example, the research literature can be searched to identify salient life history attributes associated with criterion performance.[53] Interviews that are directed toward uncovering life history experiences associated with performance can also be held with key job incumbents.

3. Forming Hypotheses of Life History Experiences After we have inferred those life history attributes believed to be important for job success, we develop life history items that will reflect those attributes. Thus, at this point, we develop hypotheses regarding the life history experiences that will measure these important attributes. If our hypotheses are correct, we should be able to identify life history items that could be used to predict success on the job, that is, our criterion.

Research by William Williams underscores the importance of forming hypotheses or a rationale for including specific items in a BIB.[54] He developed a 98-item BIB designed to predict reenlistment in the Air Force Reserve Officers'

Training Corps. During development of the measure, he formed specific hypotheses for 35 items; no specific hypotheses were given for the remaining 63 questions. Following administration, he found that 46 percent of the hypothesized items predicted reenlistment whereas only 13 percent of the nonhypothesized items served as a useful predictor. Thus, Owens recommends, "although one may include some items because they have priorly demonstrated validity in reasonably similar circumstances, biodata items are much more likely to validate if they are knowledgeably beamed at a specific target."[55] Owens's recommendation is illustrated later.

Developing hypotheses of relevant life history experiences and items to reflect these experiences obviously requires judgment. Several sources of information can be used. These may include reviews of articles published in journals such as the *Journal of Applied Psychology* or *Personnel Psychology* to identify biographical data items that are known to correlate with various criteria as well as reviews of the developmental psychology literature to identify life history attributes associated with criterion performance.

The formation of hypotheses for developing life history items is critical to the successful application of biographical data. Here we summarize a research strategy proposed by Karl Kuhnert and Craig Russel[56] and a research study by John Miner[57] to illustrate the role of hypothesis formation in developing a biographical data questionnaire. Kuhnert and Russell's suggestion attempts to tie biographical information to a theory of leadership. Although Miner's research dealt with the construction of a scoring procedure for applicant file data, his rationale also illustrates the role of hypothesis formulation in BIB development.

Kuhnert and Russell propose a research strategy for tying the content of biographical information to a theory of leader development referred to as constructive/developmental leadership theory. A model of adult development is used to describe how adults make meaning out of their life experiences. They argue that leaders derive meaning from these life experiences in different ways, and these meanings can be explained by the model of adult development. Biographical data are used to measure the important life experiences.

In designing biodata items, they propose several steps. The first one is to identify experiences that show how leaders view themselves and relate to others as leaders. Once these experiences are identified, follow-up questions are used to determine what was most significant about those experiences. Biographical items are then written to reflect these experiences. Answers to the items are used to characterize the stages of leadership development. For example, the following biodata item is suggested:

> On a school project where you were in charge of a team of fellow students, one member wasn't pulling his or her weight. You determined that you must talk to him or her about the effect of this behavior on the project. How would you approach this discussion?
>
> a.   I would let him or her know I was unhappy that he or she was putting in less effort than I was because . . .

b. I would point out how it wasn't fair to the other individuals in the group because . . .

c. I would explain how that invidual was letting him or herself down because . . .[58]

Kuhnert and Russell hypothesize that each of the response options reflects different stages in how leaders make meaning out of their life experiences. Higher-stage individuals such as those that might choose option C are proposed to have more problem-solving strategies in their repertoire than lower-stage individuals.

At this point, Kuhnert and Russell's proposal is a theoretical one; it is yet to be tested. Nevertheless, their work illustrates how a developmental theory can be used to hypothesize and develop biodata item content. Empirical support for their work would lead to a clearer understanding of the role of life history experiences in leadership development.

John Miner was interested in determining if applicant life history (developed from applicants' résumés, application forms, psychological evaluation reports, and reference letters) could be used to predict the success of management consultants in an international management consulting practice. An analysis of the consultants' jobs showed that they usually worked on project teams in large business organizations. Their principal contact was with top management. In general, the consultants tended to develop as generalists with their work being in the area of financial affairs rather than human or material resources.

Further analysis of the consultants' role within the firm suggested two hypotheses for explaining consultant success. First, it was hypothesized that an applicant's life history of outstanding accomplishments was a predictor. This rationale was characterized as the "pattern of previous success" hypothesis. Second, it was thought that successful consultants to business management come from those backgrounds that provide exposure to corporate top management culture. Individuals having such exposure were felt to possess greater interpersonal effectiveness in dealing with top executives. This second hypothesis regarding the link between life history data and consulting success was termed the "top management culture" hypothesis.

Once hypotheses for consulting success had been formulated, specific life history experiences indicative of these hypotheses were developed. Reviews of pertinent literature and research within the firm led Miner to propose a rationale for developing specific life history indicators. For instance, it was hypothesized that applicants with fathers who had high levels of education and held positions in top management would be more likely to have been exposed to top management culture. Applicants' previous business experience, use of a company officer as a reference, and undergraduate and graduate education at a prestigious college were all suggested as being indicative of exposure to top management. Similarly, military experience in the Navy or Air Force (in contrast to the Army with its lower intellectual standards and its tendency to attract lower socioeconomic personnel) were also proposed as valuable indicators.

Based on the hypotheses developed for the study, 15 life history items were prepared. Applicants' scores on these items were then related to three measures of management consulting success: performance ratings, compensation changes, and job tenure. Analyses showed that life history data were useful, and the following nine items were predictive of consultant success: (a) extent of prior business experience, (b) type of prior business experience, (c) branch of military service, (d) type of military service, (e) type of secondary schooling, (f) type of college from which graduated, (g) extent of graduate education, (h) extent of father's education, and (i) father's highest occupational attainment.

As you can tell, Miner's biographical data were limited in both number (15 items) and type (factual). His items were restricted principally because he was confined to existing application file data. Had he chosen to develop a BIB rather than use file information, other types of items would probably have been relevant. Nevertheless, his process is a useful example of the role of hypothesis formulation in the development of life history items.

4. *Developing a Pool of Biodata Items* After hypothesizing the life history experiences that may predict our identified criteria, we select or construct biodata items to reflect these experiences. Thus our hypotheses guide the selection or development of specific life history items to appear on the BIB. As we have noted, the items can be selected from previous biodata research studies or originally developed. Available publications can serve as sources of items. For example, James Glennon, Lewis Albright, and William Owens have prepared a compendium of life history items.[59] Their catalog consists of over 500 biodata items classified into the following categories: (a) habits and attitudes, (b) health, (c) human relations (d) money, (e) parental home, childhood, teens, (f) personal attributes, (g) present home, spouse, and children, (h) recreation, hobbies, and interests, (i) school and education, (j) self impressions, (k) values, opinions, and preferences, and (l) work. Items from the catalog can be selected if it appears that they may be useful in measuring the hypothesized life experiences thought to be predictive of success. In addition, research articles on biodata can also be reviewed for possible biodata item content. The *Journal of Applied Psychology* and *Personnel Psychology* are the two literature sources that have published the most on applications of biographical data. Bibliographies of biographical data research can also be a valuable source of references with potentially useful items.[60]

An excellent review of research studies investigating various aspects of writing and formatting biodata items has been provided by Michael Mumford and William Owens.[61] These investigations have important implications for the validity and reliability of biodata questionnaires. We do not review those studies per se, but we summarize some item writing guides distilled from the research. These guidelines should be followed as biodata items are formatted into a BIB. Guidelines for preparing BIB items include the following:

(1) Biodata items should principally deal with past behavior and experiences.

(2) Items dealing with family relationships are usually viewed as offensive.

(3) Specificity and brevity of items and response options are desirable.

(4) Numbers should be used to define a biodata item's options or alternatives.

(5) All possible response options or an "escape" option should be given; and, where possible, response options that form a continuum should be used.

(6) Item options should carry a neutral or pleasant connotation.

(7) Items dealing with past and present behaviors and with opinions, attitudes, and values are generally acceptable.

      Fred Mael suggests two additional guides in preparing biodata items:[62]

(8) Items should reflect historical events that are important in shaping a person's behavior and identity. (However, in contrast to Mael's recommendation, Lawrence Kleiman and Robert Faley reported that a set of biodata items measuring present behavior were as valid in predicting reenlistment in the Air National Guard as biodata items measuring past behavior.[63])

(9) In order to lessen the effect of individuals responding in ways considered to be socially desirable or faking, biodata items should reflect external events (that is, prior behaviors occurring in real-life situations), be limited to firstthand recollections, be potentially verifiable, and measure unique, discrete events (such as age when first licensed to drive).

5. Prescreening and Pilot-Testing Biodata Items   Like items appearing on other selection measures, biodata items can be objectionable and produce bias for some respondents. In this last step, the biodata items that have been developed are reviewed by a panel of judges for objectionability and potential bias against certain groups (for example, gender and ethnicity) of respondents. Item content and response option review by a panel of subject matter experts has been found to reduce objectionability and bias, and enhance the clarity, as well as job relevance of biodata items.[64]

    Once an appropriate group of items has been developed and their content prescreened, they should be tried out on an appropriate group of respondents. Roughly 100 to 200 individuals are administered the biodata questionnaire. Items exhibiting little response variance, skewed response distributions, correlation with protected group characteristics such as gender or ethnicity, or no correlation with other items thought to be measuring the same life experience are eliminated from the biodata item pool. Those biodata items passing the prescreening and pilot-testing reviews are retained for inclusion in the final version of the BIB.[65]

    The developmental approach just outlined can enhance the effectiveness of biodata as a predictor as well as our understanding of how and why biodata works. This method, or one similar to it, is also likely to be a legally defensible approach to employing biodata in HR selection.

Scoring Biodata Questionnaires

After a BIB has been developed and administered, we can score applicants who complete the questionnaire. These scores, in turn, can be used with a variety of statistical procedures to predict an applicant's probable job success. But how are these scores determined? Although several BIB scoring procedures have been developed, the various approaches tend to fall into one of two categories: (a) the calculation of a *single*, total score for BIB items that is predictive of employee success[66] or (b) the development of *multiple* scores for dimensions or groups of related items appearing on a biodata inventory.[67]

Computing a Single Biodata Score The first approach to scoring a BIB is sometimes referred to as *empirical keying*, which generally involves the computation of a single score for a biodata questionnaire. There are several methods of empirical keying available, including (a) vertical percentage,[68] (b)horizontal percentage,[69] (c) correlation,[70] (d) differential regression,[71] (e) deviant response[72], and (f) rare response.[73] Of these, the vertical percentage method has been the most popular and useful. This method of scoring is the same as that used in scoring a weighted application blank (see our earlier discussion of scoring a WAB in this chapter). That is, each item on a BIB is analyzed to determine its relation with some criterion of job success, such as job tenure or turnover. Items related to the criterion are identified, and weights are assigned to the item alternatives *empirical weights* to reflect the strength of their relationship. Scores are obtained for individuals by summing the weights corresponding to their responses. Once the keys are cross-validated, they can be used like any other selection measure.

The vertical percentage, differential regression, and correlational scoring procedures have generally been found to produce comparable results. These *unit weights* scoring methods tend to be superior to the other methods of empirical keying a biodata questionnaire.[74]

Although empirical keying represents a common method of scoring a BIB used in HR selection applications, it has many of the same problems associated with the weighted application blank. For one, the scoring of a BIB is basically limited to predictions for a specific pool of applicants and for a specific job success measure. Because of this specificity, the scoring key may not be applicable to another job, organization, or for a criterion different from the one for which the key was developed. In addition, because the total score is often composed of such a wide assortment of BIB items, there is some uncertainty about what the score really means. Although a BIB score might enhance our ability to predict employee success for a specific job, it may contribute very little to our understanding of *why* employees are successful.

Computing Multiple Biodata Scores A second approach (sometimes referred to as *homogeneous keying*) to biodata scoring involves the development of clusters or groups of related items appearing on a biodata questionnaire. Most often, statistical procedures such as factor or principal components analysis are used to identify and group related items into dimensions of life history experience.[75] The results of these procedures are a number of biodata dimensions or factors (usually 10 to 15 factors) measured by the life history questionnaire. Each biodata factor consists of a number of BIB items (usually 10 or more items) that

EXHIBIT 11.4	EXAMPLE OF THE BIOGRAPHICAL DATA FACTOR "POSITIVE ACADEMIC ATTITUDE"

Factor Name	Item Number	Biodata Item Stem
Positive Academic Attitude	29.	Did you generally expect to do well in school?
	32.	What was your approximate standing in your high school class?
	33.	Compared with your classmates in school, how hard did you try to excel?
	34.	Up to the time you left school, how did you feel about school?
	95.	When you were still in high school, what were the standards you set for yourself with regard to your studies?

SOURCE: Hubert S. Feild and William F. Giles, *Career Planning at West Point Pepperell, Inc.* Final report submitted to West Point, Ga., August 1978.

NOTE: The biographical data factor *Positive Academic Attitude* was identified through the use of a statistical technique called factor analysis. This technique can serve as a means for reducing a large number of questionnaire items to a smaller set of dimensions composed of items having similar themes. By focusing on the interrelations among biodata questionnaire items, factor analysis enables us to determine the dimensions or categories of life history experiences measured by a biodata questionnaire We can then describe and score people according to these underlying biodata dimensions. In the present example, we are illustrating only one of many possible biodata factors. Only the item stems are presented; the response options are not shown.

assess a common life experience or behavior. Scores are derived for each of the biodata factors.

Exhibit 11.4 presents as an example one biodata factor that was identified in a study by one of the authors of biodata correlates of managerial careers in a large textile firm.[76] As you look at the items shown, note that most deal with people's feelings about school and their academic performance. Thus, based on a common theme represented in the items, the name *Positive Academic Attitude* was assigned by the investigators to this biodata dimension. Rather than having one overall biodata score, scores can be obtained on each of the identified BIB factors or dimensions. For example, on the factor in Exhibit 11.4, respondents' answers to the items were added to obtain a total *Positive Academic Attitude* score. Persons scoring high on this factor were characterized as follows: always expected to do well in school, were in the upper 10 percent of their high school class, tried to excel much harder than other students, liked school very much, and set very high standards for themselves.

A study by Robert Morrison and his associates illustrates how dimensions of biodata can be used to predict and understand significant aspects of employee job performance.[77] One of the purposes of their research was to examine how dimensions of life history were related to industrial research scientists' job performance. They factor analyzed 75 biodata items and three criteria (creativity ratings, overall job performance ratings, and number of patent disclosures) collected on 418 petroleum research scientists. The five biodata dimensions identified and brief descriptions of individuals with high scores on each dimension follow:

1. **Favorable Self-Perception**
   In the top 5 percent of performance in their occupation
   Could be a highly successful supervisor if given the chance
   Work at faster pace than most people
   Desire to work independently

2. **Inquisitive Professional Orientation**
   Completed Ph.D. degree
   Belong to one or more professional organizations
   Devote much time to reading of many kinds
   Have high salary aspirations

3. **Utilitarian Drive**
   Desire extrinsic rewards from business and society
   Prefer urban dwelling
   Feel free to express self and perceive themselves as influencing others
   Do not desire to work independently

4. **Tolerance for Ambiguity**
   Desire to have many work activities
   Are not single
   Have solicited funds for charity
   Have friends with various political views

5. **General Adjustment**
   Feel that school material was adequately presented
   Came from happy homes
   Express their opinions readily; feel that they are effective in doing so

An examination of the association of the five factors with the three criteria revealed some interesting findings. *Different* biodata factors were associated with *different* types of performance on the job. For example, scientists who received high ratings on overall job performance tended to be those with high scores on the BIB factors of *Favorable Self-Perception*, *Utilitarian Drive*, and *General Adjustment*. Conversely, scientists with many patent awards had an opposite life history profile. They scored high on *Inquisitive Professional Orientation* and *Tolerance for Ambiguity*. Among others, these results suggest that different types of life experiences (that is, biodata factors) might be used to predict different types and levels of job performance (criteria). Thus, by weighting some BIB factors more than others in selection decisions, we could affect subsequent performance in our organization. For instance, in the current example, if greater weight were given to hiring applicants high in *Inquisitive Professional Orientation* and *Tolerance for Ambiguity*, we would expect higher performance in number of patents awarded than if other factors such as *General Adjustment* were emphasized.

As popularized by William Owens and Lyle Schoenfeldt, BIB scoring by identifying life history dimensions appears to be the contemporary trend.[78]

Their research program supports the idea that prediction as well as greater understanding of the relation between life history and employee job success can be enhanced by scoring biodata in terms of dimensions.

Measurement and Other Characteristics of Biodata

Reliability of Biodata   Most biodata questionnaires are developed from item pools that are composed of a wide variety of items. Because of the heterogeneity of their content, items on a biodata questionnaire typically display low intercorrelations with one another. Thus biodata questionnaires do not usually exhibit high internal consistency reliability estimates. Although the type of scoring procedure (among other factors) for a BIB can have an effect on the magnitude of a reliability coefficient, internal consistency reliability estimates (such as coefficient alpha) frequently fall in the range of .60 to .80.[79]

In contrast, average biodata test-retest reliability coefficients tend to be higher than internal consistency estimates. Although the time interval between tests and retests will have an effect on reliability, many reported coefficients fall in the range of .60 to .90.[80] For example, in a study involving test-retest reliability of a biodata questionnaire over a five-year period for 237 respondents, Garnett Shaffer and her associates reported moderate to high levels of test-retest reliability. For biodata factors where multiple items were used to compose a factor, mean reliabilities of slightly over .75 were found for both men and women. As expected, individual items on the BIB had lower test-retest estimates. For males, the average item test-retest reliability was .56 and for females, .58. It was also found that objective, verifiable biodata factors had higher test-retest reliabilities than subjective, less verifiable ones.[81]

Validity of Biodata   Several major reviews of numerous validation studies have been conducted for the purpose of examining the validity of biographical data. Investigators have reviewed these individual studies and have attempted to summarize the validity of biodata in predicting several different criteria. We do not examine each of these individual studies. However, we focus our attention on those investigations that have attempted to synthesize the validity of biodata by analyzing systematically large numbers of published and unpublished biodata validity coefficients. Because of their emphasis on multiple validation studies and the use of large samples of individuals, these studies should provide a clearer, more accurate picture of biodata validity.

Edwin Ghiselli's classic review of the validity of various types of occupational aptitude tests revealed that when averaged over a number of occupations, biographical data was the most successful predictor of job proficiency and success in job training.[82] Similarly, James Asher's reanalysis of reviews of test validation studies confirmed the predictive power of biographical data. He reported that 90 percent of biodata validity coefficients were above .30. His comparisons of life history data with tests such as finger dexterity, personality, motor ability, mechanical aptitude, intelligence, and interest led him to conclude that biodata was superior in predicting job proficiency.[83]

| TABLE 11.3 | SUMMARY OF BIOGRAPHICAL DATA VALIDATION STUDIES FOR A VARIETY OF CRITERIA |

Criterion	Investigator	Number of Validity Coefficients	Total Sample Size	Average Validity Coefficient
Performance Rating	Dunnette[a]	115	N.A.	.34
	Hunter and Hunter[b]	12	4,429	.37
	Reilly and Chao[c]	15	4,000	.36
	Schmitt et al.[d]	29	3,998	.32
Productivity	Schmitt et al.[d]	19	13,655	.20
Promotion	Hunter and Hunter[b]	17	9,024	.26
Tenure	Hunter and Hunter[b]	23	10,800	.26
Turnover	Schmitt et al.[d]	28	28,862	.21
Training Success	Hunter and Hunter[b]	11	6,139	.30

NOTE: N.A. = Data were not available.

[a]Marvin D Dunnette, *Validity Study Results for Jobs Relevant to the Petroleum Refining Industry* (Washington D.C.: American Petroleum Institute, 1972.) The data reported in the table were taken from John E. Hunter and Rhonda F. Hunter, "Validity and Utility of Alternative Predictors of Job Performance," *Psychological Bulletin* 96 (1984): 83.

[b]John E. Hunter and Rhonda F. Hunter, "Validity and Utility Of Alternative Predictors of Job Performance," *Psychological Bulletin* 96 (1984): 72–98.

[c]Richard R. Reilly and Georgia T. Chao, "Validity and Fairness of Some Alternative Employee Selection Procedures," *Personnel Psychology* 35 (1982): 1–62.

[d]Neal Schmitt, Richard Z. Gooding, Raymond A. Noe, and Michael Kirsch, "Metaanalyses of Validity Studies Published between 1964 and 1982 and the Investigation of Study Characteristics," *Personnel Psychology* 37 (1984): 407–422.

More recently, several reports have been published where newer data analytic techniques (validity generalization and metaanalysis procedures) have been used to synthesize large numbers of validation studies involving biodata.[84] Table 11.3 summarizes the validity coefficients of biodata questionnaires in predicting a variety of criteria. These coefficients were derived by investigators studying a large number of validity coefficients based on large numbers of BIB respondents (sample size). Although the investigators' methods of conducting the reviews differed among the studies, the pattern of results is reasonably consistent. As shown in Table 11.3, for criteria such as promotion, productivity, and job turnover, validity of BIB questionnaires ranged from .20 to .26. When the criterion measures of success in training programs and supervisory ratings of job performance were used in BIB validation studies, higher validity coefficients ranging from the low to upper .30s were found.

A validity generalization study by Hannah Rothstein and her colleagues showed that biodata instruments can be developed and validated so they lead to validity generalizability.[85] They selected and scored biographical items from the Supervisor Profile Record found to be related to the job performance of roughly 11,000 first-line supervisors in 79 different organizations. Mean estimated validities for the criteria of supervisory ability ratings and supervisory performance ratings were .33 and .32. These validities were judged to be stable over time and generalizable across groups based on age, gender, education, previous experience, tenure, and ethnicity. These results should not be interpreted to apply to every biodata instrument, since conventional methods of biodata construction and validation differ from Rothstein's approach. However, Rothstein's work shows that with large samples available, it is possible to produce a biographical data instrument that is predictive of performance across organizations and employee groups. Organizations without the resources to develop their own biodata questionnaires could then have access to generalizably valid ones for use in selection.

These results suggest that biodata is an effective predictor for a wide diversity of measures of job success. In fact, for entry-level selection, biodata has been found to be one of the best predictors of job performance when compared to other types of predictors such as employment interviews, training and experience ratings, reference checks, personality inventories, and some ability tests.[86]

On the other hand, there have been some reports that are not as supportive of biographical data as Ghiselli, Asher, and others' reviews. Abraham Korman's study of predictors of managerial performance concluded that the predictive utility of biographical data was lower than that for other measures. Also, he noted that biodata appeared to have less predictive power for managers at higher organizational levels than for others.[87] Donald Schwab and Richard Oliver reviewed 21 biodata studies predicting job tenure and pointed out that many of the studies reporting positive results with biodata did not incorporate cross-validation as part of their procedures.[88] Thus they argued that some of these studies' results may have been due to chance findings. Further, they suggested that biodata reports published in the professional literature are biased, since journals typically only publish articles with significant results. Because negative findings are not readily available, it would be very difficult to ascertain the true validity of biodata. Although there may be some degree of bias of professional journals against publishing nonsignificant results, the data summarized in Table 11.3 would seem to allay some of Schwab and Oliver's concerns.

In spite of these criticisms, other comprehensive reviews generally conclude that biographical data is a useful tool in human resource selection. A few summary comments from these studies will amplify this conclusion. Edwin Henry, for example, concluded that "with very few exceptions it [biodata] has been found to be the best single predictor of future behavior where the predicted behavior is of a total or complex nature.[89] Likewise, William Owens reported that "one of the unmixed and conspicuous virtues of scored autobiographical data has been its clear and recognized tendency to be an outstanding predictor of a broad spectrum of external criteria."[90] Finally, Wayne Cascio adds that "compelling evidence exists that when appropriate procedures are followed, the accuracy of biographical data as a predictor of future behavior is superior to any known alternatives."[91] Given the overwhelmingly positive results, biodata should at least be considered for adoption in many selection programs.

Accuracy of Biodata   Because a BIB is a self-report measure in which job applicants describe themselves and report their typical behaviors, the accuracy with which they make these reports is of concern. As with the application form, for biodata to be useful in selection, information collected by means of a BIB must be accurate. Proponents claim that one unique asset of biodata is its accuracy because it is subject to verification. However, all items appearing on a BIB are not verifiable because they may reflect attitudes, interests, beliefs, or other types of information that are difficult to verify. For this reason, some concern has been raised over the accuracy of biodata items that are due to selective recall by job applicants.[92]

Our earlier review of application data accuracy is relevant here. We saw that research by Irwin Goldstein[93] and David Weiss and Rene Dawis[94] revealed distortion of application data by unskilled job applicants. In contrast, James Mosel and Lee Cozan found that applicants for sales and office positions provided accurate application data.[95] These studies provide some evidence on the accuracy of verifiable data collected by an application form. But what about data collected by a BIB?

There are not a lot of published studies from which to draw definitive conclusions about biodata accuracy. The few that are available, however, shed some light on the issue. Michael Mumford and William Owens summarize two studies that examined the accuracy of nonverifiable, self-reported life histories.[96] One study showed moderate relationships between individuals' life history descriptions and psychologists' observations made 16 years later.[97] Another found moderate correlations between parents' descriptions of their children during adolescence and their children's self-descriptions for a common set of life history items.[98]

Wayne Cascio completed a study under research rather than employment conditions to test the accuracy of verifiable biodata items.[99] Cascio administered a 184-item BIB to currently employed police officers. Of 17 historical and verifiable BIB items, he found only two with substantial discrepancy: age when first married (32 percent discrepancy) and number of full-time jobs held prior to present employment (50 percent discrepancy). Finally, Garnett Shaffer and her associates explored the accuracy of a 118-item biodata form given to over 1,200 university freshmen.[100] Five years later, a sample of these students were given the same questionnaire and asked to complete it again. Parents of these students were also sent a shortened version of the life history questionnaire and asked to complete it on their children. Results showed that respondents reported objective, verifiable biodata items more consistently than subjective biodata items. Greater accuracy was also found for scores on groups of common biodata items, that is biodata factors, than for single items. Overall, the general pattern of results obtained by Shaffer's group seems to suggest that the more objective (verifiable) the biodata item or factor, the greater the degree of accuracy.

Another point relevant to the issue of accuracy is whether job applicants can fake their responses to a BIB to enhance their chances of being employed. It appears that when there is a transparent response stereotype as to how a BIB should be completed for a specific job, respondents can fake their answers to appear as a desirable applicant. When a response stereotype is not apparent, respondents have difficulty altering their responses to enhance their employability.[101] For this reason, when faking may be a problem, some writers have called for steps to be taken such as using biodata items less subject to faking, telling respondents their answers are subject to independent verification and follow-up interviews, and developing a biodata answer key to predict faking and including the key in a BIB administered to job applicants.[102]

Legality of Biodata   Our earlier comments on legal issues involved in weighted application blanks also apply to the use of biographical data. Items can be included in a BIB if it can be shown (a) that they are job related and (b) do not unfairly discriminate against protected groups of job applicants. Unfair discrimination might be established if it can be shown that a biodata item, total score on a BIB, or a score on a BIB dimension affects a group disproportionately. For example, Laurence Siegel and Irving Lane describe a situation where BIB item weights scored equally for black and white applicants would have resulted in discrimination.[103] It was discovered that the BIB item "How were you referred for a job with us?" required different weights for minority and nonminority applicants. A positive weight was assigned to a response from nonminority applicants indicating referral by one of the organization's present employees. Conversely, the item had no relationship with job performance for minority applicants because the company employed few minority group members who might make a referral. If all applicants regardless of their race had been scored on the item, then the item would have had a discriminatory impact on minority applicants.

Once a case has been established against an employer (that is, a prima facie case of discrimination), a user of a BIB must provide evidence of validity and fairness of the BIB item, total, or dimension score. If these requirements can be met, then the BIB is acceptable.

It is impossible to answer in the abstract and with complete certainty whether biodata are discriminatory or not. Previous research on the matter is far from conclusive. William Owens finds from his review that "all in all, the available evidence would seem to suggest that the major dimensions of biodata response are quite stable across cultures, age, race, and sex groups."[104] On the other hand, Richard Reilly and Georgia Chao summarize some studies reporting race and sex differences in biodata scoring keys.[105] Perhaps, the best advice that can be offered is that a user of a BIB should always check for validity and fairness. Some BIB items involving topics such as education and socioeconomic background may very well be associated with applicant gender or ethnicity. So appropriate care should be taken. Validity and fairness should not be taken for granted. Job analysis as well as other steps might be used to produce content-valid biodata measures that may have less adverse impact against protected applicant groups.[106]

Another legal issue that could arise with the use of a BIB is that of invasion of privacy. Although some writers suggest that a BIB is an innocuous selection device, some questions appearing on some biodata forms could be considered offensive. For example, items that involve relationships with siblings and parents, socioeconomic status, or self-esteem could be viewed by some respondents as highly personal. Use of rational item screening by subject matter experts for minimizing biodata item bias and objectionability is one means for handling this problem.[107] Another strategy that has been proposed is simply to have applicants omit items that they may consider highly personal or offensive. However, questions left blank by job applicants may produce negative perceptions by employers of these applicants.[108]

Invasion of privacy and job applicant rights are issues likely to grow in importance in the future. Research needs to be directed toward invasion-of-privacy implications particularly where biodata questionnaires composed of very personal items are being used as selection measures.

Why Is Biodata a Good Predictor?

If we accept the idea that biodata is a good predictor of important work behaviors, we might also ask, Why does it work? There are several plausible explanations. First, a BIB is representative of an individual's life history whereas other predictors, such as a selection interview, may only provide a caricature.[109] For example, in an unsystematic selection interview, individuals may provide a broad, perhaps distorted sketch of themselves, while in a BIB a more systematic, standardized, comprehensive, and accurate picture may be obtained.

Second, when empirical scoring keys are used, the very nature of their development ensures that only relevant items are used to predict measures of job success. In developing keys, only items that are related to job success and are cross-validated are included. Thus the final key should be a valid predictor of the criterion. In most tests, only the total test score, not individual items, is related to job success. Thus items that are not valid may lower test validity.

Third, biographical data may work because of the one-to-one correspondence between content of a BIB and the criterion being predicted. Biographical data may contain all of the important elements of consequence to the criterion. Tests generally assume that job success is determined by traits, aptitudes, abilities, or intelligence. Thus, when tests are developed, they are constructed to measure those characteristics thought to be related to job performance. Rather than use the indirect approach of tests, biodata generally attempts to measure aspects of the criterion directly. For example, high school grade point average (GPA) generally predicts college grade point average better than aptitude tests. No attempt is made to measure indirectly an abstract trait such as mathematical ability to predict college GPA. The biodata characteristic, high school GPA is used to directly predict college GPA.[110]

Fourth, performance on many criterion measures is often explained by many different variables. Most biographical data questionnaires are composed of a wide variety of items reflecting various attitudes, beliefs, interests, and behaviors. When these items are keyed to predict criterion performance, a BIB may explain aspects of a criterion that may be unaccounted for by any other single predictor.

Finally, the evidence is very persuasive that past behavior is a predictor of future behavior. Apparently, people's behavior over time is reasonably consistent in similar situations.[111] If we can accurately assess important life history experiences, then future behavior can be predicted. Because of its focus on the developmental aspects of people, a biographical data questionnaire serves as a useful vehicle for measuring associated life history experiences.

Use of Biodata

As we look at the evidence collected on the predictive power of biographical data, we have to be impressed with its applicability to a wide variety of criteria.

As we have, seen, criteria including tenure, performance in training, creativity, and productivity are within its predictive repertoire. Biodata is one of the few predictors that has been regarded as a legitimate alternative to cognitive testing in HR selection.[112]

Despite the impressive validation evidence reported on the method, biographical data are rarely used as compared to other predictors. Surveys have generally shown that fewer than 1 out of 15 employers reported they have ever used biographical information in selection.[113] Edson Hammer and Lawrence Kleiman reported that only 0.4 percent of 248 HR managers surveyed said they currently use biographical information in hiring.[114]

Obviously, a natural question is "Why?" Why should a selection method with such promise in predicting job success have such little application? Hammer and Kleiman's survey gives us some insights. Table 11.4 summarizes the percentage of HR managers indicating various reasons for not using biodata in hiring. Lack of knowledge about biodata, lack of resources such as time, money, and personnel for developing biodata forms, and perceived equal employment opportunity liability concerns from using the method were the most common important reasons given. HR managers' limited knowledge of the method suggests an educational need.

Research by James Smither and his colleagues reflects a negative attitude toward biodata by newly hired managers similar to that held by some of the managers in Hammer and Kleiman's survey.[115] Smither and associates collected data on newly hired entry-level managers and recruiting employment managers. Among other rating criteria, they were asked to judge the job relatedness of 14 predictors. Of the ratings given, biographical data along with personality inventories received some of the lowest perceived job relatedness ratings. Like the HR managers (see Table 11.4), face validity of biodata forms appears to be a significant concern among job applicants as well.

Criticisms of Biodata

So, where does this leave us? It seems that applicants are likely to provide generally accurate answers to BIB items that are at least somewhat verifiable. They *may* also give accurate responses to items that cannot be verified. However, *if* applicants want to distort or fake their responses to a BIB to enhance their employability, they may be able to do so. To what extent distortion actually occurs in such cases, we do not know.

We can see from our earlier discussion that biographical data offer outstanding potential as a predictor in our selection program. But, as with all measures, there are pitfalls or limitations that any potential user would be wise to consider. For one, biodata scoring keys have not been considered to be transferable from one organization to another. Because scoring keys are typically developed for a distinct criterion involving a specific job in a specific organization, different keys have been recommended for various jobs and organizations.[116] However, research by Hannah Rothstein and others, which we reviewed earlier, indicates that it is possible to develop a generalizable biodata form and scoring key that can be used in a variety of settings and with a variety of employee

TABLE 11.4	HR MANAGERS' REASONS FOR NOT USING BIOGRAPHICAL DATA IN SELECTION	

Reason for Not Using Biographical Data	Number of HR Managers	Percentage of HR Managers
Don't know much about biodata	129	52.2
Top management would not support	68	27.3
Lack of statistical/methodological expertise	98	39.4
Lack of resources (time, money, personnel)	155	62.6
Suitable criterion not available	79	31.9
Large enough sample of people is not available	78	31.1
Unsuccessful past experience with biodata	4	1.4
Not a valid selection tool	66	26.5
Biodata has low face validity	59	23.8
Responses to biographical data form easily faked	47	18.9
Method has EEO risks	113	45.7
Method is an invasion of privacy	98	39 5

NOTE: The percentages are based on responses of 248 HR managers who indicated that a reason was important for not using biographical data.

SOURCE: Based on Edson G. Hammer and Lawrence S. Kleiman, "Getting to Know You," *Personnel Administrator* 34 (1988): 88.

groups.[117] The problem is that most biodata forms that have been produced have not been developed in this manner. Thus they may very well suffer from the situational specificity criticism.

Another limitation is that in order to avoid the effects of chance on scoring keys, large samples of workers are needed to develop as well as validate the keys.[118] Additional samples may also be needed to monitor the future validity of the keys as well. Only sizable organizations or those organizations willing to work jointly in a consortium may be able to develop useful biodata keys.

Several additional criticisms have also been made against the use of biographical data in selection. One criticism is that biographical data are deterministic in nature. That is, those individuals who do not have the "correct" life history background will be excluded from a job, and there is little they can do about their past. Regardless of individual effort, motivation, or intervening circumstances, an applicant cannot change those life experiences that may be considered indicative of job success. Like all selection measures, biodata are an indicator of behavior. We should be sensitive to the fact that people may be excluded who have not had the opportunity to obtain the "right" life history experiences. Of course, we should have the same sensitivity for all of our selection measures.[119]

Another criticism is that use of life history data in prediction is nothing more than "dustbowl empiricism; it may work, but who knows why?" If we choose to use biodata or any measure for that matter, we should be careful to understand how our scored life histories are related to job success. William Ennis raises this question: "Does it make sense (assuming validity for such items) to give a job candidate minus or plus values on a background questionnaire simply because he had few (or many) books in his home as a child or had no father (or mother) in the home, even though other factors point to good potential?[120] Sometimes selection managers in their desire to apply objective standards in selection can be seduced by the attractiveness of a number assigned to a job applicant. However, a blind approach to scoring and using biodata, without understanding what that score represents and how it rationally relates to the job, can lead to unintentional biases against some job applicants. Robert Travers reports one instance where blind empirical scoring of a BIB led to such biases.[121] A study was conducted to identify life history predictors of the success of research scientists as administrators. The criterion to be predicted by the biodata questionnaire was the scientists' job performance ratings. Biodata variables that were positively related with success were those of (a) having a rural background and (b) coming from a family of skilled craftsworkers. Characteristics negatively correlated with success were (a) having a large city background and (b) coming from a retail-merchant family. Clearly, those characteristics were immutable, but the findings did not make sense rationally. Further research revealed the explanation. It was discovered that many of the urban-reared scientists were Jewish, and the performance evaluations used to define job success had an anti-Semitic cast. That is, the criterion to be predicted by the biodata measure being developed was found to be discriminatory. Blind application of the apparently "valid" scoring system would simply have perpetuated the bias. If we use biodata, we should always ask, "Do these results make sense?" Our job analysis results and the formation of rational hypotheses in selecting the content of our biographical inventories can help us in answering this question.

The "deterministic flavor" and "dustbowl empiricism" criticisms of biodata may have some merit. However, work by William Owens,[122] Lyle Schoenfeldt,[123] and their colleagues,[124] in their derivation of a developmental-integrative model based on biodata to predict behavior, has helped to dispel some of the criticisms. Their research has clarified our thinking with regard to understanding what biodata measures and how it can be used. To date, many of the studies employing the developmental-integrative model are promising. Future research will help to further clarify the meaning of biodata and its effectiveness as a human resource selection measure. In the mean time, biodata should continue to be considered a viable selection alternative.

References

[1] As quoted in William A. Owens, "Background Data," *in Handbook of Industrial and Organizational Psychology*, ed. Marvin Dunnette (Chicago: Rand-McNally, 1976), p. 610.

[2] For additional information, see Leonard W. Ferguson, "The Development of Industrial Psychology," in *Industrial Psychology*, ed. Byron H. Gilmer (New York: McGrawHill, 1961), pp. 18–37.

[3] George W. England, *Development and Use of Weighted Application Blanks* (Minneapolis: Industrial Relations Center, University of Minnesota, 1971), pp. 53–63.

[4] William D. Buel, "Voluntary Female Clerical Turnover, the Concurrent and Predictive Validity of a Weighted Application Blank," *Journal of Applied Psychology* 48 (1964): 180–182.

[5]James N. Mosel, "Prediction of Department Store Sales Performance from Personal Data," *Journal of Applied Psychology* 36 (1952): 8–10.

[6]N. Friedman and Ernest J. McCormick, "A Study of Personal Data as Predictors of the Job Behavior of Telephone Operators," in *Proceedings of the Indiana Academy of Science* 62 (1952): 293–294.

[7]H. C. Lockwood and S. O. Parsons, "Relationship of Personal History Information to the Performance of Production Supervisors," *Engineering Industrial Psychology* 2 (1960): 20–26.

[8]Lewis E. Albright, Wallace J. Smith, J. R. Glennon, and William A. Owens, "The Prediction of Research Competence and Creativity from Personal History," *Journal of Applied Psychology* 45 (1961): 59–62.

[9]John M. Malouff and Nicola S. Schutte, "Using Biographical Information to Hire the Best New Police Officers: Research Findings," *Journal of Police Science and Administration* 14 (1986): 175–177.

[10]Raymond Lee and Jerome M. Booth, "A Utility Analysis of a Weighted Application Blank Designed to Predict Turnover for Clerical Employees," *Journal of Applied Psychology* 59 (1974): 516–518.

[11]England, *Development and Use of Weighted Application Blanks*, pp. 4, 40.

[12]Ibid.

[13]Michael G. Aamodt and Walter L. Pierce, "Comparison of the Rare Response and Vertical Percent Methods for Scoring the Biographical Information Blank," *Educational and Psychological Measurement* 47 (1987): 506.

[14] England, *Development and Use of Weighted Application Blanks*, pp. 27–28.

[15] Edward E. Cureton, "Validity, Reliability, and Baloney," *Educational and Psychological Measurement* 10 (1950): 94–96.

[16]England, *Development and Use of Weighted Application Blanks*, p. 30.

[17]Ibid., p. 36.

[18]Ibid., p. 40.

[19]Marilyn K. Quaintance, *Development of a Weighted Application Blank to Predict Managerial Assessment Center Performance* (doctoral dissertation, George Washington University, Washington, D.C., 1981).

[20]England, *Development and Use of Weighted Application Blanks*, p. 42.

[21]Roger Bellows, *Psychology of Personnel in Business and Industry* (New York: Prentice-Hall, 1961).

[22]Morris Viteles, *Industrial Psychology* (New York: Norton, 1932).

[23]England, *Development and Use of Weighted Application Blanks*, p. 43.

[24]Marvin D. Dunnette, Wayne K. Kirchner, James R. Erickson, and Paul A. Banas, "Predicting Turnover among Female Office Workers," *Personnel Administration* 23 (1960): 45–50.

[25]Paul Wernimont, "Re-evaluation of a Weighted Application Blank for Office Personnel," *Journal of Applied Psychology* 46 (1962): 417–419.

[26]Steven H. Brown, "Long-Term Validity of a Personal History Item Scoring Procedure," *Journal of Applied Psychology* 63 (1978): 673–676.

[27]Darrell E. Roach, "Double Cross-Validation of a Weighted Application Blank over Time," *Journal of Applied Psychology* 55 (1971): 157–160.

[28]Larry A. Pace and Lyle F. Schoenfeldt, "Legal Concerns in the Use of Weighted Applications," *Personnel Psychology* 30 (1977): 159–166.

[29]Richard W. Rosenbaum, "Predictability of Employee Theft Using Weighted Application Blanks," *Journal of Applied Psychology* 61 (1976): 94–98.

[30]Wayne F. Cascio, "Turnover, Biographical Data, and Fair Employment Practice," *Journal of Applied Psychology* 61 (1976): 576–580.

[31]Bureau of National Affairs, *Employee Selection Procedures* (ASPA-BNA *Survey No. 45*) (Washington, D.C.: The Bureau of National Affairs, May 5, 1983).

[32]Owens, "Background Data," pp. 609–644.

[33]Fred A Mael, "A Conceptual Rationale for the Domain and Attributes of Biodata Items," *Personnel Psychology* 44(1991): 763–792.

[34]Craig J. Russell, "Selecting Top Corporate Leaders: An Example of Biographical Information," *Journal of Management* 6 (1990): 73–86.

[35]Craig J. Russell, J. Mattson, S.E. Devlin, and D. Atwater, "Predictive Validity of Biodata Items Generated from Retrospective Life Experience Essays," *Journal of Applied Psychology* 75 (1990): 569–580.

[36]Owens, "Background Data," pp. 612–613.

[37]Ibid.

[38]Ibid, p.613.

[39]James J. Asher, "The Biographical Item: Can It Be Improved?" *Personnel Psychology* 25 (1972): 252.

[40]Owens, "Background Data," pp. 611–612.

[41]William A. Owens, "Toward One Discipline of Scientific Psychology," *American Psychologist* 23 (1968): 782–785.

[42]Edward E. Cureton, "Comment," in Edwin R. Henry, *Research Conference on the Use of Autobiographical Data as Psychological Predictors* (Greensboro, N.C.: The Richardson Foundation, 1965), p. 13.

[43]Anne Hoiberg and William M. Pugh, "Predicting Navy Effectiveness: Expectations, Motivation, Personality, Aptitude, and Background Variables," *Personnel Psychology* 31 (1978): 841–852.

[44]William A. Owens and Edwin R. Henry, *Biographical Data in Industrial Psychology: A Review and Evaluation* (Greensboro, N.C.: The Richardson Foundation, 1966).

[45]Michael D. Mumford and William A. Owens, "Methodology Review: Principles, Procedures, and Findings in the Application of Background Data Measures," *Applied Psychological Measurement* 11 (1987): 2, 6.

[46]Abraham K. Korman, *Industrial and Organizational Psychology* (New York: Prentice-Hall, 1971), p. 239.

[47]William A. Owens, "A Quasi-Actuarial Basis for Individual Assessment," *American Psychologist* 26 (1971): 992–999.

[48]Korman, *Industrial and Organizational Psychology*, p. 239.

[49]For examples of studies involving the use of a BIB in a wide variety of occupations, see Richard R. Reilly and Georgia T. Chao, "Validity and Fairness of Some Alternative Employee Selection Procedures," *Personnel Psychology* 35 (1982): 1–63.

[50]Edwin A. Fleishman, "Some New Frontiers in Personnel Selection Research," *Personnel Psychology* 41 (1988): 685.

[51]James W. Smither, Richard R. Reilly, Roger Millsap, Kenneth Pearlman, and Ronald W. Stoffey, "Applicant Reactions to Selection Procedures," *Personnel Psychology* 46 (1993): 58–60.

[52]Mumford and Owens, "Methodology Review: Principles, Procedures, and Findings in the Application of Background Data Measures," p. 5.

[53]Terry W. Mitchell and Richard J. Klimoski, "Is It Rational to Be Empirical? A Test of Methods for Scoring Biographical Data," *Journal of Applied Psychology* 67 (1982): 4l1–418.

[54]William E. Williams, "Life History Antecedents of Volunteers versus Nonvolunteers for an AFROTC Program." Paper presented at the Midwestern Psychological Association, Chicago, 1961.

[55]Owens, "Background Data," p. 613.

[56]Karl Kuhnert and Craig J. Russell, "Using Constructive Developmental Theory and Biodata to Bridge the Gap between Personnel Selection and Leadership," *Journal of Management* 16 (1990): 595–607.

[57]John B. Miner, "Success in Management Consulting and the Concept of Eliteness Motivation," *Academy of Management Journal* 14 (1971): 367–378. Examples of the development of a content valid biodata questionnaire designed for predicting test performance of electrician job applicants can be found in Ronald D. Pannone, "Predicting Test Performance: A Content Valid Approach to Screening Applicants," *Personnel Psychology* 37 (1984): 507–514 and Michael D. Mumford, M. Cooper, and

F. M. Schemmer, *Development of a Content Valid Set of Background Data Measures* (Bethesda, Md.: Advanced Research Resources Organization, 1983).

[58]Kuhnert and Russell, "Using Constructive Developmental Theory and Biodata to Bridge the Gap between Personnel Selection and Leadership," pp. 602–603.

[59]James R. Glennon, Lewis E. Albright, and William A. Owens, *A Catalog of Life History Items* (Greensboro, N.C.: The Richardson Foundation, 1966). See also Owens and Henry, *Biographical Data in Industrial Psychology.*

[60]W. M. Brodie, William A. Owens, and M. F. Britt, *Annotated Bibliography on Biographical Data* (Greensboro, N.C.: The Richardson Foundation, 1968). See also Owens and Henry, *Biographical Data in Industrial Psychology.*

[61]Mumford and Owens, "Methodology Review: Principles, Procedures, and Findings in the Application of Background Data Measures," pp. 6–8. For a somewhat different approach to the collection of important life history accomplishments from professional job applicants, see Leaetta M. Hough, "Development and Evaluation of the 'Accomplishment Record' Method of Selecting and Promoting Professionals," *Journal of Applied Psychology* 69 (1984): 135–146 and Leaetta M. Hough, Margaret A. Keyes, and Marvin D. Dunnette, "An Evaluation of Three 'Alternative' Selection Procedures," *Personnel Psychology* 36 (1983): 261–276.

[62]Mael, "A Conceptual Rationale for the Domain and Attributes of Biodata Items."

[63]Lawrence S. Kleiman and Robert Faley, "A Comparative Analysis of the Empirical Validity of Past and Present-Oriented Biographical Items," *Journal of Business and Psychology* 4 (1990): 431–437.

[64]Williams, "Life History Antecedents of Volunteers versus Nonvolunteers for and AFROTC Program," p. 8.

[65]William A. Owens and Lyle F. Schoenfeldt, "Toward a Classification of Persons," *Journal of Applied Psychology Monograph* 64 (1979): 569–607.

[66]See, for example, Sam C. Webb, "The Comparative Validity of Two Biographical Inventory Keys," *Journal of Applied Psychology* 44 (1960): 177–183; Raymond E. Christal and Robert A. Bottenberg, *Procedure for Keying Self-Report Test Items* (Lackland Air Force Base, Tex.: Personnel Research Laboratory, 1964); William H. Clark and Bruce L. Margolis, "A Revised Procedure for the Analysis of Biographical Information," *Educational and Psychological Measurement* 31 (1971): 461–464.

[67]See, for example, Owens and Schoenfeldt, "Toward a Classification of Persons," pp. 569–607; Michael T. Matteson, "An Alternative Approach to Using Biographical Data for Predicting Job Success," *Journal of Occupational Psychology* 51 (1978): 155–162; Michael T. Matteson, "A FORTRAN Program Series for Generating Relatively Independent and Homogeneous Keys for Scoring Biographical Inventories," *Educational and Psychological Measurement* 30 (1970): 137–139; Mitchell and Klimoski, "Is It Rational to Be Empirical? A Test of Methods for Scoring Biographical Data."

[68]England, *Development and Use of Weighted Application Blanks.*

[69]William H. Stead and Carol L. Shartle, *Occupational Counseling Techniques* (New York: American Book., 1940).

[70]William B. Lecznar and John T. Dailey, "Keying Biographical Inventories in Classification Test Batteries," *American Psychologist* 5 (1950): 279.

[71]Michael P. Malone, *Predictive Efficiency and Discriminatory Impact of Verifiable Biographical Data as a Function of Data Analysis Procedure* (doctoral dissertation, University of Minnesota, Minneapolis, 1978).

[72]Webb, "The Comparative Validity of Two Biographical Inventory Keys."

[73]Paul A. Telenson, Ralph A. Alexander, and Gerald V. Barrett, "Scoring the Biographical Information Blank: A Comparison of Three Weighting Techniques," *Applied Psychological Measurement* 7 (1983): 73–80.

[74]Mumford and Owens, "Methodology Review: Principles, Procedures, and Findings in the Application of Background Data Measures," p. 12.

[75]Mumford and Owens (ibid., pp. 15–17) also discuss rational scaling procedures as a means for clustering biodata items into dimensions. However, since rational scaling approaches are used less frequently than factor analytic methods, they are omitted from this discussion.

[76]Hubert S. Feild and William F. Giles, *Career Planning at West Point Pepperell: A Strategy for Matching People with Jobs* (Auburn, Ala.: Auburn Technical Assistance Center, 1980).

[77]Robert F. Morrison, William A. Owens, J. R. Glennon, and Lewis E. Albright, "Factored Life History Antecedents of Industrial Research Performance," Journal *of Applied Psychology* 46 (1962): 281–284.

[78]Owens and Schoenfeldt, "Toward a Classification of Persons," pp. 569–607.

[79]See, for example, John R. Hinrichs, S. Haanpera, and L. Sonkin, "Validity of a Biographical Information Blank across National Boundaries," *Personnel Psychology* 29 (1976): 417–421; Owens, "Background Data"; Mumford and Owens, "Methodology Review: Principles, Procedures, and Findings in the Application of Background Data Measures," p. 9.

[80]"See, for example, Garnett S. Shaffer, Vickie Saunders, and William A. Owens, "Additional Evidence for the Accuracy of Biographical Data: Long-Term Retest and Observer Ratings," *Personnel Psychology* 39 (1986): 791–809.

[81]Ibid.

[82]Edwin E. Ghiselli, *The Validity of Occupational Aptitude Tests* (New York: Wiley, 1966).

[83]Asher, "The Biographical Item: Can It Be Improved?" pp. 251–269.

[84]John E. Hunter and Rhonda F. Hunter, "Validity and Utility of Alternative Predictors of Job Performance," *Psychological Bulletin* 96 (1984): 72–98 and Neal Schmitt, Richard Z. Gooding, Raymond A. Noe, and Michael Kirsch, "Metaanalyses of Validity Studies Published between 1964 and 1982 and the Investigation of Study Characteristics," *Personnel Psychology* 37 (1984): 407–422.

[85]Hannah R. Rothstein, Frank L. Schmidt, Frank W. Erwin, William A. Owens, and C. Paul Sparks, "Biographical Data in Employment Selection: Can Validities Be Made Generalizable? *Journal of Applied Psychology* 75 (1990): 175–184.

[86]Hunter and Hunter, "Validity and Utility of Alternative Predictors of Performance."

[87]Abraham K. Korman, "The Prediction of Managerial Performance," *Personnel Psychology* 21 (1968): 295–322.

[88]Donald P. Schwab and Richard L. Oliver, "Predicting Tenure with Biographical Data: Exhuming Buried Evidence," *Personnel Psychology* 27 (1974): 125–128.

[89]Edwin R. Henry, "Conference on the Use of Biographical Data in Psychology," *American Psychologist* 21 (1966): 248.

[90]Owens, "Background Data," p. 617.

[91]Wayne F. Cascio, "Turnover, Biographical Data, and Fair Employment Practice," p. 576.

[92]P. Van Rijn, *Biographical Questionnaires and Scored Application Blanks in Personnel Selection* (Washington, D.C.: U. S. Office of Personnel Management, Personnel Research and Development Center, 1980).

[93]Irwin L. Goldstein, "The Application Blank: How Honest Are the Responses?" *Journal of Applied Psychology* 55 (1971): 491–492.

[94]David J. Weiss and Rene V. Dawis, "An Objective Validation of Factual Interview Data," *Journal of Applied Psychology* 40 (1960): 381–385.

[95]James N. Mosel and Lee W. Cozan, "The Accuracy of Application Blank Work Histories," *Journal of Applied Psychology* 36 (1952): 365–369.

[96]Mumford and Owens, "Methodology Review: Principles, Procedures, and Findings in the Application of Background Data Measures," p. 8.

[97]Wanda C. Bronson, Edith S. Katten, and Norman Livson, "Patterns of Authority and Affection in Two Generations," *Journal of Abnormal and Social Psychology* 58 (1959): 143–152.

[98]Vickie C. Saunders, *Verification of Responses to an Autobiographical Data Form* (master's thesis, University of Georgia, Athens, Ga., 1983).

[99]Wayne F. Cascio, "Accuracy of Verifiable Biographical Information Blank Responses," *Journal of Applied Psychology* 60 (1975): 767–769.

[100]Shaffer, Saunders, and Owens, "Additional Evidence for the Accuracy of Biographical Data: Long-Term Retest and Observer Ratings."

[101]Alec D. Schrader and H. G. Osburn, "Biodata Faking: Effects of Induced Subtlety and Position Specificity," *Personnel Psychology* 30 (1977): 395–404; Gary L. Lautenschlager, "Within Subject Measures for the Assessment of Individual Differences in Faking," *Educational and Psychological Measurement* 46 (1985): 309–316. See also Cathy D. Anderson, Jack L. Warner, and Cassie C. Spencer, "Inflation Bias in Self Assessment Examinations: Implications for Valid Employee Selection," *Journal of Applied Psychology* 69 (1984): 574–580.

[102]Mumford and Owens, "Methodology Review: Principles, Procedures, and Findings in the Application of Background Data Measures," p. 9.

[103]Laurence Siegel and Irving Lane, *Personnel and Organizational Psychology* (Homewood, Ill.: Irwin, 1969).

[104]Owens, "Background Data," p. 620.

[105]Reilly and Chao, "Validity and Fairness of Some Alternative Employee Selection Procedures," pp. 1–62.

[106]Pannone, "Predicting Test Performance: A Content Valid Approach to Screening Applicants" and Mumford, Cooper, and Schemmer, *Development of a Content Valid Set of Background Data Measures.*

[107]Mumford, Cooper, and Schemmer, *Development of a Content Valid Set of Background Data Measures.*

[108]Dianna L. Stone and Eugene F. Stone, "Effects of Missing Application Blank Information on Personnel Selection Decisions: Do Privacy Protection Strategies Bias the Outcome?" *Journal of Applied Psychology* 72 (1987): 452–456.

[109]Asher, "The Biographical Item: Can It Be Improved?" p. 258.

[110]Ibid., pp. 259–260.

[111]Shaffer, Saunders, and Owens, "Additional Evidence for the Accuracy of Biographical Data: Long-Term Retest and Observer Ratings."

[112]Reilly and Chao, "Validity and Fairness of Some Alternative Employee Selection Procedures."

[113]Edson G. Hammer and Lawrence S. Kleiman, "Getting to Know You," *Personnel Administrator* 34 (1988): 86–92.

[114]Ibid.

[115]Smither, Reilly, Millsap, Pearlman, and Stoffey, "Applicant Reactions to Selection Procedures," p. 60.

[116]Michael F. Tucker, Victor B. Cline, and James R. Schmitt, "Prediction of Creativity and Other Performance Measures form Biographical Information among Pharmaceutical Scientists," *Journal of Applied Psychology* 51 (1967): 131–138.

[117]Rothstein, Schmidt, Erwin, Owens, and Sparks, "Biographical Data in Employment Selection: Can Validities Be Made Generalizable?"

[118]Hunter and Hunter, "Validity and Utility of Alternative Predictors of Job Performance," p. 88.

[119]Leaetta Hough, Margaret Keyes, and Marvin Dunnette ("An Evaluation of Three 'Alternative' Selection Procedures") have suggested the use of the Accomplishment Record inventory as one means for addressing the "deterministic flavor" argument against biodata. Because the Accomplishment Record focuses on individuals' accomplishments, individuals scoring low on the Accomplishment Record can be given feedback on areas of inadequacy. This feedback information can be used by the individuals to formulate future plans for performance in order to enhance their eligibility for promotion, selection, etc.

[120]William H Ennis, "Use of Nontest Variables in the Government Employment Setting." Paper presented as part of a symposium, *Use of Nontest Variables in Admission, Selection, and Classification Operations*, American Psychological Association, Miami Beach, September 8, 1970, pp. 11–12.

[121]Robert M. Travers, "Rational Hypotheses in the Construction of Tests," *Educational and Psychological Measurement* 11 (1951): 128–137.

[122]For a review of studies incorporating the developmental-integrative model, see Owens, "Background Data," pp. 609–644.

[123]Lyle F. Schoenfeldt, "Utilization of Manpower: Development and Evaluation of an Assessment-Classification Model for Matching Individuals with Jobs," *Journal of Applied Psychology* 59 (1974): 583–595.

[124]For example, see Michael D. Mumford, *Patterns of Life History: The Ecology of Human Individuality* (Hillsdale, N.J.: Erlbaum, 1990); Michael D. Mumford and Garnett S. Stokes, *Advances in Biodata Research* (Palo Alto, Calif.: Consulting Psychologists Press, in press);Donald R. Brush and William A. Owens, "Implementation and Evaluation of an Assessment Classification Model for Manpower Utilization," *Personnel Psychology* 32 (1979): 369–383; Andrew G. Niener and William A. Owens, "Relationships between Two Sets of Biodata with Seven Years Separation," *Journal of Applied Psychology* 67 (1982): 146–150; Kermit R. Davis, "A Longitudinal Analysis of Biographical Subgroups Using Owens' Developmental-Integrative Model," *Personnel Psychology* 37 (1984): 1–14; Bruce Eberhardt and Paul Muchinsky, "An Empirical Investigation of the Factor Stability of Owens' Biographical Questionnaire," *Journal of Applied Psychology* 67 (1982): 138–145; Andrew G. Niener and William A. Owens, "Using Biodata to Predict Job Choice among College Graduates,"*Journal of Applied Psychology* 70 (1985): 127–136; Garnett S. Shaffer, "Patterns of Work and Nonwork Satisfaction," 72 (1987): 115–124; Shaffer, Saunders, and Owens, "Additional Evidence for the Accuracy of Biographical Data: Long-Term Retest and Observer Ratings"; Gary L. Lautenschlager and Garnett S. Shaffer, "Reexamining the Component Stability of Owens' Biographical Questionnaire,"*Journal of Applied Psychology* 72 (1987): 149–152.

12

The Selection Interview

The interview has long been acknowledged as the most frequently used selection device. A reasonable case can also be made that it is the most important device in many selection decisions because it is given the most weight.[1] It is also a fairly time-consuming and expensive selection tool as a survey of members of the Society of Human Resource Managers indicates.[2] Nearly 88 percent of respondents reported having on-site interviews with between three and ten applicants for each open position. Approximately 70 percent of the companies paid all expenses associated with these visits. In the majority of companies, each applicant interviewed with two to six members of the host organization with 83 percent of the interviews lasting between 36 and 60 minutes. Based on these data, a rough estimate of staff cost is between one and a half and two days per open position just for interviews.

Partially because of its widespread use and cost, selection researchers have studied the interview for over 70 years. Until recently, these studies have resulted in pessimistic evaluations about the validity and the general usefulness of the interview. It was commonly agreed that the low validity was due to inappropriate questions being asked applicants and extraneous factors affecting interviewer decision making.[3] These studies also led to specific recommendations on how the interview might be improved. One example is the use of behavioral, job-related interview questions. The two most recognized methods that use such questions are the situational interview and the behavioral description interview.[4] Both methods have consistently demonstrated validity in selection programs covering a variety of jobs.

One type of recent research that has supported the validity of the interview has been validity generalization studies. (Quick, go back and read the validity generalization section in Chapter 5!) One of these studies, based on results from 150 correlations and a total sample size of 51,459, found a corrected validity coefficient of $r = .47$ for the interview. Moreover, structured interviews were found to be more valid than unstructured interviews, $r = .62$ versus $r = .31$.[5] This was an important finding because it had long been recommended that selection interviews be structured, that is, use a predetermined format for all interviewees.

A second study supported these findings.[6] Corrected validity coefficients were .47 for structured interviews (65 correlations, n = 9,008) and .40 for unstructured interviews (27 correlations, n = 2,799). What is surprising from these two studies is the size of the corrected validity coefficient for unstructured interviews. It had generally been thought that such instruments were useless, totally lacking in validity. It might be the case, however, that the studies identified as unstructured really were structured to some extent. At least each had a formal scoring system from which the validity coefficient was calculated. Such scoring is usually not part of typical unstructured interviews that rely on the intuition, hunch, or impression of the interviewer. A third study also found a corrected r = .49 for structured interviews (153 correlations, n = 14,298).[7] In addition, this study provided other useful information by identifying moderator variables that can increase the validity of the structured interview: single interviewers, situational questions, global rating scales, and avoiding ancillary data about applicants. We discuss these variables in detail at the end of this chapter when we summarize recommendations that have been useful in designing interviews. In summary, we refer to Michael Harris's statements in his review of the research on the interview.[8] He points out that the corrected validity coefficients from these validity generalization studies are comparable to a similar coefficient determined for cognitive ability tests (.53) and higher than one determined for assessment centers (.36). Both cognitive ability tests and assessment centers have long been recommended for selection.

In this chapter we summarize what is currently known about the selection interview by stressing the results of empirical studies. We also discuss procedures that have been demonstrated through this research to improve the interview. We hope to provide sufficient information so you will be able to design and implement this important selection device. If you wish more information, we recommend two books: Robert Dipboye's *Selection Interviews: Process Perspectives* and Robert Eder and Gerald Ferris's *The Employment Interview: Theory, Research, and Practice.*[9]

Uses of the Interview in Selection

A first step in understanding the appropriate use of the interview is a discussion of the major advantages that have been offered for its value in selection. Generally these fall into three main categories: (a) the interview provides an opportunity for the organization to recruit good candidates; (b) the interview is an efficient and practical method for measuring a number of different KSAs of an applicant; and (c) the decision about the acceptability of the applicant is made by a member of the organization who should be able to judge the match of the applicant and the job. We discuss each of these supposed advantages in the next sections. Our general conclusion is that these issues must be correctly incorporated into the interview to become advantageous to the organization. If improperly managed, these issues can detract from the usefulness of the selection interview.

Recruiting the Applicant to the Organization

Providing Job Information: Consider the Alternatives   In almost all employment situations the applicant will have questions about the conditions of employment. The selection interview has frequently been the vehicle used for answering these questions because it allows for a give-and-take between the two parties, with the clarification of misunderstandings. While the interview can be used for these purposes, some limiting factors should be noted. Both personal anecdotes and communication research studies provide many examples of oral information between two individuals subsequently being recalled differently by the two. While not all aspects of working conditions can be placed in written form, there is good reason for a written job description to be given to applicants that would convey much of the information often transmitted in the interview. One advantage would be a permanent statement that could easily be referred to by the applicant after the interview has been concluded. Also part of the time allocated for the interview could be saved and used for more direct selection purposes.

There is another factor to consider. It has been hypothesized that the interviewer's behavior changes, depending on how much recruitment is emphasized over selection. As the recruitment function increases, there is evidence that the interviewer places relatively more emphasis on job rather than applicant characteristics, describes vacant positions in more favorable terms, and asks questions that are less likely to lead to applicant disqualification.[10] Logically, this change in emphasis has costs in terms of the amount and quality of pertinent information that is gathered for selection.

Effect on Applicants: Not Always Positive   It is commonly assumed that the interview has value as a public relations device. That is, the personal contact between organizational member and applicant positively affects the attitudes of the applicant. This is not always the case. Applicants are influenced by many factors in the interview, not all of which are clearly understood. There is ample evidence that applicants often come from interviews with negative images of the interviewer and the company. An interviewer must be carefully coached if the interview is to have value.

For example, it has consistently been found that applicants' attraction to an organization is positively related to the extent of job-related questions used by the interviewer.[11] Interviewer style is also important, especially the demonstration of a friendly interest in the applicant, empathy, and providing specific information about the job.[12] Nonverbal behavior such as smiling, nodding, eye contact, and other indications of approval are also positively received.[13] Two researchers have described a dynamic in which the applicant perceives that the interviewer likes him or her and reciprocates this liking.[14] These findings serve to emphasize that the interview is a complex interaction which can have both positive and negative effects on applicants depending on its content and process.

Increasing Job Acceptance: Not!   Not surprisingly, there is consistent evidence that the most important information used in applicants' decisions to accept or reject a job offer is that of job characteristics: salary, tasks, advancement, travel, and so on.[15] Recruitment interviewers generally have not been found to have much of an effect on job choice decisions. Even those studies which have found that recruiters do have an effect on job choice decisions can be interpreted as damning with faint praise. For example, one study identified a set of specific interviewer actions that were related to the applicant's willingness to accept a job offer.[16] However, this relationship held for those interviewers who were believed to be representative of the company's employees. Not all interviewers were believed to be representative, and it was not clear what variables caused such a belief.

Another study divided the recruitment process into five stages.[17] Interviewers were only found to have an effect on applicant decisions at the early stages. Even then, this effect was restricted to those applicants who had not received any job-related information. The evidence seems clear that interviews used for recruitment have minimal influence on the job choice decisions of the applicants.

Measuring Applicant KSAs

More Is Not Better   This issue is concerned with the number and type of applicant characteristics that interviewers often attempt to measure. During the early 1970s, there was a general decrease in the use of scored ability and performance selection tests in favor of unscored interviews. In part this was attributable to a misconception regarding the EEOC's review of selection programs. Early selection discrimination cases revolved around the use of written mental and special ability tests, with the conclusion that these must be validated before they could be used for selection. It was not until recently that it was expressly clear that the selection interview was viewed as a selection test and must also be validated before use. In the interim period, however, the interview was used to assess a wide variety of applicant characteristics. The result is superficial data of limited value. Another problem is that by substituting the interview for other assessment devices that more effectively measure particular applicant characteristics, an HR specialist may be collecting less accurate, more expensive data than is necessary.

Most of the major studies that have reviewed the use of the interview have come to the same conclusions. For example, Lynn Ulrich and Don Trumbo state that "the interviewer is all too frequently asked to do the impossible because of limitations on the time, information, or both, available to him. . . . When the interviewer's task was limited to rating a single trait, acceptable validity was achieved."[18] They further point out that even when the interviewer concentrates on only a few characteristics, there are some that are not profitably addressed. For example, they contend that all too often a conclusion about the applicant's mental ability, arrived at during a 30-minute interview, may be less efficient and accurate than one based on the administration of a 10-minute test, the use of which would leave the interviewer time to assess those areas in which his or her judgment was more effective.

Appropriate KSAs   The question, therefore, is which specific characteristics are best assessed in the interview? Here the major reviews are in general agreement. There are two main types of characteristics: *personal relations*, such as sociability and verbal fluency; and *good citizenship*, such as dependability, conscientiousness, stability, and perseverance.[19] Furthermore, it appears that the interview is better suited to measure these characteristics than are other assessment methods. Personal relations in this sense usually means characteristics important for successful personal interaction in short-term or initial meetings. The interview, by its very nature, is an example of such a situation and, therefore, should be an accurate indicator of ability in these areas. The good citizenship characteristics are often evaluated after discussion of work habits, tasks completed, and work environments. Such discussions usually require clarification or elaboration of statements made by the respondent. The interview, because of its interactive nature, is suitable for such probing by the interviewer.

Studies have demonstrated these points. In one, an interview designed to measure interpersonal skills successfully predicted job performance of two sets of retail clerks.[20] Another study found that interviewers could more accurately judge the social skills of applicants for a research assistant position than they could motivation to work.[21]

A third characteristic, *job knowledge*, has also been evaluated in interviews. There are some guidelines on when an interview would usefully assess this characteristic. If there is to be a large number of job knowledge questions and especially if the answers are fairly short and routine, a written test would be preferable. Such a test would usually be less expensive to administer and score, would provide a permanent record, and would often be a more familiar format for the applicant. If interview questions ask about complex behaviors such as diagnosis of defects, operation of equipment, and manipulation of data or information, job simulation instruments usually would be more appropriate. One situation that would certainly argue for the use of job knowledge questions in the interview is when the applicant has serious reading or writing deficiencies that would impede selection evaluation but not job performance. The interviewer would be able to determine if the question is understood and to clarify unclear or poorly worded responses. Another condition would be selection situations for jobs that require the verbalization of technical information and work procedures, for example advisory or consulting jobs in which most of the requests for service are oral. In such situations, the interview approximates a job simulation selection device.

Selection Evaluation by an Organization Member

Theoretically, one advantage of the interview over other selection instruments is that the data gatherer and interpreter is a human being who understands the job and the organization. The interviewer can vary questions or methods as the situation demands, thereby obtaining more appropriate information from each applicant. Other instruments do not have such adaptable characteristics. It seems probable that given these characteristics the match between applicant and position requirements could effectively be made.

As we mentioned previously, there has been much study of factors that influence the decision making of interviewers. In this section we briefly summarize some of this work. Evidence seems to substantiate that when the interview is appropriately designed, the interviewer can, in fact, make valid predictions about job performance. The results of the validity generalization studies, which we referred to at the beginning of this chapter, concerning the increased validity associated with the use of job analysis and structured format are indications of this. However, without an appropriate design, the interviewer can become his or her own worst enemy. An interviewer's decisions can be influenced by factors that seemingly have little to do with job activities. The following section describes some of these extraneous factors and serves as a background for your better understanding of the purposes of the recommended interview features discussed later in the chapter.

Questions Used Logically, the nature of the questions asked are critical to the reliability and validity of the interview. If the questions are not related to the job, we should not expect validity to be high. If the questions used are not consistent among interviewers, we should not expect them necessarily to agree on their evaluations of applicants because each interviewer has, in fact, collected different information about the applicants.

What, would you guess, has often been found when interviewers' questions have been examined? You're right! Susan Taylor and Janet Sniezek found that interviewers often disagreed among themselves on which topics should be covered in an interview.[22] These differences seemed to be related more to individual preferences than differences in job requirements. Interviewers also consistently failed to cover topics that they themselves believed to be important, with the applicants reporting that the most frequently covered topics were the relatively unimportant ones of university life and extracurricular activities. One survey reported that fewer than 33 percent of companies used a structured format, that is, a predetermined set of interviewer questions, as a means for conducting the interview.[23] It is reasonable to assume that one would not find questions that were consistently asked of all applicants under these circumstances.

Applicant Characteristics An applicant's physical attractiveness, especially facial attractiveness, has consistently been related to interviewers' evaluations.[24] However, the strength of this relationship was found to be less than that between interviewers' evaluations and applicants' intelligence or skill.[25] Similarly, grooming (style of hair, clothing, makeup, and jewelry) was related to evaluations of female applicants.[26] Another study of clothing worn during an interview found that female applicants were perceived as more forceful and received more favorable selection recommendations when wearing masculine-type clothing, for example, a tailored navy suit versus a soft beige dress.[27]

The effect of the interviewer's personal liking of the applicant has consistently been found to be related to interviewers' evaluations. For example, as a result of the interaction between the two parties during the interview, the interviewer may develop stronger feelings about the applicant than is evoked in reviewing only the paper credentials of the applicant. The interviewer's perception of similarity to the applicant in attitudes, demographics, and other characteristics is also clearly related to his or her evaluation of the applicant.[28] However, it has been shown that this similar-to-me effect is much less pronounced when the interview is structured and job requirements are clear.[29]

Nonverbal Behaviors An area that has received much recent attention has been the relationship of the applicant's nonverbal characteristics with the interviewer's decisions. While there has not been unanimous agreement, most studies have concluded that nonverbal cues are, in fact, related to evaluations. A variety of cues have been studied but the ones investigated the most often are eye contact, head movement, smiling, hand movement, and general body posture (rigidity versus movement). It appears that high levels of these cues are related to favorable interview decisions.[30] These decisions have included overall judgments of appropriateness for employment, salary recommendations, and specific ratings of such characteristics as assertiveness, motivation, self-confidence, enthusiasm, and sociability. In many of these studies the interviewee has been trained to demonstrate various levels of these cues. One can conclude, therefore, that these nonverbal cues do indeed affect the interviewer's decision. Further, these studies lend support to the idea that an interviewee can manipulate the outcome of the interview through learned behaviors. Such manipulation is part of what is termed "impression management." This obviously brings into question the advisability of using such data in making evaluations of applicants. Also, the gender and ethnicity of applicants have been found to be related to interviewer evaluations of nonverbal behavior, opening the issue of adverse impact.[31]

Weighting Information Somewhat surprisingly, it has been found that relatively larger weight has been given to negative information over positive information in the interviewer's decision, even for experienced interviewers.[32] For example, in one study unfavorable ratings on only one of several characteristics resulted in the rejection of the applicant in over 90 percent of the cases.[33] Related work has found that interviewers could usually specify why a rejected applicant was not likely to be a good employee but could not clearly articulate reasons why acceptable applicants would be satisfactory, indicating a clearer use of negative data.[34] In some cases, it is not definite what the source of these negative judgments is. There is evidence that impressionistic information rather than actual facts gathered in the interview are related to these judgments. Such decision making would clearly be at odds with the stated purpose of the interview but consistent with the evidence that physical attractiveness, liking, and nonverbal cues affect the decision. We can explain this emphasis on negative information by thinking about the costs of various outcomes of the interview. The greatest cost to the interviewer is making the mistake of selecting an applicant who fails on the job. Professional reputation and company expenditures suffer. On the other hand, rejecting an applicant who would, in fact, be a successful performer if selected has no real costs. Who is to know? Therefore, cost is lowered by rejecting all marginal or doubtful candidates.

Finally, the pre-interview expectations of the interviewer about the applicant has a small, but measurable effect on the evaluations made of the applicant at the completion of the interview. For example, one study had 34 interviewers evaluate the qualifications of candidates for stockbroker positions before the interview on the basis of their applications and test scores, and then after the interview. A correlation of .63 was found between the two evaluations.[35] In a similar study, 120 recruiters in a university placement center were asked to evaluate the qualifications of college students both before and after interviews. Despite the fact that these recruiters received very little information about the students before the interview, for example, types of courses taken, major, work experience, but not GPA, the correlation between the evaluations was .54.[36]

Conclusions about the Use of the Interview

It seems to us that some of the often found deficiencies in the interview can be directly attributed to misperceptions about its use in selection. Our examination indicates that it is not appropriate to use a significant portion of the selection interview for attracting applicants, providing detailed employment information, and developing the company's image. We do not intend this to mean that these activities are unimportant. We are simply saying that spending a significant portion of a 30 to 40 minute interview, a common time for first and second round interviews, on these activities limits the effectiveness of this device in its primary purpose: that is, evaluating the characteristics of applicants. Alternate activities that are primarily designed for providing information and promoting a positive image would be more effective.

It is also clear that the validity of the interview is improved when a limited number of specific applicant characteristics are measured. In reality, this is only designing the interview in the same manner as other selection devices. It is generally held that application blanks, tests, and work samples can measure a few applicant characteristics each. Selection programs are designed taking this into account. However for some reason, the selection interview is often viewed as a general measuring device. Possibly this is because interviewers feel that they can make judgments about a diverse variety of applicant characteristics. The social-perception literature tells us that such judgments are a common part of initial personal interaction. However, it also tells us that such judgments are often made on very little data and are often inaccurate.

A third conclusion is that *there are many factors only marginally related to job activities that often influence an interviewer's evaluation, even if the interviewer is experienced.* One might argue that some of these, for example appearance, liking, and nonverbal behavior, are important personal characteristics that affect interaction with others. Since most jobs require some personal interaction, these cues are important for at least those aspects of job performance. We disagree with this conclusion. One problem with such an argument is that these characteristics can be learned by interviewees specifically for the interview and may not be representative of their behavior in other situations. Second, the lack of agreement in evaluating such applicant characteristics as appearance and liking limit the usefulness of these factors. How could an interviewer be certain as to whether or not the company members who would be working with the applicant would respond to the applicant in the same favorable or unfavorable way?

Does this all mean that the interview is worthless? Of course not—some recent studies have demonstrated the validity of this device. However, these studies have been conducted on interviews in which consideration of the findings of studies such as the ones referred to here have been taken into account. The last section of this chapter discusses recommendations for the design of the interview that reflect these points.

Discrimination and the Interview

Our viewpoint of the legal issues relative to the interview is similar to our viewpoint about its validity—the interviewer (and organization) could be in big trouble if specific features that closely tie the interview to job activities are not incorporated. Recalling material in Chapter 2, an organization would be in a vulnerable position in a question of discrimination if two conditions occurred: (1) decisions of the selection interview led, or assisted in leading, to disparate treatment or a pattern of adverse impact; and (2) the interview could not be defended in terms of job relatedness.

Court Cases

As we discussed in Chapter 2, the *Watson v. Ft. Worth Bank & Trust* case has had a major impact on the manner in which the selection interview is treated by courts and companies in discrimination cases.[37] Previous to this decision, interview cases were most often heard as disparate treatment issues because unscored interviews were considered to be subjective selection devices. Adverse impact cases usually were associated with formally scored, objective devices such as tests. As we have noted, defending a disparate treatment charge by an organization is easier than the defense of an adverse impact charge. It was, therefore, in the best interest of companies, in terms of legal defense, to keep the interview as an unscored selection instrument. Because of this, a conflict existed between the most effective use of the interview (scoring applicants) and ease of defense in a discrimination charge (not scoring applicants).

The *Watson v. Ft. Worth Bank & Trust* decision changed this by stating that a case in which the selection interview is central to the charge of discrimination could be heard as an adverse impact case if the appropriate data were presented. Because validation is the most common defense of adverse impact, and such a defense commonly requires statistical data, many companies are changing to a scored interview.

While the *Watson v. Ft. Worth Bank & Trust* case addresses an important legal procedural issue, other cases have focused on specific practices used by companies in conducting the selection interview. We discuss some of the more important of these cases in the next paragraphs. Table 12.1 contains a summary of these cases. You should also examine Richard Arvey and Robert Faley's *Fairness in Selecting Employees* 2d ed. for more detailed information about the interview.[38]

In *Stamps v. Detroit Edison Co.*, the court noted that adverse impact had occurred and the interview was a subjective process which unnecessarily contributed to this impact.[39] The interviewers had not been given specific job-related questions to follow nor had they been instructed in either the proper

· TABLE 12.1	SELECTED COURT CASES TREATING THE SELECTION INTERVIEW

Cases in Which Discrimination Found	Court Comments
Stamps v. Detroit Edison (1973)	All interviewers were white Interviewers made subjective judgments about applicant's personality No structured or written interview format No objective criteria for employment decisions
Weiner v. County of Oakland (1976)	All interviewers were male Interview questions suggested bias against females Selection decision rule not clearly specified
King v. TWA (1984)	Female applicant did not receive same questions as males History of interviewer's sexual bias
Robbins v. White-Wilson Medical Clinic (1981)	No guidelines for conducting or scoring interview Interviewer's evaluation seemed racially biased based on own comments
Gilbert v. City of Little Rock, Ark. (1986)	Content validity inappropriate defense for measurement of mental processes Failure to operationally define KSAs Dissimilarity between exam questions and actual work situations
Bailey et al. v. Southeastern Area Joint Apprenticeship (1983)	Content of questions discriminatory toward women Defense did not conform with EEOC Uniform Guidelines Unclear instructions for rating applicant performance
Jones v. Mississippi Dept. of Corrections (1985)	Little evidence of specific questions used No scoring standards No cutoff score for selection

Cases in Which Discrimination Not Found	
Harless v. Duck (1977)	Adverse impact relative to women Structured questionnaire Questions based on job analysis Relationship between interview performance and training
Maine Human Rights Commission v. Dept. of Corrections (1984)	Measurement of personality-related variables permitted KSAs listed Formal scoring system used
Minneapolis Comm. on Civil Rights v. Minnesota Chemical Dependency Assoc. (1981)	Permissible to use subjective measures of certain applicant characteristics that cannot be fully measured with objective tests Additional questions asked only of this applicant were appropriate Qualifications for job were posted A set of formal questions was asked of all applicants
Allesberry v. Commonwealth of Penn. (1981)	Nonscored questions used Written qualifications available to interviewer Posted notice of required qualifications Permissible to use subjective measures of administrative ability that cannot be fully measured with objective tests

weights to apply to specific pieces of information or the decision rules for evaluating the applicant as acceptable or unacceptable. In addition, all interviewers were white in contrast to a high percentage of blacks in the applicant pool. In *Weiner v. County of Oakland,* the issues of the preceding case were partially addressed by the organization, in that the interview was scored in a systematic fashion.[40] However, the questions asked in the interview were specifically reviewed by the court. The court ruled that questions such as whether Mrs. Weiner could work with aggressive young men, whether her husband approved of her working, and whether her family would be burdened if she altered her normal household chores were not sufficiently job-related to warrant their use in the interview.

King v. TWA dealt with disparate treatment in terms of the questions asked males and females for a job of kitchen helper.[41] A black woman was asked about her recent pregnancy, her marital status, and her relationship with another TWA employee, who had previously filed an EEOC complaint against the company. The interviewer also inquired about her future childbearing plans and arrangements for child care. The company claimed other reasons for her rejection, but the court did not agree for two reasons: (1) the questions at issue were not asked of anyone else, and (2) a previous TWA HR specialist testified that the interviewer in this case had a history of discriminating against women because he felt child-care problems created a high rate of absenteeism.

Robbins v. White-Wilson Medical Clinic was a case of racial discrimination in an unscored interview that was intended to measure a pleasant personality and the ability to work with others.[42] The court tentatively accepted the requirement of personality as legitimate but found the rejection of the plaintiff to be on racial grounds. Two crucial pieces of evidence were (1) a written comment in the margin of the application blank, "has a bad attitude—has called and asked many questions. She is a black girl. Could cause trouble"; and (2) a response given by the interviewer in cross-examination about a black woman who was employed by the clinic that "she's more white than she is black."

There have also been cases in which discrimination has been found despite the use of structured or scored interviews. In *Gilbert v. City of Little rock*, a formal oral interview was scored, weighted, and combined with scores on other promotion devices.[43] The court ruled that the interview resulted in adverse impact against black officers in promotion evaluations. The police department attempted to justify the interview by content validity showing that it measured attributes important to the position of sergeant. The court rejected this by pointing out that content validity is normally appropriate to justify specific tasks called for on the job. This interview required inferences to be made about mental processes and failed to define operationally the KSAs it purportedly measured.

A formally scored interview was also the focus of *Bailey v. Southeastern Area Joint Apprenticeship.*[44] In this case formal scored questions were asked of each applicant. These dealt with education, military service, work history, interests, and personal activities and attitudes. Interviewers summarized responses and assigned points to applicants based on these responses. The court held that sex discrimination had occurred despite these formal procedures. Questions involving prior military service, prior vocational training, shop classes, and prior work experience in boilermaking caused adverse impact. The defendant did not show the business necessity of these questions. Also interviewers were inexperienced and used ambivalent instructions in rating applicant performance.

Another related case was *Jones v. Mississippi Department of Corrections.*[45] A scored oral interview was given by members of a promotion interview panel. Questions were asked about job duties and prison rules and regulations. Each interviewee was rated on a five-point scale for the following characteristics: attendance and punctuality, self-improvement efforts, prior performance of duties, current job knowledge, knowledge of new grade responsibilities, command presence/leadership qualities, personal appearance, overall manner, and educational level. This interview was ruled to be racially discriminating because the department could not provide it to be job-related. Insufficient data were available concerning the actual questions used to measure these characteristics or standards to be used in scoring responses.

The interview has also been upheld in a number of court cases. In *Harless v. Duck*, the police department used an interview board to gather responses to approximately 30 questions asked of applicants. These questions tapped such KSAs as the applicant's communication skills, decision-making and problem-solving skills, and reactions to stress situations.[46] The court accepted the defendant's arguments that the interview was valid because the questions were based on dimensions identified through job analysis and that interview performance was related to performance in training at the police academy.

Maine Human Rights Commission v. Department of Corrections reviewed an interview designed to measure general appearance, self-expression, alertness, personality, interest in work, public relations ability, and leadership ability.[47] This interview was used for selection for the position of Juvenile Court Intake Worker. Multiple interviewers used a Department of Personnel Form that included a numerical grade for each of seven characteristics. The court regarded personality and the other variables to be acceptable in selection for this position. A major portion of the department's defense of its procedures was a job description for the position that listed necessary entry-level KSAs, such as ability to maintain composure in stressful situations, ability to exercise judgment in interpersonal situations, ability to relate to a variety of people, and the ability to listen and act appropriately in counseling relationships.

In *Minneapolis Commission on Civil Rights v. Minnesota Chemical Dependency Association*, the plaintiff, who had a history of gay rights activism, was asked additional questions that were not asked other applicants.[48] Included among these was the comment, "The one thing that bothers me [the interviewer] about it is this, that in this position, . . . it seems to be that although you have special interests or anyone that took this position would have some special interests, that this job requires someone else to carry the ball of those special interests." While acknowledging that the plaintiff was asked additional questions, the court found that the previous history of extensive involvement in outside activities was a legitimate concern and this justified the additional questions. The fact that the plaintiff indicated that, in his opinion, neutrality might unfairly suppress his interests and that he would resign if the agency's decisions were insensitive to these interests was held to support the use of the additional questions and to properly serve as a basis of rejection.

In *Allesberry v. Commonwealth of Pennsylvania*, an unscored interview was one of several complaints referred to by the black plaintiff, who was not hired when two white applicants were.[49] The court did not find discrimination, judging that the two white applicants were better qualified and citing educational degrees and previous work history in support of this position. In addressing the interview specifically, the court said that "decisions about hiring in supervisory jobs and managerial jobs cannot realistically be made using objective standards alone." Subjective measures were, therefore, acceptable. In this case the interviewer had access to a posted notice of the KSAs required for the position for the interview. Included in this notice were statements such as "ability to plan, organize, and direct specialized programs" and "ability to establish and maintain effect working relationships."

Because court cases address the circumstances in a particular organization, they do not produce a list of legally appropriate practices regarding the use of the selection interview. However, Laura Gollub and James Campion have analyzed 91 federal district court decisions and discussed a series of recommendations on which the following is based.[50] Interviews should use a job analysis and a specification of KSAs. These KSAs should be the criteria against which applicants are judged. Ensure that these KSAs are described in terms of behaviors rather than personal traits. However, it seems to be permissible in higher level jobs, for example, manager, to use personal traits as a portion of the criteria. It is important that the questions be job-related and avoid any topic that can be viewed as discriminatory. Finally, use a structured interview format, and a demographically mixed set of experienced or trained interviewers.

A Model of Interviewer Decision Making

An important recent trend in the study of the interview has been the development of cognitive models of the interview process and interviewer decision making. As we mentioned previously, early research on the interview pointed out deficiencies in the reliability and validity of this device. Therefore, subsequent research attempted to identify characteristics of the interviewer, the applicant, or the interview process that were related to low reliability and validity. While such research produced some interesting and useful results, as a whole it was disorganized. Many characteristics were unsystematically studied, often because they were easily measured rather than because they were rationally important. Results of various studies often were inconsistent.

Cognitive models of the interview provide a necessary organization for the conduct of research and the interpretation of results. Basically such models assume that the interviewer is gathering and processing information about the applicant for the purpose of assessing the applicant's fit with a job. Research in cognitive and social psychology becomes the basis for many of the propositions of such models. Two of the more completely described models are one by George Dreher and Paul Sackett and another by Robert Dipboye.[51] Both are similar in that they begin with factors before the interview interaction starts and conclude with factors which influence the interviewer's evaluation after the interview interaction has ended. We briefly describe Dipboye's model. We hope familiarity with this model will help explain the recommendations we make at the end of the chapter.

Central to Dipboye's model is the construct of *knowledge structures.* These are the interviewer's beliefs about the requirements of the job and the characteristics of applicants. Knowledge structures are the product of the previous education, training, and experience of the interviewer. Their influence on the interviewer's impressions, actions, and decision making are depicted in Exhibit 12.1. In the initial portion of the interview, the pre-interview phase, the interviewer uses these knowledge structures together with the information available to him or her about the candidate to form initial impressions. The interviewer's knowledge structures appear in the form of stereotypes, categories, and implicit personality theories. There is evidence that these initial impressions may fall into the following six categories: physical appearance, behavior, social relationships, context of behaviors, personal origins, and internal characteristics. This categorization forms a partial explanation of a finding we discussed previously—physical appearance is important in interviewers' evaluations. The representation of the applicant on these categories guides the comparison of the applicant against the interviewer's knowledge structures of the ideal or the typical applicant. This comparison is made on the basis of the initial information that is available about the applicant, even if that information is limited.

During the interview phase the interviewer categorizes and recategorizes the applicant in an attempt to answer these questions: Who is the applicant? What does the job require? Does the applicant fit the job? His or her knowledge structures and resulting impressions influence both the conduct of the interview and the interpretation of information gathered during this phase. For example, it has been found that interviewers have categories of "male" jobs and "female" jobs. Men and women with approximately the same qualifications are often evaluated differently depending on which type of job is being staffed.[52]

There is evidence that the interviewer will conduct the interview based on these pre-interview impressions of the applicant. Information is sought to confirm impressions in the six categories just described. There are differences among interviewers in terms of the importance and the number of categories used in this confirmation process. To the extent that data are encountered which are inconsistent with initial categorization, interviewers will attempt to account for these inconsistencies and will process information in a much more conscious and deliberate fashion. This is the reason for the recategorization of the applicant in these six categories. Of particular importance in this process is the interviewer's attributions of applicant behavior. That is, the interviewer makes a decision as to what extent the behaviors described by the applicant are caused by personal traits of the applicant or by the situational circumstances in which the applicant's behavior occurred. This is why, for example, behaviors leading to a high GPA for an applicant may be regarded by one interviewer as an indication of responsibility and perseverance and by another as an indication of parental and peer pressure.

EXHIBIT 12.1   **MULTIPLE PHASES OF THE SELECTION INTERVIEW**

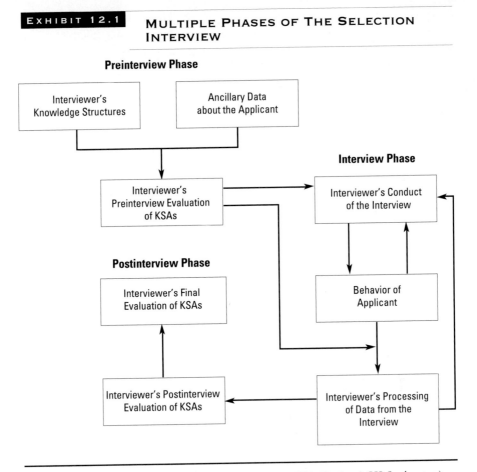

SOURCE: Robert L. Dipboye. *Selection Interviews: Process Perspectives*, 1992. (Cincinnati, OH: Southwestern).

There are several factors that make this attribution very complex. First, research shows that the first reaction of interviewers is to attribute the applicant's behavior to traits. Then, during the course of the interview, the interviewer adjusts this attribution on the basis of information gathered about factors external to the applicant. However, a large amount of information can be presented during the interview, some of which may be inconsistent. The interviewer's knowledge structures guide the interpretation of these data. Also the behavior of the interviewer toward the applicant both in terms of questions asked and nonverbal behavior affect the information that the applicant supplies. Therefore, the interviewer could be making attributions of the applicant's behavior partially based on biased information caused by the interviewer's conduct of the interview.

In the third part of the interview, the post-interview phase, the interviewer uses his or her interpretation of the information gathered from the applicant to make an evaluation of and a decision about the applicant. Knowledge structures are active in this phase also. Interviewers simply cannot remember everything and, consequently, rely on these structures to organize the information on the applicant. The most important task of the interviewer is to judge the fit between the applicant and the job. There is evidence that the amount and clarity of evidence about the job requirements and the applicant's characteristics influence this judgmental process. Interviewers are thought to rely more on knowledge structures when such information is unclear and on direct evaluation of the applicant when both job requirements and the interviewee's characteristics are clear. This explains the importance of job-related interview questions and the use of a structured format to ensure that all topics are covered for all applicants.

Even this brief description shows that the interview is a complex process which requires an interviewer to evaluate a large amount of information. Much of the research on the interview may be viewed as attempts to learn more about this evaluation. We know the interview must be carefully constructed and carried out in order to maximize its usefulness. An unplanned interview seemingly forces an interviewer to rely on the stereotypes, impressions, and implicit theories of his or her knowledge structures and reduces the importance of the information that can be gained from the interview process, thus decreasing the validity of the interview.

Attempts to Improve the Interview

As we mentioned earlier in the chapter, the deficiencies of the selection interview in terms of reliability and validity have been documented since the early part of the century. For almost as long a period of time, HR specialists have attempted to improve these deficiencies. The most frequent efforts have been in the training of interviewers and the development of appropriate questions to be asked in the interview.

Training of Interviewers

Up until the recent development of models of the total interview process, such as the one we have just discussed, the interview was thought of primarily in terms of the interaction between interviewer and interviewee. The factors and linkages that occur before the face-to-face exchange were not considered in any depth. Therefore, almost all of the attempts to train interviewers to be better at what they did focused on improving either the interpersonal skills of the interviewer or his or her ability to evaluate applicants with a minimum of interference from extraneous factors that occurred during the interview.

Much research has found that interviewers commit numerous errors in conducting the interview and evaluating applicants. Among these are the following:

1. Excessive talking by the interviewer that limits the amount of job-related information obtained from interviewees

2. Inconsistency in the questions used with applicants, which results in different types of information being gathered from each applicant

3. Asking questions that are either unrelated or only slightly related to performance on the job

4. Inability to put the interviewee at ease during the interview, making it very difficult to gather spontaneous or follow-up information

5. Overconfidence in the interviewer's ability to evaluate applicants, which results in hasty decisions

6. Stereotyping applicants and allowing personal bias to influence evaluations

7. Being influenced by the nonverbal behavior of applicants

8. Rating many applicants the same in evaluations, either superior (leniency error) or average (central tendency error) or poor (stringency error)

9. Allowing one or two either good or bad characteristics of an applicant to influence the evaluation of all other characteristics (halo effect)

10. Allowing the quality of the applicants who preceded the present applicant to influence the ratings of the present applicant (contrast effect)

11. Making an evaluation of the applicant within the first minutes of the interview (first impression error)

12. Favorably evaluating an applicant because he or she is similar to the interviewer in some way (similar-to-me error)

The Structured Interview A great many training programs have been developed to overcome these and similar deficiencies. Obviously it would be impossible to summarize the characteristics of all of these programs. There have, however, been recurrent themes, which we discuss. One major theme is the development of structured interviews. Interviews are commonly grouped into two categories: structured and unstructured. The terms refer to the use by the interviewer of predetermined questions. As you can guess, structured interviews make use of such questions and unstructured do not. In reality, there is variation among structured interviews in the percentage of use of non-predetermined questions. For our purposes, however, we follow the common practice of distinguishing between two general types and labeling all interviews with any preplanned questions as structured.

There are many arguments for using a structured rather than an unstructured interview. In an unstructured interview the interviewer can ask any question that he or she wishes. The logic of the questions is up to the interviewer. From our previous discussion about Dipboye's model of the interview, we can immediately point out the potential problems of such a strategy. In essence the extraneous factors that affect an interviewer's decisions are given free rein. Research has supported this notion—many of the problems of the selection interview have been identified in unstructured situations. Unfortunately, this type of interview is still commonly used.

The structured interview is based on key topics that should be job-related. For example, persistence in completing unstructured tasks may be important for the job under consideration. The structured interview provides questions to gather information about such persistence, such as "Have you every worked on a project in which it was not clear what exactly should be done or how the project should be completed?" These questions are asked of all applicants. Probing questions, which are not predetermined, are asked by the interviewer until enough information is obtained about the topic. These probe questions, of course, depend on the nature of the conversation between the interviewer and the applicant.

The main advantage of a structured interview is that information about the same topics is collected from all applicants. This makes the comparison of applicants easier. In an unstructured interview usually this does not happen and comparison among applicants is subject to impressions and guesses. Additionally, information about all major job topics is more assured. Several studies have indicated that the validity of structured interviews is comparable to that of other recommended selection instruments. As we mentioned earlier, recent meta-analyses have estimated the validity of structured interviews at .47, .49, and .62 for different groups of studies.[53]

A technological twist to this has been the development of computer-aided questions about an applicant's work experience, education, skills, and attitudes relative to a specific job. Frequently up to 100 questions are asked. The questions are presented one at a time on a computer monitor, usually in a multiple-choice format, and the applicant responds by pressing the appropriate key. An applicant is not allowed to scroll either backward or forward through the questions; rather each must be answered as it appears on the screen. When the applicant has completed the interview, a printout is provided to the interviewer who may use the results as a part of the personal interview. This printout contains each question and the applicant's response. Depending on the scoring program developed, responses can be compared against a key to indicate superior/deficient areas or contradictions in responses to similar questions. Another use of technology is to videotape interviews to allow for repeated viewing and comparison among applicants by interviewers.[54]

The Interview Process   A second theme in interview training programs addresses how to conduct successfully the interviewer-interviewee interaction process itself. The central issues are usually the following:

1.   Creating an open-communication atmosphere

2.   Delivering questions consistently

3.   Maintaining control of the interview

4.   Developing good speech behavior

5.   Learning listening skills

6. Taking appropriate notes

7. Keeping the conversation flowing and avoiding leading or intimidating the interviewee

8. Interpreting, ignoring, or controlling the nonverbal cues of the interview

One purpose of this work is to create an interview situation in which the interviewee feels relaxed and comfortable. Logically this should make it easier for the interviewee to think of difficult to remember information and provide complete answers about the topics asked. Another purpose is to minimize what may be called administrative errors that can occur in the interview. These are such events as misunderstanding what was said, not correctly remembering information provided, tipping off the applicant as to the "best" answers to a questions, and using time foolishly so as not to cover all topics. The general effect of such training is to increase the amount of information obtained in the interview and to ensure its accuracy.

Decision-Making Methods A third theme has been instruction in decision-making methods. One frequently used technique is to explain and demonstrate the most common rating errors: contrast effects, halo, leniency, and central tendency. Practice is then given in recognizing how these errors may influence the interviewer's own decision making. Other techniques have attempted to model the way information is weighted by the interviewer in reaching final overall judgments about applicants. Frequently, models are also built that weigh the same information more appropriately, and the interviewer is trained to imitate this model and, thereby, increase the validity of his or her evaluations.[55] Such programs frequently focus on interviewee appearance and mannerisms, and interviewer stereotypes and biases as causes of inappropriate weighting. The major point of training in decision making is that learning the nature of such errors will result in minimizing the distortion caused by these errors in actual interviews.

Systematic Scoring A fourth theme advocates systematic scoring of the interview. It is almost universally recognized that the intuitive evaluation of an applicant by an interviewer, still very common in interviewing, is to be avoided if carefully determined evaluations are desirable. Formal evaluation forms usually contain a number of defined applicant characteristics, all preferably related to job performance, a separate rating scale for each characteristic, and a rating of the overall acceptability of the applicant.

Results of Training How much improvement have these changes made in the use of the interview? The results have generally been encouraging but have not meant that all problems have been corrected. For the most part, the various training programs have reduced some of the more common rater errors: contrast, halo, leniency, and stringency. There is also evidence that training programs such as the five-day University of Houston Interviewing Institute can produce significant changes in the actual interviewing behaviors of participants.[56] This institute uses presentations, demonstrations, exercises, and videotaped practice to improve the skills of professional interviewers. After training, participants have demonstrated significant improvements in questioning techniques, interview structure, interviewing supportiveness, techniques of rapport, active listening skills, and attention to relevant materials. However, other studies have demonstrated few, if any, effects of training on interviewer behavior when shorter training programs are examined.[57] This is of importance because one report indicates the median length of interview training to be six hours.[58] Finally, structuring of the interview questions and systematic scoring has generally improved the reliability of evaluations among sets of interviewers.

Developing Appropriate Interview Questions

It can logically be argued that one way to improve the reliability and validity of the interview is to ensure that the questions used are specific and job-related. That is, if more information is obtained from the applicant about job knowledge or the performance of job activities, the interviewer's estimate of the capability of the applicant to do the job should be better. This having been said, until recently there has been little explicit direction about how to develop specific job-related questions. Interviewers, therefore, had been forced to devise their own questions or to rely heavily on questions which gather information about general characteristics of applicants that are thought to be important for job success, for example, initiative, judgment, persistence, and attitude.

In recent years, however, three similar methods for developing specific questions have been described. In the next sections, we discuss each of these.

The Situational Interview   This method was developed by Gary Latham, Lise Saari, Elliot Pursell, and Michael Campion.[59] Its basic intent is first to identify specific activities representative of the job and then to use this information to form questions that ask applicants how they would behave in the situation.

The first step is to do a job analysis of the position using the *critical-incidents technique*. Critical incidents are descriptions of work behaviors that have actually occurred and are examples of particularly good or particularly poor job performance. A well-written incident is a description, not an evaluation, of the action which includes the circumstances that lead up to the incident, what actually happened, and the result. These incidents are gathered from both job incumbents and supervisors. They can be gathered either through personal interviews or questionnaires. Both methods require that the term *critical incident* be defined and examples provided to focus the thinking of the respondents.

Typically, several hundred incidents are obtained for a single job, especially if more than 15 to 20 respondents are used, or if the respondents are not directed to limit the information provided. These incidents are then sorted into groups of similar behaviors, referred to as *behavioral dimensions*, by a small group of judges. Only those behaviors that are reliably sorted are retained. These behavioral dimensions are then named according to the content of the similar behaviors, for example, technical skills, diagnosing defects, customer service, and so on.

The next step is to review the incidents for each behavioral dimension, select a small number of the most appropriate incidents, and use these to write interview questions. There appears to be no one best way of selecting the small number of appropriate incidents. Frequently, the judgments of supervisors who are also experienced in interviewing for the job are used. The exact number of incidents that are chosen depends on the planned time of the interview and the number of dimensions to be addressed. At least two incidents per dimension is common.

These incidents are than rephrased in terms of an interview question appropriate for applicants for the job. Table 12.2 contains examples of such questions. This rephrasing is fairly straightforward as it usually requires a brief description of the circumstances of the incident and the question "What would you do?" Here's an example: "You are to start your shift as convenience store manager at 5 A.M. When you attempt to start your car at 4:45, you realize that your husband left the gas tank nearly empty. What would you do?"

Scoring of applicants' responses to these questions is simplified by the development of scales for each question. Usually, these are five-point scales on which examples of low, average, and high responses are written. Table 12.2 also contains examples of such a scale for each question. The development of the examples for each scale also uses the judgment of supervisors of the job of interest. Either the supervisors are asked to write actual behaviors that they have observed, or they are asked to write responses that they have heard in an interview. Again, only those examples for which there is agreement that they are low, average, and high behaviors are used in the scale. This scale is not revealed to the applicant, but is used only by the interviewer. In scoring the interview, the interviewer places a check on the scale using the example responses as a frame of reference. If the example responses have been carefully prepared, it is common for the applicants' responses to be very similar to the examples. A total score for the interview can be obtained by summing the ratings for each scale, or a series of separate scores can be generated by treating each scale score independently.

Various single studies have reported validity coefficients ranging from .30 to .46. Interrater reliability estimates were between .76 and .87.[60]

Behavior Description Interviewing   This method, first described by Tom Janz, is very similar to the situational interview and uses many of the same steps.[61] It starts with the generation of critical incidents and the identification of behavioral dimensions in the same manner as we described for the situational interview. However, unlike the situational interview, it calls for a review of these behavioral dimensions and the identification of each dimension as essentially describing either maximum or typical performance of the individual. The difference between these two types is described as follows:

> If how much the applicant *knows* or *can do* is critical to job performance, the dimension tends toward maximum performance. If what the applicant *typically will do* relates more closely to job performance, the dimension tends toward typical performance.[62]

TABLE 12.2	EXAMPLES OF SITUATIONAL INTERVIEW QUESTIONS AND SCORING SCALES

1. Your spouse and two teenage children are sick in bed with colds. There are no relatives or friends available to look in on them. Your shift starts in 3 hours. What would you do in this situation?

   1 (low)   I'd stay home—my family comes first.
   3 (average)   I'd phone my supervisor and explain my situation.
   5 (high)   Since they only have colds, I'd come to work.[a]

2. A customer comes into the store to pick up a watch he had left for repair. The repair was supposed to have been completed a week ago, but the watch is not back yet from the repair shop. The customer is very angry. How would you handle the situation?

   1 (low)   Tell the customer the watch is not back yet and ask him to check back with you later.
   3 (average)   Apologize, tell the customer that you will check into the problem, and call him or her back later.
   5 (high)   Put the customer at ease and call the repair shop while the customer waits.[b]

3. For the past week you have been consistently getting the jobs that are the most time consuming (e.g., poor handwriting, complex statistical work). You know it's nobody's fault because you have been taking the jobs in priority order. You have just picked your fourth job of the day and it's another "loser." What would you do?

   1 (low)   Thumb through the pile and take another job.
   3 (average)   Complain to the coordinator, but do the job.
   5 (high)   Take the job without complaining and do it.[c]

---

[a] SOURCE: Gary P. Latham, Lise M. Saari, Elliot D. Pursell, and Michael A. Campion, "The Situational Interview," *Journal of Applied Psychology* 4 (1980): 422–427.

[b] SOURCE: Jeff A. Weekley and Joseph A. Gier, "Reliability and Validity of the Situational Interview for a Sales Position," *Journal of Applied Psychology* 3 (1987): 484–487.

[c] SOURCE: Gary P. Latham and Lise M. Saari, "Do People Do What They Say? Further Studies on the Situational Interview," *Journal of Applied Psychology* 4 (1984): 569–573.

Maximum performance dimensions usually deal with technical skills and knowledge. Typical performance dimensions deal with getting along with others, working hard versus wasting time, and being organized, courteous, or punctual. The importance of this distinction is that, for the *behavior description interview*, it is recommended that maximum performance dimensions be omitted from the interview and almost complete emphasis placed on typical performance dimensions.

The development of questions is essentially the same as discussed previously. However, two aspects are different from the situational interview. First, each question is formed with appropriate probes (follow-up questions). The main question serves to locate a particular instance from the applicant's past and focus the applicant on that type of event. Probes seek out exactly how the applicant behaved and what the consequences of that behavior were. Second, a distinction is made between questions appropriate for applicants with work experience related to the job of interest and applicants without such experience. The latter type of question should focus on the same behavior as the former, except the situation is more general and need not be part of a job at all. For example, a question asked of an experienced salesperson might be "Tell me about the most difficult new client contact you made in the last six months." An equivalent question for an applicant with no sales experience might be "We have all tried to convince someone we did not know well of the merits of a product or idea we were promoting. I would like you to tell me of a time when this was especially tough for you." Table 12.3 contains examples of the basic and accompanying probe questions using behavior description interviewing.

Scoring is done for each of the behavioral dimensions separately. It is recommended that after the interview is completed, the interviewer reviews his or her notes or the tape recording if one has been used. Based on the judged quality of their responses, applicants are placed in one of five rank-order groups for each dimension (see Table 12.3). Each group on the scale represents 20 percent of all applicants; that is, a score of "1" indicates that the applicant ranks in the bottom 20 percent and a score of "5" means that he or she ranks in the top 20 percent of all applicants. Each dimension is also assigned a weight, derived from judgments made by the interviewers, which reflects its importance to overall job performance. It is advised that dimensions not be differentially weighted unless some dimensions are at least two to three times more important than other dimensions. If this is not the case, equal unit weights are recommended. The dimension score described previously is multiplied by this dimension weight to obtain the total score for the dimension. Total score for the interview is obtained by summing all the dimension total scores.

Empirical tests of this type of interview have involved relatively small samples. Validity coefficients of .54 and .48 have been reported for two recent studies.[63]

Job Content Method   The third technique for developing interview questions is the *job content method* recently described by the authors.[64] For that reason, you should not be surprised to find that it reflects some of the ideas we have already discussed. One main difference between this technique and the previous two is that it does not use critical incidents as the major job analysis method. Instead the steps discussed in previous chapters, especially Chapters 8 and 9, are used. That is, the following are accomplished:

1.   Identifying and rating critical job tasks.

2.   Identifying and rating KSAs necessary for task performance.

3.   Linking KSAs to job tasks.

4.   Choosing selection measures appropriate for the KSAs to be measured.

TABLE 12.3	EXAMPLES OF BEHAVIORAL DESCRIPTION INTERVIEWING QUESTIONS AND SCORING

1. It is often necessary to work together in a group to accomplish a task. Can you tell me about the most recent experience you had working as part of a group?
(The following are probe questions.)
   1. What was the task?
   2. How many people were in the group?
   3. What difficulties arose as a result of working as a group?
   4. What role did you play in resolving these difficulties?
   5. How successful was the group in completing its task?
   6. How often do you work as part of a group?

2. Tell me about a time when you aided an employee in understanding a difficult policy.
(The following are probe questions).)
   1. What was the policy?
   2. How did you know that the employee was having trouble understanding?
   3. What did you do or say that helped?
   4. How did you know that you had been successful?
   5. What steps did you take to change the policy?

Applicant Assessment Form for Scoring Behavioral Description Interview

Dimension	1 Bottom 20%	2 Next 20%	3 Middle 20%	4 Next 20%	5 Top 20%
1. Working with group					X
2.					
•					
•					
•					
10.			X		

Dimension	Dimension Score		Weight (optional)		Cumulative Total
1	5	×	25	=	125
•	•		•		
•	•		•		
•	•		•		
10	3	×	10	=	325

SOURCE: Based on Tom Janz, Lowell Hellervik, and David C. Gilmore, *Behavior Description Interviewing* (Boston: Allyn & Bacon, 1986).

The completion of these four steps results in the listing of those KSAs that should be measured by an interview and those that should be measured by other instruments. As suggested by the discussion in the first part of this chapter, that means that the interview primarily would be used for what we have defined as *personal relations, good citizenship,* and *job knowledge*. After the scope of the interview has been narrowed to specific KSAs, the critical-incidents technique is used to gather information to form questions only for these KSAs. In other words, supervisors and job incumbents are asked to write incidents for only those few (usually three to five) dimensions appropriate for the interview. It is recommended that questions measuring KSAs that reflect good citizenship and personal relations be phrased so that the answers do not require specific experience in a job very similar to the one of interest. For example, instead of "Tell me about working with a small group that is developing a compensation system for skilled crafts," the statement could be "Tell me about a time you worked with a small group on any project that required frequent interaction over a period of time." Follow-up questions should be used when appropriate. These should stress the personal decisions and actions of the interviewee in the situation. Multiple questions for each KSA to be measured in the interview are recommended.

Scoring is a two-step process. As in the situational interview, the interviewer first rates the interviewee on scales with scale points representing job behaviors. These scales are developed through discussion with job supervisors. The ratings for each question, then, are used by the interviewer to make a final rating on a five-point scale on each KSA to be measured in the interview. These final ratings are based on the responses of the applicant to the multiple questions for that KSA. Table 12.4 contains examples of questions and scoring scales.

Recommendations for Interview Use: An Example

We have discussed a lot of information about the selection interview. Let's put this information to use by discussing specific recommendations for how to build a better interview. These recommendations are summarized in Table 12.5.

Restrict the Scope of the Interview

We believe one of the major weaknesses in the use of the interview is that it is often used to accomplish too many purposes. As we discussed, frequently the interview is used simultaneously as a public relations vehicle to project an image of the organization, as a recruitment vehicle to convey job description and organization information to potential applicants, and as a selection vehicle to evaluate the job-related KSAs of the applicants. The interview is essentially a verbal process. It is used in a variety of other HR functions as well: performance appraisal, training, disciplinary hearings, and so on. However, no one recommends that it be used simultaneously for all of these functions. Of course, all of these HR functions do not usually occur at the same time for an employer, whereas recruitment, selection, and projecting a good public image do. However, we ought not to confuse time similarity with function similarity. Just because these three functions are compressed into a short period at the beginning of the HR management cycle does not mean they should be addressed at the same time. The purposes of and the data for public relations, recruitment, and selection are simply not the same.

We think that recruitment and selection should by systematically reviewed. If it is decided that the interview, as a process, should be used in either one of these functions, then each separate interview process ought to be planned according to the models for effective use that have been developed for that

TABLE 12.4	EXAMPLES OF JOB CONTENT METHOD QUESTIONS AND SCORING

KSA #1: Verbal ability to discuss compensation system with nonpersonnel managers of the company.

1. Describe a time when you explained technical features of a project or an object to someone who had a limited background in the area which you described.

    1 (low)   does not describe such an experience

    3 (average) provides a general description but few details

    5 (high)   describes situation in detail including questions asked and appropriate information provided

2. Assume that I am an inventory supervisor. I tell you that I think I am not paid as well as some individuals who have the same job in other companies. What do you say to me?

    1 (low)   asks supervisor to come back with names of specific companies and approximate pay levels

    3 (average) generally discusses how wage surveys are conducted every other year

    5 (high)   provides information about job evaluation method, most similar key job, and results of wage survey

KSA Overall Rating

1	2	3	4	5
(low)				(high)

Comments about responses to questions:

_____

_____

_____

function. In this way, the selection interview becomes focused, and is not a multiple-purpose hybrid activity. This should substantially increase its usefulness.

There is a second way in which the interview suffers from a multiple-purpose use. Earlier in this chapter we noted that it is the conclusion of several writers that often too many KSAs are evaluated in the interview. It has been recommended that the scope of the interview be limited to a much narrower band of applicant characteristics: *job knowledge, sociability* and *related interpersonal abilities,* and *corporate citizenship* (work habits, dependability, compliance, cooperation, adaptability, etc).

Let us use the information presented in Table 12.6 to demonstrate the appropriate use of the interview in a selection program. Through the procedures previously described in Chapter 9, we have completed a job analysis of the job of maintenance supervisor. The KSAs listed in Table 12.6 have been derived from this job analysis. The remainder of the table presents the appropriate use of various selection instruments for the measurement of the KSAs by presenting the

TABLE 12.5	RECOMMENDATIONS FOR INTERVIEW USE

1. Restrict the use of the interview to the most job-relevant KSAs.
2. Limit the use of pre-interview data about applicants.
3. Adopt a structured format by predetermining major questions to be asked.
4. Use job-related questions.
5. Use multiple questions for each KSA.
6. Apply a formal scoring that allows for the evaluation of each KSA separately.
7. Train interviewers in the process of the selection interview.

TABLE 12.6	SELECTION PLAN FOR THE JOB OF MAINTENANCE SUPERVISOR

		Selection Instruments			
Job: Maintenance Foreman	KSA Importance	Application Form	Interview	Performance Test	Ability Test
KSA					
Knowledge of construction principles of small buildings	15%	3%			12%
Knowledge of building systems: heating, electrical, plumbing	15	3			12
Knowledge of inventory control methods	10	3			7
Skill in performing basic carpentry, plumbing, electrical wiring operations	5			5%	
Ability to diagnose defects in building and building systems	10			10	
Verbal ability to give work instructions to laborers regarding construction and repair	20		20%		
Ability to schedule work crews for specific tasks	10		10		
Ability to direct multiple work crews and work projects simultaneously	15		15		
	100%	9%	45%	15%	31%

percentage of the selection program that should be devoted to each of the selection instruments.

Our judgment is that only three of these KSAs are appropriate for assessment in the interview, and that the interview should comprise 45 percent of the selection program to measure these adequately. "Verbal ability to give work instructions to laborers regarding construction and repair" is best demonstrated through a verbal exchange process like the interview. Measurement of the "ability to schedule work crews for specific tasks" would frequently entail the exchange of information about specific characteristics of tasks and also an explanation of the reasoning used in making specific assignments. Such an exchange is more appropriate for an interview than for a written test. The "ability to direct multiple work crews and work projects simultaneously" is, perhaps, the most difficult of the KSAs to measure accurately. Ideally, we would use a simulation that creates several situations and evaluates the applicant's responses. However, to be accurate, the simulation should be carried out for an extended period of time. This would not usually be feasible. Our approach, therefore, would be to view this ability as a work habit, a facet of corporate citizenship, and use the interview to determine information about the applicant's behavior in similar, previous situations.

We thus conclude that of the eight KSAs to be measured in this selection program, only these three should be assessed by the interview. As Table 12.6 indicates, three other KSAs are tapped by a combination of the application form and ability tests. The remaining two KSAs are best measured by performance tests.

Limit the Use of Pre-Interview Data

Perhaps the most common sequence of steps in selection programs is that the applicant completes an application form or provides a résumé and then participates in the employment interview. In most cases the interviewer has access to this information and uses it, at least initially, to formulate questions and direct conversation during the interview.

There is a question as to whether or not this pre-interview information is of real benefit to the interviewer. Many argue that pre-interview information is essential to good interviewing. It provides basic information about previous work and educational experience that can be developed in the interview. Some interview guides even recommend that interviewers develop hypotheses about the type of KSAs possessed by a specific applicant based on application information and then use the interview to test these hypotheses.

Recent work, however, that has closely studied this issue has not supported these proposed advantages of using pre-interview data and has found some detrimental effects. We have already presented the model developed by Dipboye which emphasizes that pre-interview information is used to develop assessments of applicants before the interview is conducted. These assessments affect the interview process itself and can serve as sources of error in the evaluation of applicants. For example, in one study, Robert Dipboye, Gail Fontelle, and Kathleen Garner carefully compared the interviewing methods and decision-making results of one group of interviewers who had application material prior to the interview with those of another group of interviewers who did not have such information.[65] They found that interviewers with this information asked more questions and gathered more nonapplication form information than did the interviewers who did not have the pre-interview data. However, this had no advantage in terms of the quality of the interviewers' decisions. In fact, the interviewers using application information demonstrated less accuracy in estimating personal characteristics of applicants and also less reliability in the ratings of both applicant performance in the interview and goodness to fit to the job than did interviewers who did not use pre-interview data. Another study found a positive relationship between interviewers' pre-interview impressions of applicants and the amount of time spent in the interview.[66] Obviously, this result places a premium on the accuracy of the impressions and lessens the informational value of the interview.

Our recommendation about the use of pre-interview data is, therefore, based on a combination of research and common sense. An important point would seem to be the completeness of the pre-interview data that is available to the interviewer. If it is a personnel file, as may be the case in selection among applicants already in the organization, such data may provide relatively extensive and useful information about the applicant's ability to perform certain tasks. This could definitely be helpful to the interviewer for developing probing questions. The problem may come when very sketchy information is obtained, for example only job titles or education degrees or brief verbal statements. As we know, there is a common inclination for the interviewer to weave this information together to form an impression of the applicant. Impressions formed on such little data could easily be inaccurate.

Assuming that the interview focuses on a small number of KSAs, our recommendation is to limit the pre-interview information that is provided interviewers to two types. The first type is *relatively complete data about any of the KSAs to be covered in the interview*. This could save time or allow for more detailed questioning. The second type would be the *incomplete or contradictory statements presented on the application blank or other similar instruments:* such items as employment gaps, overlapping full-time positions, a nonregular career movement pattern, and so on. This kind of irregularity could be clarified in the interview.

There is enough evidence to indicate that access to data not directly relevant to the purposes of the interview only contributes to deficiencies in interviewers' decisions. Therefore, these other data, for example, ability test scores, letters of reference, and brief reactions of others, should be withheld until after the interview is completed.

Adopt a Structured Format

One of the most consistent recommendations made by those who have written about ways to improve the use of the interview in selection has been to impose structure on the verbal exchange between the parties. This is done by providing the interviewer with a set of questions that must be asked of all interviewees.

In this format *a set of questions should be formulated for each KSA* identified as appropriate for the interview. Referring to the previous example of the maintenance supervisor job, this would mean a set of questions concerning each of the three KSAs: "verbal ability to give instructions," "ability to schedule work crews," and "ability to direct multiple work crews simultaneously." These questions must be asked of each applicant. However, the interviewers are also permitted to go beyond these questions as they feel necessary, either to clarify a given response, to seek other important details, or to pursue a closely related area.

The logic behind imposing this structure is to build consistency in the interview regarding essential information. This means ensuring that the interviewer consistently gathers information about each of the appropriate KSAs from each applicant. Structuring the interview helps to develop this consistency either across a set of interviewers or with one interviewer who is examining a set of applicants and must choose among them. The major benefit of this consistency in questioning is that it makes comparisons among applicants much easier. If done properly the HR specialist would have information from each applicant on the same KSAs. This would facilitate the identification of those applicants most suitable for the job.

Use Job-Related Questions

Having an appropriate structured format for the interview is only of limited value if the predetermined set of questions provides information that is only marginally related to job performance. Therefore, another concern in the interview is to ensure that the questions used are job-related, that is, information gathered is useful in measuring the appropriate KSAs identified for each job.

We have already discussed three techniques that have been used to develop job-related questions: the *situational interview, behavior description interviewing,* and the *job content method.* In these next paragraphs, we discuss questions that are useful for each of the three types of KSAs we think are appropriately measured in an interview. The three techniques described previously can be used for the development of specific questions for each type of KSA.

Questions of Job Knowledge   This is the most straightforward KSA to measure and for which to develop interview questions. Basically, the interviewer is trying to find out whether or not the applicant knows some specific information. Appropriate questions could be the following:

Could you tell me the steps in performing an empirical validation study?

How do you string a 220v electric cable in a laboratory building that is under construction?

What are the current tax laws regarding setting up a Clifford Trust?

There are a number of important points to remember in using this type of question, however. The first is that the knowledge should be important to the overall performance of the job. It should not be information that is difficult but only peripheral to the job. Asking an applicant for a production supervisor's job about the principles of Just-In-Time management is appropriate. Asking about the programming features of *Lotus 1-2-3* software, which might be used in scheduling, usually would not be appropriate. The second is that the question should not ask about material easily learned on the job or material taught as part of a training program for the job. Third, as was mentioned previously, it is not useful to ask questions about a series of specific facts or operations. A written test would be more appropriate.

Commonly, interviewers phrase would-be job knowledge questions in something like the following way:

Have you ever directed a construction crew?

If so, for how long and what kind of jobs did you do?

Did you take any courses in accounting?

What kind of courses did you enjoy in college?

Questions of this type are not very useful for measuring job knowledge because they require the interviewer to make many inferences in order to evaluate the answer. For example, if the applicant responds that he or she had two accounting courses, the interviewer normally would ask what the courses were, what grades were received, and so on. Even at this point, however, there is no direct evidence that the applicant knows specific information necessary for the job. All accounting courses with the same name do not cover the same material. All grades of "B" do not mean the same mastery of material. The interviewer has to infer the knowledge of the applicant from this circumstantial data. A better method is to ask questions directly about material that is important for the job and then to judge whether the answer given is correct or not. Little inference is necessary; the applicant indicates directly whether he or she has the knowledge or not.

In practice, this type of interview question requires the selection specialist to work with technical specialists in various parts of the organization. This is because the selection specialist usually does not have enough technical knowledge of accounting, engineering, maintenance, and so on, to properly evaluate answers to this type of question. Therefore, it is necessary to train persons working in the functional area in how to develop and score interview questions.

Questions of Social Interaction   The measurement of KSAs related to sociability and initial interpersonal interaction seem to be especially dependent on how they are stated. For example, an office receptionist position usually requires short-term, nonrecurring interaction with individuals. The worker KSAs necessary for such behavior would be appropriate for evaluation through an interview. However, if these KSAs are specified in terms of general personality characteristics such as "poise," "friendliness," "pleasantness," or "professional bearing," assessment becomes more difficult because of the ambiguity of these terms.

A better tactic would be to try to phrase the relevant worker attributes in terms of abilities and skills. For example, the receptionist's position may require "the ability to provide preliminary information to angry customers about the resolution of product defects" or "the ability to query customers regarding the exact nature of complaints in order to route them to appropriate personnel." Phrased in this manner, it is easier to develop questions that require the demonstration of these skills and abilities. *Situational interview* questions would be appropriate.

Questions of Corporate Citizenship   The group of KSAs identified as corporate citizenship is, perhaps, the most difficult to assess accurately in applicants. It might include work habits such as persistence in completing assignments, ability to work on multiple tasks simultaneously, and ability to plan future actions. Frequently these are referred to under the very general term of *motivation*. Another set of attributes included in this category are "helping coworkers with job-related problems, accepting orders without a fuss, tolerating temporary impositions without a complaint, and making timely and constructive statements about the work unit."[67]

One method frequently used in the attempt to measure these attributes is to ask the applicant in various ways whether he or she has worked or is willing to work in circumstances requiring these habits. The limitation with this type of question is that the information is virtually unverifiable and subject to distortion by the respondent who wishes to portray generally favorable characteristics. Most job applicants, especially experienced ones, know that almost all organizations desire employees who cooperate with other workers, can plan ahead, accept orders, and tolerate impositions. It is in the self-interest of the applicant to portray him or herself as having demonstrated, or being willing to demonstrate, these characteristics.

A strategy that is increasingly being used to at least partially avoid this situation is to question the applicant in detail about participation in activities that are similar to those of the job under consideration. David Grove has described such an interview used by the Procter & Gamble Company for entry-level selection.[68] This interview is aimed at forming judgments of the applicant in terms of five factors that are important for effectiveness in beginning production work in P&G plants: stamina and agility, willingness to work hard, working well with others, learning the work, and initiative. The applicant is asked to write answers to "experience items" on a special form. These experience items ask the applicant to describe several relevant experiences which may have occurred in either a work or nonwork setting for each of the five factors. For example, one experience item for assessing the factor "working well with others" may be "Describe a situation in which you had to work closely with a small group of others to complete a project." Responses to these experience items are then probed in each of two separate interviews. The interviews are conducted separately by a member of the plant employment group and a line manager, and each independently rates the applicant on a seven-point scale for each of the five factors.

We have developed a list of questions that could be used in a selection interview for the job of maintenance supervisor that we mentioned previously. These questions, presented in Table 12.7, are intended to gather information about the three KSAs that were identified in Table 12.6 as appropriate to be measured with the interview. The number of questions used for each KSA was determined from the importance assigned to each KSA in Table 12.6.

Use Multiple Questions for Each KSA

A basic psychological measurement principle that we discussed in Chapter 4 was that an *assessment device should contain several items or parts that gather answers about the same variable in order for the assessment device to be a useful instrument.* The reason is, to a certain extent, that both reliability and validity of measurement are generally related to the number of items on the measuring device. In selection this means that, all else being equal, the more items an assessment device possesses that measure the same KSA, the greater is its reliability and validity.

As we have already seen, the principle of multiple items is used in both biodata and training-and-experience evaluation forms. In later chapters, we show how special ability tests (e.g., mathematical knowledge, verbal reasoning, etc.), performance tests (e.g., typing, carpentry, welding, etc.), and situations (e.g., assessment centers) all are developed with multiple measures of each KSA.

The interview should be developed and used in the same manner. As we have already mentioned, interviews, in attempting to measure corporate citizenship attributes of applicants, often request the interviewee to describe several examples of specified work situations. The same principle should be incorporated into the measurement of each KSA that is specified as being appropriate for the interview.

Returning once more to our example of the maintenance supervisor in Table 12.7, the use of this principle of multiple questions would mean that applicants would be asked to respond to four questions to provide examples if instructions given to work crews, to two questions to measure ability to schedule work crews for specific tasks, and three questions to measure the ability to direct multiple work crews and work projects simultaneously. There is no rule for the exact number of questions to be asked. This is primarily a function of two factors: (1) the information developed from the job analysis and (2) the time available for each applicant. Concerning the information developed from the job analysis, it is necessary to consider first the relative importance of the KSAs to be measured in the interview. In our previous example in Table 12.6, "verbal ability to give work instructions" had the highest weight [20], followed by "ability to coordinate and direct multiple work crews" [15], and "ability to schedule work crews" [10]. The number of questions listed in Table 12.7 for each of these KSAs generally reflects these weights. The second consideration is the diversity of the tasks that relate to each KSA to be assessed in the interview. If the maintenance supervisor must give instructions about many different types of tasks, then it may

TABLE 12.7	SELECTION INTERVIEW QUESTIONS FOR THE JOB OF MAINTENANCE SUPERVISOR

KSA #1: Verbal ability to give work instructions to laborers regarding construction and repair.

1. What instructions would you give a work crew that was about to string a 220 volt electric cable in a laboratory building under construction?
2. Two laborers, with limited experience, ask about the procedures for tuck-pointing and restoring a damaged brick wall. What instructions would you give them regarding what equipment they should use and how they should operate it?
3. You assign a group of four to inspect the flat tar-and-gravel roofs on four buildings. They are also to make minor repairs and describe major repairs to you for future action. What instructions do you give them? (You can assume that each one knows how to operate any necessary equipment.)
4. You will use eight summer employees to do the repainting of the third floor hall, ten private offices, and two public restrooms. What instructions do you give them about both general work and specific painting procedures?

KSA #2: Ability to schedule work crews for specific tasks.

1. You need to send a work crew to the far part of the industrial park to inspect and (if necessary) repair a 40' × 10' brick wall and to prepare a 40' × 60' flower bed. It is Monday morning. Rain is expected Tuesday afternoon. How many people do you assign to which tasks? How long should each task take?
2. You are in charge of a work crew of 12. Included in this are four experienced carpenters and two electricians. These six are also permitted to do other jobs. You are to finish a 100' × 200' area that will have five separate offices and a general meeting room. Tell me the first five tasks that you would assign your crew and how many people you would put on each task. How long should each task take?

KSA #3: Ability to direct multiple work crews and work projects simultaneously.

1. Go back to the situation in the previous question. Tell me which tasks you would try to complete in the first two days. Which sequence of tasks would you schedule? How would your work crews know when to start a new task?
2. Describe a specific experience in the past few years in which you had at least five people reporting to you who were performing different parts of a bigger project. This could either be in work, school, community activities, or the military.
3. Describe a specific experience in the past few years in which you and a group of others were working under a tight deadline on a project that had several parts. This could either be in work, school, community activities, or the military.

take more questions to have a representative sample than if these are very similar tasks.

The total amount of time available for the interview is, in some cases, beyond the control of the interviewer, for example in on-campus interviews or in many job fair situations. In these cases an estimate should be made before the interview of the number of questions possible based on the total time allocated for the interview and the estimated length of time required to answer each question.

Apply a Formal Scoring Format

The study of the interview has consistently concluded that an interview format which provides a formal defined scoring system is superior in many ways to a format that does not. This is in terms of legal defensibility, reliability and validity of judgment by the interviewer, and acceptance by the interviewee. Based on a variety of material, it is easy to understand such findings. We have made the point that measurement is the essence of a selection program. Without measurement of the KSAs of applicants, any comparison of these applicants becomes too complex to be done accurately. It is simply not possible for a selection specialist to retain all relevant information, weigh it appropriately, and use it to compare a number of individuals—at least in a consistent and effective manner. The issue, therefore, becomes not whether to score the interview but rather how best to score it.

The most commonly used systems require the interviewer to rate the interviewee on a series of interval measurement scales. The number of rating points on such scales varies but usually consists of between four and seven scale points. These scale points have a number at each point that is used to reflect various degrees of the applicant characteristics being judged. These scale points also usually have either a set of adjectives describing differences among them, for example, not acceptable, marginal, minimal, good, superior, or a brief definition for each scale point, for example instructions given were not understandable, instructions given were understandable but mainly incorrect, instructions were understandable and generally correct.

A second aspect of scoring concerns the dimensions to be scored. Table 12.8 contains an example of a scoring form that can be used in interviews for the position of maintenance supervisor discussed previously. It seems best to rate the applicant directly on the KSAs for which the interview was intended and for which the questions were designed. If the questions are developed in the manner previously described, the information provided by the applicant should quite easily be used to make judgments about these dimensions.

The rating form should also provide space for comments about the applicant's performance on the KSA being rated. These comments are usually examples of summaries of the responses provided by the applicant to the questions that were designed to assess the KSA. The purpose of the comments is to provide both documentation to support the rating, if it is questioned in the future, and more information that can be used to compare a series of applicants.

TABLE 12.8	AN EXAMPLE OF INTERVIEW RATING SCALES USING KSAs

Job Analysis KSAs	Unsatisfactory	Minimal	Average	Good	Superior
1. Verbal ability to give instructions.	1	2	3	4	5

Comments: <u>Generally accurate instructions given. However, instructions lacked specificity as to worker assignment and standard of performance.</u>

Job Analysis KSAs	Unsatisfactory	Minimal	Average	Good	Superior
2. Ability to coordinate and direct multiple crews and projects.	1	2	3	4	5

Comments: <u>Previous situations indicate difficulty in setting priorities among tasks. Also poor evaluation of adequacy of completed tasks.</u>

Job Analysis KSAs	Unsatisfactory	Minimal	Average	Good	Superior
3. Ability to schedule work crews.	1	2	3	4	5

Comments: <u>Responses correctly estimated appropriate crew size and length of time needed to complete project.</u>

There is evidence that when an overall score is sought it is preferable to have this rating provided by the interviewer as an independent score rather than as a summation of the ratings of the individual KSAs.[69] That is, the interviewer should score the applicant on the basis of his or her total judgment across all factors of the interview.

Train the Interviewer

Another point important to reiterate is the value of training the interviewer. It is commonly agreed that the focal skills of an interviewer are the abilities to (a) accurately receive information (b) critically evaluate the information received, and (c) regulate his or her own behavior in delivering questions.[70] Most training programs focus on at least one of these areas; many address all three. While it is not within the scope of this book to present the specific features of such training programs, the following characteristics have frequently been included in successful programs.

Receiving Information In training interviewers to receive information accurately, instruction has concentrated on factors that influence hearing what the respondent has said, observing the applicant's behavior, and remembering the information received. In accomplishing this, programs frequently address such topics as taking notes, reducing the anxiety of the interviewee, establishing rapport with the interviewee, taking measures to reduce fatigue and loss of interest by the interviewer, and minimizing the effect of interviewer expectations on perceiving what the applicant says.

In addition, many training programs have recently focused on the nonverbal behavior of the applicant. There seems to be more difference of opinion about this topic, however, than about the others. While there is general agreement that nonverbal behavior can greatly affect the actions and judgment of the interviewer, the difference of opinion is whether this is a positive or negative factor. Some training programs, in essence, treat nonverbal behavior as a source of error in interviewer decision making that is unrelated to any future job performance by the applicant. Therefore, the interviewer is instructed on methods of reducing the effect of such cues. On the other hand, there are training programs that treat nonverbal behavior as an indicant of the applicant's attitude and personality and as useful information to the interviewer for evaluating the capability of the individual. Even among these programs, there are differences as to which behaviors are regarded as important for the interviewer. A critical issue, for which there is little data, is whether the nonverbal behavior of applicants, especially inexperienced ones, is specific to the interview situation or whether it is indicative of long-term job behavior.

Evaluation of Information   Training interviewers in the critical evaluation of information obtained from the interviewee usually focuses on improving the decision-making process of the interviewer by pointing out common decision errors and methods of overcoming these errors. For example, one workshop training program included videotapes of a simulation of job candidates being appraised by a manager. The trainees used a rating scale to estimate how they thought the manager would evaluate the applicant and how they themselves would assess him or her.[71] Group discussion followed on the reasons for each trainee's rating of both the manager's evaluation and his or her own evaluation. Four exercises were used that concentrated on the halo effect, the similar-to-me effect, the contrast effect, and the first impressions error. Another type of training program emphasizes how an interviewer weighs various pieces of information about the applicant in making judgments. In one study, a multiple regression model was developed and used in training a set of three interviewers. The training significantly improved their predictive validities, often with $r_{xy} =$ .40 or higher.[72]

Interviewing Behavior   As mentioned previously, the Interviewing Institute of the Department of Psychology at the University of Houston offers a five-day program that addresses skills related to regulating behavior in the delivery of questions. The program is 40 hours in length and consists of videotaped practice interviews on the first, third, and fourth days. Each interview lasts up to 30 minutes. Training sessions address topics of questioning techniques and interview structure. Three group playback sessions of the videotapes are also conducted in which three interviewers review the videotape of their interviews with a member of the institute's staff, whose duty it is to critique each interviewer's performance.

As an overall summary, it seems that the critical components of training are to identify the specific behavioral objectives to be addressed in the training program, to provide the trainees with opportunities to demonstrate and review their skills, and to have a method of evaluating the trainees' demonstrated behavior and offering suggestions for change. As a final point Raymond Gordon observes that although practice and analysis can quickly improve performance skills, these skills deteriorate over time through disuse or lack of critical self-analysis.[73] This implies that interviewers should attend training sessions on a regular basis to maintain the necessary skills.

References

[1] Angelo J. Kinicki, Chris A. Lockwood, Peter W. Hom, and Rodger W. Griffeth, "Interviewer Predictions of Applicant Qualifications and Interviewer Validity: Aggregate and Individual Analysis," *Journal of Applied Psychology* 75 (1990): 477–486.

[2] Joe A. Cox, David W. Schlueter, Kris K. Moore, and Debbie Sullivan, "A Look behind Corporate Doors," *Personnel Administrator*, March 1989: 56–59.

[3] Lynn Ulrich and Don Trumbo, "The Selection Interview Since 1949," Psychological Bulletin, 63 (1965): 100–116. See also Neal Schmitt, "Social and Situational Determinants of Interview Decisions: Implications for the Employment Interview," *Personnel Psychology* 29 (1976): 79–101.

[4] Gary P. Latham, Lise M. Saari, Elliott D. Pursell, and Michael A. Campion, "The Situational Interview," *Journal of Applied Psychology* 65 (1980): 422–427. See also Tom Janz, Lowell Hellervik, and David C. Gilmore, *Behavior Description Interviewing* (Boston: Allyn & Bacon, 1986).

[5] Willi H. Wiesner and Steven F. Cronshaw, "A Meta-Analytic Investigation of the Impact of Interview Format and Degree of Structure on the Validity of the Employment Interview," *Journal of Occupational Psychology* 61 (1988): 275–290.

[6] Michael A. McDaniel, Deborah L. Whetzel, Frank L. Schmidt, and Steven D. Maurer, *The Validity of Employment Interviews: A Comprehensive Review and Meta-Analysis*. Unpublished Manuscript.

[7] Cynthia Searcy, Patty Nio Woods, Robert D. Gatewood, and Charles F. Lance, "The Structured Interview: A Meta-Analytic Search for Moderators." Paper presented at the Society of Industrial and Organizational Psychology, 1993.

[8] Michael M. Harris, "Reconsidering the Employment Interview: A Review of Recent Literature and Suggestions for Future Research," *Personnel Psychology* 42 (1989): 691–726.

[9] Robert L. Dipboye, *Selection Interviews: Process Perspectives* (Cincinatti SouthWestern 1992). See also Robert W. Eder and Gerald R. Ferris, eds., *The Employment Interview* (Newbury Park, Calif.: Sage 1989).

[10] Sara L. Rynes, "The Employment Interview as a Recruitment Device" in Eder and Ferris, eds., *The Employment Interview*, 127–142.

[11] Robert L. Dipboye, *Selection Interviews: Process Perspectives*, 228.

[12] Neil Schmitt and Bryan Coylel, "Applicant Decisions in the Employment Interview," *Journal of Applied Psychology* 61 (1976): 184-192.

[13] Sara L. Rynes and H. E. Miller, "Recruiter and Job Influences on Candidates for Employment," *Journal of Applied Psychology* 68 (1983): 147–154.

[14] Michael A. Campion, "Relationship between Interviewers' and Applicants' Reciprocal Evaluations," *Psychological Reports* 42 (1978): 947–952. See also A. Keenan, "The

Selection Interview: Candidates' Reactions and Interviewers' Judgments," *British Journal of Social and Clinical Psychology* 17 (1978): 201–209.

15 Sara L. Rynes, "Recruitment, Job Choice, and Post-Hire Consequences: A Call for New Research Directions," in *Handbook of Industrial and Organizational Psychology*, ed., Vol. 2, eds. M. D. Dunnette and L. M. Hough (Palo Alto, Calif.: Consulting Psychologists Press, 1991).

16 Thomas J. Harn and George C. Thornton III, "Recruiting Counseling Behaviors and Applicant Impressions," *Journal of Occupational Psychology* 58 (1985): 57–65.

17 Susan M. Taylor and T. J. Bergmann, "Organizational Recruitment Activities and Applicants' Reactions at Different Stages of the Recruitment Processes," *Personnel Psychology* 40 (1987): 261–283.

18 Lynn Ulrich and Don Trumbo, "The Selection Interview Since 1949," *Psychological Bulletin* 63 (1965): 100–116.

19 Neal Schmitt, "Social and Situational Determinants of Interview Decisions: Implications for the Employment Interview," *Personnel Psychology* 29 (1976): 79–101.

20 Richard D. Avery, Howard E. Miller, Richard Gould, and Phillip Burch, "Interview Validity for Selecting Sales Clerks," *Personnel Psychology* 40 (1987): 1–12.

21 Robert Gifford, Cheuk Fan Ng, and Margaret Wilkinson, "Nonverbal Cues in the Employment Interview: Links between Applicant Qualities and Interviewer Judgments," *Journal of Applied Psychology* 70 (1985): 729–736.

22 Susan M. Taylor and Janet A. Sniezek, "The College Recruitment Interview: Topical Content and Applicant Reactions," *Journal of Occupational Psychology* 57 (1984): 157–168.

23 The Bureau of National Affairs, *PPF Survey No. 146—Recruiting and Selection Procedures*.

24 Paula C. Morrow, "Physical Attractiveness and Selection Decision Making," *Journal of Management* 16 (1990): 45–60.

25 Susan Raza and Bruce Carpenter, "A Model of Hiring Decisions in Real Employment Interviews," *Journal of Applied Psychology* 72 (1987): 596–603.

26 Denise Mack and David Rainey, "Female Applicants' Grooming and Personnel Selection," *Journal of Social Behavior and Personality* 5 (1990): 399–407.

27 Sandra M. Forsythe, "Effect of Applicant's Clothing on Interviewer's Decision to Hire," *Journal of Applied Social Psychology* 20 (1990): 1579–1595.

28 Robert L. Dipboye, *Selection Interviews: Process Perspectives*, p. 118.

29 A. Dalessio and A. S. Imada, "Relationship between Interview Selection Decisions and Perceptions of Applicant Similarity to an Ideal Employment and Self: A Field Study," *Human Relations* 37 (1984): 67–80.

30 Jurdee K. Burgeon, Valarie Manusou, Paul Mineo, and Jerold L. Hale, "Effects of Gaze on Hiring, Credibility, Attraction, and Relational Message Interpretation," *Journal of Nonverbal Behavior* 9 (1985): 133–146.

31 Charles K. Parsons and Robert G. Liden, "Interviewer Perceptions of Applicant Qualifications: A Multivariate Field Study of Demographic Characteristics and Nonverbal Cues," *Journal of Applied Psychology* (1984): 557–568.

32 Patricia Rowe, "Individual Differences in Selection Decisions," *Journal of Applied Psychology* 47 (1963): 305–307.

33 B. Bolster and B. Springbett, "The Reaction of Interviewers to Favorable and Unfavorable Information," *Journal of Applied Psychology* 45 (1961): 97–103.

34 Thomas Hollman, "Employment Interviewers' Errors in Processing Positive and Negative Information," *Journal of Applied Psychology* 56 (1972): 130–134.

35 Amanda P. Phillips and Robert L. Dipboye, "Correlational Tests of Predictors from a Process Model of the Interview," *Journal of Applied Psychology* 74 (1989): 41–52.

36 Theresa H. Macan and Robert L. Dipboye, "The Effects of Interviewers' Initial Impressions on Information Gathering," *Organizational Behavior and Human Decision Processes* 42 (1988): 364–387.

37 *Watson v. Ft. Worth Bank & Trust*, 47 FEP Cases 102 (1988).

[38] Richard D. Arvey and Robert H. Faley, *Fairness in Selecting Employees*, 2d ed. (Reading, Mass.: Addison-Wesley, 1988).

[39] *Stamps v. Detroit Edison Co.*, 6 FEP 612 (1973).

[40] *Weiner v. County of Oakland*, 14 FEP 380 (1976).

[41] *King v. TWA*, 35 EPD 34, 588 (1984).

[42] *Robbins v. White-Wilson Medical Clinic*, 660 F.2nd 1210(1981).

[43] *Gilbert v. City of Little Rock, Ark.*, 799 F.2nd 1210 (1986).

[44] *Bailey v. Southeastern Area Joint Apprenticeship*, 561 F. Supp. 895 (1983).

[45] *Jones v. Mississippi Department of Corrections*, 615 F. Supp. 456 (1985).

[46] *Harless v. Duck*, 14 FEP 1,616 (1977).

[47] *Maine Human Rights Commission v. Department of Correction*, 474, A.2d 860 (1984).

[48] *Minneapolis Commission on Civil Rights v. Minnesota Chemical Dependency Association*, 310 N.W.2d 497 (1981).

[49] *Allesberry v. Commonwealth of Pennsylvania*, 30 FEP 1634 (1981).

[50] Laura R. Gollub and James E. Campion, "The Employment Interview on Trial." Paper presented at the Society of Industrial and Organizational Psychology annual meeting, 1991.

[51] George Dreher and Paul Sackett, *Perspective on Employee Staffing and Selection* (Homewood, Ill.: Richard D. Irwin, 1983). See also Robert L. Dipboye, *Selection Interviews: Process Perspectives*.

[52] James E. Campion and Richard D. Arvey, "Unfair Discrimination in the Interview," in *The Employment Interview*, eds. R. W. Eder and G. R. Ferris (Newbury Park, Calif.: Sage 1989).

[53] Patrick M. Wright, Philip A. Lichtenfels and Elliot D. Pursell, "The Structured Interview: Additional Studies and Meta-Analysis," *Journal of Occupational Psychology* 62 (1989): 191–199. Also Cynthia Searcy et al., "The Structured Interview: A Meta-Analytic Search for Moderators" and Willi Wiesner and Steven Cronshaw, "A Meta-Analytic Investigation of the Impact of Interview Format and Degree of Structure on the Validity of the Employment Interview."

[54] Neil Schmitt and Walter C. Borman, *Personnel Selection in Organization* (San Francisco: Josey-Bass, 1993).

[55] Thomas W. Dougherty, Ronald J. Ebert, and John C. Callender, "Policy Capturing in the Employment Interview," *Journal of Applied Psychology* 71 (1986): 9–15.

[56] George Howard and Patrick Dailey, "Response-Shift Bias: A Source of Contamination of Self-Report Measures," *Journal of Applied Psychology* 64 (1979): 144–150.

[57] Steven D. Maurer and Charles Fay, "Effect of Situational Interviews, Conventional Structured Interviews, and Training on Interview Rating Agreement: An Experimental Analysis," *Personnel Psychology* 41 (1988): 329–344. See also Michael A. Campion and James E. Campion, "Evaluation of an Interviewee Skills Training Program in a Natural Field Experiment," *Personnel Psychology* 40 (1987): 675–691.

[58] The Bureau of National Affairs, Inc., *PPF Survey No. 146—Recruiting and Selection Procedures* (Washington, D.C.: Bureau of National Affairs, Inc., May 1988).

[59] Gary P. Latham, Lise M. Saari, Elliott D. Pursell, and Michael A. Campion, "The Situational Interview," *Journal of Applied Psychology* 65 (1980): 422–427.

[60] Michael M. Harris, "Reconsidering the Employment Interview: A Review of Recent Literature and Suggestions for Future Research."

[61] Tom Janz, "Initial Comparisons of Patterned Behavior Description Interviews versus Unstructured Interviews," *Journal of Applied Psychology* 67 (1982): 577–580.

[62] Tom Janz, Lowell Hellervik, and David C. Gilmore, *Behavior Description Interviewing* (Boston: Allyn & Bacon, 1986), 62.

[63] Michael M. Harris, "Reconsidering the Employment Interview: A Review of Recent Literature and Suggestions for Future Research."

[64] Hubert S. Feild and Robert D. Gatewood, "Development of a Selection Interview: A Job Content Method," in *The Employment Interview: Theory, Research, and Practice*, ed. Robert W. Eder and Gerald R. Ferris (Beverly Hills, Calif.: Sage, 1989).

[65] Robert L. Dipboye, Gail A. Fontelle, and Kathleen Garner, "Effects of Previewing the Application on Interview Process and Outcomes," *Journal of Applied Psychology* 69 (1984): 118–128.

[66] Amanda Phillips and Robert L. Dipboye, "Correlational Tests of Predictors from a Process Model of the Interview."

[67] Thomas S. Bateman and Dennis W. Organ, "Job Satisfaction and the Good Soldier: The Relationship between Affect and Employee 'Citizenship,'" *Academy of Management Journal* 26 (1983): 587–595.

[68] David Grove, "A Behavioral Consistency Approach to Decision Making in Employment Selection,' *Personnel Psychology* 34 (1981): 55–64.

[69] Cynthia Searcy et al., "The Structured Interview: A Meta–Analytic Search for Moderators."

[70] Raymond L. Gordon, *Interviewing: Strategy, Techniques, and Tactics*, 3d ed. (Homewood, Ill.: Dorsey Press, 1980), 480.

[71] Gary Latham, Kenneth Wexley, and Elliott Pursell, "Training Managers to Minimize Rating Errors in Observation of Behavior," *Journal of Applied Psychology* 60 (1975): 550–555.

[72] Dougherty, Ebert, and Callender, "Policy Capturing in the Employment Interview," 9–15.

[73] Gordon, *Interviewing*, 486.

13

Ability Tests

History of Ability Tests in Selection

The history of the use of ability tests in selection is almost as old as the fields of industrial psychology and HR management. Par Lahy described his work in 1908 of developing tests for use in the selection of street car operators for the Paris Transportation Society.[1] Among the abilities he measured in applicants were reaction time, speed and distance estimating, and choosing correct driving behavior in reaction to street incidents. All of these tests were administered in a laboratory, using specially designed equipment, and given to each applicant individually. The following nine years saw this type of ability test used in selection for other jobs such as telegraph and telephone operators, chauffeurs, typists, and stenographers.

World War I, with its need for rapid mobilization of military manpower, became a major impetus in the development of other tests used in selection. In 1917, a five-man Psychology Committee of the National Research Council was formed and chaired by Robert Yerkes. The group decided that the development and use of tests was the greatest contribution that psychology could offer to military efficiency. The immediate objectives of this committee were to quickly develop tests that could be simultaneously administered to a large number of military recruits and would provide scores which could be used to reject recruits who were thought to be unfit for military service.

The first ability test, as we would know it today, developed by this group was a mental ability or intelligence test. The committee required that this test correlate with existing individually administered tests of intelligence, have objective scoring methods, be rapidly scored, have alternate forms to discourage coaching, require a minimum of writing that was necessary in making responses, and be economical in the use of time.[2] These same requirements have characterized industrial ability tests ever since. The result of the committee's work was the famous (at least among test specialists) Army Alpha. Five forms were developed, each containing 212 items and taking about 28 minutes to administer. Approximately 1.25 million men were tested in 35 examining units located across the United States.

The conspicuous use of this program generated interest in the development of other ability tests for use in vocational counseling and industrial selection. The next two decades saw the development of mechanical, motor, clerical, and spatial relations ability tests among others. World War II provided another boost to test development as all three U.S. military organizations had extensive psychological testing programs. One emphasis was on the development of specialized tests to assist in placing recruits in the most appropriate jobs. Remember that by this time the military had tremendously increased both the technical complexity and the diversity of its jobs. Similar tests were used extensively by industrial organizations after the war, partially because many jobs in these organizations closely resembled military jobs and also because a large number of war veterans suddenly became available as applicants and efficient selection devices were needed.

The growing use of ability tests halted abruptly in the late 1960's and 1970's mainly because of EEO laws and early Supreme Court decisions that specifically addressed a few of the most popular of these tests (see Chapter two).

In this chapter, we discuss the nature of the major types of ability tests that have been used in selection and describe a few representative tests in some detail to show what these tests actually measure. We also discuss their usefulness in present-day selection. Much recent work has been done which indicates that these tests, when used appropriately, are valid selection measures, can be nondiscriminatory in their effects, and can cut costs significantly when used in employment decision making.

Definition of Ability Test

As a first step, we need to discuss briefly what we mean when we use the term *ability test*. Generally, these tests, except for physical ability tests, measure some form of knowledge. In this chapter, we discuss devices that measure mental, mechanical, clerical, and physical abilities. While these are the most often used, there are other ability tests, for example, musical and artistic tests, that have been included in selection programs. Space, however, does not permit our discussion of them all. Except for the physical tests, in industrial settings ability tests are almost always paper-and-pencil tests administered to applicants in a standardized manner. In addition, they are developed to be given to several applicants at the same time. Tests of physical abilities, as the name implies, measure muscular strength, cardiovascular endurance, and movement coordination. Usually special equipment is required for these measurements.

The devices we are calling ability tests have often been referred to as *aptitude* or *achievement* tests. These two terms have been employed to connote slight differences in uses of the two types of test even though, in fact, both types have been used for the same basic purpose—prediction of job performance. Ability tests were thought to measure the effects of formal learning experiences such as courses in English grammar or computer programming. Scores were interpreted to be a measure of how much an individual knew as a result of the learning experience. Aptitude tests, on the other hand, were thought to measure the accumulation of learning from a number of diverse and, usually, nonformalized, learning experiences. For example, aptitude tests were used to determine basic artistic, musical, or mechanical ability.

In reality, such distinctions between achievement and aptitude tests are arbitrary. All tests measure what a person has learned up to that point in time when he or she takes the test. No test can truly measure "future capacity" to learn. This is because all tests measure some type of current behavior, for example, writing of answers, verbal responses, or actions in simulated situations. A test respondent necessarily must have learned what to write, say, or do before being able to respond on the test. There must be previous information or acquired actions to draw on. Psychologists agree that test behaviors reflect a large degree of previous learning. Therefore, tests cannot be pure measures of "innate" or unlearned capacity.[3]

For these reasons, terms such as *aptitude* and *achievement* are being replaced by the term *ability*. Ability tests are differentiated by the nature of the content they measure (e.g., mechanical, mental, clerical, etc.) and the breadth of topics covered (specific, general). We now take a look at some of the major types of ability tests that have been used in selection.

Mental Ability Tests

Mental ability tests were at the center of many of the early critical Supreme Court decisions regarding the discriminatory effects of the use of tests in selection. Given their extensive use after World War II, it is not surprising that these tests were included in early selection cases. As we mentioned previously, after the initial Supreme Court decisions of the early 1970's, the use of mental ability tests in selection dropped drastically. HR managers were reluctant to risk using tests that had already been implicated in adverse impact situations. However, recent work in selection has indicated that mental ability tests are related to job performance for a number of jobs. Because of their previous wide use in selection and the fact that many of the principles governing the appropriate use of ability tests in general have been developed for mental ability tests, we spend more time discussing mental ability tests than we do other types of ability tests.

Development of Mental Ability Tests

To fully understand the use of mental ability tests in selection, it is important to know something of the history of their development. What is generally thought to be the first work on mental ability or intelligence tests, as we currently know them, was done by the French psychologists Alfred Binet and Theodore Simon in the years 1905 to 1911. They attempted to develop tests that would identify mentally retarded children in the French school system who should be assigned to special education classes. Most of the items that made up the tests were composed through consultation with teachers in the school system. Binet and Simon sought to develop an age scale for each year between three and adulthood. An age scale contained those curriculum items that were appropriate for instruction at each academic grade level. For example, if the average age for children in grade 1 was six years, then the six-year age scale would be composed of items learned in grade 1.

A child's mental age was based on correct answers to the various grade-level scales. For example, if a child correctly answered the items for the first grade and incorrectly answered the items on the second-grade scale, the child's mental age would be estimated at six years (average age of first-grade students). Mentally retarded students were identified as those whose calculated mental age was substantially below their chronological age.[4] Binet and Simon's test items included material such as indicating omissions in a drawing, copying written sentences, drawing figures from memory, repeating a series of numbers, composing a sentence containing three given words, giving differences between pairs of abstract terms, and interpreting given facts.[5] This mental ability test was designed to be administered by a trained professional to one individual at a time. In 1916, this test was modified for use in the United States and published as the *Stanford-Binet Intelligence Scale*. It is modified periodically and is still extensively used today.

The first group-administered mental ability test to have widespread use in industry was the *Otis Self-Administering Test of Mental Ability*. This test took approximately 30 minutes to complete and consisted of written, multiple-choice questions that measured such abilities as numerical fluency, verbal comprehension, general reasoning, and spatial orientation. The Otis served as the model for the development of several other mental ability tests that have been used in HR selection.[6]

What is Measured

There are three points about the early mental ability tests that are important for understanding this type of test. The first is the close association between the content of these tests and academic material. The first mental ability test was developed using formal educational materials. Many later tests have closely followed the same strategy. Moreover, mental ability tests have commonly been validated using educational achievement as a criterion measure. Early studies correlated scores on a mental ability test with such measures as amount of education completed, degrees obtained, or, occasionally, grade point average.[7] The rationale was that mental ability should be related to success in school. Robert Guion has commented that it seems acceptable to equate this type of test with scholastic aptitude, meaning that an adequate definition of what is measured by these tests is the ability to learn in formal education and training situations.[8]

The second point is that mental ability tests actually measure several distinct abilities (see Table 13.1 for a list). As we can see, the main abilities included are some form of verbal, mathematical, memory, and reasoning abilities. This clearly indicates that mental ability tests can actually differ greatly form one to another in what is measured. All of the topics in Table 13.1 are mental abilities. However, they obviously are not the same ability. What this means to the specialist is that *all mental ability tests are not interchangeable just because they have similar names or are described as being mental ability or intelligence tests.*

| TABLE 13.1 | ABILITIES MEASURED BY VARIOUS MENTAL ABILITY TESTS |

Memory Span	Figural Classification
Numerical Fluency	Spatial Orientation
Verbal Comprehension	Visualization
Conceptual Classification	Conceptual Correlates
Semantic Relations	Ordering
General Reasoning	Figural Identification
Conceptual Foresight	Logical Evaluation

Third, a variety of scores can be obtained from tests called mental ability tests. General mental ability tests measure several of these abilities and combine scores on all items into one total score that is , theoretically, indicative of overall mental ability. Other tests provide separate scores on each of the tested abilities and then add these scores together to report a general ability total score. A third type of test concentrates on one or more separate abilities and does not combine scores into a general ability measure. We now discuss one of the more famous and widely used mental ability tests in order to illustrate the concepts we have discussed.

The Wonderlic Personnel Test

The Wonderlic Personnel Test was first developed in 1938 and is still widely used. It was also the mental ability test used by the Duke Power Company that was questioned by Griggs in the landmark EEO selection case. The *Wonderlic* is a 12-minute multiple-choice test that consists of 50 items. The items covered include areas of vocabulary, "commonsense" reasoning, formal syllogisms, arithmetic reasoning and computation, analogies, perceptual skill, spatial relations, number series, scrambled sentences, and knowledge of proverbs. Table 13.2 contains items that are similar to those used in the *Wonderlic* to illustrate the kinds of items contained in the test. They are not part of the test itself. Statistical analysis has found that the primary factor measured by the test is verbal comprehension, with deduction and numerical fluency being the next two factors in order of importance.[9]

Over the years, 14 different forms of the *Wonderlic* have been developed and published. The forms are said by the publisher to be "equal and similar to a very high degree."[10] However, the forms are not perfectly equal, and an individual's score can vary depending on which of the forms is taken. For this reason a conversion table is provided to test users that indicates how many score points should be added or subtracted to equate scores on all possible pairs of forms. This conversion is usually necessary because it is recommended that organizations alternate the use of two or more forms of the tests to maintain the security of the items. This adjustment is of three points at the maximum. All forms of the test are easily scored by counting the number of correct answers out of the total of 50 items. No attempt is made to convert this score to an I.Q. score, even though the *Wonderlic* is purportedly a test of general mental ability. On all forms

TABLE 13.2	EXAMPLE ITEMS SIMILAR TO ITEMS ON THE WONDERLIC PERSONNEL TEST

1. Which of the following months has 30 days?
   (a) February   *(b) June   (c) August   (d) December

2. Alone is the opposite of:
   (a) happy   *(b) together   (c) single   (d) joyful

3. Which is the next number in this series: 1, 4, 16, 4, 16, 64, 16, 64, 256,
   (a) 4   (b)16   *(c) 64   (d) 1024

4. Twilight is to dawn as autumn is to:
   (a) winter   *(b) spring   (c) hot   (d) cold

5. If Nat can outrun Gui by 2 feet in every 5 yards of a race, how much ahead will Nat be at 45 yards?
   (a) 5 yards   *(b) 6 yards   (c) 10 feet   (d) 90 feet

6. The two words relevant and immaterial mean:
   (a) the same   *(b) the opposite   (c) neither same nor opposite

NOTE: An (*) indicates the correct response.

the 50 items are arranged in order of ascending difficulty. These items range form quite easy to fairly difficult with the average difficulty being at a level at which approximately 60 percent of the test takers would answer the item correctly.

One very appealing feature of the test is the extensive set of norm scores that has been developed through its long use. The test publisher provides tables indicating the distribution of scores by education level of applicants, position applied for, region of the country, gender, age, and ethnicity. In addition, parallel form reliability among the forms is given and ranges from .82 to.94.[11] During the almost 50 years of its use, many selection programs have been described in various journals that have used the *Wonderlic* as a predictor device. Some data within these journal articles have become part of validity generalization studies, which we discuss later in the chapter. These studies have been used to examine some critical selection issues.

General Comments about Mental Ability Tests

As is obvious from the preceding sections, mental ability tests and those that have been called intelligence, or I.Q., tests are the same type of tests. We think that because of widespread misconceptions about the terms *intelligence* and *I.Q.*, selection specialists can more appropriately conceptualize these tests as mental ability. The term *mental ability* makes explicit that these tests measure various cognitive abilities of the applicant. These cognitive abilities can most directly be identified by the general factors that compose the test or, in some cases, from the content of the items themselves. These cognitive abilities should really be thought of in the same manner as the abilities we have discussed in other parts of this book, abilities that primarily indicate the individual's level of mental manipulation of words, figures, numbers, symbols, and logical order.

Following from this, it is fairly easy to understand the strong relationship between mental ability test scores and academic performance. Formal education primarily stresses cognitive exercises and memorization of facts, and these are the components that make up a large part of most mental ability tests. Also, many mental ability tests have been validated against educational achievement because it is sensible to think that, in general, those with the greatest mental ability will progress farther and do better in school situations than those with lesser ability. It is for these reasons that it has been said that these tests measure basic academic ability. This, however, does not mean that mental ability is only useful for academic selection. There are many jobs in organizations that demand the use of the same abilities, such as managerial, technical, and some clerical jobs to name but a few. We develop this later in the chapter when we discuss the validity of ability tests.

Mechanical Ability Tests

There is not a strict definition of the construct of mechanical ability, even though it is a term that has long been used by testing specialists. For the most part mechanical ability refers to characteristics that tend to make for success in work with machines and equipment.[12] One of the earliest tests of this type was the *Stenquist Mechanical Assembly Test*, developed in 1923 by John Stenquist. It consisted of a long narrow box with ten compartments. Each compartment had a simple mechanical apparatus (e.g., mousetrap, push button, etc.) that had to be assembled by the test taker. Stenquist also developed two picture tests that were designed to measure the same abilities. The *Stenquist* thus demonstrated the two testing methods that have been generally used in mechanical ability tests: Performance and written problems. Early tests like the *Stenquist* and the *Minnesota Mechanical Assembly Test* (1930) emphasized actual mechanical assembly or manipulation. However, the cost and time involved in administering and scoring such tests with large numbers of individuals can quickly become prohibitive. Therefore, the group-administered paper-and-pencil tests that attempted to present problems of mechanical work through pictures and statements were developed. Over the last 30 years the use of paper-and-pencil tests has greatly exceeded the use of performance tests.

Attempts have been made to determine more precisely the abilities measured by mechanical ability tests. As with mental ability tests, these vary test to test, but, in general, the main factors are spatial visualization, perceptual speed and accuracy, and mechanical information.[13] Mechanical ability tests can also be though of as measuring general or specific abilities. We discuss two of the most frequently used general ability tests, the *Bennet Mechanical Comprehension Test* and the *MacQuarrie Test for Mechanical Ability*. These tests have been utilized for a large number of different jobs. Specific ability tests have been developed and used for jobs such as carpenter, engine lathe operator, welder, electrician, and so on.

The Bennet Mechanical Comprehension Test

There have been six different forms of this paper-and-pencil test plus a Spanish language edition. The first three forms that were developed were AA, BB, and W-1. Each had 60 items and was designed to have a different level of difficulty and, therefore, applicability. Form AA was the easiest and was designed for essentially untrained and inexperienced groups. Form CC was the most difficult and was designed for use with engineering students. Items on all forms are of general mechanical situations common to shop and garage activities. Form W-1 was developed expressly for testing women and drew its items primarily from situations in the kitchen and sewing room. As you can guess, these tests were developed during the 1940s and reflect some of the cultural differences between men and women that were more common then than now. The two most recent forms, S and T, were developed in 1969 and are parallel forms of 68 items each. For the most part these forms use many questions from the previous forms AA, BB, and W-1, with approximately 11 new items added.

The items of the Bennett contain objects that are generally familiar in American culture: airplanes, carts, steps, pulleys, seesaws, and gears. The questions measure the respondent's ability to perceive and understand the relationship of physical forces and mechanical elements in practical situations. While requiring some familiarity with common tools and objects, the questions purportedly assume no more technical knowledge than can be acquired through everyday experience in an industrial society such as ours. Partially supporting this assumption is evidence that formal training in physics only slightly increases test scores. Items are pictures with a brief accompanying question. For example, a sample item is a picture of two men carrying a weighted object hanging down from a plank and it asks, "Which man carries more weight?" Each figure has a letter below its base. Because the object is closer to one man than to the other, the correct answer is the letter of the closer man. Another item has two pictures of the same room of a house. In one picture the room contains several pieces of furniture, carpeting, and objects on the wall. In the other picture the room contains only a minimum of objects and no carpeting. The question is, "Which room has an echo?" Given some basic knowledge or experience, the question can be answered by logical analysis of the problem rather than the mastery of detailed and specific facts.

The tests have no time limit, and usually 30 minutes is ample for most individuals to complete the items. A score is the number of items answered correctly. The manuals for the different forms give percentile norms for various groups of industrial applicants, industrial employees, and students. Reported reliabilities are in the .80s. Studies have correlated scores on the older forms of the *Bennett* with scores on other ability tests to further understand the abilities being measured. Results indicate a moderate correlation with both verbal and mathematical mental ability tests and tests of spatial visualization. The relationship to verbal ability and spatial visualization can partially be explained in that it is a written test with pictures as items.

The MacQuarrie Test for Mechanical Ability

The *MacQuarrie* is a paper-and-pencil group test that requires about 30 minutes to administer. The seven subtests are called tracing, tapping, dotting, copying, location, blocks, and pursuit. Examples of items similar to items on three of these subtests are contained in Exhibit 13.1. The tracing test requires the test taker to draw a line through small openings in a series of vertical lines. The tapping test requires making pencil dots inside of figures as rapidly as possible. The dotting test requires placing one dot n each of a series of small squares spaced irregularly. The copying test requires the copying of series of simple designs. In the location test, the test taker locates points drawn on a large scale and transposes them onto an area drawn on a smaller scale. The blocks test requires spatial visualization by asking how many blocks in a pile touch a given block. The pursuit test requires following a line using only the eye.

Reported reliabilities for these subtests range from .72 to .90. Norms, based on scores of 1,000 males and 1,000 females 16 years and over, are given. Additional norms are supplied for school-age children of 14 to 16. Not surprisingly, this test appears to measure manipulative ability involving finger and hand dexterity, visual acuity, muscle control, and spatial relationship among figures, rather than the understanding of mechanical or physical principles as does the *Bennett*. However, correlations of .40 to .48 have consistently been found between the MacQuarrie and the Bennett.[14] Also the subtests of copying, location, pursuit, and blocks have been found to correlate in the .30s and .40s with the Otis Self-Administering Test of Mental Ability presumably indicating the ability to learn mechanical principles.[15]

Clerical Ability

Traditionally, clerical jobs have been thought of as similar to bookkeeping, typing, filing, and record-keeping positions. Early job analyses of these types of jobs indicated that they consist of extensive checking or copying of words and numbers and the movement and placement of objects such as office equipment, files, and reports. It was, therefore, thought that clerical jobs required perceptual speed and accuracy and also manual dexterity. However, research has not supported the importance of manual dexterity. One conclusion has been that the degree of manual dexterity necessary to perform these jobs is so low that almost all individuals qualified in other abilities possess enough of this to perform adequately. Therefore, clerical ability tests have predominantly measured perceptual speed and accuracy in processing verbal and numerical data.

The Minnesota Clerical Test

Developed in 1933, the *Minnesota Clerical Test* is generally regarded as the prototype of clerical ability tests and has been the most widely used of these tests for much of its existence. The test is a brief, easily administered, and easily scored instrument. It has two separately timed and scored subtests: number checking and name checking. In each subtest, there are 200 items. Each item consists of a

EXHIBIT 13.1 ITEMS SIMILAR TO ITEMS OF THE MACQUARRIE TEST FOR MENTAL ABILITY

1. Tracing: draw a continuous line through each space without touching the lines.

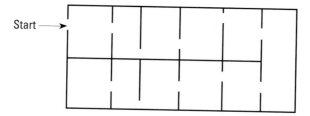

Start ⟶

2. Tapping: put three dots in each triangle as quickly as you can.

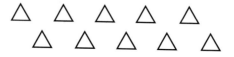

3. Dotting: put one dot in each square as quickly as you can.

Begin

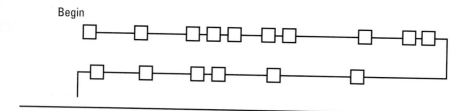

pair of numbers or names. The respondent is to compare the pair and place a check on a line between the two entries of the pair if these two entries are identical. If the two entries are different, no mark is placed on the line. The entries in the numbers subtest range from 3 through 12 digits; the entries in the names subtest range from 7 through 16 letters. The tests are timed separately at 8 minutes for numbers and 7 minutes for names. The score is the number right minus the number wrong, and scores are determined for each subtest separately as well as for the total score of both. Table 13.3 contains items similar to those used in both of these subtests.

Although the two subtests are related, they do measure separate abilities. The names subtest has been found to be correlated with speed of reading, spelling, and group measures of intelligence. The numbers subtest has been related to the verification of arithmetic computations.[16] Scores on the subtests are only slightly related to either education level or experience in clerical posi-

TABLE 13.3	EXAMPLE ITEMS SIMILAR TO ITEMS ON THE MINNESOTA CLERICAL TEST

Name Comparison

Vida Scarpello	_____	Vida Gulbanis
Diana Deadrick	_____	Deedee Deedrick
Christine Marie	_____	Tina Marie
Harry Connick, Jr.	_____	Harry Connick, Jr.
Bob Carti	_____	Greg Dobbins

Number Comparison

84644	_____	84464
179854	_____	176845
123457	_____	12457
987342	_____	987342
8877665994	_____	8876659954

tions. Reliability has been estimated as .90 for parallel forms and .85 for test-retest. Norm group scores are provided for various job groups for each sex.

Physical Abilities

Another area of importance for selection specialists is the testing of physical abilities of applicants for placement into manual labor and physically demanding jobs. As Michael Campion points out, there are three reasons for this type of testing.[17] First, EEO legislation has prompted an increase of women applicants for traditionally male-dominated physical labor jobs. Although as a group women score lower than men on many physical ability tests, we have previously discussed that all applicants must be evaluated as individuals, not as members of a group. Often the presence of female applicants has prompted a more complete analysis of physical requirements for jobs. The same comment pertains to disabled applicants.

Second, the use of appropriate selection devices for physically demanding jobs can reduce the incidence of work-related injuries. The insurance, compensation, and therapy costs associated with back, knee, and shoulder injuries continue to rise dramatically. Tests should improve the selection of individuals who are better suited to job demands. Third, the pre-employment medical examinations that have often been used for selection into physically demanding jobs do not usually focus specifically on physical requirements associated with jobs. Instead, these medical examinations have yielded a general assessment of physical fitness. General fitness is not the same as the physical abilities necessary for work activities.

As background for understanding the use of physical ability tests, we now present a brief lecture in physiology. (You do not have to read this if you are a premed major or can get one to explain this stuff.)

Performing physical work depends on the ability of the muscle cells to transform chemically bound energy in food into mechanical energy. This most directly involves the nervous system, muscular system, respiratory system, and cardiac system. The nervous system initiates and controls muscles responsible for movement. The chief agent of physical work is skeletal muscle, which exerts force to move objects. Skeletal muscle, however, is primarily dependent on the circulatory and respiratory systems that service the muscles. The respiratory system provides air to the lungs and is responsible for the exchange of oxygen and carbon dioxide between the air and the blood. The heart and the vascular system deliver the oxygen and nutrients to the active muscle tissues that are necessary for the continued operation of the muscle. This removes the metabolic waste products that inhibit muscle operation when they accumulate. Energy for the body's cells is provided through the process of metabolism, which increases directly with work intensity until exhaustion is reached.[18]

Because these physiological processes are the basis for physical activity, it follows that many physical ability tests require demonstrations of strength, oxygen intake, and coordination. For example, one approach to selection for the physically demanding jobs is to measure the aerobic power necessary for the job and select those whose tested maximum aerobic power is great enough to do the job without undue fatigue. Sometimes the rule is used that the maximum power of the individual should be two and a half times the maximum demand of the job. However, this rule is a simplistic approach to a complicated topic. Selection for physical ability has evolved so there are batteries of tests that evaluate applicants comprehensively for job activities. In the next sections we summarize the work of two experts who have identified such test batteries, Edwin Fleishman and Joyce Hogan.

Physical Abilities Analysis

Edwin Fleishman and his colleagues have developed a taxonomy of approximately 50 different abilities, both physical and nonphysical, that are necessary for performing work activities.[19] *Ability Requirements Scales* measure to what degree each of these 50 abilities is necessary for performing either a specific job or job task.

The *Ability Requirements Scales* are 7-point scales that are anchored at three points, (high, medium, and low) by tasks. For example, the 7-point *Static Strength Scale* has "Lift one package of bond paper" as a low anchor, "Walk a few steps on flat terrain carrying a 50-pound back pack" as a high anchor. The job analyst reads each of the scales and checks the scale point that correctly represents the job activity being studied.

Fleishman has identified the following nine physical abilities that have been extensively used to select employees for physically demanding jobs:[20]

1. *Static strength*—maximum force that can be exerted against external objects. Tested by lifting weights.

2. *Dynamic strength*—muscular endurance in exerting force continuously. Tested by pull-ups.

3. *Explosive strength*—ability to mobilize energy effectively for bursts of muscular effort. Tested by sprints or jumps.

4. *Trunk strength*—limited dynamic strength specific to trunk muscles. Tested by leg lifts or sit-ups.

5. *Extent flexibility*—ability to flex or stretch trunk and back muscles. Tested by twist and touch test.

6. *Dynamic flexibility*—ability to make repeated, rapid, flexing trunk movements. Tested by rapid repeated bending over and touching floor.

7. *Gross body coordination*—ability to coordinated action of several parts of body while body is in motion. Tested by cable jump test.

8. *Gross body equilibrium*—ability to maintain balance with non visual cues. Tested by rail walk test.

9. *Stamina*—capacity to sustain maximum effort requiring cardiovascular exertion. Tested by 600-yard run-walk.

The following validity coefficients for specific jobs are among the results reported by Fleishman for the use of these abilities in selection: pipeline workers (.63); correctional officers (.64); warehouse workers (.39); electrical workers (.53); and enlisted army men (.87).[21] All coefficients represent the correlation of a battery of two to four physical abilities with job performance.

Three Components of Physical Performance

The extensive work of Joyce Hogan has produced the three components of physical performance described in Table 13.4. She combined two lines of research in the development of this taxonomy. The first was data about physical requirements that were derived from job analysis. The second was data based on physical ability tests already developed for selection. Her idea was that by examining these two sources of information about physical work performance a comprehensive model of physical abilities may be developed.

Factor analyses were performed on several sets of data. Results consistently identified three factors, or components, of physical abilities.[22] The first, *muscular strength*, is the ability to apply or resist force through muscular contraction. Within this component are three, more specific subelements: muscular tension, muscular power, and muscular endurance. The second component is *cardiovascular endurance*, which refers to the capacity to sustain gross (as contrasted with localized) muscular activity over prolonged periods. It is aerobic capacity and general systemic fitness involving the large muscles. The third component, *movement quality*, concerns characteristics that contribute to skilled performance. This component also has three subelements: flexibility, balance, and muscular integration. Hogan has concluded that this three-component model

TABLE 13.4		THREE COMPONENTS OF PHYSICAL PERFORMANCE	
Component	**Subelement**	**Sample Work Activities**	**Sample Tests**
Muscular Strength	Muscular tension	activities of pushing, pulling, lifting, lowering or carrying a heavy object	handgrip strength, dynamometer (scores in pounds/kilos)
	Muscular power	use of hand tools, raising a section of a ladder with a halyard	ergometer, medicine ball put (scores in pounds)
	Muscular endurance	repetitions of tool use, loading materials onto pallets	push-ups, arm ergometer, (scores in number of repetitions)
Cardiovascular Endurance	None	search and rescue, climbing stairs, wearing protective equipment	step-up time, distance run (scores of amount of time taken)
Movement Quality	Flexibility	mining operations, installing light fixtures	sit and reach, twist and touch (scores of distance of limb displacement, repetitions)
	Balance	pole climbing, ladder usage, elevated construction	static rail balance (scores in time or distance)
	Neuromuscular integration	accessing an offshore platform, intercepting an object	Minnesota rate manipulation (scores in lapsed time or target error)

SOURCE: Based on Joyce C. Hogan, "Physical Abilities," in *Handbook of Industrial & Organizational Psychology*, 2d ed., Vol. 2, eds. Marvin Dunnette and Leatta Hough. (Palo Alto, Calif.: Consulting Psychologists Press, 1991).

describes the true structure of physical abilities necessary for work activities.[23] As such, the model could be used as the basis for selection. The major issue in developing a selection program would be to determine which subset of abilities correlates with job performance for the job under study.

Legal Issues

Selection specialists working with physically demanding jobs must be especially concerned with three groups of applicants: females, disabled, and older workers. Adverse impact for scores on physical ability tests is a common occurrence for each group. Because physical ability tests stress strength, aerobic power, and coordination, frequently males will score higher than females, nondisabled higher than disabled, and younger higher than older. The essential issue, therefore, is that the tests must clearly be linked to critical job tasks which *require* physical abilities in their completion. However, even this statement is complicated by the question of whether the tasks can be modified to reduce or eliminate these physical demands. Such modification can occur either through the use of additional equipment or personnel. If such modifications can be made, the use of the physical ability test appropriate for the original tasks may be unwarranted. We now briefly discuss some of the main legal issues that have been raised relative to selection for each of these three groups.

Two selection requirements regarding females that have been treated in court cases are state laws prohibiting women lifting over a certain amount of weight and height/weight standards. In *Weeks v. Southern Bell*, the court ruled than even though Georgia had protective legislation prohibiting women from lifting 30 pounds. ". . . Title VII rejects just this type of romantic paternalism as unduly Victorian and instead vests individual women with the power to decide whether or not to take on unromantic tasks."[24] Similarly height and weight standards have been equally hard to defend. Usually the argument has been advanced that height and weight are surrogate measures of strength that are necessary for many jobs. Courts have consistently held that if measuring strength is the objective, then selection requirements should assess that directly rather than using secondary indicators.

There are muscle strength tests which demonstrate relatively less adverse impact against females: those that measure lower body strength, for example, leg dynamometer. For tests of muscular power and endurance, vertical jumps and sit-ups have shown smaller differences between males and females than other tests. Cardiovascular endurance measures demonstrate mean scores for females that are about two-thirds those of men. For that reason, cutoff scores must be well documented. Tests of flexibility, balance, and coordination usually show little or no adverse impact.

It should be noted, however, that it is unrealistic, and perhaps undesirable, to develop a selection program for physical abilities that eliminates test score differences between men and women. The general evidence is that while women score lower than men on strength and endurance tests, they also demonstrate lower performance on jobs that require these abilities.[25] In such cases, the adverse impact may be inherent in the job activities, not in the content of the test. In order to reduce male-female differences, the appropriate strategy would be to alter the job tasks rather than the tests that are used for selection.

As discussed in Chapter 2, the Americans with Disabilities Act of 1991 prohibits discrimination on the basis of disability and requires employers to take action to hire and advance the disabled. Such action includes "reasonable accommodation" of the disabled worker in the work processes and physical setting of the job. This has generally been interpreted to mean that adjustments should be made for the known physical and mental limitations of an otherwise qualified disabled applicant or employee unless the organization can demonstrate that the accommodation would cause undue hardship on the firm. Both financial and safety costs are weighed in this consideration of undue hardship.

An employer is not justified in presuming that a disabled worker is unable to perform a job. It is necessary that a thorough job analysis be conducted and physical ability tests be identified for important corresponding job tasks. Even if this is done, the job tasks may still be subject to the reasonable accommodation directive. In general, courts have placed a more stringent demand for reasonable accommodation on employers when the disabled individuals are employees who are returning to work after illness or injury than when they are new workers. Of direct importance for physical ability testing is the ruling in *E. E. Black, Ltd. v. Marshall*.[26] In this case the plaintiff was rejected for the job of apprentice carpenter, which required a good deal of lifting and carrying, because of a back condition detected in the medical screening for the job. The court ruled, based on other evidence including the examination of an orthopedist, that even though the plaintiff should be considered disabled (the back condition), he still could perform the job. The court expressly disagreed with the company's position that the plaintiff should be denied employment because he constituted a future risk for injury. In this case, an employment decision made on the basis of a valid physical ability test rather than a medical screening test, which had no demonstrated job relatedness, may have avoided the confrontation.

No general presumptions can be made about the physical abilities of older applicants, either. That is, an organization cannot assume that an applicant in the 40 to 70 age range (specified by age discrimination in the Employment Act of 1967) is incapable of any physical demands of the job. However, the use of physical ability tests that validly correspond to job requirements should be an acceptable basis for selection decisions. It is reasonable to expect that there will be an increase in court cases of age discrimination in the future as the labor force "grays."

The Validity of Ability Tests

Now that we have a better idea of what ability tests measure and how they are constructed, let us turn our attention to their actual use in selection. One advantage of having as long a history as ability tests do is that there is a large number of selection programs that have used this type of test. There have also been a number of studies that have attempted to synthesize the results of these selection programs. In this section, we discuss the findings of the most extensive of these studies.

Project A

Project A was a seven-year effort to develop a selection system appropriate for all entry-level positions in the U.S. army. John P. Campbell and his associates describe some of the findings of Project A that are important for our discussion of the validity of mental ability tests.[27]

One of the major tasks of this project was the development of 65 predictor tests that could be used as selection instruments. Statistical analyses were applied to the scores on these tests of 4.039 incumbents of entry-level army jobs. These analyses resulted in six domains of predictor instruments: general cognitive ability, spatial ability, perceptual-psychomotor ability, temperament/personality, vocational interest, and job reward preference. Another major task was the development of components of work performance across entry-level jobs. Five components were determined: core technical task proficiency; general task proficiency; peer support and leadership, effort, and self-development; maintaining personal discipline; and physical fitness and military bearing.[28]

You can probably guess what a group of selection specialists would do if they found themselves with six predictors and five measures of job performance for 4,000 people. Yep, they conducted a giant validity study. Table 13.5 presents only a small part of the results. The validity coefficients are corrected for range restriction and adjusted for shrinkage. The general cognitive ability predictor domain correlated .63 and .65 with the two job performance factors that most directly measured job task performance. Spatial ability, a second ability domain, that sometimes has been included in measures of general cognitive ability, had almost equally high validity coefficients. It is important to remember that these data were calculated across all entry-level jobs in the army. Our conclusion is that these data indicate that general mental ability tests are valid selection instruments across a large variety of jobs.

TABLE 13.5 PROJECT A VALIDITY COEFFICIENTS

Predictor

Job Performance Factor	General Cognitive Ability	Spacial Ability	Perceptual Psychomotor Ability	Temperament/ Personality	Vocational Interest	Job Reward Preference
Core Technical Proficiency	.63	.56	.53	.26	.35	.29
General Task Proficiency	.65	.63	.57	.25	.34	.30

SOURCE: Jeffrey J. McHenry, Laetta M. Hough, Jody L. Toquam, Mary A. Hanson, and Steven Ashworth, "Project A Validity Results: The Relationship between Predictor and Criterion Domains," *Personnel Psychology*, 43 (1990), 335–354.

Validity Generalization Studies

We discussed validity generalization previously in Chapter 5. Without going over the details of this concept, we discuss the implications of the work for our question about the validity of ability tests in selection. For many years, selection specialists had noted that validity coefficients for the same combination of selection instruments and criteria measures differed greatly for studies in different organizations. This was even true when the jobs for which the selection program was designed were very similar. Selection specialists explained these differences in terms of undetermined organizational factors that affected the correlation between selection instruments and criteria. The standard recommendation was that it was necessary to conduct a validation study for each selection program that was developed. This was the only way to be sure that validity could be demonstrated and that these undetermined organizational factors did not have a large adverse effect on the validity correlations.

Importance in Selection The validity generalization studies conducted by Frank Schmidt and John Hunter have *totally disagreed* with these previous conclusions and have suggested a much different use for ability tests in selection. Schmidt and Hunter's point is that the differences in validity coefficients for the same selection instruments for similar jobs is not a function of unknown organizational factors. Rather these differences are due to methodological deficiencies in the validation studies themselves (see Chapter 5). When these deficiencies are corrected, the differences among these validity coefficients should really be close to zero. Validity generalization studies apply these corrections to validation works that have been conducted previously. Some of these studies have corrected for differences in sample size, reliability of criterion measures, reliability of predictor measures, and restriction in range. Other recent validity generalization studies only correct for differences in sample size because there is evidence that this correction accounts for most of the differences among the previous validity studies.[29] Schmidt and Hunter have adapted as a decision rule that if these corrections account for 75 percent or more of the variance among the validity coefficients in the sample of works being analyzed, then the conclusion should be that all differences among the coefficients is due to measurement error. This means that situation specificity is not present.[30]

Validity Generalization for the Same Job One approach of validity generalization studies has been to analyze data from validity studies conducted for the same job, for example, computer programmers, that all used the same type of a test as a predictor. Table 13.6 summarizes the corrected mean validity coefficients of some of these studies. The most prominent finding of these studies is that, as Schmidt and Hunter hypothesized, there is evidence that the differences among studies in terms of validity coefficients are greatly reduced; in some instances, all differences have been eliminated. This is interpreted as meaning that the validity coefficient for the predictor and criterion measures is stable across organizations.

TABLE 13.6 **SELECTED VALIDITY GENERALIZATION RESULTS FOR VARIOUS JOBS**

Job	Test Type	Estimated Average Validity Coefficient	
		Performance Criteria	Training Criteria
Computer programmer[a]	Figure analogies	.46	—
	Arithmetic reasoning	.57	—
	Total score all tests	.73	.91
Mechanical repairman[b]	Mechanical principles	—	.78
First-line supervisor[b]	General mental ability	.64	—
	Mechanical comprehension	.48	—
	Spatial ability	.43	—
Computing and account-recording clerks[c]	General mental ability	.49	.66
	Verbal ability	.41	.62
	Quantitative ability	.52	.66
	Reasoning ability	.63	—
	Perceptual speed	.50	.38
	Memory	.42	—
	Spatial/mechanical	.42	.36
	Motor	.30	—
	Clerical ability	.53	.62
Operator (petroleum[d] industry)	Mechanical comprehension	.33	—
	Chemical comprehension	.30	—
	General intelligence	.26	—
	Arithmetic reasoning	.26	—
Police and detectives[e]	Memory	—	.41
	Quantitative ability	.26	.63
	Reasoning	.17	.61
	Spatial/mechanical ability	.17	.50
	Verbal ability	—	.64

[a] SOURCE: Frank Schmidt, Ilene Gast-Rosenbery, and John Hunter, "Validity Generalization for Computer Programmers," *Journal of Applied Psychology* 65 (1980): 643–661.

[b] SOURCE: Frank Schmidt, John Hunter, Kenneth Pearlman, and Guy Shane, "Further Tests of the Schmidt-Hunter Bayesian Validity Generalization Procedure," *Personnel Psychology* 32 (1979): 257–281.

[c] SOURCE: Kenneth Pearlman, Frank Schmidt, and John Hunter, "Validity Generalization Results for Tests Used to Predict Job Proficiency and Training Success in Clerical Occupations," *Journal of Applied Psychology* 65 (1980): 373–406.

[d] SOURCE: Frank Schmidt, John Hunter, and James Caplan, "Validity Generalization Results for Two Job Groups in the Petroleum Industry," *Journal of Applied Psychology* 66 (1981): 261–273.

[e] SOURCE: Hannah Rothstein Hirsh, Lois Northrup, and Frank Schmidt, "Validity Generalization Results for Law Enforcement Occupations," *Personnel Psychology* 39 (1986): 399–420.

NOTE: Data for missing cells are not reported.

A second finding of these studies has been that the corrections to the validity coefficients have raised the magnitude of these coefficients. This is the same concept we discussed in Chapter 5 regarding the factors that may artificially reduce a validity coefficient. Many validity coefficients are understatements of the true relationships between predictors and criteria because they are affected by factors that are corrected in validity generalization studies. As Table 13.6 indicates, some of these corrected coefficients are relatively high, in the .50s and .60s. Such coefficients demonstrate a much stronger relationship between selection and performance than was previously thought. This increases the importance of selection in maintaining high productivity within organizations.

A third finding refers to previous statements we have made that selection instruments can predict training results very well. The coefficients for training criteria in Table 13.6 are, as a whole, higher than those for performance, sometimes reaching .70 to .90.

Validity across Jobs   A second tactic of validity generalization studies has been to examine differences in validity coefficients for the same set of predictor-criterion measures across different jobs. This can be regarded as a logical extension of the previously described studies. If situation specificity within organizations is false, perhaps specificity within jobs is too. The validity generalization studies that have examined this issue have almost exclusively used mental ability tests as the predictor. As you might guess from our previous comments, the conclusion of these validity generalization studies has been that mental ability tests are valid across a large variety of jobs and can serve as very useful selection instruments.[31] Table 13.7 presents some results, as obtained by John Hunter, that are representative of these studies.

The first part of this table presents the results of the validity correction formulas applied to studies within each of nine occupations. The argument for the validity of mental ability tests is strongly made as the average coefficient presented in the table is significant for each occupation. Therefore, one conclusion is that mental ability tests are valid for each of these occupations, although there are differences in the magnitude of the coefficients among the occupations. This may mean that such tests are not equally valid among occupations and that other selection instruments can be useful in selection

The second part of Table 13.7 extends these conclusions. This part is based on 515 validation studies conducted by the U.S. Employment Service on the validity of the General Aptitude Test Battery (GATB), a mental ability test battery. Data on jobs were reported using six different job analysis systems. All systems, however, had one dimension that measured complexity. Jobs in these 515 validation studies were grouped into low, medium, and high complexity based on their scores on this dimension. A second method of grouping jobs on complexity level was used for jobs in industrial families. Using the "things" scale of the *Dictionary of Occupational Titles* published by the Department of Labor, these jobs were grouped into setup work (more complex) and feeding/offbearing (less complex).

Validity generalization analyses were applied to the studies within each complexity level. This meant that many different jobs were grouped together within each of these five complexity categories. As Table 13.7 shows, the GATB

TABLE 13.7	SELECTED VALIDITY GENERALIZATION RESULTS ACROSS JOBS	

Occupations	Validity Performance	Validity Training
Manager	.53	.51
Clerical	.54	.71
Salesperson	.61	—
Sales clerk	.27	—
Protective professions	.42	.87
Service workers	.48	.66
Vehicle operators	.28	.37
Trades and crafts	.46	.65
Industrial	.37	.61

Job Families	Validity Performance	Validity Training
General job families		
high complexity	.58	.50
medium complexity	.51	.57
low complexity	.40	.54
Industrial families		
setup work	.56	.65
feeding/offbearing	.23	—

SOURCE: John Hunter, "Cognitive Ability, Cognitive Aptitudes, Job Knowledge, and Job Performance," *Journal of Vocational Behavior* 29 (1986): 340–362.

NOTE: Data for empty cells are not reported.

was valid for each category with both performance and training criterion measures. However, there are differences among the performance validity coefficients, with those for more complex jobs being higher than those for less complex jobs. Coefficients for training criteria are uniformly high. These results are interpreted to mean that mental ability tests are valid for a great many jobs, and increase in predictability of job performance as the job becomes more complex. For training success, these tests are consistently very high in validity.

Conclusions from Validity Generalization Studies Hunter and Schmidt have used results of these and similar analyses to draw some far-reaching conclusions. The first is that often it is no longer necessary to conduct validity studies within each organization. If the job of interest for the selection program is one of those for which validity generalization data have been reported, then the selection instruments reported in the validity generalization study can be used in the organization for selection.[32] This is because there are no organizational effects on validity; therefore, the same predictor can be used across all organizations. To set up the selection program, all that is necessary is to demonstrate through job analysis that the job within the organization is similar to the job in the validity generalization study. Obviously, this reduces the time, effort, and cost of establishing a valid selection program.

A second conclusion is that task differences among jobs have very little effect on the magnitude of the validity coefficients of mental ability tests.[33] In other words, mental ability tests are valid predictors for a wide variety of jobs. The variable that moderates the relationship between mental ability and job performance is most likely the differing information-processing and problem-solving demands of the job, not task differences themselves.[34] That is, jobs that differ in these demands may differ in the validity of the mental ability test. Even in such cases, however, the mental ability test should be valid for all jobs; it just has "more predictability" for jobs with greater information-processing and problem-solving demands than for those jobs with less of these characteristics.

One explanation for this is that cognitive ability is highly correlated with job knowledge, and job knowledge is highly correlated with job performance. Moreover, cognitive ability is related to job performance itself, not just to job knowledge. Hunter writes:

> This may be because high ability workers are faster at cognitive operations on the job, are better able to prioritize between conflicting rules, are better able to adapt old procedures to altered situations, are better able to innovate to meet unexpected problems, and are better able to learn new procedures quickly as the job changes over time.[35]

A third conclusion is that a score obtained from a general mental ability test is as good a predictor of job performance as is a composite score obtained from a test with multiple scales of different abilities.[36] In support of this, Hunter analyzed data obtained from military validity studies. He grouped jobs into four categories: mechanical, electronic, skilled services, and clerical. Five tests were examined: general mental ability, and four separate composite tests tailored to each job group—mechanical composite, electrical composite, skilled service composite, and clerical composite. Results indicated very little difference between the magnitude of the validity coefficient of the general mental ability test and the appropriate composite test for each of the four job groups. In fact, the coefficient for the general mental ability test was higher than the validity for the composite in three of the four jobs.

Criticisms of Validity Generalization   As we have mentioned previously, validity generalization studies apply correction formulas to the results of previous validity studies to correct the measurement deficiencies of these studies. Conclusions regarding the validity of the predictor and the generalizability of this validity estimate across organizations are based on the results of these correction formulas. Ideally, these corrections should be made to each study in the validity generalization analyses using data supplied by that study. However, the validity studies usually do not report enough data to permit the corrections to be made in this manner. Instead, correction formulas use hypothetical values derived from other research work that are assumed to be appropriate for validity generalization analyses.

For the most part, criticisms of validity generalization studies have focused on the appropriateness of the correction formulas. Many of these critical studies have used computer simulation as the method for examining appropriateness. In doing this, samples of validity studies are generated from various populations. For example, the population could be of studies in which the difference in validity coefficients among studies is actually zero; all differences are actually due to measurement errors. In other cases, the validity studies used for analyses are drawn from two populations that, in fact, differ in terms of the magnitude of the validity coefficient. In this way, the researcher knows at the start of the study whether or not the validity coefficients are the same or different across situations (e.g., organizations). The correction formulas are then applied to the data generated by the simulation model. The researcher can then determine if the results of the correction formulas agree with what is already known about the validity coefficients being tested. If agreement exists, the formulas are thought to be appropriate; if disagreement exists, the formulas are thought to be in error.

As an overall summary, it has been a common finding of these simulation studies that, under many conditions, the validity generalization correction formulas overestimate the amount of variance attributable to study deficiencies. The result of overestimates may be the rejection of the concept that there are organizational differences which affect validity coefficients more often than would be appropriate. The authors of these simulation studies, therefore, have generally cautioned restraint in the interpretation of the results of validity generalization studies and careful consideration of the conclusions that have been drawn from them. It should be noted, however, that none of these authors has concluded that the essential concept of validity generalization analyses is flawed or that all the conclusions drawn from these studies are incorrect. We briefly summarize some of the points made in these critical studies. To obtain a more complete idea of the nature and extent of the criticism, it is necessary to read directly.

Recent studies have investigated the power of validity generalization analyses and/or the related concept of Type II error associated with these procedures. Power refers to the property of the statistical test to identify differences when they do exist. In the case of validity generalization, power refers to the rejection of generalizability and the determination of effects of organizational variables on the validity coefficients among the data. Type II error refers to the failure to determine situation specificity when it exists and, therefore, finding no differences among the validity coefficients under study.

Two variables that seemingly affect the power of validity generalization analysis are the number of coefficients that are used in the analysis and the size of the samples on which these coefficients are calculated. Paul Sackett, Michael Harris, and John Orr concluded that "true population differences of .1 will not be consistently detected regardless of [sample size and number of correlations], and differences of .2 will, not be consistently detected at small values [of these same two variables].[37]

Edward Kemery, Kevin Mossholder, and Lawrence Roth have found that this lack of power may be partially attributable to the tendency of the Schmidt-Hunter procedures to overestimate the variance among validity coefficients that is due to sampling error variance.[38] By overestimating this variance, an incorrectly high proportion of differences among studies would be explained by sample size differences. This becomes especially important in that, as we mentioned earlier, sample size differences are thought to he the single most important factor to correct, and several validity generalization studies have only corrected for this. Paul Paese and Fred Switzer examined the influence of reliability of predictor and criterion measures on calculations.[39] They found that the assumed hypothetical reliability distributions used in the correction formulas consistently overestimated the variance that was due to differences in reliability among the studies. They recommend altering the decision rule used by Schmidt and Hunter [reject situation specificity if 75 percent or more variance is accounted for] depending on the suspected differences in reliability of the measures. If differences are small, the rule should be more stringent and if differences are large, the rule should be relaxed.

Other studies have questioned whether the use of certain terms and the conclusions drawn from the statistical formulas of the Schmidt-Hunter procedures are appropriate. For example, Lawrence James and his associates have criticized a number of aspects of the Schmidt-Hunter procedures.[40] Included are that the lines of evidence arguing for validity generalization are not nearly as strong as stated by Schmidt and Hunter, that the procedures call for double corrections for some measurement deficiencies, and that the use of sample validity coefficients in several formulas as opposed to the Fischer z-transformations for these coefficients is inappropriate. They conclude that "the prudent scientist/practitioner should be circumspect in interpreting results of [validity generalization] studies, especially those that support an inference of cross-situational consistency."

In partial response to some of these criticisms, Larry Hedges developed an unbiased alternate correction for sampling error.[41] Central to this correction is the use of unbiased estimators of the population validity parameters that had been developed in previous research. Hedges demonstrated that while the correction formula for sampling error used in the Schmidt and Hunter technique is biased, the bias is usually quite small. Consequently, there is little reason to discount the results of existing validity generalization studies solely because of the bias in the correction of sampling error.

Obviously, much more research is necessary before the issues concerning assumptions and procedures of validity generalization studies can be clearly evaluated. Nonetheless, these studies have produced some of the most important statements regarding selection in recent years. The work promises to have far-reaching effects on both research and implementation of selection procedures.

Ability Tests and Discrimination

As we mentioned previously, the widespread use of ability tests that has characterized selection programs since the 1920s has diminished considerably since the early 1970s. Partially, this is the direct result of the court rulings in early EEO selection cases. Ability tests were specifically singled out and found to be discriminatory. In the preceding section, we pointed out that the extensive validity data that have accumulated about ability tests were analyzed to study their effectiveness in selection programs. Similarly, these data were used to study more fully the issue of discriminatory effects of ability tests in selection. In this section, we summarize this work.

Differential Validity

Differential Validity is a term that was used to describe the hypothesis that employment tests are less valid for minority group members than nonminority. The situation is one in which the validities for the same selection test in the two groups is statistically significant but unequal. For example, the test may be significantly more valid for whites than for blacks. In many ways, this term is related to the issue of test bias that has often been addressed regarding ability tests.

Most explanations of test bias include hypotheses of differential validity. The argument is generally that the actual content of ability tests (especially mental ability tests) is based on the content of white middle-class culture and, therefore, does not mean the same thing to other groups as it does to whites. Nonwhite middle-class respondents use different terms and symbols, and, in essence, this difference reduces the score achieved on the test. The test scores will not have the same meaning for whites and nonwhites nor will the pattern of validity coefficients with other measures, such as job performance, or school grades, be the same for the two groups. This different pattern of validity coefficients is what is meant by differential validity. Taken a step further, the presence of differential validity would imply that selection managers should develop separate selection programs for each applicant group for each job. This would be necessary to control the differences in terms and symbols of selection tests among the various cultures.

To examine the problem more closely, recent studies have analyzed data collected from several selection programs simultaneously. It has been a consistent conclusion of these studies that *differential validity does not exist.* Those few selection programs in which differential validity has been observed have been characterized by methodological limitations that seem to account for the observed differences. For example, one investigation examined 31 studies in which 583 validity coefficients were reported.[42] These studies were also scored on methodological characteristics such as sample size, use of criteria measures that were identified as being for research purposes only, and use of a predictor chosen for its theoretical relationship to the criterion measures. For the most part, differential validity was only observed in those studies with several methodological limitations. For the methodologically sound studies, no differences in validity coefficients between black and white groups were observed.

Another study used 781 pairs of validity coefficients. The pairs were made up of the correlation between the same predictor variable (commonly an ability test) and criterion variable for both a white and a black group of workers.[43] These correlations ranged from approximately –.37 to +.55. Exhibit 13.2 is part of this study and shows the result of graphing these pairs of validity coefficients. As you can see, the two curves, one composed of validity coefficients for black workers and one of corresponding validity coefficients for white workers, look

EXHIBIT 13.2 GRAPH OF 781 PAIRS OF VALIDITY
COEFFICIENTS

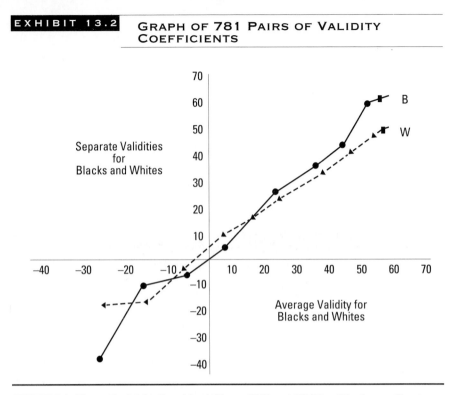

SOURCE: John Hunter, Frank Schmidt, and Ronda Hunter, "Differential Validity of Employment Tests by Race: A Comprehensive Review and Analysis," *Psychological Bulletin* 85 (1979): pp. 721–735. Copyright 1979 by the American Psychological Association. Reprinted by permission.

almost identical. This means that these tests acted in the same manner for both blacks and whites. The major conclusion of the study was that differential validity was not demonstrated and that tests that ordered whites successfully with respect to some given job criterion *also* ordered blacks with equal success.

Comparison of Ability Tests and Other Selection Instruments

Another way of studying the usefulness of ability tests in selection was undertaken by Richard Reilly and Michael Warech.[44] They grouped selection instruments into 18 types and examined the data for each type with regard to validity, adverse impact, feasibility (cost of development and use), and fairness to applicant. They also compared each of the 18 types of instruments with the use of cognitive ability tests in selection. While it is not possible to report their findings for all 18 types of instruments, Table 13.8 presents their major findings for 8 commonly used types.

Since we consider validity to be a fundamental property of selection tests, we present the comparisons of validity first. Only four of the eight types are approximately equal to cognitive ability tests: assessment centers, biographical data, trainability tests, and work samples. The other four types, academic performance, interview, personality inventories, and projective techniques, are generally less

TABLE 13.8 COMPARISON OF EIGHT SELECTION METHODS WITH COGNITIVE ABILITY TESTS

Selection Methods

	Academic Performance	Assessment Center	Biographical Data	Interview	Personality Inventories	Projective Techniques	Trainability	Work Sample
Validity	Less	Equal	Equal	Less	Less	Less	Equal	Equal
Adverse Impact	Equal	Less	Less	Less	Less	Less	Less	Less
Feasability	Less	Less	Equal	Equal/Less	Less	Less	Less	Less

SOURCE: Richard Reilly and Michael Warech, "The Validity and Fairness of Alternatives to Cognitive Tests," in Linda Wing, ed. *Employment Testing and Public Policy* (Boston, Kluwer, in press).

valid. Regarding differences between demographic groups in test scores, all types except academic performance have demonstrated less adverse impact than have cognitive ability tests.

Regarding feasibility of use, large differences are demonstrated between cognitive ability tests and other types. Usually these differences are clearly in favor of cognitive ability tests. Of the four types that have approximately equal validity and less adverse impact, only biographical data is as inexpensive and easy to administer and score as cognitive ability tests. Even so, the development of biodata requires a large-scale empirical study and may need periodic rekeying to avoid deterioration in validity. Assessment centers are among the most expensive of selection devices because they require extensive training for assessors, special physical facilities, and excessive time from assessors and participants. Work samples are only appropriate for experienced applicants. Trainability tests are expensive to administer because if necessary skills for test performance are lacking they allow time for the applicant to learn these. Valid interviews usually require extensive training. Personality inventories and projective techniques can also be expensive to administer and require a trained psychologist to interpret the applicant's responses.

The findings regarding fairness to the applicant of each type of test is very difficult to summarize briefly. Reilly and Warech's discussion addressed three dimensions. The first was false rejection rates for which trainability tests, work samples, biodata, and assessment centers were all judged to have rates equal to or less than cognitive ability tests. The second dimension was perceived relevance by the applicant of test material to the job. Work samples, trainability tests, and assessment centers were all thought to be superior. On the third dimension, potential for improvement of employability for the rejected applicant, trainability tests and work samples allow for improvement through job-related training. Cognitive ability and biodata permit no such improvement.

Based on Reilly and Warech's report, we conclude that cognitive ability tests are very viable selection instruments because of their high validity and low cost. However, biodata, trainability, work samples, and assessment centers all demonstrate almost equal validity, less adverse impact, and more fairness to the applicant. However, each has major deficiencies in terms of cost and ease of development and implementation. For many small-and medium-sized companies, these last two issues are frequently of critical importance.

Conclusions

How should we interpret the findings of these various studies in light of the specific statements of discriminatory effect in the EEO court decisions? One thing to remember is that the court decisions and the studies summarized here have two different bases of analysis. The court decisions have focused on selection programs in one specific organization. The studies summarized in this section have tried to accumulate data across many organizations. Even though ability tests have been demonstrably valid in many situations, this does not mean that ability tests will be valid no matter how they are used in all organizations. As a general rule, the organizations that were found guilty of discrimination in the use of ability tests in selection had taken only superficial steps in the development of their selection programs. More complete development procedures might have yielded different results.

Second, the analyses reviewed in this section were completed after many of the court decisions regarding the discriminatory use of ability tests were handed down. It is fair to assume that both plaintiffs and defendants were using the traditional viewpoint of the necessity of demonstrating validity for a selection device for the job in the organization under question. As we have said previously, the results of recent validity generalization studies could radically change this perspective. Not only would the concept of validity generalization shift the chief concern to an accumulation of validity results, but it argues that studies within a single organization may not be interpretable. This would especially be true if the study was limited by small sample size, restriction of range, or some of the other statistical artifacts that were mentioned. Aspects of validity generalization were an issue in one court case and were supported.[45]

The general conclusion for us is that ability tests have proved to be valid selection devices for a number years in a number of different jobs. A close look at the validity of these tests indicates that when properly used, differences between nonminority an minority groups are minimized when the relationship of scores to job criteria measures is taken into account. Moreover, few alternative selection methods can match ability tests in terms of overall validity, lack of adverse impact, and feasibility of use. Thus the markedly diminished use of these tests in the 1970s and early 1980s seems to be unfounded.

On Using Ability Tests in Selection

In this chapter we have presented brief descriptions of a few tests that are representative of ability tests. These tests were included because of their extensive use in selection over several years. However, be aware that there are a large number of other ability tests that are available to HR specialists that have not been described in this chapter. For example, the 1992 volume of *The Eleventh Mental Measurements Yearbook* contains descriptive information about 477 tests as well as 703 test reviews.[46]

The sheer number of these tests creates a difficult situation for HR specialists. What is needed is a way to evaluate an ability test to assess its potential usefulness. Obviously the best method of doing this would be to become very familiar with the principles of psychological test construction and measurement. We have already presented some, but not nearly all, of these principles in Chapters 3 through 5, which were devoted to the role of measurement in selection. We now apply these concepts to the problem of assessing the potential usefulness of available ability tests.

Review Reliability Data

Our primary assumption is that a useful ability test should have development information available to users. One part of such information should be work done to estimate the reliability of the test. As we discussed previously, reliability is a necessary characteristic of a selection test. High reliability is an indication that the test can be expected to yield consistent scores for applicants and uncontrolled factors which might affect the score of applicants are minimized. Therefore, information about the method of estimating reliability, the size of the sample used to collect these data, and the magnitude of the reliability estimate should all be fully presented to users.

As we know, each of the four major ways of estimating reliability is appropriate for specific circumstances and inappropriate for others. For example, test-retest reliability calculated with a very short intervening period of time, such as a few hours or even a few days, may be an inflated estimate because of the effect of memory factors. So it is necessary for the test user to determine if the appropriate method of estimating reliability was employed and if this method was carried out correctly. It is generally thought that the use of larger samples (200+) yields better estimates of reliability than do smaller samples. Occasionally samples of 30 to 50 respondents have been used in reliability studies. We discussed the limitations of small sample correlation estimates when we discussed validity generalization. Essentially the same limitations exist when reliability is calculated.

It is also desirable for the sample to be similar to the individuals for whom the HR specialist intends to use the test. Perhaps the most common way of judging similarity is on the basis of demographic characteristics such as ethnicity, gender, average age, average education level, and occupational background. One can argue that these are not the most accurate indicants of similarity because similarity between two groups actually means that the test is interpreted and answered in the same fashion by the two groups. However, collecting such data would require work far beyond that normally done in test development. Information about demographic characteristics allows the user to at least note major differences and form hypotheses about the meaning of such differences. For example, if the reliability of a test of English grammar and writing has been estimated using a sample of college students and the applicant pool in the selection situation is mainly high school students, the reliability may not be the same for the two groups. If the test is of moderate difficulty for the college students, it may be very difficult for individuals with less formal training in reading and writing tasks. Difficult tests often have low reliability because respondents frequently guess in making their responses and such guesses are really sources of error of measurement. Therefore, the stated reliability of the test may not be accurate for the applicant pool. The same argument can be applied to many craft or mechanical ability tests that have used experienced workers rather than inexperienced ones in reliability estimates.

We have indicated that a minimum reliability estimate of .85 is commonly thought to be necessary for selection use. This is because selection involves making a decision for each applicant about whether to extend a job offer or not. This decision is based on the scores of the selection tests used. If the test is not highly reliable, the large standard error of measurement accompanying a test score would make choosing among applicants very uncertain. For example, using the standard error of measurement information contained in Chapter 4, we would estimate that the range of true scores for a test with an estimated reliability of .60

and a standard deviation of 15 is ± 9.5 points with a 68 percent confidence level. If an applicant scores an 80 on this test, the true score realistically could be anywhere between 70 and 90. With such a large range, identifying meaningful differences among applicants is very difficult. However, if the same test has a reliability of .90, then the standard error becomes ± 4.7 points with the same confidence level. The range of probable true scores becomes much smaller, and the test results are more precise and easier for the selection specialist to use.

Review Validity Data

The second major kind of information that should be made available to test users is validity data accumulated during test development and use. Two kinds of validity data are desirable. One kind is data that aid in determining that the ability test measures what it is said to measure. Frequently this kind of information is reported in terms of statistical analyses of the scores. Two of the most common types of analyses are (a) correlational analyses of the scores of the test with other psychological measures and (b) factor analyses of the items of the test or of the test with other tests. We mentioned examples of such correlational analyses when we discussed mental ability tests. To know that scores on mental ability tests are correlated with various measures of educational achievement greatly improves our understanding of what these tests measure. In some cases correlations with other tests are conducted. For example, we noted that the *Bennett Mechanical Comprehension Test* was correlated with verbal ability and spatial visualization tests. This indicates that the test measures more than mechanical concepts.

Factor analysis is a technique for analyzing the interrelationships among several tests or a set of test items. For example, if 20 test items have been given to 400 individuals, the first step is to correlate each item with every other item. Further statistical manipulations attempt to identify small groups of items that are highly correlated with one another and minimally correlated with other groups of items. Each group of items is called a *factor* and is named by the common psychological characteristic measured. For example, on this 20 item test, one group of ten basic arithmetic problems might be identified as being one factor and ten vocabulary questions might be indentified as a second factor. This test can then be said to measure arithmetic ability and vocabulary. The ability that is measured is identified from the common content of the items that make up the factor. The importance of this type of information is that the HR specialist can examine the correspondence between the factors that are identified and the abilities that are to be tested in the selection program. It is necessary that the test, in fact, match the abilities identified from the job analysis.

The second type of validity information that can be provided is the correlation of the test scores with some measure of training or job proficiency. This is the classic test validity to which we have frequently referred. Demonstration of validity for jobs similar to the one of interest to the test specialist is, obviously, the most desirable data.

Our opinion is that this information about reliability and validity of the ability test, at minimum, must be available to the user. Other test construction data, such as norm group scores, difficulty levels of items, and whether the test measures one or multiple topics, can also be useful. However, such data are usually of secondary importance compared to basic reliability and validity information. If reliability and validity data are not provided or are inappropriately calculated, the HR specialist should be wary of using the ability test. It is not a difficult task physically to construct a purported ability test. Most intelligent individuals, with a few friends and a long weekend, could write 50 multiple-choice test items that were intended to measure any of several abilities, for example, mathematics, English, logical reasoning, or given enough reference books, some technical areas like computer programming, football analysis, and carpentry. The trick is to make sure that the test is what it is intended to be. The only way that a HR specialist who is considering using an ability test can tell this is by examining the reliability and validity information. *No amount of verbal assurance provided by the test seller can substitute for such information.* After all, the test seller has a vested interest in describing the test in favorable terms.

Our last comment on the use of ability tests is on a theme that has conspicuously run throughout the chapter. Well-developed ability tests have *consistently demonstrated their usefulness in selection.* Generally, ability tests are efficient and fairly inexpensive selection devices. The secret to using them successfully is to match the test to the ability you want to measure. Frequently an ability test is the only feasible way of measuring the characteristics of applicants. Recent trends in avoiding the use of ability tests and relying excessively on other selection devices, especially interviews, may not be wise. As we have discussed, there is a growing body of studies supporting both the validity and the minimization of adverse impact with the use of ability tests. Also, if the trends in the early work in validity generalization continue, the use of ability tests for selection for many jobs will be greatly simplified. These trends would allow for a relatively easy improvement in selection programs.

References

[1] Par Lahy, "La selection psycho-physiologique des machinistes de la société des transports en commun do la région parisienne," *L'Année Pschologique* 25 (1924): 106–172.
[2] Philip DuBois, *A History of Psychological Testing* (Boston: Allyn & Bacon, 1970).
[3] Anne Anastasi, *Psychological Testing*, 5th ed. (London: Macmillan, 1982), p. 393.
[4] Lewis Aiken, *Psychological Testing and Assessment*, 2d ed. (Boston: Allyn & Bacon, 1988), p.107.
[5] Ibid., pp. 108–109.
[6] Anastasi, *Psychological Testing*, p. 387.
[7] Donald E. Super and John O. Crites, *Appraising Vocational Fitness*, rev. ed. (New York: Harper & Row, 1962), pp. 87–88.
[8] Robert Guion, *Personnel Testing* (New York: McGraw-Hill, 1965), p. 234.
[9] Ibid., pp. 221.
[10] John Foley, "Review of the Wonderlic Personnel Test," *The Seventh Mental Measurements Yearbook*, ed. Oscar K. Boros (Highland Park, N.J.: Gryphon Press, 1972), pp. 401–403.
[11] Ibid., p. 402.
[12] Donald E. Super and John O. Crites, *Appraising Vocational Fitness*, P. 219.
[13] Ibid., pp. 220–221.

[14] Ibid., p. 262.

[15] Ibid., p. 261; John Kinzer, "Review of MacQuarrie Test for Mechanical Ability," *The Third Mental Measurements Yearbook*, ed. Oscar K. Buros (New Brunswick, N. J.: Rutgers University Press, 1949), p. 661.

[16] R. B. Selover, "Review of the Minnesota Clerical Test," *The Third Mental Measurements Yearbook*, ed. Oscar K. Buros (New Brunswick, N. J.: Rutgers University Press, 1949), pp. 635–636.

[17] Michael A. Campion, "Personnel Selection for Physically Demanding Jobs: Review and Recommendations," *Personnel Psychology* 36 (1983): 527–550.

[18] Joyce Hogan, "Physical Abilities," in Marvin D. Dunnette and Leaetta M. Hough, eds., *Handbook of Industrial & Psychology*, 2d ed., Vol. 2 (Palo Alto, Calif.: Consulting Psychologists Press, 1991).

[19] Edwin A. Fleishman & Michael D. Mumford, "Ability Requirement Scales" in *Job Analysis Handbook for Business, Industry, and Government*, Vol 2, ed. Sidney Gael (New York: Wiley, 1988).

[20] Edwin A. Fleishman, *Physical Abilities Analysis Manual*, rev. ed. (Palo Alto, Calif.: Consulting Psychologists Press, 1992).

[21] Fleishman and Mumford, "Ability Requirement Scales."

[22] Joyce Hogan, "Structure of Physical Performance in Occupational Tasks," *Journal of Applied Psychology* 76 (1991): 495–507.

[23] Ibid.

[24] *Weeks v. Southern Bell Telephone & Telegraph Co.*, 408 F.2d 228, 1 Empl. Prac. Dec. (CCH) 9970 (5th Cir. 1969).

[25] Hogan, "Physical Abilities."

[26] *E. E. Black, Ltd. v. Marshall*, 24 Empl. Prac. Dec. (CCH) 31260 (D. Haw. 1980).

[27] John Campbell, "An Overview of the Army Selection and Classification Project (Project A)," *Personnel Psychology* 43 (1990): 243–257.

[28] Jeffrey J. McHenry, Laetta M. Hough, Jody L. Toquam, Mary Ann Hanson, and Steven Ashworth, "Project A Validity Results: The Relationship between Predictor and Criterion Domains," *Personnel Psychology* 43 (1990): 335–354.

[29] Frank L. Schmidt, Ilene Gast-Rosenberg, and John E. Hunter, "Validity Generalization Results for Computer Programmers," *Journal of Applied Psychology* 65 (1980): 643–661.

[30] Frank L. Schmidt and John E. Hunter, "The Future of Criterion-Related Validity," *Personnel Psychology* 33 (1980): 41–60.

[31] John E. Hunter, "Cognitive Ability, Cognitive Attitudes, Job Knowledge, and Job Performance," *Journal of Vocational Behavior* 29 (1986): 340–362.

[32] Frank L. Schmidt and John E. Hunter, "The Future of Criterion-Related Validity."

[33] Frank L. Schmidt, John E. Hunter, and Kenneth Pearlman, "Task Differences as Moderators of Aptitude Test Validity in Selection: A Red Herring," *Journal of Applied Psychology* 66 (1981): 166–185.

[34] Ibid.

[35] John E. Hunter, "Cognitive Ability, Cognitive Attitudes, Job Knowledge, and Job Performance," P. 354.

[36] Ibid.

[37] Paul R. Sackett, Michael M. Harris, and John M. Orr, "On Seeking Moderator Variables in the Meta-Analysis of Correlational Data: A Monte Carlo Investigation of Statistical Power and Resistance to Type 1 Error," *Journal of Applied Psychology* 71 (1986): 302–310.

[38] Edward R. Kemery, Kevin W. Mossholder, and Lawrence Roth, "The Power of the Schmidt and Hunter Additive Model of Validity Generalization," *Journal of Applied Psychology* 72 (1987): 30–37.

[39] Paul W. Paese and Fred S. Switzer III, "Validity Generalization and Hypothetical Reliability Distributions: A Test of the Schmidt-Hunter Procedure," *Journal of Applied Psychology* 73 (1988): 267–274.

[40] Lawrence R. James, Robert G. Demaree, Stanley A. Mulaik, and Michael D. Mumford, "Validity Generalization: Rejoinder to Scmidt, Hunter, and Raju (1988)," *Journal of Applied Psychology* 73 (1988): 673–678.

[41] Larry Hedges, "An Unbiased Correction for Sampling Error in Validity Generalization Studies," *Journal of Applied Psychology* 74 (1989): 469–477.

[42] Virginia Boehm, "Different Validity: A Methodological Artifact:" *Journal of Applied Psychology* 62 (1977): 146–154.

[43] John Hunter, Frank Schmidt, and Ronda Hunter, "Differential Validity of Employment Tests by Race: A Comprehensive Review and Analysis," *Psychological Bulletin* 85 (1979): 721–735.

[44] Richard R. Reilly and Michael A Warech, "The Validity and Fairness of Alternatives to Cognitive Tests" in Linda Wing, ed. *Employment Testing and Public Policy.* (Boston: Kluwer, in press).

[45] *Pegues v. Mississippi State Employment Service* (N. D. Miss.) 22 FEP Case 392, 488 F. Supp. 239.

[46] Jack J. Kramer and Jane Close Conoley, eds. *The Eleventh Mental Measurement Yearbook*. (Lincoln, Neb: The University of Nebraska Press, 1992).

14

Personality Assessment

Now that you are well on your way to becoming an expert in selection (which must be true because there are only four chapters left, and we know what kind of student you are), you will be fascinated to learn about the use of personality measures in selection, one of the most complex and rapidly changing topics in the field. The use of personality data in making selection decisions has been marked by widely different opinions between researchers and practitioners. The former have usually disdained their use in making selection decisions because of the lack of consistent empirical support for such use. The latter have often used such data anyway, gathered in a variety of methods that, at times make researchers shudder.

Recently, however, many selection researchers have found that personality data, when gathered appropriately, can be valid information for selection decisions.[1] In this chapter we summarize the major issues in the use of personality data along with the relevant research. We conclude that personality data can make an independent contribution to selection decisions. Moreover, there is no evidence that only people with so-called great personalities succeed. That gives both of us authors hope. If you knew us, you would understand why.

Definition and Use of Personality in Selection

In popular usage, personality is often equated with social skill. It is thought of as the ability to elicit positive reactions from others in one's typical dealings with them. Psychologists who study personality professionally have a slightly different concept. Although there is not one standard definition of the term *personality*, most formal definitions agree that personality refers to the unique organization of characteristics which define an individual and determine that person's pattern of interaction with the environment.[2] The term *characteristics* is usually interpreted to include thoughts, feelings, and behaviors that are combined distinctly in each individual. The environment includes both human and nonhuman (organizations, governments, physical property, etc.) elements. We can see, then, that personality involves much more than social skill; in fact, many believe that no other area of psychology encompasses as broad a topic as personality.[3]

Arguments For and Against Use in Selection

Personality would seem, therefore, to be critically important to selection. If we were to review job analysis information, especially for jobs above entry-level positions, we would find many occasions when the personality characteristics of the worker seem to be essential for job performance. For example, many jobs require the incumbent to interact with others. Some, such as receptionist, salesperson, and customer service representative, emphasize interaction with people. Other jobs—air traffic controller, law enforcement officer, high school principal—require individuals to cope with the stress of hazardous conditions and demands from parties with conflicting interests. In addition to these observations, there are studies that attempt to identify distinct personality characteristics for various jobs. One such study found consistent patterns of agreement among 132 professional employment interviewers on the degree to which 20 personality characteristics were descriptive of a typical person in each of 15 occupations, including carpenter, orchestral librarian, and purchasing agent.[4] Two researchers, Glenn Grimsley and Hilton Jarrett, have concluded there are testable personality differences between more and less successful managers. These differences are in the characteristics of *drive, energy, social adjustment, self-confidence, social aggressiveness,* and *emotional stability.*[5] Similarly, a longitudinal study of managers at AT&T found personality differences between those managers who had been promoted to middle management positions and those who remained at lower managerial levels during an eight-year period. Among these differences were that the more successful had become more work-oriented whereas the less successful became more involved in their families and in their religious, recreational, and social activities.[6]

Given these findings, we should expect to find evidence that personality data are valid for selection. However, this has not often proved to be the case. In the mid-1960s, several individuals reviewed the use of personality data in selection. The following comments by Robert Guion and Richard Gottier are typical of the conclusions of this work:

> It cannot be said that any of the conventional personality measures have demonstrated really general usefulness as selection tools in employment practice. . . . The number of tests resulting in acceptable statements of validity is greater than might be expected by pure chance—but not much. The best that can be said is that in *some* situations, for *some* purposes, *some* personality measures can offer helpful predictions.[7]

One of their observations noted a tendency for tailored personality measures that were carefully and competently developed for a specific situation to be more successful for prediction than a standard existing personality measure with a standard system of scoring.

Some recent studies generally agree with these earlier conclusions. For example, one meta-analysis calculated the average validity coefficient for eight types of predictors reported in selection studies from 1962 to 1984. Of these eight, the average for personality measures, .15, was the lowest.[8]

But other work has offered evidence supporting the use of personality data in selection decisions. We borrow from Robert Hogan's writing, who has summarized this evidence.[9] First, there is growing agreement among researchers that personality characteristics can be grouped into five broad dimensions, referred to as the *Big Five*. This agreement allows for consistency among research efforts and a direct way of synthesizing results. It also calls attention to general personality characteristics which, we argue later, are more strongly related to job performance than more narrow, specific dimensions. Second, studies that are methodologically sound often yield significant uncorrected validity coefficients of .30 and higher. Third, personality data are usually uncorrelated with cognitive ability and, therefore, have been found to increase the prediction of job performance above that predicted by cognitive ability tests alone. [10]

We discuss each of these points in more detail. As a start we present background information addressed in personality theory.

Personality Traits

The use of personality data in selection requires the labeling, classifying, and measuring of individuals according to some set of personality characteristics. Over the years, there have been numerous approaches to these tasks using such individual characteristics as body size, handwriting, and shape of head as a basis. At present the scientific study of personality generally uses the concept of trait as the key feature of personality assessment. A *trait* is a continuous dimension on which individual differences may be arranged quantitatively in terms of the amount of the characteristic the individual exhibits.[11] *Sociability, independence,* and *need for achievement* are all examples of traits. Individuals show large differences in the degree to which they demonstrate such traits.

The concept of traits begins with the common observation that individuals may differ sharply in their reactions to the same situation. For example, one individual enjoys the routine of an assembly line job while another is quite unhappy about the same task features. Similarly, one person is very verbal and argumentative in a committee meeting while another is reticent. The concept of trait is used to explain these different reactions to the same situation. In these cases, individuals are thought to have different amounts of traits that could be referred to as *need for structure* and *social aggressiveness*, respectively. Traits are used to explain the consistency of one individual's behavior over a variety of situations. It has been observed that an individual who is socially aggressive in a committee meeting frequently acts similarly in other group interaction situations. From this brief description, we can understand that some psychologists and many nonpsychologists frequently regard traits as the cause of a person's reactions to situations.[12] The essence of traits has been conceptualized in many ways, for example, as biophysical (Gordon Allport) and as mental structure (Raymond B. Cattell). There is no general agreement on this issue.

Identifying Traits The use of personality data in selection requires first the specification of job tasks and second the identification of traits that are linked to these tasks. Table 14.1, which is derived from several studies, provides some examples of personality traits that have been used in selection based on these steps. In previous chapters, we discussed the difficulties associated with the specification of employee KSAs in general. The first problem with specifying employee personality traits in particular is determining which personality traits to use. In reviewing the traits in Table 14.1, note that they differ in their exactness of statement and their common usage in the English language. Partially, this is because the different studies used in the table rely on different lists of trait names.

In the English language, there are over 18,000 trait terms or names.[13] Personality psychologists have tried to reduce this to a manageable number in a variety of ways. One method has been to follow a particular personality theory. For example, David McClelland has specified that *needs for achievement, power*, and *affiliation* are essential traits for job performance, especially for managers.[14] Another method has been to use statistical analyses to determine a small number of traits. Raymond B. Cattell used correlational analyses to identify 16 traits that have been used in selection.[15]

Core versus Surface Traits   The second problem in using traits for selection is very much related to this issue of overabundance of traits: the question of which traits are related to many aspects of behavior and which are related to only a few. The significance here is that it would be more efficient to make selection decisions using those traits that are important for multiple work performance behaviors. Personality psychologists have addressed this issue also. For example, Gordon Allport makes a distinction among *cardinal, central*, and *secondary* traits.[16] *Cardinal* traits are the most generalized and seem to organize a person's whole life. Less pervasive but still quite generalized are *central* traits. Allport thought that many people are broadly influenced by central traits. Finally, more specific, narrow traits are called *secondary* traits or "attitudes." These are thought to have very limited effect on behavior. In general, trait psychologists agree that there are differences in the degree to which traits are related to different behaviors. It would seem logical to assume, therefore, that not all traits would be of equal value in selection decisions. Differences in central or basic traits would seem to be more generally related to work performance differences. Differences in surface or limited traits would seem to have less generalizability to work behaviors.

It is in this regard that the recent work in the Big Five, which we referred to previously, is important. Generally, personality psychologists now agree there are five general factors of personality that can serve as a meaningful taxonomy for describing traits. In other words, these five factors can be thought of as the five central or core traits that influence behavior.[17]

Typically, the research that has led to the development of the Big Five has involved collecting vast amounts of data. For example, a large sample of subjects may complete several personality questionnaires, each of which is designed to measure multiple personality traits. Statistical analyses, such as factor analyses, are then used to determine if all of these measured personality traits can be reduced to a smaller number. Such analyses have consistently identified five traits, each of which is comprised of several related traits measured by the various personality questionnaires. The same five traits have been identified using

| TABLE 14.1 | PERSONALITY TRAITS FOR A SAMPLE OF JOBS STUDIED IN SELECTION |

Job	Personality Trait
Executive	Cooperativeness
Foreman	Succor, nurturance, endurance
Engineer	Tolerance, social presence, intellectual efficiency
Sales Person	Order, dominance, friendliness, thoughtfulness
Secretary	General activity, emotional stability
Electronic technician	Aggression, deference, order
Computer programmer	Original thinking
Insurance agent	Original thinking, personal relations
Newspaper writer	Ascendancy

different instruments, in different cultures, and using data obtained from different sources.[18]

We describe each of these five traits and how they are measured in some detail when we discuss personality instruments in a later section.

Interaction of Personality Traits and Situations

As we have described, an underlying assumption regarding traits is that they are stable characteristics related to an individual's actions in various situations. However, when psychologists began to study this assumption more closely, they soon realized that individuals tended to show variability in their behavior even across seemingly similar conditions. To be sure, behavior is not random; but the consistency was less than many trait psychologists believed. Some of the studies of the consistency of trait behavior across different situations is represented by the early work of Hugh Hartshorne and Mark May. Investigating the honesty and deception of children in varied conditions, these researchers concluded that children's behavior was less a function of any internalized predisposition to be honest (trait) and more a function of the particular situation.[19]

Powerful and Weak Situations   Psychologists have turned their attention to the interaction of traits and situations. The reasoning is that neither can be offered as the major determiner of behavior in all cases; rather they interact with each other, exerting a different influence on behavior depending on the circumstances.[20] Following this reasoning, one line of work has labeled situations as either powerful or weak. Situations are *powerful to the degree that they lead individuals to interpret particular events in the same way, create uniform expectancies regarding the most appropriate behavior, provide adequate incentives for the performance of that behavior, and require skills that everyone possesses roughly to the same extent.* Peter Herriot has discussed the selection interview in this fashion noting that roles of both the interviewer and interviewee are frequently well known and individuals often behave very similarly in these situations.[21] *A weak situation is one with opposite characteristics: it is not uniformly interpreted, does not generate uniform expectations concerning desired behavior, does not offer sufficient incentives for one type of behavior, and is one in which a variety of skills may produce acceptable behavior.* Some sales situations could be classified as weak because of the differences in the expectations and knowledge of customers and differences in the characteristics of products or services.

The general conclusion is that in powerful situations individual behavior is more attributable to the known situational roles that to individual traits. In our example, knowing that the interview is for an entry-level managerial position in a large financial institution may better explain an interviewee's behavior than inferences about his or her responsibility, levelheadedness, or other traits. Herriot points out that the many of the differences in the behavior of interviewees can be explained in terms of inconsistency in perceptions of the proper role rather than trait differences. In weak situations, on the other hand, traits would seem to be important explanations of behavior. In these situations if individuals are uncertain about appropriate behavior, the individual is assumed to interpret the situation and act in accordance with his or her own personality traits. In our sales example, there are noticeable behavioral differences among sales personnel in friendliness, aggressiveness, and persistence, and these differences could be thought of as related to different levels of these traits.

Situation Type and Selection   These concepts have major implications for the use of personality in selection. For a job in a powerful work situation, personality may not be an important dimension for selection purposes. For example, one study found that the validities of two of the Big Five personality dimensions were significantly higher for those managers in jobs high in autonomy compared with those jobs low in autonomy.[22] Perhaps concentration on identifying the abilities necessary to perform the job may be more advantageous in powerful work situations. Second, personality data drawn from powerful testing situations would not seem to yield accurate personality information about the applicant. We have mentioned the interview as an example. Very often these interviews are short, highly structured interactions about which the interviewees have been well coached from classes, articles, and friends. Accordingly, applicant behavior could be more a function of the applicant learning what behavior and responses are appropriate in these sessions than a function of his or her personality traits. We hypothesize, therefore, that personality characteristics are more important for weak situation selection devices and job assignments than for powerful ones.

One way that has been used to identify situations as powerful or weak has been to ask a number of individuals to rate the appropriateness of a variety of behaviors for a specific situation.[23] If one or a very small number of behaviors are rated as appropriate, this would constitute a powerful situation. The rating of many behaviors as appropriate would indicate a weak situation. Such a strategy could presumably be used in organizational situations to identify powerful and weak job performance situations. Related work has attempted to characterize the appropriate personality traits for a situation.[24] In one method, children were exposed to a controlled situation in which each had a chance to delay taking an immediate, smaller reward in order to obtain a preferred reward later. The researchers measured how long each child waited and also asked parents to judge their child on various personality traits. These judgments were used to make a personality profile of the traits of the ideally performing child in this situation. Again, such a methodology would seem feasible in organizations by obtaining personality judgments of superiors and/or coworkers of the more successful workers in a specific job.

Conclusions We have introduced much information from the field of personality psychology and have drawn implications from this work to the use of personality in organizations. We have done this because it is obvious that simply administering personality instruments to applicants and attempting to relate the scores on these to job performance is not a worthwhile strategy. Instead, the appropriate use of personality data calls for an understanding of important findings in personality research. First is the observation that traits vary greatly in the extent to which they influence behavior. A seemingly small number of core traits have strong influence on behavior. A larger number of traits have limited or superficial influence. The other major observation is that the circumstances of some situations apparently have a greater influence on individual behavior than do traits. These two observations offer a partial explanation for the lack of positive findings in the use of personality data for selection and also some implications for improvement.

Personality Measurement Methods

We stated in Chapters 1 and 3 that accurate measurement of many human characteristics important for selection is a difficult task because we are trying to quantify intangible constructs through the use of inferred data. This is especially true in the measurement of personality. To fully understand the use of personality in selection, it is necessary to understand the nature and characteristics of these measurement methods. The three most commonly used methods in selection are inventories, judgment of interviewers, and behavioral observation. We discuss each of these separately.

Inventories in Personality Measurement

Inventories use the written responses of an individual as the information to determine personality. There are literally hundreds of such measures, all differing substantially in their characteristics. Many can be found in the test sources that we mentioned in Chapter 3, for example the Buros Institute's *Mental Measurements Yearbook*. Some of these are designed to measure abnormal personality traits while others measure normal traits; some devices measure several personality dimensions while others measure only one. It would obviously be impossible to discuss each one of these devices. Instead, we discuss only two major types of inventories to illustrate their principle characteristics: self-report questionnaires and projective techniques.

Self-Report Questionnaires   These instruments consist of a series of usually brief questions asking the respondent to use a multiple-choice answer format to indicate personal information about thoughts, emotions, and past experiences. Typical questions are "I am happy" or "I enjoy going to small parties" or "I think good things happen to those that work hard." The respondent is frequently given only three response categories: agree, undecided, or disagree. These questionnaires assume that a correspondence exists between what a person says about himself or herself and what is actually true. Moreover, the assumption is also made that the individual is aware of his or her thoughts and emotions and is willing to openly share them.

The Big Five   We mentioned the Big Five earlier. Actually there are several different measuring devices of the five central personality dimensions. We discuss the one developed by Murray Barrick and Michael Mount because it has been used in several selection studies.

The instrument has 200 multiple-choice items derived from empirical research using several self-report inventories. Each of the questions has three possible responses: "agree," "?," and "disagree." Typically it takes 45 minutes to complete the instrument. The five personality dimensions that are measured together with examples of typical questions (not actual questions) are presented in Table 14.2. Each of the Big Five can best be understood in terms of more specific related traits that characterize the broad trait.[25] Think of each of these traits as bipolar: Opposite extreme scores on each dimension represent opposite behaviors of the trait measured.

The first dimension is *Extraversion*. Traits frequently associated together to form this dimension include (from the positive pole) being sociable, gregarious, assertive, talkative, and active. Some personality specialists have interpreted this dimension to represent two basic components: ambition and sociability.[26] The second dimension is called *Emotional Stability*. Traits usually associated with it (from the negative pole) are being emotional, tense, insecure, nervous, excitable, apprehensive, and easily upset. The third dimension is usually interpreted as *Agreeableness* and is made up (positive pole) of being courteous, flexible, trusting, good-natured, cooperative, forgiving, softhearted, and tolerant. The fourth dimension is labeled *Conscientiousness*, which is characterized (positive pole) by being responsible, organized, dependable, planful, willing to achieve, and persevering. The fifth dimension is labeled *Openness to Experience*, although it also has been referred to as *Intellect* or *Culture*.[27] This dimension includes (positive pole) being imaginative, cultured, curious, intelligent, artistically sensitive, original, and broad-minded.

Barrick and Mount conducted an important meta-analytic study to test the validity of the Big Five in selection.[28] They used 117 validity studies across five occupational groups and three different criteria. Upon reviewing these studies, they estimated the mean reliability of the predictor scales to be .76. Results of the validity analyses indicated the following:

1. The *Conscientiousness* dimension was a valid predictor for all occupational groups (corrected *r* range was .20 to .23).

TABLE 14.2	SCALES AND REPRESENTATIVE ITEMS OF BIG FIVE PERSONALITY DIMENSIONS*

Personality Scale	*Typical Question*
Extraversion	I tend not to say what I think about things
Agreeableness	I tend to be trusting of others
Conscientiousness	I approach most of my work steadily and persistently
Emotional Stability	Whenever I'm by myself, I feel vulnerable
Openness to Experience	I enjoy eating in new restaurants I know nothing about

* Based on the Revised Personality Characteristics Inventory by Murray P. Barrick and Michael K. Mount.

2. *Extraversion and Emotional Stability* were valid predictors for some, but not all, of the occupations.

3. *Agreeableness and Openness to Experience* showed minimal validity, although several analyses were performed with a small number of studies.

4. *Conscientiousness* was a valid predictor across all three types of criteria. The four other personality dimensions were related to only some of the criteria.

The two authors indicate that some methodological features of the study probably resulted in an underestimate of the validities of the Big Five dimensions. Even so, the consistent significance of *conscientiousness* and the differential validity of other dimensions is important evidence of the usefulness of personality data in selection decisions. We conclude that unlike evidence for cognitive ability tests, which we discussed in Chapter 13, the same personality dimensions are not related to performance in jobs. Rather, specific personality dimensions appear to be related to specific jobs and criteria. This conclusion follows from our previous discussion of the interaction of traits and situations.

Another study grouped scales on two personality inventories, frequently used for selection for police jobs, into measures of the Big Five dimensions.[29] Correlations among these scales and six measures of performance indicated differential validity among scales and criteria with *Conscientiousness* being more consistently correlated with the measures of performance than the other dimensions. However, the scales did not provide additional predictability above that given by a cognitive ability test.

Two other studies have provided some evidence that personality data may add validity above that associated with cognitive ability, although neither study used the complete dimensions of the Big Five. One study found that *Work Orientation, Ascendancy*, and *Interpersonal Orientation*, related to the Big Five, did explain variance in the job performance over that explained by a cognitive measure.[30] A second study found that the personality dimension *Need for Achievement*, which is typically classified as part of the dimension *Conscientiousness*, interacted with cognitive ability to significantly increase the predictability of job performance. [31] *Need for achievement* alone, however, was not significantly related to performance. The authors concluded that further research should examine the interaction of cognitive ability and personality data on performance. The former may indicate ability to perform and the latter the motivation to perform. Together the two constructs may account for a more complete explanation of performance.

California Psychological Inventory   Another inventory used in selection is the *California Psychological Inventory (CPI)*.[32] The CPI has 480 items that require answers of "true" or "false." Typical questions are items such as "I enjoy going to parties at which I know very few people," and "I can work on several projects at the same time." Eighteen scale scores are developed, 15 of which are trait scales; the remaining scales are used to assess the general credibility of the responses. Table 14.3 lists the scales of the CPI. As is apparent, these personality scales are frequently used in organizational studies.

These scales are characterized as empirically valid. That is, criterion-related studies were conducted in the development of this instrument. For example, in the development of the *Sociability* scale, differences in responses were examined between two groups. One group was composed of individuals who had demonstrated behaviors that were indicative of the construct of sociability, for example, frequent attendance at social gatherings, membership in several organizations, interaction with several "good" friends. The other group was of individuals who did not demonstrate these frequent behaviors. Items of the *Sociability* scale were those on which the two groups responded significantly differently. A score on this scale indicates how closely the respondent's answers reflect those of the group that were identified as engaging in frequent social behaviors.

It is estimated that reliabilities (internal, test/retest, and parallel forms) of the scales range from .70 to .90.[33] While CPI manual data reports somewhat lower reliability estimates, the length of the scales and stringent test conditions lead some researchers to place more confidence in CPI score profile accuracy than the manual suggests. Standard errors of measurement are not, unfortunately, reported for the scales. As for validity, the CPI has demonstrated fairly high predictive validity for academic achievement, creativity, occupational performance, personal and social problems, and other behaviors such as leadership. Moreover, validity studies using actual descriptions by observers who were familiar with respondents produced correlations in the .40s to .60s range.[34]

The Myers-Briggs Type Indicator (MBTI)   Although we have not found any validity studies involving the MBTI in selection nor do we advocate its use for selection, we include it here because it is used in many organizations for leadership training, work group development, or career counseling. We also are betting that some organizations use it for selection decisions. Because of its popularity, we think a brief description is appropriate.

The MBTI is based on the theory of psychological types developed by C. J. Jung. The term *type* in personality theory refers to groups of individuals who roughly share the same amount of common traits. Because these individuals are common in traits they are expected to be similar in their reactions and behaviors.

TABLE 14.3	**CALIFORNIA PSYCHOLOGICAL INVENTORY SCALES**

Clinical Scales	*Validity Scales*
Dominance	Sense of well-being
Capacity for status	Good impression
Sociability	Commonality
Social presence	
Self-acceptance	
Responsibility	
Socialization	
Self-control	
Tolerance	
Achievement via conformance	
Achievement via independence	
Intellectual efficiency	
Psychological mindedness	
Flexibility	
Femininity	

TABLE 14.4	**MBTI SCALES**

EI SCALE

Extraversion (E)	Oriented primarily toward the outer world; focus on people and objects.
Introversion (I)	Oriented primarily toward the inner world; focus on concepts and ideas.

SN SCALE

Sensing (S)	Individual reports observable facts through one or more of the five senses.
Intuition (N)	reports meanings, relationships and/or possibilities that have been worked out beyond the reach of the conscious mind.

TF SCALE

Thinking (T)	Judgment is impersonally based on logical consequences.
Feeling (F)	Judgment primarily based on personal or social values

JP SCALE

Judgment (J)	Preference for using a judgment process for dealing with the outer world.
Perception (P)	Preference for using a perceptive process for dealing with the outer world.

SOURCE: Isabel B. Myers & Mary H. McCaulley, *A Guide to the Development and Use of the Meyers-Briggs Type Indicator* (Palo Alto, Calif.: Consulting Psychologists Press, 1985), pp. 2–3.

In the MBTI, 16 types are formed from four basic scales. Each scale is divided into two psychological preferences (see Table 14.4).

According to theory, one pole of each of the four scales is characteristic of an individual. Therefore, there are 16 different combinations (types) generated from the scales.

Each type is designated by the four letters that indicate the preferences within each scale. An ENTJ is a person who is characterized by extraversion, intuition, thinking, and judgment. Each type has a characteristic description associated with it. Here is part of the description associated with the ENTJ:

> Hearty, frank, able in studies, leaders in activities. Usually good in anything that requires reasoning and intelligent talk, such as public speaking. Are well-informed and keep adding to their fund of knowledge. May sometimes be more positive and confident than their experience in an area warrants.[35]

The MBTI is published in three forms—Form F (166 items), Form G (126 items), and Form AV (50 items). The items of each form are presented in forced-choice format, that is, the respondent is asked which of two alternatives he or she prefers. Each alternative is scored on a different scale. The respondent, therefore, is forced to chose the scale of preference. Scores for the four scales are related to the number of times the scales are chosen. Scores for each of the two poles of each scale are also reflective of times chosen. A respondent is classified into one of the 16 types based on the pattern of scores.

A fundamental limitation of using the MBTI in selection is that given this type of scoring system it is not meaningful to calculate validity coefficients between MBTI scales and job performance measures. The forced-choice format yields what is referred to as *ipsative* scores: The scores represent the preference of the individual among alternatives. The scores are only meaningful when making comparisons within the respondent. That is, one can say the respondent chose more E items than I items and, therefore, is more outer directed than inner directed. However, because the responses to the items are not independent (choosing one alternative prevents any score on the other even if the activity in question is representative of the respondent), the scale scores cannot be meaningfully correlated with other measures.[36] Ipsative scales do not meet the psychometric assumptions necessary for correlational analysis. Therefore, it is not possible to conduct common criterion-related validation.

Limitations of Self-Report Questionnaires   The instruments we discussed are only three of a very large number of self-report inventories used in selection. Many of them, like the *Edward's Personal Preference Schedule, Cattell's Sixteen Personality Factor Test*, the *California F Scale*, the *Thurstone Temperament Schedule*, and the *Guilford-Zimmerman Temperament Survey*, are products of extensive pretesting and developmental work.

The first major limitation in the use of self-report inventories in selection is that many others lack adequate developmental work and overstate their ability to measure personality. This is especially common for instruments used among management consulting firms that specialize in executive selection. It is common for such firms to use an inventory developed by the firm itself. The glaring limitation of many such instruments is that they lack any developmental or measurement information. At the very least, data should be provided on the reliability of the test, the group that serves as the norm or reference group to enable interpretation of any particular score, and the basis or evidence supporting the selection of the items on the scale(s). Obviously if such information is either lacking or not appropriate for the intended use of the test in the organization, one should be very skeptical of the usefulness of the instrument despite its publicity brochures.

Other issues commonly regarded as serious limitations in the use of self-report inventories have been addressed favorably by recent work. The first is faking responses. Several studies have found that respondents have been able to change their scale profiles on personality questionnaires after "fake good" instructions. This led to the conclusion that many applicants would distort responses to improve their chances of being selected. Two recent large sample empirical studies, however, disagree with this conclusion.[37] Instead, the authors conclude that even though distortion is certainly possible, such distortion did not occur very often among applicants. Even when it did occur, it did not significantly distort validity coefficients; further, it is possible to detect such distortion through the derivation of strategies derived from analyses of large databases.

A second issue is the frequently observed low correlation (usually of .20 to .30) between responses to self-report scales and other behavior indicative of the trait being measured.[38] Such modest correlations between measures of the same construct naturally introduces doubt as to the extent of correlation of the personality scale with measures of job performance. Recently, Robert Hogan has pointed out that these modest validity coefficients are not as common as suspected, with many studies reporting much higher coefficients.[39] Also such validities are uncorrected estimates, meaning that the true correlation should be higher. Finally, these low correlations are derived from the use of an individual scale when, in fact, the use of personality usually incorporates several scales. If the low correlations are associated with the use of a subscale of the Big Five, we would expect that the validity would increase with the use of the global dimension.

Based on the data, our conclusion is that self-report personality inventories which are psychometrically sound and measure broad personality traits, such as the Big Five, can be useful for selection.

Projective Techniques These devices are similar to self-report questionnaires in that they require verbal responses which are scored to obtain measures of personality characteristics. However, they differ noticeably on several other important aspects. In contrast to the structure of both the questions and the answers of self-report questionnaires, projective techniques are intentionally ambiguous. For example, the respondent is presented with a series of inkblots or pictures and asked to make up a story about each one. Instructions are usually kept brief and vague. Another frequently used technique is to present the respondent with a series of sentence stems such as "My father. . . ," or "My favorite. . . ," and ask the respondent to complete each sentence. In both types, the respondent is encouraged to say whatever he or she wishes. The inkblots, pictures, or sentence stems are purposefully chosen to be open to a wide variety of reasonable answers.

The assumption underlying projective techniques is that they allow the respondent to expose central ways of "organizing experience and structuring life" as meanings are imposed on a stimulus having "relatively little structure and cultural patterning."[40] In this sense these devices might be classified as "weak testing situations" in which individual differences in personality strongly account for the differences in responses among people. These techniques are called "projective" because, given the ambiguity of the items, the respondent must project his or her interpretation and organization on them. This interpretation and organization is an extension of the personality of the individual. The proposed advantage of these devices for obtaining clear data on personality is that the respondent is not supposed to realize the possible interpretation of the information provided. This encourages the respondent to make public certain information that he or she might otherwise not provide. For example, a subject might interpret a picture of two interacting people as a violent argument which will lead to one individual physically assaulting the other. According to the theory of projective techniques, the aggression expressed in this story is more a function of the aggressive impulses of the individual than the context of the picture, because the picture was chosen to be deliberately ambiguous. It would then be hypothesized, given additional data, that the respondent is an angry person with a predisposition to experience his world as peopled by hostile individuals.[41]

Thematic Apperception Test (TAT)   In the TAT the respondent is asked to tell a story about each of 19 cards that depict one or more human beings in a variety of ambiguous situations. A 20th card—a totally white blank card—is also frequently used. It is assumed that the content of the individual's stories about these cards will reveal unconscious desires, inner tendencies, attitudes, and conflicts. The cards are administered individually in two 1-hour sessions. The TAT can be scored in a variety of ways, all of which are complex systems. The most popular is Henry Murray's system, which analyzes several aspects of the stories, including the following: *the hero* (the leading character in each story), *the needs of the hero* (such as achievement, order, and aggression), *press* (the pressures operating on the hero), and *themes* (the interplay between needs and press and resolution of conflict.) [42]

David McClelland has developed a variation of the TAT that also has been used extensively.[43] In this system six cards, similar to those of the original TAT set, are administered. The respondent sees a card for no more than 20 seconds and then is asked to write a story that includes information on what is happening, who the people are, what led up to the situation, what is wanted, and what will happen. McClelland has developed a scoring system that primarily evaluates the content of the stories for three distinct needs: *power* (concern about getting or maintaining control of the means of influencing others), *achievement* (concern about a standard of excellence, long-term goal, or a unique accomplishment), and *affiliation* (concern with emotional relationships). Much work has been done by McClelland and his associates to study the job behavior of managers with various amounts of these three needs or motives. For example, they have identified the Leadership Motive Pattern, which is defined as being at least moderately high in need for *power*, lower in need for *affiliation*, and high in the additional personality trait of *self-control*.[44] This is explained as follows: High need for power is important because it means the person is interested in the "influence game," in having impact on others; lower need for affiliation is important because it enables the manager to make difficult decisions without worrying unduly about being disliked; and high self-control is important because it means the person is likely to be concerned with maintaining organizational systems and following orderly procedures.

Miner Sentence Completion Scale (MSCS)   The MSCS was developed by John Miner specifically for the assessment of motives that are characteristically manifested at work and in the managerial role.[45] The respondent is presented with 40 items or sentences and asked to complete each. Only 35 of the items are scored to form measures on seven different motivation scales. Table 14.5 contains these scales and some similar items. Many of the specific items of this instrument refer to situations that are either outside the work environment entirely or are not specifically related to the managerial job. This is done to minimize the ability of respondents to distort their responses to present a particular image of themselves. Each of the seven scales has been developed to measure a particular managerial motive. *Authority Figures* provides a measure of the subject's capacity to meet role requirements in the area of relationships with his superior. *Competitive Games* and *Competitive Situations* both focus on occupational or work-related competition. The *Assertive Role* generally reflects confidence in one's ability to perform well and a wish to participate in activities. *Imposing Wishes* refers to controlling or directing the behavior of others. The *Standing Out from the Group* scale uses items in which an individual is highly visible and serves to measure the desire to assume a somewhat deviant position as compared with subordinates. The last scale, *Routine Administrative Functions*, is used as an indicant of the desire to meet job requirements related to day-to-day administrative work.

A complete scoring guide has been developed. Using this, each individual response is scored as positive, neutral, or negative according to whether or not the response is a positive or negative emotion in association with the content of the item. In addition, various overall scores can be obtained, one of which compares the respondent's answers to those of a normative sample of 160 individuals. Work with the MSCS has generally focused on describing managerial motivation and success within large, bureaucratic organizations. Test-retest correlations indicate acceptable levels of reliability (about .80) for the MSCS. Furthermore, evidence of both construct and criterion-related validation has been reported.

Limitations of Projective Techniques   On the surface, it would seem that projective techniques could provide more beneficial information than self-report questionnaires in assessing personality. One would expect that socially

TABLE 14.5	SCALES AND EXAMPLE ITEMS FROM THE MINER SENTENCE COMPLETION SCALE
Authority Figures	My family doctor. . . Policemen. . .
Competitive Games	Playing golf. . . When playing cards, I. . .
Competitive Situations	Running for political office. . . Final examinations. . .
Assertive Role	Shooting a rifle. . . Wearing a necktie. . .
Imposing Wishes	Punishing children. . . When one of my men asks me for advice
Standing Out from the Group	Presenting a report at a staff meeting. . . Making introductions. . .
Routine Administrative Functions	Dictating letters. . . Decisions. . .

SOURCE: John B Miner, *Studies in Management Education* (New York: Springer, 1965).

appropriate answers would not be as evident as in the responses to personality self-report questionnaires and that responses would be reflective of personality characteristics of the respondent. This is, in fact, the basic assumption of projective techniques. However, various issues have arisen concerning the scoring and use of the information obtained from projective instruments that have questioned their general usefulness in selection. The following points are addressed to these techniques in general.

The first issue is the reliability of an individual's responses at two different times. In all other selection devices it is assumed that the characteristic demonstrated by the respondent is consistently measured. The scores derived from projective tests, however, often have low reliabilities.[46] There is a question about the proper measurement of reliability and if, in fact, this is a useful concept for these techniques. It has been thought that observed changes in test responses over time reflect real changes in the individual, since many of the characteristics measured, like emotion and mood, change over time. The problem this causes for HR selection decisions is significant. Usually, the applicant only completes a projective test once. The information obtained is then generalized to descriptions of the applicant. Even if changes in response patterns are indicative of real changes in the individual, the selection specialist can have little confidence in the usefulness of such personality data in predicting long-term job performance.

The second issue in the use of projective techniques is the impact on the score of an individual of the total number of responses given. This is not a major issue for some devices, such as the MSCS, that limit responses to a relatively constant number for all subjects. However, for those instruments that encourage free response, there is evidence the scores of personality characteristics are related to the volume of information given.[47] The problem here is that the number of responses given may not be a function of personality but rather specific skills such as verbal or test-taking skills. If this is the case, the accuracy of the personality data would be reduced as would be its usefulness in selection.

A third major concern is the scoring of the information provided. In this, the proposed benefit of projective instruments becomes a liability. The quantity and complexity of the responses make scoring, even using a designated scoring manual, very difficult. This is a greater problem for those instruments that encourage free response and less of a problem for those that limit response. The result is that at times the same answers have not been scored and interpreted identically by different scorers.[48] Such findings cloud the usefulness of the resulting personality scores for selection because it would appear that the scoring of the information is indicative of the examiners particular scoring system and judgment as well as the individual's responses. This adds error to the scores as far as HR specialists are concerned because they want the scores to be reflective of the applicant only, since the selection decision is to be made about this individual.

A fourth concern is that few HR specialists are trained in administering, scoring, and interpreting data from projective tests. This means that consultants must be hired to administer and score them. At times such consultants are not familiar with the job under consideration and evaluate the candidate in comparison to a general profile of a good worker. In many cases, this profile is based only on the opinion of the consultant. However, given the complexity of projective test data and the unfamiliarity of the HR specialist with scoring, it is difficult to find an alternative route. As a result, the personality description is often accepted by the specialist but actually is of little value.

Taking the other side of these issues, Ed Cornelius wrote a strong defense of the use of projective instruments for selection.[49] Among the several points he discussed and supported with empirical evidence from previous work are the following:

1. The reliability of projective instruments is frequently .80 or higher. The more psychometrically sound instruments have defined scoring systems that greatly reduce differences in interpretation among clinicians.

2. Often clinicians will use more than one projective instrument to assess an applicant. The accuracy of the description is strengthened by looking at the correspondence between the various test results.

3. A review of 34 articles appearing in major empirical journals between 1960 and 1981 indicated 14 "prediction studies." Ten of these reported significant validity coefficients.

We tend to agree with Cornelius's arguments. Much of the historic criticism has been based on poorly developed instruments and poorly conducted validity studies. However, there are psychometrically sound instruments and well-done studies. Evidence from these two sources argues for the use of projective techniques.

The Interview in Personality Measurement

We discussed the selection interview in Chapter 12 as a device to predict productivity through the assessment of applicant characteristics. We do not repeat that information, and, therefore, this section is brief. However, it is known that the interview also serves as a primary device for estimating personality characteristics of applicants. In this use the emphasis is on determining whether an applicant is the type of person who can be expected to fit in and get along in a particular firm. This is probably the most widespread use of the interview.[50]

As was the case in the use of the interview to predict job performance, there is little evidence to demonstrate generally the usefulness of the interview in making these personality judgments. Recently, psychologists and HR managers have studied this personality assessment process extensively and have come up with several important findings.

Linking Traits to Individuals One important finding is that interviewers tend to overemphasize personality traits in making causal attributions about behavior. For example, an interviewer wishes to know why an applicant has changed employment twice in five years. In this situation, interviewers generally assign personality causes to the behavior of applicants rather than situational causes—the job moves would more likely be attributed to the "restlessness" of the person rather than to any factors of the work situation. This can occur even after discussion of the topic between the interviewer and the interviewee. Such an attribution contrasts to the analysis of our own behavior in which the conditions of a situation are more often held to be the determinants of our action than are personality traits.[51]

Second, researchers have found that individuals tend to interpret even the simplest behaviors as signs of underlying traits and motives.[52] The obvious problem with such attribution is that, as we discussed earlier in this chapter, behavior is the product of the interaction of individual traits and situational factors. To assume that traits are the primary facet of observed behavior and to infer traits of an applicant from extremely limited information is very uncertain. Some psychologists have thought that a more useful way of judging the personality of another would be to view their actions in the same fashion that we view our own actions. As noted previously, we frequently judge our own behaviors in light of situational factors that we think affect our behaviors. It may be more useful in making judgments about the personality of others to take into account the situational characteristics of actions.

Third, interviewers tend to rely on a few central traits in forming their impressions of others. That is, certain pieces of information are given greater weight than others and are used to organize impressions. For example, it has been found that if the trait of "warmth" is attributed to an individual, frequently he or she will also be assigned the traits of being generous, good-natured, happy, sociable, and wise. On the other hand, it the individual is thought of as being "cold," the traits of being ungenerous, unhappy, irritable, and humorless are often quickly assigned.[53] There appears to be three kinds of these central traits: *evaluations* (like warmth), in which we organize trait judgments around a good-bad dimension; *potency*, in which we use a strong-weak dimension; and *activity*, in which we use an energetic-lazy dimension. In essence, this implies that in an interview situation once one or more of these central trait dimensions is attributed by the interviewer to the interviewee a number of other traits are assigned to the individual. More than likely, these additional traits will be uniformly positive or negative depending on the nature of the judged central trait. The difficulty with this process, however, is that traits are not usually so highly interrelated. It is possible for a person to be warm but not necessarily generous or wise. To the extent that the association of secondary traits to a central trait is made without actually basing the secondary trait on information of its own, the probability of incorrect judgments about the personality of another is increased.

Questions Used to Measure Personality   Often the inaccuracies in forming impressions of personality through an interview are compounded by the questions asked by the interviewer. Many of the most popular questions asked in interviews almost resemble projective techniques of personality assessment. Such as "What are your strengths?" and "What was your home life like as you grew up?" They are very open-ended, nonstructured questions that can be answered with a wide variety of responses.

Because there are not obvious right or wrong answers to these questions, the responses given, theoretically, are prompted by the interviewee's own personality and should serve as accurate indicators of it. However, there seem to be three problems with these types of questions that would severely limit their usefulness. The first is that there has not been systematic analysis of responses in order to develop scoring keys, as has happened in the case of projective techniques. Instead, each interviewer is usually left to his or her own system of scoring. The second problem is the large number of interview preparation programs that have recently been developed. Private companies, universities, and social service agencies all regularly conduct interview training sessions for a variety of audiences. In addition, many books and newspaper articles have been published to advise individuals on appropriate actions and answers in interviews. Whether advice given from these sources is accurate or not is almost irrelevant to the intended use of these questions. If the interviewee's response is prompted by learned behavior from these various programs, then the response is no longer determined by the personality of the respondent. The response may indicate nothing more than what is developed in an interview training program. Moreover, the impression formed by the interviewer on the basis of the interviewee's responses could mainly be a function of the chance agreement between the interview training course and the implicit personality theory of the interviewer. Actually, very little information about the interviewee could be obtained.

Third is the fact that for questions of this type there is very little other information that can be gathered to either support or contradict the statement of the interviewee. For example, in response to the question "What are your future vocational plans," an applicant may describe a steady progression through an organization, stressing increased skill development and responsibility in areas compatible with his or her abilities. In reality, the person wishes to start his or her own small business and feels that the management experience to be gained from two years with a large company would be valuable training. There is no feasible way for the interviewer to develop much other information to relate to this response; and, therefore, any assessment of traits of motivation or compatibility with the organization would be incorrect.

The Appropriate Use of the Interview   Saying all this, what statements can we make about the use of the interview in personality assessment? Recall that in Chapter 12 we concluded the interview is an appropriate way for assessing interpersonal skills and work habits, both of which reflect personality traits. Our first recommendation to measure these is that the scope of the interview be limited. Instead of attempting to assess the complete personality of applicants, it would be more feasible to measure social interaction patterns and work patterns (such as attention to detail, meeting difficult objectives, etc.) based on job analysis information. This would limit the number of personality characteristics that must be judged and identify more carefully the ones that are to be assessed. For example, attention to detail may be an important personal characteristic for many clerical or computer system jobs within organizations. The interviewer should, therefore, attempt to find information about this trait rather than attempt a more complete personality description that would include traits such as *ambition, aggressiveness,* and *sociability* that may seem desirable but are not directly related to job activities.

The obvious problem, however, is how to accomplish even this limited objective successfully. From our discussion, it should be clear there is no certain way to obtain accurate personality assessment data from interviews. However, one tactic that might serve to minimize errors is to concentrate on previous behaviors that would seem to be dependent on the same personality trait. In this case, questions and discussion could be addressed to previous instances in which the interviewee demonstrated behaviors requiring attention to detail. The *Behavior Description Interview* discussed in Chapter 12 is appropriate here. It is not necessary that these be employment activities. Possibilities might include hobbies and academic behaviors as well as employment. It is hoped that information could be obtained about the nature of the behavior or activity, length of time involved, situational determinants of behavior (weak or powerful situation), and whether one or multiple instances of the behavior can be cited. In interviews, the interviewer is the measuring device. One hopes that by limiting the scope of the decisions that the interviewer must make and also by maximizing the correspondence between the information gathered and the type of assessment that must be made, errors in personality assessment will be reduced.

Behavioral Assessment in Personality Measurement

The third major method of personality assessment is behavioral assessment. In this technique the emphasis is on trained individuals using judgments about the actual behavior of others to estimate personality characteristics. If we go back to our original definition of personality as the unique organization of characteristics which defines an individual and determines that person's pattern of interaction with the environment, the information gathered in this manner would seem to be very compatible with this definition. This is in contrast to self-report inventories that focus on limited written indicants of behavior, and interviews that, while capturing some behavior of the interviewee, primarily focus on verbal descriptions of behavior.

The classic studies of Hartshorne and May used behaviors to assess such traits as *honesty, truthfulness, self-control,* and *persistence* in children.[54] For example, in assessing honesty with money, children were given boxes of coins which had been secretly identified so that the experimenters could later determine which child had a particular box. Since the children were unaware of this arrangement, their honesty in handling money could be determined without their knowledge, using their behaviors as data. In another case children were given an impossible task to perform and then asked to report their own scores.

Methods of Behavioral Assessment In HR selection, behavioral assessment has been referred to as situational, work sample, or simulation problems and has been used to assess job-related KSAs as well as personality characteristics. Chapter 15 addresses these types of instruments and goes into detail on the nature, construction, scoring, and interpretation of these techniques. Therefore, we limit our comments at this point to the use of behavior tests to measure personality without going into detail in describing these devices.

There are two basic methods that have been used to gather such data for selection. In one of these, the HR specialist develops structured situations that are similar to important job situations. These situations require the interaction of a small number of individuals whose places are filled by job applicants. Trained company members observe, record, and interpret what goes on among these groups of applicants and use these data to make judgments about personality characteristics. One such method that is described further in Chapter 15 is the Leaderless Group Discussion (LGD). In this situation applicants usually interact in groups of six. The group is presented with an organizational problem that frequently requires the division of scarce resources, for example, money for raises. Each member is given the information to play a certain role. Usually this calls for the applicant to be an advocate for a particular department or subordinate and prompts the applicant to attempt to persuade the other group members to agree with his or her point of view. Trained judges view the interaction of the applicants and rate them on a variety of traits such as *persuasiveness, persistence, stress maintenance,* and *conflict management.*

The second behavioral method is used when existing organizational members are being considered for other positions in the company. In one application, the supervisors of these people are trained and asked to record and interpret certain behaviors thought to be closely related to actions of the job being considered. In another application, the *critical incident technique,* the supervisor systematically records extremely good or poor instances of work performance or, in some cases, a particular personality trait, like persuasiveness. To do this the supervisor must make a detailed description of the incident that occurred, including behaviors and circumstances. These written incidents are then used as the data for forming impressions of the individual. Both methods have had reported success within organizations and if performed correctly would appear to be superior to other methods of personality assessment in terms of the nature of the information produced.[55]

Limitations of Behavioral Assessment   There are three potential limitations in behavioral assessment that must be addressed to ensure its accuracy. The first is the situation(s) in which the individuals are placed. The essential characteristic of these situations is that they be representative of situations of the job being considered. We have observed previously that behavior is a product of the interaction of traits and situations and concluded that behavior is prompted by different mixes of these two. It is necessary that the selection situation(s) and the job situation(s) be closely related so we can generalize from the judgments of personality characteristics. For example, stressful demands are part of many jobs, and an individual's reaction to stress is important to successful performance. However, all stressful job aspects are not the same; and an individual's reactions to different types of stress is not necessarily the same. If a particular middle management job is characterized by stress attributable to several conflicting project demands, all with short time deadlines, it is not justifiable to develop a selection situation in which the applicant faces stress caused by an antagonistic interviewer or an embarrassing social situation.

   The second limitation is that the behavior to be recorded or rated should be defined as clearly as possible. Being "persuasive" or "sociable" are complex sets of behavior that can be confused or misinterpreted. If *persuasiveness* is to be defined as getting another to change his or her own verbal or physical behavior through any means other than force, then this definition should be communicated to the judges. Examples should also be provided of specific actions that demonstrate various levels of *persuasiveness.*

   The third limitation is the training of the judges. Those evaluating the actions of applicants in these behavior situations are subject to the same problems of impression formation as interviewers. To limit these distortions judges should be extensively trained in observation techniques and should practice making judgments about personality characteristics. In addition, in many cases multiple judges are used and the personality assessment is a product of the judgment of them all. More detail about each of these points will be presented in Chapter 15 in the discussion of assessment centers.

Factors in the Appropriate Use of Personality Data

We started this chapter with a discussion about the apparent contradiction of using personality data in selection programs. There is ample evidence that personality should be a worker characteristic related to performance in many jobs. This type of data conceivably should be as useful in selection decisions as data about applicant KSAs which have been stressed in other chapters. The evidence, however, does not totally support this conclusion. The demonstrated usefulness of personality data in selection programs is at best inconsistent. A possible explanation of this dilemma is that the methods of personality assessment in selection have usually been inadequate. To many working in selection, this would seem more probable than the conclusion that personality data are simply not related to job performance. The major focus of the chapter, therefore, has been on the definition and measurement methods of personality assessment. Much of the information has been drawn from psychology because personality psychologists have studied these topics in much more depth than HR specialists. At this point there are no certain directives that can be made to ensure the accurate collection and use of personality data. However, given the material available, it is possible to draw some conclusions that should be useful to selection managers.

Define Personality Traits in Terms of Job Behaviors

Of fundamental importance is the definition of what personality characteristic should be used in a selection program. We are reminded of the saying "If you don't know where you are going, any way will take you there." Obviously, the definition of important worker attributes is something we mentioned before as being necessary for all selection measures. However the lack of definition seems to be more common with personality measurement in selection than with other types of worker attributes.

The lack of definition usually takes one of two forms. In the first, a personality instrument is used without much attention paid to the specific traits being measured. The instrument is used because of someone's recommendation that it is effective or even because it has been used in previous selection work. Such reasons are not proper justification for use. As we have said before (now we're sounding like your mother!), it is necessary to have a job-related basis for whatever KSAs are measured in selection. Personality characteristics should be thought of as another type of KSA.

The second form of lack of definition is the use of very general statements of personality traits,for example, "a manager that fits in well with our staff" or a "salesperson who has a good personality." Given this impreciseness, it would be unlikely to have agreement among different selection specialists about what particular personality traits should be evaluated. Even if only one specialist is involved, there is little assurance the personality traits that are evaluated are, in fact, the appropriate ones.

There seem to be two ways that job analysis information could supply information to generate adequate definitions. The first is through the task approach described in Chapter 9. If this approach is carried out completely, it should yield information about job tasks, interaction patterns among the incumbent and others, working conditions, equipment used, and work patterns. From these data a HR specialist should be able to infer personality traits in much the same way that other KSAs are inferred. That is, for example, traits such as "control of stress caused by steady demands of users for quick answers to programming difficulties" and "diligence in review of details of complex programs" could be identified for a computer programmer's job. The second is by means of those job analysis methods that directly produce worker attributes, some of which are personality dimensions. One such method is the PAQ's "attributes of an interest or temperament nature" that we presented in Chapter 9. Included in these were *working alone, pressure of time, empathy, influencing people*, and so on. Another job analysis method is the Job Element Method (Appendix 8A) in which the job analyst leads a discussion of groups of workers to specify KSAs directly. Among these KSAs, personality traits will commonly be specified.

Basing the identification of personality traits for selection on such job analysis data could also serve another important purpose. Given all that has been said about personality measurement, it should be apparent that the use of personality data could leave a company vulnerable in a discrimination charge. Such charges, under law, are initiated by applicants who feel they have been inappropriately treated in selection. Using personality traits carefully identified by job analysis could be beneficial to the company in two ways. First, the traits measured could appear to have "face validity" to the applicant, that is, appear to be reasonable for the job being considered. This "face-validity" may reduce the inclination of the applicant to initiate a charge. Second, and perhaps more importantly, being able to justify the personality traits through the evidence of job analysis is absolutely *essential* to being able to defend the selection program in the face of a charge. It will not assure that the use of personality will be defended; but without such data, any successful defense would be highly unlikely.

The Appropriateness of the Selection Instrument

From our previous discussion, it should be clear that we feel there are two important characteristics of the selection measure of personality to consider. The first is the breadth of the personality trait being measured. This reflects the previous discussion of core versus surface traits. Remember, the conclusion of this discussion was that it would seemingly be more effective in selection to use traits which affected a wide set of behaviors rather than a narrow set.

The obvious difficulty in doing this is that personality theorists have not identified a set of traits which most can agree are appropriate. Our thought, therefore, is to use only those instruments for which enough test-construction information is available to indicate that the instrument was designed to measure broadly defined personality traits. This, of course, means that data regarding reliability, item statistics, and statistical analysis of each of the scales measuring a personality dimension should be provided. Given the extreme difficulty in constructing personality instruments, it would be foolhardy to use any personality devise in selection which does not have supporting information. An instrument without such information can really only be considered a theory of the writer without any supporting data. Therefore, the value of such an instrument is unknown and undocumented. The reason we stress this point is that there are numerous instruments of this type being sold to organizations for managerial and executive selection. Often these instruments are quite costly. We think they are often bought by selection specialists because the use of personality data is very complex even for those who have been trained in psychology. It can be over-whelming (many even say it should be avoided) for HR managers who have little formal training.

Some recent works provide examples of appropriate personality instru-ments. We have already discussed The Big Five as one example. There are others. James Browne and Edgar Howarth developed a pool of 1,726 items taken from a variety of personality inventories.[56] Various analyses reduced this num-ber into the dimensions of *adjustment, prudence, ambition, sociability*, and *likability*. Each of these is composed of several more specific traits. Studies of these scales have reported significant validity correlations of these dimensions with both peer ratings of performance for volunteers at a navy research base and supervisory rat-ings of performance for secretarial/clerical and also professional/technical employees. Using a similar approach, Walter Borman, Rodney Rosse, and Nor-man Abrahams also combined items from several sources to develop 17 person-ality scales of which 7 demonstrated significant relationships with job performance.[57]

The second important characteristic of a personality instrument in selection is whether or not "correct" responses to the instrument can be learned by the respondents. This topic was part of our discussion about weak and powerful measuring devices. It is our opinion that instruments for which appropriate responses are not apparent are preferable to those for which answers are appar-ent. We have mentioned the limitations in this regard with the interview, as it is commonly used, and many self-report, multiple-choice inventories. As we have also discussed, the reported validity data for such devices are usually quite low.

There are data which support the contention that devices for which appro-priate responses are not clear can be useful. As mentioned previously, Edwin Cornelius has reported that 10 of 14 studies using projective instruments which have been published in leading academic journals have demonstrated significant validity coefficients.[58] Similarly, John Miner reviewed several studies that he concluded supported the validity of his *Miner Sentence Completion Scale*.[59] Finally, in the use of assessment centers, it has been found that individual dimensions such as *creativity, sensitivity, flexibility*, and *initiative* correlate significantly with various job criteria.[60]

The Nature of Job Performance

We have discussed previously that personality may be less important in the per-formance of jobs that require technical solutions to many work situations and more important in the performance of jobs that are nontechnical. Similarly, per-formance in jobs that are very structured in terms of work behaviors would seem to be less related to personality than those that are unstructured. This is just another way of saying that for some jobs it appears the application of knowledge and predetermined actions are critical to successful job performance. For these jobs, cognitively based KSAs would seem more important for selection. There are other jobs that rely less on specific knowledge and procedures and have a number of acceptable ways to produce desired performance. It is for these jobs that personality would seem to be clearly related to job performance.

Of the concepts we have discussed, this distinction between the predominance of personality versus cognitive ability is the most tentative. However, some recent research is relevant for this point. For example, a longitudinal study reported that personality was related to managerial success after 8 and 16 years for a group of nontechnical managers but not for a group of technical managers.[61] The chief difference between the two was that the latter's operational responsibilities focused on construction, installation, maintenance, or repair of telephone equipment. The former group, on the other hand, were predominantly in such areas as customer service, marketing, and personnel services. Miner has also found that the MSCS predicts job performance better for what he refers to as nonbureaucratic situations than bureaucratic ones in which the criterion for success is some factor other than managerial ability.[62] Such results have prompted Ed Cornelius and Frank Lane to conclude that "a general theory is emerging. . . . to suggest that both the need for power and the willingness to exert power may be important for managerial success in only situations in which technical expertise is not critical. . . ." [63] These are the types of studies on which we base our conclusion that the nature of the job under consideration is important in the decision of whether to use personality measures in the selection program.

References

[1] Robert T. Hogan, "Personality and Personality Measurement," in *The Handbook of Industrial and Organizational Psychology*, Marvin Dunnette & Leanna Hough, 2d ed., Vol. 2, eds. (Palo Alto, Calif.: Consulting Psychologists Press, 19), 873–919

[2] Gordon W. Allport, *Pattern and Growth in Personality* (New York: Holt, Rinehart & Winston, 1961), 19.

[3] Walter Mischel, *Introduction to Personality*, 3d ed. (New York: CBS College Publishing, 1981), p. 2.

[4] Douglas N. Jackson, Andrew C. Peacock, and Ronald R. Holden, "Professional Interviewers' Trait Inferential Structures for Diverse Occupational Groups," *Organizational Behavior and Human Performance* 29 (1982): 1–20.

[5] Glen Grimsley and Hilton Jarrett, "The Relation of Past Managerial Achievement to Test Measures Obtained in the Employment Situation: Methodology and Results— II," *Personnel Psychology* 28 (1975): 215–231.

[6] Douglas W. Bray, Richard J. Campbell, and Donald L. Grant, *Formative Years in Business* (Huntington, N.Y.: Robert E. Krieger, 1979), 179.

[7] Robert M. Guion and Richard F. Gottier, "Validity of Personality Measures in Personnel Selection," *Personnel Psychology* 18 (1966): 135–164.

[8] Neal Schmitt, Richard Gooding, Raymond Noe, and Michael Kirsch, "Metaanalyses of Validity Studies Published between 1964 and 1982 and the Investigation of Study Characteristics," *Personnel Psychology* 37 (1984): 407–422.

[9] Robert T. Hogan, "Personality and Personality Measurement."

[10] David V. Day and Stanley B. Silverman, "Personality and Job Performance: Evidence of Incremental Validity," *Personnel Psychology* 42 (1989): 25–36.

[11] Mischel, *Introduction to Personality*, 18.

[12] Ibid., 19.

[13] Richard I. Lanyon and Leonard D. Goodstein, *Personality Assessment*, 2d. ed. (New York: Wiley, 1982), 28.

[14] David C. McClelland, *The Achieving Society* (Princeton, NJ.: D. Van Nostrand, Inc., 1961), 267.

15 Raymond B. Cattell, *The Scientific Analysis of Personality* (Baltimore: Penquin Books. 1965).

16 Allport, *Pattern and Growth in Personality*, 365.

17 John M. Digman and Jillian Inouye, "Further Specification of the Five Robust Factors of Personality," *Journal of Personality and Social Psychology* 50 (1986): 116–123.

18 Murray R. Barrick and Michael K. Mount, "The Big Five Personality Dimensions and Job Performance: A Meta-Analysis," *Personnel Psychology* 44 (1991): 1–26.

19 Hugh Hartshorne and Mark May, *Studies in the Nature of Character* (New York: Macmillan, 1928), 384.

20 Mark Snyder and William Ickes, "Personality and Social Behavior," in Gardner Lindsey and Ellioit Aronson eds., *The Handbook of Social Psychology, Third Edition*, Vol. II, (New York: Random House): 883–948.

21 Peter Herriot, "Towards an Attributional Theory of the Selection Interview," *Journal of Occupational Psychology* 54 (1981): 165–173.

22 Barrick and Mount, "The Big Five Personality Dimensions and Job Performance: A Meta-Analysis."

23 Richard H. Price and Dennis L. Bouffard, "Behavioral Appropriateness and Situational Constraint as Dimensions of Social Behavior," *Journal of Personality and Social Psychology* 30 (1974): 579–586.

24 Daryl J. Bem and David C. Funder, "Predicting More of the People More of the Time: Assessing the Personality of Situations," *Psychology Review* 85 (l978): 485–501.

25 Barrick and Mount, "The Big Five Personality Dimensions and Job Performance: A Meta-Analysis."

26 Robert T. Hogan, "Personality and Personality Measurement."

27 R. R. McCrae and P. T. Costa, Jr., "Updating Norman's 'adequate taxonomy': Intelligence and Personality Dimensions in Natural Language and in Questionnaires," *Journal of Personnel and Psychology* 49 (1985): 710–721. see also W. T. Norman, "Toward an Adequate Taxonomy of Personality Attributes: Replicated Factor Structure in Peer Nomination Personality Ratings," *Journal of Abnormal and Social Psychology* 66 (1963): 574–583.

28 Barrick and Mount, "The Big Five Personality Dimensions and Job Performance: A Meta-Analysis."

29 Jose M . Cortina, Mary L . Doherty, Neal Schmitt, Gary Kaufman, and Richard G . Smith, "The Big Five Personality Factors in the IPI and MMPI: Predictors of Police Performance," *Personnel Psychology* 45 (1992): 119–140.

30 Day and Silverman, "Personality and Job Performance: Evidence of Incremental Validity."

31 Patrick M . Wright, K . Michele Kacmar, Gary C . McMahan, and Kevin Deleeuw, "P=f(M x A): Cognitive Ability as a Moderator of the Relationship between Personality and Job Performance," *Proceedings of the Academy of Management*, (1992): 284–288.

32 Harrison G. Gough, *California Psychological Inventory* (Palo Alto, Calif.: Consulting Psychologists Press, 1956).

33 Brian Bolton, "Review of the California Psychological Inventory, Revised Edition," *The Eleventh Mental Measurements Yearbook*, eds. Jack J. Kramer and Jane Close Conoley (Lincoln: University of Nebraska Press, 1992), 138–139.

34 Ibid.

35 Isabel B. Myers and Mary H. McCaulley, *A Guide to the Development and Use of the Myers-Briggs Type Indicator* (Palo Alto, Calif.: Consulting Psychologists Press, 1985).

36 Charles E. Johnson, Robert Wood, and S. F. Blinkhorn, "Spuriouser and Spuriouser: The Use of Ipsative Personality Tests," *Journal of Occupational Psychology*, 61 (1988): 153–162.

37 Laetta M. Hough, Newell K. Eaton, Marvin D. Dunnette, John D. Kamp, and Rodney A. McCloy, "Criterion-Related Validities of Personality Constructs and the

[38] Effect of Response Distortion on Those Validities," *Journal of Applied Psychology* 75 (1990): 581–595. See also Kevin Lanning, "Detection of Invalid Response Patterns on the California Psychological Inventory," *Applied Psychological Measurement* 13 (1989): 45–56.

[38] Mischel, *Introduction to Personality*, 170.

[39] Robert T. Hogan, "Personality and Personality Measurement."

[40] Mark Sherman, *Personality: Inquiry and Application* (New York: Pergamon Press, 1979), 205.

[41] Ibid., p. 206.

[42] Henry A. Murray, *Thematic Apperception Test* (Cambridge: Harvard University Press, 1943).

[43] McClelland, *The Achieving Society*, 40.

[44] David C.. McClelland and Richard E. Boyatzis, "Leadership Motive Pattern and Long-term Success in Management," *Journal of Applied Psychology* (1982). 737–743.

[45] John B. Miner, *Motivation to Manage: A Ten-Year Update on the Studies In Management Education" Research* (Atlanta Ga.: Organizational Measurement Systems Press, 1977), 6.

[46] Lanyon and Goodstein, *Personality Assessment*, 144.

[47] Ibid., 145.

[48] Sherman, *Personality: Inquiry and Application*, 213.

[49] Edwin T. Cornelius III, "The Use of Projective Techniques in Personnel Selection," *Research in Personnel and Human Resource Arrangement* (Greenwich, Conn.: JAI Press, 1983).

[50] John B. Miner, "The Interview as a Selection Technique," *Contemporary Problems in Personnel*, rev. ed., ed. W. C. Hamner and F. L. Schmidt (Chicago: St. Clair Press. 1977), pp. 44–50.

[51] Mischel, *Introduction to Personality*, 490.

[52] Ibid.

[53] Solomon E. Asch, "Forming Impressions of Personality," *Journal of Abnormal and Social Psychology* 41 (1946): 258–290.

[54] Hartshorne and May, *Studies in the Nature of Character*, 49ff.

[55] Bray, Campbell, and Grant, *Formative Years in Business*, 177; John C. Flanagan, "The Critical Incident Technique," *Psychological Bulletin* 51 (1954): 327–358.

[56] James A. Browne and Edgar Howarth, "A Comprehensive Factor Analysis of Personality Questionnaire Items: A Test of Twenty Putative Factor Hypotheses," *Multivariate Behavioral Research* 12 (1977): 339–427.

[57] Walter C. Borman, Rodney L. Rosse, and Norman M. Abrahams, "An Empirical Construct Validity Approach to Studying Predictor-Job Performance Links," *Journal of Applied Psychology* 65 (1980): 662–671.

[58] Cornelius, "The Use of Projective Techniques in Personnel Selection."

[59] John B. Miner, "Twenty Years of Research on Role Motivation Theory of Managerial Effectiveness," *Personnel Psychology* 31 (1978): 739–760.

[60] George C. Thornton III and William C. Byham, *Assessment Centers and Managerial Performance* (New York: Academic Press, 1982).

[61] McClelland and Boyatzis, "Leadership Motive Pattern and Long-Term Success in Management."

[62] Miner, "Twenty Years of Research on Role-Motivation Theory of Managerial Effectiveness."

[63] Edwin T. Cornelius III and Frank B. Lane, "The Power Motive and Managerial Success in a Professionally Oriented Service Industry Organization," *Journal of Applied Psychology* 69 (1984): 32–39.

15

Performance Tests and Assessment Centers

Performance Tests

This chapter describe's selection devices that assess applicants via testing situations that closely resemble actual parts of the job being considered. In their most common form these devices are referred to as *performance* or *work sample tests* because they ask the applicant to complete some job activity, either behavioral or verbal, under structured testing conditions. Requiring applicants to write a simple computer program to solve a specific problem is one example. Performance tests are different in orientation from previously discussed selection devices, which primarily measure applicants on characteristics that are presumed to be related to job behavior instead of on-the-job behavior itself.

Differences from Other Selection Devices

It is commonly assumed that performance tests provide *direct* evidence of the applicant's ability and skill to work on the job while other selection devices provide indirect evidence. In well-constructed performance tests, the activities presented to the applicant are representative of job tasks, equipment, and so on, actually used on the job. In completing these activities the applicant, therefore, does a representative part of the job for which he or she is being evaluated.

If we consider the other types of selection devices we have discussed, we realize that these collect primarily either verbal descriptions of activities or verbal indicants of job knowledge. For example, application and biographical data forms concentrate on written descriptions of previous educational or vocational experiences. Interviews are oral exchanges that are also primarily descriptions of work and educational experiences or oral demonstration of job knowledge. Ability tests are primarily written indicants of knowledge, and personality inventories are most often written descriptions of behavior.

In most selection situations, the selection specialist must take this verbal information and make an inference about the applicant's future job performance. As we stated previously, there often are limitations to these verbal data that hinder this inference. One is that these data are subject to willful distortion or faking by the applicant. The possibility for such distortion varies—it is the greatest in the description of past experience that is difficult to verify and it is least in the demonstration of job knowledge. The second limitation is that the relationship between verbal description and job performance is not perfect. Most of us can cite personal examples in which we know the correct way of doing something, like hitting a backhand shot in tennis, tuning the motor of a car, or organizing our work and study habits more efficiently, yet do not translate that knowledge well into actual behavior. A parallel situation often exists in selection. To the extent that these two limitations occur in the collection of data from applicants, the accuracy of the selection decision becomes more tenuous.

Presumably, with performance tests the probability of both of these limitations is greatly reduced. In most cases, applicant descriptions of what to do, what equipment to use, and so on, are minimized. Instead, the applicant acts in the work situation. These actions and their results are what are important. The only time written or oral information is produced is when the actual job activity consists of written or oral components. Such as preparing a press release or answering questions posed by an assembled group of consumers.

Limitations

Looked at in this way, you might logically ask, "If performance tests are so sensible and efficient, shouldn't they be used in all selection situations?" In fact such instruments have been used widely, especially for clerical and skilled manual labor positions. Recently, performance tests have been used extensively in the form of *assessment centers* for managerial and professional selection. However, there are a number of factors that limit their use in selection programs. For one, much care must be taken in the construction of work sample tests to ensure they are representative of job activities. For many complex and multiple demand jobs this is a difficult task. We are all familiar with selection devices that may be intended as work samples but really are not. One example is the attempt by an interviewer to create a stressful situation during the interview by asking many questions rapidly, not allowing much time for the applicant's response, or acting in a cold, aloof manner. Even if the job of interest can be regarded as one of high work demands that may produce stress, the situation staged in the interview most often is not representative of those demands. Very few jobs consist of semi hostile individuals rapidly questioning the job holder. The behavior of the applicant in such an interview situation is not readily generalizable to the job and should not be used as a direct indicator of actual job behavior.

Another factor in the use of performance tests is that these devices commonly assume the applicants already have the knowledge, ability, and skill to perform the job behavior. The purpose of selection is to identify those applicants who are the most proficient in these job behaviors. Such an idea is best suited for jobs with tasks that are very similar to jobs in other organizations or tasks that can be taught in formal education programs. In other words, the most appropriate tasks are those that do not depend on specialized knowledge, abilities, or skills to use or interact with company products, personnel, materials, or customers. Performance tests, for the most part, assume that the called for job behavior has previously been learned and is in the repertoire of the applicant. To the extent that this assumption is not accurate and the performance tests would require specialized training by the company, the tests must be modified to provide instruction about equipment, and materials, before the testing can be performed.

A third factor limiting the use of performance tests is the cost. Ordinarily, performance tests are much more expensive than other selection devices if many applicants are involved. Some examples of costs are equipment and materials used only for selection, the time and facilities needed for individual or small group administration of the selection instruments, the staff time spent in detailed identification of representative tasks during job analysis, and the development of test instructions, testing situations, and scoring procedures. Some of these costs can often be reduced, however. For example, frequently existing equipment may be usable and no special facilities needed.

In the following sections, we will discuss in more detail the rationale underlying the use of performance tests, describe examples of successful tests, and present the important steps in their development for selection programs. Finally, we will describe the development and use of assessment centers for managerial selection. As we have indicated previously, these may be regarded as performance tests that are used by many organizations for this difficult selection problem.

Consistency of Behavior

Paul Wernimont and John Campbell have made the most direct statement of the principles of performance tests as selection devices.[1] Their major thesis is that the selection process benefits in those cases in which "behavioral consistency" is the major thrust of the selection program. Thus the prediction of job behavior should be the purpose of selection. To clarify their point, Wernimont and Campbell categorize all the selection devices that could be used to predict job behavior into either signs or samples.

Signs are selection tests that are used as indicators of an individual's predisposition to behave in certain ways. To the extent that these signs are different in their characteristics from the job behaviors that are being predicted, their ability to relate directly to these job behaviors is limited. *Samples*, on the other hand, are those selection tests which gather information about behaviors that are consistent with the job behavior being predicted. To the extent these samples are similar in their characteristics to the job behaviors, their ability to predict job behavior is increased.

There are two major types of instruments that are regarded as samples. One type is instruments that gather information about an applicant's work experience and educational history to determine if any of the tasks of the job of interest have been demonstrated by the applicant in the past. If so, rating methods are then developed to judge the frequency of these behaviors, the applicant's success in performing them, and the similarity of their content to the job situation addressed in the selection program. These data are used in rating the probability of relevant behavior being demonstrated by the applicant on the job. The whole process should be systematic and founded on behavior. Wernimont and Campbell do not discuss specific selection devices to do this. However, consider previous chapters. These ideas were part of discussions on the appropriate design of training and experience evaluations, biodata forms, interviews, and the gathering of behavioral descriptions in personality assessment. In each of these cases, we emphasized the gathering of several descriptions of behavior closely related to job activities.

The second type of *sample* selection instrument discussed by Wernimont and Campbell consists of work sample tests and simulation exercises. Such devices are in essence what we have called performance tests and require the applicant to complete a set of actions that demonstrate whether or not the job behavior of interest can be successfully completed. It is this second type of *sample* that we discuss in this chapter.

Examples of Performance Tests

Work-sample tests are tailor made to match the important activities of the job being considered and have been classified as either motor or verbal.[2] The term *motor* (behavioral) is used if the test requires the physical manipulation of things, for example operating a machine, installing a piece of equipment, or making a product. The term *verbal* is used if the problem situation is primarily language or people oriented, for example, simulating an interrogation editing a manuscript for grammatical errors, or explaining how to train subordinates.

Examples of various performance tests and the jobs for which they were used are presented in Table 15.1. As is evident from the table, there have been a wide variety of tests have been used, even for the same job. Traditionally, motor performance tests have been most often used for selection of skilled craftworkers, technicians, and clerical staff. These jobs usually have a large component of equipment and tool usage and, therefore, are appropriate for such tests. However, such jobs often utilize a diversity of equipment, which means that one performance test would not be appropriate for all positions. Several tests, each directed to a specific set of job tasks, have been used in selection programs for any given job. This has been especially true for the skilled craft positions such as mechanic, electrician, and machine operator.

Motor Tests The following two examples are illustrations of motor performance tests. James Campion has described the development of a motor performance test used in the selection of maintenance mechanics.[3]

> *Motor Performance Test for Maintenance Mechanics*—The development of this test began with extensive job analysis that resulted in a list of task statements which experts thought were job-related and could be performed by a large number of applicants. Thus tasks were part of the job and within the repertoire of job applicants. In addition, experts

| TABLE 15.1 | EXAMPLES OF WORK-SAMPLE TESTS USED IN SELECTION |

Test	Job
Motor:	
Lathe	Machine operator
Drill press	
Tool dexterity	
Screw board test	
Packaging	
Shorthand	Clerical worker
Stenographic	
Typing	
Blueprint reading	Mechanic
Tool identification	
Installing belts	
Repair of gearbox	
Installing a motor	
Vehicle repair	
Tracing trouble in a complex circuit	Electronics technician
Inspection of electronic defects	
Electronics test	
Verbal:	
Report of recommendations for problem solution	Manager or supervisor
Small business manufacturing game	
Judgment and decision making test	
Supervisory judgment about training, safety, performance, evaluation	
Processing of mathematical data and evaluating hypotheses	Engineer or scientist
Basic information in chemistry	
Mathematical formulation and scientific judgment	
Oral fact finding	Communication specialist
Role playing of customer contacts	
Writing business letters	
Oral directions	

identified two major work activities that differentiated good and poor job performance: use of tools and accuracy of work. Tasks included in the test were installing pulleys and belts, disassembling and repairing a gearbox, installing and aligning a motor, pressing a bushing into a sprocket, and reaming it to fit a shaft. A distinct feature of the scoring system was that experts tried to identify all possible task behaviors an applicant might demonstrate in the test. Each possible behavior was evaluated and weighted and placed on the list. The rater, therefore, only had to observe the applicant behaviors and check them off. Adding weights assigned to the checked behavior determined the applicant's overall score.

Blueprint Reading Test—David Robinson has described this test as part of a selection program for the position of construction superintendent.[4] An architect was retrained to identify common architectural errors in blueprints and to incorporate these errors in the drawings of buildings which had actually been executed by the company. Applicants were asked to review the blueprints and to mark the location of the errors with a felt-tipped pen on copies of the drawings. The test was scored by counting the number of correct markings.

Verbal Tests   Verbal performance tests used as selection programs that focus on managers, staff specialists, engineers, scientists, and similar professionals have increased. These jobs frequently require the use of spoken or written messages or interpersonal interaction to complete tasks. It is these components that are simulated in verbal performance tests. The diversity of test types that characterized the motor tests also holds true for the sample of verbal tests listed in Table 15.1.

The following two examples are illustrations of verbal performance tests. The first was also reported by David Robinson and was used in the selection of a construction superintendent.

Scrambled Subcontractor Test—In the construction business, interruption of the critical construction path can be extremely costly. The most important factor in staying on the critical path is that subcontractors appear in the right order to do their work. Knowledge of the proper order of subcontractor appearance is a prerequisite to staying on this path. In order to test this knowledge, applicants were given a list of 30 subcontractors (e.g., roofing, framing, plumbing, fencing) and were asked to list them according to order of appearance on the job site. The order of appearance given by the applicant was compared with the order of appearance agreed upon by the company managers. The applicants were given the opportunity to discuss their rationale for particular orders. Minor deviations from the managers' solution were accepted.

The second example is of a reading test developed for packers of explosive materials that was reported by Robert Gatewood and Lyle Schoenfeld.[5]

Reading Test for Chemical Packages—Reading and understanding written material was critical to the job of chemical packager because often explosive chemicals were involved. Through job analysis it was deter-

mined that 50 percent of the material read dealt with safety procedures, 30 percent with work procedures, 15 percent with daily operations, and the remaining 5 percent with miscellaneous, company
material. These four areas were referred to as content categories of
reading material. A reading test was developed that used the actual
materials read on the job. In this test the applicant read a short passage drawn from work documents. The content of these passages
appeared in the same proportions as did the content categories of the
job materials. After each passage were a few true-false and multiple-
choice items that asked about the behavior called for on the job.
Answers were scored based on their conformity to the information
contained in the passage that had been presented.

Trainability Tests   Another variation of performance tests is trainability tests.
This type of test is most often used for selection for two kinds of jobs. The first
is jobs that do not presently exist but are anticipated in the near future and for
which extensive training is necessary. The second is jobs that do exist but are so
specialized or technical that applicants could not be expected to possess the
direct knowledge or skill to complete either appropriate ability tests or common
performance tests.

Richard Reilly and Edmond Israelski describe the development and use of
trainability tests by AT&T, which are known in the company as minicourses.[6]
The major purpose of the minicourse is to place the applicant in a test situation
that closely resembles the training setting. In this way, an assessment can be
made of the applicant's ability to learn critical material and complete the necessary, extensive training program. The strategy is clearly one of selection for
performance in training. The applicant is required first to complete a standardized sample of programmed training material, the minicourse, relevant to the
target position. A typical minicourse has a 6-hour time limit, although the
range is between 2 hours and 3 days. Upon completion of the minicourse, the
applicant answers a test designed to measure learning of the material of the
minicourse. A passing score qualifies the applicant to be admitted into the
training program. He or she must then successfully complete this training to
be offered employment.

Two types of minicourses have been developed. The first type consists of
highly specific material that matches training content very closely. An example
would be a course containing material relevant to learning to use a particular
piece of equipment. The second type of minicourse consists of more general
material and is used for jobs that are expected to change frequently because of
technological advancement. The purpose of the minicourse is to present basic
information that is appropriate despite the specific technology being used
presently on the job. For example, a minicourse was developed on understanding binary, octal, hexadecimal, and decimal numbering systems. The two authors
also present data supporting the validity of trainability testing for both training
and job performance criteria.

The Development of Performance Tests

Even though performance tests vary considerably in the jobs for which they are used and the problem situations they present to applicants, they all should be similar in terms of the steps taken by HR specialists in their development. These steps are listed in Table 15.2 and have been identified as essential to the construction of performance tests that are both legally defensible and useful in selecting capable applicants.[7] This section will present the details of these steps.

Job Analysis   The material presented in Chapters 7 through 9 of this book on the methods and procedures of job analysis is relevant in developing a performance test. Special care must be taken in describing job tasks to provide enough detail to clearly identify material and equipment used (motor), or the nature of interpersonal discussion and interaction (verbal) so that this information may serve as a basis for the performance test. To maximize the likelihood that the statement of the job tasks is accurate, one should obtain information from multiple independent sources, that is, several job incumbents and supervisors. One issue in doing this is the proficiency level of the workers and supervisors who are involved. It would seem necessary to rely heavily on information supplied by individuals who perform the job well. If the information in the job analysis is to be used to design and score the performance test, accurate information about the correct method of performance is necessary.

Identification of Job Tasks   The judging of job tasks according to frequency, importance, time required, level of difficulty, and/or consequence of error is also quite important. The results of such evaluation should contribute significantly to identifying the content of a performance test. The test should be addressed to those tasks that have a strong bearing on job performance. Usually task ratings provide such information. Special attention must be paid to tasks that are seasonal or not often repeated. Such tasks may be critical and have major consequence if not performed correctly. For this reason, it is usually recommended that ratings from several individuals be obtained.

Development of Testing Procedures   Once the tasks that will serve as the basis for the performance test have been identified, another important judgment must be made as to whether an applicant can realistically be expected to perform the task or not. As we have mentioned previously, in most cases it is usually assumed that the applicant can do the task, and it is directly incorporated into the performance test. In fewer cases the job task has some idiosyncratic features and cannot be done except by experienced workers. In such cases modifications must be made in the test situation. One modification is to provide the applicant with instructions about the operation of equipment, features of special materials used, or background information about company policy before the test is given. This modification is obviously workable only in those cases in which the amount of information necessary to perform the job task is relatively simple and easy to learn. In those cases in which this preliminary information is complex or difficult, the performance test is modified to measure the ability to develop the skill to perform the task. In those cases, the test usually consists of the preliminary

TABLE 15.2	STEPS IN THE DEVELOPMENT OF PERFORMANCE TESTS

- Job analysis
- Identification of tasks to be tested
- Development of testing procedures
- Scoring test results
- Training of judges

steps of the task or of the motor or verbal processes that are fundamental to learning the task.

Selecting Tasks   Even after the most appropriate job tasks to be included in the performance test have been identified, further study of these must be done to make the most efficient use of testing time. The most important considerations in this study are the following:

1. The total time required to perform the task must be reasonable. It is expensive to administer performance tests, and the cost increases as the length of the task to be completed in the test increases.

2. Tasks that a large majority of applicants can do provide little help in discriminating among good and poor applicants.

3. If two tasks are approximately equally appropriate to include in the performance test, but one task uses less expensive materials, equipment, or facilities, usually this one is chosen.

4. Tasks should also be judged on the nature of the material that would be scored in a test. All else being equal, tasks that have standardized operations or products or have easily defined verbal or interaction components are more appropriate in performance tests than tasks not so characterized. It is usually far easier and less expensive to both develop and score the test for these types of tasks.

5. The problem presented in the tasks of the performance test should normally be representative of the job in terms of difficulty and complexity. The reason is that the testing of only very easy or very difficult material usually results in less discrimination among applicants. With very easy material almost all applicants pass and with very difficult material only very few are successful. If the purpose of using the performance test is to identify differences among applicants, the difficulty level of the performance test tasks should be more representative of the difficulty level of the tasks of the job.

Specifying Administration Procedures As with other selection tests, it is important that the performance test be consistently administered to all applicants and its grading be consistent among all scorers. Standardization of testing conditions requires that a set of instructions be developed to inform the applicant of the nature of the task, what is expected of him or her, and the materials and equipment to be used. Also, the same or identical conditions for testing should be provided each applicant. To the extent possible, information should be provided on what actions, products, or outcomes will be scored. For grading, rules must be developed to specify what constitutes a "correct" response and how many points should be deducted for various deficiencies. All scorers should be thoroughly trained in the interpretation of these rules.

Establishing Independent Test Sections In developing the task problem of the performance test, another important consideration to keep in mind is the independence of various parts of the test. All else being equal, it is preferable *not* to have the applicant's performance on one part of the test be closely tied to a previous part of the test. For example if all errors are independent of one another, it is possible to obtain a larger sample of the behavior of the applicant. If, on the other hand, the test was developed so that the identification of one or two errors would disclose the other errors, there is a greater probability of obtaining a distorted measurement of the applicant's performance. If the applicant does not recognize the one or two central errors, he or she has no opportunity to identify the remaining errors correctly; if he or she does identify the central errors, then the rest become apparent. This actually makes the test only a one- or two-item test for such applicants.

Lack of independence is most likely when the performance test is a sequence of steps in a job process like sewing a garment or constructing a small piece of apparatus. In either case, an error in measuring the materials to be used would adversely affect the remaining steps. The applicant may be able to perform these remaining steps well and, in fact, does acceptably given the starting materials. However, most scoring systems judge the accuracy of the behavior or product and do not make allowances for faulty starting materials. To avoid this problem, some tests have been designed to provide a new set of acceptable materials for each phase of the job process. For example, if the first phase of a performance test is measuring and cutting the necessary pieces, the applicant stops after this phase. The pieces are taken to be scored by the judges, and the applicant is provided with a set of acceptable pieces to use in the next phase of the construction task.

Eliminating Contaminating Factors Another important feature to keep in mind in developing a performance test is to ensure that apparatus, jargon, or other testing elements which only have a minor influence on job performance do not interfere with or limit the test performance of some applicants who are not familiar with these elements. For example, in a performance test for a HR specialist, some numerical data may be provided from a company attitude survey. The applicant is asked to make some preliminary data analyses and use these results to answer a few specific management questions about the employees' attitudes about company procedures. The data analyses are to be performed on a personal computer. A serious problem could occur if an applicant does not know how to operate the computer that is provided for the performance test. The central concept of the test is to measure the ability to choose and interpret the appropriate statistical analyses for the management questions that are asked. The skill to operate a personal computer is of almost no importance. For those who are unable to operate this particular piece of equipment efficiently, however, the equipment becomes a major component of the test. In cases such as this, it is appropriate to provide a variety of apparatuses, to train the applicant in the use of the apparatus before the performance test begins, or to provide an operator of the apparatus to carry out the requests of the applicant. From previous remarks it should be apparent that modifications such as these are not necessary if the operation of a particular apparatus is essential to the job task and not easily learned. In such a case, the apparatus becomes an essential part of the performance test.

Selecting the Number of Test Problems   The final point we address in test construction is the number of times an applicant will be asked to perform a job activity during a performance test. A trade-off usually exists between the time and cost of testing, and the increased reliability of having multiple demonstrations of the task by the applicant. The general guideline is to have the applicant repeat the task several times within cost limitations. For example, many skilled craft positions, for example, typing, sewing, maintenance, or machine operation, have short-cycle tasks. An applicant can provide several products within a relatively brief period of time by repeating the cycle of tasks. In such cases, it is desirable to design several repetitions of the task into the performance test. This would be especially true if a high degree of precision or accuracy is necessary in the product. In these cases, a larger data sample would be more useful for assessing the applicant's performance level. Obviously, if the task of the performance test is very long or costly to stage, a very limited number of trials should be scheduled.

Scoring Test Results   The scoring of the performance test must be clearly defined because the decisions facing the scorer are often very difficult. In many cases a judgment must be made about the acceptability of task performance when multiple factors are present. Scoring generally is a function of comparing the test task performance of the applicant to a standard defined by the organization as being satisfactory. Table 15.3 provides examples of several factors that have been used primarily in scoring *motor* performance tests. In this type of test, the *task process* and/or the *task product* is scored. The task process is the actions or observable behaviors that are demonstrated by the applicant in doing the task. The task product is the result of the task process. In motor performance tests, products are usually physical objects such as a typed document, a piece of sewn clothing, or a set of joined pieces of wood or other building materials. In general, a process is scored when there are clearly a small number of ways to do the job, and these ways invariably lead to an acceptable product. The operation of machinery in a continuous job process would be an example. A product is scored in those situations in which a large number of different behaviors can lead to an acceptable product.

TABLE 15.3	CRITERIA USED IN SCORING MOTOR PERFORMANCE TESTS	

Standard	Process Criteria	Product Criteria
Quality	Accuracy Error rate Choice of tools and or materials Efficiency of steps taken	Conformance to specifications Dimensions or other measures Spacing Position Strength Suitability for use General appearance
Quantity	Time to complete	Quantity of output
Learning time	Number of steps for which guidance is needed	Improvement in meeting quantity stadards Improvement in meeting quality standards
Cost	Amount of material used	Number of rejects
Safety	Handling of tools Accident rate	Safety of completed product

SOURCE: Lynnette B. Plumlee. *A short guide to the Development of Performance Tests* (Washington, D.C.: Personnel Research and Development Center. U.S. Civil Service Commission, Professional Series 75–1, January 1975).

Standards As Table 15.3 indicates, a number of separate standards can be scored for both process and product categories. Quality is vital, of course, important in almost all jobs. However, it assumes increased importance for those tasks in which time or cost to complete the task is secondary to the correctness of the task effort. Tailoring, inspection, and equipment repair are examples. Quantity is most importantly scored for those performance tests in which amount produced within a given time period is under the control of the worker and means cost savings to the organization. The review of payments made by customers is an example. Cost becomes important as a scorable standard when expensive materials are involved in constructing a product and waste should be minimized. An example would be tasks like the repair of a research apparatus in which there are several options available that vary greatly in their expense.

The remaining two standards, learning time and safety, are used much less frequently than the other standards. Learning time is a logical standard for tasks which are characterized by having a variety of novel demands placed on the incumbent; the technical repair of a variety of sophisticated, electronic equipment could be an example. In many cases, the task of repair requires the worker to learn and use new methods of diagnosis and correction constantly. The length of time that an employee takes to learn these new methods translates directly into costs for the organization. Safety is obviously an important dimension to score when physical injury can be caused by an incorrect process or product. In many cases more than one of these standards are used in scoring; for example, quantity and quality are often used together. Also, process and product can both be scored in the same performance test.

Process dimensions used in scoring can be identified by using excellent workers presently on the job. Both demonstration and descriptions of task steps given by these workers have been used. Most organizations have defined the physical dimensions or properties of satisfactory products. This information is often used in scoring product dimensions of motor performance tests. For example, the diameter of rolled wire, the strength of welds, and the location of buttons sewn on a blouse are all such standards.

Rules In the actual scoring of the motor performance test, the assignment of numbers to the applicant's test performance must have defined rules. Most often, especially if there are several repetitions or separately scored parts of the performance test, a simple "0, 1 rule" is used. Performance meeting standard is scored "1," and performance that does not is scored "0." Total .score for the test is obtained by summing across all parts of the test. For example, if ten repetitions of making a weld are required, an applicant's score could range from 0 to 10. Another scoring option is to use scales, for example I to 5. The highest number on the scale is assigned if the performance meets the desired level and other numbers are assigned to less acceptable performance, in descending order of acceptability. In doing this, however, it is necessary to determine how much of a deviation from the desired level each number on the scale represents.

If many different standards are scored in the performance test, for example, quality of the products, quantity produced, and cost of the work process, a rule must be stated to allow for the combining of these separate scores into one total score. In defining this rule, weights are assigned to each different standard scored. These weights can be determined by statistical analysis, by using cost of correction of error data compiled by the company, or judgments of relative importance of the factors by experts. For example, suppose that on each of the previously mentioned three scoring standards the highest possible score is 10, and we have determined by one of these methods that quality is four times as important as cost and quantity is twice as important as cost. An applicant's raw score on the quality standard is multiplied by 4, the raw score on quantity is multiplied by 2, and the raw score on the cost factor is left unchanged. These three adjusted scores are then added together to obtain the total score for the performance test. In those cases in which evidence cannot be determined that argues for differentially weighting the standards, each standard should remain unweighted and unadjusted scores summed for a total.

The scoring of verbal performance tests is different from that of motor performance tests. The general principle is essentially the same—the verbal performance of the applicant is compared against a standard that has been deemed satisfactory by the organization. The use of words and concepts, however, and the interaction among individuals cannot be as precisely defined as standards of motor performance tests. In many cases the scoring of verbal performance tests depends on the extensive training of judges. We discuss such scoring methods later in our discussion of assessment centers, which have a large component of verbal performance tests.

The Training of Judges   For motor performance tests, if scoring standards and rules have been well defined, training raters in how to judge applicant performance is relatively straightforward. Videotapes of applicant task behaviors have been used to train raters to make judgments about process dimensions.[8] Whether videotapes or live demonstrations are used in training, the rater is given an explanation and a description of appropriate job process behaviors including the sequence of the behaviors. Emphasis is then placed on demonstrations of appropriate and inappropriate behavior. Videotapes seemingly have an advantage in this phase because they can be used frequently, stopped at critical moments, and replayed to demonstrate specific points. Logically, it is important to present numerous inappropriate behaviors during this training to familiarize the rater with errors before actual testing begins.

Training raters to evaluate product dimensions is usually conducted by using multiple examples of actual products. The raters are instructed in the definition of the scoring dimensions and how to make measurements. Frequently, special tools such as gauges, micrometers, and electronic equipment are used in doing this. In this training, raters are required to make measurements of each product dimension, and the resulting numbers are compared to predetermined, accurate measurements. If the numerical values generated by the rater match the accurate measurements, the rater is able measure the scored product dimensions correctly. If the two sets of numbers do not match, the rater should receive more training. In addition to being able to obtain the correct measurements, raters must be trained in using the scale and assigning a score to the measured product dimension. In doing this, the rater is instructed in the decision rules of scoring, which we have discussed previously, and asked to use these rules to score several products that vary on the product dimensions. Usually these products have been scored by experts. The scores of the rater are compared with those of the experts to determine accuracy.

Reliability of measurement is important in developing a scoring system and training raters in its use. By using some measure of interrater reliability, discussed in Chapter 4, high agreement among raters in their measurement and scoring should be demonstrated. If raters do not demonstrate reliability in their judgments after training, either more training is necessary, the scoring system must be changed, or the raters replaced.

An Example of the Development of a Performance Test

Neal Schmitt and Cheri Ostroff describe the development of a performance test that was used for selection of emergency telephone operators for a police department.[9] Job analysis was conducted through two meetings with experienced workers. The first meeting, with four workers, generated a list of task statements. The second meeting, with three other workers, reviewed and revised this list. This revised list was then submitted to supervisory personnel for final revision. Seventy-eight task statements were produced that were subsequently grouped into categories based on task similarity. All workers were then reconvened in order to generate statements of the KSAs needed to perform the 78 tasks successfully. This meeting resulted in a list of 54 KSAs, which were also arranged into similar content groups. The following is an example.

Communication Skills:
1. Ability to speak on the telephone in a clearly understandable manner.
2. Ability to control conversations in order to acquire information needed to respond to emergencies.

The next step was to evaluate the importance of these tasks and KSAs to performing the job. To do this, one questionnaire was written that asked each worker to rate each task on three 7-point scales: (1) the relative time spent on the task compared to all others, (2) the relative difficulty of the task compared to all others, and (3) the criticality of the task as judged by the degree to which incorrect performance results in negative consequences. A second questionnaire asked each worker to rate each KSA on three scales: (1) the necessity for newly hired employees to possess the KSA, (2) the extent to which trouble is likely to occur if the KSA is ignored in selection, and (3) the extent to which the KSA distinguishes between superior and average workers. The first scale required simply a "yes or no" response while the other two used 7-point response formats.

Interrater reliabilities were calculated for all scales, with all but one being .87 or above. The data from these scales were then used to identify the KSAs to be measured in selection. To do this, three factors were considered: (1) being linked to important job tasks, (2) being necessary for new workers, (3) having a high score on the scale measuring likely trouble when this was ignored in selection. The resulting KSAs were grouped into six dimensions (see Table 15.4).

Three tests were developed to use in selection, an oral directions/typing test, a situational interview, and a telephone call simulation. The linkage between these devices and the KSAs is also contained in Table 15.4. To develop these tests, both important job tasks and KSAs were used. Each test measured

TABLE 15.4   KSAS AND TESTS USED FOR POLICE OPERATOR SELECTION

	Selection Test		
KSA	**Oral Directions**	**Interview**	**Simulation**
Communication skills		X	X
Emotional control		X	X
Judgment		X	X
Cooperativeness		X	X
Memory	X		
Clerical/technical skill	X		

SOURCE: Neal Schmitt and Cheri Ostroff, "Operationalizing the 'Behavioral Consistency' Approach: Selection Test Development Based on a Content-Oriented Strategy," *Personnel Psychology* 39 (1986): 91–108.

at least two KSAs and incorporated parts of the important job tasks linked to those KSAs.

Oral Directions/Typing Test   This test was designed to measure the applicant's memory and technical/clerical skills. The test consisted of four parts: (1) spelling of common street and place names, (2) recording important information from telephone calls, (3) answering questions about the location and movement of police units after monitoring conversations, and (4) typing forms required in report writing. Material for each of the four parts was obtained directly from job incidents and activities to ensure representativeness of job tasks.

Situational Interview   The development of questions for this type of interview has been described in Chapter 12. Using those procedures, critical incidents were obtained from incumbent workers. These incidents were used to form questions about how the applicant would act in specific situations. Since applicants were unlikely to have direct job experience, the questions were phrased in such a way that applicants could provide answers drawing on their own corresponding experience and knowledge. For example, a critical incident identified by the incumbent workers was:

> A caller becomes abusive when talking to the operator. The operator gets mad and verbally abuses the caller using derogatory language.

This was transformed into the following question:

> How would you react if you were a sales clerk, waitress, or service station attendant and one of your customers talked back to you, indicated you should have known something you did not, or told you that you were not waiting on them fast enough?

Seventeen such questions were developed.

Telephone Call Simulation   This test placed the job applicant in a role-playing exercise by requiring him or her to act like an operator taking calls from complainants. An experienced operator played the role of a caller. To do this, six different scripts were prepared for the operator-caller in order to ensure equality of the situation for each applicant. The callers were also trained in the presentation of their complaints. Each applicant was given one practice trial to become familiar with the test. Applicants recorded information that they gathered from the call on a standardized form used by the department to record information from such calls.

It can easily be understood that these steps resulted in a three-instrument selection program that closely resembled actual on-the-job behaviors. Moreover, development of these tests relied on the content validation procedure recommended in the *Uniform Guidelines*: They identified important tasks provided by a job analysis technique which also estimated their importance and criticality.

Major tasks were represented by the instruments. Face validity was cited as an additional benefit.

The Effectiveness of Performance Tests

Evaluations of the results of using performance tests in selection programs have almost universally been positive and have identified several benefits in this use. Not surprisingly, primary interest has been focused on the demonstrated validity of these selection tests. James Asher and James Sciarrino did an extensive review of the validities of eight different types of selection tests.[10] When a measure of job performance was used as the measure to determine validity, the motor performance tests were found to be the second best selection test, behind biographical data. Verbal performance tests ranked fourth. When a measure of success in training was used to determine validity, the pattern was reversed with verbal performance tests being superior to motor tests. These authors concluded that both types of performance tests consistently demonstrated validity, with motor tests being a better predictor of job performance (.62) than job training (.45) and the opposite being true of verbal performance tests (.55 for training and .45 for job performance). This indicates that the use of each type of performance test is affected by the measure of success that is used.

In a few cases, performance tests have been directly compared for validity with other types of tests for the same job. One study examined both a verbal performance test and an intelligence test in relationship to success in a police training program.[11] Data were collected from three different samples of cadets. The verbal performance test was found to be valid in all three cases (.52, .72, and .64); the intelligence test was valid for only one sample (.56). Moreover, when prediction of success in training was analyzed, it was determined that the work sample test gave adequate prediction and the additional information obtained from the intelligence test did not improve this predictability. Another study compared a motor performance test for maintenance mechanics with a battery of paper-and-pencil tests. Included in this battery were both mechanical comprehension and intelligence tests. All tests were evaluated against supervisors' ratings of work performance. The differences between the two types of tests were large as all of the motor performance tests were found to be valid and none of the paper-and-pencil tests were. Meta-analysis of work sample tests for use in job promotion has resulted in a corrected correlation with job performance of .54, the highest validity among seven predictors evaluated.[12] These findings of the validity of performance tests reflect our previous comments about the effectiveness of sample over sign tests.

Adverse Impact   In addition to validity, adverse impact of performance tests on minority applicants has also been examined. As we discussed in Chapter 2, adverse impact refers to the disproportionate rejection rate of one demographic group in comparison with other demographic groups. One study by a group of researchers at Michigan State University compared the scores of minority and nonminority applicants on both written and performance tests for positions such as metal trade apprentices.[13] A difference in scores between the two groups was identified for only one of three performance tests but for all five of the written tests. One conclusion was that the adverse impact of the performance test was less than one-half that of the written tests.

A related study by Wayne Cascio and Niel Phillips did a comprehensive study on the selection rates of minority and nonminority groups using performance tests for a series of city government positions.[14] Comparisons were made among white, black, and Latino applicants for 21 tests, 11 of which were motor performance and 10 of which were verbal performance, used for selection in 21 jobs. No difference in selection rates was found for any of the jobs. When comparisons were made of test scores only for the three groups, in order to study possible differences attributable only to the test, significant differences were found in 3 of the 21 tests. Each group scored significantly higher on one of the tests—there was no pattern of nonminority applicants outscoring minority applicants. Other analyses found that no gender or ethnic bias occurred among raters in scoring the performance of different applicant groups.

Other Aspects   These last two studies also found other positive results from using performance tests. One desirable condition in selection is to have applicants accept the instruments as having "face validity"—being appropriate for selection. The Michigan State study analyzed the attitudes of the applicants about different selection tests. Large percentages of both nonminority and minority applicants judged the performance tests as "about right" in difficulty. Cascio and Phillips reported that during the first 17 months that performance tests were used, no complaints about their appropriateness were lodged. This was in contrast to the previous complaint rate of 10 to 20 percent of all applicants when other types of tests were used.

Cascio and Phillips concluded that performance tests also serve as realistic job previews and can lead to the benefits we discussed in Chapter I . They cite as an example the test for sewer pumping station operator. During an initial one-hour instruction period a sewer mechanic explained and demonstrated (as if he were the applicant's supervisor) procedures for the general maintenance of sewer pipes and equipment, for example how to clean filters, grease fittings, and read a pressure chart. The test was given during the second hour, when each applicant was required to repeat the demonstration as if on the job. Follow-up interviews revealed that those who qualified for and accepted the job had an accurate idea of the job demands. For all jobs combined, the turnover rate before the use of performance tests was approximately 40 percent. During the 9 to 26 months after performance testing was started this rate dropped to less than 3 percent. It was estimated that had saved the city $336,199 in costs.

At the risk of stating the obvious, it is findings such as these that have led prominent selection researchers to highly recommend performance tests as selection devices. It is in this sense that Cascio and Phillips entitled their study, "Performance Testing: A Rose among Thorns?"

Assessment Centers
The definition of an Assessment Center (AC) that was developed by the Task Force on Assessment Center Standards is as follows:

An *assessment center* consists of a standardized evaluation of behavior on multiple inputs. Multiple trained observers and techniques are used. Judgments about behavior are made, in part, from specially developed assessment simulations These judgments are pooled by the assessors at an evaluation meeting during which assessment data are reported and discussed and the assessors agree on the evaluation of the dimension and any overall evaluation that is made.[15]

In more familiar terms, an AC is a procedure for measuring KSAs in groups of individuals (usually 12 to 24) that uses a series of devices, many of which are verbal performance tests. The KSAs are patterns of behavior that are demonstrated when the applicant completes the performance tests. The devices in an AC, usually called *exercises*, are designed so the participants have several opportunities to demonstrate each of the patterns of behavior being evaluated. The evaluators, referred to as *assessors*, are specially trained in the observing and recording of behavior of participants in the exercises. This information is used when the assessors meet as a group to share their observations of each participant and also to develop a Consensus evaluation of each.

ACs have been used for both selection and career development In selection, the emphasis is on identifying those participants that demonstrate the behaviors thought necessary to perform in the position being considered. When used for career development, the emphasis is on determining those behaviors each participant does well and those in which each is deficient. The latter are subsequently included in training programs to correct the deficiency. For our purposes, we will concentrate on the ACs used for selection. The next sections discuss in some detail the topics we have briefly introduced.

Assessment Centers in Industry

The Management Progress Study of AT&T marked the beginning of the use of the assessment center for industrial organizations.[16] This program was begun in 1956 to study the career development of men hired for managerial purposes. According to Douglas Bray, who designed the study, the general questions that prompted the study were as follows:

What significant changes take place in men as their lives develop in a business career?

Conversely, are there changes we might expect or desire that do not occur?

What are the causes of these changes or stabilities? More particularly, what are the effects of company climate, policies, and procedures?

How accurately can progress in management be predicted? What are the important indicators and how are they best measured?

The study was to provide information to be used in directing the career development of managers at AT&T.

One major focus of the study was to identify a list of personal attributes of managers that were initially thought to be related to successful career progress. In all, 25 characteristics (e.g., communication skill, goal flexibility, self-objectivity, etc.) were identified by using information drawn from research literature, industrial psychologists specializing in management career patterns, and senior executives at AT&T. The design of the study was to measure these characteristics in 274 new managers periodically over several years and to relate these data to progress through the levels of management. During this time, none of the data were made available to anyone but the researchers.

Obviously, the immediate problem for those conducting the study was to develop devices to measure the 25 characteristics of interest. It was decided that it would be necessary to examine each manager thoroughly at each testing period to obtain useful data. To do this, a 3 1/2-day assessment center was devised. Managers were brought together in groups of 12 and several methods of measuring personal characteristics were administered. These included tests of general mental ability, personality and attitude questionnaires, interviews, several group problems, an individual administrative exercise, and projective tests of personality.

It is not within the scope of this book to discuss in detail the results of the study. However, as a summary, the reports published over the years have provided much useful information about managerial careers. More importantly for us, the assessment information obtained from the various exercises was shown to be related to subsequent movement through managerial levels. This, of course, prompted much attention in the use of these types of exercises and the whole concept of assessment centers for managerial selection. The use of multiple-day, multiple-exercise testing programs quickly grew. Although there were variations among these programs, there was much similarity in the types of assessment devices used. These usually paralleled those used in the AT&T study. The next section discusses some of these types of exercises, mainly emphasizing the individual and group performance tests that were used.

Assessment Center Exercises

Dimensions   The development of an AC starts with a job analysis to identify clusters of job activities that are the important parts of the job of interest. Each cluster should be specific, observable, and consist of job tasks that can be logically related. These job clusters are referred to as *dimensions*, and it is these that are measured by the assessment center devices. Table 15.5 provides a list and brief definitions of nine dimensions that are commonly used in ACs. It is important to note that these dimensions are defined in terms of actual activities on the job. The definitions in Table 15.5 give brief summaries of the kinds of activities included. In actual use, the definitions are more detailed. For example, the dimension of *Tolerance for Stress* is often described in terms of the actions taken to meet specific multiple demands (e.g, from subordinates, superiors, outside pressure groups, etc.) and the specific multiple roles (e.g., negotiator, public relations specialist, performance evaluator, etc.) that characterize the job under study. These behaviors described for each dimension serve as the basis for the

| TABLE 15.5 | BEHAVIORAL DIMENSIONS FREQUENTLY MEASURED IN ASSESSMENT CENTERS |

Dimension	Definition
Oral Communication	Effective expression in individual or group situations (includes gestures and nonverbal communications)
Planning and Organizing	Establishing a course of action for self and/or others to accomplish a specific goal; planning proper assignments of personnel and appropriate allocation of resources
Delegation	Utilizing subordinates effectively; allocating decision making and other responsibilities to the appropriate subordinates
Control	Establishing procedures to monitor and/or regulate processes, tasks, or activities of subordinates and job activities and responsibilities; taking action to monitor the results of delegated assignments or projects
Decisiveness	Readiness to make decisions, render judgments, take action, or commit oneself
Initiative	Active attempts to influence events to achieve goals; self-starting rather than passive acceptance. Taking action to achieve goals beyond those called for; originating action
Tolerance for Stress	Stability of performance under pressure and/or opposition
Adaptability	Maintaining effectiveness in varying environments, with various tasks, responsibilities, or people
Tenacity	Staying with a position or plan of action until the desired objective is achieved or is no longer reasonably attainable

Source: George Thornton III and William Byham, *Assessment Centers and Managerial Performance* (New York: Academic Press, 1982).

development of assessment devices to measure the dimension. It is easy to understand why ACs have relied heavily on performance tests as a primary measurement device; it is usually straightforward to translate these job activities into test activities. Because of the nature of managerial work, these performance tests are usually what we have called verbal performance tests.

In looking through the list of dimensions in Table 15.5, you probably have noticed that many of them have the same title as personality dimensions we discussed in Chapter 14 . This should not be surprising. Remember that personality describes the interaction of an individual with his or her environment. Interaction is usually described in terms of activities. When AC dimensions identify either clusters of job activities completed with other organization members or activities to meet organization demands, these dimensions clearly approach the notion of personality dimensions.[17] You might also remember that in Chapter 14 we pointed out that measurement of personality characteristics with paper-and-pencil tests is tenuous because written descriptions of behavior do not always correspond to actual behavior. We went on to say that a useful measurement strategy would be to collect actual behavioral data in job situations. In essence ACs, by using performance tests, attempt to do this. It is not surprising, therefore, that there is a close similarity between personality dimensions and the behavioral dimensions of assessment centers.

Traditional Assessment Devices   Following the example of the AT&T assessment center, various types of tests and interviews are often used in ACs. We briefly describe the use of several of these types of tests, but discuss in detail only the performance tests.

Intelligence or mental ability tests have been used not only in AC,s but in several other managerial selection programs. Although results have varied somewhat depending on the specific test used, generally scores on these tests have been related to a variety of measures of managerial success and are usefully included in an AC. Personality tests both objective and projective, have not been as successful and are often omitted from recent ACs. As we mentioned previously, the measurement limitations of personality tests are great, and more useful information about the candidate's behavior is supplied by performance tests.

The interview is also employed quite often in ACs; in many ways it is similar to the selection interview we recommended using in Chapter 12. Commonly referred to as the *Background Interview*, the emphasis of the AC interview is to gather information from the candidate about job activities that represent the behavioral dimensions being evaluated in the AC. The interviewer is to gather as much information as possible about these dimensions but not to evaluate the candidate's ability to perform the job. This is quite different from the usual selection interview. Many of the recommendations made in chapter 12 for the use of the interview are incorporated in the AC Background Interview: Each interview is structured and focuses on previous job behaviors; relatively few behavioral dimensions are utilized and multiple questions are prepared to tap each dimension; interviewers are trained to record relevant job actions for each behavioral dimension; and a formal scoring system is used to evaluate each candidate on each behavioral dimension. Used in this fashion, the interview has been shown to be very effective in contributing to the information generated from other AC devices to arrive at a final evaluation of a candidate.

Performance Tests   It is the use of performance tests, sometimes referred to as *simulation tests*, that distinguishes ACs from other selection programs. We describe the most frequently used of these devices.

In-Basket   The *In-Basket* is a paper-and-pencil test that is designed to replicate administrative tasks of the job under consideration. The name of the test is taken from the "in-and out-baskets" that are on some managers' desks and are used to hold organizational memos coming to and going from the managers.

TABLE 15.6	EXAMPLES OF IN-BASKET MEMOS

TO: Ralph Alexander, Craig Russell, Jim Breaugh, Diana Stone
FROM: Susan Taylor, Division Head
RE: Annual Division Planning Meeting

      It is again time to plan for our annual division employee meeting—when we explain to our employees what we did with their invested capital. The site suggestions for the planning meeting are Buffalo or San Juan, although Craig has suggested Miami in order to relive old memories. What do you think?

TO: A. DeNisi, Head of Document Production
FROM: Larry Peters, Reviewer

      Why are you sending me all of these reports to review? I thought we agreed that I would only review those I know something about. If I remember, we discussed only those two reports on mid-life crisis. Also, why did you put L. Schoenfeldt on my review team? All he seems to know about is Japanese travel excursions.

TO: R. Klimoski and N. Schmitt
FROM: F. Schmidt
RE: Sample Size for Testing

      I have designed the upcoming exploratory study of the impact of exposure to TV soaps and the *National Enquirer* on general mental ability. However, I am really concerned about the sample size—I only have about half the population of China. Do I need the other half? What about Brazil? Please let me know.

     The content of the administrative issues contained in the set of memos that make up the *In-Basket* should be obtained from job analysis information and should be representative of the actual administrative tasks of the position. Examples of typical *In-Basket* items are presented in Table 15.6. The *In-Basket* is completed individually and usually takes two to three hours. The candidate is seated at a desk in a private area on which is found the written material of the *In-Basket*. Usually no oral directions are given by the AC staff nor is there any interaction between AC staff and the candidate while the test is being taken.

     The *In-Basket* has an introductory document that describes the hypothetical situation. This situation is some Variation of the theme that the candidate has recently been placed in a position because of the resignation, injury, vacation, or death of the previous incumbent. A number of memos, describing a variety of problems, have accumulated and must be addressed. The candidate is also informed that, unfortunately, he or she has made previous plans that cannot be changed which require leaving the company for the next several days. The candidate must, therefore, indicate what action should be taken about the issues in the memos by leaving written memos in the out-basket before departing. No other office members can be contacted. In addition to the memos, the candidate is provided with background information about the unit he or she is now managing through organization charts, mission statements, and company policy statements.

The memos themselves are presented on different types and sizes of paper and are both typed and handwritten to add realism. The candidate is to read the memos and to write his or her recommendation as to what action should be taken and which personnel should be involved. A standard time period is given each candidate in which to complete the test. After the candidate has finished, he or she may be interviewed by one of the AC staff and asked to explain the overall philosophy used in addressing the memos and the reasoning behind the specific recommendations made for each administrative problem. The written and oral information is used by the AC staff to evaluate behavioral dimensions, such as decision making, planning and organizing, ability to delegate, decisiveness, independence, and initiative.

Leaderless Group Discussion (LGD)   The *In-Basket* and the *LGD* together are probably the two most often-used performance tests in ACs. The *LGD* is designed to represent those managerial attributes that require the interaction of small groups of individuals to solve a problem successfully. In the *LGD*, participants are tested in groups of six. These six are seated around a conference table usually placed in the middle of a room. AC assessors are seated along the walls of the room to observe and record the behavior of the *LGD* participants.

The *LGD* has its name because no one member is designated as the official leader or supervisor of the group. The meeting is one of equals faced with a common problem. This problem could emphasize either cooperation or competition among the six participants. A problem describing an employment situation in which the organization must issue a statement in response to charges of discrimination in hiring or lack of control of environmental pollutants would be an example of an emphasis on cooperative actions. Competitive problems are usually characterized by a small amount of some organizational resource (e.g., money for raises or new equipment, a onetime fund for capital investment, etc.), that is not large enough to satisfy the wishes of all *LGD* members. In both cases, the group is provided with a written description of the issue together with relevant supporting material. The group is then usually charged with producing a written report that specifies the action to be taken by the company. In most cases, 1 1/2 to 2 hours is the maximum time allotted.

In addition to being classified as cooperative or competitive, the *LGD* problem can have either defined or undefined roles. Defined roles occur when each group member is given specific information, unknown to the others, that both describes his or her position in the company and provides additional information about the department or the individuals that the *LGD* participant is supposed to be representing. This information is to be used by the participant as he or she sees fit to influence the actions of the group. Unassigned roles are obviously those in which such information is not provided to each participant. Assigned roles are most commonly used in competitive *LGD* problems. Each member's role information is used to argue that the scarce resource should be allocated for that participant's purposes. Table 15.7 contains examples of a general problem

TABLE 15.7	EXAMPLES OF LEADERLESS GROUP DISCUSSION PROBLEM

Problem: Because of an unexpected resignation, your department has $5,000 available to use as onetime bonuses for department personnel. Your group is to submit a written recommendation as to how this money should be allocated.

Assigned Role# 1: George Dreher, Administrative Coordinator
Your assistant, Mick Mount has performed excellently in the last eight months. On his own time he has taken two mini-courses on office automation equipment to become familiar with differences among products that you are considering buying. His recommendations were valuable in saving $1,700 in the purchase of two electronic mail processing units. His other work is also impressive. He is currently receiving only $1,200 a year more than a senior secretary, even though you assign him much more responsibility.

Assigned Role#2: John Bouldreau, MIS Coordinator
Lynn Shore has been with the company for 18 months, coming directly from college. In the last six months she has made significant contributions to the development of an improved inventory control system. She not only wrote the programs but also led the training of the users of the system. At the most recent staff meeting, four people commented on how much time they have saved in scheduling because of the accuracy of the system. Recently Lynn has been offered a position with Auburn, Inc. at a $5,000/yr. increase. Because of several personal reasons, she has indicated that she would prefer to remain with you if the pay difference would be reduced.

and two assigned roles that could be used in such *LGD* situations. The *LGD* is used to measure behavioral dimensions such as oral communication, tolerance for stress, adaptability, resilience, energy, leadership, and persuasiveness.

Case Analysis   In case analysis exercises, each participant is provided with a long description of an organizational problem that changes according to the job being considered in the AC. For a higher level position, the case frequently describes the history of certain events in a company, with relevant financial data, marketing strategy, and organizational structure. Frequently, industry data concerning new products, consumer trends, and technology are introduced. The case focuses on a dilemma that the participant is asked to resolve. In doing so, specific recommendations must be given, supporting data presented, and any changes in company strategy detailed.

The content of the case is varied to be appropriate for the position being considered. For middle-management jobs, the major issue frequently concerns the design and implementation of operational plans or systems, for example, management information systems or job process systems. For first-level management, the focus often is either on the resolution of subordinate conflicts, subordinate nonconformity with policies, or reevaluation of specific work methods. After the candidate has been given time to read and analyze the case, he or she may be asked to prepare a written report, make an oral presentation to AC staff members, or discuss the case with other participants. The primary dimensions usually evaluated are oral and written communication, planning and organizing, control, decisiveness, resilience, and analysis.

The Training of Assessors

As we discussed previously, the scoring of the verbal performance tests that characterize ACs is usually more difficult than the scoring of motor performance tests. Therefore, for an AC to be useful as a selection device, the training of the staff members, referred to as assessors, who have the responsibility of observing and evaluating the behaviors of the participants, is crucial. As we pointed out, the focus of ACs is on the behavioral dimensions. The exercises require the participants to provide behaviors relative to these dimensions. Each dimension must be measured by more than one exercise. Also, each exercise usually measures more than one dimension. The major duty of an assessor is to record the behavior of a participant in an exercise and use the data to rate the participant on each behavioral dimension appropriate for the exercise. For example, if the *LGD* is designed to measure the dimensions of oral communication, adaptability, and persuasiveness, the assessor must use his or her observations of the actions of a participant in the *LGD* problem to rate the participant on these dimensions. Usually, the rating is done on a 5-point scale.

In most cases, there are half as many assessors in an AC as there are participants. These assessors are also usually managers within the organization who are in positions one level above the position of interest for the AC. In this way it is assumed that the assessors are very familiar with the job and the behaviors required in the job. After recording and judging the participants' behavior in the AC, and after all exercises have been completed, all of the assessors come together to discuss their observations. The ratings and data gathered by each assessor are used to develop group or consensus judgments of each participant on each behavioral dimension. These consensus ratings are then used to develop an overall rating of the acceptability of each candidate for the position of interest. The major difficulty in having managers within the organization perform these activities is that, even though they are very knowledgeable about the job behavior, they are usually unskilled in systematically observing behaviors representative of each dimension and then using the behaviors to develop ratings. The purpose of assessor training programs is to develop those skills. If assessors are not adequately trained in these observation and rating methods, the value of the AC evaluation is lessened.

TABLE 15.8	TYPES OF ABILITIES TO BE DEVELOPED IN TRAINING ASSESSORS

- Understanding the behavioral dimensions
- Observing the behavior of participants
- Categorizing participant behavior as to appropriate behavioral dimensions
- Judging the quality of participant behavior
- Determining the rating of participants on each behavioral dimension across the exercises
- Determining the overall evaluation of participants across all behavioral dimensions

William Byham has written an excellent detailed description of the training of assessors.[18] Much of the material in the following paragraphs is drawn from his ideas. Essentially, this training is to develop the six key abilities listed in Table 15.8. We describe some methods for doing this.

Understanding the Behavioral Dimensions As we mentioned, one fundamental part of an AC is the determination of which behavioral dimensions of the job are to be evaluated. These should be dimensions that are representative and important to the job. The first step in training assessors therefore, is to have them become thoroughly familiar with the dimensions. Often this is done by providing assessors with a clear and detailed definition of each one. Time is then spent discussing each dimension within the group. The major goal is to insure that all assessors have a common understanding of the dimensions. Frequently dimensions such as adaptability, decisiveness, and tolerance for stress, have different meanings for different individuals.

An example of a definition that could be used for an AC dimension focused on first-line supervisors is the following:

> *Tolerance for Stress*—stability of performance under pressure and/or opposition. A first-line supervisor finds himself/herself in a stressful situation because of three main factors: (1) multiple demands on the work unit that must be completed at approximately the same deadline, (2) the joint roles he or she must play as a representative of management to nonmanagement employees and also the representative of nonmanagement employees to management, and (3) confrontation by employees who are angry or hostile because of a work situation.

Observing the Behavior of Participants After the assessors have become familiar with the dimensions to be used in the AC, the next step is to train them to observe and record behavior. The initial tendency of most managers when they first become assessors is immediately to make evaluative judgments about the performance of participants in the AC exercises. For example, when observing a *LGD* problem, a common reaction is to make the judgment that a participant can or cannot handle stress. However, such immediate judgments are dysfunctional to the purpose of the AC. An AC, you will remember, is to provide multiple exercises or opportunities for participants to demonstrate behaviors that exemplify the dimensions under study.

These demonstrated behaviors of a participant are the crucial information collected in the AC. When the assessors come together after the exercises have been completed, they discuss the behavior of a participant and then form ratings. For this reason, if assessors make judgments about the behavior of the participant rather than record the actual behavior, the purpose of the group meeting of assessors is limited.

This step in training, therefore, is designed to overcome the tendency of assessors to form immediate judgments and instead to focus on recording the behavior of the participant. Commonly, this step has two parts. One part explains to the assessors in detail the differences between recording behavior and making judgments by providing examples of each. Often a list of statements is prepared about each of the dimensions and the assessor is asked to indicate whether the statement reflects behavior or judgment. The following provides an example:

Dimension: Tolerance for Stress

Indicate whether each of the following is a statement of a participant's behavior or a statement of an assessor's judgment.

Participant Behavior	Assessor Judgment	
	✓	Resolved the conflict quietly
✓		Listened to the explanations of both parties as to how the conflict started
✓		Offered some tentative suggestions as to changes that could be made
	✓	Broke down when the argument heated up

After the meaning of the term *behavior* is clear, the second step of training presents examples of participants' behavior in the exercises for the assessors to practice recording behaviors. These examples can be taken from either live or videotaped exercises. The advantage of a videotaped exercise is that it can be stopped at specific points, or parts can be replayed for discussion.

Categorizing Participant Behavior   The next phase of training merges the first two steps. In this phase, the assessor learns to record the behavior of the participant under the proper dimension. This ensures that assessors are consistent in recording participant behaviors that are examples of the dimensions. This consistency is also essential to the reliability and validity of the ratings.

For the most part, training in this phase centers on both descriptions and discussions of the behavior representative of each dimension and also demonstrations of these behaviors. In terms of descriptions, assessors are provided with material that briefly defines each dimension and also presents a list of behaviors that are representative of both high and low levels of the dimension. Such a list may take the following form:

> *Tolerance for Stress*—stability of performance under pressure and/or opposition.
>
> *Examples:*
> When engaging the two arguing parties, participant soon began screaming at the two.
>
> Suggested that the two arguing parties walk with him or her to an unoccupied conference room.
>
> Asked the individuals observing the arguing parties to return to work stations.
>
> Physically grabbed nearest arguing party and pulled him or her from the area.

A list of the representative behaviors is prepared for each dimension and is reviewed in group discussion among the assessors. Other example behaviors are also frequently generated during this time. In some cases, the assessors are then provided with a list of recorded behaviors that have been drawn from previous ACs and are asked to indicate which dimension is identified by the described behavior. The correct answers are reviewed by the group and differences of opinion discussed. The last part of training for this step has the assessors observe either a live set of exercises or a videotaped set and record the behaviors that demonstrate each dimension. A group discussion of the records is also conducted.

Judging the Quality of Participant Behavior   This portion of training attempts to develop consistency among assessors in the use of rating scales to evaluate the behavior of participants on the dimensions. In most ACs, each dimension is rated using the following 6-point scale:

> 5—a great deal of the dimension was shown (excellent)
> 4—quite a lot of the dimension was shown
> 3—a moderate amount of the dimension was shown (average)
> 2—only a small amount of the dimension was shown
> 1—very little was shown or this dimension was not shown at all (poor)
> 0—no opportunity existed for this dimension to be shown

The major problem in using a scale such as this is to develop a common frame of reference among assessors so that each will assign the same scale point to the same observed behaviors. This is a problem common to the use of rating scales in other HR activities (e.g., performance appraisal, scoring interviews, assessing training needs, etc.). Training in ACs revolves around providing examples of behaviors that are representative of scale points for each dimension. Frequently, these example behaviors are drawn from other ACs.

In doing this, the group of assessors is presented with either written descriptions or videotapes of examples of behaviors and asked to rate this set of behaviors on all appropriate dimensions. After each assessor has completed the ratings, a discussion follows that brings out any differences in ratings. This discussion is intended to identify common definitions of each scale point. It is usually the case that when practicing managers are used as assessors, this phase of the training is completed quite easily. Often such managers have a common viewpoint about what constitutes extremely good or extremely poor behaviors on the dimension. For example, most assessors agree that physically grabbing a person, that is, confronting the participant is an unsatisfactory demonstration of tolerance for stress. More difficulty arises in arriving at a consensus for the middle scale points. Even in this case, however, a common understanding is reached fairly quickly, owing greatly to the common work experiences of the assessors.

Determining Dimension and Overall Evaluation Ratings   We combine the discussion of the last two stages of assessor training. The training in each of these stages is similar in that it involves the use of rating scales, and it draws heavily on the training discussed in the previous stage.

After participant behaviors for any one AC exercise are described appropriately on the dimensions, the next task is to combine the data on the same dimension across two or more exercises. For example, say that planning and organization are gathered on three different exercises. Assessors must learn to combine these data into *one overall dimension rating.* Training again is primarily based both on group discussions to form a common frame of reference and several examples that serve as trials. Differences in ratings are fully discussed. Such factors as consistency of demonstrated behavior across exercises, how good each exercise is at bringing out a variety of behaviors, and the strength and duration of behaviors become relevant in forming overall dimension ratings.

The last training step is how to use the final dimension ratings to form the *overall rating* of the participant to perform the job. Job analysis information is critical for this. From the job analysis, it can be determined which dimensions are the most critical or the most frequently used in the job. The dimensions are then weighted more heavily than other dimensions in producing the overall rating of acceptability. As a means of training for these last two steps, assessor groups are often required to complete a mock assessment of a small group of candidates under the observation of experienced assessors.

The Effectiveness of Assessment Centers

Validity   As we have discussed, the major purpose of ACs is to evaluate the potential of individuals for management positions. In many organizations, the overall assessment of each AC participant is placed in corporate files, and/or summarized for the participant's current immediate supervisor, and communicated directly to the participant. When these participants are then considered for higher level positions, this information is frequently made available together with other data. Such practice, however, presents a problem in evaluating the validity of ACs in predicting managerial success. If the AC evaluations are made known, it is impossible to determine what effect these evaluations had on the selection decision. This issue is sometimes referred to as the "Crown Prince Syndrome." If the AC evaluation does affect the selection decision, then the rating creates a self-fulfilling prophecy.

There have been a few studies, most of them at AT&T, that have avoided this problem by not releasing the results of the AC to anyone, even the participants themselves. In general, these studies have been supportive of the AC's accuracy in predicting the career advancement of individuals. The most famous of such studies is the AT&T Management Progress Study we discussed previously. In this case, the AC was used to predict the advancement of each participant into middle-level management within 10 years. Eight years after the study had begun, it was shown that a significantly high percentage of those individuals who had been predicted to move into middle management had in fact done so as compared to the percentage of those who had been predicted not to move that far but who, in fact, had. When the sample was categorized into college graduates and noncollege graduates and each sample analyzed separately, the same patterns of significant differences were identified.

Other studies that also have investigated AC results have reported similar favorable findings. For example, a study of 47 IBM participants found a significant correlation between AC ratings and the level of management attained by each participant eight years later.[19] These results and those of other studies have raised the question of whether or not ACs are only useful in predicting promotions and career development. In fact, some studies have found that ACs are not related to subsequent work performance but only to promotability. Two studies have helped clarify this question.[20]

Both found that while ACs are significantly related to both promotions and job performance, they have higher validity coefficients with the former than with the latter. Meta-analysis has estimated these coefficients at .53 for predicting job potential and .36 for job performance.[21]

ACs and Managerial Behavior   There is some evidence that the experience of participating in an AC has a positive effect on both the assessors and the individuals who are being evaluated. For example, it has been shown that managers who had served as assessors in their company's AC for at least three months benefited in three ways when compared to inexperienced assessors.[22]

First, they demonstrated greater proficiency in interviewing, being able both to obtain a greater number of relevant facts and to demonstrate a more systematic approach to questioning. Second, they were also more proficient in several aspects of communicating information: orally presenting information about people to another individual, responding effectively when questioned about this information, and communicating information about people in concise written reports. Third, their assessments of the behavior of subordinates showed a decrease in the halo rating error.

Regarding assessees, it has been found that participation in an AC was related to changes in self-perceived ability ratings.[23] Data were collected from 1,693 participants who provided self-ratings on eight ability dimensions (organizing and planning, analyzing, decision making, controlling, communication, interpersonal relations, influencing others, and flexibility) both before and immediately after the AC. Results indicated significant changes in the ratings of organizing and planning, analyzing, decision making, influencing others, and flexibility. Furthermore, there was evidence that these changes could be related to specific exercises designed to measure that ability, that is, the *In-Basket* was related to changes in ratings of organizing and planning. One possible explanation for these results is that participants became sensitized to their shortcomings in the abilities tested in the exercises and were receptive to developmental ideas. Another study found that successful and unsuccessful AC candidates differed significantly. The latter group scored lower on work ethic, depressed mood, status aspiration and mastery, and acquisitiveness both before and after the AC program. Also the unsuccessful group was found to have a sharp drop in self-esteem six months after feedback on AC performance. [24]

ACs and Discrimination   Studies that have examined possible differential validity between blacks and whites or between males and females have generally failed to find such differences. One study of the performance of white females and black females in an AC did find differences in the assessors' judgments between the two groups in favor of the white females.[25] Further investigation indicated, however, that there were also differences between the two groups in job performance as rated by supervisors. The white group was rated significantly higher than the black group. In addition, there was no significant difference in the correlation between AC evaluations and job performance ratings for the two groups. The conclusion, therefore, was that even though the black females performed less well in the AC, no discrimination was evidenced because these differences were also reflected in subsequent job performance.

Another positive feature of ACs is their generally favorable support by the courts and the EEOC in alleged discrimination cases. For example, in the much publicized sex discrimination case against AT&T, ACs were identified as a method to use in changing AT&T's promotion policies.[26] The essence of the discrimination charge was the adverse impact of females in promotion through management ranks. Under the agreement between AT&T and the EEOC, ACs were to be used extensively to identify those females who were most likely to be successful in higher management positions.

There have also been a few discrimination cases that have directly evaluated the use of ACs in selection. In *Berry v. City of Omaha*, ACs were used in selection for the position of deputy police chief. The main issue was whether the three different assessor groups that evaluated candidates used different standards in evaluating participants.[27] After reviewing descriptions of the development of the AC and data analysis regarding reliability among assessors, the court upheld the use of the AC. In another case, *The Richmond Black Police Officers Association v. the City of Richmond,* the use of an AC for selection for supervisory positions in both the police and the fire departments was upheld. Of interest in this case was that a combination of written tests and the AC was used in selection. Evidence indicating that the paper-and-pencil tests were discriminatory was presented. However, final selection decisions were based on both sets of devices, and these final decisions were not discriminatory.[28] In this case, the nondiscriminatory features of the AC compensated for the discriminatory characteristics of the written tests.

Criticism of ACs   These findings of the general validity of ACs and their lack of adverse impact does not mean their use is without some criticism. Generally, such criticism has taken two forms. The first is that an AC is very expensive to develop and maintain and, if selection among applicants is its only use, there might be alternative methods that are much less expensive. John Hinrichs raised such an issue when he compared the correlation of AC evaluations with management level attained with the correlation of ratings obtained only from evaluations of personnel files with a job success measure.[29] Both correlations were statistically significant but not different from one another. If the same accuracy of prediction is possible, it would be more sensible to use the least expensive method.

Following similar reasoning, Donald Brush and Lyle Schoenfeldt have described an integrated appraisal system to generate information comparable to that yielded by assessment centers.[30] Their approach consists of the following parts: job analysis to establish the critical tasks and abilities of each managerial position, training line managers in assessing behavior of subordinates on critical dimensions identified in the job analysis, and systematic procedures for obtaining and evaluating the assessment data supplied by these line managers. Brush and Schoenfeldt explain that dimensions closely related to the behavioral dimensions measured in assessment centers can be constructed and that such actual job performance tasks as management presentations, completion of reports, unit productivity, and quality of employee performance reviews can be substituted for assessment center exercises. One advantage of this is to eliminate the coaching of participants before they attend the assessment center by colleagues who have previously completed the assessment process. Their conclusion is that it is possible to use data currently available in organizations to yield comparable selection data that is content valid at a lower cost than assessment centers. However a recent study examined the combined use of AC ratings and other commonly obtained predictors.[31] Using a criterion of supervisory job performance ratings given seven years after the AC was completed, it was found that when AC ratings were combined with other predictors the validity coefficient increased from .36 to .55. Thus AC ratings contributed substantial independent information to the prediction of job performance.

It has also been shown that both verbal and paper-and-pencil intelligence test scores predicted future performance of managers as well as or better than either individual exercises or overall assessment center ratings.[32] Obviously, such test data are easier and less expensive to collect than are AC data. Finally, one recent study explored the use of "low-fidelity" simulations, those that presented only a written or spoken description of a task.[33] Instead of a "high-fidelity," AC exercise, applicants were asked to describe how they would deal with hypothetical work situations based on the critical-incidents technique. Responses were collected by using a paper-and-pencil format with multiple-choice options. The low-fidelity simulation was not only found to be valid for entry-level management positions, with correlations ranging from .28 to .37, but was equally valid for blacks, whites, men, and women.

The second area of criticism focuses on the failure of ACs to demonstrate the pattern of correlations among dimension ratings that they were designed to produce. As we mentioned previously, ACs measure the behavioral dimensions using several devices. Logically, the ratings given for the same dimension in various exercises should be highly correlated. After all, the same characteristic is being measured. For example, if the dimension of planning and organizing is to be measured with the *In Basket*, the interview, and a case analysis, then the correlations of the ratings for participants for this dimension among these three devices should be quite high. This is commonly referred to as *convergent* validity.

The evidence is quite clear, however, that the correlations among such dimension ratings are quite low often ranging from .05 to .15).[34] This is puzzling because a lack of convergent validity indicates that either behavior on each dimension is very specific to a testing situation or is not reliably judged by assessors or both. In any case, the validity of the overall rating of the dimension, which is arrived at by the assessors through a review of the behaviors and ratings of the participants on each of the exercises, is questionable. Even more disturbing is the finding that the correlations among dimensions that are measured with the same exercise are very high.[35] This should not occur and is referred to as a lack of discriminant validity. Discriminant validity exists when relatively low correlations are found among all dimensions such as problem solving, leadership, and verbal communication within a single exercise. The dimensions are regarded as being separate characteristics of the participants. For example, an *In-Basket* may be intended to measure 12 separate dimensions of the participants. There is no reason to believe that these dimension ratings should be highly correlated. If they are indeed different dimensions, the relationship among them should be low to moderate. One interpretation of these high correlations is that the assessor ratings are, in fact, not of specific dimensions but rather of overall performance on an exercise. This is not the assessor judgment, however, that ACs were intended to gather. Possible explanations for this perplexing validity problem are, first, assessors may be required to rate several candidates on multiple dimensions that place many cognitive demands on assessors, resulting in lower accuracy and reliability.[36] Second, definitions of dimensions are typically written in general terms and not clearly related to behaviors elicited by the exercises. Third, there exists much variation between exercises in the number of opportunities for a behavior that represents a dimension to be manifested.[37] In exploring the first possible explanation, Barbara Gaugler and George Thornton found that assessors who were asked to deal with fewer dimensions made more accurate behavior classifications and more accurate ratings with greater convergent validity and less bias than assessors who dealt with a larger number of dimensions.[38] Given these findings, those who develop ACs should limit cognitive demands of assessors by attempting to minimize the number of dimensions used. Another recent study was designed to both reduce cognitive demands and eliminate the operational definition problem by stating dimensions in specific behavioral terms through the use of behavior checklists.[39] Use of these checklists increased the average convergent validity from .24 to .43 while decreasing the average discriminant validity from .47 to .41.

In addition, there are other findings that run counter to the purposes of ACs. For example, the ratings by the same assessor of the same participants in two similar *LGD* problems do not correlate very highly.[40] A related study explored how contrast effects influence assessor ratings of candidates.[41] Specifically, a low-performing candidate was rated significantly lower than he or she actually performed when evaluated in a group consisting of two similar low performers. Also, an individual's performance was rated lower when his or her prior performance was high than when his/her performance had been low. It also has been found that the correlation of assessors' ratings across exercises can be influenced by the nature of the scoring procedures.[42] Procedures can increase correlations either for the same dimension across exercises or for correlations of different dimensions within an exercise. Another study has found that assessors' overall ratings are largely explained by the interpersonal and problem solving skills of the participants even though the AC was designed to measure many more dimensions than these two.[43] Related to this, at least two recent studies have supported the notion of grouping assessment dimensions into broad categories (e.g., interpersonal and performance style or personality and intellect) based on the idea that (1) assessors usually do not utilize more than a few dimensions on deciding overall ratings, and (2) two to four factors are typically used in making ratings.[44] Finally, it has been concluded that three weeks of training for assessors does not noticeably increase their information-processing ability in comparison with two weeks of training.[45] That is, assessors are not better at producing ratings that have low correlations among dimensions even with 50 percent more training.

Thus even though there is evidence that ACs are valid in predicting both job performance and career movement we do not know why. It is not because they operate as they were intended. Assessors clearly do not gather evidence about a number of separate characteristics of participants and then use these diverse data to form an overall judgment of the future ability of the participant.

Richard Klimoski and Mary Brickner have offered some possible explanations of the validity of ACs.[46] Among these is that very often the ratings given to participants are made known to others in the organization. It could be that these ratings become a factor in other decisions made within the organization, such as promotions, pay increases, and so on. It would be expected, therefore, that the correlation between AC ratings and these measures would be very high. It would not mean, however, that ACs were doing what they were intended to do or were worth their expense. Another explanation is that, to a large extent, ACs measure cognitive abilities. There is evidence that managerial success can be predicted by cognitive ability tests (see Chapter 14). Therefore, ACs also predict managerial success. For instance, several cognitive ability measures have been found to relate strongly to performance-style AC dimension ratings.[47]

The most often discussed explanation focuses on the basis of the assessors' ratings. Instead of evaluating the participants on the dimensions intended by the AC, the assessors evaluate the participants on the behaviors that they know are favored by others in the company. That is, if it is commonly known that delegation is favorably regarded as a management strategy by many in the organization, those participants who demonstrate delegation are judged very well. The correlation between the AC rating and career development is not because the AC measures characteristics that are directly related to job performance. Instead, the assessors are able to predict which behaviors will be favorably viewed by others in making future decisions about employees. Another way of saying this is that assessors identify those participants who should do well by adhering to the corporate culture.

Not enough data exist to clearly answer all the existing questions and specify why the assessment center is a valid predictor of managerial success. Because of its promise as a predictor, future research in organizations, therefore, will have a major impact on the design and use of this device.

References

[1] Paul Wernimont and John Campbell, "Sign, Samples, and Criteria," *Journal of Applied Psychology* 52 (1968): 372–376.

[2] James Asher and James Sciarrino, "Realistic Work Sample Tests: A Review," *Personal Psychology* 27 (1974): 519–533.

[3] James E. Campion, "Work Sampling for Personnel Selection," *Journal of Applied Psychology* 56 (1972): 40–44.

[4] David Robinson, "Content-Oriented Personnel Selection in a Small Business Setting," *Personnel Psychology* 34 (1981): 77–87.

[5] Robert Gatewood and Lyle F. Schoenfeldt, "Content Validity and EEOC: A Useful Alternative for Selection," *Personnel Journal* 56 (1977): 520–528.

[6] Richard R. Reilly and Edmond W. Israelski, "Development and Validation of Minicourses in the Telecommunication Industry," *Journal of Applied Psychology* 73 (1988): 721–726.

[7] Lynnette B. Plumlee, *A Short Guide to the Development of Performance Tests* (Washington, D.C.: Personnel Research and Development Center, U.S. Civil Service Commission, Professional Series 75–1, January 1975).

[8] Joseph L. Boyd and Benjamin Shimberg, *Handbook of Performance Testing* (Princeton, N.J.: Educational Testing Service, 1971), 24.

[9] Neal Schmitt and Cheri Ostroff, "Operationalizing the 'Behavioral Consistency' Approach: Selection Test Development Based on a Content-Oriented Strategy," *Personnel Psychology* 39 (1986): 91–108.

[10] Asher and Sciarrino, "Realistic Work Sample Tests: A Review," pp. 519–533.

[11] Michael E. Gordon and Lawrence S. Kleiman, "The Prediction of Trainability Using a Work Sample Test and an Aptitude Test: A Direct Comparison" *Personnel Psychology* 29 (1976): 243–253.

[12] John E. Hunter and Ronda F. Hunter, "Validity and Utility of Alternative Predictors of Job Performance," *Psychological Bulletin* 96 (1984):72–88.

[13] Frank Schmidt, Alan Greenthol, John Hunter, John Berner, and Felicia Seaton, "Job Sample vs. Paper-and-Pencil Trade and Technical Tests: Adverse Impact and Examiner Attitudes," Personnel *Psychology* 30 (1977): 187–197.

[14] Wayne Cascio and Niel Phillips, "Performance Testing: A Rose among Thorns?" *Personnel Psychology* 32 (1979): 751–766.

[15] Task Force on Assessment Center Guidelines. "Guidelines and Ethical Considerations for Assessment Center Operations," Public Personnel Management, 18 (1989): 457–470.

[16] Douglas W. Bray, Richard J. Campbell, and Donald L. Grant, *Formative Years in Business: A Long-Term AT&T Study of Managerial Lives* (Huntington, N.Y.: Robert E., 1979), 6.

[17] Robert Guion, "Changing Views for Personnel Selection," Personnel *Psychology 18* (1987): 199–214.

[18] William C. Byham, "Assessor Selection and Training," *Applying the Assessment Center Method,* ed. J. L. Moses and W. C. Byham (New York: Pergamon Press, 1977), 89–126.

[19] John R. Hinrichs, "An Eight-Year Follow-up of a Management Assessment Center," *Journal of Applied Psychology* 63 (1978): 596–601.

[20] Richard J. Klimoski and Mary Brickner, "Why Do Assessment Centers Work? The Puzzle of Assessment Center Validity," *Personnel Psychology* 40 (1987): 243–260. See also Janet J. Turnage and Paul M. Muchinsky, "A Comparison of the Predictive Validity of Assessment Center Evaluations versus Traditional Measures in Forecasting Supervisory Job Performance: Interpretive Implications of Criterion Distortion for the Assessment Paradigm," *Journal of Applied Psychology* 69 (1984): 595–602.

[21] Barbara B. Gaugler, Douglas B. Rosenthal, George C. Thornton III, and Cynthia Bentson, "Meta-Analysis of Assessment Center Validity," *Journal of Applied Psychology* 72 (1987): 493–511.

[22] Robert V. Lorenzo, "Effects of Assessorship on Managers' Proficiency in Acquiring, Evaluating, and Communicating Information about People," *Personnel Psychology* 37 (1984): 617–634.

[23] Neal Schmitt, Kevin J. Ford, and Daniel M. Stults, "Changes in Self-Perceived Ability As a Function of Performance in an Assessment Centre," *Journal of Occupational Psychology* 74 (1986): 327–335.

[24] Clive Fletcher, "Candidates' Reactions to Assessment Centres and Their Outcomes: A Longitudinal Study," *Journal of Occupational Psychology* 64 (1991): 117–127.

[25] James R. Hock and Douglas W. Bray, "Management Assessment Center Evaluation and Subsequent Job Performance of White and Black Females," *Personnel Psychology* 29 (1976): 13–30.

[26] Landmark AT&T-EEOC Consent Agreement Increases Assessment Center Usage," *Assessment & Development* 1 (1973): 1–2.

[27] *Berry v. City of Omaha*, 14 FEP 391 (1977).

[28] Thornton and Byham, *Assessment Centers and Managerial Performance*, p. 383.

[29] Hinrichs, "An Eight-Year Follow-up of a Management Assessment Center," 596–601.

[30] Donald R. Brush and Lyle F. Schoenfeldt, "Identifying Managerial Potential: An Alternative to Assessment Centers," *Personnel* 26 (1980): 68–76.

[31] Glenn M. McEvoy and Richard W. Beatty, "Assessment Centers and Subordinate Appraisals of Managers: A Seven-Year Examination of Predictive Validity," *Personnel Psychology* 42 (1989): 37–52.

[32] Aharon Tziner and Shimon Dolan, "Validity of an Assessment Center for Identifying Future Female Officers in the Military," Journal *of Applied Psychology* 67 (1982): 728–736.

[33] Stephan J. Motowidlo, Marvin D. Dunnette, and Gary W. Carter, "An Alternative Selection Procedure: The Low-Fidelity Simulation," *Journal of Applied Psychology* 75 (1990): 640–647.

[34] Paul R. Sackett and George F. Dreher, "Constructs and Assessment Center Dimensions: Some Troubling Empirical Findings," *Journal of Applied Psychology* 67 (1982): 401–410.

[35] Peter Bycio, Kenneth M. Alvares, and June Hahn, "Situational Specificity in Assessment Center Ratings: A Confirmatory Factor Analysis," Journal *of Applied Psychology* 72 (1987): 463–474. See also Ivan Robertson, Lynda Gratton, and David Sharpley, "The Psychometric Properties and Design of Managerial Assessment Centres: Dimensions into Exercises Won't Go," *Journal of Occupational Psychology* 60 (1987): 187–195.

[36] George C. Thornton III, *Assessment Centers in Human Resource Management* (Reading, Mass.: Addison-Wesley, 1992).

[37] Richard R. Reilly, Sarah Henry, and James W. Smither, "An Examination of the Effects of Using Behavior Checklists on the Construct Validity of Assessment Center Dimensions," *Personnel Psychology* 43 (1990): 71–84; see also Sackett and Dreher, 1982 and Bycio et al., 1987.

[38] Barbara B. Gaugler and George C. Thornton III, "Number of Assessment Center Dimensions as a Determinant of Assessor Accuracy," *Journal of Applied Psychology* 74 (1989): 611–618.

[39] Richard, R. Reilly, Sarah Henry, and James W. Smither, "An Examination of the Effects of Using Behavior Checklists on the Construct Validity of Assessment Center Dimensions."

[40] Robert D. Gatewood, George Thornton III, and Harry W. Hennessey, Jr. "Reliability of Exercise Ratings in the Leaderless Group Discussion," *Journal of Occupational Psychology*, 63, (1990): 331–342.

[41] Barbara B. Gaugler and Amy S. Rudolph, "The Influence of Assessee Performance Variation on Assessors' Judgments," *Personnel Psychology* 45 (1992): 77–98.

[42] William H. Silverman, Anthony Dalessio, Steven B. Woods, and Rudolph L. Johnson, Jr., "Influence of Assessment Center Methods on Assessor's Ratings," *Personnel Psychology* 39 (1986): 565–578.

[43] Craig J. Russell, "Individual Decision Processes in an Assessment Center," *Journal of Applied Psychology* 70 (1985): 737–746.

[44] A. Jones, Peter Herriot, B. Long, and R. Drakely, "Attempting to Improve the Validity of a Well-Established Assessment Centre," *Journal of Occupational Psychology* 64 (1991): 1–21. See also Ted H. Shore, George C. Thornton III, and Lynn McFarlane Shore, "Construct Validity of Two Categories of Assessment Center Dimension Ratings," *Personnel Psychology* 43 (1990): 101–115.

[45] Beverly Dugan, "Effects of Assessor Training on Information Use," *Journal of Applied Psychology* 73 (1988): 743–748.

[46] Richard Klimoski and Mary Brickner, "Why Do Assessment Centers Work? The Puzzle of Assessment Center Validity."

[47] Ted H. Shore, George C. Thornton III, and Lynn McFarlane Shore, "Construct Validity of Two Categories of Assessment Center Dimension Ratings," *Personnel Psychology* 43 (1990) 101–115.

16

Integrity Testing, Graphology, and Drug Testing

Integrity Testing

A recent, rapidly growing cost to American business has been employee theft. Obviously, estimates of the amount of theft are unverifiable, but a common opinion is that it has grown from $1 billion in 1968 to $40 to $60 billion in 1991. The number becomes even more horrendous if one figures the volume of sales necessary to produce profits that will equal these losses. Given the pressure from international firms, often with lower labor costs, and the critical need to reduce the cost of production in order to maintain competitive positions, the interest of American firms in controlling employee theft is acute.

In the first part of this chapter we discuss two forms of tests that have been used extensively to combat this problem: polygraphs and paper-and-pencil honesty or integrity tests. In this discussion, we describe the nature of both of these forms and also present opinions about their use.

Polygraph Testing

A polygraph, or lie detector, is a machine that measures the physiological responses of an individual which accompany the verbal responses he or she makes to the direct questions of a polygraph operator. These data, in conjunction with the opinion of the polygraph operator, are used to make an evaluation of the truthfulness of the individual's responses to the questions. For all practical purposes, the use of polygraphs for selection is now illegal because of a federal law, the Employee Polygraph Protection Act of 1988.[1] However, they still may be used in some specific employment circumstances.

The most common field polygraph examination uses readings of three types of physiological data. One set of readings, the electrodermal channel, displays changes in palmar skin resistance or galvanic skin response. The second set, the "cardio" channel, records changes in upper arm volume associated with the cardiac cycle. From this channel it is possible to determine heart rate and some changes in pulse volume. The third channel is connected pneumatically or electrically to an expandable belt around the respondent's chest and records respiration. The purpose of these sets of data is to provide information to the polygraph examiner about the examinee's physiological reactions during questioning. The assumption is that lying can be detected by the specialist through detection of changes in the subject's physiological response pattern.

Procedures   In most polygraph examinations, the examiner conducts a pretest discussion with the examinee that covers all the questions to be used in the test. The purpose is to make sure the examinee understands the wording and the meaning of the questions and can answer them with a simple yes or no. After this is completed, the polygraph is attached to the examinee and the actual interview is conducted. The list of questions is then gone over again and usually repeated once or twice to obtain more reliable data. Three types of questions are usually used in the examination. One type is the irrelevant, nonemotional question, such as "Are you six feet tall?" A second type is the emotional control question. Such questions are designed to elicit an emotional reaction, preferably of guilt. Questions such as "Did you ever lie to escape punishment?" are frequently asked. The third type is specifically about the behavior of interest. In employment selection this almost always concerns stealing of company resources. To detect lying, the polygraph operator looks for evidence of autonomic disturbance associated with the answers to the last type of question.[2] When the examinee is lying, there should be a disturbance that is more intense and persistent than that associated with the other two types of questions. Most polygraph examiners make an overall judgment of lying based on the polygraph information and other data, such as the demeanor of the examinee, the examiner's knowledge of the evidence, the respondent's prior history, and so on.[3]

Limitations   One of the difficulties with such testing, however, is that other reactions besides guilt can trigger an emotional response in the examinee. Specifically, responses can be affected by the examinee's lability, the autonomic arousal threshold that differs from individual to individual. Examinees with high lability are more likely to have physiological reactions that may be interpreted as lying behavior than are respondents with low lability. Similar differences have been noted in examinees regarding their fear of the consequences of being found guilty and their confidence in the validity of the polygraph procedure.

Another difficulty is the variety of countermeasures that examinees can use to avoid detection. Any physical activity that affects physiological responses is a potential problem for interpretation of polygraph readings. Such movements as tensing muscles, biting the tongue, flexing the toes, and shifting one's position can affect physiological response.[4] In general, polygraph examiners are watchful for these movements. The use of drugs to obscure physiological reaction differences is more difficult to detect unless a urinalysis is conducted. Experience with polygraphs and biofeedback training also have had demonstrated effects on polygraph results.

The major drawback in using the polygraph in employment testing is the frequency of the false positive. The false positive is the identification of an individual as lying who, in fact, is not lying. The frequency of the false positive depends on both the validity of the test and the base rate of the lying behavior in the population. To illustrate the possible magnitude of false-positive identification we make the following assumptions: (a) that the accuracy of the polygraph is 90 percent (commonly regarded as a high estimate), and (b) that the rate of lying about company stealing is 5 percent of the working population. If 1,000 polygraph tests are conducted, we would expect that 50 of the examinees would be lying and that 45 (90 percent) of these would be detected. The serious problem concerns the remaining 950 examinees. Assuming the 90 percent accuracy rate, 95 of these (950 x .10) would be inaccurately identified as lying about their actions. Therefore, a total of 140 individuals would be identified as lying, 68 percent of which would be false positives. The consequence of such examinations is that those singled out as lying are denied employment or, if they are present employees, are commonly terminated from employment. It can be easily seen from this example that unless a polygraph test has perfect validity, a large number of false positive identifications can occur when the device is used to test for a behavior that has a low incidence in the general population. Given the limitations in validity mentioned previously, one might suppose that the actual frequency of false positives is much greater than this example would indicate.

Another group, false negatives, has also received attention. False negatives are those who are judged to be truthful when, in fact, they are not. These individuals are, understandably, of much interest to organizations because it is felt that these are the employees who are most likely to be the cause of future theft. In fact, in many ways false negatives are of more immediate concern to organizations than are false positives.

We have mentioned several times in this text that incorrect judgments about applicants occur with the use of all selection devices. That is, some applicants who are interviewed, or take paper-and-pencil mental ability tests, or who complete assessment centers are misjudged in terms of future job performance. Analogous to false positives on polygraph tests are those individuals who do not achieve scores high enough to be selected but who would perform well on the job. The group analogous to false negatives would be those applicants who do score high enough to be selected but, subsequently, do not perform well on the job. As we have said, the purpose of a well-designed selection program and selection tests is to minimize these types of erroneous decisions. However, given the inherent limitations of selection, discussed in Chapter 1, the total elimination of such errors is not possible.

The problem with misjudgments in polygraph and other forms of integrity testing is the public statement that is made about individuals who incorrectly fail these tests, the false positives. These individuals are stigmatized with an incorrect judgment about a behavior, honesty, that is highly valued in our society. It is obviously much more serious to reject an applicant because he or she has failed an honesty test than it is to reject him or her because "the applicant's knowledge and ability does not meet the demands of this job." For this reason, public outcry about false positives grew as the use of polygraphs, and the number of individuals falsely labeled, increased. This outcry resulted in the passage of the Employee Polygraph Protection Act of 1988 which, essentially, ended polygraph use in selection and greatly restricted its use in other employment situations. The following is a summary of the major parts of this act.

Under this act, it is unlawful for employers to take any of the following actions:

1. Directly or indirectly require, request, suggest or cause any employee to take or submit to any lie detector test, for example, a polygraph, deceptograph, voice-stress analyzer, psychological-stress evaluator, and any similar mechanical or electrical device used to render a diagnostic opinion about the honesty of an individual

2. Use, accept, refer to, or inquire about the results of any lie detector test of any job applicant or current employee

3. Discharge, discipline, discriminate against, or deny employment or promotion to (or threaten to take such adverse action against) any prospective or current employee who refuses, declines, or fails to take or submit to a lie detector test

However, the following employers are exempted from these prohibitions on preemployment polygraph testing:

1. Private employers whose primary business purpose is to provide security services. Prospective employees may be tested if the positions to which they are applying involve the protection of nuclear power facilities, public water supply facilities, shipments or storage of radioactive or other toxic waste materials, public transportation, or currency, negotiable securities, precious commodities, or proprietary information.

2. Employers involved in the manufacture, distribution, or dispensing of controlled substances. Employers may administer polygraph tests to applicants for positions that would provide direct access to the manufacture, storage, distribution, or sale of a controlled substance.

3. Federal, state, and local government employers. The federal government also may test private consultants or experts under contract to the Defense Department, the Energy Department, the National Security Agency, the Defense Intelligence Agency, the Central Intelligence Agency, and the Federal Bureau of Investigation.

Testing of current employees is also permitted if four conditions are met. One, the polygraph test must be administered in connection with an investigation into a workplace theft or other incident that has resulted in an economic loss to the company. Two, the employee must have had access to the property that is the subject of the investigation. Three, the employer must have a "reasonable suspicion" that the employee was involved in the incident. And four, prior to testing, the employee must have been given specific written information about the incident being investigated and the reasons for the testing.

One may conclude that the act was intended to restrict preemployment polygraph testing to only those situations that have a large public interest and the testing of current employees to those situations in which there is enough evidence to reasonably implicate an individual of a specific illegal act.

Paper-and-Pencil Integrity Tests

Before the Employee Polygraph Protection Act of 1988 was passed, more than 30 states had enacted legislation to prohibit, or severely limit, the use of polygraphs in employment decisions. Generally, these state laws were worded, as is the federal act, to address mechanical or electronic devices only. Therefore, in recent years several paper-and-pencil tests have been developed in order to accomplish the same objective as polygraphs, but provide a legal means of doing so. Given the continued problem of employee theft in organizations, we anticipate that the market for this type of test will grow steadily and that more tests will become available.

There are presently two forms of these tests that have been developed.[5] One is commonly referred to as an *overt integrity test* in that it directly asks for information about attitudes toward theft and the occurrence of previous theft behaviors. The second is commonly labeled *personality based measures* because this type of test does not ask about theft behaviors directly. Instead, it is a personality inventory that measures traits linked to several related employee behaviors that are detrimental to the organization. Theft is only one of these behaviors.

Overt Integrity Tests Examples of the first type are the *Personnel Selection Inventory* published by London House, the *Stanton Survey* published by Stanton Corporation, and the *Reid Report*, published by Reid Psychological Systems.[6] The rationale underlying this type of test is to measure a job applicant's attitudes and cognitions toward theft that might predispose him or her to steal at work, especially when both the need and the opportunity to steal are present. William Terris and John Jones have explained this testing approach in the following way:

> Past research has shown that the "typical" employee-thief (1) is more tempted to steal, (2) engages in many of the common rationalizations for theft, (3) would punish thieves less (4) often thinks about theft-related activities, (5) attributes more theft to others, (6) shows more inter-thief loyalty, and (7) is more vulnerable to peer pressure to steal than is an honest employee.[7]

Items on this type of test follow directly from these points. Some example items are the following:[8]

Most people who have had jobs where they handled money or had expense accounts have probably taken some money without their employer's permission. This includes directly taking cash, borrowing money that is not returned, or padding expense accounts. Estimate how much you have taken from all employers in the past five years.

Did you ever think about doing something which, if you had done it, would have been a crime?

In any of your other jobs did you find out a way a dishonest person could take money if a dishonest person had your job?

Do you believe that making personal phone calls from your employer's place of business without an OK is stealing?

Have you ever overcharged someone for your personal gain?

Is it true that to be human is to be dishonest?

Another type of question poses a situation that focuses on dishonest behavior. An example is "A store manager with 15 years of good work performance has an eight-year-old son who is dying of cancer. The manager takes $25/week from the store for three months in order to buy toys and games for the child. Another employee sees this behavior and tells the district manager." A number of questions follow that ask the respondent's opinions about the theft, the action of the employee who informed the district manager, and his or her choices of alternative actions that can be taken by the district manager. Recently, the concept of overt integrity testing has been extended to screening applicants for drug usage also.

Personality-Based Measures   Joyce and Robert Hogan describe the development of the second type of integrity measure, a personality inventory to measure employee reliability.[9] The rationale behind this measure is that employee theft is just one element in a larger syndrome of antisocial behavior. Therefore, tests that center only on theft overlook a number of other counterproductive behaviors that are costly to organizations: drug and alcohol abuse, vandalism, sabotage, assaultive actions, insubordination, absenteeism, excessive grievances, bogus worker compensation claims, and violence. These behaviors are elements of a syndrome labeled "organizational delinquency." The assumption is made that employees who steal, for example, are likely to engage in other delinquent acts as well. Prediction of the general pattern of behavior is both easier to accomplish and more worthwhile for the organization than is prediction any one of the behaviors in the syndrome.

To measure organizational delinquency, the authors have developed an employee reliability index which is derived from their work with the *Hogan Personality Inventory* (HPI). This instrument is a general self-report personality inventory similar in purpose, content, and items to the *California Psychological*

Inventory (CPI) described in Chapter 14. The HPI is composed of six scales that measure common personality dimensions of everyday life rather than dimensions of psychological disorders. These six are *Intellectance* (quick-witted vs. slow-witted), *Adjustment* (social shyness, mood swings), *Prudence* (superego, impulsiveness), *Ambition* (persistence), *Sociability* (social conversation), and *Likeability* (cooperative/considerate). Each of these scales is composed of a series of small and highly related subscales; a total of 43 of these exist. For example, the *Adjustment* scale is made up of the subscales of self-esteem, sense of identity, good attachment, no somatic complaint, no anxiety, no guilt, no depression, and calmness. Nine of these 43 subscales, representing parts of all six major scales, were formed to measure the reliability index.

The authors have reported test-retest reliability as high as .90 for the employee reliability index. Concurrent validity studies have been conducted with various groups of workers in a variety of jobs. Table 16.1 contains a listing of the various criteria measures that have been used in these studies. The diversity of the measures indicate two points: (1) that the index can predict employee performance as well as organizational delinquency, and (2) the scope of the employee behaviors that can be included in organizational delinquency. The authors have explained these findings in terms of the demands of particular jobs and argue for the appropriateness of the employee reliability index as a general selection device.

Another instrument of this general type is the *Employment Productivity Index* (EP1-3) published by London House, Inc.[10] This is described as a broad-based personality measure designed to predict the successful employee. The EP1-3 contains the following scales:

Dependability	—measures applicants' willingness to obey company rules while completing the work assigned, as well as the likelihood that they will show up for work on time
Drug Avoidance	—measures the likelihood that applicants will not use illegal drugs once employed
Interpersonal Cooperation	—measures the likelihood that the applicants will be courteous and cooperate with others
Validity	—detects patterns of responses which are unlikely to occur when applicants both understand the inventory and answer carefully

Another version of the inventory, the EPI-3S contains one additional scale:[11]

Safety	—measures belief in assuming personal responsibility for safety and belief in taking preventative steps to avoid accidents

TABLE 16.1	CRITERIA MEASURES CORRELATED WITH EMPLOYEE RELIABILITY INDEX	
Job	**Criteria That Are Negatively Correlated**	**Criteria That Are Positively Correlated**
Truck Driver	Discharges from work Grievances filed Claims for equipment failure	Commendations
Psychiatric counselor		Supervisor's ratings of performance
Hospital service worker	Times counseled for aberrant behavior	
Rehabilitation therapist	Injuries sustained Incidents reported to insurance fund State dollars spent for treatment	
Nuclear power plant worker		Supervisor's ratings of attitude, accuracy, punctuality
Service operations dispatchers	Absences above allowable limit	
Navy electronics students		Course time completion
Customer service representatives		Supervisor's ratings of quality, teamwork, performance
Telemarketers		Sales performance Sales lead generation

Based on: Joyce Hogan and Robert Hogan, "How to Measure Employee Reliability," in *Employee Testing: The Complete Resource Guide* (Washington, D.C.: Bureau of National Affairs, Inc., 1988).

The Usefulness and Validity of Integrity Tests

Two major points must be considered in the evaluation of integrity tests: the issue of false positives and validity. Paul Sackett, Laura Burris, and Christine Callahan did a thorough review of the published studies on integrity tests.[12] We summarize their comments in the following paragraphs.

The issue of false positives is identical to that discussed previously with polygraphs. A large percentage of applicants commonly fail the test. Estimates place this number between 40 and 70 percent. In most cases, firms that use an integrity test have a cutoff score which is supplied by the test publisher. For the most part, it is in the best interests of the test publisher to set the cutoff score high enough to reduce the number of individuals who pass the test and, subsequently, are dishonest. Therefore, it may be advantageous for the test publisher to avoid false negatives even at the cost of increased false positives.

An important issue in assessing the effect of false positives is the selection ratio. Integrity tests should, and often are, used as the final step in the selection program. Tests of the KSAs necessary for the job should have been given beforehand. Only those applicants who possess a satisfactory level of these KSAs should be given the integrity test. If more applicants than open employment positions are left prior to the administration of the integrity test, then false positives become much less of an issue as long as enough candidates pass the test to fill the open positions. Looked at another way, every selection test will have false positives. Moreover, if there are more qualified applicants remaining than positions, some qualified applicants must be rejected. It has been pointed out that it is inappropriate to compare the number of false positive decisions made by an integrity test to perfect selection. The proper comparison should be between alternative decision methods.[13] The more realistic comparison, therefore, should be between two integrity instruments or between one integrity instrument and random choice among qualified applicants. In either case, the validity of the test indicates the appropriate choice.

Another way of viewing the use of integrity tests is in reference to institutional needs rather than to the individual applicant. In any selection situation in which the number of applicants exceeds the number of open positions, the institution must reduce the number of applicants. If the integrity test is valid, then it contributes more than random selection to the reduction of applicants. Rejection of an applicant due to a low score on a personality integrity test is usually less cumbersome than when and overt integrity test is used. This is because applicants generally do not know they are being screened on an integrity test, rather than a personality measure.

Regarding the validity of integrity tests, Sackett and his colleagues reported five different categories of validity studies.

1. *Correlating integrity test scores with polygraph operators' judgments and admissions of guilt obtained during polygraph testing. Generally, positive correlations in the .4 to .5 range have been found.* However, such correlations have only been performed for overt tests not the personality instruments. Moreover, using polygraph experts' judgments as a criterion measure has doubtful usefulness.

2. *Correlating integrity tests with being discharged from employment for theft or some similar measure.* As with all integrity criteria, there are limitations with this measure. First, few instances of theft are detected. This limits sample size and variance on the measure. Second, because of the low instance of theft, a variety of measures are being used including absenteeism, turnover, grievances, and supervisory performance ratings. Comparison of validity coefficients is, therefore, somewhat difficult. However, findings form several studies indicate comparable results for overt and personality measures. Correlations with supervisory performance

ratings are usually in the .20s, and a high percentage of detected thieves fail whichever type of integrity test is used.

3. *Correlating integrity test scores with admissions of theft or dishonest actions.* (These data are collected anonymously.) High positive correlations are generally found when scores of sections of tests or complete tests are used. Much lower correlations are found between individual items and this criterion.

4. *Comparing storewide shrinkage (value of goods missing from inventory) before and after testing was begun.* Such studies usually indicate a decrease in shrinkage after testing has begun. However, it must be noted that these studies do not use control groups and often other changes addressing shrinkage are present in addition to the integrity test. Therefore, it is not possible to isolate the effect of the integrity test.

5. *Contrasting test scores between a dishonest group (convicts) and others representing the general population.* Studies have usually reported at least a 1.5 standard deviation difference in the expected direction between these groups.

In related analyses, it was found that internal consistency estimates of reliability were often .85 or higher.[14] Finally, while there is evidence that individuals can "fake good" on integrity tests, there is no evidence that this commonly happens within an applicant pool.[15] Sackett and his colleagues conclude that ". . . a more compelling case that integrity tests predict a number of outcomes of interest to organizations can be made today than (previously)."[16]

In other important research, Deniz Ones, Chockalingam Viswesvaran, and Frank Schmidt examined the validity and generalizability of integrity tests through meta-analyses. They found that these tests appear to be useful for predicting both overall job performance and counterproductive behavior. The corrected validity of all types of tests with job performance was .29. Overt integrity tests correlate higher with counterproductive behavior than do personality tests (.70 and 37, respectively).[17] In a related study, the same researchers found that integrity tests are useful for predicting voluntary absenteeism. Personality-based tests correlated .33, and overt tests showed a much lower correlation of .09.[18] Overall, these results seems to indicate that integrity tests are useful in predicting several important job behaviors.

Graphology

Graphology is the analysis of the handwriting of an individual in order to infer personality traits and behavioral tendencies. A graphologist is the individual who performs the analysis.

Graphologists link their field to the projective personality assessment devices which were discussed in Chapter 14. That is, it is thought that the idiosyncratic features of a person's handwriting serve as an expression of his or her personality in the same manner as a story that is written about ambiguous inkblots or scenes involving human beings does. All are projections of the person that are imposed on a neutral field. No standard form of expression is demanded; therefore, the result is expressive of the individual.

In HR selection, graphologists examine handwriting samples of job applicants and evaluate (a) their suitability for employment in general, and/or (b) the match of their personality traits to the demands of a specific position. This type of analysis has been in wide-spread use in Western Europe for the last three decades. Only recently has it attracted attention in the United States, with one estimate that approximately 2,500 firms are presently using graphology in selection. In this section, we will discuss the major schools of graphology, provide examples of interpretations of some of the features of handwriting, and summarize the few studies that have examined the validity of this technique in selection.

Three Schools of Graphology

The first published book on handwriting analysis was written by Camillo Baldi, an Italian physician, in 1622 and entitled *Treatise on a Method to Recognize the Nature and Quality of a Writer from His Letters*. It did not receive much attention however, partially due to the few number of people in Europe who could read and write at that time. The major impetus for graphology is generally attributed to a French priest, Abbé Jean Hippolyte Michon, who published the book *The Practical System of Graphology* in Paris in 1875. Michon asserted that in every feature of handwriting a definite trait of character was revealed which could be attributed to the writer. He described these handwriting features with such terms as "jagged as lightning," "harpoon-shaped" "coiled," and "spider-like." He used such terms as "cold," "hard," "rough," and "unpleasant" to describe personality traits. Michon's system became known as "the school of fixed signs" because of his insistence that each of hundreds of handwriting features or signs indicate a specific personality trait. Later, one of Michon's students, Crepieux-Jamin, to some extent modified the rigid one-to-one relationship between signs and traits by examining small groups or clusters of signs. Nonetheless, the emphasis on isolated handwriting features continued to be characteristic of the French school.

The German school of analysis developed at the end of the nineteenth century and became almost directly counter to the French school in its emphasis. Wilhelm Preyer examined various forms of writing, for example, handwriting, footwriting, teeth writing, and opposite-hand writing, and concluded that there was a basic similarity in the features used among these writing forms. He further concluded, therefore, that "all writing is brain writing." This expression has since served as a succinct justification for graphology.

The most influential German graphologist was Ludwig Klages who extended Preyer's concepts. Klages used the term *expressive movements* to refer to all motor activities, such as handwriting, performed habitually and automatically without conscious thought. His basic assumption was that these movements actualize the drives and tensions of the personality. Klages's method of interpretation rejected the notion that each handwriting feature always indicates the same personality trait. Instead, he emphasized the importance of the *rhythm* of the writing. Any one handwriting feature may have one of several meanings. For example, it may indicate a spirit of enterprise in one case, indolence in another, a lie in one case, diplomacy in another, depending on the rhythmic beat of the form of the handwriting.

The interpretation, therefore, of handwriting depended on the skill of the graphologist in identifying the rhythm of the writing through examination of the total writing sample. While examination of specific features of the writing is necessary in this interpretation it is not correct to make an exact interpretation of each feature and then sum these to assess the writer's personality Rather, the graphologist must determine the rhythm from the total sample of writing and then interpret specific writing features within the personality framework identified by the rhythm. Emphasis was placed on the individual expertise of the graphologist in interpreting handwriting, and it was thought that experience in analysis was the only way to develop this expertise. That is, after establishing a reservoir of past observations, the information from these accumulated data guided interpretation and analysis. In essence, the personal philosophy of the graphologist was the central element of interpretation.

The third major school is Graphoanalysis, founded by M. N. Bunker in 1929. The word *Graphoanalysis* is a registered trade name and identifies the system of handwriting analysis taught by the International Graphoanalysis Society, Inc., Chicago, Illinois. This society conducts residential and extension courses and certifies its students upon completion of training. The school is commonly regarded as holding the middle ground between the one-to-one approach of the French school and the broad generality of the German school. Graphoanalysis is based in Gestalt psychology, which focuses on the totality of the individual and studies personality as a dynamic whole. Analysis is based on the interpretation of separate writing features. However, emphasis is placed on the interplay of related traits that produces an overall personality pattern. The interpretation of specific handwriting features in relationship to others in the handwriting sample is the subject of the training courses. Such interpretation, therefore, can be learned from direct demonstration and does not depend on the personal philosophy of the analyst as does interpretation in the German school.

There are many other methods of interpretation developed by individual graphologists that are seemingly different from these three schools. For example, Jane Nugent Green, in a book entitled *You and Your Private I*,[19] describes a system based on the premise that the "ppI" (personal pronoun I) is the key to assessing the writer's intimate attitudes about himself or herself and others. How the letter is written and where it is placed on the page are important indicants. Arthur Holt, in *Handwriting in Psychological Interpretations*,[20] describes a system, which he states he personally developed, that gives specific interpretation to each stroke. This is similar in approach to the French school; however, Holt also indicates it is the sum total of all the features with their psychological interpretation that produces the complete character description.

We were not able to find many studies that systematically compared interpretations of the same samples of handwriting by analysts from the different approaches to graphology. The one study of such a comparison found the same moderate level of agreement among analysts of different schools as among those from the same school.[21] However, all analysts were required to use the same set of traits and the measured agreement was in the ratings of these traits. A more complete comparison would not restrict the traits that could be used by an analyst. We cannot, therefore, make any definite statement about the similarity of assessment across different schools of graphology.

Analysis of Handwriting Features

Although different graphological approaches exist, most of them analyze the following features of handwriting: size of letters, slant, width, zones (top, middle, and bottom) regularity of letter formation, margin, pressure, stroke, line of letters (upward, straight, downward), connections of letters, form of connection and word and line spacing. Apparently, the various approaches differ in the interpretation each assigns to these specific features and how combinations of writing features should be viewed.

The following are illustrations and comments about selected analyses provided by the International Graphoanalysis Society.[22] The writing sample should be a full page or more of spontaneous writing made with a ball-point pen or pencil on unruled paper without the subject's knowing that the sample is for analysis. The general procedure for graphoanalysis is based on the following steps. First, a *perspectograph* is developed. This is an analysis of the first one hundred *upstrokes* that occur in the writing sample according to set rules of measurement. The result is a percentage value for each of seven different degrees of slant, ranging from far forward to markedly backward. Each type of slant is indicative of a state of emotional responsiveness. In general, far-forward writing is indicative of extremely emotional individuals and backward slant of emotionally constrained ones. The percentage of each of the seven slants is plotted on a graph for reference as other traits are found.

The second step in analysis is recording the absence or presence of approximately 100 primary personality traits and 50 evaluated (secondary) traits using special worksheets. A primary trait is one that is determined from a single-stroke character. For example, *temper* is indicated by bars on the letter t made to the right of the stem of the letter. An evaluated trait is one that is identified through a combination of two or more other traits. *Timidity*, for example, is a combination of *lack of self-confidence, shyness, self-consciousness*, and *clannishness*. The intensity of both primary and evaluative traits are measured using a three-point scale.

These traits are divided into groups. Among these groups are emotions, mental processes, and social behavior. As mentioned previously, emotions are indicated by the slant of the writing. The mental process of comprehension is indicated by sharp points on the letters *m* and *n*. Rounded tops of the same letters shows logical thinking, and wedges of these two letters show investigative thinking. As an example of social behavior, tight loops on *m*'s and *n*'s indicate repression while spread loops represent uninhibition. Exhibit 16.1 presents examples of specific handwriting features and their interpretation.

EXHIBIT 16.1   SOME EXAMPLES OF HANDWRITING
FEATURES AND THEIR INTERPRETATION

Figure 1. Levels of Emotional Responsiveness

| (a)
Withdrawal | (b)
Objectiveness | (c)
Intense
Responsiveness |

Figure 2. Mental Prowess

(a)
Comprehensive
thinking

(b)
Cumulative
thinking

(c)
Exploratory or
investigative
thinking

Figure 3. Social Responsiveness

(a)
Repression

(b)
Uninhibition

Figure 4. Approach to Achievement

(a)
Lack of
self-confidence

(b)
Strong
will power

Figure 5. Levels of Social Appeal

(a)
Simplicity,
modesty

(b)
Ostentation

EXHIBIT 16.1 **(CONTINUED)**

Figure 6. Levels of Honesty

and

(a)
Frankness

and

(b)
Self-deception or
rationalization

and

(c)
Intentional
deception

Figure 7. Levels of Imagination

light

(a)
Abstract
thinking

light

(b)
Materialistic
imagination

Figure 8. Attitude toward Life

many

(a)
Depression/
Pessimism

many

(b)
Optimism

Figure 9. Levels of Determinism

many

(a)
Strong
determination

many

(b)
Weak
determination

Figure 10. Levels of Attention

in

(a)
Close attention
to detail

in

(b)
Inattention

To obtain another type of information about graphology, one of the authors of this text, Robert Gatewood, sent a writing sample to a graphologist who graduated from the program conducted by the International Graphoanalysis Society. She provided a written description of Gatewood's personality and a score for each of 88 traits. He did not know he had that much personality! (If you look at his trait ratings, the graphologist did not think so either.) Exhibit 16.2 reproduces the writing sample, the written description, and a sample of the trait ratings. Just for the fun of it, Gatewood gave the complete analysis to some of his friends. Their comments along with Gatewood's reaction are also contained in the exhibit. Part of Gatewood's final examination in his selection class asks each student to disagree with this analysis and point out specifically why he is a much better guy than described here. He is puzzled why many students do poorly on this part of the test.

Validity of Graphology in Selection

Despite the large popularity in Western Europe of graphology as a selection tool, sometimes estimated as high as 80 percent of all companies, and its growing use in the United States, there are few formal studies of the validity of the technique in selection. However, Anat Rafaeli and Richard Klimoski conducted a well-formulated study.[23] The following is a summary. Seventy real estate brokers with at least 18 months of experience in the same firm were asked to supply two samples of their handwriting: one described a neutral topic (a house description) and the second was content laden (an autobiography). For each broker, job performance data were collected in the form of supervisor's ratings and dollar level of sales. Twenty graphologists participated in the study, of which 12 had previous experience in HR selection. A group of 24 undergraduate students, untrained in graphology, served as a comparison for the graphologists and also analyzed the handwriting samples.

The graphologists were allocated ten scripts each, both the neutral and content scripts from two writers and one script each from six additional writers. Each graphologist rated each script on ten personality dimensions: *social confidence, social activity, sales drive, interpersonal communication, work management skills, decision making, health/vitality, economic maturity, empathy, and summary.* A separate overall rating of effectiveness was also obtained. The 24 students performed the same evaluation on four or five writing samples. Finally, each real estate broker rated himself or herself on the ten personality dimensions.

The first analysis examined the reliability of the ratings of two different graphologists of the same script. The median correlation for ratings of neutral scripts was low but statistically significant, .54. For content-laden scripts, the median was .34; and overall, it was .41. The authors found moderate support for the idea that different graphologists can reliably rate writing samples. They also concluded that content did not have an effect on the graphologists' assessments. It was sometimes thought these assessments would be influenced by what was said in the sample and, therefore, were not only of handwriting features.

No support, however, was found for the validity of the graphologists' ratings. None of the correlations with supervisors' ratings, sales data, or self-ratings of the brokers was significant. The same pattern held true for the student raters.

EXHIBIT 16.2	A WRITING SAMPLE AND ACCOMPANYING GRAPHOLOGICAL ANALYSIS

Dear Chris:

Want to know about my summer? Did you see the movie *Money Pit*? That's been my summer. It all started last March. I was considering selling my house. So I realized that I needed to repair two minor cracks in the ceilings of both floors of my house. Oh my nearvete! I had sprayed-on ceilings at the time — you know like a cheap motel. Well, the dimples had been sprayed on incorrectly. It was not possible to repair and repaint the ceilings. They cracked into little pieces when painted. What to do? Right, find a skilled craftsman to scrape the ceilings and make them flat. I like that better anyway, because I want to be like fashionable people in Atlanta. Trouble was the only skilled craftsman in Athens moved to Savannah. So I got a guy to do the ceilings who apparently learned from FAXes sent to him from the craftsman. Talk about dust. Talk about slow. Talk about lack of attention to detail. Talk about marks on my grass — cloth and raw cedar walls.

Graphologist's Comments

To understand personality as a whole, it is necessary to throughly explore emotional structure, for it influences the effectiveness of all your traits.

You are prone to be hightly responsive to emotional experiences. Incidents that would go unnoticed by a less emotional person may be of pronounced significance to you. There are times when you may find it difficult to control them. Though you may be

My Comments

Is this why I cry when manuscripts are rejected?

(continued)

| Ехнівіт 16.2 | (Continued) |

Graphologist's Comments	My Comments

Graphologist's Comments

acutely touched by emotional incidents, in time the memory fades.

A variety of thinking patterns exist, and that is good. When a problem exists, you are capable of breaking down information and evaluating the situation.

You have an inquiring mind, along with an interest in new things. You are selective, however, in what concepts you will accept. Your philosophical approach to life is somewhat restricted to realistic concepts. At times it is difficult for you to relate the past to the present and future. You have ideas that you do not bring to fruition. You do not use knowledge gained from past experiences.

Concentration is good. Once you focus your attention on a project or activity, you are not easily distracted. You recognize the importance of details, but do not get so involved in them that overall performance is lost.

You have the ability to structure your ideas, time and work. You are able to rank as to importance your plans and the means to get them done.

Determination is good. Generally, you are able to finish what you start. There are times, however, when your determination bends a little.

Because you mind is agile, you are able to adjust readily to new and unexpected incidents and circumstances. Because of this flexibility, you could be a writer or speaker.

There is a need to satisfy a natural urge to express yourself. You can talk big. You'll chatter about the wonderful things you are going to do.

Motivations are good. Writing shows practical goals, but some low ones are present. Have you a fear of failure in a certain area? Some insecurity and depression are present.

You do not have a realistic view of your aptitudes or talents as you overestimate what you can do. Since you fear that you will not get acceptance and affirmation, you elevate yourself above others and

My Comments

It's putting the information back together that bothers me.

What is your name and why are you in my office? . . . Oh! When did you say you joined the faculty?

This graphologist has never seen me try (for years) to do something around the yard or house.

This is easy. It's doing it that is hard.

Maybe she has seen my yard and home!

Maybe I *could* be a writer. She hasn't read this book.

Yep, I've chattered about both of the wonderful things for years. They happened when I went through puberty.

Woe is me! Will I ever finish this book?

This is wrong. If I ever do make a mistake, I will quickly admit it.

EXHIBIT 16.2	(CONTINUED)

Graphologist's Comments	**My Comments**

there you are beyond reproach. This is a form of social isolation.

It is natural and important to emotional health to express feelings without guilt or embarrassment. Excessive restraint sets up inner tensions and conflicts which damage the personality. Emotional pressure builds up to the point where it must find release, often in an explosive and uncontrollable manner.

> Did she talk to women I dated in college?

Believing that you have been unjustly imposed upon, you now are on the alert not to let it happen again. You may feel exploited by the demands that friendship or relationships impose.

> Let's see, how many pages did Feild write of this book?

If you think you are being pushed around, you are capable of making pointed remarks. These stinging remarks can keep others at a distance.

> She did talk with the women I dated in college!

One of your biggest problems is procrastination. You'll postpone decisions or actions. You delay what you are afraid to do. You may have no intention of doing something, so you put people off rather than say you won't do it.

> As soon as I get the time, I'm going to write her to tell her how wrong she is. (You knew this one was coming.)

Some stubbornness is present, but this is softened by your yieldingness. Since you are flexible, you are willing to adjust to changing conditions. This enables you to bend rather than fight. Others can convince you to change conclusions by pressure or persuasion. You'll take the path of least resistance, for good or ill.

> This is confusing! What does she want me to believe? I wish she would tell me.

In conclusion, you are an extrovert with many fine qualities. You would do well vocationally as a speaker, writer, politician, clergyman, sales, or any job where you would deal with the public. You have a great interest in others and have to be involved.

> Is she saying I run my mouth a lot?

Doing things is appealing to you. You could be an exercise fan, enjoy playing a sport or even watching a sport being played. You have a mental desire for physical movement. The brain demands that the body move, that muscles be used actively and vigorously.

> She must have seen me hanging out with Michael, Bo, Deion, and Sir Charles.

Procrastination is your biggest problem. You should belong to the DIN-DIN club (Do It Now-Do It Now). With awareness, this can be overcome.

> As soon as I finish my yard and house, I'll do something about this.

(continued)

EXHIBIT 16.2 **(CONTINUED)**

Trait Ratings

Scale: 0 (low) to 10 (high) Numbers in parentheses represent the norm for that trait as determined by a scientific study. N/A means not available; that trait was not included in the study or there is no norm.

Gatewood's Score	*Norm*	
0	(1.4)	Keen Comprehension: Grasps ideas quickly; active mind
0	(3.8)	Independence: Prefers to do things one's own way; does what is right for self; follows own ideas
5	(5.0)	Open-Minded: Listens receptively to ideas
5	(1.8)	Acquisitive: Desires objects, knowledge, and/or love
0	(1.8)	Optimism: Views life hopefully (some depression present)
6	(4.7)	Decisive: Makes choices without hesitation
5	(1.6)	Initiative: Self-starter, self-reliance
5	(1.0)	Responsible: Accepts accountability for conduct
0	(0.5)	Desire for Attention: Compensation for unmet emotional needs
0	(0.4)	Guilt: Criticizes and punishes self
0	(N/A)	Worry: Feels distress or anxiety
0	(2.2)	Argumentative: Feels a need to defend ideas or actions
5	(2.6)	Sarcasm: Sharp remarks used defensively or offensively
2	(1.0)	Stubborn: Refusal to yield saves face
6	(0.8)	Procrastinates: Puts off for fear of failure
2	(2.5)	Positive: Speaks and acts with authority
0	(N/A)	Dominating: Can take charge of people or situations
1	(2.5)	Generous: Willing to give of self—time and energy
0	(1.0)	Humor: Can find amusement in everyday happenings
7	(2.0)	Talkative: May verbalize too much without saying much

Colleagues' Comments

Colleague 1-James Lahiff

While the graphoanalyst failed to detect some significant behavioral patterns of the subject, some of the statements are highly accurate; others less so. Here are some observations based on my knowledge of the subject of the analysis.

1. The graphoanalyst failed to identify the subject as a person who cross-dresses on national holidays

2. "Some stubbornness is present" is the understatement of the analysis. Subject's behavior regularly extends beyond stubbornness toward compulsiveness. Not only does the subject believe in chewing each mouthful of food ten times, he insists on counting aloud.

3. Analysts failed to even intimate that subject is a very messy eater. He makes dining out an unusual experience (see no. 2).

EXHIBIT 16.2 (CONTINUED)

4. ". . . responsive to emotional experiences." Right! He still regularly cries over the death of Bambi's mother.
5. "You are not easily distracted." Right! He still maintains that Norman Bates was framed.
6. ". . . able to adjust readily to new and unexpected incidents." Wrong! He refuses to accept the fact that "Gilligan's Island" will not be returning to television, no matter how many petitions he circulates.
7. "Procrastination is your biggest problem." Wrong! Have you ever seen his desk?
8. " You'll chatter about the wonderful things. . . " Right!
9. ". . . an exercise fan." Right again!! Numbers 8 and 9 are both right and related. Subject runs his mouth daily for exercise.
10. "You have ideas that you do not bring to fruition." Right! And it's a good thing.

Colleague 2-Charles Lance

According to the graphologist's graphoanalysis of Dr. Bob's handwriting sample, Dr. Bob:
1. Is highly responsive to emotional experiences (Dr. Bob is a very funny guy!).
2. Has a variety of thinking patterns (which he sometimes expresses all at once).
3. Is able to structure his ideas, time, work (actually Billie, his secretary, does all this).
4. Has good concentration, motivation, and determination and an Enquiring mind (yes, he reads a lot of tabloids)
5. Is stubborn and also yielding (huh?)
6. Procrastinates (I didn't know this, but perhaps he has delayed displaying this tendency).
7. Would make a good speaker, writer, politition, clergyman, or salesperson (its nice to have options Dr. Bob).

Colleague 3-Richard Riordan

This analysis plays best as a good news/bad news story. Initially, the graphoanalyst adroitly avoids irritating Gatewood by describing him as responsive, inquiring, selective, realistic, practical, and both flexible and structured. Then the grapho begins sticking it to him. He talks big, fears failure, is insecure, depressed and socially isolated. The only think that saves him is that he procrastinates. Why not? One would have to be quite dumb not to put off until tomorrow something that might hurt today. Finally, the grapho suggests Gatewood should belong to the DIN-DIN Club. This tickles him because he is enjoying his membership in a club with the same initials—DO IT NOT-DO IT NOT!

Rafaeli and Klimoski concluded that experienced graphologists were no better than untrained students at selection and that neither group operated at better than a chance level.

Abraham Jansen reports a series of four experiments on the validity of graphology that were carried out over a period of almost ten years.[24] The first two experiments used equal numbers of raters from each of three experimental groups consisting of people who analyzed handwriting samples: graphologists, psychologists and psychologists who had had a short course in graphology. Each rater was to evaluate the writing samples as being *energetic* or *weak*. The criteria for comparison were scores on a complete psychological test. There were no differences among the three rating groups, with each group being correct in about 60 percent of the cases. This level of accuracy was statistically significant above the chance level, but was judged to have little practical import.

In the third experiment, the writers were separated into energetic and weak groups on the basis of ratings of job performance. In essence, then, this experiment became one of the concurrent validity of graphological assessments. The accuracy rate of all three groups improved to approximately 70 percent. However, again there were no differences in accuracy among the three groups of writing sample raters. In the fourth experiment, the three groups of judges were asked to rate writing samples on 18 different characteristics. All 18 were used for performance ratings of employees in a commercial-administrative contact job. This experiment may also be considered as a concurrent validity study. The 18 variables fell into groups of energy variables (6), work ability variables (9), contact variables (2), and self-control. A fourth group of judges was also used, a group of psychologists who made ratings based on typed versions of the handwriting samples. None of the three groups of handwriting analysts demonstrated significant correlations with the 18 performance ratings. In addition, the ratings of the fourth group, who used typed copy, were significantly more accurate on a number of the variables. In none of the four experiments was a very high level of reliability attained by any of the groups of analysts. The author concluded that "graphology is a diagnostic method of highly questionable and in all probability minimal, practical value."[25] Finally, a meta-analysis has been done of 17 graphology studies. Results demonstrated that graphologists were not better than non graphologists in predicting future performance based on handwritten scripts. In fact, psychologists with no knowledge of graphology outperformed graphologists on all dimensions. Also the nature of the scripts was found to be a moderating variable. Content-laden scripts had a higher validity ($r=.16$) than neutral scripts ($r=.03$).[26]

Evidence to date, therefore, does not seem to warrant the use of graphology as a selection instrument. In all fairness to its advocates, the studies supporting this conclusion are few and generally did not use large samples. We have commented several times in this text about the difficulty of making any judgments about validity based on studies with small samples. In addition, the normal use of graphology in selection does not appear to involve the use of data obtained from job analysis. There seems to be no linkage of traits to job performance. Instead, the graphologist apparently performs a general assessment of the character of the writer and uses that assessment as the basis for the selection evaluation. Such a procedure is obviously contrary to common professional selection strategy. It is unlikely, then, that the resulting ratings will be related to subsequent job performance.

Drug Testing

Substance abuse of illegal drugs has been linked to numerous problems in business, such as employee theft, violence, poor work performance, lateness, and absenteeism. The true cost of such behaviors is unknown, but is generally agreed to be considerable and increasing rapidly. Many in business fear this problem will continue in the near future because of the change in the demographics of the labor force. Drug abuse is strongly linked to certain population cohorts. Wide-scale drug usage is commonly thought to have begun with teens and young adults in the mid-1960s and to have continued in subsequent generations of these age groups. Today, these groups constitute a significant portion of the labor force and will continue to grow as a percentage as older workers retire.

Two programs have been used by business and government to combat and control this phenomena: drug education programs and drug employment testing. The first attempts to inform children and adults of the ease of developing drug addiction, the serious consequences of even limited drug use, and the opportunity for the individual to make a choice to avoid drug use. The second administers paper-and-pencil tests or clinically tests urine samples of job applicants and incumbents in the hopes of identifying those who have recently used drugs

As we discuss in this section, the testing of urine samples is legally controversial and numerous court cases are in progress at the time of this writing. Perhaps because of this, according to a recent Department of Labor survey of 7,500 private employers, only 9 percent of employers had either testing or counseling programs.[27] Mining, communications, public utilities, and transportation establishments were most likely to have drug testing programs, partly because of government regulatory requirements. Least likely to have such programs were retail trade, service, and construction firms. Size was the largest determining factor in whether an establishment had a program. Of the organizations with at least 1,000 employees, 43 percent had testing programs and 76 percent had some form of counseling or assistance. Of those organizations with fewer than 50 employees, only 2 percent had testing and only 9 percent had counseling programs.

Job applicants were far more likely to be tested than job incumbents. According to survey responses, of 3.9 million applicants who were tested, 12 percent tested positive for drug use. The industries with the highest rates of applicants testing positive were the retail sector with 24 percent and wholesale trade with 17 percent. The industries with the lowest rates for applicants were communication and public utilities with 5.5 percent.

In the following pages we describe the various major drug tests, discuss the legal issues surrounding this type of testing, and summarize some necessary features of a testing program. After reading this section, consult legal employment journals, for example, *Fair Employment Practices*, or professional associations, such as, the American Society for Personnel Administration, the American Federation of State, County, and Municipal Employees, or AFI-CI0, for further information.

Drug Tests

The simplest, and least controversial, of drug tests is the paper-and-pencil type. This test is identical in intent to the paper-and-pencil integrity tests that were discussed previously. Overt-type tests ask directly about drug usage with questions such as:

> Do you think that it is okay for workers to use "soft" drugs at work if this does not cause poor job performance?

> In the past six months, how often have you used marijuana at work?

> In the past six months, have you brought cocaine to work even though you did not use it at work?

General-purpose tests are adaptations of personality inventories, analogous to personality-based integrity measures, which are developed to identify drug users. Unlike integrity tests, however, there is almost no public literature that evaluates the reliability or the validity of this type of test. However, one court case ruled that pre-employment tests in which applicants had to indicate their use of legal and illegal drug use were unconstitutional based on the Fifth Amendment's prohibition of involuntary self incrimination.[28] Therefore, it seems that a company would be limited in its ability to force an applicant to complete at least the overt type of test. Perhaps because of this, it seems that paper-and-pencil tests are used very infrequently by organizations. Other infrequently used tests are analysis of hair and physical coordination. Urine testing is the predominant technique.

Testing of urine samples for the presence of drugs was begun in the 1960s for use in hospital emergency rooms as a way of diagnosing patients in a drug-induced coma for appropriate treatment. In the 1970s, demand for this type of testing increased with the need to monitor clients' compliance with treatment programs for methadone maintenance and other drug therapy programs. The desire of business organizations to control the problems associated with employee drug usage has further increased the demand for these tests in the 1980s, and 1990s.

Commonly in employment testing, a drug can be reported as present only if it has been detected in two separate tests, using different analytic methods. In practice this means two levels of testing, a *screening test* and a *confirmation test,* which is used only when the screening test indicates that a drug is present. If the screening tests finds no drug presence or if the confirmatory test does not agree with the results of the screening test, the decision is that no drug is present. To conduct these tests, the urine sample is divided into two parts immediately after it is collected. Identification of samples is usually by number or code rather than by name of person.

All urine tests are based on the fact that what enters the body through ingestion, injection, or inhalation must be excreted in some form. Most drugs are excreted wholly, or in part, via the liver, kidneys, and bladder, in the urine. Although some drugs are excreted unchanged (e.g., morphine), most drugs are broken down by the body, and the products, or *metabolites*, can be found in the urine. The physical evidence of drug use thus differs from drug to drug. The testing procedures, then, must also differ for the different drug families, and new tests need to be developed as new drugs come into use. To avoid error, standard thresholds (amount of drug present) of detection are set to determine the presence of a drug. If less than the threshold amount is detected, the decision is made that no drug is present. This greatly reduces the possibility of drug presence being indicated by amounts of a legally permissible drug product.

Screening Tests   The most common form of screening test is some type of *immunoassay* test. A typical immunoassay test kit contains a number of solutions (reagents) which are added to the urine sample. In the first step, a solution containing antibody against the drug in question is mixed with the urine. If there is some drug in the urine, some of this antibody immediately binds to the drug, with the rest remaining free. Other substances are also added, enzymes, enzyme substrates, and a measured amount of the drug in question. The activity between the enzyme and its substrate produces a density change in the sample. This optical density change is measured by an instrument called a spectrophotometer. When an optical density change is detected, the presence of the drug is positive. Limitations of an immunoassay test are its high sensitivity (the ability to detect small amounts of the drug) and its cross-reactivity (the ability to detect small amounts of similar drugs, some of which may not be illegal drugs). For this reason a confirmatory test is necessary when the immunoassay test produces a positive result.

Confirmatory Tests   The most often used confirmatory tests are *gas chromatography, gas chromatography with mass spectrometry,* and *thin-layer chromatography.* All tests start with the extraction of drugs or their breakdown products from the second portion of urine. The urine is passed down a column that contains silica powder or another substance that has been treated with chemicals that will bind drugs. The residue is then picked off the silica.

In gas chromatography, a tiny sample of the extracted material is injected into a long hollow glass tube that is coated with liquid silicone. The sample is vaporized and carried by a pressurized pulse of inert helium gas through the length of the tube, usually 15 to 30 meters. Each drug has its own transit time. The rate of the substance in question is then timed and this information is compared with times of known drugs. Given controlled conditions in the glass tube, there should be no variance of transit time of a drug over trials. Therefore, the identification is definite.

In gas chromatography with mass spectrometry, the vaporized drugs resulting from gas chromatography are bombarded with a stream of electrons. Each drug is unique in terms of the ratio of various-sized mass fragments that result after electron impact. This pattern is, in effect, a "molecular fingerprint" of the drug. The molecular fragment pattern of the substance in question is compared to a library of standard molecular fragmentation patterns by a computer. The drug is labeled by this comparison.

Thin layer chromatography starts with a portion of the extracted material. This is placed near the bottom edge of a thin glass plate that is coated with grains of silica. The edge of the glass is placed in a solvent, and the solvent migrates up the slide, as ink travels up a blotter. As the solvent moves up the silica, it carries the drug with it. Different drugs migrate upward at specific speeds and for specific distances. Distance traveled is measured by "developing" the glass plate like a photographic film. The plate is sprayed with various dyes that react with the drug, producing characteristic color reactions. The color and distance traveled serve to identify the drug.

Cost and Accuracy of Tests Depending on the agreement between an employer and a drug testing company or lab, the tests can range in cost from $30 to $70 per employee or applicant.

Because the physical properties of each drug are invariate, the tests should be completely accurate. False positives, individuals indicated as drug users who, in fact, are not users, may be identified with the immunoassay test because of its cross-reactivity. However, these individuals will be eliminated by any of the confirmation tests. Errors in confirmatory tests can only occur if the laboratory conducting the testing does not use standard procedures in testing. There is, however, some evidence that such errors may have occurred frequently, at least in the past. For example, the Centers for Disease Control studied the error rates of 13 laboratories over a ten-year period for simple tests designed to detect amphetamines, barbiturates, cocaine, codeine, methadone, and morphine. The range of false positives was dramatic (up to 37 percent) for amphetamines, up to 66 percent for methadone, and up to 100 percent for cocaine, codeine, morphine, and amphetamines).

Many think that such error rates are no longer common, because of the increased public concern and recent regulation of laboratory procedures. The U.S. Department of Health and Human Services, the Substance Abuse and Mental Health Services Administration, and the National Institute on Drug Abuse have issued final rules concerning standards for certification of laboratories engaged in urine drug testing federal agencies. Several states have passed similar standards.

It is also important to realize the limitations of the information obtained from these tests. A positive result means a presence of the drug above the threshold level set for detection. The result does *not* allow a determination of how much of the drug was used, how frequently it has been used, how long ago it was used, the circumstances of its use, or the level of impairment in performance caused by the drug. There are differences among individuals in absorption, metabolism, and tolerance of drugs. Also many drugs leave a metabolite trail long after any performance effects have faded; therefore, it is not accurate to assume automatically that a positive test is an infallible indicant of inability to perform. Finally, the threshold level, obviously, affects the results. While there are commonly accepted threshold levels for detection, some levels are so low that passive inhalation of marijuana can give a positive result.

Legal Issues in Employment Drug Testing

As we mentioned previously, the legal status of using drug tests in employment is unclear and is changing rapidly. However, it seems safe to say that organizations have less risk in using such tests for pre-employment selection; considerably more legal risk is associated with testing existing workers in promotion decisions or with testing employees in order to detect drug users for disciplinary or counseling purposes. This is mainly due to the fact that applicants cannot take advantage of collective bargaining or challenge employment-at-will principles as can employees who feel they have been wrongly treated. This reduced risk is undoubtedly reflected in the results of the Department of Labor's survey that was previously discussed, in which it was found that many more organizations used pre-employment testing than testing of existing employees.

A chief concern in pre-employment testing is the communication of results to those who test positive. Reckless communication can lead to a charge of defamation of character. Similarly, labeling an applicant as a "drug user" or "dope addict" can potentially subject an employer to a legal claim of "outrage" or "intentional infliction of emotional distress." It is, therefore, crucial that employers be particularly sensitive and restrained in the manner used to inform an applicant who has tested positive that employment has been denied. Generally, this includes stating that denial of employment is the consequence applied to all applicants who show a positive result and that no further judgment is made as to the typical behavior of the applicant regarding drug usage. The results of all tests should, obviously, he kept confidential. It is also important to require all applicants to take the drug test if such a program is in place. As we have mentioned, EEO laws prohibit discrimination on the basis of demographic characteristics. Failure to require the testing of all individuals may lead to the situation in which a protected group member is tested and denied employment and a few nonminority members are not tested and selected. Such circumstances could prompt a charge of disparate treatment.

Deborah Crown and Joseph Rosse have examined the major legal questions concerning drug testing programs, especially as applied to current employees.[29] The following summarizes their observations. They found that opposition to testing has centered on the following six legal arguments:

1. Testing represents an invasion of privacy.

2. It constitutes an unreasonable search and seizure.

3. Testing is a violation of due process.

4. Drug users are protected under the Americans with Disabilities Act.

5.   Testing may violate the Civil Rights Act.

6.   It may violate the National Labor Relations Act.

We briefly discuss each of these issues.

By its very nature, the collection of the urine sample for testing is intrusive. Intrusion, physically or otherwise, on the private affairs of an individual has commonly been the basis for civil suits under the doctrine of "right of privacy." However, this term offers protection only if the employer is a governmental institution or agency. Therefore, this defense is actually open to a minority of employees. It is not clear to what extent this concept can be applied to private industry, but at present it seems limited. It is possible that "right to privacy" in nongovernmental firms may apply only to confidentiality in the collection and reporting of the results of the drug test. Collection practices should include guarantees of the privacy of the individual in terms of both the facilities provided and the procedures used in monitoring the specimen collection to ensure that it has not been altered.

For certain jobs, it may be acceptable to require testing in the interests of public safety even at the cost of employee privacy. These would be jobs in which the employee could place himself or herself or others in substantial danger while under the effects of drug use. Examples of such jobs include airline pilots and other public transportation positions, chemical and nuclear power plant operators, and security officers.

The Fourth Amendment prohibits unreasonable search; the Fifth and Fourteenth Amendments guarantee the right of due process. While frequently applied in public practices, these concepts have limited application to private industry. A central issue is the reasons for the testing. It seems important that testing be linked to workplace problems such as accidents, theft, absenteeism, and sabotage. Data that indicate the existence of such problems before testing can serve as evidence the company was pursuing a legitimate self-interest. In the absence of such data, the company is at risk by seeming arbitrary in its actions with little actual justification for its claims.

The question of due process, under which a person is innocent unless proven guilty, seems to deal with the validity of drug tests. Presumably, evidence provided by professionally carried out testing would constitute evidence of guilt. As of this writing, no cases have addressed this issue directly.

The Americans With Disabilities Act of 1990 prohibits discrimination against the disabled. The act clearly protects former drug users who are in rehabilitation and excludes individuals currently using drugs.

Title VII of the *Civil Rights Act of 1964* could be a legal basis for discrimination if, as described previously, unequal treatment occurs. It is possible drug testing could also result in adverse impact if a greater percentage of minority than nonminority members are identified. The test would, then, have to be shown to be job-related. Safety of others or demonstration of previous records of high rates of damage, accidents, or absenteeism could serve as evidence. The previously noted difficulty in linking positive results of a drug test with decrements in job performance could limit an organization's defense.

Collective bargaining agreements represent one of the most significant obstacles to drug testing programs in unionized firms. Because drug testing is considered a working condition, and as such is subject to collective bargaining, employers generally cannot implement drug testing without consulting with the union. Even when such testing is accepted by both parties, disciplinary measures prompted by the results of testing can be subject to arbitration. One study reports that arbitrators have overturned more discharges than they have sustained.[30] Also pertinent are court rulings regarding employment-at-will and wrongful discharge. Traditionally management has had nearly complete discretion in terminating employees under these principles. However, some recent rulings have altered this position.

It is no surprise that drug testing has caused negative reactions among applicants as well as employees. Subsequently, it is important for selection and HR specialists to understand how applicants and existing employees may react to a drug testing program.

In general, recent research has indicated that employees and applicants react more favorably to drug testing when (1) an advance warning of the testing is given, (2) the company uses rehabilitation rather than termination when the presence of drugs is detected,[31] and (3) the drug testing adheres to fair detection procedures and explanation of results.[32] Additionally, researchers have found that employees and applicants are more positive about drug testing when there is a perceived need for the test.[33] In this research, some of the acceptable reasons for testing included perceptions of danger, contact with the public, use of spatial ability, and the performance of repetitive tasks. However, other research has provided evidence that, all in all, individuals have more positive attitudes toward companies that do not have a drug testing program, and toward those that do not need a testing program.[34]

Guidelines for Drug Testing Programs

We conclude this chapter with a brief description of the important features of a drug testing program.

1. The organization is in the most legally defensible position if it limits testing to those positions that have major safety implications or have a history of poor performance in specific areas that may be linked to drug usage. Organizations have more flexibility in such testing with applicants rather than existing employees.

2. It is necessary to use a combination of screening and confirmatory tests so the testing results will be valid. Such tests increase the cost of the program but are necessary given the seriousness of the matter.

3. The organization should obtain the written consent of the individual before testing and provide the individual with the test results afterward. Particular attention should be paid to those situations in which an individual is informed of positive results from the drug test. At a minimum, the

person should be allowed to explain positive results in terms of legal drugs that he or she may have taken. Obviously, a physician's verification may be required in such explanations. Some have also recommended that the individual who tested positive be offered the opportunity of taking part of the urine sample used in the testing and submitting it to another laboratory for additional testing. This would be done at the individual's expense.

4. Whatever procedures are used in the testing program should be applied to all individuals in the same job status. It would be inadvisable to exempt some persons from testing because it is thought to be obvious that they are not taking drugs.

5. The program should be designed and reviewed periodically to ensure that privacy is afforded to the individuals being tested. This means that urine collection procedures be standardized and attuned to the privacy of the individual. Also, all results must be kept confidential, especially from supervisors of existing employees unless there is a defined need-to-know.

6. Drug testing, especially when used for current employees, should be one part of a larger program. Other features should include some form of education, counseling, and assistance.

References

[1] FEP, section 401.

[2] David Z. Lykken, "Psychology and the Lie Detector Industry," *American Psychologist* 29 (1974): 725–739.

[3] Ibid.

[4] Leonard Saye, Denise Dougherty, and Theodore Cross, "The Validity of Polygraph Testing," *American Psychologist* 40 (1985): 355–366.

[5] Paul Sackett, Laura Burris, and Christine Callahan, "Integrity Testing for Personnel Selection: An Update," *Personnel Psychology* 42 (1989): 491–529

[6] London House, Inc., 1550 Northwest Highway, Park Ridge, IL. 60068; Reid Psychological Systems, Borg-Warner Bldg., 200 S. Michigan Ave., Chicago, IL. 60604.

[7] William Terris and John Jones, "Psychological Factors Related to Employees' Theft in the Convenience Store Industry," *Psychological Reports* 51 (1982): 1219–1238.

[8] Bureau of National Affairs, *Employee Testing: The Complete Resource Guide* (Washington, D.C.: Bureau of National Affairs, Inc., 1988).

[9] Joyce Hogan and Robert Hogan, "How to Measure Employee Reliability," *Journal of Applied Psychology* 74 (1989): 273–279

[10] London House, Inc., 1550 Northwest Highway, Park Ridge, Ill. 60068.

[11] Ibid.

[12] Paul Sackett, Laura Burris, and Christine Callahan, "Integrity Testing for the Personnel Selection: An Update," *Personnel Psychology* 42 (1989) 491–529.

[13] Scott Martin and William Terris, "Predicting Infrequent Behavior: Clarifying the Impact on False-Positives," *Journal of Applied Psychology* 76 (1991): 484–487.

[14] Fred M. Rafilson "Temporal Stability of Preemployment Integrity Test," *Psychological Reports* 65 (1989): 1384–1386.

[15] Ann M. Ryan and Paul R. Sackett, "Pre-employment Honesty Testing: Fakability, Reactions of Test Takers, and Company Image." *Journal of Business and Psychology* 1 (1987): 248–256.

[16] Paul Sackett, Laura Burris, and Christine Callahan, "Integrity Testing for Personnel Selection: An Update," *Personnel Psychology* 42 (1989): 491–529.

[17] Deniz S. Ones, Chockalingam Viswesvaran, and Frank L. Schmidt, "Integrity Test Validities: Meta-Analytic Tests of Moderator Hypotheses," paper presented at Society for Industrial/Organizational Psychologists conference St. Louis, Mo., April 27, 1991.

[18] Deniz S. Ones, Chockalingam Viswesvaran, and Frank L. Schmidt, "Meta-Analysis of Integrity Test Validities for Predicting Employee Absenteeism," paper presented at Annual meeting of Academy of Management, Personnel/HR Division, Las Vegas, August 9, 1992.

[19] Jane Nugent Green, *You and Your Private I* (St. Paul, Minn.: Llewelyn , 1975).

[20] Arthur Holt, *Handwriting in Psychological Interpretations* (Springfield, Ill.: Thomas Publishing, 1985).

[21] Richard J. Klimoski and Anat Rafaeli, "Inferring Personal Qualities through Hand writing Analysis," *Journal of Occupational Psychology* 56 (1983): 195.

[22] James C. Crumbaugh, "Graphoanalytic Cues," *Encyclopedia of Clinical Assessment*, vol. 2 (San Francisco, Calif.: Bass, 1980), 919–929.

[23] Anat Rafaeli and Richard Klimoski, "Predicting Sales Success through Handwriting Analysis: An Evaluation of the Effects of Training and Handwriting Sample Content," *Journal of Applied Psychology* 68 (1983): 212–217.

[24] Abraham Jansen, *Validation of Graphological Judgments: An Experimental Study* (The Hague, Netherlands: Mouton, 1973).

[25] Ibid., p. 126.

[26] Efrat Neter and Gershon Ben-Shakhar, "The Predictive Validity of Graphological Inferences: A Meta-Analytic," *Personality and Individual Differences* 10 (1989): 737–745.

[27] U.S. Department of Labor, Bureau of Labor Statistics, *Survey of Employer Anti-Drug Programs*, Report 760 (Washington, D.C.: U.S. Department of Labor, January 1989).

[28] *National Treasury Employees Union v. Von Raab*, 649 F. Supp 380 (1986).

[29] Deborah F. Crown and Joseph G. Rosse, "A Critical Review of Assumptions Underlying Drug Testing," in *Applying Psychology in Business: The Manager's Handbook*, Douglas W. Bray, John W. Jones, and Brian D. Steffy, eds. (Lexington, Mass.: Lexington Books; 1991).

[30] Thomas Geidt, "Drug and Alcohol Abuse in the Work Place: Balancing Employer and Employee Rights," *Employer Relations Law Journal* 11 (1985): 181–205.

[31] Dianna Stone and Debra Kotch, "Individual's Attitudes toward Organizational Drug Testing Policies and Practices," *Journal of Applied Psychology*, 74 (1989): 518–521.

[32] Mary Konovsky and Russell Cropanzano, "Perceived Fairness of Employee Drug Testing as a Predictor of Employee Attitudes and Job Performance, "*Journal of Applied Psychology*, 76 (1991): 698–707.

[33] Kevin Murphy, George Thornton, and Kristin Prue, "Influence of Job Characteristics on the Acceptability of Employee Drug Testing," 76 (1991): 447–453.

[34] J. Michael Crant and Thomas Bateman, "An experimental Test of the Impact of Drug-Testing Programs on Potential Job Applicants' Attitudes and Intentions," *Journal of Applied Psychology*, 75 (1990): 127–131.

V

Criteria Measures

As we have stated more times in this book than any of us would wish to count, the ultimate test of a selection program is how well those selected perform on the job. Just as selection instruments should be properly constructed to obtain the most useful information about applicants, job performance measures should be carefully developed to obtain accurate data. Otherwise, the adequacy of the selection program may be unduly open to criticism. The program itself could be suitable, but the data used to evaluate the job performance of those selected could be flawed. This chapter has the following objectives:

1. describe the various measures used to determine job performance;

2. discuss the appropriate use of each type of measure; and

3. detail the important characteristics of each measure.

17

Measurement of Job Performance

Well this is it. We can see the proverbial light at the end of the tunnel, the cows have left the barn, and the rolling stone has gathered moss (or whatever). Our last remaining topic is criterion data.

In previous chapters, we discussed two of the major parts of validation work: (a) the statistical procedures necessary to conduct validity studies (Chapter 5), and (b) the methods of developing predictor measures (Chapters 10 through 16). In this chapter we turn our attention to the third part of validation, the criteria measures. These are the instruments used to measure the job performance of *individual* workers. Examples of such instruments can range from a supervisor's rating of a worker's job performance to the actual number of goods produced by an individual worker.

The adequacy of the criterion measure is as important to a validation study and to the selection program as the adequacy of the predictor measures. The criterion measure defines what is meant by job performance. High scores on this measure, therefore, define what is meant by "successful" job performance. The main purpose of the selection program is to predict which applicants will be successful on the job, and thus score high on the criterion measure once they are employed by the organization. As we discuss in this chapter, many different types of criteria measures have been used in validity studies. It is up to the selection specialist to decide which of these to use in the study. The importance of this decision should be obvious. If the criterion measure chosen for the validation study is inappropriate, then the selection program may be inappropriate also. That is, the selection program may not identify those applicants who will perform well on important aspects of the job.

As is the case with the development of predictors, the information obtained from the job analysis should serve as the basis for the development of the appropriate criterion measure. For example, using the task approach for job analysis, performance of workers on those tasks that are rated as highly important or requiring the most time to complete should be measured by the criterion. The same principle applies when one of the standardized questionnaire approaches is used; those job characteristics that are rated as important should be included in the criterion measure. This chapter presents several topics essential to the development of an appropriate criterion: the strengths and limitations of the major types of job performance measures, the essential characteristics of any measure that is used, and the EEO implications for these measures.

Types of Job Performance Measures

There are a number of different types of job performance measures that can be used singly or in combination as a criterion measure. We will present an overview of each of these major types and discuss its use in selection. For a more detailed treatment of each type, books such as *The Measurement of Work Performance Methods, Theory, and Application* by Frank Landy and James Farr, *Performance Appraisal: An Organizational Perspective* by Kevin Murphy and Jeanette Cleveland, and *Performance Appraisal: Assessing Human Behavior at Work* by John Bernardin and Richard Beatty are excellent sources.[1]

One way of presenting the various types of job performance measures is to group them according to the nature of the data gathered into the following four categories:

1. Production data—quality, quantity of output, etc.

2. Personnel data—lateness, absenteeism, turnover, etc.

3. Training proficiency—a specially developed test or simulation of training information or activities

4. Judgmental data—supervisors' opinions of subordinates' performance, etc. Each of these four categories may be further subdivided, as we see in the following discussion.

Production Data

Production data consists of the results of work. The data comprise things that can be counted, seen, and compared directly from one worker to another. other terms that have been used to describe these data are *output, objective,* and *nonjudgmental performance measures.* Such measures are usually based upon the specific nature of the job tasks, and quite different measures have been used for the same job title. The variety of measures which can be used is actually so great that it is not possible to summarize them in any representative manner. Instead, Table 17.1 contains a list of job titles and some of the various production criteria measures that have been used for each title. It is apparent from the table that data about both quantity and quality of production have been used. Quantity is usually expressed in terms of the number of units produced within a specified time period. Quality is, in a way, indirectly measured by the number of defects, errors, or mistakes identified either per number of units or amount of time.

TABLE 17.1	EXAMPLES OF PRODUCTION CRITERIA MEASURES FOR VARIOUS JOBS	
	Production Measure	
Job Title	**Quantity**	**Quality**
Key punch operator	Number of data columns punched per hour	Number of errors per hour
Skilled machine operator	Number of units produced per week Weight of output per week	Number of defects Weight of scrap
Salesperson	Dollar volume of sales Number of orders	Number of cancelled orders Number of returns
Manager	Profit of unit	Number of grievances filed by subordinates

Many consider the use of production data as the most desirable type of measure for a number of reasons. First, such data are often easy to gather because they are collected routinely for business operations such as production planning and budgeting. Also, the importance of such measures is thought to be obvious and easily understood. Production data are the direct result of job actions. They are the objectives of the work process. Finally, these data are thought to be unchallengeable and easily accepted by workers. Production output can be seen and counted; and, therefore, no argument can be made about its measurement.

Our opinion is that such enthusiasm about production data as criteria measures is not entirely justified. None of these four major categories of work measurement data is without limitation. Each is appropriate in some circumstances and inappropriate in others. We will discuss some of the limitations in the use of production data to illustrate this point.

Consider first the argument of the ease of gathering the data through commonly used business operations. Frequently, such operations are concerned with the records of total work units as opposed to individuals. For example, budgeting usually compares a departmental unit's actual production and cost to a projection of these variables. Production planning frequently is concerned with the optimum movement of goods through various stages of the manufacturing process. In neither case is attention paid to the individual worker, especially if he or she frequently moves to different work stations. However, data on individuals are essential for validation. As we know, a validity coefficient correlates individual workers' selection test scores with the same individuals' performance scores. Therefore, if accurate *individual* worker data cannot be gathered, then validation cannot be performed.

The assumption that production data are countable and, therefore, indisputable, is also tenuous. As Table 17.1 indicates, there are numerous measures that are used for sales performance. All seem to be straightforward measures that would be acceptable to those concerned. However, the literature and the practice of sales management contradict such a notion. There is a consensus in sales work that the most often used measure of sales performance, dollar sales volume, is closely related to the characteristics of the territory that is worked. Such items as population, store density, socio-economic status of customers, number of competitors and amount of advertising are all relevant characteristics.

Various modifications of sales records have been suggested to control for these differences in territory. One of the most popular is to calculate monthly sales as a percentage of a quota set for the territory.[2] Quotas are usually determined by the sales manager. However, this assumes that the judgment of the sales manager is accurate and acceptable to all. Another adjustment is to divide sales volume by years that the salesperson has been in the territory.[3] The rationale is that as a salesperson learns the territory, sales should increase rather than merely staying level. This simplified judgment may not be acceptable to all.

Similar issues have been raised regarding the use of production data of managers. Several studies, especially those of assessment centers, have used rate or level of promotion or salary increase as job performance measures. The assumption is that high performance by a manager will result in promotion and salary increase. Such an assumption probably is not totally accurate because labor market availability, job tenure, and area of specialization are all known to affect compensation and promotion.

Production measures have frequently been used in validation studies and are desirable mainly because of their direct relationship to job activities. However, these measures are often limited either by lack of availability or by uncontrolled variations in the work situation. While the former may prevent measurement entirely, the latter frequently complicates validation work by requiring correction factors. Most correction factors require that a manager make a judgment about how to adjust the raw data to minimize the effect of these differences in work situations. Different correction factors can vary considerably in their effects on measurements of performance. In these cases, the objectivity of the data and its direct relationship to job activities may be questionable.

HR Data

Absenteeism, turnover, grievances, accidents, and promotions are the variables in the second type of performance data, HR data. These variables are similar in many ways to production data. They are usually collected as part of other HR data files, almost always on an individual basis. In addition, they are reflective of important aspects of work behavior—attendance, after all, seems to be a prerequisite for performance. Finally, the data for these variables are countable and seemingly objective.

There are, however, some limitations that must be considered when using these measures. The first is limited variance in the scores of employees on these measures. That is, it is common for a majority of any given group of workers to have no accidents or grievances, and to remain with the company (no turnover). This is especially true if the time period investigated is relatively brief. Even absenteeism and promotions, for many groups of workers, can be very limited.

As we discussed in Chapter 5, limited variance will lower the magnitude of the validity coefficient. The second limitation, which we discuss in the following paragraphs, is the different measures that can be used for each of these variables. The problem is that the different measures of absenteeism, for example, do not yield identical data for a group of workers. Therefore, the selection specialist must clearly evaluate the concept to be measured and the most appropriate method of doing it.

Absenteeism The most frequently used measures of absenteeism have been the following:

1. Number of separate instances

2. Total number of days absent

3. Number of short absences (one or two days)

4. Blue Mondays (occurrence of a one-day absence on a Monday)[4]

A major concern in these measures has been the distinction between voluntary and involuntary absences. Involuntary absences are usually thought of as those due to severe illness, jury duty, union activities, death in the immediate family, and vacation. Voluntary absences are all other absences. Presumably the distinction is made to differentiate between absences workers have control over and others that they do not. A high frequency of the former indicates conscious restriction of output. The latter, while not desirable, may only reflect unfortunate circumstances that affect a worker.

We can see how this distinction is reflected in the four measures just identified. Counting the number of short absences or the number of Mondays missed is clearly an attempt to measure voluntary absences. The assumption is that a majority of each type of absence is taken by the employee to avoid work. The number of separate instances of absenteeism, logically, reflects the same idea. Presumably, undesirable workers are absent more times than desirable ones. Therefore, only frequency of instances are recorded, which is now the most commonly used measure of absenteeism. The number of days missed each time is irrelevant in this measure as is the reason for absence. The measure of the total number of days absent makes a different assumption. Time off is undesirable for whatever reason. Moreover, if one assumes that illness is evenly distributed in the population of workers, much of the difference among individuals is a function of voluntary absences.

Even without spending a great deal of effort in examining these various assumptions, it is obvious that each categorizes and counts items differently. One could take the same set of employee data records and construct different sets of criteria measures by using each of the four definitions. Another problem in the use of any of the four is the length of the time period to use for measurement. In most organizations, absenteeism is controlled within specified limits. Most employees realize that flagrant or repeated absenteeism, especially within a short time period, would prompt a reaction from the organization. Therefore, it has tentatively been concluded that absence data should be accumulated over at least one year to be useful.[5]

Another difficulty in using absenteeism data as a criterion is that the distribution of scores on this variable limits its use in correlational analysis. Measures of absenteeism are almost never normally distributed due to the low base rate of absences in organizations.[6] This lack of a normal distribution severely affects correlations between absenteeism and other variables. Even statistically transformed measures of absenteeism are questionable in linear regression models because of the normality violation. In general, correlations between absences and other variables are lowered due to differences in the shapes of their distributions.[7]

Although these problems have been known for several years, the vast majority of research on absenteeism has used linear regression or product-moment correlations. Recently, however, David Harrison and Charles Hulin have proposed a set of modeling procedures known as event history analysis as a viable solution to the non-normality problem.[8] Event history analysis models focus on two states (absenteeism, continuous attendance) an individual is in now and previously, the time spent in those states, and the rates of movement from state to state. Harrison and Julin suggest using the Cox Proportional Hazard Rate Model for analysis. The central data of this model is the time between the beginning of an observation period and the occurrence of a state such as absenteeism. This model also allows many types of predictors to be examined including individual-level, group-level, and temporal characteristics. This hazard rate model is useful for both prediction and understanding absenteeism.

Turnover This is a measure of permanent separation from the organization. We have mentioned that turnover is a frequently used criterion in validation studies of weighted application blanks. In general, its use in selection is very similar to the use of absenteeism data. A primary question is how to separate turnover data into voluntary/involuntary categories. Voluntary usually means resignation despite the opportunity for continued employment; involuntary means termination by the organization for any of several reasons.

Measures of turnover can confound the two types. For example, if the company has dismissed employees because of an economic downturn, these terminations are clearly involuntary. However, it is not always clear how to classify the other cases of separation. Some workers are allowed to resign rather than be terminated. On paper these would look like incidents of voluntary turnover even though they are not. Similarly, at the perceived threat of dismissal for either financial or performance reasons, some employees may seek other jobs and resign from the company. These, too, appear to be voluntary, yet this behavior was prompted by the organization's actions and might not have occurred otherwise.

As we discussed with absenteeism as a criterion, measurement and statistical issues surrounding turnover must be addressed. Charles Williams points out that voluntary turnover measures usually represent two different theoretical constructs. One is employee tenure (the continuous variable of length of time a worker stay's with an organization) and turnover (a dichotomous variable of stay/quit behavior).[9] Because tenure is a continuous variable and turnover is dichotomous, statistical limitations arise in the use of turnover measures. Williams asserts that researchers need to realize tenure and turnover are different constructs. Although special formulas are available to correct for either artifactual dichotomization of tenure or unequal sample sizes in the distribution of turnover, Williams argues that these correctional formulas are largely insufficient. Instead, he suggests a form of event history analysis called "survival analysis" when trying to correct for dichotomization of tenure.[10] This use of event history analysis is similar to that described for use with absenteeism information.

Survival analysis allows the incorporation of time as an essential component of a measure of turnover.[11] The two important constructs of survival analysis are (1) the *survivor function*, which describes the unconditional probability of staying beyond time t for a person or group, and (2) the *hazard function*, which describes the probability of turnover during an interval of time anchored at time t. Measures of these two constructs can be compared to determine whether differences exist in the probabilities of turnover between groups of subjects. A log rank statistical test allows for these comparisons. Two methodological issues that frequently limit validity studies that use turnover as a criterion measure are the dichotomization of the variable of turnover and unequal sample sizes of the turnover and non-turnover groups. Corrections formulae for both issues are available.[12]

Grievances A grievance is an employee's complaint against some aspect of management's behavior. Grievances have been used occasionally as criteria measures for supervisory and management selection. Theoretically, a large number of grievances would indicate poor treatment of subordinates and/or inferior management decision making. Grievance systems exist almost always as part of a union-management contract. In these agreements, the steps and procedures for filing a grievance are outlined.

When grievances are used as job performance measures, the assumption must be made that the tendency to file a grievance is equal among all work groups and that the working conditions related to grievances are also equal for all work groups. In reality, neither assumption is likely to be true. For example, working conditions can vary dramatically within the same organization. Safety hazards, amount of overtime, job pressure, and ambiguity of task objectives are just a few conditions that could be correlated with grievances. Also, individuals and work groups can differ in their willingness to file grievances and engage in open confrontation. In fact, one study has found that the number of grievances is at least as much a function of the union steward's personality as it is an indication of management performance.[13] As was true in the use of turnover, it may be best to limit the use of grievances to a constant time period during a supervisor's career, job, or assignment to a new work group. For example, the first year may be used. Using a calendar year, in which the sample of managers would be at different points in their work experience, could introduce error into the measure.

Accidents Accidents are usually measured either in terms of injury to the worker or damage to the equipment being used (e.g., car, truck, etc.). In either case, some threshold of damage must be exceeded before the incident is classified as an accident. For personal injury, usually a medical determination of damage that prevents working on the job for some period of time (e.g., one day) is required. In the case of equipment damage, frequently some dollar amount of repair (e.g., $100) must be exceeded before the incident is recorded. The assumption is made that the worker's carelessness precipitated the accident.

Even more than in the use of other HR data, such assumptions are probably not valid. Jobs differ in inherent hazards, equipment differs in its operating condition, and employees differ in the amount of safety training they have received. There is no easy way to remove these factors from accident rates. The only way to overcome them is to equalize their occurrence within the sample. For example, a group of long-distance truck drivers may be measured usefully on accidents if they receive a standardized training program, drive approximately the same schedules and locations, and operate equally maintained trucks. If such conditions cannot be used, accident rates are questionable as criteria measures. This is underscored by the studies that have failed to find accident proneness as a stable worker characteristic and have concluded that a large proportion of accidents are situationally determined.

Promotions This is a measure of career progress in terms of the number of vertical job changes that an individual has experienced as a worker. The term *vertical* means the job change represents a move upward in the organization that results in increased responsibility and authority. The underlying assumption in the use of such a measure as a criterion is that high performance is a prerequisite for promotion. Those individuals who receive more promotions, therefore, have performed better than those individuals with fewer promotions. This measure is most commonly used in validation studies involving managers and professionals, frequently with an assessment center as the predictor. Conceptually, it is feasible to use this measure for lower-level jobs also. However, in actual practice many lower-level jobs have very limited career ladders and, therefore, promotions. Even in these promotions, job tenure, not performance, is often the most important factor.

There are two possible limitations in the use of promotions that we should consider. The first is the number of factors besides performance that may affect promotion opportunities. This becomes especially important if the factors differentially affect the employees in the validation study. For example, divisions within an organization grow at different rates. Presumably, managers in high-growth divisions have a much greater chance for promotion than do those with comparable performance in low-growth divisions. The same situation can also occur between functional areas within a division, that is, marketing is being enlarged while production remains the same. In such instances, promotion is not just a measure of performance; it includes factors not directly influenced by the individual and, therefore, is less useful as a criterion measure.

The second consideration is the difficulty in identifying vertical job changes from HR records. Obviously, not all job changes are promotions. The term lateral is commonly applied to those job changes that result in no change in responsibility and authority but rather a different set of tasks. In many instances, it is difficult to determine accurately if a given job change is lateral or vertical. In organizations with well-known career paths, the determination is usually straightforward. Even so, organizations occasionally obscure the true details of lateral changes to avoid embarrassing the individual involved. In new or rapidly expanding organizations, the difference between the two types of change is often not apparent or not conceptually appropriate.

Training Proficiency

Arguments for Its Use A seldom used but very desirable criterion measure is training proficiency, that is, a measure of employees' performance immediately after completing a training program. We pointed out in our discussion of ability tests in Chapter 13 that validity generalization studies found that training proficiency demonstrated higher validities than the measures of job performance.[14] In addition, the EEOC *Uniform Guidelines* explicitly state that training proficiency is legally permissible as a criterion measure. Despite these points, the reported use of this variable in recent validation studies has been infrequent.

There are strong arguments for the use of training measures as criteria. Essentially, these arguments point out the increased control of the selection specialist in the measurement process and the resulting reduction in error of measurement. This would increase reliability and, in turn, increase the magnitude of the validity coefficient.

The first source of control is the amount of standardization possible. The most common sequence of events in using training measures is to select the employees, place them in a training program, and at the end of training, but before job assignment, administer some measure(s) of mastery of training. In such a sequence, it is possible to design a formal training program that is consistent for all employees, even if they are at different physical locations. Companies commonly develop instruction booklets, films, and exercises that are sent to several cities. In addition, the training instructors can be trained in the sequencing of topics and specific instructional methodologies. Perhaps most important, standardized measures of proficiency can be developed and used. All of these factors would reduce measurement errors that affect validity coefficients adversely.

A second source of control is that validity coefficients between predictors and training measures are oftentimes more direct indicators of the relationship between KSAs and work level than are validity coefficients using other criteria measures. To explain this, let us start with a point we made in Chapter 1. In discussing the inherent limitations in developing and evaluating selection programs, we stated that the adequacy of selection is judged in terms of the level of actual job performance achieved. However, the management literature is filled with organizational factors that affect work performance, for example, leadership, specificity of objectives, amount of training, and so on. This means that performance levels could possibly be influenced by these other factors even though the selection program itself is basically sound. In measurement terms, the validity coefficient between selection devices and job performance measures could be artificially lowered by these factors. This is, in fact, the finding of the studies that we presented in Chapter 13, that validity coefficients using job performance as criteria measures were lower, often greatly lower, than coefficients using training proficiency. One explanation of these findings is that there is less opportunity for other organizational factors to operate when training proficiency is used because of the brief time that has elapsed. The training proficiency measure, therefore, is influenced more by the workers' KSAs and less by the organizational factors. This is clearly a desirable state of affairs for attempts to validate selection programs.

Measures Three basic measures can be used to quantify training proficiency. All assume that the training program is representative of the job itself. This may seem to be a superfluous statement. However, it is common to find training programs that are really orientation sessions covering general company issues, not job activities, or are improperly designed to teach the main features of the job. The first of these three measures is judgments made by the training instructor about the trainees. Judgments could be made about parts of the training program and/or a judgment of overall proficiency. In either case, this method is prone to common drawbacks of decision making. These drawbacks and appropriate corrections are discussed in the next section.

The second method uses scores on a paper-and-pencil test. To do this correctly, basic test construction principles should be followed in the development of the test. We do not elaborate on these principles, but the following issues are important. There should be a match between the extent of topic coverage in training and the number of questions asked about this topic on the test. It would make little sense, for example, to have 5 of 50 questions asked about how to operate a wine processing machine if one-half of the training program was devoted to this topic. Also, standardized administration and scoring procedures must be developed and utilized, in order to reduce errors in the measurement process.

The third measurement method uses scores on a performance test, exactly the same kind of device we described in Chapter 15. This may be confusing because in that chapter we presented performance tests as predictors. Now we introduce them as criteria measures. Remember the central characteristic of a performance test is to replicate the major tasks of the job. However, performance tests cannot be used in all selection situations, especially if the assumption cannot be made that the applicants already possess the KSAs necessary to attempt the task. In those instances in which performance tests may not be appropriate as selection devices, they could be appropriate as training proficiency measures. The training program is designed to be representative of the job activities. Performance tests are similarly designed. Therefore, a performance test should be appropriate as a measure of adequacy of training.

Sidney Gael, Donald Grant, and Richard Ritchie have described two selection programs validated at AT&T that used performance tests in this fashion.[15] One selection program for telephone operators used ten specially developed ability tests as predictors. The criterion, administered upon the completion of a formal training program, was a one-hour job simulation. In this simulation, trainers acting as customers initiated calls at a steady pace in the same way for each operator-trainee. Each operator activity that was to be performed for each call was listed on the evaluation form. Supervisors directly observed and assessed the effectiveness of trainees in processing each call during the simulation. The second selection program used ten different paper-and-pencil tests of mental ability and perceptual speed and accuracy as predictors for clerical jobs. In this case, the criterion was an extensive two day simulation that was given by a specially trained administrator. This simulation consisted of eight separate exercises. Five were timed clerical activities—filing, classifying, posting, checking, and coding. The remaining three were untimed tests covering plant repair service, punched card fundamentals, and toll fundamentals.

Judgmental Data

In the fourth type of criterion measure, judgmental data, an individual familiar with the work of another is required to judge this work. For selection, this measurement is usually obtained by using a rating scale with numerical values. In almost all cases, the individual doing the evaluation is the immediate supervisor of the worker being evaluated. The evaluation is based on the opinion or judgment of this supervisor, hence the term *judgmental* data.

Because it relies on opinion, there is a general skepticism on the part of HR specialists and managers about the use of such data. Many of the deficiencies in decision making that we described in the use of the unstructured interview have also been observed with judgmental performance data. However, as with the selection interview, much effort has been devoted to correcting these deficiencies. In reality, the use of judgmental data is unavoidable in modern business. Many jobs such as managerial, service, professional, and staff positions no longer produce tangible, easily counted products on a regular basis for which the use of production data would be appropriate. In most cases, neither HR nor training performance data are relevant or available. Almost by default, judgmental data are increasingly being used for work measurement. In addition to availability, there are other arguments for the use of this type of criterion data. The information is supplied by supervisors who should know firsthand the work and the work circumstances; and after initial development the use of the judgment scales should be relatively easy.

Types of Judgmental Instruments There are many different types of instruments that have been used to collect judgemental data. We discuss four of the most commonly used ones. All four are various forms of rating scales.

Trait Rating Scales This method requires the supervisor to evaluate subordinates on the extent to which each individual possesses personal characteristics thought to be necessary for good work performance. The evaluation uses rating scales that contain as few as three points or as many as eleven. The scale points are usually designated with integers and may also be associated with adjectives, for example, unsatisfactory, average, superior, or excellent. The personal characteristics are most often stated in terms of personality traits such as dependability, ambition, positive attitude, initiative, determination, assertiveness, and loyalty.

Even though this type of judgmental data is commonly collected in organizations, it is generally regarded as inappropriate criterion data by selection specialists. For a validation study, the criterion must be a direct measure of job performance. Trait ratings are measures of personal characteristics that have no proven relationship to performance. Moreover, the accurate assessment of such traits by a supervisor is nearly impossible. John Bernardin and Richard Beatty have summarized the common viewpoint of these scales: "If the purpose of appraisal is to evaluate *past performance*, then an evaluation of simple personality traits. . . . hardly fits the bill. . . . Trait ratings are notoriously error-prone and are usually not even measured reliably."[16] Instead of traits, therefore, acceptable judgmental measures require the evaluation of work behaviors. The following three types are examples.

Simple Behavioral Scale This type of measure is based on information about tasks determined from job analysis. The supervisor is asked to rate each subordinate on major or critical tasks of the job. For example, a manager of information systems within an organization may be evaluated by her supervisor on the task of "Developing software packages to process compensation system data." The number of tasks used in the evaluation differs according to the complexity of the job, but commonly the range is between four and ten tasks. A supervisor scores the subordinate using a rating scale similar to that described for use with *trait rating scales;* that is, usually three to seven-point scales using integers and descriptive adjectives. The following is an example of such a scale.

	Unsatisfactory		Average		Superior
Developing software packages to process compensation system data.	1	2	3	4	5

Scores can be added across all task scales to produce an overall measure of job performance, or individual task scales can be used to obtain a measure of a specific aspect of job performance. The major limitation in using this type of measure is that supervisors of the same job often disagree on what level of performance on a task is required for a score of 3 or "average."

BARS or BES Behaviorally Anchored Rating Scales (BARS) and Behavioral Expectation Scales (BES) are judgmental scales developed to define the rating points in terms of job behaviors.[17] Such definitions are intended to reduce the difficulty for supervisors, of consistently interpreting the performance associated with various scale points. Exhibit 17.1 presents an example of one scale representative of this approach. The following describes the steps necessary in developing BARS or BES scales.

1. The *Critical Incidents Technique* is used to gather data from groups of six to twelve job incumbents/supervisors. A critical incident is defined as a description of a job behavior of a worker that has four characteristics: (a) it is specific; (b) it focuses on observable behaviors that have been, or could

| EXHIBIT 17.1 | AN EXAMPLE OF A BES RATING DIMENSION FOR THE JOB OF BANK TELLER |

Dimension: Interacting with Customers

7   Employee can be expected to smile, greet customer by name as he or she approaches teller window, and ask to be service.

6

5   Employee can be expected to smile and ask to be of service to the customer.

4

3   Employee can be expected to greet customer.

2

1   Employee can be expected to remain silent until customer makes specific request.

---

be, exhibited on the job; (c) it briefly describes the context in which the behavior occurred; and (d) it indicates the consequences of the behavior. Each member of the group is asked individually to generate as many critical incidents as possible describing competent, average, and incompetent job behaviors.

2. These critical incidents are then given to other groups of incumbents/supervisors to form dimensions. A dimension is a group of critical incidents that share a common theme, such as "interacting with customers" for the job of bank teller. These dimensions are usually developed through discussion within the group.

3. Other groups of individuals are given the critical incidents and the dimensions and each individual in the group is asked to sort independently the critical incidents into the dimensions. The purpose of this is to determine which critical incidents are reliably viewed to be included in the dimensions. Usually only those incidents that are assigned to the same category by at least 80 percent of the judges are retained for further work.

4. Other groups of incumbents/supervisors are then given the list of dimensions and the critical incidents assigned to each dimension. Individuals in these groups are asked to rate each of the critical incidents on a 7-point scale ranging from poor performance (scale point of l) to outstanding performance (scale point of 7). Only those critical incidents for which there is a high agreement among judges (measured in terms of a standard deviation; the smaller the standard deviation the greater the agreement) are retained.

5. For each dimension, a set of critical incidents is selected that represents various levels of performance on the dimension. Average scores determined in the previous step are used as measures. These selected incidents are then arranged at appropriate places on the scale (see Exhibit 17.1).

The main difference in *BARS* and *BES* is in the wording of the incidents. *BARS* incidents are worded in terms of *actual* work behaviors, for example, "greets customer as he or she approaches the teller window." *BES* incidents are phrased in terms of *expected* behavior, for example, "can be expected to greet customer as he or she approaches the teller window." The wording difference points out to supervisors that the employee does not need to demonstrate the actual behavior of the incident to be scored at that level. The incident is to be interpreted as representative of the performance of the employee. Scores can be obtained for each dimension or summed for a total score of job performance.

In a study that examined behavioral anchors as a source of bias in ratings, Kevin Murphy and Joseph Constans came to the conclusion that the *appropriate behaviors to use as scale points are those representative of actual job behaviors.*[18] This could especially be true of behaviors used to anchor the high and low ends of scales. The authors' viewpoint was, for example, that poor performers probably make a series of small errors on the job. Therefore, the behaviors located on the lower end of the scale should be representative of these behaviors rather than an example of one spectacular mistake. In terms of the scale in Exhibit 17.1, the behavior associated with scale point 1 should be appropriate in that it is a behavior that frequently could be exhibited by poorly performing tellers. On the other hand, a behavior such as "Could be expected to tell customer to wait until she has finished her telephone call" would also be an example of poor behavior, but is less desirable because it occurs so infrequently that it does not describe "representative" performance.

BOS The Behavioral Observation Scales (BOS) technique is similar to the *BARS* and *BES* in that critical incidents are used to identify job dimensions to be rated by supervisors.[19] It is different from them, however, in that multiple scales are produced for each of these job dimensions. The following steps are taken in the development of *BOS:*

1. Critical incidents for the job are developed as previously described using job incumbents/supervisors.

2. Critical incidents that are similar in content are grouped together to form one behavioral item. For example, all critical incidents describing behaviors in which the supervisor points out mistakes made by the employee may be grouped to form the behavioral item "communicates mistakes in work procedures to subordinates."

3. Similar behavioral items are grouped together to form one *BOS* criterion or dimension. For example, the *BOS* criterion of "Reviews Previous Work Performance" could be made up of behavioral items such as the previously mentioned one together with "praises employees for good work behavior," "discusses hindrances in completing project," "inspects quality of output materials," and "reviews inventory of necessary parts and equipment." The procedures for grouping behavioral items into *BOS* criteria are simi-

lar to those discussed with *BARS* and *BES* in that agreement among judges is of primary importance.

4. Behavioral items are reviewed and sometimes analyzed statistically to eliminate those that have reduced variance or are highly correlated with other behavioral items.

5. Five-point rating scales measuring the frequency with which the employee engages in the behavior are written for each behavioral item on a *BOS* criterion. This results in many more rating scales being used by the supervisor than the previous methods. One study describes the formation of 92 scales that were used to judge the performance of foremen on eight *BOS* criteria.

Exhibit 17.2 presents an example of one *BOS* rating criterion and some of the behavioral item scales that could be used. In making an evaluation of each subordinate, the supervisor reads each scale and makes a rating at the appropriate scale point. Scores are summed for all behavioral items on a given criterion to obtain a total score for that criterion. An overall job performance score is determined by summing criteria scores.

Comparison of Scales Uco Wiersma and Gary Latham surveyed one sample of managers and programmer/analysts and a second sample of lawyers as to the

---

EXHIBIT 17.2   **AN EXAMPLE OF BOS**

Criterion: Reviews Previous Work Performance

1. Communicates mistakes in job activities to subordinates
    Almost Never   1   2   3   4   5   Almost Always

2. Praises subordinates for good work behavior
    Almost Never   1   2   3   4   5   Almost Always

3. Discusses hindrances in completing projects
    Almost Never   1   2   3   4   5   Almost Always

    •

    •

    •

11. Inspects quality of output materials
    Almost Never   1   2   3   4   5   Almost Always

12. Reviews inventory of necessary parts and equipment
    Almost Never   1   2   3   4   5   Almost Always

                Total Score_____

practicality of using *trait, BES,* and *BOS* scales.[20] The managers and programmer/analysts rated each of the three types of scales on factors important for the use of performance appraisal instruments. These factors included, among others, use in giving performance feedback; accurately differentiating among poor, average, and good workers; objectively measuring performance; and identifying training needs The lawyers evaluated the legal standing of the scales by rating each of the three types on seven items dealing with issues that courts might examine in legal questions concerning the use of judgmental performance data. These included the specificity of the criteria, objectivity, and resistance to bias. An eighth item was "If I were defending a company, this rating format would be an asset to my case."

Results showed an overwhelming preference by both samples for the use of *BOS.* For managers and programmer/analysts, *BOS* was preferred over the *BES* format on all of the scales measuring practicality of use, and over trait scales on six of the eight scales In general, *BES* and trait scales were judged to be comparable. The attorneys judged *BOS* to be superior to the other two types on the items treating court review issues They also judged *BES* to be superior to trait scales on these issues. Regarding the answer to the question of whether the rating format would be an asset in a case, *BOS* was again rated as being superior to the other two. There was no difference between *BES* and trait scales on responses to this question.

The authors, predictably, concluded that *BOS* was the format of choice on both employment and legal bases. This conclusion was buttressed by findings obtained a year later in the organization employing the sample of managers and programmer/analysts. The use of *BOS* was viewed positively because it minimized personality disputes, enabled appraisers to justify low ratings, and resulted in comprehensive reviews.

The Problem of Bias A possible distrust of these judgmental measures centers on the problems of intentional and inadvertent bias by the supervisor making the judgment. Intentional bias is very difficult, if not impossible, to detect accurately, especially if it is done selectively. The general feeling among selection specialists, however, is that it is not a widespread problem. As we explain later in the chapter, when criteria data are collected for validation, these data are not used for any other purpose. This creates circumstances in which there can be little profit for intentional distortion in ratings. It is thought that this minimizes the problem.

Inadvertent bias in responses is a more frequently found problem. Commonly called *rater error*, this bias most frequently is described in one of the following four ways: halo, leniency, severity, and central tendency. We described these errors in Chapter 13 when discussing the interviewer's decision-making process regarding applicants. *Halo* is rating the subordinate equally on different performance scales because of a general impression of the worker. Specific attention is not paid to each individual scale used. *Leniency* or *severity* occurs when a disproportionate number of workers receive either high or low ratings respectively. This bias is commonly attributed to distortion in the supervisor's viewpoint of what constitutes acceptable behavior. *Central tendency* occurs when a large number of subordinates receive ratings in the middle of the scale. Neither very good nor very poor performance is rated as often as it actually occurs. The effect of all these forms of bias on validation work is usually to lower the calculated correlation. Generally, bias lowers the range of scores on the criteria measures which mathematically lowers the magnitude of the validity coefficient.

Some studies have compared different judgmental rating formats on their extent of halo, leniency, restriction of range, and interrater reliability. One of these studies compared *BARS* and two other forms of rating scales that included positively and negatively worded behavioral statements. No significant differences among the three formats on these psychometric properties were found.[21]

It has been suggested by Walter Borman that a useful way to look at performance rating formats is as tools to do three things: (1) help ratees conduct an organized and efficient search for performance-related behavior of raters, (2) translate behavioral observations of raters into pertinent evidence in order to assess performance, and (3) then make accurate judgments about effectiveness levels. Thus rating formats should reflect natural cognitive processes leading to the attainment of those purposes.[22]

An interesting research topic is the similarity of ratings and objective production measures as criteria for validation. Calvin Hoffman, Barry Nathan, and Lisa Holden recently compared four criteria—two objective (production quantity and production quality) and two subjective (supervisor and self-ratings) for their predictability by a composite measure of several cognitive ability tests. While both supervisory ratings and production quantity resulted in validity coefficients of about .25, production quality and self-appraisal ratings resulted in validities of .00.[23] Another study found that the overlap in the distributions of validity coefficients between production quantities and supervisor ratings ranged from 80 to 98 percent.[24] We can conclude that despite their subjectivity, supervisor ratings are no less useful as test validation criteria than objective productivity measures.

Training Supervisors The major tactic in overcoming rater bias is to train supervisors to avoid these errors. Gary Latham, Kenneth Wexley, and Elliott Pursell describe one such program that is representative of a type of training called rater-error training.[25] This program consisted of five videotaped interactions in which a manager was to rate another person. At the end of each interaction, each individual in the training program was asked to give ratings for the following two questions: (1) How would you rate the person? and (2) How do you think the manager rated this person? Each of the five interactions demonstrated a different form of rating error. A discussion followed each interaction in which the particular rating error was pointed out and various solutions were developed to minimize this error.

Another form of training uses another tactic by stressing rater accuracy rather than avoidance of errors.[26] In this training, supervisors are first lectured on the multidimensionality of jobs and the need to pay close attention to employee performance in terms of these dimensions. Supervisors are then given rating scales and the trainer reads the general definition of each dimension as well as the scale anchors associated with varying levels of performance. The group then discusses, more specifically, the types of behavior that are indicative of various levels within each dimension, and the performance associated with each scale point. Videos and role-playing examples can be used as illustrations.

Several studies have demonstrated positive effects from training programs. For example, one study examined both types of training programs and found benefits from each.[27] Rater-error training was associated with a reduced halo effect, and rater accuracy with reduced leniency. The use of both types of training was recommended. Another study examined the use of rater-error training in conjunction with each of three types of judgmental scales, trait, *BES*, and *BOS*.[28] Training resulted in a reduction of errors regardless of the type of scale used. In addition, the two types of behavioral scales resulted in fewer rating errors than did trait scales, even without training. Perhaps the most dramatic finding was reported by Elliot Pursell, Dennis Dossett, and Gary Latham.[29] In a criterion-related validity study for journeyman electricians, the authors correlated scores from five predictors with supervisors' ratings using a 9-point scale with three behavioral anchors. The anchors were taken from job analysis information. Nonsignificant correlations were found for all of the predictors, indicating no validity for the test battery. The authors decided that this failure was due to rating errors of the supervisors rather than deficiencies in the predictors. Therefore, it was decided to give these supervisors an eight-hour, rater-error training program. New performance ratings were obtained on the same sample of journeyman electricians one month after the supervisors completed the training. A second set of analyses indicated significant validity coefficients for four of the five predictors.

Systematic Data Collection Incomplete data about the job performance of subordinates is an additional source of bias. Such incompleteness forces the manager to base judgments on partially formed impressions. One example, known as the *primacy effect*, describes situations in which judgments are based on events that occurred during the first part of the evaluation period. The term *recency effect* is used when the judgments are based on events that occurred in the latter part of the period. To avoid this source of bias, managers have been taught to record behavior systematically during the complete period of evaluation. Usually this entails making written notes at fixed intervals describing the actual work behavior of each subordinate. These notes are not summary evaluations of the goodness or badness of the behavior but, rather, nonevaluative descriptions. Often these notes are also shared with the subordinate. At the time of the appraisal, the manager reviews the file and bases his or her judgment on the total job descriptions gathered over the complete time period of evaluation.

Concluding Comments on Judgmental Scales To maximize the effectiveness of judgmental scales, the principles that were presented in this section should be kept in mind. First, the use of job-behavior scales rather than traits is recommended. The role of selection is to identify individuals who will perform well on the job, not to identify those with desirable personality characteristics. Therefore, job-behavior dimensions are the only acceptable kind.

Second, the history of selection argues that the dimensions used be fairly broad statements of performance or job behaviors.[30] We hope the following example will help to clarify what we mean by this statement. Directors of management information systems have multiple, diverse activities. If we were validating a set of selection instruments for this job, we would probably use some form of judgmental data as part of the criterion measures. Suppose that one performance dimension is the design and implementation of computer systems for various groups within the company. This behavior is actually made up of several, more specific, job behaviors, for example, the discussion of user information needs, the development of a report describing the nature of the recommended system, the design of a detailed hardware plan, the development of software packages, and the training of users in software packages. It is better to determine one rating that is a measure of the general performance dimension than it is to treat each of these separate, behavioral dimensions as a criterion measure. This is because selection measures have less ability to correlate with specific, narrow job dimensions than to correlate with broad, encompassing dimensions. For this reason, criterion data should be collected by asking the supervisor to make one judgment of the overall job dimension or, if he or she is asked to rate the more specific dimensions, they should all be combined into one single score.

Third, it is obvious that extensive training must be done with the supervisors who will use the instrument. The studies we summarized demonstrated the sometimes dramatic effect of training on reducing rater bias that masks an acceptable validity correlation. This training should address how to record and evaluate job behaviors accurately as well as the more commonly stressed topic of how to avoid the judgmental errors of halo and leniency.

Appropriate Characteristics of Selection Criteria Measures

As we have mentioned, it is possible to use each of the performance measurement devices we have presented in validity studies. It is the role of the selection specialist to choose those measures that are the most appropriate for the selection program under consideration. Partially this choice depends on how the strengths and limitations of each device match the work situation under which the validation must be carried out. In addition, this choice is dependent on the extent to which the criterion measure possesses the characteristics that we discuss in this section. Possession of these characteristics helps ensure that the criterion has the information that is necessary to conduct validation. We briefly mentioned a few of these characteristics in Chapter 3. In the following section, we discuss them more completely.

Individualization

Selection programs are designed to furnish data used in employment decisions. As we have described these programs, the applicant completes various selection instruments each of which is designed to measure specific KSAs. In validation these measures of KSAs are gathered for each member of a group and correlated with corresponding measures of job performance. The logic of this is that the job performance measure must also be a measure of the individual. If we are attempting to determine if high scores on the selection instruments are indicative of high scores on job performance, it would be dysfunctional to have the job performance be representative of anyone except the individual. This may seem obvious but many work situations create job performance outputs that violate this principle. For example, team or group tasks are becoming increasingly popular. Even traditional manufacturing operations have formed groups of 10 to 12 workers who are assigned all operations necessary for completion of the product. Workers are interchangeable and move unsystematically from work station to work station. It would not be appropriate to use the number of articles produced as a criterion measure for selection. Such a number would not measure the distinct performance of an individual and, therefore should not be correlated with individual selection instrument scores.

Controllability

The logic of selection also indicates that measuring the KSAs of applicants is important because these KSAs affect job performance. Those workers who possess more of the desirable KSAs should perform better. This can only be tested if the work performance measure is a reflection of the employee's use of these KSAs. In other words the measure of job performance should allow for differences in KSAs to be reflected in performance.

Again, many frequently used measures of job performance do not have this characteristic. For example it has been common to evaluate branch managers performance for financial service institutions partially on the basis of profits generated by the branch. Offhand this seems accurate because profits are of central importance to financial institutions, and branch managers are commonly assumed to be the chief executive of the unit and in charge of operations. But, oftentimes this assumption does not hold up. Interest rates for deposits are set by the highest level of management. Loans are also often controlled by standard policy. Loans over a certain amount must be approved by others, and guidelines concerning loan evaluation are used for smaller loans. Furthermore, other items such as size and salary of staff are dictated by company headquarters. Therefore, many of the factors that greatly affect the profits of the branch are not influenced by the branch manager. To use profits as a criterion measure in selection would be an error in such a situation. Logically, differences in the KSAs of various branch managers may be reflected in other performance aspects such as completeness and timeliness of reports. The branch manager's use of KSAs can make a difference in the reports; therefore, reports are controllable by the branch manager. The us of KSAs does not make a difference in profits—profits are not controllable by the manager.

There are other easily thought of examples. Job scheduling and quality of materials frequently affect production output of workers, even though neither may be controlled by the worker. Repair records of maintenance workers in plants are often evaluated in terms of time spent on service visits and frequency of return calls. In many instances these factors are more attributable to the performance of the operators of the machinery than they are to the maintenance worker who repairs the machine.

Relevance

Selection is designed to contribute to the productivity of the organization. Individuals are employed primarily to perform well on the critical or important parts of a job. It is these parts, therefore, that should be included in job performance measures. Sometimes it is easy to overlook this principle because other job performance aspects are easy to obtain. For example, promptness and attendance are, at times, easily obtained records. However, as we mentioned previously, in many jobs such attendance is not a critical dimension of performance. This is commonly the case for managers and professionals in an organization in which little attention is paid to coming and going or the use of company time for doctor visits. Such events are irrelevant as long as "the work gets done." Our point is that this may also be true of other jobs for which attendance records are carefully kept. Therefore, these records are not appropriate criteria measures.

The primary method of judging the relevance of a criterion measure is job analysis. Job analysis should identify the important, critical, or frequently performed job activities. The question of relevance is whether the job performance measure corresponds to this information.

Measurability

Given the nature of validation, this is one of the more obvious characteristics. It is not possible to perform an empirical validation study unless behavior on both the selection and the job performance instruments is quantified. This quantification is how we have defined measurement (see Chapter 3). As we discussed in the previous section, the source of this measurement can be production output units, an individual's judgment, training examinations work sample tests, attendance records, and so on.

The most frequently experienced difficulty in meeting this measurement characteristic is determining how to quantify a job behavior dimension. For example, a regional sales manager may be in charge of advertising for the region. Ultimately, the purpose of advertising is to increase sales. However, this end may not be achieved for a long period of time. The problem is what should be measured in place of sales that will measure the effectiveness of the advertising. In many cases, some associated measure is obtained. For example, a judgment is made about the quality of the advertising campaign based on its correspondence to accepted standards of advertising. The judgment becomes the job performance measure.

Reliability

Chapter 4 discussed in detail the importance of reliability in measurement. Frequently, HR specialists are greatly concerned with the reliability of selection instruments but pay less attention to the reliability of job performance measures.

This is unfortunate because unreliability in these measures can negatively affect validation coefficients also. As we have noted, the unreliability of supervisors' judgments of subordinates has been of great concern to selection specialists.

Unreliability in other measures is not often thought of, but does exist and must be corrected. Monthly sales volume for many jobs, such as furniture or clothing representatives, fluctuates with seasonal buying patterns. In these cases, it is necessary to accumulate sales data for a longer period of time than a month to compensate for these seasonal fluctuations. As we mentioned, a major difficulty in using absenteeism as a criterion variable has been unreliability in some forms of its measurement. This has been especially true if total days absent is used as a measure. One severe illness could distort the data.

Variance

It is conceptually useless and statistically difficult to validate a selection program in cases in which there is little, if any, variance in performance levels of workers. If every worker performs at the same level, the amount of KSAs of workers is apparently irrelevant—the difference in KSAs makes no difference in performance levels. This lack of variance can be caused by two factors: (1) standardization in output due to work process, or (2) inappropriate use of the measurement device. Output for machine-paced manufacturing is an example of the former. If an assembly line is set to move continuously at a certain speed, all workers should produce the same number. The latter case is often demonstrated in supervisors' judgments of subordinates. At one time the military experienced severe problems with its appraisal forms. Theoretically, 100 scale points were to be used for rating with a score of 70 being designated as average performance. In practice, however, the great majority of personnel were rated between 90 and 100 to ensure their chances for promotion. The same problem has been repeated in other situations in which a supervisor feels that all the subordinates are exceptionally good workers.

A problem for selection specialists is determining whether such supervisory judgments reflect actual similarity in performance or misuse of the rating instrument. After all, it is possible that members of a work group, especially one that is experienced and well trained, could all perform at the same general level. In most cases, the decision is made that the appraisal from is being used incorrectly, and a training program is implemented for its users to encourage the spread of ratings in future measurement.

Practicality

Practicality refers to the cost and logistics of gathering data. In those rare circumstances in which these factors are not constraints, this can be ignored. In most cases, however, time and money become major issues. For example, most companies that have direct sales operations feel that both sales volume and customer service are important performance dimensions. The problem is that to collect customer service data accurately, many time-consuming and costly steps must be carried out. A representative sample of customers for each salesperson must be compiled. Then, each must be contacted and questioned, using a standardized interview, about the behaviors of the salesperson and the customer's reaction to the services rendered. Obviously, this is not a practical operation in most cases. Instead, less time-consuming and costly measures are used. For example, often the number of complaints made by customers is used. To do this, however, the logical assumption must be made that the probability of customer complaints is the same for all sales personnel and the frequency of complaints is directly related to the frequency of poor customer service. If such an assumption cannot be made, then this measure is not useful as a job performance measure.

Lack of Contamination

Criterion contamination occurs when the applicants' scores on the selection instruments are used to make employment decisions about these individuals, and these employment decisions, in turn, have a bearing on criterion scores. One of the best examples has occurred in the use of assessment centers (ACs). Most often, ACs are used for internal selection for higher-level management jobs. For this example, let us assume an AC for lower-level managers that has been designed to determine their suitability for higher management positions. The lower level managers complete the AC and receive formal feedback from the assessors.

In many cases, the assessment ratings and descriptions are given to the superiors of those who have completed the AC and are also placed in central HR files. Contamination occurs when these assessment center data are used to make decisions about whom among the group should be promoted, and then promotion is used as the criterion variable. Obviously such an action would increase the magnitude of the validity coefficient artificially. These events would constitute a self-fulfilling prophecy: individuals would be promoted because they scored well at the AC and the AC scores would be validated against promotion records of individuals. Similar contamination could occur when scores on selection devices are used for placement of employees into desirable sales territories or fast-track positions.

Specificity for Selection

Selection specialists generally prefer to use job performance data in validation that is specifically collected for selection program development rather than data that is collected primarily for one of the other HRM purposes. Frank Landy and James Farr discuss this as the difference between the administrative and the research use of performance data within organizations.[31] They clearly point out that there are basic differences between the two uses. For our purposes, the major difference is that validation is impersonal. The emphasis is on using quantitative performance and predictor scores of unknown individuals. The administrative uses of performance data, in contrast, frequently emphasize the individual on whom the measurement is taken. Especially when judgmental methods are used, this sometimes means that other factors affect the measure. For example, when performance measures are used for salary increases, supervisors may consider such factors as the worker's experience, market demand, potential career, and personal relationships when making the evaluation.

What if Some of The Characteristics Aren't There?

After this discussion of characteristics the question that undoubtedly arises in your mind is "What happens if these characteristics are violated?" Without going into a long explanation, *the general conclusion is that major violations of these characteristics can lower the correlation coefficient artificially and reduce the probability of demonstrating empirical validity.* This is because such violations would introduce unsystematic errors into the measures. We said previously that the effect of unsystematic error is usually to lower both reliability and validity. We use the word *artificially* because the lowering is due to extraneous factors that could be controlled. In other words the validity coefficient provides an indication of the relationship between predictor and criterion. It should be low if no relationship exists and high if such a relationship is present. Under the circumstances we have mentioned, however, the relationship could still be high in reality but the magnitude of the validity coefficient would be low because of the presence of unsystematic error. The low correlation would not be representative of the actual relationship between predictor and criterion.

Issues in Criterion Use

Single versus Multiple Criteria

One of the most perplexing issues for selection specialists involved in validation is how to decide on the number of measures of job performance to use. This issue is commonly referred to as the choice between single or multiple criteria. In validation the use of a single measure of job performance translates into viewing it as overall or global performance. This single measure could exist in either of two forms. One form consists of a single aspect of performance. For example, for sales personnel a measure of dollar sales volume frequently has been used. For computer operators, the measure has been the number of jobs run. The second form consists of two or more measures that are combined algebraically to yield one overall measure. For example, a district sales manager's rating of quality of customer service may be combined in some manner with the sales volume figures to arrive at one total composite of job performance for sales personnel.

The argument for using a single performance measure in validation is partially based on the fact that validation procedures become more straight-forward with one criterion. The predictor(s) is correlated with this one measure in the manner we described in Chapter 5. In most instances, only one correlation coefficient would be tested to determine significance. This makes the interpretation of the findings and the judgment about the adequacy of the selection program relatively simple.

The argument for the use of multiple criteria measures is made on the basis of research findings and logic. Essentially, this argument starts with the fact that job analysis studies identify multiple tasks within jobs. Multiple tasks are indicative of the multiple aspects of job performance. Also review studies, specifically of job performance, have concluded that a global measure of performance is not an accurate description of activities even for simple entry-level jobs.[32]

Project A, which we described in Chapter 13, identified multiple components of performance for 19 entry-level army jobs. John Campbell, Jeffrey McHenry, and Lauress Wise utilized multiple job analysis methods and criterion measurement to yield more than 200 performance indicators which were further reduced to 32 criterion scores for each job.[33] The same argument can be made for other types of jobs such as manufacturing where both days present and lack of defective assembly items are, at the minimum, thought to be important. Even in typing and stenography jobs, the importance of both speed and accuracy as performance measures is obvious.

When to Use Each Wayne Cascio has presented the most straightforward solution to the dilemma and the following reflects his writings.[34] Cascio makes the distinction between using job performance measures to assist in managerial decision making or to serve research purposes. A validation study can be used for either purpose. In most cases a validity study is done to identity a set of selection devices that assist in managerial decision making. That is, the applicants' scores on the selection devices are used in making decisions about to whom to extend job offers. In these cases a composite criterion would generally be used. Managers are essentially interested in selecting individuals who, all things considered, perform well in an overall manner. The use of the composite criterion reflects this thinking.

In a few cases, a validity study is done for research purposes. For example, we may wish to study the relationship of specific mental abilities (e.g., mathematical reasoning, spatial visualization, etc.) to different parts of a research engineering job (e.g., development of research plans, preparation of technical reports, etc.). In such a case, the major emphasis is on linking a specific mental ability to each subpart of the job. Such information could later be used in selection, training, and career development work. It would therefore, be appropriate to use multiple criteria and to validate the mental ability tests against each separate measure of job performance.

Forming the Single Measure If a composite measure is desired, the immediate problem is how to combine the different measures into one. Essentially, there are three methods of doing this.

Dollar Criterion The first, which Cascio points out is the logical basis of combination, is to develop a composite that represents economic worth to the organization. This entails expressing the various job performance measures we have discussed as a monetary amount that represents the value of worker performance to the organization. Logically, this is in agreement with the concept of using validation data to assist managerial decision making. Put simply, a main management concern with selection is to improve the economic position of the firm by means of the more able workers employed through using a valid selection program. Expressing job performance in dollars would be a direct reflection of this thinking.

This line of reasoning was first expressed over 40 years ago by Hubert Brogden and Erwin Taylor, who developed the dollar criterion.[35] It has been only recently, however, that refinements have been made in how practically to estimate the monetary worth of job performance. These refinements are part of the general topic of *utility analysis* (see Chapter 5). Without going through a detailed description of this topic, there are at least three major methods of determining this dollar value of job performance. One method has job experts estimate the monetary value of various levels of job performance.[36] A second method assumes this dollar value to be a direct function of yearly salary.[37] The third method also uses employee salary but partitions this among a job's principal activities so that each activity is assigned a proportion of that salary in accord with the job analysis results.[38]

Factor Analysis The second method of combining separate criteria measures into one composite relies on statistical correlational analysis. In this approach, all individual criteria measures are correlated with one another. The intercorrelation matrix is factor analyzed which, statistically, combines these separate measures into clusters or factors. Ideally, a majority of the separate measures would be combined into one factor that would then serve as the composite performance measure. The factor analysis procedure also provides weights that could apply to each specific measure in forming the composite.

Expert Judgment A third method uses judgments of job experts to form the composite. Essentially, the problem for these judges is to identify the relative weights of the specific performance aspects. For example, let us assume that the job of laboratory technician has five components we wish to combine. The role of the job experts is to specify the numerical value that each component should be multiplied by to derive the overall performance score. This weighting should be reflective of the importance of each of the five components to overall performance. If all five components are regarded as being equally important, then all five parts carry a weight of "1" and are directly added. If the five components are thought to be unequal in importance, there are two different procedures that are often used to determine the appropriate weights. Under the first procedure, each judge is given 100 points and asked to divide these up among the five parts. The weight for each part is the average number of points assigned to it by the judges. The second procedure asks each judge to assign a value of 1.0 to the most unimportant part. The number assigned to each of the other four is to represent how many times more important each part is to this least important one. The weight is again the average of these values. Both procedures assume reliability among the judges in terms of both the ordering of the five parts and the relative importance among them. This means that if the judges do not closely agree on which components are unimportant and which are very important, the computed averages are conceptually meaningless and ought not to be used.

Another judgment method describes how a single score can be compiled by using preferences obtained from individuals, such as customers, who derive value from the organizations outputs.[39] These preference values on such variables as product or service performance can be ordered and weighted to identify critical performance criteria to be used to evaluate individual and organizational effectiveness.

It is also important to disaggregate values represented by different customers to identify these performance criteria.

Stability of Job Performance

Another important issue in developing and using a criterion measure is whether or not the measure will be stable over time. Many researchers don't agree on the prevalence of the "dynamic criteria" problem—generally defined as the variability in the relative performance of employees over time. A major reason for this disagreement probably has to do with the fact that dynamic criteria have been operationally defined differently by different researchers, Diana Deadrick and Robert Madigan separate criterion changes in three types. One type is changes in rank order differences among individuals at two times on the criterion measure, termed *performance consistency.* Another type is changes attributable to organizational contextual variables such as objectives or job design termed *evaluation consistency,* and the third is changes attributable to the measurement procedure termed *measurement reliability.*[40]

Deadrick and Madigan were particularly interested in studying performance consistency, Using weekly performance data from sewing machine operators, these two found that performance consistency was not stable over time but declined systematically as a function of time between performance measurement occasions. Moreover, this decay was found regardless of prior job experience, cognitive ability, or psychomotor ability of the employees. They interpret their results as "additional evidence for the instability of skilled performance and highlight the need for models of job performance that incorporate the phenomenon of dynamic performance."[41] One interesting but unexpected finding was that over time the validity of cognitive ability predictors increased, the validity of psychomotor ability was stable, and that of prior job experience decreased.

Another study examined dynamic criteria within an interactional psychology framework.[42] Interactional psychology maintains that behavior is determined by an interaction between personal traits and the situation, (This idea should sound familiar, as we discussed the effects of powerful versus weak situations on personality traits in Chapter 13, remember?). As it applies to performance stability, interactional psychology holds that when similar situations occur over time, considerable performance stability should be present within the same individual.

The researchers used a model of job performance that has two distinct stages.[43] The *transition stage* happens when people are new to a job or when new responsibilities are added to an existing job. At this stage individual performance differences are primarily a function of differences in cognitive ability, and because cognitive ability is a rather stable attribute, performance differences are predicted to be stable during this stage. The second stage, the *maintenance stage,* is entered once people have learned the KSAs necessary to perform their jobs. Individual differences are now more a function of variables such as motivation, personality, interests, and values that are seen as more variable over time. College student ratings of faculty teaching over 6.5 years provided the performance data that was examined. It was found that students' ratings were most stable for faculty members teaching the same course over time. In other words the interactional framework of person-in-situation indicated higher performance stability than did the ratings of the same faculty (across different courses) or ratings of the same courses (accross different faculty). A major implication of this study is that the interactional framework and the two stage model of transition and maintenance may help explain conlicting findings about performance stability.

Work Measurement and EEO Issues

The precise effect of EEO principles on work measurement is not as clear as it is for other areas of selection. Partially, this is because only a small part of the *Uniform Guidelines* explicitly treats work measurement, and it really does not fully discuss the necessary features of such systems. Similarly, while there have been a number of court cases that have addressed work measurement, there have been very few cases in which it has been the major issue in the case. Moreover, the major proportion of even this sketchy treatment has focused on judgmental data, not the complete topic of work measurement. For these reasons, it is difficult to state specifically what actions HR specialists should take to minimize the chances of having a court disagree with the nature of a performance evaluation system.

To provide an understanding of what is known about this topic, this section indicates those parts of the *Uniform Guidelines* that pertain to performance measurement, summarizes the results of relevant court decisions, and present some recommendations regarding necessary features of work measurement systems. As other authors have put it, these recommendations ought to be treated as "a set of hypotheses regarding the legal ramifications" rather than a strict set of guidelines.[44]

The Uniform Guidelines

Three sections of the *Uniform Guidelines* have the most direct statements about work measurement (see Appendix 2A). Of these, section 2.B is the most often cited. Its purpose is to make clear that any procedure that contributes to any employment decision is covered by the *Uniform Guidelines*. This is addressed by the statement, "These guidelines apply to tests and other selection procedures which are used as a basis for any employment decision."[45] To the extent that work measurement data are used in validation or for any other purpose in selection, they are covered. Some interpret this section to mean that all procedures used in these employment decisions are to be generally labeled as "tests" and subject to all the statements of the *Uniform Guidelines* directed at tests.

The second statement, section 14.B.(3) (see table 17.2), serves several purposes. For one, it makes explicit that three of the four types of data we have discussed are permissible: production data, HR data, and training proficiency. More detail is provided about training proficiency than the others. It is pointed out that the relevance of the training to actual important dimensions of job performance must be demonstrated and that various measures of training proficiency may be used including instructor evaluations, performance samples, and paper and pencil tests. The statement is also made that these three types of criteria measures may be used without a previous job analysis "if the user can show the importance of the criteria to the particular employment context." Presumably, this is done by pointing out the direct relationship of these criteria measures to the purpose of the job. Other issues in section 14 refer to some of the points we made in the previous section of this chapter, "Characteristics of Selection Criteria Measures." These include preventing contamination and ensuring relevance. A statement is also made that it is permissible to develop one overall measure of job performance. We discussed appropriate methods of doing this earlier in this chapter.

A third section, 15.B.(5) makes clear that the data used to identify and develop the criterion measure(s) of validation must be made explicit: "The bases for the selection of the criterion measures should be provided. . . ." This includes the description of the criterion and how the measure was developed and collected. Explicit statements are also made recognizing the fourth type of work measurement data, judgmental data. When this type is used, both the forms used to collect the judgments and the explicit instructions given to the judges must be provided.

Court Decisions

A comprehensive review of court decisions about judgmental performance measures, done by Hubert Feild and William Holley, examined 66 cases heard between 1966 and 1980.[46] All of the cases focused on judgmental rather than other measures. From statements in the *Uniform Guidelines* and our previous remarks, it is understandable that EEO regulatory agencies would be far more concerned with the discriminatory effects of this type of performance measure than any of the other three. Presumably, court statements about judgmental data would also be applicable to the other types.

Feild and Holley reviewed 66 cases and classified each on the 13 appraisal system characteristics shown in Table 17.3. They also divided the cases into those that were decided in favor of the plaintiff (31 cases) and those decided in favor of the defendant (35 cases). The purpose of the study was to determine how these appraisal characteristics might be related to the court decisions. As Table 17.3 indicates, 5 of the 13 characteristics were found to have a statistically significant relationship with these decisions.

These five characteristics seem to provide useful information about critical features of performance systems in discrimination cases. The most strongly related characteristic was the type of organization of the defendant. Court decisions usually went for the plaintiff in cases involving manufacturing companies and went against the plaintiff in cases within service industries, many of which were educational systems. This pattern is not explainable in terms of EEO directives, but it does reflect a viewpoint possible within the regulatory model.

The remaining characteristics provide information to form recommendations about necessary features of work measurement systems. The second characteristic is a concept explicitly mentioned in the *Uniform Guidelines*, the

TABLE 17.2   **STATEMENTS FROM THE UNIFORM GUIDELINES PERTAINING TO WORK MEASUREMENT**

Selection 14.B.(3).

(3) Criterion measures. Proper safeguards should be taken to insure that scores on selection procedures do not enter into any judgments of employee adequacy that are to be used as criterion measures. Whatever criteria are used should represent important or critical work behavior(s) or work outcomes. Certain criteria may be used without a full job analysis if the user can show the importance of the criteria to the particular employment context. These criteria include but are not limited to production rate, error rate, tardiness, absenteeism, and length of service. A standardized rating of overall work performance may be used where a study of the job shows that it is an appropriate criterion. Where performance in training is used as a criterion, success in training should be properly measured and the relevance of the training should be shown either through a comparison of the content of the training program with the critical or important work behavior(s) of the job(s), or through a demonstration of the relationship between measures of performance in training and measures of job performance. Measures of relative success in training include but are not limited to instructor evaluation, performance samples, or tests. Criterion measures consisting of paper and pencil tests will be closely reviewed for job relevance.

SOURCE: Adoption of Four Agencies of Uniform Guidelines on Employee Selection Procedures, 43 Federal Register 38, 290–315 (Aug. 25, 1978).

presence of specific written instructions given to raters describing the system of evaluation. As you might guess, the overwhelming majority of cases with specific instructions were decided in favor of the defendant; and the opposite pattern was found in those cases without such instruction. This is an expected result and also conforms with general principles about the professional development of judgmental data systems. This is also true of the remaining three critical characteristics. The plaintiff was generally upheld in cases involving trait or personal characteristic dimensions while the company was upheld when behavior-oriented dimensions were used. Similarly, the use of job analysis to establish the dimension on which judgments were made and the practice of sharing the results of the appraisal with the workers were also related to decisions made in favor of the defendant. The lack of job analysis and lack of sharing of information favored the plaintiff. Again, these practices are part of standard professional evaluation practices.

A more recent study examined 21 federal appeals court discrimination cases from 1979 to 1990. Glenn McEvoy and Caryn Beck-Dudley found four performance appraisal systems characteristics that exhibited significant relationships with the decision outcome.[47] The most significant predictor of case outcome was the provision of written instructions for raters. Plaintiffs won all five cases where written instructions weren't provided; defendants won six of seven cases where instructions were provided. Two other significant predictors were feedback and appeals channels. When feedback was provided to ratees, defendants won most cases; when it was not, they lost. Appeals channels followed the same pattern. The fourth characteristic was having multiple raters such as higher-level

| TABLE 17.3 | | CHARACTERISTICS OF JUDGMENTAL APPRAISAL SYSTEMS RELATED TO COURT DECISIONS | | |

| | | Number of Legal Cases with Decisions for | | |
Appraisal System Characteristic	N	Plaintiff	Defendant	Statistically Significant
Purpose of the appraisal system?	61			No
Promotion		18		
Other layoffs, transfers, discharges)		I0	18	
Job analysis used to develop appraisal system?	17			Yes
Yes		0	3	
No		11	3	
Type of appraisal system used?	48			Yes
Trait-oriented		17	8	
Behavior-oriented		7	I6	
Presented validity information on appraisal system?	65			No
Yes		I0	10	
No		21	24	
Presented validity information on appraisal system?	58			No
Yes		3	3	
No		28	24	
Frequency that appraisals were conducted?	19			No
Mean		3.75	3.45	
SD		.71	.93	
Number of evaluators used?	32			No
Mean		1.56	2.00	
SD		1.37	1.75	
Evaluators given formal training appraising performance?	15			No
Yes		0	1	
No		11	3	
Evaluators given specific written instructions?	27			Yes
Yes		1	11	
No		14	1	

(continued)

TABLE 17.3   (CONTINUED)

Appraisal System Characteristic	N	Number of Legal Cases with Decisions for		
		Plaintiff	Defendant	Statistically Significant
Appraisal results reviewed with employees?	12			Yes
Yes		2	7	
No		3	0	
Basis for employment discrimination charge?	55			No
Race		19	21	
Sex		8	7	
Type of organization	63			Yes
Industrial		14	4	
Nonindustrial		17	30	
Geographical location of organization	66			No
Inside the Southeast		13	8	
Outside the Southeast		19	26	

SOURCE: Hubert Feild and William Holley, "The Relationship of Performance Appraisal System Characteristics to Verdicts in Selected Employment Discrimination Cases," *Academy of Management Journal* 2 (1982): 397. Reprinted with permission from the authors.

managers. Interestingly, although Feild and Holley did not find that the number of evaluators used was significant, later in this later review defendants won eight of ten cases in which there were multiple raters and lost all cases in which there was a single rater. Based on these reviews it would seem essential to base work measurement systems on job analysis, to use job behaviors as dimensions, to provide specific instructions on the use of the system, to communicate the results to all employees, and to provide multiple raters and an appeal system.

Well, that's it. We do not know any more about selection. Ask your instructor if you want more information. We know you are now ready to be a selection specialist and earn at least $125,000 per year doing what is in this book. All we ask is 10 percent of your first year's salary. Good luck!

References

[1] Frank J. Landy and James L. Farr, *The Measurement of Worth Performance Methods, Theory, and Applications* (New York: Academic Press, 1983); Kevin R. Murphy and Jeanette N. Cleveland, *Performance Appraisal: An Organizational Perspective* (Boston: Allyn & Bacon, 1991). H. John Bernadin and Richard W. Beatty, *Performance Appraisal: Assessing Human Behavior At Work* (Boston: West Publishing, Co. 1984).

[2] William W. Ronan and Erich P. Prien, *Perspectives on the Measurement of Human Performance* (New York: Appleton-Century-Crofts, 1971), 73.

[3] Ibid., 94.

[4] Landy and Farr, *The Measurement of Work Performance Methods, Theory, and Applications*, 30.

[5] Ibid., 33.

[6] David A. Harrison and Charles L. Hulin, "Investigations of Absenteeism: Using Event History Models to Study the Absence-Taking Process," *Journal of Applied Psychology* 74 (1989): 300–316.

[7] J.B. Carroll, "The Nature of the Data, or How to Choose a Correlation Coefficient," *Psychometrika* 26 (1961): 347–372.

[8] David A. Harrison and Charles L. Hulin, *Journal of Applied Psychology* 74 (1989): 300–316.

[9] Charles Williams, "Deciding When, How, and IF to Correct Turnover Correlations," *Journal of Applied Psychology* 75 (1990): 732–737.

[10] Ibid.

[11] June Morita, Thomas W. Lee, and Richard T. Mowday, "Introducing Survival Analysis to Organizational Researchers: A Selected Application to Turnover Research," *Journal of Applied Psychology* 74 (1989): 280–292.

[12] Charles Williams, *Journal of Applied Psychology* (1990): 732–737.

[13] Dan R. Dalton and William D. Todor, "Manifest Needs of Stewards: Propensity to File a Grievance," *Journal of Applied Psychology* 64 (1979): 654–659.

[14] Hannah Rothstein Hirsh, Lois Northrup, and Frank Schmidt. "Validity Generalization Results for Law Enforcement Occupations," *Personnel Psychology* 39 (1986) 399–429.

[15] Sidney Gael, Donald L. Grant, and Richard J. Ritchie, "Employment Test Validation for Minority and Nonminority Telephone Operators," *Journal of Applied Psychology* 60 (1975) 411–419; Sidney Gael, Donald L. Grant and Richard J. Ritchie, "Employment Test Validation for Minority and Nonminority Clerks with Work Sample Criteria," *Journal of Applied Psychology* 60 (1975) 420–426.

[16] Bernardin and Beatty, *Performance Appraisal: Assessing Human Behavior at Work*, 64-65.

[17] Latham and Wexley, *Increasing Productivity through Performance Appraisal*, 51-55.

[18] Kevin Murphy and Joseph Constans, "Behavioral Anchors as a Source of Bias in Ratings," *Journal of Applied Psychology* 72 (1987): 573-577.

[19] Latham and Wexley, *Increasing Productivity through Performance Appraisal*, 55-64.

[20] Uco Wiersma and Gary P. Latham, "The Practicality of Behavioral Observation Scales, Behavioral Expectation Scales, and Trait Scales," *Personnel Psychology* 39 (1986): 619–628.

[21] H. John Bernardin, "Behavioral Expectation Scales versus Summated Scales: A Fairer Comparison," *Journal of Applied Psychology* 62 (1977): 422–427.

[22] Walter Borman, "Job Behavior, Performance, and Effectiveness," in *Handbook of Industrial and Organizational Psychology*, 2d ed., Vol. 2, eds. Marvin D. Dunnette and Leaetta M. Hough: (Palo Alto, Calif: Consulting Psychologists Press, Inc.), pp 271–326.

[23] Calvin C. Hoffman, Barry R. Nathan, and Lisa M. Holden, "A Comparison of Validation Criteria: Objective versus Subjective Performance Measures and Self versus Supervisor Ratings," *Personnel Psychology* (1991): 601–619.

[24] Barry Nathan and Ralph Alexander, "A Comparison of Criteria for Test Validation: A Meta-Analytic Investigation," *Personnel Psychology* 41 (1988): 517–535.

[25] Gary P. Latham, Kenneth N. Wexley, and Elliott Persell, "Training Managers to Minimize Rating Errors in the Observation of Behavior," *Journal of Applied Psychology* 60 (1975): 550–555.

[26] Elaine Pulakos, "A Comparison of Rater Training Programs : Error Training and Accuracy Training," *Journal of Applied Psychology* 69 (1984): 581–588.

[27] Ibid.

[28] Charles H. Fay and Gary P. Latham, "The Effects of Training and Rating Scales on Rating Errors," *Personnel Psychology* 35 (1982): 105-116.

[29] Elliot D. Pursell, Dennis L. Dossett, and Gary P. Latham, "Observing Valid Predictors by Minimizing Rating Errors in the Criterion," *Personnel Psychology* 33 (1980): 91–96.

[30] Neil Schmidt and Benjamin Schneider, "Current Issues in Personnel Selection." *Research in Personnel and Human Resources Management*, vol.1 (JAI Press, 1983), 93.

[31] Landy and Farr, *The Measurement of Work Performance Methods, Theory, and Applications*, 191–207.

[32] Wayne F. Cascio, *Applied Psychology in Personnel Management*, 3d ed. (Reston, Va.: Reston, 1987), 116-118

[33] John P. Campbell, Jeffrey J McHenry, and Lauress L. Wise, "Modeling Job Performance in a Population of Jobs," *Personnel Psychology* 43 (1990): 313–333.

[34] Wayne F. Cascio, *Applied Psychology in Personnel Management*, p. 109.

[35] Hubert E. Brogden and Erwin K. Taylor, "The Dollar Criterion—Applying the Cost Accounting Concept to Criterion Construction," *Personnel Psychology* 3 (1950): 133–154.

[36] Frank L. Schmidt, John E. Hunter, Robert C. Mckenzie, and Tressie W. Muldrow, "Impact of Personnel Programs on Workforce Productivity," *Journal of Applied Psychology* 64 (1979): 609–626.

[37] Frank L. Schmidt, John E. Hunter, Robert C. Mckenzie, and Tressie W. Muldrow, "Impact of Personnel Programs on Workforce Productivity," *Personnel Psychology* 35 (1982): 333–348.

[38] Wayne F. Cascio, *Costing Human Resources: The Financial Impact of Behavior in Organizations* (Boston: Kent, 1982), 163.

[39] Peter Villanova, "A Customer-Based Model for Developing Job Performance Criteria," *Human Resource Management Review* 2 (1992): 103–114. See also James T. Austin and Peter Villanova, "The Criterion Problem: 1917–1992," *Journal of Applied Psychology* 77 (1992): 836–874.

[40] Diana L. Deadrick and Robert M. Madigan, "Dynamic Criteria Revisited: A Longitudinal Study of Performance Stability and Predictive Validity," *Personnel Psychology* 43 (1990): 717–744.

[41] Ibid., 738.

[42] Paul J. Hanges, Benjamin Schneider, and Kathryn Niles, "Stability of Performance: An Interactionist Perspective," *Journal of Applied Psychology* 75 (1990): 658–667.

[43] Kevin R. Murphy, "Is the Relationship between Cognitive Ability and Job Performance Stable over Time?" *Human Performance* 2 (1989): 183–200.

[44] Bernardin and Beatty, *Performance Appraisal: Assessing Human Behavior at Work*, 43

[45] *Adoption of Four Agencies of Uniform Guidelines on Employee Selection Procedures*, 43 Federal Register 38, 290–38, 315 (Aug. 25, 1978).

[46] Hubert S. Feild and William H. Holley, "The Relationship of Performance Appraisal System Characteristics to Verdicts in Selected Employment Discrimination Cases," *Academy of Management Journal* 25 (1982): 392–406. Also see Hubert S. Feild and Diane Thompson, "A Study of Court Decisions in Cases Involving Performance Appraisal Systems," *The Daily Labor Report*, December 26, E1–E5

[47] Glenn M. McEvoy and Caryn L. Beck-Dudley, "Legally Defensible Performance Appraisals: A Review of Federal Appeals Court Cases," paper presented an the sixth Annual Conference of the Society for Industrial and Organizational Psychology, April 1991. St. Louis, Mo.

SUBJECT INDEX